31

COMMUNICATION
YEARBOOK

31

COMMUNICATION YEARBOOK

Edited by
CHRISTINA S. BECK

Published Annually for the
International Communication Association

LEA Lawrence Erlbaum Associates
Taylor & Francis Group

New York   London

Lawrence Erlbaum Associates
Taylor & Francis Group
270 Madison Avenue
New York, NY 10016

Lawrence Erlbaum Associates
Taylor & Francis Group
2 Park Square
Milton Park, Abingdon
Oxon OX14 4RN

© 2008 by Taylor & Francis Group, LLC
Lawrence Erlbaum Associates is an imprint of Taylor & Francis Group, an Informa business

Printed in the United States of America on acid-free paper
10 9 8 7 6 5 4 3 2 1

International Standard Book Number-13: 978-0-8058-6358-1 (Hardcover)

Visit the Taylor & Francis Web site at
http://www.taylorandfrancis.com

Contents

The International
Communication Association

The International Communication Association (ICA) was formed in 1950, bringing together academics and other professionals whose interests focus on human communication. The association maintains an active membership of more than 4,000 individuals, of whom some two thirds are teaching and conducting research in colleges, universities, and schools around the world. Other members are in government, law, medicine, and other professions. The wide professional and geographic distribution of the membership provides the basic strength of the ICA. The association is a meeting ground for sharing research and useful dialogue about communication interests.

Through its divisions and interest groups, publications, annual conferences, and relations with other associations around the world, the ICA promotes the systemic study of communication theories, processes, and skills. In addition to *Communication Yearbook*, the association publishes the *Journal of Communication, Human Communication Research, Communication Theory, Journal of Computer-Mediated Communication, A Guide to Publishing in Scholarly Communication Journals*, and the *ICA Newsletter*.

For additional information about the ICA and its activities, visit online at www.icahdq.org or contact Michael L. Haley, executive director, International Communication Association, 1730 Rhode Island Ave. NW, Suite 300, Washington, DC, 20036; phone (202) 530-9855; fax (202) 530-9851; e-mail ica@icahdq.org

Editors of the *Communication Yearbook* series:

Volumes 1 and 2, Brent D. Ruben
Volumes 3 and 4, Dan Nimmo
Volumes 5 and 6, Michael Burgoon

Volumes 7 and 8, Robert N. Bostrom
Volumes 9 and 10, Margaret L. McLaughlin
Volumes 11, 12, 13, and 14, James A. Anderson
Volumes 15, 16, and 17, Stanley A. Deetz
Volumes 18, 19, and 20, Brant R. Burleson
Volumes 21, 22, and 23, Michael E. Roloff
Volumes 24, 25, and 26, William B. Gudykunst
Volumes 27, 28, and 29, Pamela J. Kalbfleisch
Volumes 30 and 31, Christina S. Beck

International Communication Association Executive Committee

President and Chair
Ronald E. Rice
University of California, Santa Barbara

President-Elect
Sonia Livingstone
London School of Economics

Past President
Wolfgang Donsbach
University of Dresden

President-Elect Select
Patrice M. Buzzanell
Purdue University

Finance Chair
Robert T. Craig (ex-officio)
University of Colorado–Boulder

Immediate Past President
Jon F. Nussbaum
Pennsylvania State University

Executive Director
Michael L. Haley (ex-officio)
ICA Headquarters

Board of Directors

Members at Large

Sherry Lynn Ferguson,
University of Ottawa

Yu-li- Liu, *National Chengchi University*

Elena E. Pernia, *University of the Philippines, Diliman*

Karen Ross, *Coventry University*

Ted Zorn, *University of Waikato*

Student Members

Rebecca C. Hains, *Temple University*

Qi Wang, *Villanova University*

Division Chairs

Information Systems
David R. Roskos-Ewoldsen,
University of Alabama

Interpersonal Communication
Beth A. LePoire, *California Lutheran University*

Mass Communication
Holli A. Semetko, *Emory University*

Organizational Communication
Cynthia Stohl, *University of California, Santa Barbara*

Intercultural/Development Communication
Min-Sun Kim, *University of Hawaii at Manoa*

Political Communication
Patricia Moy, *University of Washington*

Instructional/Developmental Communication
Amy Nathanson, *Ohio State University*

Health Communication
Douglas Storey, *Johns Hopkins Bloomberg School of Public Health*

Philosophy of Communication
Christina Slade, *Macquarie University*

Communication and Technology
Jan A. G. M. Van Dijk, *University of Twente*

Popular Communication
Lynn Schofield Clark, *University of Denver*

Public Relations
Hochang Shin, *Sogang University*

Feminist Scholarship
Marian J. Meyers, *Georgia State University*

Communication Law and Policy
Sharon Strover, *University of Texas*

Language and Social Interaction
François Cooren, *University of Montreal*

Visual Studies
Dong Hoon Ma, *Korea University*

Journalism Studies
John E. Newhagen, *University of Maryland*

Special Interest Group Chairs

Gay, Lesbian, Bisexual, and Transgender Studies
David Phillips, *University of Toronto*

Intergroup Communication
Hiroshi Ota, *Aichi Shukutoku University*

Ethnicity and Race in Communication
Isabel Molina Guzman, *University of Illinois at Urbana-Champaign*

Game Studies
James H. Watt, *Rensselaer Polytechnic Institute*

Communication Yearbook 31
Editorial Board

Christina Holtz-Bacha	Universität Erlangen–Nürnberg
Michael Kent	Western Michigan University
Elly Konijn	Free University of Amsterdam
Eric Mark Kramer	University of Oklahoma
Wendy Leeds-Hurwitz	University of Wisconsin–Parkside
Dafna Lemish	Tel-Aviv University
Leah Anne Lievrouw	University of California, Los Angeles
John Lucaites	Indiana University
Gianpietro Mazzoleni	University of Milano
Raymie McKerrow	Ohio University
Caryn Medved	Ohio University
Paul Messaris	University of Pennsylvania
Michael D. E. Meyer	Christopher Newport University
Renee Meyers	University of Wisconsin–Milwaukee
Peter Monge	University of Southern California
Dennis Mumby	University of North Carolina at Chapel Hill
Michael Papa	Central Michigan University
Ronald Pelias	Southern Illinois University
Brian Quick	Ohio University
Sandra Ragan	University of Oklahoma
William Rawlins	Ohio University
Jeff Robinson	Rutgers University
Barbara Sharf	Texas A&M University
Christina Slade	Macquarie University
J. Michael Sproule	Saint Louis University
Maureen Taylor	Western Michigan University
Teresa Thompson	University of Dayton
Nick Trujillo	Sacramento State University
Patti Valkenburg	University of Amsterdam
Robert Westerfelhaus	College of Charleston
Andrew Wood	San José State University
Barbie Zelizer	University of Pennsylvania

Communication Yearbook 31
Guest Reviewers

Roger Aden	Ohio University
Mike Allen	University of Wisconsin–Milwaukee
Julie Andsager	University of Iowa
Robert Asen	University of Wisconsin–Madison
Betsy Bach	University of Montana–Missoula
Eileen Berlin Ray	Cleveland State University
Tom Bivins	University of Oregon
Bryna Bogoch	Bar-Ilan University
Oliver Boyd-Barrett	Bowling Green State University
Samuel D. Bradley	Ohio State University
Charles Braithwaite	University of Nebraska–Lincoln
Pablo Briñol	Universidad Autónoma de Madrid
Shannon Brogan	Ohio University–Chillicothe
Barbara Wake Carroll	McMaster University
Ling Chen	Hong Kong Baptist University
Robin Clair	Purdue University
Timothy Coombs	Eastern Illinois University
Robert T. Craig	University of Colorado at Boulder
David Croteau	Virginia Commonwealth University
Roberta Davilla	University of Northern Iowa
Estaban del Rio	University of San Diego
Stephen Depoe	University of Cincinnati
Sara DeTurk	University of Texas at San Antonio
Natalie Dollar	Oregon State University, Cascades
Jill Edy	University of Oklahoma
Peter Ehrenhaus	Pacific Lutheran University
William Eveland	Ohio State University
Jennifer Gibbs	Rutgers University
Catherine Gillotti	Purdue University, Calumet
Steve Greenfield	University of Westminster
Joshua Gunn	University of Texas at Austin
Christopher Hanson	University of Maryland
Richard Harris	Kansas State University
Zachary P. Hart	Northern Kentucky University
Keith Hearit	Western Michigan University

Steve Hoekstra	Kansas Wesleyan University
W. Wat Hopkins	Virgina Tech
Annika Hylmö	Loyola Marymount University
Robert Jackall	Williams College
J. Michael Jaffe	University of Michigan
Jessica Katz Jamison	North Carolina State University
Craig Johnson	George Fox University
David Jonassen	University of Missouri
Flora Keshishian	St. John's University
Erika Kirby	Creighton University
Jenny Kitzinger	Cardiff University
Kim Kline	Southern Illinois University
Marwan Kraidy	American University
Michael W. Kramer	University of Missouri–Columbia
Dale Kunkel	University of Arizona
Megan Lewis	RIT International
Sally J. McMillan	University of Tennessee
Miriam Metzger	University of California, Santa Barbara
Trudy Milburn	California State University, Channel Islands
Jerry L. Miller	Ohio University
Mark Morman	Baylor University
Kelly Morrison	Michigan State University
Julianne H. Newton	University of Oregon
Daniel O'Keefe	Northwestern University
Guy Osborn	University of Westminster
Trevor Parry-Giles	University of Maryland
Jennifer Peeples	Utah State University
Richard M. Perloff	Cleveland State University
Elizabeth M. Perse	University of Delaware
Kendall Phillips	Syracuse University
Patrick Plaisance	Colorado State University
David Pritchard	University of Wisconsin–Milwaukee
David E. Procter	Kansas State University
Steven M. Ralston	Northern Illinois University
Ronald E. Rice	University of California, Santa Barbara
Yeidy Rivero	Indiana University
Raul Roman	University of Southern California
Eric Rothenbuhler	Texas A&M University
Theresa A. Russell-Loretz	Millersville University
Karen Sanders	University of Sheffield
Clifford Scherer	Cornell University
Matt Seeger	Wayne State University
Susan Senecah	The State University of New York
Jan Servaes	University of Queensland

Introduction

As editor of *Communication Yearbook*, I have enjoyed amazing opportunities to interact with potential contributors and expert reviewers from varied areas of the communication discipline and, indeed, the world. Throughout those exchanges, I have marveled at the rich diversity of perspectives, focal areas, theoretical frameworks, and approaches to scholarship within our discipline, not to mention related works from noncommunication scholars that can inform and enrich our work.

The ever-expanding wealth of articles and books pertaining to communication (within and beyond our disciplinary boundaries) underscores the value of *Communication Yearbook*. Especially since *Communication Yearbook 19*, this annual publication has served as a tremendous forum for compiling, reviewing, and evaluating the status of research in our discipline, enabling us to examine what we know and what we still need to learn about important communication issues. Given the vast number of publications in a wide array of outlets, *Communication Yearbook* provides essential scholarly space to synthesize, analyze, and set agendas for future directions.

Moreover, I believe that *Communication Yearbook* can (and should) foster conversations and connections across often artificial subdisciplinary boundaries. Given the challenges of "staying current" on any given topic, we can easily become isolated and compartmentalized, even from others in our same discipline. Despite (or, perhaps, because of) the abundance of options for information, we remain necessarily constrained because we lack hours in the day to pursue them.

Yet, we can benefit greatly from intradisciplinary dialogues. For example, as a health communication scholar, I recognize the considerable (and often conflicting) influences on enacting and achieving health and wellness: interpersonal relationships, support systems, medical treatment and prevention options, diverse organizational contexts, political decisions, technological resources, mediated messages, etc. Although I try to read widely, time precludes my ability to read all potentially relevant literature. As a publication dedicated to publishing state-of-the-discipline literature reviews, *Communication Yearbook* provides snapshots of research, affording readers invaluable exposure to theoretical arguments and empirical findings that may linger beyond their specific areas of expertise.

In *Communication Yearbook 31,* I urged contributors to take one more step. Especially given my conviction about the importance of discussion across our discipline, I asked all authors to articulate the relevance of their respective chapters beyond the more narrow emphasis of their respective reviews. In so doing, I urged them to initiate scholarly dialogues about important ideas and issues with a diverse and global audience of communication researchers. Thus, each chapter in this volume highlights potential intersections between its focal topic and other areas of scholarly inquiry in communication.

Further, although incidentally, each chapter in this volume also mirrors contemporary life by wrestling to some extent with the dialectic of fluidity and stability, especially in terms of capturing meaning, understanding relationships, and defining contexts. Fluidity offers flexibility—the chance to reshape, redefine, or reposition ourselves for emergent opportunities (e.g., connecting with others, making career moves, or advancing political agendas). Stability provides security—consistency in a rapidly changing world (e.g., efforts to preserve traditions, norms, values, or "the way it is" or "has always been"). Extending from Gergen (1991), social actors in this postmodern era can embrace this paradox by desiring flexibility as well as stability, affirming either or both as they decide how to "play" particular situations.

However, as social actors, we inherently co-negotiate fluidity and stability with other co-participants in certain circumstances. As I was finishing this introduction, I happened to take a break and watch an episode of *Desperate Housewives,* a popular U.S. television show in a much improved third season. Gabrielle Solis, one of the main characters in her early 30s, recently divorced her husband. A former model, Gabrielle decided to return to the runway. Her agent agreed to represent the beautiful and shapely Gabrielle, and she sent the model to her first job—as a matronly mother in the background to a dazzling young woman. As the agent explained to a shocked and saddened

Gabrielle, the modeling world would not accept Gabrielle's preferred identity as a glamorous model. Although she playfully (and seductively) tried to reframe their perceptions of her, she had aged, and her self-image as a model could no longer remain frozen in time.

As the chapters in this volume illustrate, our lives necessarily change due to age, disease, conflict, trauma, family status, and other circumstances (such as organizational, institutional, technological, or political developments). Each new twist compels us to redefine "ordinary," "normal," "typical," or "usual," perhaps even fragmenting our existence as we continually reconsider those terms (as well as a plethora of others) through our interactions in diverse (and potentially concurrent) social circles.

Relational constraints, power structures, and institutional barriers can hinder our ability to advance personal preferences for flexibility or stability. We cannot always mandate others to interact with us as we like or to accept our alternate views, identities, or visions for how things "ought" to be in the home, workforce, or world. Yet, the ever-fluctuating tension between fluidity and stability reveals a crack in absolutism: Instead of "either/or," we might be able to snatch the possibility of "both/and." We might possess just enough agency to (re)configure ourselves (and our circumstances) creatively, perhaps even in multiple ways for diverse audiences (see related arguments by Rayner, 2006). As such, contemporary discourse involves the perpetual struggle to strike the "right" balance between postmodern fluidity and more modernist stability as we communicate with others in varied and consequential episodes during our hectic, and often frazzled, lives.

Although some chapters hint at this dialectic more overtly than others, all raise related, critical questions about our communicative choices as social actors, as citizens, and as policy makers in private and public spheres. How do we co-define the meanings of silence, openness, and conflict in a world in which such actions can be taken (and treated) in different ways? What do our communities, organizations, political parties, or media organizations communicate when members respond (or not) to large-scale disasters, personal tragedies, or initiatives to redefine policies, procedures, or perspectives (such as the conceptualization of time, attempts to fit in, or interpretations of mediated messages)? As such, these chapters tackle important issues for communication scholars in ever-changing relational, health, organizational, social, political, technological, and mediated contexts.

Overview of Chapters

In the lead chapter in this volume, Kris Acheson offers a comprehensive and eloquent examination of silence. In this outstanding chapter, Acheson details the dialectics of silence, refusing to cast it as "good" or "bad." Indeed, despite preferences by some cultures for particular enactments of silence, it can hold varied meanings for diverse individuals, especially when they juggle multiple allegiances, memberships, and, perhaps, power differentials (e.g., doctor as well as loved one, boss as well as friend, etc.). This powerful review offers considerable insight for scholars across our discipline, and it could inspire interesting new areas of exploration, including the role of silence in health care contexts, enactment of organizational roles, group participation, political involvement, international disputes, and media presentation of issues.

From silence, we turn to a chapter on openness and avoidance. In their chapter, Daena Goldsmith, Laura Miller, and John Caughlin note that avoidance does not quite constitute the same phenomenon as silence; however, their work presents an excellent companion to Acheson's contribution. After providing valuable references to research on openness and avoidance in general, the authors focus on findings that pertain to couples coping with cancer. Illness can shatter stability, and this chapter describes the ways in which openness (and avoidance) can enable couples to accomplish a "new normal" and/or to preserve pre-cancer relational dynamics. As such, this review features relevant information for scholars across communication contexts—especially for individuals in the areas of health and interpersonal communication.

As Goldsmith et al. observe, a cancer diagnosis can cause significant disruption for patients and loved ones and, occasionally, result in conflict over communicative responses to disease. Indeed, Courtney Waite Miller, Michael E. Roloff, and Rachel S. Malis emphasize that conflict constitutes a concept that crosses communication contexts, from dyadic difficulties to international disputes. In their chapter, Miller et al. concentrate on conflicts that individuals find difficult to resolve, and they provide an important synthesis of pertinent literature through narrative critique and advancement of an integrative model. This chapter also summarizes literature of cross-disciplinary significance, and it should be especially appealing to scholars with a focus on interpersonal, group, and intercultural communication.

Communication during (and about) traumatic events breeds conflict as affected parties react to natural disasters, oppression, war, disease, corporate downsizing, etc. In her chapter, Stephanie Houston Grey discusses the critical role of communication in co-defining (and often disputing) traumatic events and co-determining "appropriate" personal, political, corporate, and social responses. Grey's chapter draws together an intriguing assortment of articles and books from a wide range of scholarship, and it captures the complexities of working through trauma on varying levels—individual, institutional, societal, and political. The chapter truly spans our discipline in terms of its potential applications, particularly in the areas of interpersonal, health, organizational, intercultural, and political communication.

Notably, trauma can extend from (and profoundly affect) individual and collective identities. In her chapter, Niki Young details the opportunities for (and challenges to) enacting and revising identities in an increasingly complicated world. Young contrasts modernist and postmodernist approaches to identity, and she highlights examples from scholarly research on individuals and groups that "trans/formed" their identities for personal or political purposes. This chapter provides a valuable synthesis of literature on a significant topic with implications for a wide array of communication scholars, ranging from interpersonal through international contexts as well as mediated communication.

Many of us construct at least part of our identities through our work. Yet, as Dawna Ballard and Loril Gossett argue, we covet our time, and we crave flexibility in accomplishing our work as well as stability in our organizational and personal lives. Furthermore, as Ballard and Gossett detail in their compelling review, time defines us as much as we (both individually and collectively) enact it, and varied treatments of temporality can result in challenges and conflicts affecting our identities as legitimate organizational members, "real" moms or dads, etc. Although this chapter focuses on organizational implications of "alternative times," it also offers related insights for communication scholars in interpersonal, family, religious, and intercultural communication.

As Jennifer Waldeck and Karen Myers assert in their chapter, newcomers to organizations must ascertain the often unspoken "ground rules" for managing time as well as other delicate yet critical components of organizational life. In their chapter, Waldeck and Myers provide a compelling synthesis of organizational assimilation research. This review underscores the importance of this topic as well as the challenges for future research, especially given the diversity of contemporary organizations (and variety of individual and institutional preferences for enacting professional life) on local, national, and international levels. Further, Waldeck and Myers emphasize the relevance of this work for other areas of communication scholarship, given that individuals in contemporary life also assimilate into new family structures, groups, and communities.

Despite the fluidity of contemporary life (i.e., as we experience health problems or conflict, relocate due to traumatic incident or personal choice, alter our identities, or reconfigure jobs), the idea of community offers hope for connection and at least a bit of consistency. In their chapter, underwood and Frey share a comprehensive review of the considerable literature on community from a communication perspective. This chapter constitutes a superb discussion of major arguments on this important topic; as such, it includes relevant information for varied scholars, especially in the areas of interpersonal, group, health, organizational, political, or mediated communication.

In their chapter, Southwell and Yzer stress the salient roles of interpersonal communication within the context of social communities for potential interpretations of mass-mediated campaigns. These authors draw together important empirical and theoretical contributions from diverse areas, and they advance valuable arguments about the ways in which interpersonal communication can influence interpretation of mediated messages, especially in the context of health, science, and political campaigns. Thus, this chapter should interest interpersonal and media scholars as well as health, organizational, and political communication researchers.

Especially given advances in technology, mass-mediated messages permeate society as individuals weave them into their interpersonal interactions and allow them to influence interpretations of topics (such as health issues, organizational images, politicians, social agendas, and, perhaps, even impressions of religions and cultures). In his chapter, Roessler addresses the critical issue of mass-media diversity. He explores multiple levels of diversity, and he discusses the implications of technology and large-scale media organizations for accomplishing aspects of diversity. Although of particular interest to media scholars, this chapter offers rich, related insights to interpersonal, organizational, health, intercultural, and political communication scholars.

Summary of Process

I received 69 submissions to *Communication Yearbook 31*. Overall, reviewers applauded the outstanding quality of submissions, and competition for the possible chapter slots was intense. I selected 10 proposals for development into chapters for this volume based on reviewer feedback (during a blind, peer-review process) about the quality of the potential literature reviews and fit with the theme of *Communication Yearbook 31*. Unfortunately, schedule conflicts eventually prevented authors of one accepted proposal from completing their work. That team of authors withdrew early enough in the process to allow me to replace their chapter with one by an alternate team of authors. Thus, this volume of *Communication Yearbook* features 10 chapters by scholars from the United States and Germany, representing diverse areas in our discipline. Each selected chapter received input during at least two rounds of review from peer reviewers as well as feedback from the editor.

Grateful Acknowledgments

The submissions for *Communication Yearbook 31* exceeded my expectations in terms of quantity and diversity, resulting in a very difficult selection process. Because the variety of topics pushed my personal boundaries in terms of theoretical, empirical, and methodological expertise, I relied on trusted and valued members of my editorial board as well as over 100 guest reviewers for their wisdom and input on submissions. I thank each of them for their willingness to share their expertise and time during this important process. To their credit, I know that each of the chapters in *Communication Yearbook 31* benefited tremendously from reviewer feedback, and I believe that many potential contributors appreciated the insightful comments as well. (Indeed, I actually received thank-you messages from some individuals after they received their decision letters. Although disappointed with the outcome, they wrote to express deep gratitude to the reviewers for offering such helpful and detailed feedback on their respective submissions.)

Throughout the last two years, I have relied on the incredible support and encouragement of my "right hand" in this editorial journey: senior editorial associate Dr. Jennifer Scott. Although she began her work with me as a graduate assistant, she agreed to continue her work on *Communication Yearbook* after receiving a fellowship and then earning her doctoral degree. Nearly all of the chapters in this volume have been greatly enhanced through her dedication to tracking down potential resources and her smart ideas to develop arguments, amend chapter titles, and integrate additional citations.

I am also grateful to my editorial assistant, Stephanie Young. Stephanie assisted in the difficult chore of identifying appropriate reviewers, a task that proved to be one of the most challenging parts of this process, given the number and diversity of submissions. She also reminded reviewers about deadlines, compiled records, and chased down information. I appreciate all of her help with logistical details during the production of *Communication Yearbook 31*.

Two undergraduate communication majors also provided important research assistance during our efforts to identify additional guest reviewers. Gretchen Cataline, Ohio University and Brittany Pangburn, Saint Mary's College conducted background research on potential guest reviewers, and I am very thankful for the resources that they gathered as I considered possible reviewers for the various submissions.

I appreciate the support and encouragement of my colleagues in the School of Communication Studies at Ohio University as well as Karin Wittig Bates and Linda Bathgate at Lawrence Erlbaum Associates. Further, I continue to be very grateful to the Publications Committee of the International Communication Association for this rich opportunity. This editorial journey has been quite special and rewarding, and I thank the committee for entrusting me with this responsibility.

On a more personal note, I thank my husband, Roger C. Aden, and our girls, Brittany Nicole, Chelsea Meagan, and Emmy Grace. Although I embrace the flexible scheduling afforded by an academic lifestyle, this book still cut into some "wife" and "mom" time, and I appreciate their collective patience as I worked with authors for the past 10 months and, especially, as I put the final touches on this volume. As always, I dedicate my work to them and their profound and inspiring influences on my personal and professional life.

Christina S. Beck

References

Gergen, K. (1991). *The saturated self: Dilemmas of identity in contemporary life.* New York: Basic Books.

Rayner, P. (2006). A need for postmodern fluidity? *Critical Studies in Media Communication, 23,* 345–349.

Chapter 1 Contents

1

Silence in Dispute

Kris Acheson
Arizona State University

Over the past several decades, scholars in communication and other fields working from various paradigmatic and cultural perspectives have found themselves increasingly in opposition over the nature of silence—its meanings, the values that it holds for the people who perform and perceive it, and the ways in which it is used. This chapter reviews recent and germinal literature on silence organized according to dialectical thinking, which allows the inclusion of contradictory definitions of silence, negative and positive perceptions of silence, and performances of silence fulfilling various functions that signify both power and lack of power. The chapter demonstrates that, for a thorough understanding of the nature of silence, a "both/and" approach seems more effective than an "either/or" approach and that studies of silence must be evaluated from within the paradigm in which they were conducted.

Silence in Dispute

What silence is, what it means, and how people use it constitute questions that have long occupied many scholars; yet, no one seems to have definitively answered them. In fact, in the past two decades, scholars from different cultures,[1] various disciplines,[2] and numerous paradigmatic perspectives[3] have responded to Johannesen's (1974) call for more systematic research on silence and found themselves increasingly in opposition to one another over the nature of silence. This dialogue has resulted in a body of literature that offers much conflicting information on the definitions, values, and uses of silence.

In this chapter, I do not argue that such conflict is damaging or should be resolved by a unified theory of silence. Instead, I contend that research on silence has greatly benefited from such interdisciplinary and intercultural debates (see Zuo, 2002) and that a unified theory of silence is probably impossible, as Grabher and Jessner (1996) purported. This chapter strives to prompt greater reflexivity on the part of scholars in their treatment of silence so that they approach the theorizing and/or studying of silence from a carefully considered position with regard to a variety of issues surrounding silence.

In this chapter, I also encourage the use of dialectical ("both/ and" rather than "either/or") thinking about silences. Martin and Nakayama (1999) endorsed such a dialectical approach to research as "a way to think about different ways of knowing in a more comprehensive manner" (p. 13). They warned, however, that accepting dialectics demands an acknowledgment of plurality and messiness and that it often "requires holding two contradictory ideas simultaneously" (p. 14). A paradoxical body of knowledge can thus be built through a variety of epistemologies, provided that each piece of knowledge remains linked to the means and context of knowledge production. This chapter reviews cross-cultural, cross-disciplinary, and cross-paradigmatic literature on silence by identifying and exploring current disputes, some more overt than others, in the definitions of, values for, and uses of silence. In contrast, however, to the common conception of these questions as dichotomous (either/or) in nature, I treat them as dialectical (both/and) or dimensional (more/ less). Thus, each section discusses the complexity that recent and germinal literature reveals regarding contested conceptualizations of silence. Through the use of dialectical thinking, the validity and contributions of seemingly incongruous research on the relationship between silence and speech can be simultaneously recognized.

Definitions of Silence

The Polysemous Nature of Silence

Readers might expect a literature review on silence to begin by defining silence, but the available research is of such an incongruous nature that this seemingly simple task becomes very difficult indeed. As a religious or philosophical phenomenon, for example, silence can be conceptualized as a means of communicating with God, an appropriate way to approach God, and a space through which God speaks (Bauman, 1983; Bill, 2005; Lippard, 1988); alternatively, silence may be a controlled retreat into intrapersonal communication, a refuge in which to engage in reflection, nonverbal awareness, or meditation (A. B. Greene, 1940; Reuter, 2005).

Because silence operates as a *sign* (in a semiotic sense), dependent upon both culture and context for its meanings (Vainiomäki, 2004), it represents many different things to diverse people and even to the same individuals in varied contexts—so much so that Jaworski (1997) recommended thinking of silences metaphorically instead of attempting to delineate one precise definition for silence. The varying definitions of silence seem endless.[4] In Mildorf's (2005) treatment of abuse and power in relationships, silence is *silencing*—the imposed inability to name oneself, events, or others, and the internalization of the naming performed by others—whereas Maitra (2004) also equated silence with silencing but defined it differently as the inability to make oneself understood, such as when a man interprets a woman's *no* as a coy *yes*. Medina (2004) disagreed, arguing that a concept is not meaningful if it is inexpressible, and explored the polyphony of silence from the perspective of its interpreters rather than its performers.

In contrast, Polanyi (1962) wrote of silence as a necessary strategy for communicating the unspeakable: concepts, experience, knowledge, and relationships that defy articulation due to the natural limitations of language. Goffman (1981) separated silences into three categories: silences performed by a speaker within a conversational move, those that separate conversational moves by the same speaker, and those cooperatively performed by multiple speakers between turns, when the floor, so to speak, changes ownership (see also conversational analysts such as Sacks, Schlegloff, & Jefferson, 1974, and Wilson & Zimmerman, 1986). The one constant seems to be that silence is somehow connected to language.

The Relationship of Silence to Language

Picard (1952) claimed that "[s]ilence and language belong together" and "[s]peech must remain in relationship with silence" (pp. 16, 36). Likewise, Chafe (1985) argued that scholars now tend to recognize the inseparability of silence and language in communication research. Researchers might conceptualize silence and speech as opposites or as similarly functioning communicative acts; they might define silence as the absence of speech, or speech as an addition to silence, but they will rarely define (or study) one without the other (see Jaworski, 1998, and Philips, 1985, for examples). Even with this consensus on the relatedness of silence and speech, however, the issue of *how* the two are related remains unresolved. Yet, despite the variety of approaches to silence and researching silence, these differences are far from random. In fact, the ways in which scholars define and study silence intertwine with and often depend upon their given paradigmatic perspectives.[5]

Scholars who either espouse a functionalist point of view or simply take its underlying assumptions for granted in their work (e.g., W. A. Afifi & L. K. Guerrero, 1998; Cappella, 1979, 1980; Cappella & Planalp, 1981; Cramer, Gallant, & Langlois, 2005; Potter & Dillman Carpentier, 2005) tend to view silence as the lack of speech (see also Muñoz-Duston & Kaplan, 1985, for foundational functionalist research on silence). Despite their many differences, social scientific scholars are inclined to treat silence in their work as a *dependent* (e.g., Hasegawa & Gudykunst, 1998; Vangelisti & Caughlin, 1997) or *independent* (e.g., Höllgren, Larsby, Lyxell, & Arlinger, 2005; Johnson, Pearce, Tuten, & Sinclair, 2003; Wagener, Brand, & Kollmeier, 2006) *variable* that can be isolated, operationalized, measured, and compared.

Within the framework of interpretivism, scholars conceptualize silence, much as they do language, as both product and creator of cultural identity (e.g., Buchanan-Aruwafu, Maebiru, & Aruwafu, 2003; J. Coupland & Jaworski, 2003; Nwoye, 1985; P. Williams, 2003). This body of research strives to discover how silence functions as a cultural symbol system (see Basso, 1970, 1996; Philipsen, 1975). Some scholars who conduct research within the interpretive paradigm (e.g., Berman, 1998; Goodall, 2005; Pawelczyk, 2003; Wayne, 1996) continue to conceptualize silence as the absence of speech; others (e.g., Carbaugh, 1995, 1999; Wieder & Pratt, 1990) explicitly define speech as an addition to an active foundation of silence.

Silence from critical perspectives falls into one of two general categories. In a reversal of the traditional speech-as-figure and silence-as-background organization, scholars in the first group (e.g., Bruening, 2005; Carabas & Harter, 2005; Depelchin, 2005; Galasiński & Jaworski, 1997; Hegde, 1996; Jackson, 1998; Jaworski, 1992; Jaworski & Galasiński, 2000; Nakayama & Krizek, 1995) privilege silence over speech as an object of study, equating silence (defined as the absence of speech) either with silencing or with the rhetorical choices of the powerful, which manufactures their perception of silence as a tool of oppression. Alternatively, some scholars conceptualize silence and language as similarly functioning communicative acts and focus on the ability of silence to empower rather than oppress (e.g., Colp-Hansbury, 2004; Dalton & Fatzinger, 2003). Both groups are apt to consider silence as, if not more powerful than words, at least more telling than words.

Based on the few available examples (Clair, 1997, 1998; Scott, 1993, 2000), I would argue that postmodern scholars believe silence and speech to be dialectically related, coinciding in constant tension and thus forming a borderland in which members create culture. Neither silence nor speech is privileged from this viewpoint; they cannot be separated, and one cannot be used as a base concept by which the other is defined. Clair (1998) demonstrated that sometimes silence research is best developed through the concept of self-contained opposites—for example, through a realization that "communication can be silencing and silence can be expressive" (p. 157).

Again, based on a sadly limited set of examples, the Asiacentric and Afrocentric positions appear less concerned with defining silence and more concerned with arguing for its value and explicating ways in which it can be achieved. These scholars portray silence as necessary for balance and harmony in communication, and most portray silence as similar to but somehow above speech—as a highly valued, even superior, form of communication to which cultural members aspire (e.g., Bruneau & Ishii, 1988; Caranfa, 2006; Davies & Ikeno, 2002; Ishii & Bruneau, 1994; Liu, 2001; Matsumoto, 1988).

The complexity and diversity of silence illustrate the importance of reflexivity on the part of scholars so that they may be more aware of their own definitions as well as dissimilar ones. In addition, this same complexity and diversity should serve as motivation for researchers to be more explicit in explaining their conceptions of silence rather than assuming that others define silence in the same ways.

Values for Silence

One of the greatest disparities in research on silence involves the values that people hold for silence—whether they perceive silence as a positive or negative phenomenon. This section discusses the dialectical conception of silence as both good and bad, exploring valences for silence across disciplines such as popular culture, health, business, government, and education. I emphasize the association of silence with the related concepts of silencing, taboos, and secrets, and I offer theoretical explanations for contradictory valences. The section ends with scrutiny of a second dialectic in which silence is both culture specific and cross culturally similar.

The Mixed Valences of Silence Across Disciplines

Popular Culture   In the "West"[6] in general and in the United States in particular, silence appears to have a reputation that *belies* the adage that "silence is golden." According to Scarpi (1987), "Even the most commonplace definition of silence, such as can be found in a school dictionary, is striking in its negative connotations" (p. 21). Many "Western" cultures seem to be biased in favor of speech and against silence (Grabher & Jessner, 1996; Jaworski, 1993; Kim, 2002). Yet, while one need not look far to find examples of negative attitudes toward silence in a wide assortment of "Western" literature and popular culture, digging deeper often results in a more conflicted valuation of silence, since many contrasting positive attitudes exist as well.

Bruneau (1973) characterized the popular music of his time as filled with the "deep, deep silences" of "loneliness, isolation, despair, and rejection" (p. 41). These silences are echoed in popular literature—novels, poetry, even news articles—where authors often (but not always) associate silence with absence, loss, death, darkness, secrets, and forgetting. Berger's (1947) account of silent crowds of New Yorkers, 400,000 strong, who greeted the returning dead of World War II and Bennet's (2005) references to "haunting silence" in the *New York Times* serve as examples, as do Villegas's (2004) *In the Silence Absence Makes* and Greenberg's (2002) *The Dog of Memory: A Family Album of Secrets and Silences.*

This negativity connected with silence becomes all the more striking in contrast to silence's positive valence as present in popular literature from other parts of the world, such as Mexican author Manuel Aguilar-Moreno's (2003) *La Perfección del Silencio* and the Indian fables of the Panchatantra that teach the virtues of holding one's tongue (Kirkwood, 1987). In 1996, Mair completed a multicorpus analysis of spoken and written English to determine which types of adjectives commonly modify the word *silence*, and the results were overwhelmingly negative. With frequent negative premodifications like *awful, awkward, sepulchral,* and *uncanny,* silence was "metaphorically cast as cold, deep, and deadly ... and speaking if not roaring, screaming and deafening" (p. 21).

Despite this weighty evidence, though, the valence for silence expressed in popular "Western" literature is not homogenous. In a recent nonfictional work on solitude, Barbour (2004) discussed silence quite approvingly, portraying it as a wise and virtuous choice. Likewise, despite the frequency of negative adjectives associated with silence, others link positive modifiers like *elegant* (Nicholls, 2005), *comfortable* (Lauer, 2005), *sacred* (Moore, 2005), and *healthy* (Reuter, 2005) with silence. Notably, "Westerners" would not speak of that proverbial *golden* silence unless silence can be, at least occasionally, appropriate, valued, and desirable.

Health and Medicine   In the "West," silence also holds conflicting valences in the fields of health and medicine. Montalbano-Phelps (2003) denounced silence as unhealthy in her treatise on communication between family members. Likewise, Woodstock (2001) problematized the silences that surround suicide, juxtaposing the conception of storytelling as therapeutically rewarding and the social unacceptability of some stories (like her mother's suicide). Similarly, Carabas and Harter (2005) critiqued silent suffering in Romania, where oppressed citizens concealed their state-induced injuries and illnesses for fear of reprisal. Many researchers condemn such silencing as a cause of depression (Cramer et al., 2005; Piran & Cormier, 2005).

Zhang and Siminoff (2003), Ufema (2005), and Feldman-Stewart, Brundage, and Tishelman (2005) continued this theme of unhealthy silence, arguing that silences between oncologists and patients and between cancer patients and their families constitute (potentially harmful) cases of failed communication.[7] Furthermore, contrary to the Chinese medical practice of keeping bad news from cancer patients, codes of ethics in the United States dictate that medical practitioners should be forthright and forthcoming with their patients concerning diagnoses and prognoses, no matter how grim; a doctor's silence in such cases would be perceived by colleagues and patients as unethical (Tse, Chong, & Fok, 2003).

Psychoanalysts comprise some of the few in the field of health who acknowledge the value of silence—at least as a tool of the analyst to encourage patient talk. Yet, when the patient chooses to be silent as well (or is unable to break silence), the analyst is gripped by "the unease, the sense of impotence [of] sitting with silent patients" (Schön, 1987, p. 8), and psychoanalysts may attribute silence, once again negatively, to a defect in the communicative skill or mental health of the patient. Because of its roots in ancient Greece, "Western" medicine (psychology included) tends to equate silence with death and illness, so lack of physical voice becomes a sign of weakness and impotence (Cosi, 1987), hysteria and depression (Ciani, 1987), or mental illness (Schön, 1987). This negativity might also be linked to Descartes' metaphor of malfunction (Kim, 2002; Scollon, 1985), a metaphor evident in Palfreman's (1993) video production and the 2005 *People* article by Fields-Meyer, Duffy, and Arias that portrayed autistic children as trapped in the silence caused by their jammed communication.

A recent trend in the field of health, however, directly contradicts these portrayals of silence as unhealthy. Young (2002) encouraged nurses to honor silent patients and learn to employ silence in an ethics of caring. Subsequently, after the *Journal of the American Medical Association* published an article, "The Therapeutic Value of Silence" (2003), the health literature exploded with articles advising people to seek out silence in their lives for the sake of their health and sanity (see Lowenstein, 2005; Reuter, 2005; Wright, 2005). *Prevention* magazine printed an article that urged readers to noise-proof their homes in an attempt to boost health, claiming that shutting out exterior noise and choosing quieter appliances would prevent everything from hearing damage to overeating and chemical imbalances (Gordon, 2005). Wright also advised busy people to retreat into silence and solitude to refresh their spirits.

One distinction between these arguments and the earlier negative approaches to silence in the field of health could be the relational factor—that is, that silence between people in a relationship is unhealthy, while seeking some "alone-time" for quiet reflection is healthy. Yet, this generalization does not necessarily apply to all of the positive attitudes toward silence in the literature. Lowenstein's (2005) recent article, titled "Shut Up and Heal," also recommended dedicating a few moments each day to relational silence. In contrast to earlier arguments on the unhealthy effects of staying quiet, however, she claimed that silence is inaccurately "associated with bottled-up energy and forced-down feelings." She maintained that "silence serves not to close us down but to open us up" (p. 93). Additionally,

Reuter (2005) argued that silence functions as an effective method of protecting one's sanity and emotional health in relationships, contending that "[s]ilence introduces a delay in our actions by curbing the tendency to form rapid conclusions and inferences ... With silence, a more balanced evaluation follows; reactions [to others] based on that evaluation are more appropriate, sane, and healthy" (p. 436).

Business   Experts often give contradictory advice for business situations as well. Bogoroch-Ditkofsky (2005) claimed that there "are times when keeping quiet is simply not a sound business strategy." She dwelled on anecdotes illustrating "silences that sting, bruise and hurt, cause disappointment and even evoke feelings of despair" (p. 189). Moore (2005) told a different story, though, of becoming "a better communicator by keeping your mouth shut" (p. 8). He purported that transferring skills and practices of silence that he learned living in a monastery during his young adulthood to his family life and his corporate relationships made him not only a happier person but also a more successful executive officer. J. Taylor and Mackenzie (1983) encouraged salespeople to learn the value of silence, and Lauer (2005) concurred, exemplifying ways in which "talking too much can literally kill a business deal" and "shutting up is an art" (p. 22).

Another critical body of literature on silence versus voice in the workplace has also developed. Buzzanell (1994) offered a feminist critique of organizations that silence women while Meares, Oetzel, Torres, Derkacs, and Ginossar (2004) described silencing based on cultural rather than gendered identities. Other scholars (Brown & C. Coupland, 2005; Milliken, Morrison, & Hewlin, 2003; Pinder & Harlos, 2001) questioned silences within the hierarchy of organizations, exploring reasons for and effects of management's silencing of employees. In addition, Trethewey (1997) examined silencing of customers in the client–organization relationship, and Mumby and Putnam (1992), in their germinal research on bounded emotionality, revealed how emotional experience in traditional (patriarchal) organizational structures becomes silenced through its relegation to the private sphere and its degradation as an unfit criteria for decision making. Although many characterize silencing as harmful (see the section on silencing), Morrison and Milliken (2003) implied positive valences for other-oriented silences motivated by concern for group cohesiveness and/or individual face-saving.

Religion Turning to discourse about religion in the "Western" world, we again encounter conflicting messages about the valence of silence. At times, scholars associate silence with wrong-doing or even call it outright evil, as in all of the following books:

- *The Silence We Keep: One Nun's View of the Catholic Priest Scandal* (Jackowski, 2004)
- *In Darkness and Secrecy: The Anthropology of Assault Sorcery and Witchcraft in Amazonia* (Whitehead & Wright, 2004)
- *Sacred Silence: Denial and Crisis in the Church* (Cozzens, 2002)
- *Breaking the Conspiracy of Silence: Christian Churches and the Global AIDS Crisis* (Messer, 2004)

Yet, some religious groups, from Quakers (Bauman, 1983; Bill, 2005; Lippard, 1988) to Pentecostals (Maltz, 1985), celebrate silence and regularly use both solitary and communal silence in their worship. Moreover, Keizer (2005) recently reminded Christians of all denominations that Jesus could be a fairly silent person himself. Not only did he withhold comment regarding many topics on which modern Christians seek direction, but Biblical texts often depict Jesus as refusing to speak, answering tersely or cryptically, or replying to questions with questions. Silence is also inseparable from the spirituality of some Native American groups, as Keith Basso (1996) described in his ethnographic work with the Western Apaches, *Wisdom Sits in Places*, where the land actively, silently, and constantly reminds people of their morality.

Education The field of education also offers both negative and positive examples of silence in the "West." In the United States, some critics argue that the classroom should embody its professed democratic ideals (hooks, 1993). Our educational system apparently fails in this goal, however. Critical and feminist scholars have taken teachers to task countless times in the past two decades, pointing out problematic student silences in the classroom of women (Bell & Golombisky, 2004; Gallas, 1997; Jaworski, 1993; Julé, 2004; Rich, 1979), ethnic minorities (Carbaugh, 1995; hooks, 1993; Reyes, J. D. Scribner, & A. P. Scribner, 1999; Minh-ha, 1990), religious minorities

(Eckstein & Turman, 2002), non-native English speakers (Duncan, 2004; Nelson, 1995; Valenzuela, 1999), and queers (Anzaldúa, 1990; Duncan, 2004; Winans, 2006). Critics connect student silences with injustice, inhibition, lack of cultural knowledge or social skills, and pressure to conform to stereotypes; they frame breaking these silences as beneficial (Epstein, O'Flynn, & Telford, 2003; Langhout, 2005; Zhou, Knoke, & Sakamoto, 2005).

Students are not alone in performing or experiencing silencing. Despite current trends in the United States toward more democratic and student-centered classrooms, teachers' own silences can indicate and perpetuate a large power differential between instructor and students when silence becomes a tool of punishment or censure (Gilmore, 1985). Additionally, J. Blase and J. R. Blase (2003) portrayed teachers as silenced by administrators, and Skrla, Reyes, and Scheurich (2000) discussed instances of communities or institutional structures silencing female administrators.

Yet, a line of research rapidly growing in popularity paints quite a different portrait of silence in education—one where silence is precious, and worthy as an object of study (Caranfa, 2006; Patten, 1997) and a means of teaching/learning (Jaworski & Sachdev, 1998; Kalamaras, 1994). Patten described a course that he designed and taught on "discovering silence," in which his students explored the intersections of silence with poetry, music, and the body and learned to find and appreciate silences in their lives. Jaworski and Sachdev suggested that, from the perspective of students, silence generally seems unmarked (a normal state of being) in the classroom and operates as a useful tool for knowledge acquisition since it enables listening. Similarly, Hawk (2003) and Kameen (2000) contended that, although it may feel like silencing, demanding silent reflection after comments or performances in the classroom rather than allowing counterarguments can create a space where attempting to understand and not formulating a response becomes the purpose of listening. Based on traditions of Christian mysticism or Buddhist and Confucian philosophies, other scholars (Kalamaras, 1994; Zembylas & Pavlos, 2004) have also argued in favor of silence as an epistemology.

Government, Law, and Politics   Government (including law and politics) comprises the one area that unequivocally treats silence as negative. Many cultures in the United States, as in other "Western" countries, have developed a distrust of silence regarding the government, not surprising given the consistent connection between silence and guilt (Smith, 2001; Stroińska, 2000; Walker, 1985). Walker observed the guilt attributed to defendants when they choose to "plead the Fifth" or remain silent too long before answering questions. Another example in the courts involves the inevitable adverse inferences drawn in the "deafening" silence of inadequate supporting evidence, such as when a defendant claims to have been at a particular place at a particular time but lacks witnesses to support the statement (Morman, 2005, p. 38). Furthermore, Jaworski (1997) described the detrimental effect on one's credibility of testifying to something after remaining silent on the subject earlier, since the court may interpret the breaking of silence in such cases as a poor reflection on a witness's character.

The equation of silence with guilt also occurs in critical examinations of historical accounts, where scholars contend that guilty regimes, administrations, governments, and leaders create silence around their present and past disreputable actions (Carabas & Harter, 2005; "Palocci Under Siege," 2005; Smith, 2001; Stroińska, 2000; Tent, 2003). Valone and Kinealy's (2002) treatment of the erasure of the Irish potato famine and Wilkinson's (2002) exposé on politically motivated atrocities in Guatemala demonstrate that silences imposed by colonial rulers and military dictators, in particular, can foster suspicions of conspiracy and deception.

Even when it stems from members of the U.S. government, though, silence still carries the negative connotations of guilt (Borjesson, 2004; Stephenson, 1982), impotence (Brummett, 1980), and passivity (A. Guerrero, 2002; Pitt, 2003). For example, a recent *CQ Researcher* issue devoted to government secrecy posed and answered (affirmatively) the questions, "Is too much information kept from the public?" "Should the government classify less information?" "Has the Bush administration misused government secrecy?" and "Should Congress make it easier to obtain government records?" (Jost, 2005, pp. 1005–1006). Clearly, the U.S. media most often construe silence between governments and the public as negative.

Negative Associations of Silence

The preceding examples suggest that the valuation of some silences as negative rather than positive occurs quite commonly in the United

States and other "Western" cultures. Although I argue in this chapter that silence can carry both positive and negative valences for different people or for the same people under different circumstances, I believe that the frequency of negativity in "Western" perceptions of silence deserves further attention. What could be the reasons for this negative valence? Perhaps part of the responsibility lies in associations between silence and silencing, secrets, and taboos.

Silencing   Some scholars equate silence with silencing, transferring the negative connotations of the one to the other. Dadge (2005) discussed media silence as censorship; Leander (2002) examined classroom silence as silencing using discourse analysis, and Natapoff (2005) problematized the complexity of the U.S. legal system for silencing uneducated defendants. In addition, Bruening (2005) and Bruening, Armstrong, and Pastore (2005) interpreted the silence and invisibility of women of color in sports as systemic and discursive silencing. Scarpi (1987) maintained that such imposed silence, or "silence born of a condition of subjection," is "dangerous in that it may coincide with oblivion, negation and the loss of the individual's identity" (p. 37). Poyatos (2002) concluded that this imposed silence is so painful and the threat of it so feared that we "tend to identify silence itself with it" (p. 318).

Much communication literature equates silence with silencing as well, especially literature of a critical nature (e.g., feminist and postcolonial writings). To many critical scholars, silence symbolizes lack of voice and therefore carries the negative associations of oppression, marginalization, lack of agency, loss of culture, lack of power, and the inability to express oneself or ascribe one's own identity (Carabas & Harter, 2005; Clair, 1998; Conn, 2004; Hegde, 1996; Houppert, 1999; Jaworski, 1992, 1993; Kramarae, Schulz, & O'Barr, 1984; Raab, 1996; Rubik, 1996; Scollon, 1985; Wayne, 1996). Two recent works on African history illustrate critical scholars' interpretations of silence as a sign and means of oppression (Bailey, 2005; Depelchin, 2005). Also, based on Foucault's work on systemically imposed silence (1972, 2001), poststructuralist theorist Judith Butler (1997) explained the silencing (as lack of agency) that occurs through interpellation.[8]

A good deal of the communication literature on silencing comes from the field of rhetoric. Feminist rhetorical scholars such as Kathleen Hall Jamieson (1988) and Karlyn Kohrs Campbell (1973, 1989b, 2002) began in the 1970s and 1980s to criticize their field for silencing the voices of women. Others followed their lead—for example, Blair, Brown, and Baxter (1994), with a cutting critique of the communication academic community for its silencing of women. Campbell (1989a), as well as other feminists like K. A. Foss and S. K. Foss (1996), also published collected volumes of speeches by women, since part of their criticism of rhetoric involves the conspicuous absence of women speakers in general collections. Carlson (1994) provided another example of this attempt to introduce female rhetors as the object of the study of rhetoric. She identified Aspasia of Miletus as a female Greek philosopher and rhetor who was silenced/erased/forgotten. In addition, Campbell (2001), Dow and Condit (2005), S. K. Foss and Griffin (1995), K. A. Foss, S. K. Foss, and Griffin (2004), and Griffin (1993) have produced work on feminist rhetorical theory in an effort to counteract the dearth of such literature.

Other feminists protest the silencing of women as well. Tillie Olsen (1978) authored a landmark book on the myriad ways in which women writers experience silencing, including exhaustion from juggling the call of creativity and their responsibilities, economic realities that prevent them from writing for a living, the knife of the perfectionist attitude, and prejudices about the type of writing that women are "supposed" to produce. Audre Lorde's speech, "The Transformation of Silence to Language and Action" (1984), expressed not only ways in which she has been silenced, but also her determination to overcome this silencing.[9] Wood (1992, 1996) explored the silencing of women through acts of sexual harassment and their surrounding discourses, and many feminists (Daly, 1978, 1984; Gowen, 1991; Jamieson, 1995; Kramarae, 1981; Kramarae et al., 1984) have noted that the patriarchal nature of language itself constrains and subjugates women. They have argued for various ways of resisting this domination by exposing the silencing of women in critical analyses (Houston & Kramarae, 1991), taking control of language with creative use of existing words (Jamieson, 1995), (re)appropriating words and (re)discovering their feminine meanings (Daly & Caputi, 1987), or inventing new words that better express the experiences of women (Rakow & Kramarae, 1990).

Additionally, scholars have examined the silencing of other groups. Women of color (Bruening, 2005; Etter-Lewis, 1991; Hegde, 1998; hooks, 1984, 1993) often protest that they have been silenced, even within or by feminist and civil rights movements. Furthermore, queer writers such as Lorde (1984), Butler (1993), and Rich (1979) observed the intersectionality among the ways in which they are oppressed, or the reasons for their oppression. Scholars also demonstrate concern for silencing in cases where marginalized or colonized groups experience language domination or erasure (Adera & Ahmed, 1995; Marlow & Giles, 2006; Pratt & Buchanan, 2004) and where either censorship or self-censorship occurs (Splichal, 2006).

Moreover, Mark Orbe (1994, 1995) applied muted group theory (E. Ardener, 1975; S. Ardener, 1978)—originally constructed to explain the silencing of women—to other groups such as African-American men; Pelias (2002) demonstrated how fathers and sons can feel silenced with regard to certain subjects, and Sparkes (2002) criticized academic gatekeepers who throttle researchers' individual and cultural voices by insisting on objectivity and the removal of the self from scholarship. Finally, several decades of research contribute to a body of literature on Elisabeth Noelle-Neumann's theory of the *spiral of silence* (1974), which explains how people feel silenced when their opinions differ from those of the majority.[10]

Secrets   Silence also surfaces as a common theme, albeit with a much less critical edge, in interpersonal and family communication literature, where it may be called silencing (Solomon, Knobloch, & Fitzpatrick, 2004). However, researchers more frequently dub it secret-keeping (Bradshaw, 1995; Brown-Smith, 1998; L. K. Guerrero & W. A. Afifi, 1995; Hunt & Paine-Gernee, 1994; Imber-Black, 1998; Vangelisti, 1994; Vangelisti & Caughlin, 1997; Vangelisti, Caughlin, & Timmerman, 2001), topic avoidance (W. A. Afifi & Burgoon, 1998; Baxter & Wilmot, 1985), or nondisclosure (Cant, 2006; Derlega, Metts, Petronio, & Margulis, 1993; Dindia & Allen, 1992; K. Greene & Serovich, 1996).

Of the three, topic avoidance probably portrays silence in the least negative way as a natural phenomenon that, in moderation, does not damage interpersonal relationships (W. A. Afifi & L. K. Guerrero, 1998; see also a related review by Goldsmith, Miller, & Caughlin, this volume). Nondisclosure leans toward negativity; for example, Petronio's (1991, 2000, 2002) communication boundary management theory associates disclosure with openness and silence with closedness in relationships, implying that closedness (and therefore silence) is less healthy or desirable. Secrets, however, constitute by far the most negative of these interpersonal silences. Goodall (2005) described his family secrets as toxic, and others treated secrets within families primarily as silencing that resulted from abuse or other power dynamics (T. D. Afifi & L. N. Olson, 2005; T. D. Afifi, L. N. Olson, & Armstrong, 2005).

Taboos   Silence also takes the form of linguistic taboo, or restrictions on speech, that can affect the value of silence in cultures that champion freedom of speech and equate speech with empowerment. Early anthropologists defined taboo (then spelled *tabu*) as a negative sanction against participation in dangerous situations (Mead, 1939; Steiner, 1956). Later, taboo came to mean a linguistic prohibition of a sacred or inviolable nature (Hardin, 1973). Just as the taboos studied in early twentieth-century anthropology kept "primitive" tribes away from volcano mouths and venomous snakes, linguistic taboos in any society protect its members from some sort of danger, real or imagined.

As a general rule,[11] people do not talk about what they fear or do not understand, what might cause conflict, and what they would like to forget (Cline, 1997; Hardin, 1973; Mead, 1939; Steiner, 1956). In the United States, for example, the subject of death is "surrounded by disapproval and shame" (Feifel, 1963, p. 14). According to Cline, we fear our own deaths, our losses when people we love die, and others' reactions to our grief and pain. For these reasons, younger people often seem uneasy when the aged mention their mortality, and even medical professionals sometimes talk around rather than about death (N. Coupland & J. Coupland, 1997).

Moreover, in this day and age in the United States, people tend to treat anything that might offend other people or make them uncomfortable as taboo. Axtel (1985) gave travelers advice on international taboos—on what *not* to say in various parts of the world. Likewise, because of a fear of controversy, school boards constantly issue updated lists of banned books, restricted topics, and forbidden terms; they censure to avoid giving offense (Sanchez, 2003). Interestingly, some in the United States react to the linguistic restrictions placed upon them by rebelling, causing a backlash against political correctness and taboos of all kinds (Hardin, 1973). People now poke fun at politically correct job titles and other euphemisms, and many urge the wholesale violation of taboos surrounding everything from death (Cline, 1997) to menstruation (Houppert, 1999), sexual molestation (S. C. Taylor, 2001), and female adolescent sexual desire (Welles, 2005). Resentment toward political correctness and taboos, for some, may somehow taint silence as a whole.

Theoretical Explanations for the Valences of Silence

The interpersonal communication theory of expectancy violations (Burgoon & Hale, 1988) may shed some light on the valences of silence. Some scholars argue that "Westerners" often perceive silence to be bad because they only notice it when they expect to hear speech, such as when an ordinary pause becomes too long. Brummett (1980), Scollon (1985), and Walker (1985) all claimed that humans naturally react to such violations of expectations regarding silence with discomfort or displeasure. Regardless of a culture's general trend toward a positive or negative valence, in practice, silence can be perceived as both positive and negative in every culture, "as it is measured against what is expected in that context" (Tannen, 1985, p. 98). If interactants anticipate silence, then they will receive it positively; if they expect speech, silence in place of the appropriate speech will be viewed negatively.

Thus, if Ehrenhaus (1988) was correct in his claim that "Westerners" carry an ever present expectation "for the presence of speech, as the pervasive mode of symbolic expression," then mainstream "Western" cultures likely hold a negative valence for silence because it counters expectations (p. 42). Moreover, even for cultures that generally valuate silence positively, occurrences of silence that violate an expectation of speech might also carry a negative valence. Poyatos (1983, 2002) and Enninger (1991) described silence in place of anticipated speech as *zero-signs*, and they noted that people tend to interpret such silences unfavorably as stemming from disrespect, laziness, anger or other strong emotions, malevolency, or lack of understanding or competence.

Other scholars assert that, since "Western" societies have tended to view silence as a lack of life, sound, and other "good" things, members consider the absence as negative (Ehrenhaus, 1988; Grabher & Jessner, 1996). Poyatos (2002), in fact, offered an especially in-depth comparison of silence and stillness, which he claimed are the polar opposites of sound and movement in the same way that darkness is the opposite of light. According to Poyatos, "[Just] as we perceive light and sound as activities, as something alive, darkness and silence evoke for us the emptiness of what is dead or, at most, asleep and inactive" (p. 294).

Yet another possible reason for the generally negative valence of silence in the "West" involves "Western" culture's preference for a rather low-context communication style—performing and demanding that others perform communicative acts in fairly direct, explicit, and verbal ways (Lehtonen & Sajavaara, 1985). McKinney's (1982) finding that groups view reticent members as ineffectual and rarely offer them positions of leadership illustrates this preference for directness. Ehrenhaus (1988) observed that, unlike "verbal communication, silence cannot direct interpretation ... [it] cannot tell us what it means" (p. 42). Tannen (1985) asserted that, of all nonverbal communication, "[s]ilence is the extreme manifestation of indirectness" (p. 97). Thus, silence would naturally not be preferred as a means of communication by members of these "low-context" cultures, given its location on the indirect end of the spectrum.

Finally, some scholars have proposed that the extent to which people value silence could vary as a result of how their cultural groups use silence and what meanings they attribute to it (Lehtonen & Sajavaara, 1985). This reasoning, of course, implies that different people use and value silence in diverse ways, which scholars in the "West" did not really consider until the past few decades (Kim, 2002). Since Basso's (1970) groundbreaking[12] study on silence in a Western Apache community, though, researchers in intercultural communication have begun to explore silence in both cross-cultural and intercultural studies (Braithwaite, 1990; Enninger, 1991; Hasegawa & Gudykunst, 1998).[13]

Differing Valences for Silence Across or Within Cultures

Kim (2002) observed that the "West" holds a particular penchant for polarization, which might explain why cross-cultural studies on silence are usually conceptually organized around an "East/West" dichotomy, with Native American, East Asian, or other cultures contrasted against the "norm" of "Western" views of silence (Jaworski, 1993). Basso (1970, 1996), Braithwaite (1990), Carbaugh (1995, 1999), and Wieder and Pratt (1990) all noted that the value for silence in various Native American communities can vary dramatically from that of more mainstream U.S. cultures. Basso, for instance, portrayed silence in Western Apache culture as a much valued communicative strategy in interpersonal relationships, a facework[14] strategy that demonstrates respect for another person or functions as an appropriate response to uncertainty. Brandt (1980) described the importance of internal and external secret-keeping to the maintenance of Pueblo religion and politics.

Additionally, Carbaugh (1999) wrote that the Blackfoot culture, contrary to other "Western" cultures, "valorizes 'listening' as a communicative form" and "utilizes silence as a communal means for increasing understanding of oneself and one's environment" (p. 265). Since these communities employ silence more frequently and in varied situations, for additional (and different) purposes, and for longer periods of time than in more typical "Western" cultures, these researchers argue that alternatives exist to the "Western" perceptions of silence.

A second grouping of studies, including Bruneau and Ishii (1988), Davies and Ikeno (2002), Hasegawa and Gudykunst (1998), Ishii and Bruneau (1994), Matsumoto (1988), and Morsbach (1988), focused on the importance of silence in Japanese communication, where silence (placed in opposition to its role in "Western" cultures) comprises an essential component of being and therefore of interacting with others. Matsumoto, in defining the Japanese communication style of *haragei*, offered an excellent example of the positive valence of silence for the Japanese, noting that it constitutes "the least confrontational form of negotiation ... [an] actor's ability to express his feelings directly to his audience without doing or saying anything" (p. 23) and the minimization of "verbal exchanges in favor of 'wordy' silence or *ma* (pauses pregnant with meaning)" (p. 27). Similarly, Davies and Ikeno illustrated the Japanese communicative strategy of *chinmoku* (silence), juxtaposing Japanese concepts and uses of silence with those "in Western countries" (p. 51).

Of course, not all cross-cultural research on silence supports this "East/West" dichotomy. Intracultural studies on Finnish culture (Lehtonen & Sajavaara, 1985; Sajavaara & Lehtonen, 1997) and on intercultural interaction between Finns and foreigners (Carbaugh, 2005) demonstrate that the Finnish culture differs from other "Western" cultures regarding the specific issue of silence. This distinction is evident not only in the Finnish uses and meanings of silence (see Carbaugh for examples from ethnographic data) but also in the values for silence, since Finns appreciate silence much more highly than, say, other European groups or many U.S. Americans (see Lehtonen & Sajavaara, 1985; Sajavaara & Lehtonen, 1997). Kalamaras's (1994) application of silence as a state of knowing or learning (similar to that described in the work of Carbaugh with the Blackfoot) to the writing classroom also serves as a useful example.

Exemplifying the dialectic nature of silence marks another recent trend in communication literature: a return to intracultural examinations of silence (Clair, 1997, 1998; Huckin, 2002; Lippard, 1988). Until the 1970s, silence research in the "West" was entirely intracultural because cultural differences in the value or uses of silence remained generally unacknowledged (e.g., Newman, 1982). Once scholars began to recognize some of those differences, cross-cultural studies to explore those differences comparatively (see Sobkowiak's 1997 application of markedness theory to silence and speech) and intercultural studies to gauge the effects of those differences on intercultural communication (e.g., Dendrinos & Pedro, 1997; Enninger, 1991; Feldstein & Crown, 1990; Houck & Gass, 1997; Jaworski, 2000; Liu, 2001) grew in popularity.

However, scholars began to recognize the complexity of communicative silences even within the same culture, subsequently returning to intracultural research (e.g., N. Coupland & J. Coupland, 1997; Hall, Sarangi, & Slembrouck, 1997; Pelias, 2002). In this trend, scholars pursue varied uses of silence, carrying both negative and positive valences, within the same cultural group. Examples of this tendency include Jaska and Stech's (1978) examination of Trappist monk culture and Jaworski and Stephens's (1998) study on silence as a communicative strategy of the hearing impaired. Therefore, even when the studies focus on (or are located within) "Western" cultures, much of this work emphasizes more positive associations of silence (Acheson, 2006; Bauman, 1983; Lippard, 1988; Maltz, 1985) than does other research by "Western" scholars.

Unlike critical scholars who tend to treat silence as an oppressive state, some researchers involved in this new wave of work view silence as libratory (Duncan, 2004; C. Miller, 1996). As early as Bruneau (1973), scholars recognized the power of silence as a method of protest. Bruneau noted the persuasive strength of "the righteous indignation of persons refraining from speech who are silently resolute and convinced in their belief" (p. 35). More recently, C. Miller discussed how, in the work of African-Caribbean author Marlene Nourbese

Philip, marginalized people forced to speak a hegemonic language find silence to be empowering and meaningful. Fanon (1967) explained the hegemony of language within the context of colonization:

> The Negro of the Antilles will be proportionately whiter—that is, he will come closer to being a real human being—in direct ratio to his mastery of the French language.... Every colonized people—in other words, every people in whose soul an inferiority complex has been created by the death and burial of its local cultural originality—finds itself face to face with the language of the civilizing nation. (p. 18)

In the face of such hegemony, then, silence can become a very powerful means of protesting the elevated status of the language and culture of the colonizers. Similarly, Duncan explored the resistance of some Asian-American women to marginalization through strategic silence, which for them constitutes a refusal to participate in the roles assigned them by society. Butler (2005) described such a silence as a refusal to give an account of oneself (to tell one's story, justify one's actions, or prove one's innocence) when authority figures demand an account. Other scholars (Clair, 1997, 1998; Colp-Hansbury, 2004; Dalton & Fatzinger, 2003) have told similar tales of protest through silence. By belying some of the generalizations in this chapter concerning the generally negative valence of silence in the "West," these researchers remind us of the necessity in our postmodern world of pluralizing silence to silences (if not linguistically, at least conceptually) in recognition of its fragmented, disjointed, and contradictory nature.

Uses of Silence

This section examines how silence functions for humans as a form of communication, including silence as a (1) context-dependent communicative tool, (2) culturally dependent identity marker, and (3) form of enculturation. For each of these uses of silence, I explore a central debate vis-à-vis silence: the relationship of silence to power.

The Power of Silence

Whether scholars perceive silence as more negative or positive (or both), few deny that it is powerful (Bruneau, 1973; Ganguly, 1968;

Stephenson, 1982). Silence can, in fact, be "a virtually inviolable position of strength over the burden of talking" (Sontag, 1969, p. 17). Convinced of silence's ability to persuade and defy, Duncan (2004) and Colp-Hansbury (2004), among others, explained the power of silence in two ways. The first explanation stems from silence's ability to gain notice. According to Duncan, marginalized voices may be out-shouted until hegemonic opponents realize that those voices have "left" the argument; deliberate silence often becomes quite noticeable, especially when marginalized voices refuse to "echo" those in power. Colp-Hansbury asserted an equally important second explanation—silence's capacity for cooperative meaning construction—since the ambiguity of silence can enable individuals to disarm opponents, making them more willing to enter the discussion, and also allow multiple participants in an interaction to co-create meanings by interpreting the message in the silence for themselves.

Other scholars, even those with negative views of silence, also attribute the power of silence to its ambiguity (Jaworski, 1993; Tannen, 1985). Tannen argued that silence is polysemous. Jaworski contended that it "has many faces" (p. 24)—so many, in fact, that Minh-ha (1990) referred to silence as a distinct language. Schön (1987) agreed, asserting that "silence can have all the meanings that words have, just as in music[15] the pauses and the notes have numberless expressive functions" (p. 16). Matsumoto (1988) even purported that silence in Japan has *more* meanings than words.

Organizing Functions of Silence

Obviously, the debate surrounding power and silence does not focus on whether or not the experience of silence can be powerful. Instead, many scholars disagree over whether the use of silence indicates power or the lack thereof in those who wield silence. Shedding light on the contested relationship between silence and power, therefore, requires that we organize the uses of silence in some way. The question remains, though, of the best way to do so.

Jensen (1973) categorized silence into five functions: linking, affecting, revelational, judgmental, and activating. Saville-Troike (1985) provided another way to organize the myriad uses of silence, proposing an etic taxonomy of functions categorized into institutionally determined, group-determined, and individually determined silences (pp. 16–17).[16] Poyatos (1983, 2002) offered yet another taxonomy for organizing silence, based on semiotics rather than the functions of silence. He separated silences into *non-signs* (noncommunicative because they are not interactive), *signs proper* (signifying meaning themselves, not as a replacement for sound or word), *zero-signs* (where the absence of expected speech actually signifies), and *carriers of signs* (where silences add meaning to other signs or activities that they precede, follow, or contain).

The organization of silences in this section, however, follows none of these taxonomies. Unlike developers of taxonomies, who exhaustively attempt to classify their objects of study, I make no attempt to be comprehensive in my exploration of the uses of silence and do not claim to create categories that do not overlap. Since I aim to clarify the complex relationship between silence and power through dialectical thinking, I use a narrower, deeper, and messier organizing technique than these more familiar taxonomies. In the following section, I discuss three types of silences—context-dependent tools, markers of identity, and means of enculturation—without implying that an example of silence would necessarily fit into only one of the categories or that these types of silence represent the only ones that humans use to communicate.[17]

Situational Uses of Silence

The following six examples of silences could be deemed *situational uses* of silence. These silences comprise context-dependent communicative tools that can express emotions, relational messages, cognitive processes, and specific semantic propositions. They could affect the distance/closeness of interpersonal relationships, or they may cause change on the interactional level by affecting the speech or actions of others (e.g., demands and requests can be made or met with silence). Sometimes, they attempt or accomplish several of these purposes simultaneously. Yet, the following six groupings of situational uses of silence also tackle the question of whether or not silence stems from power. Because the capability of using silence as a communicative tool in these contexts implies some degree of agency, the silence/power relationship becomes complicated and unclear even in seemingly forced silences (Gal, 1994).

Stimulus of Expectation or Instrument of Emphasis   Alfred Hitchcock's ability to create suspense was legendary, and part of his
repertoire for creating a sense of expectation in the audience involved
a strategic use of silence (Hemmeter, 1996). Advertisers, in addition
to movie-makers, remain well aware that the use of silence comprises
a wonderfully effective way to capture an audience's attention, set
the mood of an advertisement, elicit emotion (such as sadness, peace,
or anxiety) in listeners and viewers, and improve the retention of
information offered in an ad (G. D. Olsen, 1994). In fact, G. D. Olsen
(1995) found using silence just before and after important information in an advertisement to be by far the best way of encouraging
notice and retention of that information, more so than any other
arrangement of background noise. This finding is certainly not news
to conversation and discourse analysts, who have long been aware
that people often use silence in interactions to organize and punc-
tuate discourse, to gain attention, and to emphasize specific parts
of verbal communication (Chafe, 1985; Jaworski, 1993; Meise, 1996;
Saville-Troike, 1985; Zuo, 2002). Bruneau (1973) asserted that speech
becomes meaningful when broken by silences; without pauses to
help listeners parse sounds, speech is only so much noise. Moreover, Saville-Troike argued that silence serves as an effective tool for
intensifying and/or emphasizing verbal messages. Regardless of purpose, this type of silence functions as an available tool, consciously
strategic or otherwise, for speakers actively involved in communicative interactions with others.

Display of Intense Emotion   In many cultures, intense emotions
are considered inexpressible in words. According to Bruneau (1973),
"Intense grief, sorrow, and great disappointment are quiet states—
words are difficult to find.... In short: Silence is the language of all
strong passions" (p. 34). In other cultures (e.g., South Korea, according to Kim, 1992), the expression of emotion with silence is socially
prescribed rather than linguistically impossible; for these peoples,
strong emotion constitutes a private matter whose public verbal
acknowledgment is culturally inappropriate (Wardhaugh, 2002).
Whether due to impossibility or inappropriateness, though, research
verifies that silence expresses a wide range of emotions in many different cultures, accompanied at some times by kinesthetic forms of
nonverbal communication and, at other times, only by stillness:

- anger/disapproval (Jaworski, 1993; Kim, 2002; Saunders, 1985; Saville-Troike, 1985)
- fear (Bruneau, 1973; Hemmeter, 1996)
- embarrassment/shame (Bruneau, 1973; Nwoye, 1985; Saunders, 1985; Schön, 1987)
- grief (Basso, 1970; Berger, 1947; Braithwaite, 1990; Bruneau, 1973; Clair, 1998; Cline, 1997; Fox, 1974; Nwoye, 1985; Wardhaugh, 2002; Woodstock, 2001).

These silences, like previous ones, serve as communicative tools. Since suppressing verbal, paralinguistic, and kinesthetic expressions of emotion requires effort (Buck, 2003), one could argue that people who remain silent through strong emotions possess some degree of agency.

Reaction to Uncertainty or Confusion   Subsequent to Basso's (1970) foundational work, other scholars documented the use of silence as a method of coping with uncertainty or confusion. Braithwaite (1990), for instance, conducted a cross-cultural test of Basso's hypotheses. Based on 13 ethnographic reports gathered from other studies (of Native American, East Asian, African, and African-American cultures), Braithwaite determined that members used silence as a primary management strategy when confronted with uncertain, unpredictable, or ambiguous relationships or information. Likewise, Saunders (1985) presented evidence that Italians, often stereotyped as noisy and emotional, employ silence as a tactical response to social uncertainty. In these cases, silence may indicate less power than previously discussed examples because people can experience uncertainty in interactions with others who exercise known authority over them or with strangers whose potential authority is yet undiscovered (Basso, 1970; Liu, 2001; Nwoye, 1985; Saunders, 1985).

Device of Relational Control   Because silence intersects complexly with politeness (Sifianou, 1997), it operates in multiple and contradictory ways with regard to distance in interpersonal relationships (Liu, 2001; Wardhaugh, 2002). Tannen (1985) documented that silence can stimulate and maintain a comfortable rapport between intimates as well as cause discomfort among unfamiliar persons (who react in many "Western" cultures by filling the silence with small talk). Jaworski (1993) illustrated silences that close communication channels (i.e., by giving the impression of avoidance or refusal to engage in interaction) as well as silences that keep communication channels open (e.g., by refusing to take leave verbally or by refraining from cutting off a quarrel with angry words). Moreover, according to Anderson (1998) and K. D. Williams (2001), social groups commonly utilize silence to ostracize wayward members, punishing them by controlling the closeness of their relationships with other group members through the "silent treatment."

Yet another example involves the case of linguistic taboos (silences on particular topics) that interactants can employ to create and cross boundaries in interpersonal relationships. We can keep people at a distance by speaking formally and politely and observing linguistic taboos; violating taboos, however, can work like phatic communication, rising above the meaning of the words themselves to the social function of bonding (J. Coupland & Jaworski, 2003; Jaworski, 2000). In the business world, for instance, definite rules of "professional courtesy" that involve avoiding certain topics and certain registers of speech are supposed to be followed (Hardin, 1973, p. 137), and the necessity of engaging in face-saving politeness strategies often demands silence as well (Sifianou, 1997). These silences work to maintain "professional relationships"—frequently formal, careful, and polite relationships rather than close, intimate ones.

This formula of observing taboos to maintain distance in a relationship can be read in reverse as well. When silence is expected but *not* observed, bonds form and communities strengthen. For example, the formation of a generation among the young people of the Solomon Islands has recently been aided by their creation of a new vocabulary used to discuss the topic of sex, which was formerly off-limits (Buchanan-Aruwafu et al., 2003). Yielding to linguistic temptation (Freud, 1952; Steiner, 1956) with other people enables individuals to break down barriers and bond through shared transgression. For this reason, J. Coupland and Jaworski (2003) argued that taboo-breaking (or the absence of expected silences) marks a form of phatic communication that aligns speakers with each other and against third parties.

Acceptance/Agreement Versus Refusal/Protest   Paradoxically, silence can carry precisely opposite propositional messages, such as acceptance versus protest or agreement versus refusal (Jaworski, 1993). Saville-Troike (1985) offered a pair of examples that beautifully illustrate a cross-cultural difference in the semantic content of silence. According to Saville-Troike, in Japan, if a girl remains silent in response to a marriage proposal, she gives her consent; between Igbo speakers, however, the same exact response signifies a refusal of the proposal. Even intraculturally, contradictory meanings can be attributed to silence depending on the context of the interaction, as when bullies construe silent responses (or nonresponses) as either ignoring or submitting to the maltreatment (Pörhölä, Karhunen, & Rainivaara, 2006).

Brummett (1980), for example, examined a case of strategic political silence, determining that President Carter's 10-day silence in the press in 1979, meant to imply composure and strength, backfired and was instead interpreted by the public as a sign of passivity and the acceptance of defeat. In contrast, Duncan (2004), Gilmore (1985), C. Miller (1996), and Nwoye (1985) argued that silence can function effectively as either a politely indirect refusal or a boldly defiant form of resistance. As signs representing specific semantic propositions, these silences exemplify the use of silence as a communicative tool. Refusals, especially, require power to perform, and even silent acquiescence can indicate some agency. If silent speakers had no power, they probably would be told, not asked; commanded, not requested.

Rhetorical Strategy   Some researchers (e.g., Bokser, 2006; Brummett, 1980; Crenshaw, 1997; Glenn, 2002) identified silences that function as tools to accomplish specific rhetorical goals. Interestingly, Glenn claimed that these goals could include persuasion through silence as well as rhetorical listening. Additionally, building upon earlier work by Nakayama and Krizek (1995) that explored the silence and invisibility of the rhetoric of whiteness, Crenshaw demonstrated that White people use silence about race to reify the hegemonic structure within which whiteness is normalized and nonwhiteness is "otherized." The silences behind and following[18] an invocation of ideology both validate the ideology and quell opposition to it. Thus, for scholars from this perspective, silence operates as a tool of persuasion.

Additionally, Lippard (1988) analyzed the collective silence of Quakers as a rhetorical event that promotes group unity and teaches/reinforces the values of the community. Colp-Hansbury (2004) painted another vivid portrait of silent rhetoric as employed by the Women in Black, a protest group with whom she participated during an ethnographic study. She observed that "[f]or an hour every week, four to 12 women stand in a line between the library's two main doors, dressed all in black, with black veils covering their faces. They do not speak to passers-by" (p. 3). The women believe their silence enacts invitational rhetoric (S. K. Foss & Griffin, 1995) by encouraging reflection on the issue at hand. Weber (2005) noted famous authors who stopped publishing, demonstrating that statements can be made in the silent space created by that next work that is never forthcoming. Further, in a book-length study of rhetorical silences, Glenn (2004) contributed a thoughtful synthesis of the ways in which silence constitutes a rhetoric with a critical review of historical silences, connections to an array of other research on silence, and suggestions for future research.

Silence as a Marker of Identity

Based on the preceding discussion, situational uses of silence are clearly ubiquitous. Yet, not all silences constitute a deliberately used tool. Some silences—those performed by individuals to mark their identity—fall into another category (or perhaps operate as a tool while simultaneously marking identity and, as such, occupy both categories). These silences can offer very different answers to the debates surrounding silence. They comprise displays of cultural knowledge without clear indications of power. According to Scarpi (1987), silence can be a choice or an imposition. The following four categories of silences as identity markers include instances of imposed (relatively powerless) silence and chosen (relatively powerful) silence.

Identity of Authority   Some scholars argue that language is power (Lakoff, 1990; Stroińska, 2000). Apparently, so is silence (see Brandt, 1980, for a discussion of secret-keeping and power differentials). Duez (1997) documented that people with power in an interaction often establish authority through the use of silence. Bruneau (1973) also wrote of power and silence, purporting that the "burden of speech is often the burden of the subordinate" (p. 31). Other research suggests that people without any "real" authority in an interaction can gain perceived status by mimicking this authoritative silence, thereby enacting an identity of power (J. Taylor & Mackenzie, 1983). Similarly, Watts (1997) asserted that people consciously and unconsciously shift and maintain power balances in interpersonal interactions through silences, such as in response to requests. As examples, DeFrancisco (1991) and Ragan, Aarons, and J. Taylor (1986) offered feminist critiques of male–female interactions, noting that men tend to control the topic, the pace, and the length of conversations with women through the strategic use of silences.

Another enactment of the authority identity a propos silence does not involve silence on the part of the person with power; instead, the person with authority marks the power of her or his identity by silencing the subordinate or victim involved in the interaction (Bruneau, 1973; Jaworski, 1993). This silencing may be perceived as the denial of voice (Bruening, 2005; Bruneau, 1973; Jaworski, 1992, 1993; Natapoff, 2005), status (Dendrinos & Pedro, 1997), decision-making power (Corbin, 2002), or identity self-avowal (Hegde, 1996; Mildorf, 2005) to individuals dominated by people in positions of power, and it may occur when the powerful either speak for others or do not permit others to speak for themselves (Thiesmeyer, 2003). I discuss such silencing as a marker of powerless identity in greater detail in the next section.

Authorities also use linguistic taboos as identity markers for oppressed groups. Individuals or groups of people with power impose taboos on those without power, as in Steiner's (1956) description of tribal priests outlawing "sacred" words, people, objects, and actions. Linguistic taboos, then, act as a demonstration of force—a show of power—because language creation and prohibition constitute privileges of the powerful (Wilks & Brick, 2000). Only authorities possess the right to decide what may be said—what can or cannot be uttered (Herdina, 1996). People with more power tend to create derogatory names for those with less and, as power differentials change, so does name-calling. Wachal (2002) reported that many ethnic slurs (e.g., "Spick," "Limey," and "Redskin") that used to be characterized by dictionaries as "informal" or "slang" terms are now labeled as "offensive" or "disparaging" (p. 199). The report that certain slurs have become inappropriate prompts me to wonder if the marginalized ethnic groups they refer to have gained a voice loud enough to object to defamation.

Bruneau (1973) explained that, in silencing others, authorities assign nonperson status to those who cannot speak. Schön (1987) made a similar claim regarding silence toward subordinates, for ignoring those without or with less power, intentionally or otherwise, assigns nonperson status to those not recognized or acknowledged.

This delineation between people and nonpeople resembles Goffman's (1974) concept of the *nonplayer*, an individual outside one's primary frame not noticed, listened to, or given attention. Anderson (1998) reported the deliberate creation of nonpeople in cases where social groups exert power over individuals (encouraging appropriate behavior) with social ostracism. Relatedly, Butler (1997, 2005) argued that some societies silence certain physical bodies (e.g., queer bodies) by dehumanizing them or, as she stated it, deeming them unrecognizable as subjects. Critical theorists problematize such nonperson status (Thiesmeyer, 2003), particularly feminists (Clair, 1998; Jaworski, 1992; Julé, 2004; Wayne, 1996) and postcolonialists (Duncan, 2004; Hegde, 1996, 1998; Minh-ha, 1990).

Identity of Subordinate or Victim[19]   Silence can also be an identity marker for those with relatively less power in a given situation. Subordinates often demonstrate their deference to authority by maintaining silence in the presence of those with power (Bruneau, 1973; Duncan, 2004; Jackowski, 2004; Maltz, 1985; Nwoye, 1985; Rich, 1979; Scarpi, 1987; Tannen, 1985; P. Williams, 2003). Wardhaugh (2002) reminded us that language varieties, words, topics, specific sounds or grammatical structures, and even speech itself all mark forms of linguistic taboos that function to maintain power structures in a society. In many parts of the world, for example, women have fewer choices in whom they may address (Tuite & Schulze, 1998), words that they may use (Reynolds, 1998), topics that they may discuss (Houppert, 1999), and when and where they may speak (Jaworski, 1992; Wardhaugh, 2002). Acquiescence to these imposed silences can indicate lack of agency and resignation to the role of victim or subordinate (Hegde, 1996; Sebate, 1996; Wayne, 1996).

Not all researchers, however, agree that silence signifies a lack of power, even in the oppressed or marginalized. Instead, they suggest that silence can function as a means of protest (Duncan, 2004; Ehrenhaus, 1988; Huckin, 2002; Jaworski, 1993; C. Miller, 1996; Scarpi, 1987). When oppressed people gain clout, they may break silences to illustrate a change in the power differential, as in the case of Japanese girls demonstrating empowerment in academic settings by beginning to use traditionally male language forms (Reynolds, 1998). People might even deliberately violate taboos to don a new identity of authority by that very violation. In the 1970s, under the shadow of GDR socialist ideology (*Kulturpolitik*), which strictly forbade public criticism, especially satire of the state, author Wolfgang Hilbig strove to break free of linguistic restrictions "as a means of exploding the word prison of [the GDR's] rhetorical construction of reality" (Cooke, 2000, p. 48). Stroińska (2000) provided examples of other authors, poets, and artists (for instance, George Orwell) who advocated resisting the state-imposed silences that they viewed as attempts to create reality and control thinking by manipulating language.

Yet, breaking silence is not the only method for people to protest or vie for power. Many do so by *maintaining* silence (Clair, 1997, 1998; Colp-Hansbury, 2004; Duncan, 2004; Rich, 1979). In choosing silence, they reject the identity ascribed them by those in power, either by refusing to speak a particular language or language variety (C. Miller, 1996), withdrawing from verbal battles that they feel they cannot win (Dalton & Fatzinger, 2003), or, according to Duncan, "unsaying" (i.e., declining to propagate) a history that has left them marginalized and forgotten. The Warramunga tribe of Australia requires female relatives (wives, mothers, sisters, etc.) to display their status of mourning for 2 years after a man's death (Enninger, 1991). Clair (1998) interpreted one Warramunga woman's refusal to break silence for 22 years after the imposed silence was lifted as an enactment of her identity that served simultaneously to underscore and protest her victimization. Fulton (2006) labeled such subversion "silent orality," illustrating the concept with examples from literature by African-American women (p. 66).

Gender Identity In various U.S. cultures, both masculine and feminine identities may be enacted through silence (Bell & Golombisky, 2004; Philipsen, 1975; Tannen, 1986). Women, consciously or not, often perform silences as a way to demonstrate their femininity, since some equate femininity with passivity (Julé, 2004; Pawelczyk, 2003) and propriety (Houppert, 1999). Philips (1983) provided an example of this performance of femininity through silence, describing how young women on the Warm Springs reservation in Oregon, striving to portray modesty, refrain from answering questions to which they know the answers.

On the other hand, in U.S. cultures where actions speak louder than words, men can enact a masculine identity by substituting (sometimes violent) actions for verbal communicative strategies (Philipsen, 1975; Wayne, 1996), or, as Tannen explained, they may play the part of the "strong, silent type" that has been romanticized through American film. Gendered silence exists in other cultures as well. Traditional Japanese (Bruneau & Ishii, 1988) and Indian (Hegde, 1996) cultures, for instance, expect women to perform their gender roles by keeping silent, and women around the world observe gender-specific linguistic taboos (or even complete silence) in the presence of certain other people, such as their husbands, in-laws, or men in general (Dixon, 1990; Tuite & Schulze, 1998; Wardhaugh, 2002).

Other Cultural Identities   Silence indicates cultural identities that are not necessarily gendered as well. P. Williams (2003) described the intricate norms of silence about the dead in a Gypsy community; in "On Being a Recognizable Indian Among Indians," Wieder and Pratt (1990) illustrated how some Native Americans enact cultural identity through silences. In these studies, not speaking of the dead marks the silent speaker as Gypsy-like, and Native Americans some-times evaluate a member's *Indian-ness* based upon (in)appropriate uses of silence. Using silence in culturally appropriate ways enables members of a culture to demonstrate their "insider" knowledge. Thus, learning when not to say anything, or when to say something by not saying anything, constitutes an essential skill in intercul-tural communication (Carbaugh, 2005; Enninger, 1991) and a very important aspect of learning communicative competence in accul-turation (Basso, 1970) as well as in the second (or even first) language acquisition process (Perales & Cenoz, 1996). Berman (1998) argued that such communicative competence involving silences remains essential to successful social interactions in Javanese cultures, where demonstrating respect with language use (or lack of language use) involves an unavoidable obligation in nearly every utterance.

Silence in the form of linguistic taboos also fulfills an important function for co-cultural groups, aiding in the exhibition of group membership. Observing occupational taboos in order to present one-self as a recognizable member of a certain profession exemplifies this function (Estes, 1984). Although the nature and strictness of taboos vary by community, even from ship to ship, legend suggests that fishermen all over the world share a superstition that saying certain words (e.g., pig or rabbit), making particular noises (e.g., a whistle), or mentioning specific topics (e.g., the church) on board will result in empty nets (Knipe & Bromley, 1984). Until individuals become initiated into the world of any particular profession by learning its vernacular and communicative norms, they cannot know which words are taboo. Once part of the community, however, they can mark themselves as members by appropriately performing silences.

Since these uses of silence as identity markers generally (although not always) operate below the level of consciousness as largely unnoticed discursive restrictions rather than strategic communicative tools, they address the question of silence's relationship to power differently than the first five types of silence discussed. Here, the use of silence could stem either from power (as in the enactment of an authority identity), lack of power (i.e., unquestioningly enacting a gender and/or cultural identity), or a struggle for power (e.g., when either breaking silence or keeping silent becomes a form of protest).

Silence as a Form of Enculturation

Another recurring theme in the literature on taboos is that silences aid in the process of enculturation (Bruneau, 1973; Jaworski, 1993; Saville-Troike, 1985; Wieder & Pratt, 1990; P. Williams, 2003). Older generations (Farberow, 1963) and the media (Houppert, 1999) expressly use silences to pass on cultural values and norms to younger generations. Countless words exist to label linguistic taboos: inappropriate, inapt, unacceptable, unseemly, tactless, tasteless, unbecoming, and indecent—to name a few. These same words apply to actions that we must refrain from, feelings that we must repress, or relationships that we must avoid (Freud, 1952; Mead, 1939; Steiner, 1956). Such words teach values to the young and to immigrants. Elders and peers employ these words to guide others into conformity, not just in language but in behavior. This relationship between word and act is even expressed in the degree of inappropriateness of topics. If others only mildly frown upon a behavior, then mentioning it can be treated as merely crude, offensive, or impolite; however, if it constitutes truly horrifying behavior, then it becomes unmentionable or unspeakable (Ferreira, 2001; S. C. Taylor, 2001).

In many cultures, members teach norms of morality (e.g., sexual behavior) through a topic's status as unsuitable for discussion in polite society. The Solomon Islands (Buchanan-Aruwafu et al., 2003) and Victorian England (Cline, 1997) encompass societies well known for prudishness, and in the United States, sex has also traditionally not been an appropriate topic in most public, business, academic, and other formal settings (Pomeroy, 1963). Such taboos are very effective for the purpose of enculturation because they are hard to contest. If, in a particular culture, custom dictates a certain act as taboo, then a member of that culture might feel pressure to refrain from even mentioning that act because, if someone verbalizes the taboo, others might assume that the speaker either has committed the act or condones it (Hardin, 1973). In this way, for example, taboos surrounding male/male rape work not only to silence rape victims but also to perpetuate the hegemony of heteronormative masculinity (Sivakumaran, 2005).

Hardin's description of taboo effects (1973) rings especially true when the taboo involves not what we may do but who we can be. In the United States, for instance, some topics remain off-limits simply because they can be perceived as unpatriotic. Business professionals complain of restrictions on their search for solutions to labor problems because individuals resist discussing offshore outsourcing[20] for fear of being labeled un-American, or worse yet, *anti*-American (Hayes, 2003). In academia, Robinson (1996) reported that translators in the publishing industry, which often vetoes translated texts that sound foreign (because if people can tell a book was not written in the United States they may not buy it[21]), do not wish to appear to prefer other languages or other cultures to English and the United States. These taboos support a value of being—in this case, American (good) or not (bad)—and they are powerful because they resemble a Matryoshka doll or a Chinese egg, with a silence inside a silence.

Hardin (1973) noted that "[i]nside is the primary taboo, surrounding a thing that must not be discussed; around this is the secondary taboo, a taboo against even acknowledging the existence of the primary taboo" (p. xi). Some may perceive silence as a form of enculturation in a positive light, in that it serves as a mechanism for cultures to educate new members about societal norms, helping them to adapt to the culture. Yet, because of this Chinese egg phenomenon, enculturating silences can also be oppressive. Individuals might not feel able to resist the social demand to perform silences, especially in cases where breaking taboos can hinder personal, professional, or social success (see Splichal, 2006, for a discussion of public and academic censorship and Zerubavel, 2006, for an analysis of open secrets, or sociological denial).

In previous sections, this chapter demonstrated an incredible diversity in definitions of and values for silence; the functions of silence are no less complicated or varied. Indeed, whether used as context-dependent communicative tools, markers of identity, means of enculturation, or some combination of these uses, silences do not maintain a consistent relationship to power—sometimes dimensionally indicating more or less power and, at others, dialectically signifying both power and lack of power simultaneously. Cross-cultural variations in the functionality of silences, as well as their inherently ambiguous nature, create a world of possibilities for those who would employ or interpret communicative silences and, thus, a continually changing world for scholars to explore.

Conclusion

At times, building knowledge about any particular concept or process only serves to expose more gaps in our knowledge. Such is the case with silence, which now demands exploration in many new directions based on the foundational literature explored in this chapter. Important topics related to silence await investigation, and, more importantly, many voices from around the globe remain silent (or silenced) on this subject. As a scholar fascinated by silence, I remain hopeful that future studies address these issues by involving culturally diverse participants and researchers from a variety of perspectives (not necessarily simultaneously).

In this chapter, I have embraced the cognitive dissonances apparent in research on silence, describing silence as negative and positive, as culturally specific and universal, as signifying both power and lack of power, as a communicative tool, an identity marker, and a means of enculturation, as both a foundation for language and a void created by the lack of language, and as both opposite of language and similar to it. The adoption of this "both/and" rather than "either/or" approach comes closer, I believe, to grappling with the complexity of silence and the accompanying contradictions in the definitions, values, and uses people have for silence.

Such acceptance of contradictions necessitates the use of dialectical thinking (Martin & Nakayama, 1999)—not the relinquishing of one's own perspective but the ability to cross paradigmatic lines and acknowledge ways in which research that diverges from one's own can be complementary to it, providing a more complete understanding of silence as communication. In order to accomplish this dialectical approach to silence, however, scholars must perform a process of reflexivity in which they (1) acknowledge their own assumptions about silence, (2) recognize the differences between their own and others' conceptions of silence, (3) understand the relationships between their paradigmatic perspectives and their approaches to silence, and (4) write explicitly about their reflexivity so that their readers may engage in the process with them.

I also encourage scholars to move beyond what they know about silence, both by transcending disciplinary boundaries and finding new ways to organize their knowledge. This chapter draws from many fields in its search for relevant literature, and I believe that forging connections between those diverse bodies of literature creates a richly textured portrait of silence not otherwise possible. Furthermore, rather than an acceptance of current taxonomies as complete or sufficient, silence, in all its ambiguity and polysemy, requires scholars constantly to resift ideas, relationships, and research findings. In writing this chapter, I have learned that the validity and value of past and current conceptualizations, operationalizations, and categorizations do not in any way prohibit the possibility of other ways to explore, study, or experience silence.

Acknowledgments

The author wishes to express indebtedness to the parallax collective for their support and stimulus, special appreciation to Dr. Judith Martin for her guidance and encouragement, and gratitude to Dr. Christina Beck, Dr. Jennifer Scott, Dr. Adam Jaworski, Sundae Bean, Karma Chavez, Elizabeth Richard, and two anonymous reviewers for their insightful comments on the manuscript or assistance in locating sources.

Notes

1. "Mainstream" U.S. scholars (White, middle-class males) have been joined recently by a handful of researchers from East Asia (mostly Japan and Korea) and other researchers who represent minorities in the United States. Vast areas of the world (such as Africa, Latin America, Eastern Europe, and most of Asia) remain underrepresented.

2. In addition to communication (including but not limited to the fields of rhetoric and intercultural, interpersonal, and organizational communication), research on silence can be found in most

social sciences, such as the fields of psycholinguistics, anthropology, sociolinguistics, literature, media studies, psychology, medicine (particularly audiology), and political and historical studies. See Muñoz-Duston and Kaplan (1985) for additional sources.

3. The most common perspectives taken in the study of silence seem to be social scientific or functionalist, interpretative, critical (in which I include feminist and postcolonial), Afrocentric, and Asiacentric.

4. For a detailed and systematic description of the phenomenon of silence, see Dauenhauer (1980).

5. I do not mean to imply that any and all studies of silence are valid or true, but instead that they may be useful *when considered within the contexts of their paradigms.* To engage in dialectical thinking and so to cross paradigmatic (as well as cultural and disciplinary) lines, then, we need to discuss explicitly what those contexts are.

6. I have surrounded "West" with quotes here and throughout the chapter as a recognition of the problematic ways in which a geographical label, especially one that encompasses so much of the world, becomes synonymous with one or a few dominant cultures within that geographical region, and in so doing necessarily erases the value or even the very presence of marginalized, colonized, and in other ways oppressed groups. Robin Patric Clair (1998) remarked that "this language functions to split the world in half—eastern from western. It then labels western as white European" (p. 216). In a footnote to her introduction of *Expressions of Ethnography: Novel Approaches to Qualitative Methods* (2003), she continued the conversation by adding:

> This discourse marginalizes African Americans because they have a distinct heritage that is neither eastern nor western per se and yet contains elements of both. It leaves the cultural contributions of South American cultures in question. Spanish, Hispanic, Latino, Mexican identities are placed in a precarious position. There is no clear place for the Irish who have suffered the throes of colonization for generations. Geopoliticizing under the term "western" further erases marginalized groups like people who are bi homo or a-sexuals [and] it would seem that even women of "western" origin have been constrained by colonization. (p. 20)

In addition to Clair's examples, some White Europeans/USians (see Bauman, 1983; Bill, 2005; Carbaugh, 2005; Lehtonen & Sajavaara, 1985, and Lippard, 1988) also differ greatly from so-called mainstream "Western" culture, and those differences are made invisible by the application of that label. While I do not wish to perpetuate the essentialization that seems unavoidable with these terms, I am at a loss as to how to avoid using them. Since so much of the literature that I review here invokes the "East/West" dichotomy, I set off "East" and "West" in quotes as a continual reminder that these labels are suspect.

7. See also Goldsmith, Miller, and Caughlin's chapter in this volume on avoidance and coping with cancer.

8. Butler's 1997 account, however, leaves room for the possibility of agency in interpellation:

> In being called an injurious name, one is derogated and demeaned. But the name holds out another possibility as well: by being called a name, one is also, paradoxically, given a certain possibility for social existence, initiated into a temporal life of language that exceeds the prior purposes that animate that call. Thus the injurious address may ... produce an unexpected and enabling response. If to be addressed is to be interpellated, then the offensive call runs the risk of inaugurating a subject in speech who comes to use language to counter the offensive call. (p. 2)

9. For analyses of Lorde's work, see L. C. Olson (1997, 1998). Also, Adam Jaworski's 1992 article on the silencing of women, though not written from personal experience like Lorde's work, offers a theoretical description of the process of silencing and serves as an excellent resource of other research on this topic from the 1970s and 1980s.

10. For current work on the spiral of silence, see Glynn, Hayes, and Shanahan (1997) and Scheufele and Moy (2000).

11. Despite the fact that many U.S. writers often universalize their comments based upon experiences in "Western" cultures, I hesitate to make that claim here. While common, such overgeneralization is dangerous, for it is likely to be inaccurate. Asante (1987) remarked that his colleagues "have often assumed that their 'objectivity,' a kind of collective subjectivity of European culture, should be the measure by which the world marches" (p. 3). Chuang (2003) echoed this charge, adding the postmodern critiques of essentialization and dualism to Eurocentrism, as did Hegde (1998) in her postcolonial criticism of feminism for essentializing women.

12. I use the term "groundbreaking" only in reference to "Western" communication/anthropological scholarship written (or translated into) English, due to my limited access to work published in other languages.

13. Jaworski (1993) provides an additional reference list of some important cross-cultural studies on silence (p. 22).

14. See Ting-Toomey's 1994 edited volume for more information on interpersonal facework across cultures.

15. For silence as it manifests in or relates to music, see Boykan (2004), Edgar (1997), and Picard (1952).

16. Zuo (2002) criticized Saville-Troike's taxonomy as impractical for analytical purposes: (1) since the functions of silence overlap, her categories based on functionality also overlap; (2) social, psychological, and linguistic uses of silence are all included in one taxonomy, creating confusion: and (3) silence "directly involved in the cognitive process of speech production" is missing (p. 43).

17. A caveat or two: The silences discussed here are all communicative. While silences that have no meaning certainly exist (Brummett, 1980; Saville-Troike, 1985), they are irrelevant to the current discussion. This section, therefore, focuses specifically on what Poyatos (1983) referred to as "intelligible" silence, as opposed to "sensible" silence that is unintelligible (p. 216). Also, I include both silences *from* people (only one participant in a communicative setting needs to be producing it at any given time) and silences *between* people (only occurs when everyone involved simultaneously cooperates to produce it) (Jaworski, 1993; Tannen, 1985).

18. By "behind and following", I mean the lack of justification of the ideology and the difficulty of arguing with it. See A. N. Miller and Harris's 2005 discussion of the need for explicit examinations of whiteness in mixed-race classrooms.

19. By discussing subordinates and victims together, I do not intend to imply that all subordinates (or anyone with less relative power in a particular situation) consider themselves, or should be considered by others, a victim.

20. Outsourcing in this context involves subcontracting outside the United States in order to lower the cost of human resources.

21. One anonymous reviewer noted that this claim does not always apply to the French, whose books on everything from philosophy to cooking are often popular in the United States. I suspect, however, it is no coincidence that the exception has considerable cultural capital; the French also often enjoy exemption from the handicap of foreign-accented English.

References

Acheson, K. (2006). *The birth of silences: An ethnography of communication on families of addicts.* Paper presented at the annual meeting of the National Communication Association, San Antonio, TX.

Adera, T., & Ahmed, A. J. (Eds.). (1995). *Silence is not golden: A critical anthology of Ethiopian literature.* Lawrenceville, NJ: Red Sea Press.

Afifi, T. D., & Olson, L. N. (2005). The chilling effect and the pressure to conceal secrets in families. *Communication Monographs, 72*, 192–216.

Afifi, T. D., Olson, L. N., & Armstrong, C. (2005). The chilling effect and family secrets: Examining the role of self-protection, other protection, and communication efficacy. *Human Communication Research, 31*, 564–598.

Afifi, W. A., & Burgoon, J. K. (1998). "We never talk about that": A comparison of cross-sex friendships and dating relationships on uncertainty and topic avoidance. *Personal Relationships, 5*, 255–272.

Afifi, W. A., & Guerrero, L. K. (1998). Some things are better left unsaid II: Topic avoidance in friendships. *Communication Quarterly, 46*, 231–250.

Aguilar-Moreno, M. (2003). *La perfección del silencio: el Panteón de Belén, el culto a la muerte en México* [*Death in Mexico and the cemetery of Belén: The perfection of silence*]. Guadalajara, Mexico: Gobierno del Estado de Jalisco, Secretaría de Cultura.

Anderson, I. (1998). The awful power of silence. *New Scientist, 158*, 18.

Anzaldúa, G. (Ed.). (1990). *Making face, making soul = Haciendo caras: Creative and critical perspectives by women of color.* San Francisco: Aunt Lute Books.

Ardener, E. (1975). The problem revisited. In S. Ardener (Ed.), *Perceiving women* (pp. 19–28). London: Malaby.

Ardener, S. (1978). *Defining females: The nature of women in society.* New York: Wiley Press.

Asante, M. K. (1987). *The Afrocentric idea.* Philadelphia: Temple University Press.

Axtel, R. E. (Ed.). (1985). *Do's and taboos around the world.* New York: John Wiley & Sons.

Bailey, A. C. (2005). *African voices of the Atlantic slave trade: Beyond the silence and the shame.* Boston: Beacon Press.

Barbour, J. D. (2004). *The value of solitude: The ethics and spirituality of aloneness in autobiography.* Charlottesville: University of Virginia Press.

Basso, K. H. (1970). To give up on words: Silence in Western Apache culture. *Southwest Journal of Anthropology, 26*, 213–230.

Basso, K. H. (1996). *Wisdom sits in places: Landscape and language among the Western Apache.* Albuquerque: University of New Mexico Press.

Bauman, R. (1983). *Let your words be few: Symbolism of speaking and silence among seventeenth-century Quakers.* Cambridge, England: Cambridge University Press.

Baxter, L. A., & Wilmot, W. W. (1985). Taboo topics in close relationships. *Journal of Social and Personal Relationships, 2*, 253–269.

Bell, E., & Golombisky, K. (2004). Voices and silences in our classrooms: Strategies for mapping trails among sex/gender, race, and class. *Women's Studies in Communication, 27*, 294–330.

Bennet, J. (2005, September 15). Haunting silence and berets that don't speak French. *New York Times, 154*, A21.

Berger, M. (1947, October 27). 400,000 in silent tribute as war dead come home. *New York Times*. Retrieved June 15, 2006, from http://www.nytimes.com.

Berman, L. (1998). *Speaking through the silence: Narratives, social conventions, and power in Java*. New York: Oxford University Press.

Bill, J. B. (2005). *The gift of Quaker spirituality*. Ventura, CA: Paraclete.

Blair, C., Brown, J. R., & Baxter, L. A. (1994). Disciplining the feminine. *Quarterly Journal of Speech, 80*, 383–410.

Blase, J., & Blase, J. R. (2003). *Breaking the silence: Overcoming the problem of principal mistreatment of teachers*. Thousand Oaks, CA: Corwin Press.

Bogoroch-Ditkofsky, M. (2005). The bounds of silence. *Canadian Business, 78*, 189–193.

Bokser, J. A. (2006). Sor Juana's rhetoric of silence. *Rhetoric Review, 25*, 5–21.

Borjesson, K. (Ed.). (2004). *Into the buzzsaw: Leading journalists expose the myth of a free press*. Amherst, NY: Prometheus Books.

Boykan, M. (2004). *Silence and slow time: Studies in musical narrative*. Lanham, MD: Scarecrow Press.

Bradshaw, J. (1995). *Family secrets: What you don't know can't hurt you*. New York: Bantam Books.

Braithwaite, C. A. (1990). Communicative silence: A cross cultural study of Basso's hypothesis. In D. Carbaugh (Ed.), *Cultural communication and intercultural contact* (pp. 321–328). Hillsdale, NJ: Lawrence Erlbaum Associates.

Brandt, E. (1980). On secrecy and control of knowledge. In S. Teft (Ed.), *Secrecy: A cross-cultural perspective* (pp. 123–146). New York: Human Sciences Press.

Brown, A. D., & Coupland, C. (2005). Sounds of silence: Graduate trainees, hegemony, and resistance. *Organizational Studies, 26*, 1049–1069.

Brown-Smith, N. (1998). Family secrets. *Journal of Family Issues, 19*, 20–42.

Bruening, J. E. (2005). Gender and racial analysis in sport: Are all the women white and all the blacks men? *Human Kinetics, 57*, 330–349.

Bruening, J. E., Armstrong, K. L., & Pastore, D. (2005). Listening to the voices: The experiences of African American female student athletes. *Research Quarterly for Exercise and Sport, 76*, 82–100.

Brummett, B. (1980). Towards a theory of silence as a political strategy. *Quarterly Journal of Speech, 66*, 289–303.

Bruneau, T. J. (1973). Communicative silences: Forms and functions. *Journal of Communication, 23*, 17–46.

Bruneau, T. J., & Ishii, S. (1988). Communicative silences: East and West. *World Communication, 17*, 1–33.

Buchanan-Aruwafu, H. R., Maebiru, R., & Aruwafu, F. (2003). Stiki Lole: Language and the mediation of desire in Auki, Malaita, Solomon Islands. *Culture, Health & Sexuality, 5,* 219–236.

Buck, R. (2003). Emotional expression, suppression, and control: Nonverbal communication in cultural context. *Journal of Intercultural Communication Research, 32,* 47–65.

Burgoon, J. K., & Hale, J. L. (1988). Nonverbal expectancy violations theory: Model elaboration and application to immediacy behaviors. *Communication Monographs, 55,* 58–79.

Butler, J. (1993). *Bodies that matter: On the discursive limits of "sex."* New York: Routledge.

Butler, J. (1997). *Excitable speech: A politics of the performative.* New York: Routledge.

Butler, J. (2005). *Giving an account of oneself.* New York: Fordham University Press.

Buzzanell, P. M. (1994). Gaining a voice: Feminist organizational communication theorizing. *Management Communication Quarterly, 7,* 339–383.

Campbell, K. K. (1973). The rhetoric of women's liberation: An oxymoron. *Quarterly Journal of Speech, 59,* 74–86.

Campbell, K. K. (1989a). *Man cannot speak for her* (Vol. 1). New York: Greenwood Press.

Campbell, K. K. (1989b). The sound of women's voices. *Quarterly Journal of Speech, 75,* 212–221.

Campbell, K. K. (2001). Rhetorical feminism. *Rhetoric Review, 20,* 9–13.

Campbell, K. K. (2002). Consciousness-raising: Linking theory, criticism, and practice. *Rhetoric Society Quarterly, 32,* 45–64.

Cant, B. (2006). Exploring the implications for health professionals of men coming out as gay in healthcare settings. *Health & Social Care in the Community, 14,* 9–16.

Cappella, J. N. (1979). Talk-silence sequences in informal conversations. *Human Communication Research, 6,* 3–18.

Cappella, J. N. (1980). Talk and silence sequences in informal conversations II. *Human Communication Research, 6,* 130–146.

Cappella, J. N., & Planalp, S. (1981). Talk and silence sequences in informal conversations III. *Human Communication Research, 7,* 117–133.

Carabas, T., & Harter, L. M. (2005). State-induced illness and forbidden stories: The role of storytelling in healing individual and social traumas in Romania. In L. M. Harter, P. M. Japp, & C. S. Beck (Eds.), *Narratives, health, and healing: Communication theory, research, and practice* (pp. 149–169). Mahwah, NJ: Lawrence Earlbaum Associates.

Caranfa, A. (2006). Voices of silence in pedagogy: Art, writing and self-encounter. *Journal of Philosophy of Education, 40,* 85–103.

Carbaugh, D. (1995). "I can't do that!" but I "can actually see around corners": American Indian students and the study of public "communication." In J. Lehtonen & L. Lahtinen (Eds.), *Critical perspectives on communication research and pedagogy* (pp. 215–234). St. Ingbert, Germany: Röhrig Universitätsverlag.

Carbaugh, D. (1999). "Just listen": "Listening" and landscape among the Blackfeet. *Western Journal of Communication, 63,* 250–270.

Carbaugh, D. (2005). *Cultures in conversation.* Mahwah, NJ: Lawrence Erlbaum Associates.

Carlson, A. C. (1994). Aspasia of Miletus: How one woman disappeared from the history of rhetoric. *Women's Studies in Communication, 17,* 26–44.

Chafe, W. L. (1985). Some reasons for hesitating. In D. Tannen & M. Saville-Troike (Eds.), *Perspectives on silence* (pp. 77–91). Norwood, NJ: Ablex.

Chuang, R. (2003). A postmodern critique of cross-cultural and intercultural communication research. In W. J. Starosta & G. M. Chen (Eds.), *Ferment in the intercultural field: Axiology/value/praxis* (pp. 24–53). Thousand Oaks, CA: Sage.

Ciani, M. G. (1987). The silence of the body: Defect and absence of voice in Hippocrates. In M. G. Ciani (Ed.), *The regions of silence: Studies on the difficulty of communicating* (pp. 145–160). Amsterdam: J. C. Gieben.

Clair, R. P. (1997). Organizing silence: Silence as voice and voice as silence in the narrative exploration of the Treaty of New Echota. *Western Journal of Communication, 61,* 315–338.

Clair, R. P. (1998). *Organizing silence: A world of possibilities.* New York: State University of New York Press.

Clair, R. P. (Ed.). (2003). *Expressions of ethnography: Novel approaches to qualitative methods.* Albany: State University of New York Press.

Cline, S. (1997). *Lifting the taboo: Women, death and dying.* New York: New York University Press.

Colp-Hansbury, C. (2004). *Standing their ground silently: A qualitative examination of the protest strategies of Women in Black.* Paper presented at the annual meeting of the National Communication Association, Chicago.

Conn, S. (2004). *History's shadow: Native Americans and historical consciousness in the nineteenth century.* Chicago: University of Chicago Press.

Cooke, P. (2000). *Speaking the taboo: A study of the work of Wolfgang Hilbig.* Amsterdam: Rodopi.

Corbin, C. (2002). Silence and lies: How the industrial fishery constrained voices of ecological conversation. *Canadian Journal of Communication, 27,* 7–33.

Cosi, D. M. (1987). Jammed communication: Battos, the founder of Cyrene, stammering and castrated. In M. G. Ciani (Ed.), *The regions of silence: Studies on the difficulty of communicating* (pp. 115–144). Amsterdam: J.C. Gieben.

Coupland, J., & Jaworski, A. (2003). Transgression and intimacy in recreational talk narratives. *Research on Language and Social Interaction, 36*, 85–106.

Coupland, N., & Coupland, J. (1997). Discourses of the unsayable: Death implicative talk in geriatric medical consultations. In A. Jaworski (Ed.), *Silence: Interdisciplinary perspectives* (pp. 117–151). Berlin: Mouton de Gruyter.

Cozzens, D. B. (2002). *Sacred silence: Denial and crisis in the Church.* Collegeville, MN: Liturgical Press.

Cramer, K. M., Gallant, M. D., & Langlois, M. W. (2005). Self-silencing and depression in women and men: Comparative structural equation models. *Personality & Individual Differences, 39*, 581–592.

Crenshaw, C. (1997). Resisting Whiteness' rhetorical silence. *Western Journal of Communication, 61*, 253–278.

Dadge, D. (Ed.). (2005). *Silenced: International journalists expose media censorship.* Amherst, NY: Prometheus Books.

Dalton, M. M., & Fatzinger, K. J. (2003). Choosing silence: Defiance and resistance without voice in Jane Campion's *The Piano. Women & Language, 26*, 34–40.

Daly, M. (1978). *Gyn/ecology: The meta-ethics of radical feminism.* Boston: Beacon.

Daly, M. (1984). *Pure lust: Elemental feminist philosophy.* Boston: Beacon.

Daly, M., & Caputi, J. (1987). *Websters' first new intergalactic wickedary of the English language.* Boston: Beacon Press.

Dauenhauer, B. (1980). *Silence: The phenomenon and its ontological significance.* Bloomington: Indiana University Press.

Davies, R., & Ikeno, O. (Eds.). (2002). *The Japanese mind: Understanding contemporary Japanese culture.* Boston: Tuttle.

DeFrancisco, V. L. (1991). The sounds of silence: How men silence women in marital relations. *Discourse & Society, 2*, 413–423.

Dendrinos, B., & Pedro, E. R. (1997). Giving street directions: The silent role of women. In A. Jaworski (Ed.), *Silence: Interdisciplinary perspectives* (pp. 215–237). Berlin: Mouton de Gruyter.

Depelchin, J. (2005). *Silences in African history: Between the syndromes of discovery and abolition.* Dar Es Salaam, Tanzania: Mkuki na Nyota.

Derlega, V. J., Metts, S., Petronio, S., & Margulis, S. T. (1993). *Self-disclosure.* Newbury Park, CA: Sage.

Dindia, K., & Allen, M. (1992). Sex differences in self-disclosure: A meta-analysis. *Psychological Bulletin, 112*, 106–124.

Dixon, R .M. (1990). The origin of "mother-in-law vocabulary" in two Australian languages. *Anthropological Linguistics, 32*, 1–56.

Dow, B. J., & Condit, C. M. (2005). The state of the art in feminist scholarship in communication. *Journal of Communication, 55*, 448–478.

Duez, D. (1997). Acoustic markers of political power. *Journal of Psycholinguistic Research, 26,* 641–665.

Duncan, P. (2004). *Tell this silence: Asian American women writers and the politics of speech.* Iowa City: University of Iowa Press.

Eckstein, N. J., & Turman, P. D. (2002). "Children are to be seen and not heard": Silencing students' religious voices in the university classroom. *Journal of Communication and Religion, 25,* 166–193.

Edgar, A. (1997). Music and silence. In A. Jaworski (Ed.), *Silence: Interdisciplinary perspectives* (pp. 311–327). Berlin: Mouton de Gruyter.

Ehrenhaus, P. (1988). Silence and symbolic expression. *Communication Monographs, 55,* 41–58.

Enninger, W. (1991). Focus on silence across cultures. *Intercultural Communication Studies, 1,* 1–37.

Epstein, D., O'Flynn, S., & Telford, D. (2003). *Silenced sexualities in schools and universities.* Stoke-on-Trent, England: Trentham Books.

Estes, J. (1984). Loggers can't cry: And other taboos of the Northwest woods. In R. B. Browne (Ed.), *Forbidden fruits: Taboos and tabooism in culture* (pp. 177–182). Bowling Green, OH: Bowling Green State University Popular Press.

Etter-Lewis, G. (1991). Standing up and speaking out: African American women's narrative legacy. *Discourse & Society, 2,* 425–437.

Fanon, F. (1967). *Black skin, white masks* (C. L. Markmann, Trans.). New York: Grove Press.

Farberow, N. L. (1963). Introduction. In N. L. Farberow (Ed.), *Taboo topics* (pp. 1–7). New York: Atherton Press.

Feifel, H. (1963). Death. In N. L. Farberow (Ed.), *Taboo topics* (pp. 8–21). New York: Atherton Press.

Feldman-Stewart, D., Brundage, M. D., & Tishelman, C. (2005). A conceptual framework for patient–professional communication: An application to the cancer context. *Psycho-Oncology, 14,* 801–809.

Feldstein, S., & Crown, C. (1990). Oriental and Canadian conversational interactions: Chronographic structure and interpersonal perception. *Journal of Asian Pacific Communication, 1,* 247–265.

Ferreira, A. (2001). (Unspeakable) body parts: Patchwork characters in literature and film. In A. Mills & J. Smith (Eds.), *Utter silence: Voicing the unspeakable* (pp. 109–125). New York: Peter Lang.

Fields-Meyer, T., Duffy, T., & Arias, R. (2005, April 11). Autism: Breaking the silence. *People, 63,* 83–86.

Foss, K. A., & Foss, S. K. (Eds). (1996). *Women speak: The eloquence of women's lives.* Prospect Heights, IL: Waveland Press.

Foss, K. A., Foss, S. K., & Griffin, C. L. (2004). *Readings in feminist rhetorical theory.* Thousand Oaks, CA: Sage.

Foss, S. K., & Griffin, C. L. (1995). Beyond persuasion: A proposal for an invitational rhetoric. *Communication Monographs, 62,* 2–18.

Foucault, M. (1972). *The archaeology of knowledge and the discourse on language* (A. M. Sheridan Smith, Trans.). New York: Dorset Press.

Foucault, M. (2001). *Fearless speech.* Los Angeles: Semiotext(e).

Fox, J. J. (1974). Our ancestors spoke in pairs: Rotinese views of language, dialect, and code. In R. Bauman & J. Sherzer (Eds.), *Explorations in the ethnography of speaking* (2nd ed., pp. 65–87). London: Cambridge University Press.

Freud, S. (1952). *Totem and taboo: Some points of agreement between the mental lives of savages and neurotics* (J. Strachey, Trans.). New York: Norton.

Fulton, D. S. (2006). *Speaking power: Black feminist orality in women's narratives of slavery.* Albany: State University of New York Press.

Gal, S. (1994). Between speech and silence: The problematics of research on language and gender. In C. Roman, S. Juhasz, & C. Miller (Eds.), *The women and language debate* (pp. 407–431). New Brunswick, NJ: Rutgers University Press.

Galasiński, D., & Jaworski, A. (1997). The linguistic construction of reality in the *Black Book of Polish Censorship. Discourse & Society, 8,* 341–357.

Gallas, K. (1997). Bad boys and silent girls: What children know about language and power. *Women & Language, 20,* 63–71.

Ganguly, S. N. (1968). Culture, communication, and silence. *Philosophy and Phenomenological Research, 29,* 182–200.

Gilmore, P. (1985). Silence and sulking: Emotional displays in the classroom. In D. Tannen & M. Saville-Troike (Eds.), *Perspectives on silence* (pp. 139–163). Norwood, NJ: Ablex.

Glenn, C. (2002). Silence: A rhetorical art for resisting disciplines. *JAC: A Journal of Composition Theory, 22,* 261–291.

Glenn, C. (2004). *Unspoken: A rhetoric of silence.* Carbondale: Southern Illinois University Press.

Glynn, C. J., Hayes, A. F., & Shanahan, J. (1997). Perceived support for one's opinions and willingness to speak out: A meta-analysis of survey studies on the "spiral of silence." *Public Opinion Quarterly, 61,* 452–463.

Goffman, E. (1974). *Frame analysis: An essay on the organization of experience.* Cambridge, MA: Harvard University Press.

Goffman, E. (1981). *Forms of talk.* Philadelphia: University of Pennsylvania Press.

Goldsmith, D., Miller, L., & Caughlin, J. (2007). Openness and avoidance in couples communicating about cancer. In C. S. Beck (Ed.), *Communication yearbook 31* (pp. 61–115). New York, NY: Lawrence Erlbaum Associates.

Goodall, H. L., Jr. (2005). Narrative inheritance: A nuclear family with toxic secrets. *Qualitative Inquiry, 11*, 492–513.

Gordon, S. (2005, May). Noise-proof your house. *Prevention, 57*, 141–144.

Gowen, S. G. (1991). Beliefs about literacy: Measuring women into silence/ hearing women into speech. *Discourse & Society, 2*, 439–450.

Grabher, G. M., & Jessner, U. (Eds.). (1996). *Semantics of silence in linguistics and literature.* Heidelberg, Germany: Universitätsverlag C. Winter.

Greenberg, A. (2002). *The dog of memory: A family album of secrets and silences.* Salt Lake City: University of Utah Press.

Greene, A. B. (1940). *The philosophy of silence.* New York: Richard R. Smith.

Greene, K., & Serovich, J. M. (1996). Appropriateness of disclosure of HIV testing information: The perspective of PLWAs. *Journal of Applied Communication Research, 24*, 50–65.

Griffin, C. L. (1993). Women as communicators: Mary Daly's hagiography as rhetoric. *Communication Monographs, 60*, 158–177.

Guerrero, A. (2002). *Silence at Boalt Hall: The dismantling of affirmative action.* Berkeley: University of California Press.

Guerrero, L. K., & Afifi, W. A. (1995). Some things are better left unsaid: Topic avoidance in family relationships. *Communication Quarterly, 43*, 276–296.

Hall, C., Sarangi, S., & Slembrouck, S. (1997). Silent and silenced voices: Interactional construction of audience in social work talk. In A. Jaworski (Ed.), *Silence: Interdisciplinary perspectives* (pp. 181–211). Berlin: Mouton de Gruyter.

Hardin, G. (1973). *Stalking the wild taboo.* Los Altos, CA: William Kaufmann, Inc.

Hasegawa, T., & Gudykunst, W. B. (1998). Silence in Japan and the United States. *Journal of Cross-Cultural Psychology, 29*, 668–684.

Hawk, B. (2003). A rhetoric/pedagogy of silences: Sub-version in Paul Kameen's writing/teaching. *Pedagogy, 3*, 377–397.

Hayes, M. (2003, July 28). Taboo: Outsourcing. *InformationWeek, 949*, 32–35.

Hegde, R. S. (1996). Narratives of silence: Rethinking gender, agency, and power from the communication experiences of battered women in South India. *Communication Studies, 47*, 303–318.

Hegde, R. S. (1998). A view from elsewhere: Locating difference and the politics of representation from a transnational feminist perspective. *Communication Theory, 8*, 271–297.

Hemmeter, T. (1996). Hitchcock's melodramatic silence. *Journal of Film & Video, 48*, 32–41.

Herdina, P. (1996). The manufacture of silence (or how to stop people doing things with words). In G. M. Grabher & U. Jessner (Eds.), *Semantics of silences in linguistics and literature* (pp. 29–44). Heidelberg, Germany: Universitätsverlag C. Winter.

Höllgren, M., Larsby, B., Lyxell, B., & Arlinger, S. (2005). Speech understanding in quiet and noise, with and without hearing aids. *International Journal of Audiology, 44*, 574–583.

hooks, b. (1984). *Feminist theory from margin to center.* Boston: South End Press.

hooks, b. (1993). Transformative pedagogy and multiculturalism. In T. Perry & J. Fraser (Eds.), *Freedom's plow* (pp. 91–97). New York: Routledge.

Houck, N., & Gass, S. M. (1997). Cross-cultural back channels in English refusals: A source of trouble. In A. Jaworski (Ed.), *Silence: Interdisciplinary perspectives* (pp. 285–307). Berlin: Mouton de Gruyter.

Houppert, K. (1999). *The curse. Confronting the last unmentionable taboo: Menstruation.* New York: Farrar, Straus and Giroux.

Houston, M., & Kramarae, C. (1991). Speaking from silence: Methods of silencing and of resistance. *Discourse and Society, 2*, 387–399.

Huckin, T. (2002). Textual silence and the discourse of homelessness. *Discourse and Society, 13*, 347–372.

Hunt, T., & Paine-Gernee, K. (1994). *Secrets to tell, secrets to keep.* New York: Warner Books.

Imber-Black, E. (1998). *The secret lives of families: Truth-telling, privacy, and reconciliation in a tell-all society.* New York: Bantam Books.

Ishii, S., & Bruneau, T. (1994). Silence in cross-cultural perspective: Japanese and the United States. In A. Samovar & E. Porter (Eds.), *Intercultural communication: A reader* (pp. 246–251). Belmont, CA: Wadsworth.

Jackowski, K. (2004). *The silence we keep: One nun's view of the Catholic priest scandal.* New York: Harmony Books.

Jackson, D. D. (1998). "This hole in our heart": Urban Indian identity and the power of silence. *American Indian Culture & Research Journal, 22*, 227–255.

Jamieson, K. H. (1988). *Eloquence in an electronic age: The transformation of political speechmaking.* New York: Oxford University Press.

Jamieson, K. H. (1995, July 7). Turning tables with creative tongues. *Christian Science Monitor.* Retrieved September 4, 2006, from http://www.csmonitor.com

Jaska, J. A., & Stech, E. L. (1978). Communication to enhance silence: The Trappist monk experience. *Journal of Communication, 28*, 14–18.

Jaworski, A. (1992). How to silence a minority: The case of women. *International Journal of the Sociology of Language, 94*, 27–42.

Jaworski, A. (1993). *The power of silence: Social and pragmatic perspectives.* Newbury Park, CA: Sage.

Jaworski, A. (1997). "White and white": Metacommunicative and metaphorical silences. In A. Jaworski (Ed.), *Silence: Interdisciplinary perspectives* (pp. 381–401). Berlin: Mouton de Gruyter.

Jaworski, A. (1998). Talk and silence in *The Interrogation*. *Language and Literature, 7,* 99–122.

Jaworski, A. (2000). Silence and small talk. In J. Coupland (Ed.), *Small talk* (pp. 110–152). Harlow, England: Longman.

Jaworski, A., & Galasiński, D. (2000). Strategies of silence: Omission and ambiguity in the *Black Book of Polish Censorship*. *Semiotica, 131,* 185–200.

Jaworski, A., & Sachdev, I. (1998). Beliefs about silence in the classroom. *Language and Education, 12,* 271–292.

Jaworski, A., & Stephens, D. (1998). Self-reports on silence as a face-saving strategy by people with hearing impairment. *International Journal of Applied Linguistics, 8,* 61–80.

Jensen, J. V. (1973). Communicative functions of silence. *ETC: A Review of General Semantics, 30,* 249–257.

Johannesen, R. L. (1974). The functions of silence: A plea for communication research. *Western Speech, 38,* 25–35.

Johnson, I. W., Pearce, C. G., Tuten, T. L., & Sinclair, L. (2003). Self-imposed silence and perceived listening effectiveness. *Business Communication Quarterly, 66,* 23–45.

Jost, K. (2005, December 2). Government secrecy. *CQ Researcher, 15,* 1005–1027.

Julé, A. (2004). *Gender, participation and silence in the language classroom: Shushing the girls.* New York: Palgrave Macmillan.

Kalamaras, G. (1994). *Reclaiming the tacit dimension.* Albany: State University of New York Press.

Kameen, P. (2000). *Writing/teaching: Essays toward a rhetoric of pedagogy.* Pittsburgh: University of Pittsburgh Press.

Keizer, G. (2005, April 5). Slow to answer. *Christian Century, 122,* 26–27.

Kim, M. S. (1992). A comparative analysis of nonverbal expressions as portrayed by Korean and American print-media advertising. *Howard Journal of Communications, 3,* 317–339.

Kim, M. S. (2002). *Non-western perspectives on human communication.* Thousand Oaks, CA: Sage.

Kirkwood, W. G. (1987). The turtle spoke, the donkey brayed: Fables about speech and silence in the Panchatantra. *Journal of Communication and Religion, 10,* 1–12.

Knipe, E. E., & Bromley, D. G. (1984). Speak no evil: Word taboos among Scottish fishermen. In R. B. Browne (Ed.), *Forbidden fruits: Taboos and tabooism in culture* (pp. 183–192). Bowling Green, OH: Bowling Green State University Popular Press.

Kramarae, C. (1981). *Women and men speaking: Frameworks for analysis.* Rowley, MA: Newbury House.

Kramarae, C., Schulz, M., & O'Barr, W. M. (Eds.). (1984). *Language and power.* Beverly Hills, CA: Sage.

Lakoff, R. T. (1990). *Talking power: The politics of language in our lives.* New York: Basic Books.

Langhout, R. D. (2005). Acts of resistance: Student (in)visibility. *Culture & Psychology, 11,* 123–158.

Lauer, C. S. (2005, July 18). Enjoying the silence. *Modern Healthcare, 35,* 22.

Leander, K. M. (2002). Silencing in classroom interaction: Producing and relating social spaces. *Discourse Processes, 34,* 193–235.

Lehtonen, J., & Sajavaara, K. (1985). The silent Finn. In D. Tannen & M. Saville-Troike (Eds.), *Perspectives on silence* (pp. 193–203). Norwood, NJ: Ablex.

Lippard, P. V. (1988). The rhetoric of silence: The Society of Friends' unprogrammed meeting for worship. *Communication Quarterly, 36,* 145–156.

Liu, J. (2001). *Asian students' classroom communication patterns in U.S. universities: An emic perspective.* Westport, CT: Greenwood Publishing Group.

Lorde, A. (1984). *Sister outsider: Essays and speeches by Audre Lorde.* Berkeley, CA: The Crossing Press.

Lowenstein, M. (2005, November). Shut up and heal. *Natural Health, 35,* 93.

Mair, C. (1996). The semantics of silence. In G. M. Grabher & U. Jessner (Eds.), *Semantics of silences in linguistics and literature* (pp. 19–28). Heidelberg, Germany: Universitätsverlag C. Winter.

Maitra, I. (2004). Silence and responsibility. *Philosophical Perspectives, 18,* 189–208.

Maltz, D. N. (1985). Joyful noise and reverent silence: The significance of noise in Pentecostal worship. In D. Tannen & M. Saville-Troike (Eds.), *Perspectives on silence* (pp. 113–138). Norwood, NJ: Ablex.

Marlow, M. L., & Giles, H. (2006). From the roots to the shoots: A Hawaiian case study of language revitalization and modes of communication. In C. S. Beck (Ed.), *Communication yearbook 30* (pp. 343–386). Mahwah, NJ: Lawrence Erlbaum Associates.

Martin, J. N., & Nakayama, T. K. (1999). Thinking dialectically about culture and communication. *Communication Theory, 9,* 1–25.

Matsumoto, M. (1988). *The unspoken way = Haragei: Silence in Japanese business and society.* Tokyo: Kodansha International.

McKinney, B. C. (1982). The effects of reticence on group interaction. *Communication Quarterly, 30,* 124–128.

Mead, M. (1939). *From the South Seas: Studies of adolescence and sex in primitive societies.* New York: W. Morrow & Company.

Meares, M. M., Oetzel, J. G., Torres, A., Derkacs, D., & Ginossar, T. (2004). Employee mistreatment and muted voices in the culturally diverse workplace. *Journal of Applied Communication Research, 32,* 4–27.

Medina, J. (2004). The meanings of silence: Wittgensteinian contextualism and polyphony. *Inquiry, 47,* 562–579.

Meise, K. (1996). On talking about silence in conversation and literature. In G. M. Grabher & U. Jessner (Eds.), *Semantics of silences in linguistics and literature* (pp. 45–66). Heidelberg, Germany: Universitätsverlag C. Winter.

Messer, D. E. (2004). *Breaking the conspiracy of silence: Christian churches and the global AIDS crisis.* Minneapolis, MN: Fortress Press.

Mildorf, J. (2005). Words that strike and words that comfort: Discursive dynamics of verbal abuse in Roddy Doyle's "The Woman Who Walked into Doors." *Journal of Gender Studies, 14,* 107–122.

Miller, A. N., & Harris, T. M. (2005). Communicating to develop White racial identity in an interracial communication class. *Communication Education, 54,* 223–242.

Miller, C. (1996). M. Nourbese Philip and the poetics/politics of silence. In G. M. Grabher & U. Jessner (Eds.), *Semantics of silences in linguistics and literature* (pp. 139–160). Heidelberg, Germany: Universitätsverlag C. Winter.

Milliken, F. J., Morrison, E. W., & Hewlin, P. F. (2003). An exploratory study of employee silence: Issues that employees don't communicate upward and why. *Journal of Management Studies, 40,* 1453–1476.

Minh-ha, T. T. (1990). Not you/like you: Post-colonial women and the interlocking questions of identity and difference. In G. Anzaldúa (Ed.), *Making face, making soul = Haciendo caras: Creative and critical perspectives by women of color* (pp. 371–375). San Francisco: Aunt Lute Books.

Montalbano-Phelps, L. L. (2003). Discourse of survival: Building families free of unhealthy relationships. *Journal of Family Communication, 3,* 149–178.

Moore, K. (2005). Become a better communicator by keeping your mouth shut. *Journal for Quality & Participation, 28,* 8–10.

Morman, D. (2005). The wild and wooly world of inferences and presumptions—When silence is deafening. *The Florida Bar Journal, 79,* 38–43.

Morrison, E. W., & Milliken, F. J. (2003). Speaking up, remaining silent: The dynamics of voice and silence in organizations. *Journal of Management Studies, 40,* 1353–1358.

Morsbach, H. (1988). The importance of silence and stillness in Japanese nonverbal communication: A cross-cultural approach. In F. Poyatos (Ed.), *Cross-cultural perspectives in nonverbal communication* (pp. 201–215). Lewiston, NY: Hogrefe.

Mumby, D. K., & Putnam, L. L. (1992). The politics of emotion: A feminist reading of bounded emotionality. *Academy of Management Review, 17,* 465–486.

Muñoz-Duston, E., & Kaplan, J. (1985). A sampling of sources on silence. In D. Tannen & M. Saville-Troike (Eds.), *Perspectives on silence* (pp. 235–242). Norwood, NJ: Ablex.

Nakayama, T. K., & Krizek, R. L. (1995). Whiteness: A strategic rhetoric. *Quarterly Journal of Speech, 81,* 291–309.

Natapoff, A. (2005). Speechless: The silencing of criminal defendants. *New York University Law Review, 80,* 1449–1504.

Nelson, G. (1995). Cultural differences in learning styles. In J. M. Reid (Ed.), *Learning styles in the ESL/EFL classroom* (pp. 3–18). Boston: Heinle & Heinle.

Newman, H. M. (1982). The sounds of silence in communicative encounters. *Communication Quarterly, 30,* 142–149.

Nicholls, C. (2005). Exhibition round-up. *Art & Australia, 43,* 176–179.

Noelle-Neumann, E. (1974). The spiral of silence. *Journal of Communication, 24,* 43–51.

Nwoye, G. (1985). Eloquent silences among the Igbo of Nigeria. In D. Tannen & M. Saville-Troike (Eds.), *Perspectives on silence* (pp. 185–192). Norwood, NJ: Ablex.

Olsen, G. D. (1994). Observations: The sounds of silence: Functions and use of silence in television advertising. *Journal of Advertising Research, 34,* 89–96.

Olsen, G. D. (1995). Creating the contrast: The influence of silence and sound. *Journal of Advertising, 24,* 29–45.

Olsen, T. (1978). *Silences.* New York: Delta/Seymour.

Olson, L. C. (1997). On the margins of rhetoric: Audre Lorde transforming silence into language and action. *Quarterly Journal of Speech, 83,* 49–70.

Olson, L. C. (1998). Liabilities of language: Audre Lorde reclaiming difference. *Quarterly Journal of Speech, 84,* 448–470.

Orbe, M. (1994). "Remember, it's always whites' ball": Descriptions of African American male communication. *Communication Quarterly, 42,* 287–300.

Orbe, M. (1995). African American communication research: Toward a deeper understanding of interethnic communication. *Western Journal of Communication, 59,* 61–78.

Palfreman, J. (Producer and director). (1993). *Prisoners of silence* [motion picture]. United States: PBS Video.

Palocci Under Siege. (2005, November 19). *Economist, 377,* 39–40.

Patten, K. (1997). Teaching "Discovering Silence." In A. Jaworski (Ed.), *Silence: Interdisciplinary perspectives* (pp. 369–378). Berlin: Mouton de Gruyter.

Pawelczyk, J. (2003). Redefining femininity: Call and response as gendered features in African-American discourse. *Multilingua, 22,* 415–438.

Pelias, R. J. (2002). For father and son: An ethnodrama with no catharsis. In A. P. Bochner & C. Ellis (Eds.), *Ethnographically speaking*
(pp. 35–43). Walnut Creek, CA: AltaMira Press.

Perales, J., & Cenoz, J. (1996). Silence, communicative competence and communication strategies in second language acquisition. In G. M. Grabher & U. Jessner (Eds.), *Semantics of silences in linguistics and literature*
(pp. 67–88). Heidelberg, Germany: Universitätsverlag C. Winter.

Petronio, S. (1991). Communication boundary management: A theoretical
model of managing disclosure of private information between marital couples. *Communication Theory, 1,* 311–335.

Petronio, S. (Ed.). (2000). *Balancing secrets of private disclosures.* Mahwah,
NJ: Lawrence Erlbaum Associates.

Petronio, S. (2002). *Boundaries of privacy: Dialectics of disclosure.* Albany:
State University of New York Press.

Philips, S. U. (1983). *The invisible culture: Communication in classroom and community on the Warm Springs Indian Reservation.* New York: Longman.

Philips, S. U. (1985). Interaction structured through talk and interaction
structured through silence. In D. Tannen & M. Saville-Troike (Eds.),
Perspectives on silence (pp. 205–214). Norwood, NJ: Ablex.

Philipsen, G. (1975). Speaking like a man in Teamsterville: Culture patterns of role enactment in an urban neighborhood. *Quarterly Journal
of Speech, 61,* 13–22.

Picard, M. (1952). *The world of silence.* Chicago: Henry Regnery Company.

Pinder, C. C., & Harlos, H. P. (2001). Employee silence: Quiescence and
acquiescence as responses to received injustice. *Research in Personnel
and Human Resource Management, 20,* 331–369.

Piran, N., & Cormier, H. C. (2005). The social construction of women and
disordered eating patterns. *Journal of Counseling Psychology, 52,*
549–558.

Pitt, W. R. (2003). *The greatest sedition is silence: Four years in America.*
London: Pluto Press.

Polanyi, M. (1962). *Personal knowledge: Towards a post-critical philosophy.*
London: Routledge & Kegan Paul.

Pomeroy, W. B. (1963). Human sexual behavior. In N. L. Farberow (Ed.),
Taboo topics (pp. 22–32). New York: Atherton Press.

Pörhölä, M., Karhunen, S., & Rainivaara, S. (2006). Bullying at school and
in the workplace: A challenge for communication research. In C. S.
Beck (Ed.), *Communication yearbook 30* (pp. 249–302). Mahwah, NJ:
Lawrence Erlbaum Associates.

Potter, R., & Dillman Carpentier, F. (2005). *Effects of music on physiological arousal: Explorations into genre and tempo.* Paper presented at the
annual meeting of the International Communication Association,
New York.

Poyatos, F. (1983). *New perspectives in nonverbal communication.* Oxford, England: Pergamon Press.

Poyatos, F. (2002). *Nonverbal communication across disciplines* (Vol. 2). Amsterdam: John Benjamins.

Pratt, S. B., & Buchanan, M. C. (2004). Wa-Zha-Zhe I-E: Notions on a dying ancestral language. In A. González, M. Houston, & V. Chen (Eds.), *Our voices: Essays in culture, ethnicity, and communication* (4th ed., pp. 174–182). Los Angeles: Roxbury.

Raab, J. (1996). Elizabeth Bishop's autobiographical silences. In G. M. Grabher & U. Jessner (Eds.), *Semantics of silences in linguistics and literature* (pp. 291–308). Heidelberg, Germany: Universitätsverlag C. Winter.

Ragan, S. L., Aarons, V., & Taylor, J. (1986). Women's response to men's silence: A fictional analysis. *Women's Studies in Communication, 9,* 67–89.

Rakow, L., & Kramarae, C. (Eds.). (1990). *The revolution in words: Righting women.* New York: Routledge.

Reuter, D. (2005). Silent knight: Protecting yourself with silence. *ETC: A Review of General Semantics, 62,* 433–438.

Reyes, P., Scribner, J. D., & Scribner, A. P. (1999). *Lessons from high-performing Hispanic students: Creating learning communities.* New York: Teacher's College Press.

Reynolds, K. A. (1998). Female speakers of Japanese in transition. In J. Coates (Ed.), *Language and gender: A reader* (pp. 299–308). Malden, MA: Blackwell.

Rich, A. (1979). *On lies, secrets, and silence: Selected prose, 1966–1978.* New York: W. W. Norton.

Robinson, D. (1996). *Translation and taboo.* DeKalb: Northern Illinois University Press.

Rubik, M. (1996). The silencing of women in feminist British drama. In G. M. Grabher & U. Jessner (Eds.), *Semantics of silences in linguistics and literature* (pp. 177–190). Heidelberg, Germany: Universitätsverlag C. Winter.

Sacks, H., Schegloff, E. A., & Jefferson, G. (1974). A simplest systematics for the organization of turn-taking for conversation. *Language, 50,* 696–735.

Sajavaara, K., & Lehtonen, J. (1997). The silent Finn revisited. In A. Jaworski (Ed.), *Silence: Interdisciplinary perspectives* (pp. 263–283). Berlin: Mouton de Gruyter.

Sanchez, J. (2003). Dirty words. *Reason, 35,* 15.

Saunders, G. R. (1985). Silence and noise as emotion management styles: An Italian case. In D. Tannen & M. Saville-Troike (Eds.), *Perspectives on silence* (pp. 165–184). Norwood, NJ: Ablex.

Saville-Troike, M. (1985). The place of silence in an integrated theory of communication. In D. Tannen & M. Saville-Troike (Eds.), *Perspectives on silence* (pp. 3–20). Norwood, NJ: Ablex.

Scarpi, P. (1987). The eloquence of silence: Aspects of power without words. In M. G. Ciani (Ed.), *The regions of silence: Studies on the difficulty of communicating* (pp. 19–40). Amsterdam: J. C. Gieben.

Scheufele, D. A., & Moy, P. (2000). Twenty-five years of the spiral of silence: A conceptual review and empirical outlook. *International Journal of Public Opinion Research, 12*, 3–29.

Schön, A. (1987). Silence in the myth: Psychoanalytical observations. In M. G. Ciani (Ed.), *The regions of silence: Studies on the difficulty of communicating* (pp. 5–18). Amsterdam: J.C. Gieben.

Scollon, R. (1985). The machine stops: Silence in the metaphor of malfunction. In D. Tannen & M. Saville-Troike (Eds.), *Perspectives on silence* (pp. 21–30). Norwood, NJ: Ablex.

Scott, R. L. (1993). Dialectical tensions of speaking and silence. *Quarterly Journal of Speech, 79*, 1–18.

Scott, R. L. (2000). Between silence and certainty: A codicil to "Dialectical Tensions of Speaking and Silence." *Quarterly Journal of Speech, 86*, 108–111.

Sebate, P. M. (1996). The role of silence in the modern Tswana short story. *South African Journal of African Languages, 16*, 67–73.

Sifianou, M. (1997). Silence and politeness. In A. Jaworski (Ed.), *Silence: Interdisciplinary perspectives* (pp. 63–84). Berlin: Mouton de Gruyter.

Sivakumaran, S. (2005). Male/male rape and the "taint" of homosexuality. *Human Rights Quarterly, 27*, 1274–1306.

Skrla, L., Reyes, P., & Scheurich, J. J. (2000). Sexism, silence, and solutions: Women superintendents speak up and out. *Educational Administration Quarterly, 36*, 44–75

Smith, J. (2001). The visible and the vanished: Taboos in Japan. In A. Mills & J. Smith (Eds.), *Utter silence: Voicing the unspeakable* (pp. 31–50). New York: Peter Lang.

Sobkowiak, W. (1997). Silence and markedness theory. In A. Jaworski (Ed.), *Silence: Interdisciplinary perspectives* (pp. 39–61). Berlin: Mouton de Gruyter.

Solomon, D. H., Knobloch, L. K., & Fitzpatrick, M. A. (2004). Relational power, marital schema, and decisions to withhold complaints: An investigation of the chilling effect on confrontation in marriage. *Communication Studies, 55*, 146–171.

Sontag, S. (1969). *Styles of radical will.* New York: Farrar, Straus, and Giroux.

Sparkes, A. C. (2002). Autoethnography: Self-indulgence or something more? In A. P. Bochner & C. Ellis (Eds.), *Ethnographically speaking* (pp. 209–232). Walnut Creek, CA: AltaMira Press.

Splichal, S. (2006). Manufacturing the (in)visible: Power to communicate, power to silence. *Communication and Critical/Cultural Studies, 3*, 95–115.

Steiner, F. B. (1956). *Taboo*. London: Cohen & West.

Stephenson, D. R. (1982). How to turn pitfalls into opportunities in crisis situations. *Public Opinion Quarterly, 27,* 11–16.

Stroińska, M. (2000). Forbidden reality: The language and functions of propaganda. In F. Lloyd & C. O'Brien (Eds.), *Secret spaces, forbidden places: Rethinking culture* (pp. 121–132). New York: Berghahn Books.

Tannen, D. (1985). Silence: Anything but. In D. Tannen & M. Saville-Troike (Eds.), *Perspectives on silence* (pp. 93–112). Norwood, NJ: Ablex.

Tannen, D. (1986). *That's not what I meant: How conversational style makes or breaks your relations with others*. London: J. M. Dent & Sons.

Taylor, J., & Mackenzie, R. A. (1983). The power of silence in selling. *Business Quarterly, 48,* 38–41.

Taylor, S. C. (2001). A name by any other word does not necessarily make it merely another rose. In A. Mills & J. Smith (Eds.), *Utter silence: Voicing the unspeakable* (pp. 211–228). New York: Peter Lang.

Tent, J. F. (2003). *In the shadow of the Holocaust: Nazi persecution of Jewish–Christian Germans*. Lawrence: University Press of Kansas.

The therapeutic value of silence. (2003). *Journal of the American Medical Association, 294,* 112.

Thiesmeyer, L. (Ed.). (2003). *Discourse and silencing: Representation and the language of displacement*. Amsterdam: J. Benjamins.

Ting-Toomey, S. (Ed.). (1994). *The challenge of facework: Cross-cultural and interpersonal issues*. Albany: State University of New York Press.

Trethewey, A. (1997). Resistance, identity, and empowerment: A postmodern feminist analysis of clients in a human services organization. *Communication Monographs, 64,* 281–301.

Tse, C. Y., Chong, A., & Fok, S. Y. (2003). Breaking bad news: A Chinese perspective. *Palliative Medicine, 17,* 339–343.

Tuite, K., & Schulze, W. (1998). A case of taboo-motivated lexical replacement in the indigenous languages of the Caucasus. *Anthropological Linguistics, 40,* 363–383.

Ufema, J. (2005, October). Terminal illness: Conspiracy of silence. *Nursing, 35,* 21.

Vainiomäki, T. (2004). Silence as a cultural sign. *Semiotica, 150,* 347–362.

Valenzuela, A. (1999). *Subtractive schooling: U.S.–Mexican youth and the politics of caring*. New York: State University of New York Press.

Valone, D. A., & Kinealy, C. (Eds.). (2002). *Ireland's great hunger: Silence, memory, and commemoration*. Lanham, MD: University Press of America.

Vangelisti, A. L. (1994). Family secrets: Forms, functions, and correlates. *Journal of Social and Personal Relationships, 11,* 113–135.

Vangelisti, A. L., & Caughlin, J. P. (1997). Revealing family secrets: The influence of topic, function, and relationships. *Journal of Social and Personal Relationships, 14,* 679–705.

Vangelisti, A. L., Caughlin, J. P., & Timmerman, L. (2001). Criteria for revealing family secrets. *Communication Monographs, 68,* 1–17.

Villegas, H. (2004). *In the silence absence makes.* Toronto, Canada: Guernica Editions.

Wachal, R. S. (2002). Taboo or not taboo: That is the question. *American Speech, 77,* 195–206.

Wagener, K. C., Brand, T., & Kollmeier, B. (2006). The role of silent intervals for sentence intelligibility in fluctuating noise in hearing-impaired listeners. *International Journal of Audiology, 45,* 26–33.

Walker, A. G. (1985). The two faces of silence: The effect of witness hesitancy on lawyer's impressions. In D. Tannen & M. Saville-Troike (Eds.), *Perspectives on silence* (pp. 55–76). Norwood, NJ: Ablex.

Wardhaugh, R. (2002). *An introduction to sociolinguistics* (4th ed.). Malden, MA: Blackwell.

Watts, R. J. (1997). Silence and the acquisition of status in verbal interaction. In A. Jaworski (Ed.), *Silence: Interdisciplinary perspectives* (pp. 87–115). Berlin: Mouton de Gruyter.

Wayne, L. D. (1996). Silence and violence: The woman behind the wall. *Women & Language, 19,* 1–7.

Weber, M. (2005). *Consuming silences: How we read authors who don't publish.* Athens: University of Georgia Press.

Welles, C. E. (2005). Breaking the silence surrounding female adolescent sexual desire. *Women & Therapy, 28,* 31–45.

Whitehead, N. L., & Wright, R. (Eds.). (2004). *In darkness and secrecy: The anthropology of assault sorcery and witchcraft in Amazonia.* Durham, NC: Duke University Press.

Wieder, D. L., & Pratt, S. (1990). On being a recognizable Indian among Indians. In D. Carbaugh (Ed.), *Cultural communication and intercultural contact* (pp. 45–64). Hillsdale, NJ: Lawrence Erlbaum Associates.

Wilkinson, D. (2002). *Silence on the mountain: Stories of terror, betrayal, and forgetting in Guatemala.* Boston: Houghton Mifflin.

Wilks, C., & Brick, N. (2000). Naming and exclusion: The politics of language in contemporary France. In F. Lloyd & C. O'Brien (Eds.), *Secret spaces, forbidden places: Rethinking culture* (pp. 145–153). New York: Berghahn Books.

Williams, K. D. (2001). *Ostracism: The power of silence.* New York: Guilford Press.

Williams, P. (2003). *Gypsy world: The silence of the living and the voices of the dead.* Chicago: University of Chicago Press.

Wilson, T. P., & Zimmerman, D. H. (1986). The structure of silence between turns in two-party conversation. *Discourse Processes, 9,* 375–390.

Winans, A. (2006). Queering pedagogy in the English classroom: Engaging with the places where thinking stops. *Pedagogy, 6,* 103–122.

Wood, J. T. (1992). Telling our stories: Narratives as a basis for theorizing sexual harrassment. *Journal of Applied Communication Research, 20,* 349–363.

Wood, J. T. (1996). Dominant and muted discourses in popular representations of feminism. *Quarterly Journal of Speech, 82,* 171–186.

Woodstock, L. (2001). Hide and seek: The paradox of documenting a suicide. *Text & Performance Quarterly, 21,* 247–261.

Wright, S. (2005, September 21). Away from it all. *Nursing Standard, 20,* 30–31.

Young, V. (2002). Pieces of time. *Nursing Philosophy, 3,* 90–108.

Zembylas, M., & Pavlos, M. (2004). The sounds of silence in pedagogy. *Educational Theory, 54,* 193–210.

Zerubavel, E. (2006). *The elephant in the room: Silence and denial in everyday life.* New York: Oxford University Press.

Zhang, A. Y., & Siminoff, L. A. (2003). Silence and cancer: Why do patients and families fail to communicate? *Health Communication, 15,* 415–430.

Zhou, Y. R., Knoke, D., & Sakamoto, I. (2005). Rethinking silence in the classroom: Chinese students' experiences of sharing indigenous knowledge. *International Journal of Inclusive Education, 9,* 287–311.

Zuo, Y. (2002). *The golden silence: A pragmatic study on silence in dyadic English conversation.* Munich, Germany: Lincom Europa.

Chapter 2 Contents

2

Openness and Avoidance in Couples Communicating About Cancer

Daena J. Goldsmith
Lews and Clark College

Laura E. Miller and John P. Caughlin
University of Illinois at Urbana-Champaign

Open communication and avoidance are fundamental communication processes that have been studied across a range of communication contexts. Couples in which one person has cancer are a theoretically and practically important site for examining openness and avoidance. We review the cancer-related topics that couples find challenging, couples' reasons for communicating openly or avoiding talk about cancer-related topics, outcomes of communication, features and strategies of communication, and individual, relational, and illness-related factors that may influence communication. The application of theories of open and avoidant communication suggests new directions for cancer research and has practical implications for interventions designed to assist couples. We also discuss needed changes in how we conceptualize and measure openness and avoidance. These suggested refinements are relevant across a wide range of contexts in which researchers study openness and avoidance.

Openness and Avoidance in Couples Communicating About Cancer

Open communication (i.e., disclosure of thoughts, information, and/or feelings) and avoidance of communication (i.e., deciding not to discuss particular issues and/or withholding some details of particular issues) fascinate scholars across the communication discipline. Scholars have delineated the importance of secrecy, privacy, and discretion for individual and relational well-being (Bochner, 1982; Parks, 1982) and theorized the tensions between and management of openness and closedness (Baxter & Montgomery, 1996; Petronio, 2002). Eisenberg and Witten (1987) proposed that individual, relational, organizational, and environmental contingencies shape the usefulness of open communication in organizations, and research on "the subtle boundaries and conditions of disclosure" (Duggan, 2006, p. 101) is a central issue for future health communication research.

A cursory sampling of studies reveals the breadth of interest, including studies of nursing home patient privacy (Petronio & Kovach, 1997); the forms, functions, and correlates of family secrets (Vangelisti, 1994); nurses' avoidance behaviors in hospitals with different organizational structures (Marin, Sherblom, & Shipps, 1994), and cultural variation in avoiding communication to manage face (Oetzel et al., 2001). In this volume, chapters on silence (Acheson), identity (Young), organizational assimilation (Waldeck & Myers), community (underwood & Frey), and media content diversity (Roessler) likewise attest to the salience of open communication and avoidance across an array of theoretical concerns. This widespread scholarly interest is justified because openness and avoidance connect with important individual, relational, and social outcomes. Openness and avoidance also entail fundamental processes (including privacy regulation, uncertainty management, expression of feelings, and information seeking and provision) that cut across communication contexts.

In this chapter, we examine openness and avoidance as couples cope with one person's cancer. Cancer is a prevalent illness worldwide (e.g., Parkin, Bray, Ferlay, & Pisani, 2005), and scholars across disciplines are interested in how patients and their loved ones manage not only physical effects, but also psychosocial ramifications. Communication between a patient and his or her spouse or partner shapes psychosocial, physical, and relational well-being (e.g., Manne, 1998). We synthesize a sizable body of work addressing partners' open communication and avoidance of communication about cancer-related topics. Most of this research has proceeded without grounding in communication theory (P. G. Northouse & L. Northouse, 1987). Embedding our interest in this context within broader questions about open and avoidant communication enables us to make sense of the available literature and suggest directions for future research that will inform our understanding of the cancer experience and of open and avoidant communication more generally. Accordingly, we begin with an overview of research on open and avoidant communication. The remainder of the chapter demonstrates how these general concepts and principles take shape in couple communication about cancer.

Open Communication and Communication Avoidance

An enormous amount of scholarship has addressed these concepts, and an exhaustive summary of this literature is beyond the scope of the current chapter (for reviews, see T. D. Afifi, Caughlin, & W. A. Afifi, in press; Caughlin & Petronio, 2004; Derlega, Metts, Petronio, & Margulis, 1993; Petronio, 2002; Rosenfeld, 2000). Instead, we extract key theoretical principles that may be applied widely. We have drawn most extensively from the research on personal relationships because of our interest in couples' coping. Three issues provide a synthetic framework for interpreting research on couple communication about cancer: (a) predictors of openness or avoidance, (b) consequences of openness or avoidance, and (c) factors influencing the consequences of openness or avoidance.

What Predicts Openness or Avoidance?

A main research question concerns when and why individuals communicate openly or avoid communication. One way of approaching this question emphasizes observable disclosure patterns and proclivities. For example, individuals from diverse cultures differ in their tendency to self-disclose (Gudykunst & Nishida, 1984; Petronio, 2000; Rosenfeld, 2000), and women generally disclose more than do men (though the difference is small; see Dindia & Allen, 1992). According to Petronio, differences in the tendency to disclose may arise because sociocultural groups have different criteria for determining when to be open or when to avoid.

Researchers have also explored predictors of openness or avoidance by asking individuals about their reasons for disclosing or concealing information (e.g., Golish & Caughlin, 2002; Rosenfeld, 1979; Vangelisti, 1994). Two crucial conceptual conclusions can be drawn from this research. First, rationales for avoidance or openness vary in terms of specificity. Some reasons seem to be broadly relevant; others are situated in particular circumstances. Second, individuals often have multiple, and potentially competing, explanations for avoiding or openly communicating. To illustrate these points and their theoretical implications, we briefly review common general reasons for avoidance, common general reasons for communicating openly, and reasons for openness or avoidance that are shaped by particular contexts.

Reasons for Avoiding Communication

Perhaps the most widely cited rationale for withholding information involves trying to prevent others from forming a negative impression (W. A. Afifi & Guerrero, 2000; Greene & Faulkner, 2002; Petronio,

2002; Rosenfeld, 1979). This reason has been cited in a wide variety of contexts, including family members who worry that outsiders might judge their family if they learned their secrets (Vangelisti, 1994), people living with HIV who worry about the stigma associated with it (Greene & Faulkner, 2002), sexual abuse victims who fear blame and stigma (Paine & Hansen, 2002), and members of a university search committee who omit negative information when speaking publicly (Eisenberg, Murphy, & Andrews, 1998).

People also conceal information due to a desire to protect themselves from people who might use the information against them or pass it on to third parties (Greene & Faulkner, 2002; Vangelisti, 1994). In other cases, individuals express concern that the other person would not be appropriately responsive or discuss the information in a constructive manner (Caughlin & Golish, 2002; Guerrero & W. A. Afifi, 1995; Roloff & Ifert, 2000). Some people avoid communication to protect others; for instance, parents with HIV may try to protect their children from stress by concealing their health status (Schrimshaw & Siegel, 2002). Additionally, individuals often give relationship-based explanations for avoiding communication (T. D. Afifi, Olson, & Armstrong, 2005), such as preventing unwanted conflicts (Guerrero & W. A. Afifi, 1995; Roloff & Ifert, 2000) or not delving into topics that might lead to deterioration of the relationship (Caughlin & Golish, 2002; Guerrero & W. A. Afifi, 1995).

Reasons for Communicating Openly

A largely separate literature addresses reasons for being open. Researchers have long noted the association between relational closeness and disclosure (Derlega et al., 1993). Individuals reveal private information because they perceive sufficient trust and closeness in the relationship to warrant such revelations (Vangelisti, Caughlin, & Timmerman, 2001). However, open communication also occurs outside of close relationships. For example, people may disclose a family secret without being close to the other person, if they perceive an urgent need (e.g., helping somebody in a crisis; Vangelisti et al., 2001). Stiles (1987) suggested that avoiding communication can cause distress and that people may feel compelled to disclose to relieve such distress. Consistent with the notion of disclosing to relieve distress, women who told others they had HIV often did so because they desired catharsis (Kimberly, Serovich, & Greene, 1995).

Context-Specific Reasons   Although not intended to provide an exhaustive list (see Caughlin & Petronio, 2004), the aforementioned examples illustrate some of the variety in explanations that people give for avoiding or being open. Even more diversity becomes evident when considering specific circumstances. Research on topic avoidance by adolescents in stepfamilies, for instance, suggests that they avoid communicating for reasons related to their unique family dynamics, including (a) trying not to take sides in conflicts between their custodial and noncustodial parents, (b) not recognizing the authority of a stepparent to discuss an issue, and (c) concerns that a stepparent sides with his or her children from a previous marriage (Golish & Caughlin, 2002).

Individuals may also have context-specific reasons when they avoid health-related topics. In a study of heart disease patients, Goldsmith, Gumminger, and Bute (2006) found that some people did not discuss the illness because talking about it would imply that the patient was still sick. That is, avoiding this topic allows spouses to construct a healthy—or at least non-ill—identity for the patient (for a related review of identity research, see Young, this volume). As Goldsmith, Gumminger, et al. explained, although these couples' identity management related to the broader goal of minimizing negative impressions, it had to do with collusion in ignoring rather than individual efforts to conceal. In short, despite broad commonalities in reasons for avoiding or being open, specific circumstances also influence individuals' reasons for withholding or revealing information.

What Are the Consequences of Openness or Avoidance?

North American culture tends to favor openness over avoidance (Bochner, 1982; Katriel & Philipsen, 1981; for a review on silence, see Acheson, this volume). Much early research focused on benefits of disclosure, such as the potential for closer relationships (for review, see Parks, 1982). Many scholars continue to treat openness as inherently desirable and avoidance as inherently problematic (T. D. Afifi et al., in press). Some evidence supports this bias. Avoiding topics in close relationships, for instance, generally predicts dissatisfaction (Caughlin & Golish, 2002). Nevertheless, theory and research indicate openness is not always good and avoidance is not always bad. Various theories, most notably dialectical theories (e.g., Baxter & Montgomery, 1996) and communication privacy management theory (Petronio, 2002), posit that both openness and avoidance can be useful in relationships and that each has risks and benefits.

Self-disclosure correlates with satisfaction in romantic relationships (for reviews, see Collins & Miller, 1994; Dindia, 2000), and it can improve mental and physical health (for reviews, see Kelly, 2002; Smyth & Pennebaker, 2001). Open communication also can let others know that one needs comforting (Derlega et al., 1993) or tangible support (Gewirtz & Gossart-Walker, 2000). Such unquestionable benefits of openness must be weighed against various risks involved. As noted earlier, people often avoid certain disclosures because they worry about impression management—a legitimate concern because sometimes others do express disapproval (Caughlin, W. A. Afifi, Carpenter-Theune, & Miller, 2005). Moreover, although disclosures of traumatic events can yield mental and physical health benefits, such revelations can be harmful to the confidant's mental state (Frawley, 1990; Pennebaker, 1997; for a related review of research on trauma, see Grey, this volume), and an unsupportive confidant can make the person who discloses feel worse (Petrie, Booth, & Davison, 1995).

Some of the risks and benefits of avoidance parallel those of openness. Whereas openness appears to offer certain mental and physical health benefits, research links keeping secrets with tension, loneliness, behavioral impulsiveness, and stress-related physical health problems (Kelly, 2002). Whereas disclosure generally correlates with satisfaction in relationships, avoiding topics generally is linked to dissatisfaction (Caughlin & Golish, 2002). However, some consequences of avoiding cannot easily be inferred from the literature on open communication. Secret keeping can actually enhance relationships, such as when individuals collaborate to keep information from others (Bok, 1983; Vangelisti, 1994). Additionally, restricting some information facilitates establishing functional boundaries in families (Caughlin & Petronio, 2004). Parents who do not avoid certain topics with their children may experience problematic intergeneration cohesion, such as a parent–child bond that excludes the other parent (Minuchin, 1974).

In short, neither openness nor avoidance is entirely good or bad. Both pose risks and potential benefits. However, the particular mix of risks and potential benefits varies across situations. In some instances, openness might be very risky, but not in others. In some cases, keeping a secret may yield benefits; in other situations, revelation may prove more desirable.

Factors Influencing the Consequences of Openness or Avoidance

Other factors moderate the effects of openness and avoidance. The topic of information is one such factor. Despite the connection between disclosure and relational satisfaction, revealing negative thoughts about one's partner more often indicates dissatisfaction (Caughlin & Petronio, 2004). Not all disclosures of negative information are bad, however. For example, disclosing negative emotions about somebody outside the relationship (e.g., hostile feelings toward a co-worker) can be viewed favorably in relationships (Shimanoff, 1987). Perceptions of a topic matter as well. Greene (2000), for example, found that people revealed a cancer diagnosis more readily than an HIV diagnosis, probably due to the greater stigma associated with HIV. Vangelisti and Caughlin (1997) concluded that perceptions of secrets (e.g., the centrality of the information to identity) predicted family satisfaction better than the topic of the secret per se.

Variations in perceptions influence the impact of openness and avoidance. For example, people hold different standards for communication (i.e., beliefs about what counts as good communication). Although individuals generally view avoidance as dissatisfying, avoidance does not bother others because their beliefs about and expectations for relationships do not require disclosure (Caughlin, 2003). Also, the reasons that people attribute to openness or avoidance likely moderate their impact. For example, believing one's partner avoids topics to protect the relationship makes topic avoidance less dissatisfying, but assuming one's partner avoids for self-protection amplifies the avoidance–dissatisfaction connection (Caughlin & T. D. Afifi, 2004).

Additionally, the effects of openness or avoidance depend on relationship factors. Being less powerful in relationships can exacerbate the association between avoidance and dissatisfaction (Caughlin & T. D. Afifi, 2004). Also, openness and avoidance function differently in various types of couples; those who emphasize autonomy and emotional distance actually may be more satisfied when they avoid conflict than when they disclose openly during conflict discussions (Sillars, Pike, Jones, & Redmon, 1983).

Sociocultural differences may moderate effects of openness and avoidance. North American culture tends to value openness (Gudykunst & Nishida, 1984; Petronio, 2000), probably contributing to the dissatisfaction often connected with avoidance. Cohort studies show that couples married in recent decades prefer open and frank discussions more than couples from previous generations (Zietlow & Sillars, 1988).

Finally, the particular messages used to reveal or avoid information are important. Many degrees lie in between openness and avoidance, and one can also be open about certain aspects of a topic but avoid others. Messages vary in directness; for instance, Greene, Derlega, Yep, and Petronio (2003) noted that people disclosing their HIV status sometimes do so directly (e.g., by saying, "I have HIV") but also often do so indirectly (e.g., by discussing a related topic like visiting a physician). Indirect messages cannot be considered completely open or avoidant.

Individuals can be open or avoidant in various ways. Scholars have described different tactics for avoiding (e.g., Dailey & Palomares, 2004; Sillars et al., 1983) and for managing conflicting desires for openness and avoidance (Baxter & Montgomery, 1996). More important, diverse ways of avoiding probably result in different impacts. For example, hostile avoidance indicates marital dissatisfaction more than affectively neutral avoidance (Roberts, 2000).

The relationship between reasons for avoidance or openness and actual behavior is not a simple one in which a person has a single reason for acting and then follows the obvious course of action. Instead, individuals may possess various (and, occasionally, conflicting) reasons for being open or for avoiding. Thus, it is useful to conceptualize openness and avoidance from a multiple goals perspective (e.g., Dillard, 1990; Goldsmith, 2004; O'Keefe, 1988), in which the consequences of openness or avoidance depend on the extent to which (and competence with which) individuals manage multiple goals. To illustrate, Goldsmith, Lindholm, and Bute (2006) reported that some heart patients and their partners avoided talking about lifestyle changes because discussion might imply that the patient could not enact the changes alone. This concern could be a reason for avoiding talk, but, if other factors lead a couple to talk about the issue, the most effective ways of discussing lifestyle changes would likely be responsive to these identity concerns. For instance, some partners respected patient autonomy by letting the patient initiate the topic and by expressing their concerns once, then letting it go (Goldsmith, Gumminger, et al., 2006). In short, individuals' approaches for addressing multiple goals pertaining to openness and avoidance could mitigate the effects of revealing or concealing certain information.

Summary

Couples may possess multiple reasons for communicating openly or avoiding communication. Some of these reasons spring from general processes (e.g., managing privacy, uncertainty, or affect), but others pertain to specific situations. Open and avoidant communication can be consequential for individuals and for their relationships. Yet, the realization of these consequences depends upon features of the communication itself, communicators, their relationships, and the broader sociocultural context. Next, we examine how general principles of communication illuminate our understanding of the experiences of couples communicating about one person's cancer.

Open and Avoidant Couple Communication About Cancer

Cancer will affect most of us at some time, either through direct personal experience or through contact with others in our social network. The American Cancer Society (ACS) (2006) reported that an estimated 10.1 million U.S. residents have a history of cancer, and the ACS predicted 1.4 million new cases in 2006. Worldwide statistics for the year 2002 indicate 10.9 million new cases, 6.7 million deaths, and 24.6 million people living within 3 years of a cancer diagnosis (Parkin et al., 2005). Cancer may be a terminal condition, but more individuals now live with cancer, its treatments, and its aftermath for extended periods of time. For example, in the United States, the 5-year survival rate for people diagnosed with cancer between 1995 and 2001 was 65% across all types of cancer.

The cancer experience involves physical and psychosocial challenges that arise during treatment and beyond. Cancer affects both patients and their life partners, and partners may experience distress as much as or more than patients (for reviews, see Blanchard, Albrecht, & Ruckdeschel, 1997; Lewis, 1986; Manne, 1998; L. Northouse, 1984; Pitceathly & Maguire, 2003). As Hilton (1993) explained, "Learning to live with cancer is no easy task. Learning to live with someone else's cancer may be even more difficult" (p. 88). In turn, partners can significantly influence how patients experience and manage illness (e.g., Giese-Davis, Hermanson, Koopman, Weibel, & Spiegel, 2000; Manne, 1998; Manne, Pape, Taylor, & Dougherty, 1999; Pistrang & Barker, 1995).

As a complex experience that impacts individual and relational well-being, cancer entails several processes that make it theoretically interesting for communication scholars, including meaning-making, social support, decision-making, and uncertainty management. Do couples use communication to manage the ominous connotations of "cancer"? Does communication play a role in deciding upon and coping with difficult treatments with lingering effects on body and psyche? Is communication one of the ways that couples resolve uncertainty about cause and trajectory? Do couples use talk to make sense of "why me?" and decide "what now?"

Communication is an important process through which couples cope and coordinate their coping, but talking about cancer-related issues can be challenging, even for couples who remain otherwise satisfied with their relationship (de Boer et al., 1995; Friedman, Lehane, Weinberg, Mirabi, & Cooper, 1993; Harrison, Maguire, & Pitceathly, 1995; Heinrich, Schag, & Ganz, 1984; Holmberg, Scott, Alexy, & Fife, 2001; Lichtman, Taylor, & Wood, 1987; Rapoport, Kreitler, Chaitchik, Algor, & Weissler, 1993). Couples coping with cancer often report difficulty communicating and cite ineffective communication as a primary concern (Hodgson, Shields, & Rousseau, 2003; Howell, 1986; L. Northouse, Cracchiolo-Caraway, & Appel, 1991).

Openness and avoidance of communication are salient concerns in this body of research. However, researchers disagree on the relative advantages of couple openness or avoidance about cancer-related issues. Some scholars conclude that open communication is beneficial, even if difficult, and should be encouraged. For example, in their review of factors that affect partner adjustment, Carlson, Bultz, Speca, and St. Pierre (2000) concluded:

> What is most striking in the accumulated literature is the near consensus regarding the importance of communication between partners about the cancer experience. Virtually every article we reviewed stressed the important role that communication plays ... In no instance were partners who communicated less more well adjusted. (p. 56)

Other scholars note that, although evidence supports a link between open communication and adjustment, the association must be viewed with caution (Sales, Schultz, & Biegel, 1992) and that not all families benefit from open communication (Pederson & Valanis, 1988). Another recent review concluded that the evidence for benefits of openness remains unclear (Pitceathly & Maguire, 2003). P. G.

Northouse and L. Northouse (1987) noted the lack of theoretically based research that could account for variability in findings.

Previous reviews have treated couple communication as one topic among many psychosocial issues. In contrast, our review provides a focused and comprehensive look at openness and avoidance of communication about cancer-related issues among couples coping with one person's cancer. Using various combinations of the search terms *cancer, communication, social support, marital, spouse,* and *partner,* we searched through May, 2005, in PsycINFO (189 items), Medline (238 items), and Cumulative Index to Nursing and Allied Health Literature (123 items). After eliminating duplicate citations, we retrieved and read all articles to identify those that pertained to our review. We gleaned additional citations from article bibliographies. We targeted studies specific to communication with a partner or spouse; we indicate when we report results of studies that did not exclusively focus on a partner/spouse but in which a majority of respondents identified the partner/spouse as the focal person. We did not obtain translations of three studies published in languages other than English. The final corpus included 279 articles or chapters and 12 dissertations.

Our review is also distinctive in drawing on theory and research on open communication and topic avoidance to order and explain previous empirical findings. This foundation directed us to the following issues in the literature on couples coping with cancer. First, we explore the topics of cancer-related communication for insight into the context-specific dynamics of communication. Second, we distill reasons for disclosing or avoiding because they may explain couple behavior and influence the outcomes of communicating. Third, we look at individual and relational outcomes of communication. Fourth, we explore the strategies that couples employ and the features of their talk. Finally, we examine how openness or avoidance and the outcomes of communication may be shaped by individual, relational, and illness-related factors.

Topics of Cancer-Related Communication

Even within a circumstance such as "one person in the couple has cancer," different topics may pose specific challenges and elicit particular patterns of response. For example, the topic of death inspires some of the greatest variability in communication, from full truth to full concealment (Hinton, 1998). Feelings about cancer may pose different challenges than talk about medical treatments. The degree to which couples agree on the quality of their communication varies by topic (Baider & Sarell, 1984). Topics of cancer-related communication include the connotations of "cancer," death, future plans, treatments and side effects, bodily changes and sex, daily life, feelings and fears, and communication practices.

The word "cancer" has ominous connotations, and couples report difficulty in discussing the patient's diagnosis and prognosis (e.g., Hannah et al., 1992; Vess, Moreland, Schwebel, & Kraut, 1988; Walsh, Manuel, & Avis, 2005). Some couples report trouble even mentioning the word "cancer" (Salander & Spetz, 2002; van der Does & Duyvis, 1989). A recurrence of cancer may be especially difficult to confront (Lewis & Deal, 1995; Pistrang & Barker, 1992; Wilson & Morse, 1991). Partners may experience difficulty in finding the "right" words when communicating with their ill spouse (Johnston & Abraham, 2000), or they could fear saying the wrong thing (Wortman & Dunkel-Schetter, 1979).

A majority of respondents in several studies voiced concerns about how to talk about death (Howell, 1986; Walsh et al., 2005). Women with breast cancer discuss death significantly less than other cancer-related topics (e.g., Pistrang & Barker, 1992), and both women and their partners acknowledge death is the most difficult topic to discuss (e.g., Lewis & Deal, 1995). Wilson and Morse (1991) described a "mutual conspiracy of silence" (p. 82), to the point that some couples coping with recurrence never interacted about death.

Future plans and arrangements may also be particularly challenging to discuss (Skerrett, 1998; Walsh et al., 2005). Some couples address future arrangements in indirect ways. One respondent shared how her husband "took me to see the house and how it worked—'You must do like this, and that,' he told me. Then he showed me the boundary lines of our property … We never overtly talked about death and the funeral" (Salander & Spetz, 2002, p. 309). Despite the difficulty in discussing such issues, couples commented on the importance of preparation (Vess et al., 1988). Partners may differ in their willingness to discuss arrangements, and this hesitancy can be an added source of distress (Kagawa-Singer & Wellisch, 2003; Wilson & Morse, 1991).

Talking about the medical aspects of cancer is sometimes easier than discussing meanings and feelings (Hinton, 1998; Lewis & Deal, 1995; Pistrang & Barker, 1992). Nonetheless, diagnosis, treatment, and side effects pose challenges to patients and partners, including uncertainty about treatment efficacy and prognosis, lack of knowledge about cancer and treatment, learning how to obtain needed information, choosing among alternative treatments, knowing what to do about unsatisfactory medical care, and anticipating and coping with side effects (Hilton, 1993). For participants in Hilton's study, negotiating treatment decisions became tough when families felt that they received divergent opinions from health care professionals or when partners disagreed with one another or with their physician about how to proceed. Talking about treatments may be especially hard when the prognosis is poor. Zhang and Siminoff (2003) found that 65% of families coping with lung cancer reported disputes about routine treatment decisions, trade-offs involved in discontinuation of curative treatment, and consideration of hospice care.

Adequacy of information from health care professionals affects couple talk about treatments and side effects. Women with gynecological cancer who felt uninformed or uncertain had more difficulty with telling their husbands about what physicians said and what would happen (A. Lalos, Jacobsson, O. Lalos, & Stendahl, 1995). Differing desires for information (and strategies for pursuing it) can create problems; for example, one partner may see no reason for the couple to talk, preferring to trust physicians for information, while the other partner may want the couple to discuss second opinions and information from other sources (Lindholm, Bute, Tassio, & Goldsmith, 2004). Women with breast cancer are more likely to talk with their partners about the disease and its treatment when they share similar information needs (Rees & Bath, 2000).

Cancer treatment and side effects can alter the body and influence sexual desire and performance. Sex, sexuality, and body image are sensitive topics for many couples (Boehmer & Clark, 2001; Gilbar & Ben-Zur, 2002; L. Northouse et al., 1991; Skerrett, 1998). For example, husbands of women treated for breast cancer reported reluctance to express negative reactions to their wives' appearance (Wilson & Morse, 1991), and husbands of women with gynecological cancer revealed difficulty in discussing sex (Maughan, Heyman, & Matthews, 2002; van der Does & Duyvis, 1989). Fewer expressions of sexual intimacy may perpetuate communication problems and increase emotional distance (O'Mahoney & Carroll, 1997).

Couples face difficulties in talking about the added stressors and responsibilities that an illness can bring to their daily lives (Keller,

Henrich, Sellschopp, & Beutel, 1996; Vess, Moreland, & Schwebel, 1985). The experience of cancer, its treatments, and side effects can result in reallocation of household roles and responsibilities and changes in leisure time and social activities (Keller et al., 1996; L. Northouse et al., 1991; Oberst & James, 1985). L. Northouse and Swain (1987) found that husbands of hospitalized breast cancer patients experienced exhaustion, depressed moods, and increased distress as they juggled work responsibilities, household responsibilities, and visits to their wives. Couples have concerns about the inequitable distribution of responsibilities that cancer and its treatment can entail (Kuijer, Buunk, & Ybema, 2001), yet it can be hard to talk about feelings of guilt, resentment, and loss.

Partners rank feelings and fears among the most difficult topics of talk (L. Northouse, 1994; Walsh et al., 2005), and patients also report reluctance in sharing distressing feelings (Gray, Fitch, Phillips, Labrecque, & Klotz, 1999). Guilt, anger, and frustration are especially troubling (A. Lalos et al., 1995). In one study, 57% of women with breast cancer could talk openly about their fears; 73% expressed joy openly, and 24% revealed guilt openly (Spiegel, Bloom, & Gottheil, 1983). In their study of women undergoing chemotherapy, Wilson and Morse (1991) reported that husbands' success in dealing with anger played a major role in determining successful couple communication.

Relational communication may be complicated. For example, engaging in conflict may become more difficult (Giese-Davis et al., 2000), and partners worry that expressing concerns will come across as complaining about the patient (Payne, Smith, & Dean, 1999). Partners may be hesitant to ask for support because they do not know what to ask and fear burdening the patient (Oberst & James, 1985; Persson, Rasmusson, & Hallberg, 1998). One husband of a woman with breast cancer explained that his "needs or feelings were irrelevant compared to what she was going through" (Lethborg, Kissane, & Burns, 2003, p. 74).

Reasons for Talking or Avoiding Talk

Partners' reasons for talking or not talking may moderate the effects of communication choices, and understanding them can indicate how partners choose and/or justify their communication practices. Couples' reasons for talking openly about cancer-related topics include talking to coordinate and to affirm commitment and closeness. In contrast, couples withhold their thoughts and feelings for reasons of protection, reluctance to express feelings, desire for privacy, sustaining hope and normalcy, avoiding the unnecessary, and preserving identities and relational qualities.

Reasons for Talking   Coordination. Open communication helps couples coordinate coping and support. Gray, Fitch, Phillips, Labrecque, and Fergus (2000) found talking was part of facing prostate cancer as a team, enabling couples to reassure one another about their capacity to deal with whatever might happen. Avoiding communication can leave each person to suffer alone and miss opportunities to voice preferences about end-of-life issues (Vess et al., 1988). Carers of persons with cancer (most of them spouses or partners) felt "facing this together" involved negotiating and interactively constructing the cancer experience (Thomas, Morris, & Harman, 2002, p. 538).

Commitment and closeness. Talking can renew commitment and affirm closeness. Among couples coping with prostate cancer, open communication led to an appraisal of the crisis as shared (Gray et al., 1999). Communicating openly about death did not remove the pain of imminent separation, but it did enable advanced stage patients and their families to experience peace, closure, and closeness (Johnston & Abraham, 2000). In a study by Maughan and colleagues (2002), one man said he felt excluded when his wife discussed her diagnosis with her sister before telling him.

Reasons for Not Talking   Protection. Protecting the other from distress is one of the most commonly reported reasons for not talking. Vess and colleagues (1988) found more than two thirds of patients who wanted more open communication with their spouse claimed a desire to protect their spouse constrained them from talking. Men with prostate cancer and their wives withheld thoughts and feelings to be strong for one another and protect each other from distress (Boehmer & Clark, 2001; Gray et al., 1999). Boehmer and Clark suggested cancer's association with death explains why talk about cancer-related issues can be so distressing. Johnston and Abraham (2000) noted similar concerns among patients who were terminally ill. Many partners in their study did, in fact, understand the patients' fears but felt unable to find a way to broach the topic. Husbands of women who had had a mastectomy sometimes discussed their wives' concerns about breast loss and dying, but they refrained from expressing their own intense emotions to allay their wives' fears of rejection and further illness (Sabo, Brown, & Smith, 1986).

Partners also try to shield patients from everyday concerns. Wives of men with bone or lung cancer acknowledged considerable stress from working, maintaining a household, and providing care or visitation, but they felt unwilling to express these difficulties to their husbands (Kalayjian, 1989). Oberst and James (1985) found that some partners did not want to burden ill spouses, and some patients were too preoccupied with cancer to notice. Husbands who believed that stress contributed to the onset of their wives' breast cancer said they tried to avoid minor conflicts and disagreements with their wives (Holmberg et al., 2001).

Avoiding talk about cancer-related issues can arise from self-protective motives as well as other-oriented reasons. Some prostate cancer patients and partners avoid talking so that they do not have to see their partners in distress, while others' own intense emotion and uncertainty make them unwilling to talk (Boehmer & Clark, 2001; Lavery & Clark, 1999). A few of the wives in another study of couples coping with prostate cancer feared what might be revealed if their husbands did speak (Gray et al., 2000). Among couples confronting the patient's terminal diagnosis, Hinton (1981) speculated that patients and partners who claimed to be sheltering the other from distress could be protecting themselves as well.

Reluctance to express feelings. Patients and partners may be unsure how to express strong emotions such as uncertainty and suffering (Kalayjian, 1989). In their review of research on spouses' experiences, Keitel, Cramer, and Zevon (1990) described spouses' apprehensions of further burdening patients by saying the wrong thing. They also discovered that spouses may experience negative feelings toward patients such as resentment or anger for personal difficulties and for an increased share of household responsibilities; yet, they may struggle to acknowledge, much less speak of, negative feelings toward someone who is ill. When men suspected their own past sexual history put their partners at risk for gynecological cancer, they struggled to communicate feelings of guilt and responsibility (A. Lalos et al., 1995).

Desire for privacy. Couples may avoid talking due to a desire for privacy or in deference to the other person's wishes. Elal-Lawrence and Celikoglu (1995) found that a small number of women with breast cancer felt their thoughts and feelings were their own and did not want others to know about them. One person may give up trying to discuss topics to honor the other's wishes (Hinton, 1981; Lavery & Clark, 1999). Salander and Spetz (2002) identified couples in which a spouse was aware of the patient's poor prognosis for malignant glioma but pretended not to be after realizing the patient did not wish to communicate about the prospect of death.

Maintaining hope or normalcy. Not talking can be an attempt to maintain hope, optimism, and a sense of normalcy. When couples perceive a prognosis as threatening, limiting talk about cancer can be a way of "balancing [their] lives" (Lewis & Deal, 1995, p. 943) so that they can enjoy their remaining time and be themselves (Rose, Webb, & Waters, 1997). Even couples with good prognoses may wish to refrain from dwelling on the disease (Boehmer & Clark, 2001; Gray et al., 2000). Hinton (1981) noted that a common reaction to a terminal prognosis involved "the almost automatic response to communicate hope and encourage the patient to fight the disease" (p. 342; see also Salander & Spetz, 2002). Physicians' encouragement to fight cancer and keep a positive attitude may be interpreted by patients as constraining emotional expression (Byrne, Ellershaw, Holcombe, & Salmon, 2002), and some couples believe that concentrating on the disease increases the chance of recurrence (Lichtman et al., 1987).

Avoiding talk is a component of coping styles that seek to distract self and other from cancer (Lethborg et al., 2003), minimize the problem (Lavery & Clark, 1999), maintain hope (Thomas et al., 2002), or encourage a fighting spirit (Reardon & Buck, 1989). These beliefs complicate situations when one person expresses hopelessness or wants to talk about a poor prognosis; others may be uncertain if they should allow expression of negative thoughts or may not know how to talk about cancer while still remaining hopeful, optimistic, and determined to fight (Pederson & Valanis, 1988).

Avoiding the unnecessary. Some couples feel talk is unnecessary or unproductive. For example, couples may feel that nothing remains to be discussed after deciding on a prostate cancer treatment (Gray et al., 2000). To continue to talk or think about cancer would be pointless until (or unless) something further happened that required them to problem-solve or reassure one another. Relatedly, two studies of couples with varied types of cancer (Chaitchik, Kreitler, Rapoport, & Algor, 1992; Hilton, 1993) concluded that couples could be quite satisfied with mutually agreeing on off-limit topics. A patient with malignant glioma explained, "We have sort of finished our talk about the disease. I am not so fond of dwelling on it. It doesn't make you healthier" (Salander & Spetz, 2002, p. 309). Men with prostate cancer may assume that their spouses must not have any questions or need to talk if they do not voice concerns (Arrington, 2005; Boehmer & Clark, 2001). Boehmer and Clark's study included wives of men with prostate cancer who feared that talking might create problems where none existed for their partners. For example, wives feared commenting on sexual functioning would make their husbands start worrying about their wives' sexual dissatisfaction. For some men in Arrington's study, not talking constituted their wives handling it beautifully.

Preserving identities and relational qualities. Avoiding talk about cancer may be a way to enact valued identities and relational definitions. Male withdrawal comprised part of a masculine identity for some men with prostate cancer, who, in turn, appreciated their wives respecting their wishes not to talk (Gray et al., 2000). Their wives often felt talking about the cancer would be more consistent with their own coping style, and they feared leaving their husbands uncommunicative for too long. This circumstance presented the wives with a dilemma between respecting their husbands' masculine self-reliance versus enacting their own preferred identity and relational definitions through supportive talk. Strong identification with a masculine gender identity led some husbands of women with breast cancer to flee from intimate exchange of feelings into caretaking (Sabo et al., 1986). People can perceive talking or not talking as part of a lifelong pattern for an individual or a relationship, so they justify their orientation toward communication about cancer by the reasoning, "that's just how he/she/we is/are" (Gray et al., 2000; Hinton, 1981; Pederson & Valanis, 1988). Reardon and Buck (1989) suggested various coping styles can be healthy if patients experience them as consistent with their respective identities and if supported by significant others.

Outcomes of Talking

Although couples describe a complex constellation of reasons for openness and avoidance, studies show couples who are able to talk openly tend to have better outcomes. Manne and her colleagues (Manne, Ostroff, Winkel, et al., 2004) suggested several mechanisms that might explain why talking could benefit couples, including preventing suppression of intrusive memories so that they can be processed, aiding the search for reasons for the cancer so that the event can be assimilated, and giving meaning to the experience. Cognitive and behavioral avoidance of cancer and emotional nonexpression may even be associated with cancer progression (e.g., Epping-Jordan, Compas, & Howell, 1994; Gross, 1989). Couples bemoan that a lack of openness can hurt relationships too. Failing to communicate feelings can impair intimacy, create dissonance, hinder mutual support, and leave partners uncertain about one another's feelings (Boehmer & Clark, 2001; Gray et al., 1999). As we shall see, studies that go beyond assessing degree or amount of openness show that the character of talk is a crucial determinant of outcomes. If partners interpret talk as supportive, it is more beneficial than if they experience talk as conflictive, critical, or unsupportive. We organize our review of findings around individual outcomes, relational outcomes, and the pivotal importance of differentiating open expression of support versus conflict.

Individual Outcomes   The patient's psychological distress is the most frequently measured outcome of openness. Research findings link open communication of concerns, feelings, and problems between breast cancer patients and their husbands with better psychological adjustment (Lichtman et al., 1987) and enhanced social adjustment, emotional adjustment, and self-esteem (Zemore & Shepel, 1989). In their study of 49 women receiving treatment for various forms of cancer, Kayser, Sormanti, and Strainchamps (1999) did not find a connection between engaging in open discussions and any outcome. However, women enjoyed better quality of life, greater self-care agency, and less depression when they perceived that their relationships involved reciprocal expression of feelings, thoughts, and activities. Several studies linked open family communication (including partner communication) with less patient distress (de Boer et al., 1995; Giese-Davis et al., 2000; Mesters et al., 1997).

Death is one of the most challenging cancer-related topics that couples confront, and several studies have examined the outcomes of open communication among patients with terminal cancer. Hinton (1981) compared couples who had said nothing about death, had limited communication, or discussed death openly. Hinton discovered that anxiety and depression did not relate to patterns of communication (perhaps due to small sample size), but those with limited communication experienced greater distress than those with full or no communication. In a subsequent study of 76 patients and caregiving relatives (64 were spouses), patients who talked more openly about their feelings about death expressed more anxiety and depression (Hinton, 1998); however, distress could have emerged from or motivated conversation about death. Vachon and colleagues (1977) discovered that 81% of widows who spoke with their husbands about death felt that it helped them cope with bereavement. In contrast, among those who had not talked about death, 59% perceived no difference in their adjustment to bereavement; 36% felt guilt and doubt about not talking, and they indicated that avoidance made their bereavement more difficult.

Most studies of the outcomes of open communication are cross-sectional, raising the possibility that people are reluctant to talk when they have more distress to express. Consequently, the findings of longitudinal studies are particularly useful. Among 86 women with breast cancer (42 of whom were partnered), those who reported more expressiveness and less conflict experienced less mood disturbance one year later (controlling for baseline mood; Spiegel et al., 1983). Women treated for breast or colon cancer (75 of 97 were married) who were more optimistic after surgery said three months later that they felt more able to disclose concerns to others and, in turn, reported improved affect (Lepore & Ituarte, 1999). Women with breast cancer who felt their spouse had met their needs for communication in the seven to ten days following surgery adjusted better to illness and were less distressed one year later (Hoskins, Baker, Sherman, et al., 1996). Hoskins, Baker, Budin, and colleagues (1996) observed a similar pattern for husbands.

A few studies have observed couples communicating about cancer-related issues in a laboratory setting. In one study, self-disclosure in couples' conversations about breast cancer did not significantly correlate with patient or partner reports of distress (Manne, Ostroff, Sherman, et al., 2004). Hannum, Giese-Davis, Harding, and Hatfield (1991) combined observation of couple conversations about breast cancer and each person's reports of self and partner coping. Women with breast cancer were less distressed when (a) their husbands reported that the women coped by confronting the illness, and (b) the women's own behavior in the observed conversation involved less confrontation of illness. Hannum and colleagues reported that husbands felt better when (a) their wives reported that husbands coped by denying the illness, and (b) they engaged in more confrontation of illness in the observed conversation. Findings in this study must be interpreted with caution due to sample size and the uncertain correspondence between coping measures and inferences about communication; nonetheless, these findings suggest that how we assess openness or avoidance (and especially from whose point of view) may reveal quite different patterns of outcome.

Even when dealing with cancer causes distress, couples may simultaneously report personal growth as they discover individual and relational strengths and new appreciation for life and for each other. Communication may facilitate these positive outcomes. Head and neck cancer patients who could openly discuss their illness with their families had more confidence in their social functioning and ability to perform, felt more in control, and experienced less uncertainty about their access to help and problem-solving and their ability to handle practical and emotional consequences of the illness (de Boer et al., 1995). In another study, patients who expressed more emotion reported more growth (i.e., discovering personal strength, appreciation for life, spiritual change, and new interests) 18 months later (Manne, Ostroff, Winkel, et al., 2004). However, the effect was not significant for partners, and their measure included expression to all sources, not just one's partner. Manne and colleagues' intervention for wives of prostate cancer patients that included communication training did not reduce the wives' distress, but it did improve their growth and coping one month later (Manne, Babb, Pinover, Horwitz, & Ebbert, 2004).

Relationship Outcomes   Relatively few couples separate or divorce following one person's diagnosis of cancer, and many couples report drawing closer together as a result of their experience (for reviews, see L. Northouse et al., 1991; O'Mahoney & Carroll, 1997; Taylor-Brown, Kilpatrick, Maunsell, & Dorval, 2000). Yet, couples who struggle and those who grow closer recognize threats to satisfaction (e.g., Holmberg et al., 2001). In Walsh and colleagues' (2005) study of women with breast cancer, 75% felt closer to partners, and 7% of those who felt closer mentioned the importance of emotional support and open communication. In contrast, 25% of the women felt relational strain, which they attributed to communication avoidance. Another 35% wanted to discuss their feelings but felt partners were unwilling. Twelve percent had separated from partners or terminated their relationships, and 3% said they actively contemplated separation because of communication difficulties. In their review, Taylor-Brown and colleagues concluded that little empirical support exists for the lay belief that cancer frequently breaks up marriages. However, breakups that do occur may be related to ineffective communication, and cancer could magnify pre-existing problems.

Couples who had talked about cancer recurrence were no more satisfied than those who had not in a study by Chekryn (1984), though sample and cell sizes were small. Among couples coping with terminal illness, those who characterized their marriages as just average had engaged in more discussion of patient prognosis than highly satisfied couples (Hinton, 1981). In contrast, Vess and colleagues (1985) linked open communication with perceptions of more cohesion and spousal role competence and less family conflict, role conflict, and role strain. Women treated for breast cancer were most satisfied with their relationship when they had communicated the most concern about recurrence or death (Lichtman et al., 1987). In this study, husbands who worried about emotional reactions from their wives or rated them as highly anxious and fearful were in the best adjusted marriages.

Manne and her colleagues (Manne, Ostroff, Rini, et al., 2004; Manne, Ostroff, Sherman, et al., 2004) linked couples' perceptions of their communication and relationship to their laboratory interaction. Patient and partner disclosure were significantly correlated, and greater disclosure corresponded to feelings of intimacy, particularly when the patient perceived the partner as responsive (Manne, Ostroff, Rini, et al., 2004). Self-disclosure (coded by observers) correlated with couples' relational satisfaction (Manne, Ostroff, Sherman, et al., 2004).

Supportive Versus Conflictual Talk   The benefits of couple communication depend not only upon the frequency or degree of openness but also on topics and interpretation of talk. Patients and partners who find one another responsive to disclosures and who interpret their talk as supportive attain better outcomes than those who report open expression of conflict, hostility, and criticism.

Social support and cancer have been widely studied (see Blanchard, Albrecht, Ruckdeschel, Grant, & Hemmick, 1995, for a review); we focused on studies that measured couple communication. Among 113 women with breast cancer (68 of whom were partnered), patients felt less anxious, depressed, and hostile when they perceived disclosure to their partner as more helpful; helpful conversations displayed greater empathy and less withdrawal (Pistrang & Barker, 1995). Elal-Lawrence and Celikoglu (1995) linked supportive communication about breast cancer and positive reactions to mastectomy with less depression and anxiety. Gotcher (1992, 1993, 1995) examined communication between breast or prostate cancer patients and a family member (65% reported on a spouse). Patients indicated better psychosocial adjustment to illness when they experienced frequent, honest, and encouraging communication that included discussion of unpleasant topics. Of the various features of communication that Gotcher examined, emotional supportiveness of communication most strongly predicted adjustment to illness.

Scholars have also compared the effects of openly expressing support versus conflict. In their longitudinal study of women with breast cancer, Spiegel and colleagues (1983) concluded:

> These data provide objective support for the contention that conspiracies of silence can have destructive consequences for patients, while at the same time underscoring that it is the type of expression that is crucial since the presence of conflict is directly predictive of mood disturbance to the same extent that the presence of expressiveness is inversely predictive of mood disturbance over the course of the year. (p. 42)

Manne and colleagues (1999) learned that supportive conversations with one's spouse produced more constructive coping by the patient, which positively impacted patient mood. In contrast, negative interactions between spouses prompted escape and avoidance coping, resulting in worse mood (an alternative model that coping influenced communication did not fit the data as well). A subsequent study of women with breast cancer (Manne et al., 2003) explored whether high levels of support from family and friends might offset the negative effects of an unsupportive partner. Women with low family and friend support and a negative partner engaged in more avoidant coping and appraised their own coping efficacy negatively. Even when support from friends and family was high, partner unsupportive behavior had a direct negative effect on patient distress.

The benefit of talking also depends upon the responsiveness of the other person. Lepore (2001) explained this relationship by examining how feeling constrained from talking may prevent patients from working through intrusive thoughts to understand the meaning of the cancer experience. For example, Lepore and Helgeson (1998) found that, when men with prostate cancer felt constrained from talking with their wives, intrusive thoughts about cancer were linked to poorer mental health. Lepore obtained similar results with breast cancer patients. This study also indicated that the experience of intrusive thoughts prompted more frequent communication for women who could converse with their spouses. In contrast, women who felt constrained from talking did not share their intrusive thoughts, and this avoidance may explain their higher levels of negative affect.

A few studies have examined the effects of positive and negative talk by observing couples' interactions in a lab. Hodgson and colleagues (2003) found that, although behaviors coded as disengaging or lacking interest were infrequent among breast cancer patients and spouses (fewer than 2% of all comments), one person's disengagement was linked to less marital satisfaction for the other partner. Manne, Ostroff, Sherman, and colleagues (2004) observed couples discussing the woman's breast cancer. Distressed patients communicated accordingly with more distress-maintaining attributions, more dysphoric affect, and less problem discussion; their partners also expressed more dysphoric affect. Maritally dissatisfied patients showed more hostility than satisfied patients, and dissatisfied partners expressed distress-maintaining attributions, hostility, and dysphoric affect more often than satisfied partners. Dissatisfied patients were also more likely than satisfied patients to be part of a pattern in which patient disclosure met with a hostile partner response.

Features and Strategies of Talk

An interesting pattern emerges from the juxtaposition of research on reasons (i.e., asking people what they do and why and using qualitative methods to analyze their responses) and research on outcomes (in which the researcher demonstrates a statistical linkage between measures of openness and outcomes). Participants perceive that openness and avoidance hold both risks and benefits; yet, when researchers assess the association of openness and outcomes, the findings seem to favor openness. A bias toward publishing significant findings might under-represent findings of a nonsignificant relationship between openness and outcomes (though significant negative effects of openness would be newsworthy).

This pattern of results could indicate that open communication is beneficial, though potentially difficult to do. Those couples who find ways to manage the dilemmas of openness may experience the benefits of talk; those who cannot find a way to talk may be less able to reap those benefits but can, at least, minimize the risks and avoid an even worse outcome. If this interpretation is correct, then we should attend to strategies (i.e., efforts that couples undertake to achieve some openness but also some protection) and features of talk (i.e., aspects of a couple's interaction that may or may not be intentional but nonetheless could function to achieve some openness but also some protection). We should also consider how couples vary in their preferred patterns of interaction and the importance of congruency between partners in their approach.

Balancing Strategies   Couples try to achieve the benefits of openness while avoiding risks by moderating how often they discuss cancer-related issues. Lewis and Deal (1995) proposed "balancing our lives" (p. 943) as a central theme among women with recurring breast cancer and their husbands. Couples put boundaries on the frequency, form, and amount of time that they discussed cancer-related issues, and they avoided discussion of what recurrence meant. They felt that limiting their communication kept them from dwelling on the illness so that they could focus instead on surviving, healing, containing the cancer, and living their lives. Likewise, Gray et al. (2000) found that couples coping with prostate cancer said that they acknowledged the possibility of death but did not dwell on it. Even many couples facing a terminal prognosis reported that they had one significant discussion of death and then spoke of it only rarely after that (Hinton, 1981). According to Skerrett (1998), the most resilient couples practiced selective disclosure, talking about the illness but not letting it dominate daily life. In contrast, couples encountered difficulties when they completely avoided talk or talked excessively in an anxious and unproductive manner.

Couples can practice selective communication by openly discussing factual issues (such as treatments and symptom management) while withholding discussion of feelings. Talking about illness facts may feel safe compared to discussing the feelings associated with the prospect of death (Lewis & Deal, 1995). However, this strategy could be isolating for partners when "repetitive conversations about certain symptoms or episodes sometimes supplanted frankness about other matters that needed discussion ... significant items were often minimized or left unmentioned, just things to be silently endured" (Hinton, 1998, p. 17).

Some partners refrain from talking until patients raise a cancer-related topic. Some husbands felt confident that their wives with breast cancer would eventually bring up any concerns and reasoned that, if their wives were not talking, they did not feel up to it at that particular time (Skerrett, 1998). These men believed that they could practice sensitivity and restraint by "keeping the conversation light" and not "pushing" their wives to talk (p. 288). This pattern poses risks, however, if wives do not realize their husbands' willingness to talk. For example, some women with breast cancer did not bring up important topics because they assumed their husbands would not understand and could not cope with their feelings (Pistrang & Barker, 1992). Likewise, wives of prostate cancer patients feared that discussing their sex life would create concerns that their husbands did not have; the wives' silence led the men to assume that their wives had no concerns so the men did not bring up the topic either (Boehmer & Clark, 2001). Some wives resolved this dilemma by leaving their husbands alone for awhile but monitoring their emotional state for signs of depression or "festering" (Gray et al., 2000, p. 542).

Although the term "balancing" holds positive connotations, we lack conclusive evidence about whether these strategies optimize the risks and benefits of openness or whether balancing entails risks of its own. Wortman and Dunkel-Schetter (1979) described the confusion and hurt that cancer patients may feel when communication seems inconsistent or ambivalent. In one study, 50% of patients recognized others pretending to be cheerful, and 34% said that others told them that they looked good when they knew they did not (Gotcher, 1993). Rose and colleagues (1997) observed several useful distinctions in evaluating the functionality of balancing strategies. They differentiated couples who refrained from discussion because they were denying a terminal prognosis from those couples who had made peace with the prognosis and wished to normalize their remaining time. Similarly, according to Rose and colleagues, some couples experienced solitary denial and withholding from one another, whereas others experienced togetherness in a mutual denial of reality. Survivors who had coped together with a dying patient expressed greater satisfaction and less distress after the patient's death than those who felt unable to cope together. Couples who vacillated between acceptance and denial seemed more distressed than those who consistently accepted or denied death.

Stylistic Features   Next, we review those few studies that have probed the details of how couples talk about cancer-related issues. Although balancing exemplifies a pattern that lies between openness and avoidance, the concept still focuses on talking or not talking rather than the character of the conversation when it occurs. Stylistic features include nonverbal communication and humor.

Nonverbal communication. Nonverbal communication can accompany verbal disclosure or can replace explicit verbal communication. While their wives went through chemotherapy, husbands attempted to "soften the blow" and "cherish" their wives by being there, being supportive but not hovering, nurturing, listening, touching, humoring, and assisting (Wilson & Morse, 1991, p. 80). Touching is obviously nonverbal and it seems likely that nonverbal communication is central to nurturing, not hovering, listening, and being there as well.

Nonverbal communication may substitute for verbal communication in some couples. In the absence of talk about physical changes, wives of men with prostate cancer depended upon nonverbal communication and close observation to monitor their husbands (Boehmer & Clark, 2001). Some couples' sense of knowing one another and communicating nonverbally enabled them to feel intimate with little explicit communication (Gray et al., 1999). In their review of how breast cancer affects families, Pederson and Valanis (1988) concluded:

> Although stress-related issues can be resolved by open communication and disclosure of feelings, the ability of a family to use these means of coping varies widely and depends upon already established patterns.... Some families find that focusing conversation on other subjects and communicating their feelings in nonverbal ways are effective strategies for them. (p. 105)

Studies that emphasize only explicit verbal discussion may miss some of the important ways families cope with cancer. Likewise, when family members respond to global, abstract communication measures (e.g., we show our affection, we let each other know how we feel), they may have nonverbal means of expression in mind. Scholars who assume that agreement with these items reveals high levels of verbal disclosure may mistakenly draw conclusions about the frequency or effects of talk and thus underestimate the value of other expressive modes.

Humor. Humor can help couples broach challenging topics. Wives of prostate cancer patients reported joking and teasing to build up their husbands' morale while husbands couched expression of their own fears in humorous comments (Boehmer & Clark, 2001). In another sample of couples coping with prostate cancer (Gray et al., 1999, 2000), couples used humor to counteract negative feelings, generate positive feelings, prevent strain, and gauge the other person's feelings. Husbands of wives undergoing chemotherapy employed humor to comfort their wives and to counteract their feelings of humiliation and fear (Wilson & Morse, 1991). Even among those facing a terminal diagnosis, engaging in black humor and continuing to be the sort of person who "see[s] the funny side" served to normalize the period at the end of life (Rose et al., 1997, p. 129).

Variation Among Couples   Although most research has examined the practice and effects of communication across couples, evidence exists for different types of preferences and patterns (and perhaps different outcomes) of communication. For example, Reynolds and Perrin (2004) clustered women with breast cancer (71% of whom identified their husband or partner as their chief supporter) into four groups based on their needs and preferences for social support. One group wanted many types of support but especially desired reassurance that "things would be OK" (p. 427) and would eventually return to normal. Another group needed very few kinds of support, preferring to be treated "normally" and to avoid talking about cancer with their main supporter. A third group sought facts, information, and advice, and a fourth group appreciated talk about cancer but disliked receiving advice. Reynolds and Perrin concluded that the match between what a woman wanted and what she received predicted psychosocial adjustment better than the amount of or overall satisfaction with supportive communication.

Hilton (1994) identified five couple types in her study of families coping with the woman's breast cancer. Both members of *talker* couples agreed on the importance of frequent talk, though they sometimes kept private thoughts, withheld feelings, or "softened the blow" (p. 374) for one another. These couples relied on knowledge of one another and short forms of communicating but also verbally checked interpretations. In addition to explicit talk, these couples reported staying close by simply enjoying one another's company, using humor, and expressing affection. *Medium talkers* spoke freely about concrete things and day-to-day issues but shared less about feelings. Although important, communication was not their main coping strategy. These couples felt close, and they occasionally exhibited affection overtly. Yet, more often, they conveyed caring nonverbally and through considerate gestures (e.g., bringing needed items to the hospital without being asked, bringing flowers). *Nontalkers* engaged in little or no conversation about cancer-related issues except for factual matters (e.g., treatments), and they believed that discussing fears and emotional issues would only make things worse. They occasionally expressed negative views very bluntly. These couples did not need to talk a lot to feel close or to know what their partner thought because they had been together for so long.

These three couple types tended to agree about communication and their patterns predated the cancer diagnosis. Hilton (1994) also specified two other couple types with disagreements about communication. Among *"minorly" discrepant talkers,* the woman wanted more communication than the man, and they engaged in little or one-sided talk about cancer-related issues. Although they cared for one another, their discrepant expectations made sharing difficult. For some, the discrepancy lessened after the initial shock of diagnosis; for others, difficulties persisted but became less of a concern as the need to talk subsided. *"Majorly" discrepant talkers* expressed very different needs for communication, difficulty talking, and dissatisfaction with communication. The women felt unsupported and experienced adjustment problems. Communication entailed conflict, argumentativeness, and insensitivity. Cancer seemed to have magnified pre-existing problems in the relationship.

Hilton's (1994) couple types illustrate how reasons, features, and strategies may co-occur in systematic ways with implications for the outcomes couple experience. Although talkers tended to be more relationally satisfied than other types, Hilton concluded that congruence in preferences and patterns best predicted individual adjustment and relational satisfaction. Likewise, patients in Reynolds and Perrin's (2004) study expressed the most distress when they experienced a discrepancy between what they wanted and what they received from significant others. Absolute amount of openness may be less important than whether a couple develops a coherent combination of beliefs about communication and features of interaction, including not only openness but also expression of affection, nonverbal communication, considerate gestures, companionship, and humor.

Thorne (1985) identified some families who attributed successful coping to open communication; others said the secret to their success was never to discuss cancer. She proposed that families succeeded to the extent that they interpreted coping choices within a pre-existing family philosophy (e.g., "we're fighters," "we always look on the bright side") that "allowed them to develop a sense of normalcy and dignity within their experiences with cancer" (p. 289). Thorne concluded that "the challenge, then, is that of re-evaluating our assumptions about what we think is best for cancer families, and, instead, helping families rediscover what is best for themselves" (p. 290).

Contextual Factors That May Shape Reasons, Features, and Outcomes

Although open communication about cancer-related issues may benefit individuals and relationships, the effect sizes are modest. Differences in how couples talk or avoid talking may account for some of the unexplained variability. Individual, relational, and illness-related variables may moderate the effects of openness and avoidance. Consequently, we lack conclusive evidence about the benefits of openness across different circumstances. We explore this possibility by examining studies of the moderators of the effects of openness, including culture, gender, patient or partner role, age, relationship length, and illness characteristics.

Cultural Differences   Culture shapes the meaning and practice of communication for couples (Bloom, 2000; Molassiotis, C. W. Chan, Yam, E. S. Chan, & Lam, 2002; Salander & Spetz, 2002). For example, Kagawa-Singer and Wellisch (2003) compared Japanese-American, Chinese-American, and European-American breast cancer patients. According to these researchers, Japanese-American and Chinese-American women valued nonverbal more than verbal communication and preferred indirect styles in which "people are sensitive enough to understand the other's emotional state without words or open expression" (p. 33). In contrast, European-American women valued verbal over nonverbal expression. Japanese-American women reported that their husbands turned for support to their families of origin, instead of their wives; European-American women felt that their husbands became more openly expressive with them.

In Sarell and Baider's (1984) study of Jewish Israelis, those from a European or American background ("moderns") noted improvement in communication about feelings with partners since the illness, and most (85%) reported communicating with their partner. In contrast, immigrants from Africa or the Middle East ("traditionals") acknowledged some deterioration in communication about feelings with the partner, and only 28% had spoken with their partner about feelings related to cancer. Racial/ethnic groups differed significantly in how much they disclosed (traditionals least, moderns most, Israeli-born in between), and those who considered themselves religious disclosed less than those who said that they were not religious. Among Turkish breast cancer patients, 93% wished to discuss their illness, but only 68% did; those who did not disclose, even though they wished to, noted traditional Turkish culture as a reason (Elal-Lawrence & Celikoglu, 1995).

Gender and Patient/Partner Differences   Men and women may differ in the tendency to be open and the perceived benefits of doing so. However, findings are inconsistent, and explanations for differences usually rely upon gender stereotypes (women like to talk, men do not) without systematic exploration of the meaning and effect of gender. In addition, studies often confound gender with patient/partner status (e.g., in studies of prostate cancer, none of the patients are women) or with different types of cancer (e.g., a sample that compares patient/partner dynamics for breast and prostate cancer may inadvertently confound potential differences in the age of the cohort affected, meanings of the disease, and types of treatments and side effects).

Male prostate cancer patients had more mood disturbance and intrusive thoughts when they felt they could not talk to their spouse; in contrast, female gynecological patients were not more distressed when they felt constrained from talking (Zakowski et al., 2003). Among partners of patients treated for breast or prostate cancer, men (but not women) felt more satisfied with their spouse's support and were better adjusted and more relationally satisfied when they received more support (J. T. Ptacek, Pierce, Dodge, & J. J. Ptacek, 1997). In Manne and colleagues' (1999) study, women (whether patients or partners) felt more distressed when they avoided talking to protect their partners. In contrast, male patients and partners did more protective withholding than women (see also Lavery & Clarke, 1999), yet this pattern did not lead them to feel more distressed.

According to Carlson, Ottenbriet, St. Pierre, and Bultz (2001), female partners understood male prostate cancer patients' experiences better than male partners grasped female breast cancer patients' experiences; prostate cancer couples were more likely than breast cancer couples to agree on perceptions of support and the cancer experience. The authors noted that their findings may reveal gender differences, but they could also reflect differences in age and the length of time that couples had been together, which was twice as long for their prostate couples. To specify how gender shapes the practice and benefits of open communication or avoidance, future studies should measure the processes presumed to account for gender differences (e.g., gender role identification, different expectations for communication). We must also differentiate gender from patient/partner status; for example, patients tend to assess communication more positively than partners (Baider & Sarrell, 1984; Douglass, 1997), and scholars could mistakenly attribute this discrepancy in a study with only patients of one gender and partners of another.

Age and Relationship Length   The practice and effects of open communication or avoidance may vary with age. O'Mahoney and Carroll (1997) reviewed studies indicating that younger couples typically experience more emotional distress and marital conflict than older couples, and L. Northouse (1994) summarized studies showing that age relates to distress as well as difficulties in family interaction. Among Hilton's (1994) couple types, talkers tended to be younger than nontalkers or medium talkers; younger families were more often discrepant or medium talkers; whereas, retired couples were more likely to be nontalkers.

The length of the couple's relationship may also predict adjustment and expressive patterns. O'Mahoney and Carroll (1997) proposed that established relationships buffer the negative effects of the initial stress of diagnosis. Conversely, less established couples may need more supportive interventions after surgery (L. Northouse & Swain, 1987). Partners in established relationships may have more congruent perceptions of support (Carlson et al., 2001). In Hilton's (1994) study, nontalkers had been together longer.

Research on the effects of communication should account for age, relational length, and the processes associated with these variables (i.e., expectations, experience). Age differences may reflect diverse beliefs about the value of open communication or different experiences of cancer (e.g., due to previous experience with illness or different expectations for having a life-threatening illness). Age may also correlate with relationship length because older individuals could potentially be in a longer relationship. Couples in longer term relationships may have routines to help them cope, and they may have weathered other crises together.

Illness Characteristics   Some types of cancer could pose greater communication challenges than others. For example, partners of Hodgkin's disease survivors reported more communication difficulties than partners of testicular cancer survivors (Hannah et al., 1992), and larynegectomy patients experienced heightened difficulties in effective communication with others (including spouses), compared to patients with T1 carcinoma of the glottic larynx (de Boer et al., 1995).

The outcomes of communication may depend upon disease severity (Manne, 1994; O'Mahoney & Carroll, 1997). In a study by Hagedoorn and colleagues (2000), open discussion benefited relationships most among patients with greater physical limitations and poorer psychological adjustment. Likewise, protective withholding reduced marital satisfaction only when patients were highly distressed and physically limited.

Adaptation and distress could vary over the illness trajectory (e.g., Bloom, 2000; Hoskins, Baker, Budin et al., 1996); correspondingly, the amount, effects, and necessity of communication may change (Juraskova et al., 2003). For example, many couples avoided talk about emotional aspects of a mastectomy until the women returned home after surgery (Jamison, Wellisch, & Pasnau, 1978). In one study, patients and relatives talked most openly about death during the patients' final 6 weeks (Hinton, 1998). Conversely, patients with malignant glioma and their spouses discussed the possibility of death early on, then left the topic alone (Salander & Spetz, 2002).

Problems can arise if patients and partners have different views about the need to communicate across the illness trajectory. One breast cancer patient asserted, "Now that I'm getting better he doesn't want to think about it, but I don't think that's how it should be run … it should be discussed once in a while" (Hilton, 1993, p. 96). After completing treatment, some women with breast cancer still want to discuss certain issues; whereas, their husbands may resist talking about cancer because they want to "get back to normal" (Lethborg et al., 2003, p. 79).

Conclusions and Implications

Based on this review, we add our voices to a chorus across the discipline, questioning whether open communication is unequivocally beneficial. Several scholars have suggested the value placed on open communication may represent an American cultural ideology (Goldsmith, 2001; Katriel & Philipsen, 1981). Even Americans do not uniformly prefer open communication. If we accept that both openness and avoidance have benefits and risks under particular circumstances, then we need to theorize these contingencies as well as the features and strategies of communication that constitute openness, avoidance, and the various other ways of communicating that fall in between. Couple communication about cancer provides a theoretically rich and practically important context in which to pursue these issues. We conclude our review by summarizing the major themes pertaining to couples and cancer and the practical implications of these findings. We then turn to methodological and theoretical implications for research—not only in the cancer context but also in other areas.

Couple Communication About Cancer

Cancer-related topics of talk (or avoidance) include the meaning of cancer, death, future plans, treatment, symptoms, side-effects of treatment, sex, sexuality, body image, household burdens, changes in daily life, feelings, and relationship issues. Individuals find some topics to be especially challenging (e.g., death), and topics may vary in salience over the course of the illness. The degree of openness or avoidance can differ from one topic to another. For example, some couples find it easier to discuss factual aspects of cancer than feelings about the experience.

Couples talk about cancer-related topics to coordinate coping and affirm closeness. Reasons not to talk vary, including protecting self and/or other from distress, shielding the patient from everyday concerns, uncertainty about how to express strong emotions, respect for self or other's privacy, maintaining hope, restoring normalcy, perceiving talk as unnecessary or unproductive, and enacting valued identities and relational qualities. Researchers report contradictions in couples' rationales for talking or not (Hinton, 1998; Thorne, 1985).

For example, couples may say that "we talk about everything (or we could)" but then describe reasons why they actively avoid some topics. Reasons for openness and avoidance can co-occur within individuals or couples to create dilemmas, inconsistencies, or variation across topics.

Some studies summarized in this review associate open communication about cancer-related issues with reduced distress, individual growth, and relational satisfaction. However, because so many studies have utilized cross-sectional designs, we must consider the competing explanations that feeling distressed or dissatisfied with a relationship makes it more difficult to talk or that the benefits of talking are less certain when a couple has more intense, negative material to disclose. Another limitation occurs in studies that do not differentiate openness with a partner from openness with family, friends, and others. As long as a patient can find one person in whom he or she can confide, perhaps it does not need to be his or her partner. Pressure to confide in the partner (whether from cultural norms, relational expectations, or the design of an intervention) may not improve outcomes if that particular partner cannot communicate openly or that particular relationship does not include a history of doing so. Alternatively, talking freely with one's partner may confer distinctive benefits (Manne et al., 2003; Pistrang & Barker, 1995). We need research to determine how different sources of disclosure may contribute to patient well-being and to understand how couples negotiate disclosure within and outside the couple. Finally, we must consider what partners communicate (support or negativity) and how they receive disclosures (responsively or with hostility).

Features and strategies of communication about cancer have seldom been a primary focus of research. We gleaned findings from brief passages in qualitative studies. Future research should examine how couples communicate and whether different strategies or features are useful in addressing the conflicting reasons for talk or avoidance. For example, Baxter and Montgomery (1996) described segmentation (talking openly on some topics and not others), cyclic alternation (being open on some occasions and closed on others), moderation (being somewhat open and somewhat closed), and reframing (interpreting openness and avoidance in such a way that dyads minimize or transform risks). These concepts could provide further specification of the "balancing" reported in studies of cancer. Similarly, multiple goals perspectives (e.g., Dillard, 1990; Goldsmith,

2004; O'Keefe, 1988) point to features of language such as directness, indirectness, face work, and reframing as potentially useful ways in which individuals can manage risks and benefits of communicating. Beach and Anderson (2003, p. 4) called for study of "how families *interactively* accomplish" patterns of communication about cancer-related issues and proposed conversation analysis as another theoretical and methodological framework that has been underutilized in studies of family talk about cancer.

Communication about cancer may differ as a function of culture, gender, patient/partner role, age, relationship length, type of cancer, illness intrusiveness, prognosis, and stage/trajectory. However, few studies test whether these variables moderate the influence of communication on outcomes. Many studies examine a single type of cancer (typically breast or prostate). Future research should establish whether communication processes are similar across types of cancer. Within and across types of cancer, we also need to consider variability in intrusiveness, prognosis, and stage. When scholars have taken these variables into account, they have usually treated them as inclusion/exclusion criteria or control variables; we should also theorize how these features may shape communication and its effects. Is avoidance of communication most detrimental for later stage patients or those facing death? Alternatively, is it equally critical for an early stage patient with a good prognosis? Do intrusive symptoms or side effects require more discussion, or do they justify couples' desires not to dwell on the illness?

People in different cultural groups, age groups, or relational contexts may have different preferences for talk, but it is unclear whether different groups benefit more or less from talk. White participants dominate study samples. Age of participants and length of relationship vary across samples, but researchers seldom examine them for their potential moderating effects. Patients and partners may have different preferences for talk and diverse constellations of risks and benefits. However, the confounding of gender with patient/partner status in most studies complicates our ability to determine the source of these variations. Theories of gender identity (Deaux & Major, 1990), illness identity (Charmaz, 1991), and caregiver identity (Hagedoorn, Sanderman, Buunk, & Wobbes, 2002) could provide needed explanations for differences and enrich our understanding of the varied needs and perspectives of each member of a couple. Research among same-sex couples could also offer important comparative data.

Practical Implications

Our findings can inform interventions designed to assist couples and serve as a basis for developing educational materials about couple communication. The evidence for universal benefits of openness is not conclusive, and couples' reports of the reasons for not talking should not be too readily dismissed. Young healthy adults who avoid topics usually express less relational satisfaction; however, the strength of this association depends upon the perceived reason for topic avoidance (for a review, see T. D. Afifi et al., in press). Studies have also found that individuals who avoid discussing a topic, and then later disclose it, often do incur costs and risks associated with the disclosure (Caughlin et al., 2005). It remains to be seen if these results occur in the context of cancer and if the variable benefits of openness extend beyond relational satisfaction to individual distress. For example, even if avoiding talk does not necessarily harm the relationship, it might, nonetheless, deprive individuals of opportunities for improved adjustment and emotional relief.

If, in fact, avoiding talk about cancer-related topics is detrimental no matter what the reason, then we need to study how couples can overcome barriers and successfully manage risks. Many interventions reported in the literature cover numerous topics (e.g., information about treatments, side effects, body image and sexuality, individual coping) with only a single session or part of a session devoted to couple communication. This approach seems unlikely to be sufficient for changing long-standing relational patterns or overcoming deep-seated reasons for avoiding talk, perhaps accounting for the mixed results of these interventions (for review, see Pitceathly & Maguire, 2000).

Methodological Implications

We should seek greater precision in the measure of open communication about cancer-related issues and reflect upon what we mean by "openness." Too often, researchers assess "openness" in global, abstract ways. When interpreting findings, researchers tend to assume that participant responses reflect explicit verbal communication about cancer, but global items (e.g., if couples are open, if they express themselves, and if they understand one another) do not necessarily differentiate between verbal and nonverbal expressions, between understandings achieved through talk versus those presumed from shared history, between open talk about treatment facts versus discussion of distressing feelings, or between a socially desirable perception that "we can talk" and the practice of frequent discussion. Asking couples about the extent of openness solicits a relative judgment: Is a couple open if they have had only one significant discussion of death but that one talk was deep and meaningful? Are they open if they thoroughly discussed the pros and cons of prostate surgery prior to treatment but have refrained from talk about their sex life since surgery? Are they open if they believe they could talk but do not because they feel it is not necessary at the moment?

The topics of talk and avoidance that we have generated could be used to develop more precise measurement. Couples could reflect upon various topics and respond to distinct questions about how often they talk, the need to talk, perception of constraint from talk, and satisfaction with talk about each topic. Compared to abstract, global measures of openness, this approach gets us closer to behavior, and it can also reveal important information about whether frequency, perceived availability, unmet need, or satisfaction is the most important determinant of the benefits of communication.

This observation has broader implications as well. For example, researchers widely mention open communication as a key to successful family relations, but as in the studies about couples coping with cancer, they typically assess it in a very global way (for a review, see Kirkman, Rosenthal, & Feldman, 2005). Often, they fail to define openness, implying that openness is a simple and self-evident construct that can be assessed by general perceptions that one's family is responsive and understanding (Kirkman et al., 2005). Too often, researchers conceptualize openness as a unidimensional feature that varies only in amount or degree (T. D. Afifi et al., in press). Research has not adequately examined the possibility that couples can be open in some respects or on some topics and avoidant on others.

Theoretical Implications

Our review provides a basis for comparison of communication about other illnesses and in other relationships. Research on the psychosocial aspects of chronic illness usually focuses on a particular illness, so little comparative work has been conducted. The concepts that we have discussed constitute a common set of issues for comparative study of illnesses with different prognoses, meanings, stigmas, and so on. This framework could also be used to study other relationships (e.g., family, friends, health care providers) to determine how patients coordinate their communication across their social network. For example, communication with health care providers may facilitate couple coping (Blanchard et al., 1997).

Couples around the globe experience cancer, and, although most of the research we reviewed came from the United States, our sample also included studies from Australia, Belgium, Britain, Canada, Hong Kong, Germany, Israel, Japan, The Netherlands, South Africa, Spain, Sweden, and Turkey. Perhaps not surprisingly, these studies show that, regardless of country of origin, it is distressing for patient and partner to go through the cancer experience, and communicating about these issues can be challenging. Most international studies have not been undertaken with the intention of examining cultural difference, and they have utilized measures, concepts, and theories that are also employed in the United States. We summarized the few studies that have focused on cultural comparison in this chapter; they indicate that, while cancer and communication about it may be universally challenging for couples, the particular challenges and preferred ways of coping can take culturally specific forms. In addition, these studies point to important within-nation variability; for example, Sarell and Baider (1984) found significant variability among Israelis depending upon racial and religious background. Future research should be conducted in varying nations and sociocultural groups within nations, and they should employ research designs that are sensitive to the possibility of cultural nuances.

Many unanswered questions about couples' openness or avoidance of talk remain. For example, do the outcomes of communication differ for different topics? Does the functionality of avoidance depend upon the reasons couples have for avoiding talk? Are couples who choose not to talk for various reasons simply misguided as to the "real" beneficial outcomes of communicating openly, or do couples who communicate openly tend to have less problematic circumstances than those who give reasons for not talking? In this chapter, we offer concepts and theories that hold great potential for guiding future research about the features and strategies of couples' talk about cancer-related topics that can enable them to manage conflicting reasons for openness and avoidance so they can achieve positive outcomes.

Although we could readily classify findings according to topic, reasons, outcomes, or strategies/features, we found few studies that examine the interrelationship among these constructs. For example, no studies have pursued how reasons for talking may create dilemmas that could then be managed more or less effectively by strategies or features of talk. Further, we did not locate any studies comparing the outcomes of openness for different topics. As already noted, few studies have examined moderators of effects. The multiple goals framework prominent in communication research holds promise for helping us understand whether communication is beneficial as well as how, why, and when.

Each of these theoretical issues is relevant, not only to couples coping with cancer, but also for scholars interested in openness and avoidance as communication processes. For example, does it matter what particular topics are discussed openly or avoided or is the overall degree of openness what matters for individual well-being and relational satisfaction? Is openness objectively better for individuals, their relationships, their workplaces, and their public image even if people have fears about, concerns for, and difficulty being open? Are reasons for seeking avoidance grounded in fact, such that the benefits of openness depend upon reasons that people can recognize and articulate? Scholars have begun to address this issue (e.g., Caughlin & T. D. Afifi, 2004), but too often research that documents outcomes of openness does not inquire into participants' reasons and vice versa.

Our review of couple openness and avoidance about cancer-related issues also suggests how the application of theories of openness and avoidance to various contexts can refine and extend these theories. For example, motives (such as building closeness and protecting self or other) resemble reasons found in previous research on openness and avoidance generally (for a review, see Caughlin & Petronio, 2004); however, some reasons may be distinctive to longer term relationships coping with a distressing life event. For example, previous research has emphasized concerns for protecting self and preventing information from being misused by third parties (e.g., Vangelisti, 1994); in contrast, the kinds of protection most often desired by couples coping with cancer involved avoiding distress. Perhaps because few relationships break up as a result of cancer, protecting the relationship seldom emerged as a reason. Avoiding a negative impression is another reason prominent in previous research (e.g., W. A. Afifi & Guerrero, 2000), but among couples coping with cancer, identity concerns were subtly different. Rather than one person concealing information to sustain an image in the other's eyes, we located more reports of partners colluding to prop up a performance or respecting a long-standing personal preference.

Much previous work on openness and avoidance has focused on situations in which information one might consider disclosing is not otherwise known to the target of disclosure (e.g., disclosure of secrets, getting to know one another in a developing relationship, or revealing private information); in contrast, much of what couples coping with cancer did not discuss was known (or perhaps suspected) but not explicitly mentioned. Rather than withholding facts about one of them, couples were more likely to withhold the feelings and meanings associated with facts known to both. Likewise, previous research has often concentrated on openness or avoidance as individual choices about the management of personal information (e.g., Greene et al., 2003; Kelly, 2002); in contrast, couples coping with cancer frequently coordinate choices about the attention given to issues that affect both parties. The cancer context offers opportunities to expand our conceptualization of reasons for openness and avoidance. More generally, examining these phenomena in a wide range of relationship types and life circumstances should strengthen our understanding of these processes and enable us to distinguish between context-specific and more general characteristics of openness and avoidance.

Conclusion

Research on openness and avoidance in relationships has often occurred among young healthy adults in developing relationships in which the topics of and motivations for disclosing or avoiding often stem from everyday concerns. Exceptions to this generalization exist, but they only make clear the fruitfulness of examining communication in ongoing relationships, in noncollege populations, and for quite serious, sensitive, and potentially stigmatizing topics. We have already noted that motives (such as protection of self or impression management) take on a different salience and import in enduring relationships with the prospect of physical limitations, diminished identity, or even death. We should also explore questions such as: Are the mental health benefits of disclosing about stressful experiences greater when the population is at greater risk due to physical illness? How are privacy issues understood and managed during treatment periods when one partner must depend upon the other for assistance with activities of daily living? The manifestation of relational dialectics (Baxter & Montgomery, 1996) or privacy management rules (Petronio, 2000) can take on situation-specific dimensions, and application of these theories in a diverse range of relational contexts remains vital to testing and advancing these theories.

Openness and avoidance matter across a range of communication contexts, from interpersonal to organizational settings, on topics ranging from health to politics, and in varying cultures and media. Applying communication theories to the case of couples and cancer highlights particular issues (e.g., the word "cancer" has particular connotations), but this review can also benefit scholars beyond that specific circumstance. Our suggestions for refinements to the conceptualization and measurement of openness and avoidance (as well as the questions that we posed about the relationships among topics, reasons, outcomes, strategies, and situational contingencies) also pertain to the broader literature on openness and avoidance.

References

Acheson, K. (2007). Silence in dispute. In C. S. Beck (Ed.), *Communication yearbook 31* (pp. 1–59). New York, NY: Lawrence Erlbaum Associates.

Afifi, T. D., Caughlin, J. P., & Afifi, W. A. (in press). The dark side (and light side) of avoidance and secrets. In B. H. Spitzberg & W. R. Cupach (Eds.), *The dark side of interpersonal communication* (2nd ed.). Mahwah, NJ: Lawrence Erlbaum Associates.

Afifi, T. D., Olson, L., & Armstrong, C. (2005). The chilling effect and family secrets: Examining the role of self-protection, other protection, and communication efficacy. *Human Communication Research, 31,* 564–598.

Afifi, W. A., & Guerrero, L. K. (2000). Motivations underlying topic avoidance in close relationships. In S. Petronio (Ed.), *Balancing the secrets of private disclosures* (pp. 165–179). Mahwah, NJ: Lawrence Erlbaum Associates.

American Cancer Society. (2006). *Cancer facts and figures.* Atlanta, GA: American Cancer Society.

Arrington, M. I. (2005). "She's right behind me all the way": An analysis of prostate cancer narratives and changes in family relationships. *Journal of Family Communication, 5*, 141–162.

Baider, L., & Sarell, M. (1984). Couples in crisis: Patient–spouse differences in perception of interaction patterns and the illness situation. *Family Therapy, 11*, 115–122.

Baxter, L. A., & Montgomery, B. M. (1996). *Relating: Dialogues & dialectics.* New York: Guilford Press.

Beach, W. A., & Anderson, J. K. (2003). Communication and cancer? Part I: The noticeable absence of interactional research. *Journal of Psychosocial Oncology, 21*(3), 1–23.

Blanchard, C. G., Albrecht, T. L., & Ruckdeschel, J. C. (1997). The crisis of cancer: Psychological impact on families. *Oncology, 11*, 189–194.

Blanchard, C. G., Albrecht, T. L., Ruckdeschel, J. C., Grant, C. H., & Hemmick, R. M. (1995). The role of social support in adaptation to cancer and to survival. *Journal of Psychosocial Oncology, 13*(1/2), 75–95.

Bloom, J. R. (2000). The role of family support in cancer control. In L. Baider, C. L. Cooper, & A. K. DeNour (Eds.), *Cancer and the family* (pp. 55–71). Chichester, England: John Wiley.

Bochner, A. P. (1982). On the efficacy of openness in close relationships. In M. Burgoon (Ed.), *Communication yearbook 6* (pp. 109–123). Beverly Hills, CA: Sage.

Boehmer, U., & Clark, J. A. (2001). Communication about prostate cancer between men and their wives. *The Journal of Family Practice, 50*, 226–231.

Bok, S. (1983). *Secrets: On the ethics of concealment and revelation.* New York: Vintage Books.

Byrne, A., Ellershaw, J., Holcombe, C., & Salmon, P. (2002). Patients' experience of cancer: Evidence of the role of "fighting" in collusive clinical communication. *Patient Education and Counseling, 48*, 15–21.

Carlson, L. E., Bultz, B. D., Speca, M., & St. Pierre, M. (2000). Partners of cancer patients: Part I. Impact, adjustment, and coping across the illness trajectory. *Journal of Psychosocial Oncology, 18*(2), 39–63.

Carlson, L. E., Ottenbriet, N., St. Pierre, M., & Bultz, B. D. (2001). Partner understanding of the breast and prostate cancer experience. *Cancer Nursing, 24*, 231–239.

Caughlin, J. P. (2003). Family communication standards: What counts as excellent family communication and how are such standards associated with family satisfaction? *Human Communication Research, 29*, 5–40.

Caughlin, J., & Afifi, T. D. (2004). When is topic avoidance unsatisfying? Examining moderators of the association between avoidance and dissatisfaction. *Human Communication Research, 30*, 479–513.

Caughlin J. P., Afifi, W. A., Carpenter-Theune K. E., & Miller, L. E. (2005). Reasons for, and consequences of, revealing personal secrets in close relationships: A longitudinal study. *Personal Relationships, 12,* 43–59.

Caughlin, J. P., & Golish, T. (2002). An analysis of the association between topic avoidance and dissatisfaction: Comparing perceptual and interpersonal explanations. *Communication Monographs, 69,* 275–296.

Caughlin, J. P., & Petronio, S. (2004). Privacy in families. In A. L. Vangelisti (Ed.), *Handbook of family communication* (pp. 379–412). Mahwah, NJ: Lawrence Erlbaum Associates.

Chaitchik, S., Kreitler, S., Rapoport, Y., & Algor, R. (1992). What do cancer patients' spouses know about the patients? *Cancer Nursing, 15,* 353–362.

Charmaz, K. (1991). *Good days and bad days: The self in chronic illness and time.* New Brunswick, NJ: Rutgers University Press.

Chekryn, J. (1984). Cancer recurrence: Personal meaning, communication, and marital adjustment. *Cancer Nursing, 7,* 491–498.

Collins, N. L., & Miller, L. C. (1994) Self-disclosure and liking: A meta-analytic review. *Psychological Bulletin, 116,* 457–475.

Dailey, R. M., & Palomares, N. A. (2004). Strategic topic avoidance: An investigation of topic avoidance frequency, strategies used, and relational correlates. *Communication Monographs, 71,* 471–496.

Deaux, K., & Major, B. (1990). A social-psychological model of gender. In D. L. Rhode (Ed.), *Theoretical perspectives on sexual difference* (pp. 89–99). New Haven, CT: Yale University Press.

de Boer, M. F., Pruyn, J. F., van den Borne, B., Knegt, P. P., Ryckman, R. M., & Verwoerd, C. D. (1995). Rehabilitation outcomes of long-term survivors treated for head and neck cancer. *Head & Neck, 17,* 503–515.

Derlega, V. J., Metts, S., Petronio, S., & Margulis, S. T. (1993). *Self-disclosure.* Newbury Park, CA: Sage.

Dillard, J. P. (1990). A goal-driven model of interpersonal influence. In J. P. Dillard (Ed.), *Seeking compliance: The production of interpersonal influence messages* (pp. 41–56). Scottsdale, AZ: Gorsuch Scarisbrick.

Dindia, K. (2000). Sex differences in self-disclosure, reciprocity of self-disclosure, and self-disclosure and liking: Three meta-analyses reviewed. In S. Petronio (Ed.), *Balancing the secrets of private disclosures* (pp. 21–35). Mahwah, NJ: Lawrence Erlbaum Associates.

Dindia, K., & Allen, M. (1992). Sex differences in self-disclosure: A meta-analysis. *Psychological Bulletin, 112,* 106–124.

Douglass, L. G. (1997). Reciprocal support in the context of cancer: Perspectives of the patient and spouse. *Oncology Nursing Forum, 24,* 1529–1536.

Duggan, A. (2006). Understanding interpersonal communication processes across health contexts: Advances in the last decade and challenges for the next decade. *Journal of Health Communication, 11,* 93–108.

Eisenberg, E. M., Murphy, A., & Andrews, L. (1998). Openness and decision making in the search for a university provost. *Communication Monographs, 65,* 1–23.

Eisenberg, E. M., & Witten, M. G. (1987). Reconsidering openness in organizational communication. *Academy of Management Review, 12,* 418–426.

Elal-Lawrence, G., & Celikoglu, P. (1995). Social support and psychological well-being in breast cancer patients. *Health and Social Care in the Community, 3,* 1–7.

Epping-Jordan, J. E., Compas, B. E., & Howell, D. C. (1994). Predictors of cancer progression in young adult men and women: Avoidance, intrusive thoughts, and psychological symptoms. *Health Psychology, 13,* 539–547.

Frawley, M. G. (1990). From secrecy to self-disclosure: Healing the scars of incest. In G. Stricker & M. Fisher (Eds.), *Self-disclosure in the therapeutic relationship* (pp. 247–259). New York: Plenum Press.

Friedman, L. C., Lehane, D., Weinberg, A. D., Mirabi, M., & Cooper, H. P. (1993). Physical and psychosocial needs of cancer patients. *Texas Medicine, 89*(7), 61–64.

Gewirtz, A., & Gossart-Walker, S. (2000). Home-based treatment for children and families affected by HIV and AIDS: Dealing with stigma, secrecy, disclosure, and loss. *Child and Adolescent Psychiatric Clinics of North America, 9,* 313–330.

Giese-Davis, J., Hermanson, K., Koopman, C., Weibel, D., & Spiegel, D. (2000). Quality of couples' relationship and adjustment to metastatic breast cancer. *Journal of Family Psychology, 14,* 251–266.

Gilbar, O. l., & Ben-Zur, H. (2002). *Cancer and the family caregiver: Distress and coping.* Springfield, IL: Thomas.

Goldsmith, D. J. (2001). A normative approach to the study of uncertainty and communication. *Journal of Communication, 51,* 514–533.

Goldsmith, D. J. (2004). *Communicating social support.* New York: Cambridge University Press.

Goldsmith, D. J., Gumminger, K. L., & Bute, J. (2006). Couple communication and recovery from a cardiac event. In B. LePoire & R. M. Dailey (Eds.), *Socially meaningful applied research in interpersonal communication* (pp. 95–117). New York: Peter Lang.

Goldsmith, D. J., Lindholm, K., & Bute, J. (2006). Dilemmas of talking about lifestyle changes among couples coping with a cardiac event. *Social Science and Medicine, 63,* 2079–2090.

Golish, T. D., & Caughlin, J. P. (2002). "I'd rather not talk about it:" Adolescents' and young adults' use of topic avoidance in stepfamilies. *Journal of Applied Communication Research, 30,* 78–106.

Gotcher, J. M. (1992). Interpersonal communication and psychosocial adjustment. *Journal of Psychosocial Oncology, 10*(3), 21–39.

Gotcher, J. M. (1993). The effects of family communication on psychosocial adjustment of cancer patients. *Journal of Applied Communication Research, 21,* 176–188.

Gotcher, J. M. (1995). Well-adjusted and maladjusted cancer patients: An examination of communication variables. *Health Communication, 7,* 21–33.

Gray, R., Fitch, M., Phillips, C., Labrecque, M., & Fergus, K. (2000). Managing the impact of illness: The experiences of men with prostate cancer and their spouses. *Journal of Health Psychology, 5,* 531–548.

Gray, R., Fitch, M. I., Phillips, C., Labrecque, M., & Klotz, L. (1999). Presurgery experiences of prostate cancer patients and their spouses. *Cancer Practice, 7,* 130–135.

Greene, K. (2000). Disclosure of chronic illness varies by topic and target: The role of stigma and boundaries in willingness to disclose. In S. Petronio (Ed.), *Balancing the secrets of private disclosures* (pp. 123–135). Mahwah, NJ: Lawrence Erlbaum Associates.

Greene, K., Derlega, V. J., Yep, G. A., & Petronio, S. (2003). *Privacy and disclosure of HIV in interpersonal relationships: A sourcebook for researchers and practitioners.* Mahwah, NJ: Lawrence Erlbaum Associates.

Greene, K., & Faulkner, S. L. (2002). Expected versus actual responses to disclosure in relationships of HIV-positive African American adolescent females. *Communication Studies, 53,* 297–317.

Grey, S. (2007). Wounds not easily healed: Exploring trauma in communication studies. In C. S. Beck (Ed.), *Communication yearbook 31* (pp. 173–222). New York, NY: Lawrence Erlbaum Associates.

Gross, J. (1989). Emotional expression in cancer onset and progression. *Social Science and Medicine, 28,* 1239–1248.

Gudykunst, W. B., & Nishida, T. (1984). Individual and cultural influences on uncertainty reduction. *Communication Monographs, 51,* 23–36.

Guerrero, L. K., & Afifi, W. A. (1995). What parents don't know: Topic avoidance in parent–child relationships. In T. Socha & G. Stamp (Eds.), *Parents, children, and communication: Frontiers of theory and research* (pp. 219–247). Mahwah, NJ: Lawrence Erlbaum Associates.

Hagedoorn, M., Kuijer, R. G., Buunk, B. P., DeJong, G. M., Wobbes, T., & Sanderman, R. (2000). Marital satisfaction in patients with cancer: Does support from intimate partners particularly affect those who need it most? *Health Psychology, 19,* 274–282.

Hagedoorn, M., Sanderman, R., Buunk, B. P., & Wobbes, T. (2002). Failing in spousal caregiving: The "identity-relevant stress" hypothesis to explain sex differences in caregiver distress. *British Journal of Health Psychology, 7,* 481–494.

Hannah, M. T., Gritz, E. R., Wellisch, D. K., Fobair, P., Hoppe, R. T., Bloom, J. R., et al. (1992). Changes in marital and sexual functions of long-term survivors and their spouses: Testicular cancer versus Hodgkin's disease. *Psycho-Oncology, 1*, 89–103.

Hannum, J. W., Giese-Davis, J., Harding, K., & Hatfield, A. K. (1991). Effects of individual and marital variables on coping with cancer. *Journal of Psychosocial Oncology, 9*(2), 1–20.

Harrison, J., Maguire, P., & Pitceathly, C. (1995). Confiding in crisis: Gender differences in pattern of confiding among cancer patients. *Social Science and Medicine, 41*, 1255–1260.

Heinrich, R. L., Schag, C. C., & Ganz, P. A. (1984). Living with cancer: The inventory of problem situations. *Journal of Clinical Psychology, 40*, 972–980.

Hilton, B. A. (1993). Issues, problems, and challenges for families coping with breast cancer. *Seminars in Oncology Nursing, 9*, 88–100.

Hilton, B. A. (1994). Family communication patterns in coping with early breast cancer. *Western Journal of Nursing Research, 16*, 366–391.

Hinton, J. (1981). Sharing or withholding awareness of dying between husband and wife. *Journal of Psychosomatic Research, 25*, 337–343.

Hinton, J. (1998). An assessment of open communication between people with terminal cancer, caring relatives, and others during home care. *Journal of Palliative Care, 14*(3), 15–23.

Hodgson, J. H., Shields, C.G., & Rousseau, S.L. (2003). Disengaging communication in later-life couples coping with breast cancer. *Families, Systems, and Health, 21*, 145–163.

Holmberg, S. K., Scott, L. L., Alexy, W., & Fife, B. L. (2001). Relationship issues of women with breast cancer. *Cancer Nursing, 24*, 53–60.

Hoskins, C. N., Baker, S., Budin, W., Edkstrom, D., Maislin, G., Sherman, D., et al. (1996). Adjustment among husbands of women with breast cancer. *Journal of Psychosocial Oncology, 14*(1), 41–69.

Hoskins, C. N., Baker, S., Sherman, D., Bohlander, J., Bookbinder, M., Budin, W., et al. (1996). Social support and patterns of adjustment to breast cancer. *Scholarly Inquiry for Nursing Practice, 10*, 99–123.

Howell, D. (1986). The impact of terminal illness on the spouse. *Journal of Palliative Care, 2*, 22–30.

Jamison, K. R., Wellisch, D., & Pasnau, R. O. (1978). Psychosocial aspects of mastectomy: The woman's perspective. *American Journal of Psychiatry, 134*, 432–436.

Johnston, G., & Abraham, C. (2000). Managing awareness: Negotiating and coping with a terminal prognosis. *International Journal of Palliative Nursing, 6*, 485–494.

Juraskova, I., Butow, P., Robertson, R., Sharpe, L., McLeod, C., & Hacker, N. (2003). Post-treatment sexual adjustment following cervical and endometrial cancer: A qualitative insight. *Psycho-Oncology, 12*, 267–279.

Kagawa-Singer, M., & Wellisch, D. K. (2003). Breast cancer patients' perceptions of their husbands' support in a cross-cultural context. *Psycho-Oncology, 12*, 24–37.

Kalayjian, A. (1989). Coping with cancer: The spouse's perspective. *Archives of Psychiatric Nursing, 3*, 166–172.

Katriel, T., & Philipsen, G. (1981). "What we need is communication": "Communication" as a cultural category in some American speech. *Communication Monographs, 48*, 301–317.

Kayser, K., Sormanti, M. E., & Strainchamps, E. (1999). Women coping with cancer: The influence of relationship factors on psychosocial adjustment. *Psychology of Women Quarterly, 23*, 725–739.

Keitel, M. A., Cramer, S. H., & Zevon, M. A. (1990). Spouses of cancer patients: A review of the literature. *Journal of Counseling and Development, 69*, 163–166.

Keller, M., Henrich, G., Sellschopp, A., & Beutel, M. (1996). Between distress and support: Spouses of cancer patients. In L. Baider, C. L. Cooper, & A. Kaplan de-Nour (Eds.), *Cancer and the family* (pp. 187–223). Chichester, England: Wiley.

Kelly, A. E. (2002). *The psychology of secrets.* New York: Kluwer Academic/Plenum.

Kimberly, J. A., Serovich, J. M., & Greene, K. (1995). Disclosure of HIV-positive status: Five women's stories. *Family Relations, 44*, 316–322.

Kirkman, M., Rosenthal, D. A., & Feldman, S. S. (2005). Being open with your mouth shut: The meaning of "openness" in family communication about sexuality. *Sex Education, 5*, 49–66.

Kuijer, R. G., Buunk, B. P., & Ybema, J. F. (2001). Justice of give-and-take in the intimate relationship: When one partner of a couple is diagnosed with cancer. *Personal Relationships, 8*, 75–92.

Lalos, A., Jacobsson, L., Lalos, O., & Stendahl, U. (1995). Experiences of the male partner in cervical and endometrial cancer: A prospective interview study. *Journal of Psychosomatic Obstetric Gynaecology, 16*, 153–165.

Lavery, J. F., & Clarke, V. A. (1999). Prostate cancer: Patients' and spouses' coping and marital adjustment. *Psychology, Health, and Medicine, 4*, 289–302.

Lepore, S. J. (2001). A social-cognitive processing model of emotional adjustment to cancer. In A. Baum & B. L. Anderson (Eds.), *Psychosocial interventions for cancer* (pp. 99–116). Washington, DC: American Psychological Association.

Lepore, S. J., & Helgeson, V. S. (1998). Social constraints, intrusive thoughts, and mental health after prostate cancer. *Journal of Social and Clinical Psychology, 17,* 89–106.

Lepore, S. J., & Ituarte, P. H. G. (1999). Optimism about cancer enhances mood by reducing negative social relations. *Cancer Research Therapy and Control, 8,* 165–174.

Lethborg, C. E., Kissane, D., & Burns, W. I. (2003). "It's not the easy part": The experience of significant others of women with early stage breast cancer, at treatment completion. *Social Work in Health Care, 37*(1), 63–85.

Lewis, F. M. (1986). The impact of cancer on the family: A critical analysis of the research literature. *Patient Education and Counseling, 8,* 269–289.

Lewis, F. M., & Deal, L. W. (1995). Balancing our lives: A study of the married couple's experience with breast cancer recurrence. *Oncology Nursing Forum, 22,* 943–953.

Lichtman, R. R., Taylor, S. E., & Wood, J. V. (1987). Social support and marital adjustment after breast cancer. *Journal of Psychosocial Oncology, 5*(3), 47–74.

Lindholm, K. A., Bute, J., Tassio, G. M., & Goldsmith, D. J. (2004, November). *Reasons people with cancer and their partners find information helpful or unhelpful.* Paper presented at the annual meeting of the National Communication Association, Chicago.

Manne, S. (1994). Couples coping with cancer: Research issues and recent findings. *Journal of Clinical Psychology in Medical Settings, 1,* 317–330.

Manne, S. (1998). Cancer in the marital context: A review of the literature. *Cancer Investigation, 16,* 188–202.

Manne, S., Babb, J., Pinover, W., Horwitz, E., & Ebbert, J. (2004). Psycho-educational group intervention for wives of men with prostate cancer. *Psycho-Oncology, 13,* 37–46.

Manne, S., Ostroff, J., Rini, C., Fox, K., Goldstein, L., & Grana, G. (2004). The interpersonal process model of intimacy: The role of self-disclosure, partner disclosure, and partner responsiveness in interactions between breast cancer patients and their partners. *Journal of Family Psychology, 18,* 589–599.

Manne, S., Ostroff, J., Sherman, M., Glassman, M., Ross, S., Goldstein, L., et al. (2003). Buffering effects of family and friend support on associations between partner unsupportive behaviors and coping among women with breast cancer. *Journal of Social and Personal Relationships, 20,* 771–792.

Manne, S., Ostroff, J., Sherman, M., Heyman, R. E., Ross, S., & Fox, K. (2004). Couples' support-related communication, psychological distress, and relationship satisfaction among women with early stage breast cancer. *Journal of Consulting and Clinical Psychology, 72,* 660–670.

Manne, S., Ostroff, J., Winkel, G., Goldstein, L., Fox, K., & Grana, G. (2004). Posttraumatic growth after breast cancer: Patient, partner, and couple perspectives. *Psychosomatic Medicine, 66,* 442–454.

Manne, S., Pape, S. J., Taylor, K. L., & Dougherty, J. (1999). Spouse support, coping, and mood among individuals with cancer. *Annals of Behavioral Medicine, 21,* 111–121.

Marin, M. J., Sherblom, J. C., & Shipps, T. B. (1994). Contextual influences on nurses' conflict management strategies. *Western Journal of Communication, 58,* 201–228.

Maughan, K., Heyman, B., & Matthews, M. (2002). In the shadow of risk: How men cope with a partner's gynecological cancer. *International Journal of Nursing Studies, 39,* 27–34.

Mesters, I., van den Borne, H. G., McCormick, L., Pruyn, J., de Boer, M., & Imbos, T. (1997). Openness to discuss cancer in the nuclear family: Scale, development, and validation. *Psychosomatic Medicine, 59,* 269–279.

Minuchin, S. (1974). *Families and family therapy.* Cambridge, MA: Harvard University Press.

Molassiotis, A., Chan, C. W., Yam, B. M., Chan, E. S., & Lam, C. S. (2002). Life after cancer: Adaptation issues faced by Chinese gynaecological cancer survivors in Hong Kong. *Psycho-Oncology, 11,* 114–123.

Northouse, L. (1984). The impact of cancer on the family: An overview. *International Journal of Psychiatry in Medicine, 14,* 215–242.

Northouse, L. (1994). Breast cancer in younger women: Effects on interpersonal and family relations. *Journal of the National Cancer Institute Monographs, 16,* 183–190.

Northouse, L., Cracchiolo-Caraway, A., & Appel, C. (1991). Psychologic consequences of breast cancer on partner and family. *Seminars in Oncology Nursing, 7,* 216–223.

Northouse, L., & Swain, M. A. (1987). Adjustment of patients and spouses to initial impact of breast cancer. *Nursing Research, 36,* 221–225.

Northouse, P. G., & Northouse, L. (1987). Communication and cancer: Issues confronting patients, health professionals, and family members. *Journal of Psychosocial Oncology, 5*(3), 17–46.

Oberst, M. T., & James, R. H. (1985, April). Going home: Patient and spouse following cancer surgery. *Topics in Clinical Nursing, 7,* 46–57.

Oetzel, J., Ting-Toomey, S., Masumoto, T., Yokochi, Y., Pan, X., Takai, J., et al. (2001). Face and facework in conflict: A cross-cultural comparison of China, Germany, Japan, and the United States. *Communication Monographs, 68,* 235–258.

O'Keefe, B. J. (1988). The logic of message design: Individual differences in reasoning about communication. *Communication Monographs, 55,* 80–103.

O'Mahoney, J. M., & Carroll, R. A. (1997). The impact of breast cancer and its treatment on marital functioning. *Journal of Clinical Psychology in Medical Settings, 4,* 397–415.

Paine, M. L., & Hansen, D. J. (2002). Factors influencing children to self-disclose sexual abuse. *Clinical Psychology Review, 22,* 271–295.

Parkin, D. M., Bray, F., Ferlay, J., & Pisani, P. (2005). Global cancer statistics, 2002. *CA: A Cancer Journal for Clinicians, 55,* 74–108.

Parks, M. R. (1982). Ideology in interpersonal communication: Off the couch and into the world. In M. Burgoon (Ed.), *Communication yearbook 6* (pp. 79–107). Beverly Hills, CA: Sage.

Payne, S., Smith, S. P., & Dean, S. (1999). Identifying the concerns of informal carers in palliative care. *Palliative Medicine, 13,* 37–44.

Pederson, L. M., & Valanis, B. G. (1988). The effects of breast cancer on the family: A review of the literature. *Journal of Psychosocial Oncology, 6*(1/2), 95–118.

Pennebaker, J. W. (1997). *Opening up: The healing power of expressing emotions* (Rev. ed.). New York: Guilford Press.

Persson, L., Rasmusson, M., & Hallberg, I. R. (1998). Spouses' view during their partner's illness and treatment. *Cancer Nursing, 21,* 97–105.

Petrie, K. J., Booth, R. J., & Davison, K. P. (1995). Repression, disclosure, and immune function: Recent findings and methodological issues. In J. W. Pennebaker (Ed.), *Emotion, disclosure, and health* (pp. 223–240). Washington, DC: American Psychological Association.

Petronio, S. (2000). The boundaries of privacy: Praxis of everyday life. In S. Petronio (Ed.), *Balancing the secrets of private disclosures* (pp. 37–49). Mahwah, NJ: Lawrence Erlbaum Associates.

Petronio, S. (2002). *Boundaries of privacy: Dialectics of disclosure.* Albany, NY: SUNY Press.

Petronio, S., & Kovach, S. (1997). Managing privacy boundaries: Health providers' perceptions of resident care in Scottish nursing homes. *Journal of Applied Communication Research, 25,* 115–131.

Pistrang, N., & Barker, C. (1992). Disclosure of concerns in breast cancer. *Psycho-Oncology, 1,* 182–192.

Pistrang, N., & Barker, C. (1995). The partner relationship in psychological response to breast cancer. *Social Science and Medicine, 40,* 789–797.

Pitceathly, C., & Maguire, P. (2000). Preventing affective disorders in partners of cancer patients: An intervention study. In L. Baider, C. L. Cooper, & A. De-Nour (Eds.), *Cancer and the family* (2nd ed., pp. 137–154). Chichester, England: Wiley.

Pitceathly, C., & Maguire, P. (2003). The psychological impact of cancer on patients' partners and other relatives: A review. *European Journal of Cancer, 39,* 1517–1524.

Ptacek, J. T., Pierce, G. R., Dodge, K. L., & Ptacek, J. J. (1997). Social support in spouses of cancer patients: What do they get and to what end? *Personal Relationships, 4,* 431–449.

Rapoport, Y., Kreitler, S., Chaitchik, S., Algor, R., & Weissler, K. (1993). Psychosocial problems in head-and-neck cancer patients and their change with time since diagnosis. *Annals of Oncology, 4,* 69–73.

Reardon, K., & Buck, R. (1989). Emotion, reason, and communication in coping with cancer. *Health Communication, 1,* 41–54.

Rees, C. E., & Bath, P. A. (2000). Exploring the information flow: Partners of women with breast cancer, patients, and healthcare professionals. *Oncology Nursing Forum, 27,* 1267–1275.

Reynolds, J. S., & Perrin, N. A. (2004). Mismatches in social support and psychosocial adjustment to breast cancer. *Health Psychology, 23,* 425–430.

Roberts, L. J. (2000). Fire and ice in marital communication: Hostile and distancing behaviors as predictors of marital distress. *Journal of Marriage and the Family, 62,* 693–707.

Roessler, P. (2007). Media content diversity: Conceptual issues and future directions for communication research. In C. S. Beck (Ed.), *Communication yearbook 31* (pp. 463–520). New York, NY: Lawrence Erlbaum Associates.

Roloff, M. E., & Ifert, D. E. (2000). Conflict management through avoidance: Withholding complaints, suppressing arguments, and declaring topics taboo. In S. Petronio (Ed.), *Balancing the secrets of private disclosures* (pp. 151–179). Mahwah, NJ: Lawrence Erlbaum Associates.

Rose, K. E., Webb, C., & Waters, K. (1997). Coping strategies employed by informal carers of terminally ill cancer patients. *Journal of Cancer Nursing, 1,* 126–133.

Rosenfeld, L. B. (1979). Self-disclosure avoidance: Why am I afraid to tell you who I am? *Communication Monographs, 46,* 63–74.

Rosenfeld, L. B. (2000). Overview of the ways privacy, secrecy, and disclosure are balanced in today's society. In S. Petronio (Ed.), *Balancing the secrets of private disclosures* (pp. 3–17). Mahwah, NJ: Lawrence Erlbaum Associates.

Sabo, D., Brown, J., & Smith, C. (1986). The male role and mastectomy: Support groups as men's adjustment. *Journal of Psychosocial Oncology, 4*(1/2), 19–31.

Salander, P., & Spetz, A. (2002). How do patients and spouses deal with the serious facts of malignant glioma? *Palliative Medicine, 16,* 305–313.

Sales, E., Schulz, R., & Biegel, D. (1992). Predictors of strain in families of cancer patients: A review of the literature. *Journal of Psychosocial Oncology, 10*(2), 1–26.

Sarell, M., & Baider, L. (1984). The effects of cultural background on communication patterns of Israeli cancer patients. *Psychopathology, 17,* 17–23.

Schrimshaw, E. W., & Siegel, K. (2002). HIV-infected mothers' disclosure to their uninfected children: Rates, reasons, and reactions. *Journal of Social and Personal Relationships, 19,* 19–43.

Shimanoff, S. B. (1987). Types of emotional disclosures and request compliance between spouses. *Communication Monographs, 54,* 86–100.

Sillars, A. L., Pike, G. R., Jones, T. S., & Redmon, K. (1983). Communication and conflict in marriage. In R. Bostrom (Ed.), *Communication yearbook 7* (pp. 414–429). Beverly Hills, CA: Sage.

Skerrett, K. (1998). Couple adjustment to the experience of breast cancer. *Families, Systems, and Health, 16,* 281–297.

Smyth, J. M., & Pennebaker, J. W. (2001). What are the health effects of disclosure? In A. Baum, T. A. Revenson, & J. E. Singer (Eds.), *Handbook of health psychology* (pp. 339–348). Mahwah, NJ: Lawrence Erlbaum Associates.

Spiegel, D., Bloom, J. R., & Gottheil, E. (1983). Family environment as a predictor of adjustment to metastatic breast carcinoma. *Journal of Psychosocial Oncology, 1*(1), 33–44.

Stiles, W. B. (1987). "I have to talk to somebody": A fever model of disclosure. In V. Derlega & J. Berg (Eds.), *Self-disclosure: Theory, research, and therapy* (pp. 257–282). New York: Plenum Press.

Taylor-Brown, J., Kilpatrick, M., Maunsell, E., & Dorval, M. (2000). Partner abandonment of women with breast cancer: Myth or reality? *Cancer Practice, 8,* 160–164.

Thomas, C., Morris, S. M., & Harman, J. C. (2002). Companions through cancer: The care given by informal carers in cancer contexts. *Social Science and Medicine, 54,* 529–544.

Thorne, S. (1985). The family cancer experience. *Cancer Nursing, 8,* 285–291.

underwood, e. d., & Frey, L. R. (2007). Communication and community: Clarifying the connection across the communication community. In C. S. Beck (Ed.), *Communication yearbook 31* (pp. 369–418). New York, NY: Lawrence Erlbaum Associates.

Vachon, M. L. S., Freedman, K., Formo, A., Rogers, J., Lyall, W. A. L., & Freeman, S. J. J. (1977). The final illness in cancer: The widow's perspective. *Canadian Medical Association Journal, 117,* 1151–1154.

van der Does, J. V. S., & Duyvis, D. J. (1989). Psychosocial adjustment of spouses of cervical carcinoma patients. *Journal of Psychosomatics in Obstetrics and Gynecology, 19,* 163–171.

Vangelisti, A. L. (1994). Family secrets: Forms, functions, and correlates. *Journal of Social and Personal Relationships, 11,* 113–135.

Vangelisti, A. L., & Caughlin J. P. (1997). Revealing family secrets: The influence of topic, function, and relationships. *Journal of Social and Personal Relationships, 14,* 679–705.

Vangelisti, A. L., Caughlin, J. P., & Timmerman, L. M. (2001). Criteria for revealing family secrets. *Communication Monographs, 68,* 1–27.

Vess, J. D. J., Moreland, J. R., & Schwebel, A. I. (1985). An empirical assessment of the effects of cancer on family role functioning. *Journal of Psychosocial Oncology, 3*(1), 1–16.

Vess, J. D., Moreland, J. R., Schwebel, A. I., & Kraut, E. (1988). Psychosocial needs of cancer patients: Learning from patients and their spouses. *Journal of Psychosocial Oncology, 6*(1/2), 31–51.

Waldeck, J., & Myers, K. (2007). Organizational assimilation theory, research, and implications for multiple areas of the discipline: A state of the art review. In C. S. Beck (Ed.), *Communication yearbook 31* (pp. 321–367). New York, NY: Lawrence Erlbaum Associates.

Walsh, S. R., Manuel, J. C., & Avis, N. E. (2005). The impact of breast cancer on younger women's relationships with their partner and children. *Families, Systems, and Health, 23,* 80–93.

Wilson, S., & Morse, J. M. (1991). Living with a wife undergoing chemotherapy. *Image: Journal of Nursing Scholarship, 23,* 78–84.

Wortman, C. B., & Dunkel-Schetter, C. (1979). Interpersonal relationships and cancer: A theoretical analysis. *Journal of Social Issues, 35,* 120–155.

Young, N. (2007). Identity trans/formations. In C. S. Beck (Ed.), *Communication yearbook 31* (pp. 223–272). New York, NY: Lawrence Erlbaum Associates.

Zakowski, S. G., Harris, C., Krueger, N., Laubmeier, K. K., Garrett, S., Flanigan, R., et al. (2003). Social barriers to emotional expression and their relations to distress in male and female cancer patients. *British Journal of Health Psychology, 8,* 271–286.

Zemore, R., & Shepel, L. F. (1989). Effects of breast cancer and mastectomy on emotional support and adjustment. *Social Science and Medicine, 28,* 19–27.

Zhang, A. Y., & Siminoff, L. A. (2003). The role of family in treatment decision making by patients with cancer. *Oncology Nursing Forum, 30,* 1022–1028.

Zietlow, P. H., & Sillars, A. L. (1988). Life-stage differences in communication during marital conflicts. *Journal of Social and Personal Relationships, 5,* 223–245.

Chapter 3 Contents

3

Understanding Interpersonal Conflicts That Are Difficult to Resolve: A Review of Literature and Presentation of an Integrated Model

Courtney Waite Miller
Elmhurst College

Michael E. Roloff
Northwestern University

Rachel S. Malis
Elmhurst College

Our review summarizes and integrates existing research on interpersonal conflicts that are difficult to resolve. Research indicates that interpersonal conflicts can adversely impact families, individual health, team functioning, and intercultural relations. Hence, we need to better understand protracted disputes. We focus on two research programs directly related to interpersonal conflict (serial arguments and perpetual problems) and a third area of research that takes a macro approach to studying intractable conflict. We combine elements of the three approaches into an integrative framework that suggests nine questions worthy of future research.

Significance of Review

Conflict arises from incompatible activity (Deutsch, 1973) and comprises a frequent form of human interaction. Researchers have studied it in a variety of contexts (see Oetzel & Ting-Toomey, 2006), focusing on units of analysis ranging from the individual to the culture (see Roloff, 1988). This review concentrates on research regarding interpersonal conflicts that are difficult to resolve. Although a great deal of research on interpersonal conflict has been conducted in the context of close relationships (see Roloff & Soule, 2002), as Roloff noted, it has also been explored in other contexts such as group, organizational, and intercultural settings. Consequently, this topic interests many scholars across varied research specializations. Furthermore, research demonstrates that interpersonal conflict can have serious effects. Although scholars have long argued that interpersonal conflict can be functional (e.g., Wilmot & Hocker, 2001), evidence suggests that participants often characterize interpersonal conflict as a negative event (e.g., McCorkle & Mills, 1992). Ongoing, irresolvable interpersonal disputes can be especially problematic. We will briefly illustrate the negative outcomes in the following contexts: families, health care, organizations, intercultural contacts, religion, and political and ethnonational conflicts.

Family conflict can negatively affect the entire family. Marital arguments can be stressful for spouses (see Kiecolt-Glaser & Newton, 2001) and for children who observe the arguments (see Davies & Cummings, 1998). Marital conflict can adversely impact parenting behaviors (Krishnakumar & Buehler, 2000) and everyday interactions with children (Almeida, Wethington, & Chandler, 1999). Sibling conflict commonly occurs, even into adulthood (Bedford, 1998; Stewart, Verbrugge, & Beilfuss, 1998). Adolescent sibling conflict has been linked to increased risk of anxiety, depression, and delinquent behavior (Stocker, Burwell, & Briggs, 2002). Caughlin and Vangelisti (2006) and Sillars, Canary, and Tafoya (2004) provided recent reviews of conflict communication in dating and marital relationships, and Koerner and Fitzpatrick (2006) reviewed research on family conflict communication.

Health communication researchers are increasingly interested in the aversive health effects of arguing. Conflict poses negative implications for individuals' psychological (e.g., Bolger, DeLongis, Kessler, & Schilling, 1989; Finch & Zautra, 1992) and physical well-being (e.g., Kiecolt-Glaser et al., 1993). For example, conflict can result in decreased vitality, increased physical symptoms (Reis, Sheldon, Gable, Roscoe, & Ryan, 2000), and anxiety and depression (Abbey, Abramis, & Caplan, 1985). According to Kiecolt-Glaser et al., intense negative affect expressed during conflict has been directly connected to decreases in immune functioning as well as increases in blood pressure. More specifically, irresolvable conflicts can harm individuals' health. Malis and Roloff (2006b) found that individuals who tended to believe that an ongoing argument in their relationship was not likely to be solved more likely experienced negative health consequences.

Health communication scholars also have discussed the difficult conflicts that can occur over decisions about limiting or withholding life-sustaining treatments (e.g., Breen, Abernethy, Abbott, & Tulsky,

2001) and deciding appropriate treatment plans (e.g., Back & Arnold, 2005; Iecovich, 2000). For example, in Breen and colleagues' study, health care providers perceived conflict in 78% of decisions regarding life-sustaining treatments for critically ill patients. Iecovich argued that patients' families often disagree with the treatment and care that their elderly family members receive in health care settings.

Furthermore, these conflicts can be exacerbated by cultural differences. For example, in a study of Chinese immigrants in Canada with medically unexplained chronic fatigue and weakness, the majority of respondents reported that they did not want others to know about their experiences of chronic fatigue (Lee, Rodin, Devins, & Weiss, 2001). Participants referenced a cultural rule against disclosing failures to others. They feared being labeled as lazy as opposed to suffering from a medical condition. Respondents also reported that disclosure of their symptoms could result in difficulty finding mates and disgrace their entire families, especially if others defined their conditions as mental problems. According to Lee et al., this conflict intensified patients' distress levels and prevented them from utilizing some treatment options, such as mental health services.

Further, prior research has demonstrated negative outcomes of interpersonal conflict in work groups and management teams, especially those conflicts that are perceived as unresolved (Gayle & Preiss, 1998). For example, Jehn and Chatman (2000) discovered that relationship and process conflict within management teams negatively relate to commitment, cohesiveness, satisfaction, and individual performance. Relationship conflict centers on personal and social issues not tied to work. Process conflict focuses on issues such as task strategy and delegation of duties. Furthermore, a recent meta-analysis determined that task conflict arising from group consideration of alternative solutions to a problem also can impede group performance (De Dreu & Weingart, 2003). Additionally, lengthy disputes in work groups and management teams cost considerable time and effort because conflict impedes group members' abilities to gather, integrate, and adequately assess valuable information (Jehn, 1995). Poole and Garner (2006), Nicotera and Dorsey (2006), and Lipsky and Seeber (2006) have offered reviews of organizational conflict and communication.

Intercultural conflicts can be particularly difficult to manage because "misunderstanding, and from this counterproductive pseudoconflict, arises when members of one culture are unable to understand culturally determined differences in communication practices, traditions, and thought processing" (Borisoff & Victor, 1998, p. 152). For example, in a comparative study of China, Germany, Japan, and the United States, Oetzel and Ting-Toomey (2003) found that the degree to which a culture is individualistic or collectivistic directly and indirectly influences the conflict management styles that cultures tend to favor. Face concerns accounted for much of the variance in conflict management styles. Meanings of particular styles of conflict management differ across cultures (Kozan, 1997), and such differences can lead to or exacerbate negative intergroup encounters resulting in negative stereotypes (e.g., Stephan, Diaz-Loving, & Duran, 2000). Oetzel, Arcos, Mabizela, Weinman, and Zhang (2006) and Ting-Toomey and Takai (2006) provided reviews of intercultural conflict communication.

Conflicts centered on religion can also hurt relationships (e.g., Hughes, 2004), nations (e.g., Rouhana & Bar-Tal, 1998), and the world (e.g., Coleman, 2000). For example, Sternberg and Beier (1977) found that newlywed husbands often clashed with their wives about religion. According to Hughes, couples in interfaith marriages face higher than average risk for divorce and might exhibit strained communication. Hughes concluded that religious orientation corresponded to communication processes during conflicts. Intrinsically religious persons tend to view religion as a primary feature of their lives. They perceive religion as a unifying principle in their lives, attend church often, and exhibit tolerance toward varying viewpoints. Extrinsically oriented religious persons tend to perceive religion as a means of attaining personal benefits, such as social connections. They go to church irregularly, show dependence or a need for comfort and security, and demonstrate prejudice. According to Hughes, an extrinsic orientation to religion negatively relates to mutual constructive communication and positively relates to demand/withdrawal cycles; an intrinsic orientation to religion correlated positively with mutual constructive communication and negatively to demand/withdrawal patterns.

The effects of political and ethnonational conflicts range from economic costs (e.g., Coleman, 2000) to violence (e.g., Albeck, Adwan, & Bar-On, 2002) to negative mental health effects (Montiel, 2000). Ellis (2005) asserted that public figures and groups (such as politicians, public policy officials, institutes, and the like) traditionally study political and ethnonational conflicts. He argued that such perspectives on these conflicts should be complemented by intercultural communication scholars with the aim of designing communication experiences that could transform the relationships between hostile groups. Indeed, factors that promote positive everyday contact between different groups can reduce prejudice (Pettigrew & Tropp, 2006). However, negative intergroup encounters can increase anxiety that promotes negative outgroup attitudes (Corenblum & Stephan, 2001; Stephan et al., 2002) and avoidance of further contact (Plant, 2004; Plant & Devine, 2003).

Introduction to Difficult Conflicts

As mentioned previously, disputes occur commonly in interpersonal relationships (e.g., W. L. Benoit & P. J. Benoit, 1987; Miller, 1997). For example, Averill (1982) reported that a majority of people (66%) become angry with someone in any given week; on any given day, 44% of people become annoyed by a relational partner. Many everyday disputes end quickly (e.g., Vuchinich, 1987), but some end without resolution (e.g., W. L. Benoit & P. J. Benoit, 1987; Gottman, 1999; Johnson & Roloff, 1998; Lloyd, 1987; Montemayor & Hanson, 1985; Raffaelli, 1992; Trapp & Hoff, 1985; Vuchinich, 1987, 1990). For example, W. L. Benoit and P. J. Benoit stated that approximately 40% of the everyday argumentative episodes described by college students ended when the interactants stopped arguing or when one interactant left the scene.

Similarly, Lloyd (1987) found that 32% of disagreements described by dating couples stopped when one partner left the scene or refused to continue discussion of the issue. Vuchinich (1990) concluded that 66% of family dinner table quarrels concluded in a standoff in which the participants implicitly agreed to disagree; 2% halted with one party leaving the dinner table or refusing to continue arguing. In Raffaelli's (1992) study of sibling disputes, 37% of conflicts ended without a resolution. According to Montemayor & Hanson (1985), adolescents reported that 50% of arguments with parents or siblings finished with the interactants withdrawing without resolution. Finally, 79% of Gayle and Preiss's (1998) participants responded that their workplace conflicts were not resolved.

When a dispute ends without resolution, it might re-emerge (W. L. Benoit & P. J. Benoit, 1987; Roloff & Johnson, 2002). In fact, almost half of the college students in W. L. Benoit and P. J. Benoit's study reported that they had the same argument with the same person fairly often. Respondents in Johnson and Roloff's (1998) study described disagreeing with a romantic partner an average of 13 times on a particular issue.

Repeated disputes can negatively impact individuals and their relationships. Relational conflicts that extend over several days adversely impact a person's mood state (Bolger et al., 1989). Moreover, individuals in distressed marriages report more ongoing conflicts than do those in nondistressed marriages (Birchler & Webb, 1977), and frequent arguing positively relates to relational termination (McGonagle, Kessler, & Gotlib, 1993). Furthermore, after multiple arguments on the same topic without progress toward a resolution, individuals often conclude that they cannot resolve a conflict (Johnson & Roloff, 1998). Such beliefs and attempts to manage perceived irresolvable conflict hinder relational satisfaction (see related arguments by Gottman, 1999; Metts & Cupach, 1990).

Consequently, we must explore the nature of and reasons for unresolved and irresolvable interpersonal conflicts. A better understanding of conflicts that are difficult to resolve will be helpful to scholars in a variety of areas.

Goals of the Present Review

Although research clearly indicates that some interpersonal conflicts are difficult to resolve, much of the scholarship is scattered, and findings lack integration into a coherent perspective. In order to rectify this problem, we review two research programs focused on conflicts that are not easily resolved (serial arguing and perpetual conflict). Serial arguing involves repetitive arguments on the same topic (Trapp & Hoff, 1985), and perpetual conflict encompasses arguments that will not be resolved (Gottman, 1999). We provide more detailed definitions later in the chapter.

We supplement this knowledge base by examining research focused on intractable conflict. In short, intractable conflicts comprise intense conflicts that individuals struggle to resolve (Coleman, 2000). A more comprehensive definition will follow. Although scholars often conduct research on intractable conflict in large-scale contexts (e.g., intergroup, political, and international conflict), many of the findings remain relevant for understanding interpersonal disagreements. Indeed, research on interpersonal conflict may provide useful insight into more macro conflicts as well.

We chose to limit our review in this way in order to focus on research programs that specifically examine conflicts that are difficult to resolve. As mentioned previously, these conflicts can seriously affect individuals, workplaces, communities, and nations. Thus, they warrant particular attention focused on promoting a better understanding of these complicated conflicts.

Taken together, research on serial arguing, perpetual problems, and intractable conflict constitutes a substantial body of literature. As we detail, literature on intractable conflict is well developed, and many researchers have been studying this topic for decades. Research on serial arguing and perpetual problems is fairly new and, so far, only conducted by a handful of scholars. Thus, it is limited. For this reason, the reader will notice a bit of an imbalance in our discussion of serial arguing and perpetual problems when compared to our review of intractable conflict literature.

In limiting our review to research focused on conflicts that are difficult to resolve, we do not discount the usefulness of prior research in interpersonal conflict. Such research enhances understanding of these types of conflicts. We selectively incorporate examples of this research to provide additional depth when needed. Research on interpersonal conflict entails a vast topic worthy of several literature reviews by subtopic and therefore could not be fully incorporated here. For a more complete picture of interpersonal conflict research, readers should see reviews of interpersonal conflict (e.g., Caughlin & Vangelisti, 2006; Roloff & Soule, 2002) and the reviews suggested in the previous section. Readers also might want to consult textbooks on conflict communication (e.g., Cupach & Canary, 2000; Folger, Poole, & Stutman, 2005; Wilmot & Hocker, 2001).

This chapter includes four sections. The first three sections review relevant research on serial arguing, perpetual conflict, and intractable conflict. The fourth section combines the key contributions of each research area into a single model. Based on the model, we identify future research directions.

Review of Serial Arguing Research

Generally speaking, when scholars study arguing, they typically investigate a dyad's behavior at one point in time (Johnson & Roloff, 1998). This method provides rich information about a particular encounter, but it does not capture the nature of all types of disagreements that couples encounter. Sometimes couples cannot resolve their arguments in a single episode and therefore extend arguments over a period of time. This practice results in recurring argumentative episodes known as serial arguments (Trapp & Hoff, 1985). According to Johnson and Roloff, "A serial argument exists when individuals argue or engage in conflict about the same topic over time, during which they participate in several (at least two) arguments about the topic" (p. 333). Research on serial arguing has focused on (a) the characteristics of serial arguments, (b) goals of serial arguing, (c) the impact of serial arguing on individual well-being, and (d) the impact of serial arguing on relational quality.

Characteristics of Serial Arguments

Argumentative Episodes   Serial arguments consist of linked argumentative episodes (Roloff & Johnson, 2002). Individuals might be motivated to end disagreements (Katz, Jones, & Beach, 2000); however, they do not always do so in one episode (Trapp & Hoff, 1985). Episodes often start when one partner engages in a provocative action, is challenged by his or her partner, and then resists that challenge (Vuchinich, 1987). Newell and Stutman (1988) advanced a model of social confrontation in which a person expresses to another that his or her behavior "has violated (or is violating) a rule or expectation for appropriate conduct within the relationship or situation" (p. 271). A central issue involves the legitimacy of a complaint. According to Newell and Stutman, individuals discuss whether the target's behavior has violated a rule and whether they can mutually agree about the rule's legitimacy. Confrontations provide a means of resolving differences and establish expectations for future behavior (see also Newell & Stutman, 1989/90). Although many argumentative episodes are short, Vuchinich asserted that they sometimes extend into lengthy disputes as one partner pressures the other to change.

Many argumentative episodes end unresolved. Not surprisingly, individuals report that they frequently argue with the same person about the same issue (W. L. Benoit & P. J. Benoit, 1987). Indeed, the vast majority of participants in Trapp and Hoff's (1985) study perceived an argument in their relationship as serial. Additionally, all of the participants in Johnson and Roloff's (1998) study described at least one serial argument currently occurring in their dating relationships.

Issue Focused   Serial arguments focus on a single issue. For example, Johnson and Roloff (1998) reported three issue types common in serial arguments. Of respondents, 63% revealed differences in perspectives on the relationship as a reason why the serial argument was problematic. The differences tended to center on issues such as whether the relationship was exclusive and whether the relationship was progressing toward marriage. Violated expectations were described by 33% of participants. Such violations included relational transgressions such as lying or failure to follow through with promises or commitments. Conflicting values or beliefs were described by 33% of respondents as the source of the serial argument on which they were reporting. Beliefs tended to conflict on religious, political, or social issues, and personal tastes in music, art, or movies.

Consequently, many individuals report that, during typical argumentative episodes, the same person initiates the disagreement while the other partner resists (Johnson & Roloff, 2000b). *Demand/withdraw* describes a pattern in which one partner pressures for change by demanding, complaining, nagging, or criticizing while the other partner resists this pressure by withdrawing or trying to avoid the issue (Caughlin, 2002; Eldridge & Christensen, 2002). Johnson and Roloff (2000b) observed that, when individuals assumed an initiator role in the serial argument, they engaged in more demanding behavior while their partners tended to withdraw from the interaction. In that same study, resistors confirmed that their partners were more demanding and that they themselves were likely to withdraw. Furthermore, some individuals reported the existence of conditions that set off argumentative episodes (Johnson & Roloff, 1998), predictable content of the episodes, and a tendency to follow a script (Johnson & Roloff, 2000b).

Recurrence   Although argumentative episodes in a serial argument can be spread out over time (Trapp & Hoff, 1985), they are repeated, by definition. Johnson and Roloff (2000a) explained that "the nature of serial arguing inherently implies that individuals have not been able to bring their opinions, values, and behaviors into alignment after a single confrontation" (p. 677). The ongoing nature of a serial argument lends itself to negatively impacting individuals' relationships. For both men and women, frequency of relational conflict deterred satisfaction with each other (Lloyd, 1987). According to Lloyd, frequency of relational conflict resulted in men feeling less love and women experiencing less commitment. Furthermore, relational quality negatively relates to the total number of argumentative episodes (Johnson & Roloff, 2000b).

Goals of Serial Arguing

Although not yet as extensive as other areas of research on serial arguing, several researchers have studied the objectives that individuals want to achieve by engaging in repeated argumentative episodes. Bevan, Hale, and Williams (2004) solicited undergraduates' goals of a current serial argument. A cluster analysis of their responses yielded ten goal clusters, four of which occurred with sufficient frequency that these researchers considered them to be major. The most common cluster involved reaching mutual understanding/resolution. In effect, the respondents wanted to comprehend their partners' viewpoints and to end the disputes. The second major cluster entailed fighting to fight. Individuals with this goal sought to enrage their partners. The third cluster focused on achieving relational progression or continuation. In a sense, individuals with these goals wanted to assess the future of their relationships. The final major goal encompassed achieving dominance/control. This objective reflected a power structure.

Clearly, the goals reveal a range of possible effects of serial arguing. According to Bevan et al. (2004), seeking greater understanding and resolution seems very task oriented, given the desire to accomplish a mutually satisfactory end to the dispute. However, fighting to fight and seeking dominance/control imply a more contentious and potentially negative consequence. Interestingly, seeking information about the relationship's future suggests that serial arguing might not always reflect the desire to resolve a given issue but could be a test of the relationship.

According to Bevan and colleagues (2004), minor goals included expressing positivity, expressing negative emotions, winning at all costs, achieving personal benefits, derogating the partner, and changing the partner. These goals, both major and minor, indicate that individuals involved in serial arguing often seek self-oriented or negative objectives rather than positive ones. Indeed, these researchers noted that the content of the goals was more negative than the general conflict goals that other researchers discovered (see Canary, Cunningham, & Cody, 1988).

Individual Well-Being

By investigating the link between conflict and individuals' well-being, researchers have identified nonverbal behaviors that indicate stress during arguments (e.g., Sillars & Parry, 1982). Reis et al. (2000) asserted that relational conflicts are generally stressful. Experimental research using physiological measures shows that participating in an argumentative episode can be traumatic, especially for women (see Kiecolt-Glaser & Newton, 2001). Wives whose husbands responded to their complaints by withdrawing had elevated levels of stress hormones later in the day (Kiecolt-Glaser et al., 1996). Gottman (1994) explained that the husbands' withdrawal resulted from efforts to reduce their physiological arousal.

Conflict also positively relates to psychological distress. Bolger and colleagues' (1989) diary study examined the impact of daily stressors on mood and determined that conflicts that occur on consecutive days are the most distressing. Particular conflict styles can also be connected to individuals experiencing work-related stress (Friedman, Tidd, Currall, & Tsai, 2000). Specifically, Friedman et al. concluded that using a more integrative style corresponded to less work stress as a result of a decline in relational conflict. Conversely, they linked more dominating or avoiding styles to more work stress as a result of increases in relational conflict. However, social support in one relational context can help buffer the deleterious effects of conflict in another relational context (Lepore, 1992). Consequently, serial arguing research has examined the impact of serial arguing on stress and stress-related symptoms. This research has examined how the characteristics of serial arguing relate to stress and individual coping with stressful reactions.

Serial Arguments as a Stressor

Malis and Roloff (2006b) described serial arguments as a chronic stressor based on Segerstrom and Miller's (2004) meta-analysis examining the impact of stressors on immune-system functioning. Segerstrom and Miller highlighted three characteristics of chronic stressors: duration (the length of time that the stressor has been occurring), persistence (the frequency of the stressor), and stability (akin to resolvability). Malis and Roloff examined how these three aspects of serial arguments intersected with stress and stress-related symptoms that occurred after an argumentative episode. They found that the perceived resolvability of a serial argument negatively impacts individuals' stress levels and stress-related problems such as eating problems, anxiety, and hyperarousal. However, neither duration nor persistence of the serial argument consistently influenced any stress-related variables.

In a second study, Malis and Roloff (2006a) explored how demand/withdraw patterns typically enacted during argumentative episodes affected stress and stress-related symptoms. This asymmetrical approach/avoidance pattern typifies dissatisfied couples (Sillars & Wilmot, 1994). Malis and Roloff discovered that the degree to which individuals typically make demands and their partners withdraw positively relates to postepisode stress reactions such as intrusive thoughts and feelings about the episode, attempts to avoid such thoughts and feelings, a hyperaroused state, and disruption of everyday activities. Interestingly, the degree to which individuals reported that their partners typically are demanding and they respond by withdrawing positively correlates with stress but not significantly with most indicators of postepisode stress. Thus, individuals somewhat successfully control the stress of being confronted by withdrawing. However, their behavior increases their partners' stress.

Coping with Serial Arguments

Individuals often engage in behaviors that help them cope with stress, and such strategies occur during serial arguments. Participants in Johnson and Roloff's (2000a) study engaged in three individual coping strategies after an argumentative episode ended. First, some individuals coped with their serial arguments through selective ignoring (i.e., overlooking a partner's faults, reasoning that the difficulties are not important, and focusing on the positive aspects of the relationship). Second, some individuals coped by taking a resigned stance (i.e., waiting for time to remedy the problem, keeping hurt feelings inside, staying out of a partner's way, and giving in to a partner). Finally, other individuals made optimistic comparisons between their own relational problems and those experienced by others in similar relationships or they related their current experiences to earlier points in their own relational histories.

Malis and Roloff (2006b) investigated how these coping strategies correlated with stress and stress-related symptoms. They reported that taking a resigned stance is an ineffective strategy because it was linked to greater stress and stress-related problems. Making optimistic comparisons was unrelated to most of the outcome variables. Although unexpected, Malis and Roloff found that selective ignoring serves as a beneficial coping strategy for reducing stress because it related negatively to intrusive thoughts, hyperarousal, sleeping problems, anxiety, and eating problems.

This finding mirrors other coping research. In a study of healthy and unhealthy individuals, Badr (2004) examined the interpersonal style of protective buffering, including being "extra patient and tolerant" (p. 203) with one's spouse and acting more positive than one feels. Protective buffering somewhat resembles selective ignoring. Badr found that ill husbands less likely engaged in protective buffering when compared to healthy husbands.

Relational Quality

Serial arguing can impact relational quality. We discuss the relational effects of perceived resolvability and several communication patterns common in serial arguments.

Perceived Resolvability   Research indicates that features of serial arguing can threaten relational quality. In particular, the perceived resolvability of a serial argument positively relates to relational satisfaction and commitment and negatively relates to relational harm (Johnson & Roloff, 1998). Furthermore, according to Johnson and Roloff, perceived resolvability is more predictive of relational harm than frequency of the argumentative episodes. They concluded that the more an individual perceived his or her serial argument as resolvable, the more likely it was that his or her relationship still existed. In subsequent work, Johnson and Roloff (2000a) defined perceived resolvability as "the degree to which partners perceive that they are making progress toward resolution" and characterized it as "the most important feature of serial arguing" (p. 677). Lloyd (1987) found that stable conflict issues were associated with decreases in the couple's relational quality, as indexed by the partners' love and commitment for each other. Thus, the most crucial factor for relationships involves individuals' perceptions of potential resolution sometime in the future rather than whether partners raise the issues frequently or infrequently (Johnson & Roloff, 2000a).

Communication Patterns During Argumentative Episodes   Communication patterns enacted during serial arguments can impact relational quality. We discuss such patterns as the form of serial arguments.

"Form" refers to the content of the communication in the argumentative episodes. Words spoken during argumentative episodes impact perceived resolvability and relational quality. Although serial argument episodes address the same issue, the content can vary across episodes (Roloff & Johnson, 2002). Johnson and Roloff (2000a) explicated three patterns that might emerge during argumentative episodes. Individuals might repeat what has been said during previous episodes, engage in mutual hostility, or confirm commitments. They classified a serial argument as repetitious if the participants indicated that the content of a typical argumentative episode tended to recur. Hostility included communication behaviors such as insults, threats, or negative emotions such as anger. Finally, Johnson and Roloff determined that relational confirmation included communication that expressed love or commitment. Repetition did not impact perceived resolvability or relational harm.

Hostility in serial arguments correlated positively with relational harm (Johnson & Roloff, 2000a). Mutual hostility in the form of cross-complaining in which both partners blame, threaten, and criticize each other negatively related to perceived resolvability (Johnson & Roloff, 1998). Conversely, serial arguing was not as detrimental to a relationship if the individuals employed relationally confirming behaviors during argumentative episodes compared to when they did not engage in confirming communication (Johnson & Roloff, 2000a). This finding coincides with Gottman's (1993) conclusion that stable couples maintained about a 5:1 ratio of positivity to negativity.

Constructive communication during arguments also positively corresponded to perceiving that the argument could be resolved, and it provides a better predictor of resolvability than destructive communication (Johnson & Roloff, 1998).

Despite the links to negativity and harmful outcomes, Johnson and Roloff (2000a) found that only relationally confirming behaviors significantly predicted relational harm using both hostility and confirming behaviors in a regression equation. The authors speculate that the presence of confirming behaviors might make negative behaviors less likely to occur during argumentative episodes. A limitation of this research is that repetition, relational confirmation, and mutual hostility do not exhaust all of the possible communication patterns enacted in serial arguments. Demand/withdraw comprises another such pattern. Sillars, Roberts, Leonard, and Dun (2000) described couples as engaging in problem solving, negativity, and withdrawing, and Sillars et al. (2004) provided a summary of conflict strategies in observational marital research. Additionally, many interpersonal communication skills intersect with relational quality (see Spitzberg & Cupach, 2002).

In summary, interactants do not resolve all conflicts in a single episode. Taken together, considerable evidence suggests that ongoing arguments impact individuals' health and well-being as well as their relational quality. Johnson and Roloff's (1998, 2000a, 2000b) research indicates that the degree to which partners perceive progress toward a resolution constitutes one of the most important factors of serial arguing. Malis and Roloff (2006b) found that resolvability contributes to well-being more than the frequency of the episodes and duration of the arguments.

Communication during the episodes (as well as the coping strategies that individuals employ to deal with the argument) impacts well-being. According to Johnson and Roloff (1998), individuals who chose to cope by taking a resigned stance experienced decreased well-being. Also, the serial arguing literature suggests the significance of positive and confirming content. Johnson and Roloff found that relational-confirming behavior facilitated relational quality and resolvability more than hostility. They also discovered that individual well-being benefited when participants did not engage in the demand/withdraw pattern.

Studies (Johnson & Roloff, 1998, 2000a, 2000b; Malis & Roloff, 2006a, 2006b) have begun to investigate the consequences of various aspects of serial arguing and individual well-being, but more work is needed. Thus far, most research (Johnson & Roloff, 1998, 2000a, 2000b; Malis & Roloff, 2006a, 2006b) utilizing the serial arguing framework has only examined one relational partner's self-reported perceptions of the arguments. In the future, both partners' thoughts and behaviors should be taken into account using a combination of methodologies, including observational measures and self-report, to corroborate the results. Gottman's (1999) program of research on perpetual problems addresses these methodological limitations by using questionnaires and observations. We discuss perpetual problems next.

Review of Perpetual Problems Research

In this section, we discuss perpetual problems in marriages. We describe the occurrence of perpetual problems and detail the role of communication in the effect of perpetual problems on relationships.

Occurrence of Perpetual Problems

Even though perceived resolvability comprises an important feature of serial arguing (Johnson & Roloff, 1998), some conflicts will not be resolved. Irresolvable conflicts are fairly common. Gottman (1999) contended that very few marital problems are ever truly resolved and most become perpetual problems. Gottman defined perpetual problems as "issues with no resolution that the couple has been dealing with for many years" (p. 96). He reported that 69% of couples involved in his research experienced perpetual problems. These perpetual problems often occur as a result of fundamental differences in personality, culture, or religion or because each partner has different needs (Driver, Tabares, Shapiro, Nahm, & Gottman, 2003). Perpetual problems generate serial arguments.

Communication and the Relational Impact of Perpetual Problems

Gottman (1999) asserted that the presence of perpetual problems in marriages is not necessarily problematic. The affect expressed when couples talk about perpetual problems should be considered more important. When couples achieve an ongoing dialogue (e.g., Lewis, 2006) about a perpetual problem and retain some positive affect and little or no negative affect, the perpetual problem is not gridlocked. According to Gottman, perpetual problems are gridlocked if individuals feel unaccepted and attacked when they discuss their thoughts and opinions.

Couples with a good-natured attitude and a sense of humor about their perpetual problems can avoid becoming overwhelmed by them (Gottman & Silver, 1999). This acceptance of a partner's shortcomings and ability to avoid becoming enraged contributes to dialogues about perpetual problems (Gottman, 1999).

If, however, couples cannot cope effectively (Gottman & Silver, 1999) or discuss the problem without high levels of negative affect, feelings of attack, or nonacceptance, the problem becomes gridlocked (Gottman, 1999). Gottman and Silver determined that discussions between such partners become repetitive and make no progress toward resolution. Couples grappling with gridlock most likely pass through four stages.

First, couples experience dreams in opposition. Gottman and Silver (1999) argued that everyone has profound hopes and goals for the future, such as knowing one's family, becoming more powerful, getting over past hurts, exploring an old part of oneself that is lost, having quietness, or building something important. Most of these dreams extend from childhood and tend to center on positive aspects of life. None of these issues is inherently problematic for marriages. These issues become problematic when spouses hide their own dreams or disrespect their partner's dreams.

When dreams clash, couples commonly become entrenched in their respective positions (Gottman, 1999). Without an understanding of the importance of each other's dreams and how the dreams impact their relationship, spouses often experience a sense of fear. During this phase, each spouse becomes even more committed to his or her position (Gottman & Silver, 1999).

In the third phase, the couple dreads accepting influence (Gottman, 1999). Gottman and Silver (1999) reported that many men become afraid to let their wives influence their behavior and decisions and tend to resist sharing power with their wives. Such behavior is predictive of divorce. In the happiest and most stable marriages, husbands treat wives with respect, and they share power and decision making. In general, Gottman and Silver contended that wives tend to accept influence from husbands.

In the fourth and fifth stages, couples tend to feel vilification and emotional disengagement. Couples will eventually exhibit one of two states of gridlock. In the *hot* state, criticism, contempt, defensiveness, and stonewalling regularly occur (Gottman, 1999). According to Gottman, in the state of *affective death*, "Partners exhibit high levels of fatigue and emotional distance and apathy and low levels of humor and affection" (p. 235). Gottman considered the state of affective death to be the more dangerous. Over time, these couples might "feel rejected, overwhelmed, and hopeless about ever reaching any sort of a compromise" (Driver et al., 2003, pp. 500–501).

Summary of Serial Arguing and Perpetual Problems Research

Research on perpetual problems facilitates understanding how individuals communicate when discussing an irresolvable problem and grasping the importance of communication on the relational effects of the perpetual problem. This research provides some insight into the types of issues that become irresolvable and highlights the widespread nature of such problems in marriages. Gottman and his colleagues (Driver et al., 2003; Gottman, 1999; Gottman & Silver, 1999) also make a unique contribution to the interpersonal conflict literature by conceding that perpetual problems likely will not be resolved.

Although useful insights have occurred, the two approaches— serial arguing and perpetual problems—have focused on a limited number of issues and types of relationships. Gottman and his colleagues study perpetual problems exclusively within marital relationships. Likewise, serial arguing research has concentrated solely on romantic relationships. Likely, perpetual problems and the resulting serial arguments occur in other relationships. Effective communication might differ by relationship. Future research should address this issue.

Additionally, research on serial arguing and perpetual problems does not investigate the reason that some issues remain irresolvable and the factors that contribute to irresolvability. This limitation restricts its utility. Fortunately, research focused on intractable conflict provides some insight into these questions. Before we examine this literature, we differentiate serial arguments, perpetual problems, and intractable conflicts.

As a review, repetition characterizes serial arguments (Trapp & Hoff, 1985). Gottman (1999) asserted that the issues involved in a perpetual conflict likely will not be resolved. Intractable conflicts are typified by their volatile and extremely recalcitrant nature (Coleman, 2000).

However, applying these definitions to categorize a particular conflict can be a difficult, complicated task. For example, the existence of a perpetual problem likely involves serial arguments (Gottman, 1999). However, we argue that does not have to be the case. It is possible, albeit unlikely, for an individual to argue about an issue once and declare that the issue will never be resolved. Likewise, some serial arguments might become perpetual problems, but not all serial arguments comprise perpetual problems. Some individuals believe that their serial arguments will be resolved (Johnson & Roloff, 1998). Finally, an intractable conflict usually involves serial arguments (Coleman, 2000). However, we allow that a conflict can become intractable after one argument and not involve future arguments.

A low likelihood of resolution marks both perpetual problems and intractable conflicts (Coleman, 2000; Gottman, 1999). However, individuals generally experience intractable conflicts more intensely than they perceive most perpetual problems (Coleman, 2000; Gottman, 1999). In addition, because the current study of perpetual problems focuses on those within marriages, its applicability is limited. Intractable conflict literature has explored many different types of relationships and contexts (e.g., Gray, 1997; LeBaron & Carstarphen, 1997; Rouhana & Bar-Tal, 1998; Wynn, 1989), thus making its findings easier to apply in a variety of settings. Next, we review research focused on intractable conflicts.

Review of Intractable Conflict Literature[1]

This section contains three parts. First, we discuss various definitions of the term "intractable conflict." Second, we examine defining characteristics of intractable conflicts. Finally, we review causes and contributing factors of intractability.

Definition

Conflict scholars have provided numerous characterizations and definitions of intractable conflict. We include several examples. Northrup (1989) defined an intractable conflict as:

> [a] prolonged conflictual psychosocial process between (or among) parties that has three primary characteristics: (1) it is resistant to being resolved, (2) it has some conflict-intensifying features not related to the initial issues in contention, (3) it involves attempts (and/or successes) to harm the other party, by at least one of the parties. (p. 62)

Thorson (1989) summarized intractable conflicts as stubborn, and Kriesberg (1993) characterized an intractable conflict as a "self-perpetuating, mutually reinforcing, violent antagonism" (p. 417). Coleman (2000) described an intractable conflict as "one that is recalcitrant, intense, deadlocked, and extremely difficult to resolve" (p. 429). Finally, Putnam and Wondolleck (2003) illustrated intractable conflicts as "messy," "hard to pin down," "frustrating," "complex," and "with no readily conceived solutions" (p. 37). By definition, intractable conflicts resist repeated attempts at resolution (Coleman, 2000; Putnam & Wondolleck, 2003). In many cases, mediation and other alternative dispute-resolution techniques do not succeed (H. Burgess & G. Burgess, 1996).

Scholars consistently assert that intractable conflicts are long-standing (e.g., Coleman, 2000, 2003; Putnam & Wondolleck, 2003; Rouhana & Bar-Tal, 1998). Protracted social or international conflicts, such as the Israeli–Palestinian conflict, tend to last at least a generation, and some last many generations (Coleman, 2000; Rouhana & Bar-Tal, 1998). The amount of time that a conflict must persist to be considered intractable depends on the type of conflict and the normal amount of time that such a conflict tends to last before resolution (Kriesberg, 1989).

Intractable conflicts usually go through cycles of inactivity with sporadic increases in intensity and possible occasional outbreaks of violence (Coleman, 2000; Kriesberg, 1982). During inactive periods, these conflicts can appear to be resolved. However, if stakeholders do not address root causes, these conflicts will reemerge and intensify, especially if external circumstances allow or encourage conflict or violence (Coleman, 2003). As a hypothetical example, a married couple cannot agree on whether one set of in-laws should be allowed to discipline their children. The in-laws live across the country so this argument only becomes an issue when the in-laws visit. The argument appears resolved during the long periods of time between the in-laws' visits. However, because the couple fails to resolve the argument, it likely re-emerges and intensifies when the in-laws visit. The in-laws might permit marital fighting or bickering in their presence and encourage marital fighting by disciplining the children even though they know this issue constitutes a sore spot. They also might encourage their son or daughter to confront his or her spouse about the issue.

All of these definitions also highlight the difficult, complicated, and intransigent nature of intractable conflicts. As a result, communication in intractable conflicts tends to be poor or nonexistent and exhibits a high degree of hostility (Northrup, 1989). However, even highly competent communication might not be enough to overcome conflicts centered on objectively incompatible interests, such as in real conflicts (Deutsch, 1969). In contrast, tractable conflicts involve incompatible or divergent interests, goals, beliefs, activities, etc., and hold the potential and incentive for resolution (Putnam & Wondolleck, 2003). A tractable conflict also exhibits conflict-mitigating features, such as open communication, goodwill between parties, and a desire to find a resolution that meets the needs of both (or all) parties.

However, Nagle (1989) and other conflict scholars caution us about conceptualizing a conflict as either tractable or intractable. Instead, intractability is more accurately represented as existing in degrees along a continuum (Thorson, 1989). According to Putnam and Wondolleck (2003), the poles of this continuum include problem solving and common ground on the far left side and intractability and eluding resolution on the far right side. Tractable disputes are in the middle of this continuum. Intractable conflicts vary along the middle to right side of this continuum. They tend to change and evolve over time. In other words, intractability is not a static state but a dynamic one (Putnam & Wondolleck, 2003; Thorson, 1989).

Intractable conflicts occur commonly (Coleman, 2003) and between two or more individuals, within or between groups, and within or between nations (H. Burgess & G. Burgess, 1996; Coleman, 2000). Examples include custody disputes in divorce negotiations (Wynn, 1989); local, regional, national, international, and global environmental issues (Gray, 1997, 2004); abortion rights in the United States and

Canada (LeBaron & Carstarphen, 1997), and the Israeli–Palestinian conflict (Rouhana & Bar-Tal, 1998).

These definitions provide useful and uncomplicated ways of characterizing intractable conflicts in a broad sense. However, intractable conflicts are more complex than the aforementioned definitions might suggest. As such, conflict scholars have identified characteristics that distinguish intractable conflicts from those that are more tractable. We discuss these characteristics next.

Distinguishing Characteristics of Intractable Conflicts

Through theorizing and prior research, scholars have identified a number of complex and interrelated characteristics that distinguish intractable conflicts (Coleman, 2003). In describing these characteristics, several points must be considered.

First, not all intractable conflicts are the same (Kriesberg, 2003; Salomon, 2004). These characteristics can be present in varying degrees across different types of intractable conflicts (Coleman, 2003; Kriesberg, 1998; Putnam & Wondolleck, 2003). Second, to allow for maximum application of these characteristics to intractable conflicts in a variety of contexts and to provide the most utility to communication scholars, we present characteristics that conflict scholars mentioned repeatedly across a variety of contexts. Third, we chose to collapse individual models of distinguishing characteristics (e.g., Bar-Tal, 1998; Northrup, 1989; Putnam & Wondolleck, 2003; Rouhana & Bar-Tal, 1998) in order to present a cohesive model that is widely applicable and useful to scholars in diverse areas. Fourth, due to the complexity of intractable conflict systems, a distinguishing feature of an intractable conflict might also lend to its intractability. For example, if an individual labels an intractable conflict as hopeless with regard to the likelihood of resolution, this label probably discourages resolution attempts, thereby contributing to intractability. Therefore, according to Coleman, the distinction between a distinguishing factor and a cause or contributing factor might be "fuzzy" or somewhat overlapping (p. 7).

We propose that the following four characteristics can be used to distinguish intractable conflicts from tractable ones: hopelessness, intense emotionality, pervasiveness, and complexity. We address each characteristic individually.

Hopelessness   In many cases, the parties involved in the dispute come to feel hopeless about the potential for resolution (Coleman, 2000; Fisher & Keashly, 1990; Pruitt & Olczak, 1995). The parties view their goals as radically opposite and, therefore, eventually expect that the conflict will last indefinitely (Kriesberg, 1995, as cited in Bar-Tal, 1998). In contrast, individuals entangled in tractable disputes do not have such a perception.

Intense Emotionality   Intractable conflicts feature emotionality and hostility in varying degrees (Coleman, 2003; Northrup, 1989; Putnam & Wondolleck, 2003; Retzinger & Scheff, 2000; Salomon, 2004). Intense negative emotions such as humiliation, frustration, rage, and resentment combined with feelings of pride, esteem, and dignity can elicit extreme reactions in intractable conflicts. Such emotions can blind parties from the actual issues encompassed in a conflict and complicate an already complex situation. In contrast, as Coleman noted, tractable conflicts can include periods of escalation and even violence but tend to exhibit low to moderate intensity overall.

Pervasiveness   In many intractable conflicts, such as social or political conflicts, the threats involved can be so extreme that the conflict begins to affect most aspects of a person's or group's day-to-day life (Azar, 1986; Coleman, 2000; Rouhana & Bar-Tal, 1998). Individuals commonly perceive such conflicts as traumatic (for a review of literature focused on trauma, see Grey in this volume). For example, in an intractable international conflict, interested parties can easily access relevant perspectives of the conflict within each society. These thoughts can affect a wide variety of decisions—from ones that public officials make on policy issues to ones that citizens make on whether to shop and eat in public places. Israelis and Palestinians struggle with such choices on a day-to-day basis (Bar-Tal, Raviv, & Freund, 1994; Coleman, 2003).

An irresolvable interpersonal conflict also can be perceived as pervasive. For example, individuals experiencing interpersonal problems often engage in cognitive activity aimed at making sense of the problem (Cloven & Roloff, 1991), including rehearsing arguments prior to confrontation (Stutman & Newell, 1990) or imagining interactions with other individuals (Honeycutt, Zagacki, & Edwards,

1990). Cloven and Roloff identified an association between such cognitive activity and increased distress, and Lyubomirsky, Tucker, Caldwell, and Berg (1999) connected it with decreased likelihood of solving interpersonal problems.

In contrast, tractable conflicts tend to have clear boundaries that identify the issues, the parties involved, and the time and location of appropriate conflict engagements (Coleman, 2003). Thus, tractable conflicts do not often affect individuals' day-to-day lives for long periods of time.

Complexity   Intractable conflicts vary in the degree of complexity involved (Putnam & Wondolleck, 2003), and multiple levels exist in every intractable conflict (Northrup, 1989). Northrup explained:

> Intrapersonal processes of the individuals who are involved in a conflict interact with social processes which occur in the course of a relationship. Further, the social and psychological processes are affected by the greater social, cultural, historical and political context of the conflict. (pp. 58–59)

These levels interact in complex ways that often result in confusion and an inability to separate the issues and concerns of each party involved (Coleman, 2003; Putnam & Wondolleck, 2003). When intractable conflicts occur on multiple levels, they usually involve many people and groups in various roles (Coleman, 2003; Kriesberg, 1982). As Putnam and Wondolleck argued, no one level can effectively manage all of the issues and parties involved in a conflict.

All conflicts also contain a subjective component, and most conflicts include some objective component. Both of these factors play an important role in most conflicts (Northrup, 1989). However, the subjective component primarily drives reactions and behavior (Pruitt & Kim, 2004).

Summary   In summary, four characteristics distinguish intractable conflicts from tractable ones: hopelessness, intense emotionality, pervasiveness, and complexity. Importantly, these factors interrelate and work together to capture the complex and diverse nature of intractable conflicts. These characteristics also can act as causes or contributing factors in intractable conflicts. We discuss causes and contributing factors next.

Causes and Contributing Factors of Intractable Conflicts

No single reason can explain all intractable conflicts (Hunter, 1989). As a result, conflict scholars have provided an abundance of reasons for the existence of intractable conflicts (Putnam & Wondolleck, 2003). In order to provide maximum application and utility in this review, we chose to present causes and contributing factors that have been identified repeatedly across a variety of contexts. We somewhat adopted the framework provided by Coleman (2003), but we also integrated individual models of causes and contributing factors developed by other scholars (e.g., Kriesberg, 1998; Northrup, 1989; Putnam & Wondolleck, 2003). Again, notably, as Coleman stressed, intractable conflicts vary and can be or become intractable for a variety of reasons. Further, as Putnam and Wondolleck indicated, not all conflicts share the same causes or contributing factors. Their origins differ (Kriesberg, 2003). In addition, Coleman contended that these causes and contributing factors interrelate and likely interact in a pattern of circular causality such that each cause or contributing factor can influence and be influenced by another cause or contributing factor.

As Coleman (2003) argued, "The phenomenon of intractable conflict is best characterized as a complex, dynamic, nonlinear system with a core set of interrelated and mutually influential variables" (p. 7). Consequently, it is necessary to provide an analysis of the variables in such a system, but the nature of such a "messy," "hard to pin down" (Putnam & Wondolleck, 2003, p. 37) system muddles this process. Therefore, even though we describe categories individually in order to provide some clarity of definition, we acknowledge that the categories presented are not clean or mutually exclusive. We recognize that categories overlap and are mutually influential. We present the following five causes and contributing factors of intractability: issues, contexts, relationships, conflict processes, and conflict frames.

Issues   Intractable conflicts often entail one or more interrelated issues such as resources, values, beliefs, power, or basic needs. Most conflicts encompass more than one type of issue either directly or indirectly (Coleman, 2000). Issues usually exhibit a depth of symbolic meaning, interconnectedness with other difficult issues, and a higher centrality of meaning than the issues involved in tractable disputes (Coleman, 2003).

At least four issue-based factors cause or contribute to intractability. We discuss common issues in intractable disputes, divisible resource issues and identity issues, relational messages, and conflict overlays. We discuss these factors individually to aid in clarity of presentation. However, we acknowledge that these factors overlap, especially when a conflict involves several issues, as commonly occurs.

Common intractable issues. H. Burgess and G. Burgess (1996) identified three types of issues that strongly resist resolution: (1) irreconcilable moral differences, defined by Coleman (2000) as conflicts regarding questions of fundamental moral, religious, or personal values that do not have verifiable answers and, as a result, are not easily changed or compromised; (2) high-stakes distributional conflicts regarding finite or scarce resources; and (3) domination conflicts, defined by Coleman as conflicts pertaining to power, ranking, or dominance. Threats to health and human safety also lead to intractable conflict. For example, environmental conflicts over toxic waste, nuclear power, and pollution center on issues with implications for health and human safety (Putnam & Wondolleck, 2003). These conflicts can be treated separately from the three issue types identified by H. Burgess and G. Burgess or as centered on the elements at stake in the issues that they described. For example, the cover-up of a toxic waste spill might involve a moral issue, destruction of a finite or scarce resource, and domination by the group that covered up the incident. However, the health issues might also stand alone as a distinct issue. Conflict comprises a subjective experience (Northup, 1989), so much of its definition lies in the eye of the beholder (Pinkley, 1990). Individual perceptions of conflict also can vary culturally (e.g., Gelfand et al., 2001).

Coleman (2003) also argued that intractable conflicts tend to focus on central human and social polarities that are paradoxical in nature and not resolvable in the traditional sense. He identified seven such dilemmas: stability versus change, identity (integrity versus complexity), interdependence versus security, power (efficient versus inclusive), time (short-term versus long-term goals), capital (profits versus costs), and coping versus adapting.[2] Coleman cautioned that the presence of these polarities drives and sustains an intractable conflict as well as the unintended consequences of attempts to manage these dilemmas.

Divisible resource issues and identity issues. Rothman (1997), Burton (1987), Lederach (1997), and Retzinger and Scheff (2000) distinguished between issues that concern resources that can be divided (such as time, money, or land) and less tangible ones that focus on issues of personal and group identity. Northrup (1989) defined identity as "the tendency for human beings, individually and in groups, to establish, maintain, and protect a sense of self-meaning, predictability and purpose" (p. 63). A sense of self also serves a crucial human need to avert anxiety. The world is an uncertain place, and a sense of self constitutes an essential coping mechanism (Smyth, 2002). Individuals often experience or perceive conflicts involving identity as threatening their existence (Coleman, 2000; for a communication-centered review of identity research, see Young, this volume).

Accordingly, identity issues tend to be more significant in intractable disputes, even though most intractable disputes involve both resource and identity issues. Rothman (1997) also warned that identity issues can be difficult to recognize in conflict situations because they are obscured by a focus on tangible, resource-based issues. Consequently, identity disputes must be handled carefully, and they often require a different resolution approach than resource-based conflicts do (Coleman, 2000).

Relational messages. All messages contain two levels of meaning: the content level and the relational level (Watzlawick, Beavin, & Jackson, 1967). The content level includes the actual information conveyed; the relational level contains information about how the message should be interpreted or understood. In other words, according to Watzlawick et al., the relational message provides information about the nature of the relationship between interactants.

Interpersonal conflicts tend to be most affected by relational messages. Unfortunately, we cannot know the other person's exact perceptions of a relational message (Wilmot & Hocker, 2001). For example, in a study of cognition during marital conflict, Sillars et al. (2000) reported that wives concentrated more on the relational level of meaning, whereas husbands focused more on the content level. This pattern can cause confusion when the husband is not aware of the relational meaning assigned by the wife. The use of conflict strategies also contains relational messages (e.g., Pawlowski, Myers, & Rocca, 2000). For example, Pawlowski et al. found that siblings who used the relational communication themes of immediacy, similarity, receptivity, composure, and equality reported using an integrative conflict strategy.

Conflict overlays. In highly escalated conflicts, a complex web of latent and manifest subissues can develop (Coleman, 2000; Northrup, 1989). As a result, core aspects of conflicts become harder to address due to what H. Burgess and G. Burgess (1996) called *conflict overlays.* Conflict overlays encompass "extraneous problems in the conflict process that get 'laid over' the core, making the core issues harder to see and address" (p. 308). Burgess and Burgess described five types of overlay problems: framing problems, misunderstanding, procedural problems, fact-finding problems, and escalation and polarization.[3] According to Coleman, the destructive processes encompassed in conflicts also can generate new areas of conflict regarding the negative or immoral conduct of the individuals or groups involved in the conflict.

Contexts   Intractable conflicts must be investigated in a highly contextual manner (Thorson, 1989). The embedded context or social system sometimes serves as the source of an intractable conflict (Kriesberg, 1998; Putnam & Wondolleck, 2003). In order to understand an intractable conflict, Thorson contended that we must investigate the historical and social development of a conflict. At least two context-based causes or contributing factors contribute to intractable disputes: power imbalances and conditions of change, ambiguity, or anarchy.

Power imbalances. Intractable conflicts commonly happen in situations in which a severe imbalance of power exists and the party with more power uses it to exploit, control, or abuse the less powerful party (Coleman, 2000; Kriesberg, 1998). Many intractable conflicts, especially those involving groups or nations, are embedded in a history of colonialism, ethnocentrism, racism, sexism, or human rights abuses (Azar, 1986). Instances of relational dominance and injustice also transpire frequently. These practices occur both formally and informally and purposefully and unwittingly (Baumeister, Stillwell, & Wotman, 1990; Coleman, 2003). For example, parents often dominate children in unjust ways. If a parent is physically or verbally abusive, most young children must accept the abuse because they have few other options. Children whose parents use physical punishment reported that they hated the parent for punishing them in that way (Straus, 1998). Individuals also are bullied in workplaces and schools, often with little recourse (Pörhölä, Karhunen, & Rainivaara, 2006).

The distribution of power between or among parties can significantly impact an intractable conflict. Outcomes differ greatly between situations with unequal versus equal power (Northrup, 1989). In general, lasting settlements are extremely difficult to achieve when opponents have unequal power (Kriesberg, 1993).

Conditions of change, ambiguity, or anarchy. When a conflict develops in a system with formal or informal conflict resolution procedures, it is more likely to be tractable (Putnam & Wondolleck, 2003). However, a substantial change—such as the divorce of two parents, a death, a catastrophic natural disaster, the failure of a state, or the collapse of a superpower—can greatly disrupt a once stable, well-functioning system and generate latent intractable conflicts. Coleman (2003) argued that changes, particularly sudden ones, weaken normative influences that suppress the expression of individual and subgroup concerns. Changes can encourage the expression of these issues.

Conflicts frequently surface in ambiguous social systems (Putnam & Wondolleck, 2003). Uncertainty regarding rank and power fuels power struggles among opponents as they attempt to determine who has or should have control (Smyth, 1994). Ambiguity regarding rank and power also can motivate an individual's or group's aggressive behavior aimed at gaining power or protecting power (Coleman, 2003).

Additionally, anarchical situations can foster intractable conflicts (Coleman, 2003; Putnam & Wondolleck, 2003). In these cases, Putnam and Wondolleck noted that opponents do not agree on methods for managing disputes. Such situations can produce a focus on short-term security needs, worst-case scenarios, power struggles, and the use of threat and coercion (Levy, 1996). Crocker, Hampson, and Aall (1996) contended that chaotic situations contribute to violent international conflicts.

Relationships   Some intractable conflicts exist due to fundamental tensions or the relationship between opponents (Kriesberg, 1998; Putnam & Wondolleck, 2003). At least three relationship-based sources cause or facilitate intractability: destructive relationships, polarized group identities, and internal dynamics.

Destructive relationships. Intractable conflicts tend to be embedded in destructive and inescapable relationships. Coleman (2003) advanced several reasons. First, in many intractable conflicts, the nature of their relationship and social structures limit contact between opponents and isolate groups and individuals (Coleman,

2003; Northrup, 1989). This constrained contact fosters negative stereotypical perceptions of the opponent (Fisher & Keashly, 1990) and, according to Coleman, promotes hostility and violence. Second, individuals in tractable conflicts can often terminate a relationship without severe consequences as a means of ending a conflict. Coleman noted that, in intractable conflicts, opponents usually perceive their relationships as inescapable due to the stakes involved or geographical, financial, moral, or psychological factors. Third, as Coleman asserted, opponents often share an interdependent relationship focused on an inescapable combination of cooperative and competitive goals that center on irreconcilable or non-negotiable issues.

To illustrate this idea, we offer the following hypothetical scenario of a married couple experiencing a perpetual problem regarding how to invest their money. The wife would like to invest the couple's savings in stocks with the hope that they will "hit it big" and be able to retire early. The husband prefers "safer" investments such as bonds. Both spouses agree that they would like some return on their investment, so they share a cooperative goal in this sense. However, the argument stems from an investment strategy that each believes to be incompatible and non-negotiable. Neither spouse sees the value of the other spouse's investment strategy. Choosing stocks represents a loss of a "safe" investment for the husband, and choosing bonds means the loss of growth potential for the wife. In other words, their goals are competitive. Competitive processes tend to produce destructive communication (Deutsch, 1969). Protracted intractable conflicts damage the trust, faith, and cooperative potential necessary for constructive or even tolerant relationships (Coleman, 2003). As the reader will recall, the presence of a perpetual problem is not problematic for marital relationships. Instead, the difficulty results from couple communication about such problems (Gottman, 1999).

Polarized group identities. Intractable conflicts vary in the degree to which the conflict divides people and parties (Putnam & Wondolleck, 2003). As conflicts progress, individuals take sides and become more identified with and committed to allies. Individuals and groups also organize against their opponents. As conflicts escalate, opposing groups grow increasingly polarized and develop polarized collective identities aimed at negating and disparaging the opponent (Coleman, 2003). A lack of communication between opponents can reinforce these negative perceptions and further hinder communication

(Fisher & Keashly, 1990). When identity intersects with group membership, Putnam and Wondolleck found that individuals or groups can impact the intractability of a conflict by staking their identities on the outcome of the dispute.

Internal dynamics. Internal dynamics also can exacerbate the impossible nature of intractable conflicts (Coleman, 2003; Kriesberg, 1998). According to Coleman, the complex nature of intractable conflicts "consists of both implicit and explicit issues, formal and informal agendas, and deliberate and unconscious processes" (p. 23). Groups or individuals involved in intractable conflicts often suppress or channel internal conflicts into the intractable conflict (Deutsch, 2002, as cited in Coleman). A conflict can serve many purposes for an individual or group. A conflict can provide a needed distraction, serve as a reasonable excuse for other problems, or offer a sense of excitement. For example, it is not unusual for siblings to fight over assets or other issues after the death of a parent. Fighting can distract individuals from the sadness, regret, or other negative emotions that they might feel after the death of a parent. Protracted disputes also can serve as an excuse for missing time at work, shirking responsibilities at home, or withdrawing from relationships while affording a sense of excitement or anticipation about what might happen next. Individuals also might enjoy the attention and social support received during such conflicts. As a result, Kriesberg argued that individuals and groups often commit to continuing the conflict because it fulfills some underlying needs. According to Coleman, intractable international conflicts also have been used to unify nations or to provide distraction from domestic issues.

Conflict Processes   The processes encompassed in intractable conflicts can facilitate their intractability (Putnam & Wondolleck, 2003), including cycles of escalation and other conflict behaviors.

Cycles of escalation. Based on studies of third-party consultation and the contributions of other scholars,[4] Fisher and Keashly (1990) suggested a stage model of conflict escalation. This model includes four stages: discussion, polarization, segregation, and destruction. Fisher and Keashly identified the stages by changes in communication, perceptions, overt issues in the dispute, perceived possible outcomes, and the appropriate approach to managing the conflict. These researchers described the changes in communication:

As conflict escalates, communication moves from direct discussion and debate between the parties to reliance on the interpretation of actions rather than words, to the use of threats, and finally to direct attacks. Thus, communication is carried out through increasingly aggressive forms of interaction between the parties. Accompanying this breakdown in open and direct communication is the replacement of accurate perceptions with negative and simplified stereotypes to the point where the other party is regarded as evil and nonhuman. The relationship moves from one of trust, respect, and commitment to one of mistrust, disrespect, and finally, hopelessness in terms of possible improvements. (p. 236)

In an escalated conflict, each party holds an overall negative attitude toward the other (Pruitt & Kim, 2004). Pruitt and Kim specified seven ways that negative attitudes and perceptions escalate conflict and discouragement settlement. Negative attitudes and perceptions (1) make it easier to place blame on the other person or group involved in the conflict for unpleasant experiences, (2) lead to mistrust and viewing ambiguous actions as threatening, (3) can cause decreased inhibitions against retaliation when provoked, (4) interfere with communication such that the parties involved in the conflict strive to avoid communicating with each other, (5) reduce empathy for the opposing party, (6) engender zero-sum thinking, and (7) encourage viewing the other individual or group as a "diabolical enemy" (White, 1984, p. 109).

Due to the negative consequence of arguing, disputes also stimulate cognitive activity (for a review of social cognition approaches to conflict and communication, see Roloff & Miller, 2006). When individuals experience negative events, they often engage in attribution-making to grasp why the events occurred (Wong & Weiner, 1981). The way an individual assigns attributions can impact conflict efficacy (Fincham, Harold, & Gano-Phillips, 2000), communication strategies that individuals employ during conflicts (e.g., Canary & Spitzberg, 1990; Sillars, 1980), and the communication behaviors used to negotiate forgiveness (e.g., Kelley & Waldron, 2006).

Conflict behavior and perceptions. Conflict behaviors such as violence can frame the ongoing nature of intractable disputes. Acts of violence ranging from property destruction, intimidation, and physical violence to terrorism, genocide, and war ensure the deterioration of intractable conflicts (Coleman, 2003). Additionally, violence can generate new areas of conflict (Coleman, 2000).

Misunderstanding fuels intractability. Sillars (1998) described understanding as "highly abstract, subject to various interpretations, and difficult to operationalize. Any difficulties encountered in identifying a person's perspective are multiplied when considering mutual understanding" (p. 75). As a result, misunderstanding commonly occurs in conflict situations. Misunderstanding especially transpires during conflict due to the nature of communication during disputes and the inherent ambiguity, disorganization, and confusion involved (Sillars et al., 2000). As examples, Sillars et al. found that spouses often perceive marital conflicts in incongruous manners, and Baumeister et al. (1990) reported that victims and perpetrators tend to offer very different descriptions of the experience. Indeed, even silence during disputes can be perceived in different and conflicting ways (see Acheson, this volume).

H. Burgess and G. Burgess (1996) argued that individuals embrace the worst-case bias toward their opponents during conflicts and described several types of misunderstandings that parties commonly experience during conflict. Anger-induced misunderstanding comprises a common problem. Because very few angry people communicate effectively, they can say things that they do not mean or things that they would not say if they had been thinking clearly when communicating with their opponent (Baumeister et al., 1990; Canary, Spitzberg, & Semic, 1998). This problem becomes compounded by the fact that individuals tend to misinterpret, usually for the worse, comments made by their opponents. Intense emotion takes away an individual's ability to tolerate his or her opponent, rationally judge the opponent's position, and perceive the position in a less negative and threatening manner (Salomon, 2004).

Angry individuals also tend to see issues in a one-sided manner with a focus on the incomprehensible, unjustifiable, immoral, and deliberately cruel and harmful nature of the opponent's intentions and actions. Researchers associate this tunnel vision with lasting consequences, continued anger, and relationship damage (Baumeister et al., 1990). H. Burgess and G. Burgess (1996) argued that, in some disputes, individuals become so angry that they exhibit the *primal scream syndrome*. In these cases, individuals vent their frustrations without considering how the other side will respond or what is necessary to achieve their goals. Other negative emotions (such as jealousy, hurt, and guilt) can play a large role in how individuals interact during disputes. Negative emotion and destructive communication often sabotage opportunities for resolution (Guerrero & La Valley, 2006; also see this chapter for a recent review of conflict, emotion, and communication).

H. Burgess and G. Burgess (1996) labeled the "*I already know*" syndrome as another source of misunderstanding. Once an individual makes up his or her mind on an issue, he or she often refuses to reconsider the issue or listen to any new arguments because of thinking that he or she has heard everything necessary. Individuals' tendency to interpret ambiguous inferences with certainty, especially within interpersonal relationships, exacerbates this situation (Sillars, 1998). In coding thoughts during marital conflict, Sillars et al. (2000) found that partners frequently make attributions without accounting for the possibility of error. Sillars asserted that the repetitious and anxiety-producing nature of marital conflicts encourages spouses to fit each other's comments into existing categories, limiting their ability to learn new perspectives or information during arguments.

H. Burgess and G. Burgess (1996) also maintained that problems of misunderstanding are worsened by the *recreational complaint syndrome*. This syndrome involves gossip with friends or allies that portrays the opponent as evil while reaffirming the complaining individual's superiority and morality. Such gossip solidifies a one-sided view of events that friends and allies are not likely to challenge.

Conflict Frames   When individuals or groups are in a conflict, each side develops an interpretation about the conflict, reasons for it, participant motivations, and ideas for resolution (Gray, 2003). Drake and Donohue (1996) conceptualized frames as "communicative structures disputants build around conflict issues during each turn at talk" (p. 302) and emphasized the importance of language in the verbal highlighting of the issue.

The framing of conflicts contributes to intractability. Putnam and Wondolleck (2003) asserted:

> Framing is an overarching feature of a conflict that feeds into intractability in a reflexive way.... The more disputants [that] frame a conflict as intense and eluding resolution, the more framing feeds into polarization and other conflict processes that perpetuate intractability. Thus the overall relationship between framing and intractability is reflexive in that framing both contributes to and signals the development of intractability. (p. 53)

Many types of frames exist. For example, Gray (2003) described the relevance of identity frames, characterization frames, conflict management frames, whole-story frames, power frames, risk frames, and gain-versus-loss frames in understanding environmental disputes (see also related review by O'Keefe & Jensen, 2006). Conflict management frames can be particularly important for perceptions of intractability. Conflict frames associated with avoidance/passivity, settlement, and struggle/sabotage often escalate conflict. Putnam and Wondolleck (2003) argued that relying on an avoidance frame in an intense conflict can delay confrontation and, in turn, increase the intensity of the next confrontation. In some cases, when individuals avoid conflict, the conflict builds until it grows out of control and must be confronted. In many cases, the confrontation intensifies due to the built-up anger during the periods of avoidance. Avoidance of conflict often leads to a self-perpetuating cycle (Wilmot & Hocker, 2001).

In addition, framing an intractable dispute comprises a complex and messy process, and individuals and practitioners do not always frame conflicts accurately (H. Burgess & G. Burgess, 1996). When stakeholders make framing errors, H. Burgess and G. Burgess noted that muddled framing occurs, and it can lead individuals to pursue arguments and positions that do not advance their interests in the dispute. Opponents also do not always frame a dispute in the same manner. Framing inconsistencies can produce intractability because mismatches in frames equate to mismatches in understanding the issues involved in the dispute (Putnam & Wondolleck, 2003).

Summary

In summary, issues, contexts, relationships, conflict processes, and conflict frames can cause or contribute to intractability. However, notably, not all conflicts share the same causes, contributing factors (Putnam & Wondolleck, 2003), or origins (Kriesberg, 2003). These factors interrelate and likely interact in a pattern of circular causality (Coleman, 2003).

Intractable conflict research provides many useful insights into why irresolvable conflicts occur and the factors that shape perceptions of intractability. However, very little of this research specifically focuses on the communication between conflict parties, resulting in a huge limitation of this body of research. Research on serial arguing and perpetual problems fills some of the gaps regarding how individuals communicate during conflicts that are difficult to resolve and the most effective strategies.

The next section combines the key contributions of each of these three research areas into a single model. Based on this model, we identify future research directions.

Synthesis and Future Research Directions

Although the research that we reviewed is diverse in conceptual frameworks, units of analysis studied, and methods, we believe that some important commonalities emerge. Figure 3.1 contains a diagram that illustrates these commonalities.

This model focuses on six different sets of variables. First, researchers (e.g., H. Burgess & G. Burgess, 1996; Burton, 1987; Coleman, 2000, 2003; Lederach, 1997; Northrup, 1989; Putnam & Wondolleck, 2003; Rothman, 1997) have attempted to identify the factors that impede resolution. These factors reflect differences in values, scarce resources, and identity threats. Individuals consider each of these factors to be sufficiently important that they will not (or cannot) compromise. Second, researchers (e.g., Bar-Tal, 1998; Cloven & Roloff, 1991; Coleman, 2000) have argued that individuals involved in unresolved conflicts attempt to make sense of the conflicts. This sense-making activity includes negative processes such as mulling

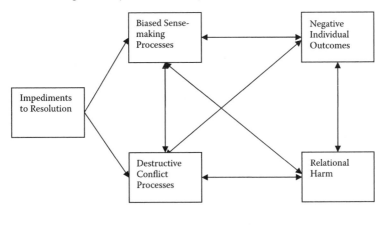

Figure 3.1   Integrated model.

over causes or solutions, making negative attributions about the causes of a partner's behavior, adopting an egocentric frame, creating pessimistic expectations about what will occur in future episodes, and believing the conflict will never be resolved.

Third, researchers (e.g., Coleman, 2000, 2003; Putnam & Wondolleck, 2003; Rouhana & Bar-Tal, 1998) have investigated conflict in particular situations as well as more generally. These processes include the prolonged duration and persistence of conflict episodes. Researchers (e.g., Caughlin, 2002; Eldridge & Christensen, 2002; Johnson & Roloff, 2000a, 2000b) studied dysfunctional patterns related to repetitive arguments, escalation, and demand/withdraw within particular episodes. Fourth, researchers (Malis & Roloff, 2006a, 2006b) have noted that unresolved conflicts can influence a person's well-being. Most research has focused on stress and stress-related symptoms. Fifth, researchers (Gottman, 1999; Johnson & Roloff, 1998, 2000a, 2000b; Lloyd, 1987; Malis & Roloff, 2006a, 2006b) have studied the relational impact of unresolved conflict, including its impact on relational quality and termination. Finally, researchers (e.g., Coleman, 2000, 2003; Driver et al., 2003; Gottman, 1999; Johnson & Roloff, 1998, 2000a, 2000b) recognize that protracted conflict usually involves a series of interconnected episodes. Hence, a current episode consists of an ongoing set of confrontations with a history and future.

Within the figure, each of the nine links identifies a research question worthy of future research. First, to what extent do the various impediments to resolution spark sense-making activity? Although a variety of features characterize irresolvable conflicts, some potentially stimulate certain types of sense-making more than others. For example, the impediments might vary with regard to how much they reflect underlying personal rather than situational causes for the dispute. Hence, the impediments might bias the degree to which partners blame each other for conflict episodes. Differences in fundamental values might prompt partners to blame each other for the problem to a greater extent than differences regarding scarce resources.

Second, to what extent do the various impediments to resolution generate destructive conflict processes? Just as some impediments initiate sense-making, some might generate conflict processes that ensure the conflict will not be resolved. For example, identity threats might be especially likely to foster escalation; whereas, problems focused on differing values might result in avoidance, especially if neither party believes that he or she can persuade the other to change.

Third, what sense-making activities correlate most with destructive conflict processes? It seems reasonable that sense-making activities could stimulate destructive conflict processes and that, as a result of destructive processes, individuals engage in more sense-making activities. Hence, as individuals increasingly mull over the conflict or frame it in a manner that stresses the correctness of their position, they might be even more willing to escalate the dispute. This escalation might reinforce the sense-making activity.

Fourth, what sense-making activities interrelate with negative individual outcomes? Potentially, the way in which individuals construe a conflict makes them feel even greater distress, resulting in even more negative construal. For example, a person who engages in negative sense-making might feel worse afterward (e.g., become stressed or depressed). His or her negative feelings might be associated with increased sense-making behavior.

Fifth, what sense-making activities correspond to particular relational outcomes? Although a variety of conflict factors can attenuate relational damage, sense-making activity about irresolvable conflict could also influence relational quality. As noted in our review, prolonged thinking about the irresolvable nature of the conflict seems to negatively impact relational quality.

Sixth, what conflict processes relate to individual outcomes? Destructive conflict behaviors seem especially stressful, potentially prompting individuals to engage in destructive behaviors. We noted earlier that destructive patterns enacted during argumentative episodes can be stressful for the individual.

Seventh, what conflict processes impact certain relational outcomes? This question has generated the greatest research attention thus far. As noted earlier, evidence suggests that factors such as demand/withdraw patterns correlate negatively with relational outcomes. Although not studied, reductions in positive relational processes also could reinforce or prompt negative conflict processes. Hence, as a person becomes less satisfied with the relationship, he or she might withdraw from it.

Eighth, to what extent are individual and relational outcomes correlated? A person's stress level could possibly reduce relational quality and vice versa. One could argue that prolonged conflict can deplete a person's personal resources and disrupt other aspects of his or her life (e.g., job). As the person becomes tired or depressed and/or the conflict intrudes on many aspects of his or her life, it would not be surprising to see relational quality erode. This erosion in the relationship could yield even greater stress.

Ninth, what complex relationships exist among the variables in the model? We simplified the model by specifying additive relationships among the variables that predict individual and relational outcomes. Mediating relationships might be uncovered among some of them. For example, in their review of social cognition approaches to the study of interpersonal conflict, Roloff and Miller (2006) noted that researchers have treated cognitive processes (such as attribution-making) as mediators of the effect that conflict behaviors have on individual and relational outcomes. Other cognitive processes, such as rumination, have been characterized as directly affecting individual and relational outcomes.

Finally, to what extent do the linkages among the variables change across conflict episodes? Most often, researchers (e.g., Johnson & Roloff, 1998, 2000a, 2000b; Malis & Roloff, 2006a, 2006b) study protracted conflict at a single point in time rather than employing a longitudinal design. Although providing useful information, studying a single episode of a protracted conflict affords little insight into the degree to which key variables in protracted conflicts intersect across episodes or the degree to which the linkages within episodes change over time.

Because of the limited nature of research focused on conflicts that are difficult to resolve, we cannot be highly specific about possible hypotheses related to the questions. To provide guidance for future research, it might be useful to build upon extant models of conflict communication. For example, a body of research on perceptions of conflict competence (Cupach & Canary, 2000; Spitzberg, Canary, & Cupach, 1994) includes variables associated with disputes that are difficult to resolve. Because conflict competence relates to episodic outcomes, this framework might provide insight into conflicts that are not resolved after repeated episodes. In other words, does repeated conflict result from deficient knowledge, motivation, and skills to resolve a dispute in a single episode, or does something new emerge during the course of repeated conflict that prevents resolution?

An alternative approach to studying protracted conflict highlights the decision to continue the engagement. Unlike spontaneously occurring events, the repeated nature of protracted disputes permits participants time to consider whether they wish to extend the conflicts. Vuchinich and Teachman (1993) used utility theory to predict the duration of a variety of types of conflicts, including wars, strikes, riots, and family disagreements. Essentially, they argued that, as conflict continues, the costs of engagement rise, but the benefits derived from winning remain relatively constant. For example, as wars continue, fatalities and material costs increase, but the benefits from winning the war stay approximately the same. This pattern holds true in family conflicts as well. As family conflicts continue, relational quality likely decreases while health and psychological problems possibly increase. However, the benefits of winning the family conflict potentially remain the same.

To offset such losses, participants must have an ample supply of resources as well as means to bolster sagging morale. If they do not, they will look for a way of bringing the disagreement to a close. In their analysis, Vuchinich and Teachman (1993) found that larger and rigidly organized groups (i.e., nations, businesses, unions) possess the wherewithal to counter their losses, and their conflicts typically last longer. On the other hand, rioting groups and families can draw from fewer resources, and they might be less organized. Thus, their disputes tend to end much faster. However, exceptions exist. As the number of people involved in a riot or family disagreement increases, Vuchinich and Teachman argued that the length of the dispute also increases because bigger groups share greater collective resources and can spread the costs among a larger number of people. Furthermore, according to Vuchinich and Teachman, additional individuals become a source of support for one's cause.

This model advances some important and potentially counterintuitive insights about protracted interpersonal conflict. It suggests that protracted conflicts end because individuals lack resources and morale to continue the fight. If so, resource exhaustion and demoralization comprise a necessary condition for the parties to disengage. In other words, a prolonged conflict is not ripe for resolution until both parties find it too painful to continue (Zartman, 2001). This notion has three implications.

First, when others provide disputants with financial and emotional support, they prolong the dispute rather than moving it toward resolution. Although such support might be well intentioned and appreciated by the participants, it also might lock them into a dysfunctional pattern of disagreement.

Second, to reduce the costs of continued fighting, disputants might attempt to avoid prolonged and frequent episodes that could seriously diminish their resources. Rather than arguing all of the time, participants might go through relatively peaceful times during which they replenish their resources and plan for the next encounter.

Third, although optimism about conflict resolution attempts might guard against relational harm and health-related problems, it could bind individuals into prolonged conflict. In other words, in some cases, optimism might be unrealistic. Optimism might cause individuals to continue the struggle instead of changing their course of action to be more conciliatory or accepting.

Although we have emphasized the importance of this framework for generating useful research, it can also be beneficial for professionals who deal with interpersonal conflict. For example, the model might inform therapists about how best to approach couples who struggle with conflicts that are difficult to resolve. The model suggests that some specific conflict processes, such as demand/withdraw, might be harmful to relational well-being but that other factors might stimulate such behaviors (e.g., how couples construe the problem and the very nature of the problem itself). Hence, negative conflict behaviors are merely symptoms of other problems that might become manifested in other ways if individuals eliminate the targeted negative behavior. Indeed, a therapist might find it useful to attack the issue that makes the conflict difficult to resolve (e.g., identity threats, discrepant values) rather than the symptoms arising from the conflict.

The model also might serve as a framework for a hospital social worker who is working with a family conflict regarding treatment options for an ill family member. The social worker might be able to tease out the issues in conflict by asking family members about their sense of what is causing the conflict, perceived individual outcomes, and perceived relational harm. In that way, the social worker might be able to control destructive conflict processes that can make a difficult situation worse.

Finally, the model also might serve as a guideline for making sense of an intercultural conflict. For example, perceptions regarding the destructiveness of conflict might vary across cultures (e.g., Gelfand et al., 2001). These views might influence sense-making behaviors. Clarifying each party's cultural views on conflict might ease relations between parties and decrease destructive conflict processes.

Conclusion

Although interpersonal relationships provide individuals with many benefits, they sometimes serve as a source of disagreement. In some cases, the disputes are very difficult to resolve, with the potential to erode individual and relational well-being. Our review indicates that useful insights can be derived by studying serial arguing and persistent problems as well as borrowing from macro perspectives such as intractable conflict. Indeed, by integrating features of each of the aforementioned perspectives, we propose an overall framework that could guide future conflict communication research in small group communication, organizational communication, family communication, health communication, intercultural communication, religious communication, political communication, and international communication.

Acknowledgments

The authors wish to thank Christina Beck and three anonymous reviewers for their insightful feedback on drafts of this chapter. We also would like to thank Jennifer Scott for her helpful research assistance.

Notes

1. Because our review focuses on the characteristics and causes of irresolvable interpersonal disputes, we did not review intractable conflict literature focused on management or resolution strategies for intractable conflicts. Much of this research is contextual and/or focuses on international conflicts (e.g., Albeck et al., 2002; Azar, 1986; Bar-Tal, 2000, 2004; Benson, Moore, & Kapur, 2005; Friedman, 2005; Gray, 1997, 2004; Greig, 2001; Horton-Deutsch & Horton, 2003; Jameson, 2003; Kriesberg, 1989; Kriesberg & Thorson, 1991; LeBaron & Carstarphen, 1997; Pruitt & Olczak, 1995; Retzinger & Scheff, 2000; Salomon, 2004; Weiss, 2003; Zartman, 2001) and therefore is outside the scope of our review. See Coleman (2004) for a review of five major

paradigms employed in intervention research and practice of intractable conflicts. For the same reason, we also did not address costs of intractable conflict (see Azar, 1986; Coleman, 2000, 2003).
2. Please see Coleman (2003) for a more in-depth description of each dilemma.
3. Please see H. Burgess and G. Burgess (1996) for a detailed description of each conflict overlay.
4. Please see Fisher and Keashly (1990) for a detailed description of the contributions other scholars made to this model.

References

Abbey, A., Abramis, D. J., & Caplan, R. D. (1985). Effects of different sources of social support and social conflict on emotional well-being. *Basic and Applied Social Psychology, 6,* 111–129.

Acheson, K. (2007) Silence in dispute. In C. S. Beck (Ed.), *Communication yearbook 31* (pp. 1–59). New York, NY: Lawrence Erlbaum Associates.

Albeck, J. H., Adwan, S., & Bar-On, D. (2002). Dialogue groups: TRT's guidelines for working through intractable conflicts by personal storytelling. *Peace and Conflict: Journal of Peace Psychology, 8,* 301–322.

Almeida, D. M., Wethington, E., & Chandler, A. L. (1999). Daily transmission of tensions between marital dyads and parent–child dyads. *Journal of Marriage and the Family, 61,* 49–61.

Averill, J. R. (1982). *Anger and aggression: An essay on emotion.* New York: Springer.

Azar, E. E. (1986). Management of protracted social conflict in the Third World. *Ethnic Studies Report, 4*(2), 1–17.

Back, A., & Arnold, R. (2005). Dealing with conflict in caring for the seriously ill: "It was just out of the question." *Journal of the American Medical Association, 293,* 1374–1381.

Badr, H. (2004). Coping marital dyads: A contextual perspective on the role of gender and health. *Personal Relationships, 11,* 197–211.

Bar-Tal, D. (1998). Societal beliefs in times of intractable conflict: The Israeli case. *International Journal of Conflict Management, 9*(1), 22–50.

Bar-Tal, D. (2000). From intractable conflict through conflict resolution to reconciliation: Psychological analysis. *Political Psychology, 21,* 351–365.

Bar-Tal, D. (2004). Nature, rationale, and effectiveness of education for coexistence. *Journal of Social Issues, 60,* 253–271.

Bar-Tal, D., Raviv, A., & Freund, T. (1994). An anatomy of political beliefs: A study of their centrality, confidence, contents, and epistemic authority. *Journal of Applied Social Psychology, 24,* 849–872.

Baumeister, R. F., Stillwell, A., & Wotman, S. R. (1990). Victim and perpetrator accounts of interpersonal conflict: Autobiographical narratives about anger. *Journal of Personality and Social Psychology, 59,* 994–1005.

Bedford, V. H. (1998). Sibling relationship troubles and well-being in middle and old age. *Family Relations, 47,* 369–376.

Benoit, W. L., & Benoit, P. J. (1987). Everyday argument practices of naïve social actors. In J. W. Wentzel (Ed.), *Argument and critical practices: Proceedings of the Fifth SCA/AFA Conference on Argumentation* (pp. 465–473). Annandale, VA: Speech Communication Association.

Benson, J. F., Moore, R., & Kapur, R. (2005). Management of intense countertransference in group psychotherapy conducted in situations of civic conflict. *International Journal of Group Psychotherapy, 55,* 63–86.

Bevan, J. L., Hale, J. L., & Williams, S. L. (2004). Identifying and characterizing goals of dating partners engaging in serial argumentation. *Argumentation and Advocacy, 41,* 28–40.

Birchler, G. R., & Webb, L. J. (1977). Discriminating interaction behaviors in happy and unhappy marriages. *Journal of Consulting and Clinical Psychology, 45,* 494–495.

Bolger, N., DeLongis, A., Kessler, R. C., & Schilling, E. A. (1989). Effects of daily stress on negative mood. *Journal of Personality and Social Psychology, 57,* 808–818.

Borisoff, D., & Victor, D. A. (1998). *Conflict management: A communication skills approach* (2nd ed.). Needham Heights, MA: Allyn & Bacon.

Breen, C., Abernethy, A., Abbott, K, & Tulsky, J. (2001). Conflict associated with decisions to limit life-sustaining treatment in intensive care units. *Journal of General Internal Medicine, 16,* 283–289.

Burgess, H., & Burgess, G. (1996). Constructive confrontation: A transformative approach to intractable conflicts. *Mediation Quarterly, 13,* 305–322.

Burton, J. (1987). *Resolving deep-rooted conflict: A handbook.* Lanham, MD: University Press of America.

Canary, D. J., Cunningham, E. M., & Cody, M. J. (1988). Goal types, gender, and locus of control in managing interpersonal conflict. *Communication Research, 15,* 426–446.

Canary, D. J, & Spitzberg, B. H. (1990). Attribution biases and associations between conflict strategies and competence judgments. *Communication Monographs, 57,* 139–151.

Canary, D. J., Spitzberg, B. H., & Semic, B. A. (1998). The experience and expression of anger in interpersonal settings. In P. A. Andersen & L. K. Guerrero (Eds.), *Handbook of communication and emotion: Research, theory, applications, and contexts* (pp. 189–213). San Diego, CA: Academic Press.

Caughlin, J. P. (2002). The demand/withdraw pattern of communication as a predictor of marital satisfaction over time: Unresolved issues and future directions. *Human Communication Research, 28,* 49–85.

Caughlin, J. P., & Vangelisti, A. L. (2006). Conflict in dating and marital relationships. In J. Oetzel & S. Ting-Toomey (Eds.), *The Sage handbook of conflict communication: Integrating theory, research, and practice* (pp. 129–157). Thousand Oaks, CA: Sage.

Cloven, D. H., & Roloff, M. E. (1991). Sense-making activities and interpersonal conflict: Communicative cures for the mulling blues. *Western Journal of Speech Communication, 55,* 134–158.

Coleman, P. T. (2000). Intractable conflict. In M. Deutsch & P. T. Coleman (Eds.), *The handbook of conflict resolution: Theory and practice* (pp. 428–450). San Francisco: Jossey–Bass.

Coleman, P. T. (2003). Characteristics of protracted, intractable conflict: Towards the development of a meta framework—I. *Peace and Conflict. Journal of Peace Psychology, 9,* 1–37.

Coleman, P. T. (2004). Paradigmatic framing of protracted, intractable conflict: Toward the development of a meta-framework—II. *Peace and Conflict: Journal of Peace Psychology, 10,* 197–235.

Corenblum, B., & Stephan, W. G. (2001). White fears and native apprehensions: An integrated threat theory approach to intergroup attitudes. *Canadian Journal of Behavioral Sciences, 33,* 251–268.

Crocker, C. A., Hampson, F. O., & Aall, P. (1996). Introduction. In C. A. Crocker, F. O. Hampson, & P. Aall (Eds.), *Managing global chaos: Sources of and responses to international conflict* (pp. xiii–xix). Washington, DC: United States Institute of Peace Press.

Cupach, W. R., & Canary, D. J. (2000). *Competence in interpersonal conflict.* Long Grove, IL; Waveland Press Inc.

Davies, P. T., & Cummings, E. M. (1998). Exploring children's emotional security as a mediator of the link between marital relations and child adjustment. *Child Development, 69,* 124–139.

De Dreu, C. K. W., & Weingart, L. R. (2003). Task versus relationship conflict, team performance, and team member satisfaction: A meta-analysis. *Journal of Applied Psychology, 88,* 741–749.

Deutsch, M. (1969). Conflicts: Productive and destructive. *Journal of Social Issues, 25,* 7–41.

Deutsch, M. (1973). *The resolution of conflict: Constructive and destructive processes.* New Haven, CT: Yale University Press.

Drake, L. E., & Donohue, W. A. (1996). Communication framing theory in conflict resolution. *Communication Research, 23,* 297–322.

Driver, J., Tabares, A., Shapiro, A., Nahm, E. Y., & Gottman, J. M. (2003). Interactional patterns in marital success and failure: Gottman laboratory studies. In F. Walsh (Ed.), *Normal family processes: Growing diversity and complexity* (3rd ed., pp. 493–513). New York: Guilford Press.

Eldridge, K. A., & Christensen, A. (2002). Demand–withdraw communication during couple conflict: A review and analysis. In P. Noller & J. A. Feeney (Eds.), *Understanding marriage: Developments in the study of couple interaction* (pp. 289–322). Cambridge, England: Cambridge University Press.

Ellis, D. G. (2005). Intercultural communication in intractable ethnopolitical conflicts. *International and Intercultural Communication Annual, 28,* 45–69.

Finch, J. F., & Zautra, A. J. (1992). Testing latent longitudinal models of social ties and depression among the elderly: A comparison of distribution-free and maximum likelihood estimates with nonnormal data. *Psychology and Aging, 7,* 107–118.

Fincham, F. D., Harold, G. T., & Gano-Phillips, S. (2000). The longitudinal association between attributions and marital satisfaction: Direction of effects and role of efficacy expectations. *Journal of Family Psychology, 14,* 267–285.

Fisher, R. J., & Keashly, L. (1990). Third-party consultation as a method of intergroup and international conflict resolution. In R. J. Fisher (Ed.), *The social psychology of intergroup and international conflict resolution* (pp. 211–238). New York: Springer-Verlag.

Folger, J. P., Poole, M. S., & Stutman, R. K. (2005). *Working through conflict: Strategies for relationships, groups, and organizations* (5th ed.). Boston: Allyn & Bacon.

Friedman, G. (2005). Commercial pacifism and protracted conflict: Models from the Palestinian–Israeli case. *Journal of Conflict Resolution, 49,* 360–382.

Friedman, R. A., Tidd, S. A., Currall, S. C., & Tsai, J. C. (2000). What goes around comes around: The impact of personal conflict style on work conflict and stress. *The International Journal of Conflict Management, 11,* 32–55.

Gayle, B. M., & Preiss, R. W. (1998). Assessing emotionality in organizational conflicts. *Management Communication Quarterly, 12,* 280–302.

Gelfand, M. J., Nishii, L. H., Holcombe, K. M., Dyer, N., Ohbuchi, K., & Fukuno, M. (2001). Cultural influences on cognitive representations of conflict: Interpretations of conflict episodes in the U.S. and Japan. *Journal of Applied Psychology, 86,* 1059–1074.

Gottman, J. M. (1993). The roles of conflict engagement, escalation, and avoidance in marital interaction: A longitudinal view of five types of couples. *Journal of Consulting and Clinical Psychology, 61*, 6–15.

Gottman, J. M. (1994). *What predicts divorce: The relationship between marital processes and marital outcomes.* Hillsdale, NJ: Lawrence Erlbaum Associates.

Gottman, J. M. (1999). *The marriage clinic: A scientifically based marital therapy.* New York: W. W. Norton.

Gottman, J. M., & Silver, N. (1999). *The seven principles for making marriage work.* New York: Crown Publishers.

Gray, B. (1997). Framing and reframing of intractable environmental disputes. In R. J. Lewicki, R. J. Bies, & B. H. Sheppard (Eds.), *Research on negotiation in organizations* (Vol. 6, pp. 163–188). Greenwich, CT: JAI Press.

Gray, B. (2003). Framing of environmental disputes. In R. Lewicki, B. Gray, & M. Elliott (Eds.), *Making sense of intractable environmental disputes: Concepts and cases* (pp. 11–34). Washington, DC: Island Press.

Gray, B. (2004). Strong opposition: Frame-based resistance to collaboration. *Journal of Community and Applied Social Psychology, 14*, 166–176.

Greig, J. M. (2001). Moments of opportunity: Recognizing conditions of ripeness for international mediation between enduring rivals. *Journal of Conflict Resolution, 45*, 691–718.

Grey, S. H. (2007). Wounds not easily healed: Exploring trauma in communication studies. In C. S. Beck (Ed.), *Communication yearbook 31* (pp. 173–222). New York, NY: Lawrence Erlbaum Associates.

Guerrero, L. K., & La Valley, A. G. (2006). Conflict, emotion, and communication. In J. Oetzel & S. Ting-Toomey (Eds.), *The Sage handbook of conflict communication: Integrating theory, research, and practice* (pp. 69–96). Thousand Oaks, CA: Sage.

Honeycutt, J. M., Zagacki, K. S., & Edwards, R. (1990). Imagined interaction and interpersonal communication. *Communication Reports, 3*, 1–8.

Horton-Deutsch, S. L., & Horton, J. M. (2003). Mindfulness: Overcoming intractable conflict. *Archives of Psychiatric Nursing, 17*, 186–193.

Hughes, P. C. (2004). The influence of religious orientation on conflict tactics in interfaith marriages. *Journal of Communication and Religion, 27*, 245–267.

Hunter, S. (1989). The roots of environmental conflict in the Tahoe Basin. In L. Kriesberg, T. A. Northrup, & S. J. Johnson (Eds.), *Intractable conflicts and their transformation* (pp. 25–40). Syracuse, NY: Syracuse University Press.

Iecovich, E. (2000). Sources of stress and conflicts between elderly patients, their family members, and personnel in care settings. *Journal of Gerontological Social Work, 34*(2), 73–88.

Jameson, J. K. (2003). Transcending intractable conflict in health care: An exploratory study of communication and conflict management among anesthesia providers. *Journal of Health Communication, 8*, 563–581.

Jehn, K. A. (1995). A multimethod examination of the benefits and detriments of intragroup conflict. *Administrative Science Quarterly, 40*, 256–282.

Jehn, K. A., & Chatman, J. A. (2000). The influence of proportional and perceptual conflict composition on team performance. *The International Journal of Conflict Management, 11*, 56–73.

Johnson, K. L., & Roloff, M. E. (1998). Serial arguing and relational quality: Determinants and consequences of perceived resolvability. *Communication Research, 25*, 327–343.

Johnson, K. L., & Roloff, M. E. (2000a). Correlates of the perceived resolvability and relational consequences of serial arguing in dating relationships: Argumentative features and the use of coping strategies. *Journal of Social and Personal Relationships, 17*, 676–686.

Johnson, K. L., & Roloff, M. E. (2000b). The influences of argumentative role (initiator vs. resistor) on perceptions of serial argument resolvability and relational harm. *Argumentation, 14*, 1–15.

Katz, J., Jones, D. J., & Beach, S. R. H. (2000). Distress and aggression during dating conflict: A test of the coercion hypothesis. *Personal Relationships, 7*, 391–402.

Kelley, D. L., & Waldron, V. R. (2006). Forgiveness: Communicative implications for social relationships. In C. S. Beck (Ed.), *Communication yearbook 30* (pp. 303–342). Mahwah, NJ: Lawrence Erlbaum Associates.

Kiecolt-Glaser, J. K., Malarkey, W. B., Chee, M. A., Newton, T., Cacioppo, J. T., Mao, H. Y., et al. (1993). Negative behavior during marital conflict is associated with immunological down-regulation. *Psychosomatic Medicine, 55*, 395–409.

Kiecolt-Glaser, J. K., & Newton, T. L. (2001). Marriage and health: His and hers. *Psychological Bulletin, 127*, 472–503.

Kiecolt-Glaser, J. K., Newton, T., Cacioppo, J. T., MacCallum, R. C., Glaser, R., & Malarkey, W. B. (1996). Marital conflict and endocrine function: Are men really more physiologically affected than women? *Journal of Counseling and Clinical Psychology, 64*, 324–332.

Koerner, A. F., & Fitzpatrick, M. A. (2006). Family conflict communication. In J. Oetzel & S. Ting-Toomey (Eds.), *The Sage handbook of conflict communication: Integrating theory, research, and practice* (pp. 159–183). Thousand Oaks, CA: Sage.

Kozan, M. K. (1997). Culture and conflict management: A theoretical framework. *International Journal of Conflict Management, 8*, 338–360.

Kriesberg, L. (1982). *Social conflicts* (2nd ed.). Englewood Cliffs, NJ: Prentice Hall.

Kriesberg, L. (1989). Transforming conflicts in the Middle East and Central Europe. In L. Kriesberg, T. A. Northrup, & S. J. Johnson (Eds.), *Intractable conflicts and their transformation* (pp. 109–131). Syracuse, NY: Syracuse University Press.

Kriesberg, L. (1993). Intractable conflicts. *Peace Review, 5,* 417–421.

Kriesberg, L. (1998). Intractable conflicts. In E. Weiner & A. B. Slifka (Eds.), *The handbook of interethnic coexistence* (pp. 332–342). New York: Continuum.

Kriesberg, L. (2003). *Constructive conflict: From escalation to resolution* (2nd ed.). Oxford, England: Rowman & Littlefield.

Kriesberg, L., & Thorson, S. J. (Eds.). (1991). *Timing the de-escalation of international conflicts.* Syracuse, NY: Syracuse University Press.

Krishnakumar, A., & Buehler, C. (2000). Interparental conflict and parenting behaviors: A meta-analytic review. *Family Relations, 49,* 25–44.

LeBaron, M., & Carstarphen, N. (1997). Negotiating intractable conflict: The common ground dialogue process and abortion. *Negotiation Journal, 13,* 341–361.

Lederach, J. P. (1997). *Building peace: Sustainable reconciliation in divided societies.* Washington, DC: United States Institute of Peace Press.

Lee, R., Rodin, G., Devins, G., & Weiss, M.G. (2001). Illness experience, meaning and help-seeking among Chinese immigrants in Canada with chronic fatigue and weakness. *Anthropology & Medicine, 8,* 89–107.

Lepore, S. J. (1992). Social conflict, social support, and psychological distress: Evidence of cross-domain buffering effects. *Journal of Personality and Social Psychology, 63,* 857–867.

Levy, J. S. (1996). Contending theories of international conflict: A levels-of-analysis approach. In C. A. Crocker, F. O. Hampson, & P. Aall (Eds.), *Managing global chaos: Sources of and responses to international conflict* (pp. 3–24). Washington, DC: United States Institute of Peace Press.

Lewis, L. K. (2006). Collaborative interaction: Review of communication scholarship and a research agenda. In C. S. Beck (Ed.), *Communication yearbook 30* (pp. 197–248). Mahwah, NJ: Lawrence Erlbaum Associates.

Lipsky, D. B., & Seeber, R. L. (2006). Managing organizational conflicts. In J. Oetzel & S. Ting-Toomey (Eds.), *The Sage handbook of conflict communication: Integrating theory, research, and practice* (pp. 359–390). Thousand Oaks, CA: Sage.

Lloyd, S. A. (1987). Conflict in premarital relationships: Differential perceptions of males and females. *Family Relations, 36,* 290–294.

Lyubomirsky, S., Tucker, K. L., Caldwell, N. D., & Berg, K. (1999). Why ruminators are poor problem solvers: Clues from the phenomenology of dysphoric rumination. *Journal of Personality and Social Psychology, 77,* 1014–1060.

Malis, R. S., & Roloff, M. E. (2006a). Demand/withdraw patterns in serial arguing: Implications for well-being. *Human Communication Research, 32,* 198–216.

Malis, R. S., & Roloff, M. E. (2006b). Features of serial arguing and coping strategies: Links with stress and well-being. In R. M. Dailey & B. A. Le Poire (Eds.), *Applied interpersonal communication matters: Family, health, and community relations* (pp. 39–65). New York: Peter Lang.

McCorkle, S., & Mills, J. L. (1992). Rowboat in a hurricane: Metaphors of interpersonal conflict management. *Communication Reports, 5,* 57–66.

McGonagle, K. A., Kessler, R. C., & Gotlib, I. H. (1993). The effects of marital disagreement style, frequency, and outcome on marital disruption. *Journal of Social and Personal Relationships, 10,* 385–404.

Metts, S., & Cupach, W. R. (1990). The influence of relationship beliefs and problem-solving responses on satisfaction in romantic relationships. *Human Communication Research, 17,* 170–185.

Miller, R. S. (1997). We always hurt the ones we love: Aversive interactions in close relationships. In R. M. Kowalski (Ed.), *Aversive interpersonal behaviors* (pp. 11–29). New York: Plenum Press.

Montemayor, R., & Hanson, E. (1985). A naturalistic view of conflict between adolescents and their parents and siblings. *Journal of Early Adolescence, 5,* 23–30.

Montiel, C. J. (2000). Political trauma and recovery in a protracted conflict: Understanding contextual effects. *Peace and Conflict: Journal of Peace Psychology, 6,* 93–111.

Nagle, J. D. (1989). The West German Greens: An evolving response to political conflict. In L. Kriesberg, T. A. Northrup, & S. J. Johnson (Eds.), *Intractable conflicts and their transformation* (pp. 132–155). Syracuse, NY: Syracuse University Press.

Newell, S. E., & Stutman, R. K. (1988). The social confrontation episode. *Communication Monographs, 55,* 266–285.

Newell, S. E., & Stutman, R. K. (1989/90). Negotiating confrontation: The problematic nature of initiation and response. *Research on Language and Social Interaction, 23,* 139–162.

Nicotera, A. M., & Dorsey, L. K. (2006). Individual and interactive processes in organizational conflict. In J. Oetzel & S. Ting-Toomey (Eds.), *The Sage handbook of conflict communication: Integrating theory, research, and practice* (pp. 293–325). Thousand Oaks, CA: Sage.

Northrup, T. A. (1989). The dynamic of identity in personal and social conflict. In L. Kriesberg, T. A. Northrup, & S. J. Johnson (Eds.), *Intractable conflicts and their transformation* (pp. 55–82). Syracuse, NY: Syracuse University Press.

Oetzel, J. G., Arcos, B., Mabizela, P., Weinman, A. M., & Zhang, Q. (2006). Historical, political, and spiritual factors of conflict: Understanding conflict perspectives and communication in the Muslim world, China, Colombia, and South Africa. In J. Oetzel & S. Ting-Toomey (Eds.), *The Sage handbook of conflict communication: Integrating theory, research, and practice* (pp. 549–574). Thousand Oaks, CA: Sage.

Oetzel, J. G., & Ting-Toomey, S. (2003). Face concerns in interpersonal conflict: A cross-cultural empirical test of the face negotiation theory. *Communication Research, 30,* 599–624.

Oetzel, J. G., & Ting-Toomey, S. (Eds.). (2006). *The Sage handbook of conflict communication: Integrating theory, research, and practice.* Thousand Oaks, CA: Sage.

O'Keefe, D. J., & Jensen, J. D. (2006). The disadvantages of compliance or the disadvantages of noncompliance? A meta-analytic review of the relative persuasive effectiveness of gain-framed and loss-framed messages. In C. S. Beck (Ed.), *Communication yearbook 30* (pp. 1–44). Mahwah, NJ: Lawrence Erlbaum Associates.

Pawlowski, D. R., Myers, S. A., & Rocca, K. A. (2000). Relational messages in conflict situations among siblings. *Communication Research Reports, 17,* 271–277.

Pettigrew, T. F., & Tropp, L. R. (2006). A meta-analytic test of intergroup contact theory. *Journal of Personality and Social Psychology, 90,* 751–783.

Pinkley, R. L. (1990). Dimensions of conflict frame: Disputant interpretations of conflict. *Journal of Applied Psychology, 75,* 117–126.

Plant, E. A. (2004). Responses to interracial interactions over time. *Personality and Social Psychology Bulletin, 30,* 1458–1471.

Plant, E. A., & Devine, P. G. (2003). The antecedents and implications of interracial anxiety. *Personality and Social Psychology Bulletin, 29,* 790–801.

Poole, M. S., & Garner, J. T. (2006). Perspectives on workgroup conflict and communication. In J. Oetzel & S. Ting-Toomey (Eds.), *The Sage handbook of conflict communication: Integrating theory, research, and practice* (pp. 267–292). Thousand Oaks, CA: Sage.

Pörhölä, M., Karhunen, S., & Rainivaara, S. (2006). Bullying at school and in the workplace: A challenge for communication research. In C. S. Beck (Ed.), *Communication yearbook 30* (pp. 249–302). Mahwah, NJ: Lawrence Erlbaum Associates.

Pruitt, D. G., & Kim, S. H. (2004). *Social conflict: Escalation, stalemate, and resolution* (3rd ed.). New York: McGraw–Hill.

Pruitt, D. G., & Olczak, P. V. (1995). Beyond hope: Approaches to resolving seemingly intractable conflict. In B. B. Bunker & J. Z. Rubin (Eds.), *Conflict, cooperation, and justice: Essays inspired by the work of Morton Deutsch* (pp. 59–92). San Francisco: Jossey–Bass.

Putnam, L. L., & Wondolleck, J. M. (2003). Intractability: Definitions, dimensions, and distinctions. In R. Lewicki, B. Gray, & M. Elliott (Eds.), *Making sense of intractable environmental disputes: Concepts and cases* (pp. 35–59). Washington, DC: Island Press.

Raffaelli, M. (1992). Sibling conflict in early adolescence. *Journal of Marriage and the Family, 54,* 652–663.

Reis, H. T., Sheldon, K. M., Gable, S. L., Roscoe, R., & Ryan, R. (2000). Daily well being: The role of autonomy, competence, and relatedness. *Personality and Social Psychology Bulletin, 26,* 419–435.

Retzinger, S., & Scheff, T. (2000). Emotion, alienation, and narratives: Resolving intractable conflict. *Mediation Quarterly, 18,* 71–85.

Roloff, M. E. (1988). Communication and conflict. In C. R. Berger & S. H. Chaffee (Eds.), *Handbook of communication science* (pp. 484–534). Thousand Oaks, CA: Sage.

Roloff, M. E., & Johnson, K. L. (2002). Serial arguing over the relational life course: Antecedents and consequences. In A. L. Vangelisti, H. T. Reis, & M. A. Fitzpatrick (Eds.), *Stability and change in relationships* (pp. 107–128). New York: Cambridge University Press.

Roloff, M. E., & Miller, C. W. (2006). Social cognition approaches to understanding interpersonal conflict and communication. In J. Oetzel & S. Ting-Toomey (Eds.), *The Sage handbook of conflict communication: Integrating theory, research, and practice* (pp. 97–128). Thousand Oaks, CA: Sage.

Roloff, M. E., & Soule, K. P. (2002). Interpersonal conflict: A review. In M. L. Knapp & J. A. Daly (Eds.), *Handbook of interpersonal communication* (pp. 475–528). Thousand Oaks, CA: Sage.

Rothman, J. (1997). Resolving identity-based conflict in nations, organizations, and communities. San Francisco: Jossey–Bass.

Rouhana, N. N., & Bar-Tal, D. (1998). Psychological dynamics of intractable ethnonational conflicts: The Israeli–Palestinian case. *American Psychologist, 53,* 761–770.

Salomon, G. (2004). Does peace education make a difference in the context of an intractable conflict? *Peace and Conflict: Journal of Peace Psychology, 10,* 257–274.

Segerstrom, S. C., & Miller, G. E. (2004). Psychological stress and the human immune system: A meta-analytic study of 30 years of inquiry. *Psychological Bulletin, 130,* 601–630.

Sillars, A. L. (1980). Attributions and communication in roommate conflicts. *Communication Monographs, 47,* 180–200.

Sillars, A. L. (1998). (Mis)understanding. In B. H. Spitzberg & W. R. Cupach (Eds.), *The dark side of close relationships* (pp. 73–102). Mahwah, NJ: Lawrence Erlbaum Associates.

Sillars, A. L., Canary, D. J., & Tafoya, M. (2004). Communication, conflict, and the quality of family relationships. In A. Vangelisti (Ed.), *Handbook of family communication* (pp. 413–446). Mahwah, NJ: Lawrence Erlbaum Associates.

Sillars, A., & Parry, D. (1982). Stress, cognition, and communication in interpersonal conflicts. *Communication Research, 9,* 201–226.

Sillars, A., Roberts, L. J., Leonard, K. E. & Dun, T. (2000). Cognition during marital conflict: The relationship of thought and talk. *Journal of Social and Personal Relationships, 17,* 479–502.

Sillars, A. L., & Wilmot, W. W. (1994). Communication strategies in conflict and mediation. In J. Wiemann & J. Daly (Eds.), *Communicating strategically: Strategies in interpersonal communication* (pp. 163–190). Hillsdale, NJ: Lawrence Erlbaum Associates.

Smyth, L. F. (1994). Intractable conflicts and the role of identity. *Negotiation Journal, 10,* 311–321.

Smyth, L. F. (2002). Identity-based conflicts: A systemic approach. *Negotiation Journal, 18,* 147–161.

Spitzberg, B. H., Canary, D.J., & Cupach, W. R. (1994). A competence-based approach to the study of interpersonal conflict. In D. D. Cahn (Ed.), *Conflict in personal relationships* (pp. 183–202). Hillsdale, NJ: Lawrence Erlbaum Associates.

Spitzberg, B. H., & Cupach, W. R. (2002). Interpersonal skills. In M. L. Knapp & J. A. Daly (Eds.), *Handbook of interpersonal communication* (3rd ed., pp. 564–611). Thousand Oaks, CA: Sage.

Stephan, W. G., Boniecki, K. A., Ybarra, O., Bettencourt, A., Ervin, K. S., Jackson, L. A., et al. (2002). The role of threats in the racial attitudes of Blacks and Whites. *Personality and Social Psychology Bulletin, 28,* 1242–1254.

Stephan, W. G., Diaz-Loving, R., & Duran, A. (2000). Integrated threat theory and intercultural attitudes: Mexico and the United States. *Journal of Cross-Cultural Psychology, 31,* 240–249.

Sternberg, D. P., & Beier, E. G. (1977). Changing patterns of conflict. *Journal of Communication, 27,* 97–103.

Stewart, R. B., Verbrugge, K. M., & Beilfuss, M. C. (1998). Sibling relationship in early adulthood: A typology. *Personal Relationships, 5,* 59–74.

Stocker, C. M., Burwell, R. A., & Briggs, M. L. (2002). Sibling conflict in middle childhood predicts children's adjustment in early adolescence. *Journal of Family Psychology, 16,* 50–57.

Straus, M. A. (1998). Ten myths that perpetuate corporal punishment. In K. V. Hansen & A. I. Garey (Eds.), *Families in the U.S.* (pp. 641–650). Philadelphia: Temple University Press.

Stutman, R. K., & Newell, S. E. (1990). Rehearsing for confrontation. *Argumentation, 4,* 185–198.

Thorson, S. J. (1989). Introduction: Conceptual issues. In L. Kriesberg, T. A. Northrup, & S. J. Johnson (Eds.), *Intractable conflicts and their transformation* (pp. 1–10). Syracuse, NY: Syracuse University Press.

Ting-Toomey, S., & Takai, J. (2006). Explaining intercultural conflict: Promising approaches and directions. In J. Oetzel & S. Ting-Toomey (Eds.), *The Sage handbook of conflict communication: Integrating theory, research, and practice* (pp. 691–723). Thousand Oaks, CA: Sage.

Trapp, R., & Hoff, N. (1985). A model of serial argument in interpersonal relationships. *Journal of the American Forensic Association, 22,* 1–11.

Vuchinich, S. (1987). Starting and stopping spontaneous family conflicts. *Journal of Marriage and the Family, 49,* 591–601.

Vuchinich, S. (1990). The sequential organization of closing in verbal family conflict. In A. D. Grimshaw (Ed.), *Conflict talk: Sociolinguistic investigations of arguments in conversations* (pp.118–138). Cambridge, NY: Cambridge University Press.

Vuchinich, S., & Teachman, J. (1993). Influence on the duration of wars, strikes, riots, and family arguments. *Journal of Conflict Resolution, 37,* 544–568.

Watzlawick, P., Beavin, J., & Jackson, D. D. (1967). *Pragmatics of human communication: A study of interactional patterns, pathologies, and paradoxes.* New York: Norton.

Weiss, J. N. (2003). Trajectories toward peace: Mediator sequencing strategies in intractable communal conflicts. *Negotiation Journal, 19,* 109–115.

White, R. K. (1984). *Fearful warriors: A psychological profile of U.S.–Soviet relations.* New York: Free Press.

Wilmot, W. W., & Hocker, J. L. (2001). *Interpersonal conflict* (6th ed.). New York: McGraw-Hill.

Wong, P. T. P., & Weiner, B. (1981). When people ask "why" questions, and the heuristics of attributional search. *Journal of Personality and Social Psychology, 40,* 650–663.

Wynn, R. L. (1989). Custody disputes and the victims. In L. Kriesberg, T. A. Northrup, & S. J. Johnson (Eds.), *Intractable conflicts and their transformation* (pp. 83–92). Syracuse, NY: Syracuse University Press.

Young, N. (2007). Identity trans/formations. In C. S. Beck (Ed.), *Communication yearbook 31* (pp. 223–272). New York, NY: Lawrence Erlbaum Associates.

Zartman, I. W. (2001). Negotiating internal conflict: Incentives and intractability. *International Negotiation, 6,* 297–302.

Chapter 4 Contents

4

Wounds Not Easily Healed: Exploring Trauma in Communication Studies

Stephanie Houston Grey
Louisiana University

The study of trauma, a pervasive subtext throughout the field of communication, runs like an invisible thread that links the research of scholars who study a diverse range of discursive activities. It connects the work of researchers interested in the analysis of interpersonal, family, and organizational communication to critical theorists and historians who explore the symbolic dynamics that bind cultures in times of stress and political contest. This chapter attempts to expose these threads and develop a heuristic vocabulary for foregrounding these research practices and perspectives. The first half of the chapter explores the impact of trauma upon local peer communities—the way that it both binds and fragments people as they grapple with the wounds left by disaster, war, and disease. Issues of authority and stigma remain central to these discussions as the traumatized individual searches for a legitimate vocabulary through which to make sense of these experiences. The second half of this chapter explores the impact of trauma on collective identity and representation, particularly in the fields of history and popular culture. Here trauma can be addressed overtly through mass-mediated spectacles or run as an unconscious thread through the accumulated images and texts that constitute the fabric of society. By recognizing the symbolic dissonance produced by traumatic memory, exposing the complexities of these discursive practices provides insight into individual, national, and global responses to tragedy.

Dissonant Echoes: The Cultural Reverberations of Trauma

Communication drives our capacity to constitute past experiences through discursive practice and project our respective identities through language. The effects of external crises on our behavior, identity, and policy can be traced through the scars that they leave upon the symbolic universe that forms the basis for our cultural consciousness. When individuals or societies undergo stressful events, whether generated by internal violence or driven by natural catastrophe, these occurrences become integral to the collective histories of those who shared them. *Trauma* denotes the impact of events that produce severe ruptures in social cohesion and threaten the stability of these cultural narratives. As the social fabric abruptly tears in the face of tragedy, subsequent symbolic activity must address these openings—both their impact on individuals and the long-term consequences for entire societies.

Stemming from the Greek term used to describe a severe wound, trauma originally appears in Hippocratic texts instructing the surgeons of antiquity in the appropriate means for treating injuries that opened the interior of the body to external inspection (Agelarakis, 2006). These treatments often required the physician to invade the body in carefully choreographed procedures designed to repair the wounds of war or mishap. One of these practices involved physicians opening the skull along its natural sutures to relieve cerebral swelling. The study of trauma expanded during the nineteenth century when doctors realized that head wounds often manifested symptoms throughout the entire body via the central nervous system. Thus, the term shifted from its more visceral meaning to signify those injuries that tended to originate in the brain, setting the stage for the psychoanalytic detour from anatomy into the interpretive science of the psyche (Higonnet, 2002). During the course of the last century, accounts of war veterans, victims of genocide, and survivors of catastrophes further expanded our understanding of trauma as a wound that cannot be seen but often profoundly impacts individuals and their social networks. Filtered through the templates of the therapeutic sciences, trauma encompasses a phenomenon known, experienced, and interpreted through symbolic activity (Laplanche & Pontalis, 1973).

This chapter provides a navigational guide through literature dealing with trauma. Given that the residue of traumatic experiences reverberates throughout individual lives, local peer networks, institutions, and mass-mediated narratives that form the basis for national and international consciousness, these events and their aftershocks span the entire discipline of communication. Through the humanities and the social sciences, scholars have attempted to understand and represent the contours of trauma using a diverse range of methodologies and theoretical perspectives. These studies comprise the disciplinary topography of the entire field, beginning at the interpersonal level of therapy and counseling, moving through the management of these events within institutions, and eventually ending in the study of trauma at the cultural level.

Following this spatial logic, the present discussion begins with the study of trauma within local contexts, exploring the dynamic tensions that emerge between traumatized individuals or subgroups and their immediate culture. The second half of the chapter examines scholarly attempts to articulate how trauma is represented at the broadest cultural levels—a discussion that involves questions of epistemology, history, and aesthetics. Traumatized groups continue to challenge dominant understandings of their experiences; thus, the ambiguity left in the wake of these cultural exchanges constitutes a rich avenue for those who explore discursive activities from a variety of perspectives to enter this terrain and shed light on one of the most troubling cultural dynamics to capture the intellectual imagination in recent decades.

Traumatized Individuals and Their Communities

When Alexander of Macedon conquered Egypt, legend has it that he encountered what is known today as the Gordian knot, a great mass of rope and twine that had baffled rulers, philosophers, and mystics for decades. With his usual linear decisiveness, Alexander solved the riddle by cutting it in two (see Burke, 2001). This event can serve as a metaphor for how trauma often entangles individuals in a massive knot involving psychology, culture, experience, relationships, history, and communication. Not only does this knot bind individuals, but it also can fragment them from some allegiances while meshing them with others as their recollections of these traumatic events collide with their local cultures, diverse encounters, and disparate beliefs. Drawing from the work of psychoanalyst Jacques Lacan, Ragland-Sullivan (2001) argued that traumatic manifestations present us with a tension between the real and the imagined:

> The symptom knots together each individual unit of real/symbolic/imaginary material into a vast, elaborate signifying necklace of associated images, words and affect that produce the meanings we live by. Thus the knot would be central to any interpretation of trauma, insofar as it ultimately resides in the real, while retaining properties of each of the other orders of meaning. (p. 2)

Even after the event ends, the memory reverberates across time and place. Drawing heavily from the work of Sigmund Freud, Laplanche and Pontalis (1973) codified the modern definition of trauma for the field of psychoanalysis by creating a theory accounting for the complex and often indirect expression of trauma through language. Laplanche and Pontalis acknowledged that trauma includes a spatial dimension—a material ontology that could be mapped at a particular historical moment and that also continues to echo across time. This form of psychoanalytic reasoning combines science and interpretation to focus attention on the communicative process through which the minds of individuals intersect with a broader social universe where their identities are shaped. In a subsequent interview, Laplanche used the metaphor of the envelope to describe the process whereby individuals create unique identities as a protective barrier against the disorientation produced by interactions with estranged others (Caruth, 2001). In other words, the social formation of the self during times of crisis constitutes a symptom of trauma (for a related discussion of identity and communication, please see Young, this volume).

As I will detail in the following sections, though, the dialectic of trauma as both an individual and societal concern pervades theoretical discussions of this important issue. Through our discourse, we construct trauma as a private and public event; we determine how trauma can authorize individuals, peer groups, and social networks to stigmatize traumatized individuals and communities.

Tracing the Boundaries of Traumatic Experience

Trauma has become a ubiquitous phenomenon throughout the lived experience of our society, evidenced by the resources spent training health professionals to cope with the victims of disease and violence (Harris, 1998). As one moves through the communicative contexts that range from the private realm to the public sphere, this section examines the way that individuals express and manage trauma through a variety of practices and settings. These events can begin at the personal or local level and then, through the process of symbolic interaction, emanate outward to reverberate throughout the community. Further, this section illustrates that people often understand trauma only after they articulate it. Affected individuals and communities seek either comfort or redress within their immediate interpersonal and institutional contexts—externalizing their internal dissonance and presenting it as an experience for others to consume or reject.

Cathartic Expressions of Trauma   The desire to share and express pain links the traumatized subject to the broader human condition. When experiences such as violence or disease leave a jagged mark upon the psyche, these memories necessitate some form of self-expression as they drive interlocutors to seek out others and manufacture resolution through a variety of comfort networks. Following the conventional wisdom that "confession is good for the soul," some researchers have found evidence that discussing problems (such as the passing of family members or divorce) can be managed or lessened through talking about them (Pennebaker & Beall, 1986). Pennebaker and O'Heeron (1984) suggested that, while these confessional moments may only result in minor improvements in the immediate prognosis, they can have beneficial effects on the long-term physical and psychological health of the individual.

Following the traditional dynamics of *catharsis*, the psychological dissonance that builds within the mind of the traumatized subject creates an unmanageable tension that must be released. To avoid destructive or unhealthy manifestations, such feelings must be channeled in positive ways where the act of self-expression becomes an avenue toward resolution. In his book, *The Wounded Storyteller: Body, Illness and Ethics* (1995), A. W. Frank noted that individuals who are diagnosed with various illnesses find that they are better able to cope with these conditions by "hearing themselves tell their stories, absorbing others' reactions, and experiencing their stories being shared" (p. 1). Thus, the process of encoding traumatic experiences into narratives that can be expressed and shared seems to play an important role in the management of these conditions. As such, communication becomes a channel for individual catharsis as individuals release unwanted emotional tensions via language.

The responses by some of the family members who lost loved ones in the World Trade Center attacks exemplify the benefit of confiding personal narratives to those who have had similar life experiences. In their recent book, *Love You, Mean It: A True Story of Love, Loss, and Friendship*, four women who lost their husbands during the 9/11 attacks described "The Widow's Club," a bond that enabled them to continue beyond the horrible tragedy (Carrington, Collins, Gerbasi, Haynes, & Charles, 2006). According to a review in *Publishers Weekly*, "True, they found sympathy everywhere—from in-laws, co-workers, friends, grief professionals—but even their dearest intimates couldn't offer the absolutely unconditional acceptance and understanding of a sister sufferer (vol. 253, p. 40)." The stories told by these individuals do not emerge from a vacuum. Instead, they unfold out of the intense personal experiences that they share—that only one who has walked in similar shoes can really grasp the enormity of this type of loss.

Ideally, the narratives that emerge from these contexts (while certainly expressing pain, grief, and anger) ultimately should conclude with some life-enhancing goal. McAdams and Bowman (2001) argued that redemptive life stories remain crucial to facilitating the healing and comfort of those individuals who experience life-changing catastrophe. They explained that "narratives in which negative scenes are transformed into positive outcomes ... are strongly linked to feeling satisfied and fulfilled in life" (p. 28). These individuals do not engage in purely instrumental speech, but they attempt to manage their experiences by externalizing them through language and developing strategies for moving forward into a productive future. At its core, traumatic experience necessitates communication as a byproduct of the instability that it produces within individual consciousness.

Collective Responses to Trauma   Traumatic events often produce ripples (as consensus and clashes) throughout symbolic societal networks. Through interpersonal interactions, new social realities evolve from the traumatic memories of individuals and their immediate peer groups, causing social networks to shift and adjust. While such events may be localized, they quickly spread through the intersubjective universe as the psychological shockwaves reverberate outward. In some cases, well-known or well-liked individuals bring their own struggles with trauma to the forefront of public consciousness. For example, Michael J. Fox began his struggle with Parkinson's disease quite privately, sharing the news only with his wife and close friends. However, his public disclosure and subsequent congressional testimony prompted considerable reactions from fans and media discussion (see Beck, 2005). When these accounts of physical trauma filter into the public arena, they generate and encourage an ongoing dialogue that projects outward from their immediate family circle and into the media spotlight. Much as Fox became the face of Parkinson's, fans connect Lance Armstrong with cancer and Christopher Reeve with spinal paralysis. As such, these narratives shape the broader understanding of these conditions.

Some of the most compelling instances where one can trace the anatomy of a collective response to trauma involve those instances where catastrophe strikes a discreet geographical locale or social/religious community. The terrorist attacks of 9/11 provide a rich source of information concerning how traumatic events can begin at "ground zero" and then echo to the margins of society. Starting with the assessment of those who directly experienced the event, Sattler (2002) described the social stresses and bonding behaviors that emerge during natural disasters or acts of terror. Sattler explained that victims and rescuers frequently created a powerful relationship with the event and the individuals with whom they shared it during the aftermath of the terror attacks on 9/11.

However, traumatic events—particularly those that rise to the level of catastrophe—are not restricted to those individuals who immediately experience them. Such events impact not only those at "ground zero," but also those who aid in the activities of rescue, recovery, and even information gathering. As individuals mutually encounter such events, they generate a psychological shockwave that emanates from this point of origin throughout the culture (Place, 1992). In the case of 9/11, extensive electronic networks, such as cell phones, linked the disaster sites to surrounding communities (Dutta-Bergman, 2004). Thus, individuals form a sense of community in the face of catastrophe as direct participants as well as indirect witnesses. In an analysis of the 9/11 obituaries that appeared in the *New York Times*, Miller (2003) noted that these accounts, though repetitive, provided necessary insight into the event because they captured its human essence, explaining that "like the snapshot, the anecdote through the brevity of its narrative catches life in its everyday dimensions" (p. 115). Through these accounts, the deaths of innocent citizens impacted others far beyond the scope of their immediate families, comprising a national tragedy.

While communities may confront tragedy as an external threat, violence can also create trauma. While not rising to the level of catastrophe, these events may nonetheless generate a shockwave of despair, horror, or revulsion. One study of the dragging death of James Byrd in Jasper, Texas, explored how individuals within the community came to terms with their shock and guilt as well as how the story evolved over time in the local newspapers (Ainslie & Brabeck, 2003). While the event did not produce a national sense of despair, the graphic accounts of a man being dragged to his death because of his skin color opened the still oozing wounds of repressed racism. This situation exemplifies the powerful connections that individuals can form between themselves and the subjects about which they read— allowing the horror of something outside their own immediate social network to profoundly influence their individual sense of well-being.

In a more extensive study of Laramie, Wyoming, the town where Matthew Shepard was brutally murdered for being an openly gay teen, Loffreda (2000) outlined the way that the community responded to his death by closing off its social borders with outsiders. A media circus descended upon the town, coupled with the disruptive influence of Reverend Phelps (a Baptist minister who openly protests at the funerals of gay individuals and U.S. servicemen killed in Iraq). However, citizens in Laramie attempted to maintain their stability by minimizing the impact that the story about their community had upon their culture. Such collective responses reflect the power that traumatic experiences have to foster powerful bonding experiences in the face of horror and violence.

The Amish community suffered a tremendous tragedy in October, 2006, when a gunman stormed into a school house and killed five girls (see Anderson, 2006; Dewan & Hamill, 2006; Hastings, 2006). Although this traditionally isolated religious community asked only for privacy and prayer, others across the nation reached out and offered support. One small school district in Albany, Ohio, sent a gift of 2,000 daffodil bulbs because they understand shattering loss. According to Gallagher (2006), "Over the past several years, five students have died in accidents, bringing the devastation that the loss of a bright young life can cause" (p. A1). As teacher Lois Harkins stressed, "With each of our losses, we received so many acts of kindness from people we will never know. It helps you heal, helps when you understand that other people grieve your loss" (Gallagher, p. A1).

Institutional Influences   Institutions can also participate in discourse surrounding trauma. For example, public relations scholars note the institutional pressures on corporations when reporting traumatic events such as plane crashes. Englehardt, Sallot, and Springston (2004) described this process in their analysis of the postcrash communication from Valujet, which attempted to manage public panic by providing comforting messages that, at the same time, deflected blame. In this case, the company balanced the therapeutic desire to console with the corporate imperative to avoid legal responsibility, serving both to distance the organization from and to embrace the victims' families.

Political figures also employ a similar type of grief management when either circumstances or policies produce deadly consequences with national resonance. Mister (1986) discussed such political therapy through an analysis of Reagan's *Challenger* tribute, a speech in which Reagan attempted to facilitate the national grieving process while reaffirming NASA's role as a viable institution.

Both governments and organizations recognize the potential that traumatic events possess to produce shifts in consciousness—an often violent and unpredictable process that must be harnessed and controlled. This research demonstrates that institutional strategists are becoming more adept at channeling anxieties rather than dismissing or repressing them.

The maintenance of national and community ethos can become particularly problematic when the institution itself has played a significant role in inflicting trauma upon a particular group. From 1932 to 1972, the Tuskegee syphilis studies—an experiment that traced the effects of the disease on African-American men who were placed under observation and left untreated—constitutes one such breech. Soloman (1985) described the treatment of these men as an example of rhetorical dehumanization where their identity as test subjects superseded their ontology as human beings. Such a breech in experimental ethics has created ongoing distrust within the African-American community, creating a situation in which illnesses such as AIDS become the fodder for rumors of conspiracy (Jones, 1993). In their analysis of Bill Clinton's apology to the Tuskegee survivors, Harter, Stephens, and Japp (2000) suggested that Clinton sought to offer a clear invitation to healing, while at the same time softening the blame that might be levied at the Tuskegee Institute itself.

Reincorporating a population that has been victimized by a governing culture back into the national community can be difficult when deceit or the repression of information plays a key role in the ongoing history of the event. In an interesting ethnography, Trujillo (1993) traveled to Dealey Plaza 25 years after the assassination of John F. Kennedy. Trujillo argued that the site has emerged as a sphere of resistance to the dominant cultural narrative due to lingering suspicion about the official account for the event. When a culture undergoes a trauma that is perpetrated by an institution such as its own government, it is difficult to rebuild these bonds of trust.

The Truth and Reconciliation Commission in South Africa, a government-sponsored tribunal, manages memories of violence and oppression through a series of public displays that function as theatres of mutual recognition and community building. In these moments of testimony and display, private and public spheres intersect as years of violence surge into the national consciousness. These public performances become critical in managing the fear and hatred generated by the violent history of repression that threatened to rip the culture apart. In her work on the use of testimonials to address the symptoms of trauma in South Africa, Laub (2005) suggested that the Truth Commission facilitates healing by affording a public space through which the public and private selves of these individuals can be fused.

Feldman (2004) also noted that these trials often exhibit a dynamic of antiphonic discourse where interaction is invited rather than repressed. According to Feldman, these performances "[take] on the atmosphere of Church witnessing call and response call-outs, choral singing and the dancing of the toi-toi, as other survivors in the audience [support] the witnesses through public expressions of feeling" (p. 175). These rituals, now considered among the most successful in the world at bringing perpetrators and victims together, derive power from their ability to link the spectacle and the audience through a common discursive activity where a higher order of truth—one that links the facts to associated pain—can be expressed. Uniquely, the rituals do not minimize traumatic experience or transform it into a media spectacle, but they connect diverse social actors through the dynamics of conflict and dialogue using the antiphonic form to reestablish national equilibrium.

As compelling as these performances are in creating social bonds, the reverberations of trauma do more than foster intimacy. They can also prompt dissonance. In a collection of essays edited by Greenberg (2003), one of the latent effects of 9/11 entails the extent to which terror attacks not only shape the lives of those directly affected by them but also reinforce particular modes of governance that permanently change the way that the entire culture lives. Anxiety and fear can greatly impact public policies. For example, McMahon (1999) identified unresolved tensions of the Vietnam War as causal agents in the policies that guided future international conflicts and set the stage for repressive policies in the domestic sphere. More recently, Haridakis and Rubin (2005) observed the influence of 9/11 on the policy of fear that has defined American society since these attacks.

Media Influences on Community Responses   Whenever a subgroup within a particular culture perceives that it has been traumatized, the act of public storytelling can play a significant role in manufacturing healing. In a discussion of the relationship between cancer survivors

and public advocacy, Sharf (1997) argued that "personal breast cancer stories have inspired efforts by citizens, advocates, and legislators
to provide better care and more resources for the disease" (p. 217).
As these individuals use their experiences to raise the consciousness
level of their broader communities, they sometimes discover a sense
of peace or resolution in the knowledge that their pain and suffering has not been without some benefit. In these cases, information
and entertainment media can shape public agendas—particularly
through fictional and reality television series that dramatize the
after-effects of personal tragedy. Sharf, Freimuth, Greenspon, and
Plotnick (1993) contended:

> The potential of the mass media to set public health agendas and model
> healthy behaviors (while biographical or fictional television portrayals
> of serious illness) provides illustrations for problem solving and oppor-
> tunities for viewers to think about how they would handle the dilemmas
> attendant to such situations. (pp. 157–158)

However, this sheer glut of information, images, and accounts can
be overwhelming, deterring our ability to empathize with others and
gradually desensitizing us to violence and suffering. Moeller (1999)
questioned the journalistic exhibition of trauma because it causes a
systematic deadening of the audience's emotional responses, a condition that she calls "compassion fatigue" (p. 3). As the media steadily
bombards audiences with images of death and suffering, Moeller
asserted that individuals eventually lose their capacity to respond to
them sympathetically.

These observations raise important questions about the extent to
which information overload heightens viewer ability to identify with
the victims of trauma, especially as one set of visual atrocities accu-
mulates on the heels of another. Coming as it did in the wake of the
tsunami that struck the South Pacific, was the audience already desensitized to the images that they saw in the wake of Hurricane Katrina,
the most destructive storm ever to hit the United States? For Moeller
(1999), the most destructive byproduct of the media obsession with
death and violence is social apathy. As such, according to Moeller,
reporters must look for increasingly sensationalistic ways to convey
trauma in order to sustain audience interest by, for example, catching
the reaction shot of the president after a natural disaster or terrorist
attack (Bucy, 2003) or incessantly portraying narratives of grief and
loss when public figures die (Brown, Basil, & Bocarnea, 2003).

The problem that compassion fatigue presents to the survivors of trauma is that they must strive to be heard amid the existing cultural noise. Vanderford and Smith (1996) used the case of defective breast implants to suggest that the media exploited the panic surrounding these devices to create a culture of fear that obsessed on the personal suffering of these victims. Exploiting emotions for ratings or economic gain creates a society that vacillates between panic and cynicism. Cultural member immunity to images of disease, violence, and torture becomes particularly problematic when the culture itself perpetrates these transgressions (see, for example, Carabas & Harter, 2005). In these cases, the social upheaval produced by the conflict between the wounded victim and the transgressor must be carefully negotiated, particularly when they occupy the same cultural topography.

I suggest the term "cultural topography" as a means of capturing the constellation of ideas and values that comprise a culture—a terrain that can shift and adjust over time as material circumstances change. It also entails exploring the conditions that must be met for the traumatized subject to reenter the society without creating unproductive divisions (Vansant, 2001). In a society that has become desensitized to mediated violence and disease, this process of reconciliation can be impeded by the countervailing forces of apathy bred by the media spectacle.

The Authority to Articulate Trauma

Given the hyper-reality that trauma produces in both individual memory and cultural narratives, it can become the lynchpin of one's identity. Proceeding from this assumption, the question of who is authorized to translate the traumatic experience becomes a point of conflict as those who have experienced these events directly and those who have not struggle to establish parameters of authenticity. Scarry (1985) observed that torture or bodily pain compels victims to identify with the event as well as generates ruptures in the surrounding symbolic universe. In other words, the symbolic dynamics of stress, rupture, transition, and eventual stabilization frame how lingering pain impacts individuals and their social networks. This section explores how stakeholders negotiate, articulate, and contest authority within a variety of institutional contexts.

Trauma as a Form of Political Authenticity   In the wake of 9/11, many family members of individuals who were killed used their status as the bereaved to bring political pressure upon the federal government. Breitweiser's (2006) narrative detailing the events surrounding the "Jersey Widows," a group of women whose efforts eventually led to the creation of the 9/11 Commission, explored the political relationship between the bereaved seeking justice and the realities of American political culture. This group has recently come under fire from conservative ideologue Ann Coulter (2006), who argued that these women unfairly used their position as widows to enter into the public arena, deploying their grief as a shield to deflect political attacks. Coulter's account descended into a scathing *ad hominem* attack, characterizing the Jersey Widows as "harpies" having fun in the wake of their husbands' deaths.

Yet, the depth of Coulter's anger belies the point that traumatized subjects can sometimes achieve an elevated status in our culture. Similar groups, such as MADD (Mothers Against Drunk Driving), continue to demonstrate the profound power that the grief-stricken voice can have when confronting institutional authority. When these grieving subjects are afforded this authority, others cannot easily challenge them.

In societies where traumatized individuals remain isolated, the discursive field can become rich with performances that resist strategic forgetfulness in often surprising ways. Foss and Domenici (2001) provided a compelling portrayal of mothers in Buenos Aires who march daily for their lost children, attempting to gain social legitimacy for the pain and suffering that their families have endured. This refusal to retreat into the private sphere and grieve quietly constitutes a social transgression as these women use the public stage as a platform to advance the legitimacy of their experiences.

The question of legitimacy and institutional authority remains central to understanding the dynamics of trauma and its impact on individual and subcultural identities (see, for example, related arguments by Carabas & Harter, 2005). One of the key factors in the success of the South African Truth Commission stems from its ability to legitimate the voices of those who have been victimized and set them in dialogue with the larger culture. In these cases, the social networks that are necessary to maintain a productive society can be reopened and maintained as the reverberations of trauma are acknowledged publicly and the victims' experiences incorporated into the community's collective history.

Performance can become a powerful force in articulating a shared traumatic experience, reinforcing mutually binding narratives through a series of creative and resistant acts. Researchers in this area have noticed, for example, that singing accesses collective experience and fosters internal cohesion against the dominant culture (Segall, 2005). Certainly, the prevalence of slave spirituals illustrates one of the most compelling examples of this form of oral performance where counter-histories emerge to affirm a sense of authority among those suffering political oppression (Eyerman, 2001). Within these types of communicative contexts, the voice can be used to craft a sense of togetherness and maintain focus on a joint counter-history absent from the broader culture. As such, singing became integral to the Civil Rights movement, especially when individuals were jailed for participating in freedom marches and employed this technique to maintain their spirits in the face of legal persecution (see, e.g., G. Carawan & C. Carawan (1990). Because it is so difficult to censor, this sphere enables the repressed voice to pass these memories across transgenerational boundaries. The recognition of this cultural process brings Foss and Domenici's (2001) observations into finer relief by extracting individual psychological experiences from the private sphere and deploying them as voices that possess unique authority in public life.

The Challenge to Psychiatric Authority   The emergence of posttraumatic stress disorders among the returning veterans of foreign wars exemplifies a battle for legitimacy that revolves around the ability to know, articulate, and speak from the position of a traumatized individual or group. For example, doctors have been unable to locate a discreet medical cause of Gulf War syndrome, a collection of physical symptoms reported by many returning soldiers, thus resulting in a political contest over defining these symptoms as essentially real or imagined (Mahoney, 2001). This struggle between patients and doctors has led some researchers to suggest that physicians must try to avoid challenging these experiences by labeling them phantom illnesses—deploying instead models of medical uncertainly to manage cases and prevent potential political activism (Zavestoki et al., 2004). Hence, it may not be productive for those in the therapeutic community to engage in an epistemic contest with those in the traumatized subculture regarding respective ability to author experiences from an authentic standpoint. Instead, new interpretive frameworks can be embraced that allow these individuals to articulate their own experiences in a way that does not conflict with the medical community.

In his classic polemic against certain institutionalized practices within the field of medicine, Illich (1976) asserted that the medical culture often reinforces its own societal authority by laying claim to medical terminologies, diagnoses, and the assessment of symptoms. The necessity that some traumatized individuals feel to speak and author their own experience propels them into dispute with their care providers—a power-laden situation over authenticity, authority, and agency.

The Immediacy of Traumatic Experience   Proceeding from Scarry's (1995) observation that the traumatized subject often identifies with its point of origin at a visceral level, this moment can become a form of rebirth. In these cases, the traumatic event becomes the lynchpin around which individuals symbolically negotiate issues of social legitimacy and identity. Thus, access to a community that marks itself by a shared sense of trauma can be difficult. Braithwaite (1997) examined the social dynamics that underscore legitimacy as a survivor of the Vietnam War, particularly how the level of trauma (measured by the intensity and duration of exposure to combat) enhances an individual's authenticity to speak about certain events. The idea of "being there" provides one way to think about this phenomenon—that ultimate sense of having experienced certain conditions, such as combat, that sets one apart from the rest of the community.

Along the same lines, Chaitin (2002) identified similar dynamics among survivors of the Holocaust who, rather than seeking social support from the broader community, withdrew into subgroups who distrust outsiders. In these circumstances, the intimacy established by the traumatic event may, in fact, form the basis for their fragmentation from the larger culture as they seek legitimacy by withdrawing into peer groups rather than demanding public recognition. Traumatized groups (such as the survivors of war, violence, or health problems) cocoon themselves rather than establishing their authority through an outside source, such as the medical community.

This focus upon "being there" creates certain boundaries between those who are and are not authorized to speak. In an interesting investigation of how trauma can be excavated historically, J. Frank

(2003) presented the letters of her father, who was a GI during World War II. She wrote extensively about the atrocities that he witnessed while liberating the death camps in Europe. Using his letters as a meditation on the relationship of experience, knowledge, and witnessing, she grappled with these issues by positioning herself as a mediating agent for her father and the outside world. If the event represents truth, then the social layers intervening between witness and reader become barriers to understanding this truth. As J. Frank's work attests, individuals who speak from the standpoint of "not being there" must necessarily justify why they have elected to speak at all. The drive for authenticity necessitates that secondary witnesses locate themselves at the periphery of the event and, in some way, address the standards of legitimacy that guide social and political presumptions about the trauma.

One related set of questions revolves around the capacity of individuals to communicate experiences as persuasive in a legal context. For example, the institutional systems must gauge particular levels of trauma in order to assign legal status to the individuals who have undergone political repression. Shuman and Bohmer (2004) examined the stories told by seekers of political asylum within the United States and the evolving standards used by review committees that must determine whether these individuals actually present a compelling case. The authors discovered that individuals soon became aware that certain elements of their personal narrative must be accentuated, such as accounts of forced detainment or torture, to meet the standards established by these committees. The authors then noticed that accounts followed a standardized format as their trauma was coded according to what the applicants hoped would be a legitimate framework. As the symbolic reality of the event evolves to meet these standards, officials evaluate its legitimacy through a set of governing procedures to determine access, or lack thereof, to the formal experience of trauma and, thus, the legal status that it can afford (Cvetkovich, 2003).

Trauma and Stigma

Early in his career, Foucault (1965) speculated that the apparatuses of mental health function to maintain institutional control over those who were housed in these facilities. Social stigma ensured that those who strayed from the confines of reason could be marked and contained. In more recent decades, the marginalization of traumatized subjects has produced a different form of backlash to therapeutic vocabularies. Farrell (1998) observed that we currently live in an age obsessed with post-traumatic language where accounts of wounding have become so pervasive that trauma is rendered virtually meaningless. Because so many individuals call for public support through the popular and health media, Farrell argued that trauma now permeates the very fabric of human social activity and serves as a generative force in a modern culture obsessed with psychoanalytic interpretation. Rather than the direct institutional control described by Foucault, the accounts of traumatized individuals can be dismissed as symptoms of collective fantasy. The following section explores the way that the conditions that generate trauma and the designation of trauma itself can lead to social isolation and shame.

Internal Stigmata   In his account of his life in the concentration camps, entitled *The Drowned and the Saved*, Primo Levi (1988) noted that the dynamics of trauma, particularly those dealing with victims and victimizers, include *shame* and *guilt*. While the survivor was not *guilty* of any crime, he or she can feel *shame*. For Levi, this process revolves around the recognition of self via the other. When the camps were liberated by the American troops, he experienced shame when he projected how the soldiers who witnessed the degraded state of the camp and its occupants must have viewed the survivors. He continued to be plagued by the memories of the inherent competition among those with whom he was imprisoned and the way that they sometimes compromised their own moral codes to survive. Using his own personal experience as a point of reference, Levi systematically addressed the manner in which the victims of violence can be subject to the dynamics of self-blame.

When individuals define themselves (or others do so) by their history or an illness, they enter the cultural sphere as marked subjects that must incorporate a sense of stigma into their performances of their public identities (Langellier, 2001). This marking can profoundly impact how individuals perceive themselves and interact with the broader culture.

In an interesting study of the stories used in legal settings to shift the grounds for empathy within the courtroom, Coates and Wade (2004) explained that the strategic reversal of blame can be used as a defense strategy. These authors examined the tendency of lawyers to portray the perpetrators of violent crimes as victims of social deprivation, thus deflecting legitimacy away from those who have been harmed by these defendants. Is everyone traumatized by bad parenting or economic circumstance? Can even aggressors be traumatized by the aggression of their victim's culture (see Colley, 2005)? Experiencing profound violence does not guarantee that social support or empathy will be forthcoming. For example, Horvitz (2000) explored how erotica can turn sexual violence against women into a fetish, noting that "powerlessness becomes eroticized, then entrenched within the victim's self-identity" (p. 21).

Such social frameworks constitute a means for revising violence in a way that re-establishes the presence of the traumatized subject within an ideological construct that allows it to be consumed while also providing a compromised form of legitimacy to the individual as a sexual object. In an analysis of how victims of sexual violence articulate their experiences, Hesford (2004) explained that these testimonies represent an "act that involves the negotiation of available cultural and national scripts and truth-telling conventions" (p. 108). Disturbingly, many sexual violence victims tend to adopt these vocabularies to downplay or rationalize the event. Fusing the traumatized subject with a less challenging mode of representation masks the ruptures that his or her subjectivity creates for the larger symbolic network. Rather than face the reality of sexual violence, these symbolic constructions enable society to dismiss or eroticize it.

Communication researchers recognize that those who work with the victims of trauma must address stigma associated with disease or social circumstances (see, for example, Berman, 2000). In the case of people living with HIV/AIDS, individuals and their support networks must deal with the potential for physical deterioration as well as the damaging stigma that threatens to increase the strain already experienced by these communities (Greene, Frey, & Derlega, 2002).

Communication theories (such as uncertainty reduction theory and boundary management theory) can provide valuable insight into the ways that comfort networks can reduce stigma and reincorporate these individuals into the larger community (Petronio, 2002, 2004; Planalp, Rutherford, & Honeycutt, 1988). In particular, boundary management theory facilitates understanding the reticence to reveal stigmatizing experiences such as sexual violence, etc. (see, e.g., Petronio, Reeder, Hecht, & Ros-Mendoza, 1996). For example, when an individual comes forward with testimony of sexual abuse, the backlash often resonates throughout his or her social spheres, producing a condition where defensive borders are deployed to protect the individual from further harm or stigma.

Projecting Shame   The stigma associated with trauma can become particularly acute when the label of "victim" challenges some widely held social prescription—that the wound itself becomes a mark of shame. Some researchers have noticed that professionals such as law enforcement officers, who must manage stressful situations where they are forced to witness or experience violence for long periods of time, will frequently avoid counseling and actively resist being labeled a traumatized individual (Howard, Tuffin, & Stephens, 2000).

In recent years, a debate has emerged over whether trauma comprises a real condition or a fabrication of the psychiatric community. Farrell (1998) suggested that we live in a culture obsessed with this lexicon. He contended that conditions such as post-traumatic stress disorder (PTSD) have become symptoms of a social malaise rather than an actual response to prior events. This perception is reinforced by the dominant codes of appropriate behavior and response to stressful conditions associated with gender—particularly codes of masculinity. Higonnet (2002) contended that, early in this century, "PTSD was understood by the military as a failure of masculinity—a failure of hardness, courage, or willpower—and a manifestation of latent effeminacy or immaturity" (p. 93). These studies stem from the early analysis of the battle fatigue experience of WWI troops, who were subjected to prolonged periods of artillery fire and developed chronic psychiatric disability (Lerner, 2003). Extending the logic of these complaints, if a man identifies himself as traumatized, he demonstrates effeminate weakness to shirk responsibility.

In a provocative work entitled *Achilles in Vietnam*, Shay (1994) explored the myth of the "berserker" as an outgrowth of trauma. The assumption that those who returned from this conflict experienced violent pathologies and delusions inscribed itself into the mass consciousness of American culture in unpredictable ways. In this case, the anecdotes derived from these narratives shifted the terms to describe a soldier's experience in combat from a transcendent sphere (where courage finds its ultimate expression) to one where latent insanity plagues individuals for the duration of their lives. In the Republican presidential primaries of 2000, push polls used in South Carolina portrayed Governor Bush's opponent, Senator John McCain, as an ex-prisoner of war whose trauma might influence his ability to conduct the office of the presidency in a rational fashion (Moore & Slater, 2003). Recent elections such as the presidential campaign of 2004, with its Swift Boat ads, vividly affirmed that military service, particularly exposure to prolonged combat, no longer serves as a stepping stone to political legitimacy and that it can be turned into a liability if political opponents use military service as an avenue of attack.

While therapeutic contexts provide a legitimate avenue for the expression of trauma, they also contain a double-edged sword. Some individuals will avoid treatment rather than being subjected to scrutiny or labeled neurotic. Belau (2001) argued that the traumatic event plays a significant role in the formation of both individual and group history, emphasizing:

> The signifier marks the subject twice. It marks the subject as the primordial cut where the signifier carves the subject out of the body, and it also marks the subject in its failure to cover the void opened by that very cut. (p. 5)

Thus, the pain and wounding of trauma produce a fragmented subject, and, due to their inability to authenticate the social networks around them, these individuals can be labeled as contaminants, forced into a position where they must create counter-narratives to resist being characterized in such a demeaning way (Nelson, 2001). When they seem to be unable to authenticate the preferred symbolic network around them, the victims of trauma can be marginalized as symptoms of an age obsessed with the language of psychology and personal tragedy.

Representing Trauma in History, Art, and Popular Culture

As societies attempt to grapple with their collective histories, they create a discursive culture through which they express and negotiate tensions and ruptures through politics, art, and popular culture. Caruth (1996) extended the work of Laplanche by suggesting that philosophical, literary, and, in particular, historical endeavors comprise responses to traumatic experiences. Where events or objects cannot be known, history emerges to explain and provide meaning to what would otherwise be a destabilizing event. Caruth (1995) asserted that these events encompass "not so much a symptom of the unconscious, as a symptom of history. The traumatized, we might say, carry an impossible history within them, or they become themselves the symptom of a history that they cannot entirely possess" (p. 5).

A more traditional psychoanalytic theorist, Leys (2000) challenged Caruth's interpretations of psychoanalytic history and her claim that trauma—once it reaches the field of representation—can impact an entire culture as a material presence. While Leys's cautions are well-founded, the focus upon symbolic systems inevitably leads to the investigation of trauma as a textual phenomenon that has an undeniable presence upon the cultural landscape. Tracing these symbolic activities requires sensitivity to the ways in which representations constitute the basis for mass consciousness and, by extension, national and international pathologies. This literature review suggests that trauma often emerges as an acoustic event that resounds throughout the cultural economy, regardless of how historically distant.

In a discussion of the role that history plays in shaping present and future action, Friedrich Nietzsche contended that memory can function as an eternal return through the medium of language—that it betrays us by bringing the forgotten into the present. Ramadanovic (2001) noted that Nietzsche viewed forgetting as essential to human existence:

> Active forgetting is selective remembering, the recognition that not all past forms of knowledge and not all experiences are beneficial for present and future life. Active forgetting is then part of a more general attempt to rationalize the relation to the past and to render conscious—in order to overcome—all those haunting events that return to disturb the calm of a later moment. (p. 1)

Thus, repression is not altogether undesirable and is to some extent inescapable. Yet, if the traumatic event demands expression as argued in the previous section, we can expect these repressions and silences to make significant impacts once they reach the cultural level, especially as the energy generated by these symbolic ruptures begins to emerge within the mass culture in surprising ways.

These eruptions within the mass consciousness may not always return in a direct manner, but they can find indirect expressions in ways for which even Caruth's model cannot fully account. Sturken (1992) argued:

> The Vietnam War and the AIDS epidemic [must be viewed] in the context of postmodern culture not only because they have disrupted previously held truths but [also] because they force a rethinking of the process of memory itself. Both the Vietnam War and the AIDS epidemic can be said to disrupt master narratives, those of American imperialism, technology, science, and masculinity. (p. 16)

Thus, these events do not always find expression in direct and literal ways. This process involves more than repression and, in fact, proceeds according to a much deeper exchange between the event and its subsequent inscription into the cultural terrain. Through such trauma, the dynamics of knowledge, history, and representation circulate to craft a complex exchange between that which a society articulates and that which is left unsaid. To explore this dynamic fully, one must understand the way that epistemic questions of trauma are negotiated through the telling of history, the way that artists attempt to capture the traumatic experience through literature and performance, and the unconscious eruptions of trauma within the mass culture.

Nostalgia, Truth, and Knowing the Traumatic Event

History comprises a contested terrain where narratives and accounts of the past emerge as embodiments of guilt, accusation, and denial. For example, in their analysis of the relationship of slavery, race, and trauma in American history, Alexander, Eyerman, Giesen, Smelser, and Sztompka (2004) argued that slavery did not become traumatic until the nation entered the period of Reconstruction. Thus, it was not the material event itself that produced negative ramifications for the African-American community but rather the way that the event became coded as traumatic experience within collective memory. In an earlier work, Eyerman (2001) described a dichotomy between physical and cultural trauma:

> As opposed to psychological or physical trauma, which involves a wound and the experience of great emotional anguish by an individual, cultural trauma refers to a less dramatic loss of identity and meaning, a tear in the social fabric, affecting a group of people that has achieved some degree of cohesion. (p. 2)

Alexander and colleagues (2004) did not argue that trauma constitutes a phantom experience. Instead, they asserted that cultural trauma forms the basis for identity. As the traumatic event enters into the cultural memory of a particular group, it can function as a powerful counterweight to the forces that might seek to delegitimate their cultural experiences. While shame can motivate the victim to search for some public acknowledgment to abate his or her sense of helplessness, the perpetrator likely resists this exposure, preferring to expunge history of the event in order to emerge blameless (see related argument by Carabas & Harter, 2005). The following sections explore the manner in which these debates implicate more than just ethical justification and strike at the very foundations of history and our ability to know and articulate the past.

Politics of Silence and Division   Whenever a country is accused of war crimes, the dynamics of guilt can lead to sustained counter-campaigns that reduce the aggressor's perceived guilt or responsibility in order to preserve the national *ethos* (Steyn, 2004). Given that nations generally adhere to principles of ethical coherence, governments must often justify brutal actions as being somehow consistent with these moral frameworks. Eyal (2004) divided the field of traumatic representation into two distinct political camps—those who seek to excavate violent memories and those who hold a vested interest in managing or limiting this flow, noting that "those who invest memory with the function of overcoming trauma and protecting society from repetition generate the sense of an unstable memory" (p. 7).

When history becomes a site of contest or repression, the culture itself must deal with the social divisions created when these counter-narratives emerge and the traumatized subject attempts to speak through its wound. In such struggles, the dynamics of shame and guilt become particularly salient, dictating the direction that these political struggles for authenticity will take. In cases where this repression of memory is very acute, entire subcultures will emerge where historians and autobiographical writers will strive to express the experiences that the perpetrator culture wishes to forget or censor (Gilmore, 2001b). This battle for the right to represent history becomes an epistemic issue where stakeholders clearly understand the past as a rhetorical moment when competing accounts challenge one another for exclusive ownership of this terrain.

In an account of the phenomenon of postmemory, Sicher (2001) noted that the past always becomes legible through a collection of screens or fictions that challenge the very notion that the event can ever be truly known, providing instead an illusion of this connection. He argued that these postmemories create a sense of common bond by "accommodating a personal connection with collective trauma" (p. 80). To understand and know trauma through its representation means looking for the indirect pathways that it creates through language. If individuals code these wounds through symbolic screens, then the psychoanalytic insists these memories constitute a fantasy that functions to create epistemic distance between the observer and the event (Rauch, 1998).

In some cases, society views the narratives related by the traumatized subject as historical fictions or reconstructions of the past that serve a particular need in the present (Homans, 2006). One can observe the powerful denial that circumvented the politics of healing in post-apartheid South Africa or the responses to the genocide in Rwanda. From an epistemic standpoint, the very authenticity of victim accounts and whether they can be transmitted as cultural knowledge remain at stake. When testimony of oppression and violence renders history ambiguous, the subsequent struggle for legitimacy can provoke conflicts that divide societies along epistemic axes. This unresolved conflict perpetuates trauma, particularly in situations where competing groups maintain a vested interest in controlling the stories or fictions that constitute their collective history. These narratives impact political cultures where cultural legitimacy determines how particular memories transgress the legitimate boundaries of history and challenge the wall of silence.

The amount of political tension produced by a rupture in history can be measured by determining the amount of energy generated to manage it. These manifestations of trauma can be demonstrated as much through the absence or presence of silence as through counter-representations (Acton, 2004). Thus, the politically sensitive event becomes a nonevent in cases where exposure may produce ongoing violence—a silence that has been associated with many genocides over the past 50 years (Kennerly, 1987). Absence contributes to identity formation—the ego that is both spoken and establishes itself against the borders of the unspoken *other*. As such, the traumatized subject becomes the embodiment of this perpetual wounding within the mass-mediated sphere that must be either silenced or resolved (see related arguments by Acheson, this volume).

The contest that these silences produce can be evidenced by the continuing struggle over Turkey's perpetuation of the Armenian genocide, a historical conflict that is rife with denial and claims of counter genocide (Balakian, 2003). According to Balakian, this selective history exceeds traditional denial as both groups now attempt to occupy the terrain of traumatized constituency, leaving these cultures permanently divided. While history must be a sphere through which groups can establish dialogue, the epistemic questions about its function as knowledge or a political tool hinder dialogue.

Because trauma forces cultural actors to participate in a culturally exclusive terrain or operate in multiple spheres at once, cultural divisions can impact identity. Traumatized subject positions exist in a state of divided memory—particularly in cases where brutalized minority populations produce a double consciousness that extends throughout the society's literary culture (Du Bois, 1903). Within certain cultural and political performances, this divided subject becomes a source of tremendous cultural anxiety as it continually searches for ways to express itself in this hostile climate. In an analysis that uses the template of trauma to understand the concept of double consciousness in the work of W. E. B. Du Bois, Zwarg (2002) argued, "The double-consciousness trauma imposed on minorities through this segregation shadows forth the double-consciousness that trauma begins to assume for a more privileged population" (p. 3).

In this way, the fragmented subject wrestles with what can and cannot be said. In an analysis of Barack Obama's address to the 2000 Democratic Convention, D. A. Frank and McPhail (2005) demonstrated this tension. In his portion of that article, D. A. Frank noted that the speech appealed to a legacy "of shared purpose and coalition and embraced a vision of America grounded in the enlightened ideals of a social contract that espoused human equality, dignity, and justice regardless or race, class status, or ethnic origin" (p. 576). McPhail interpreted the text less hopefully, describing it as one that glosses over the material inequality currently faced by African Americans with a false sense of community and shared purpose. This article itself demonstrates the legacy of silence and the divisions in perspective and identity that emerge from systematic repression and invisibility.

The violent ruptures created by traumatic echoes reverberate through political spheres, creating rifts not only among affected individuals but also between social groups. The narration of trauma contributes to historical templates that define the ethical consistency with which a society will constitute itself. The subsequent repression or reconfiguration of this shared past shapes how productively these rifts will be negotiated—sometimes involving both the aggressor and the victim. As Clark (2005) contended:

> The project of memory, which is central to the process of oral history, is the idea of restoring something that has been lost not only for the self, but for the other—so that what is needed to do the work of memory is to link the processes of telling and hearing or to restore the capacity for dialogue. (p. 294)

When traumatic experience is lost or repressed, its social impact clearly contributes to shifting the grounds of authority away from victim experiences, particularly those who have suffered under systematic political oppression. In these cases, the entire culture becomes heir to the grave of silence in which survivors bury accounts and, potentially, subsequent divisions.

The Memorial as Contested Memory   The management of history illustrates the power of events to divide societies as they negotiate the distance between the experience of trauma and the artifacts used to express it. Ragland-Sullivan (2001) reduced this question to an issue of knowledge production by noting that "when the real elements of a trauma appear as artifacts in a museum, or as literary or artistic representations, they dramatize the paradox. Distance from the real—from its traumatic properties of loss, suffering, and anxiety—enables the looker or hearer to not see or not hear" (p. 12). Rather than coding cultural trauma as a study in the neurotic, a reinvestment in the interactive components of identity formation moves the discussion from ontological questions dealing with the essential division between the symbolic and the real. When one examines a frozen timepiece in a Hiroshima exhibit, the object's ontology as an artifact means that it is removed from the event in such a way that it does not connect the viewer with the reality of the past but negotiates the gaps between the viewer and the differing accounts that comprise his or her cultural experience. Because it extends from history, it becomes subject to interpretations that may reflect discontinuity rather than the seamless merger with a real and knowable past.

One can see this contest enacted repeatedly when Holocaust memorials are constructed in key sites such as the one currently under development in Berlin in view of the old Reichstag. These global events provide insight into museum designers' attempts to render these atrocities meaningful by using them as moral warrants (Hasian, 2004). Museums and memorials possess cultural authority because these sites frame the accepted version of history for a particular society and then, sometimes quite literally, set such accounts in stone (see, for example, Blair, Jeppeson, & Pucci, 1991; Carlson & Hocking, 1988; Ehrenhaus, 1988; Foss, 1986).

These sites have spawned a subset of analyses that examine the way in which particular media such as visual, audio, and digital technology enhance and shape the rhetorical experience of trauma (Cohen & Willis, 2004; Jorgensen-Earp & Lanzilotti, 1998; Reading, 2003; Zelizer, 1998). Notably, they encode the material experience of the traumatized subject into the dominant culture—a culture that may itself be monitoring its own guilt in conducting this violence. These memorials, along with heritage museums, create the grounds upon which the dialogic tensions between competing groups can be accentuated rather than obfuscated through complex, performative interactions (Armada, 1998; Katriel, 1993, 1994). Temporality factors into these performances. Prosise (2003) discussed the concept of liminality, which suggests that these sites must often resolve the events of a gruesome and violent past with visions of progress into a brighter and more humane future. Holocaust museums, for example, deal with events that can be repeated, but they must also pose warnings in a way that does not paralyze their audiences with fear.

Rhetorical scholars can also bring insight into initial phases of design for memorials and exhibits, particularly when stakeholders contest these performances. Taylor (1998) provided an excellent example of dialogues failing with the 1995 exhibition of the *Enola Gay* in the Smithsonian, where original displays included visual depictions of the bomb's aftereffects. In cultural sites associated with the perpetration of mass violence, such as the Holocaust in Berlin, the atomic bombing in Washington, DC, or the rape of Nanjing in Tokyo, the struggle for the traumatized subject to be heard produces a counter-dynamic of containment to prevent it from disrupting the collective history upon which the culture bases its own moral authority (Hubbard & Hassian, 1998; Linenthal & Englehardt, 1996; Prosise, 1998).

In the case of the *Enola Gay* exhibit, historians and politicians found themselves at a deadlock about representing the trauma, especially given the tendency to vilify the Japanese universally for their role during World War II. Here the original script, which contained some focus on the effects of the bomb on the civilian population, was essentially scrapped for a more limited version. In an analysis of another exhibit that depicted the experiences of Japanese civilians who were placed in concentration camps in America, Yoo (1996) argued that these accounts brought a sense of balance to a culture rather than viewing them in terms of contest. However, because it exists with an aura of permanence, dialogue frequently degenerates into political contest.

Pornography of Grief   One of the primary critiques of modern journalism stems from the way that reporters sometimes turn violent events into a type of visual fetish (see related argument by Moeller, 1999). When reporters cover a tragedy such as a school shooting, how many interviews with the families of the victims are necessary to convey the story and when does that coverage become morbid speculation (Berrington & Jemphrey, 2003)? Brown (1987) referred to this type of voyeurism as the "pornography of grief" (p. 75), a process whereby reporters exploit traumatized individuals by turning their pain into a form of exhibition. Given the media's reliance upon spectacle to capture the gaze of the viewer, trauma can be contextualized as entertainment that excites or stimulates an otherwise apathetic public.

These same concerns also emerge in the production of history and its narration at cultural sites such as museums and memorials. Rather than healing, these attempts to fuse the wounds of the past can also function to reopen political conflict, particularly in cases where the victims of trauma view the memorial process as politically unfair or exhibitionist (Taylor, 2003). When the museum becomes a pornographic site for the perverse exhibition of pain and mutilation, the traumatized subject may challenge the very nature and wisdom of the exhibition itself.

Through violent spectacles, the public can constitute itself as an entity that witnesses the event but is not really affected by it. Warner (1993) asserted that "transitive pleasure of witnessing/injuring makes available our translation into the disembodied publicity of the mass subject. By injuring a mass body—preferably a really massive body, somewhere—we constitute ourselves as a corporeal mass subject" (p. 250). From this standpoint, displaying the violated bodies may not necessarily serve the function of fusing the fragmented subject. In fact, the damaged body can become a perverse form of unifying desire. Instead, the wounding depicted in these representations may serve more to foster a sense of pleasure and bonding as those individuals who consume these violent images do so without incorporating them into their cultural epistemology or experiencing any type of connection with those subjected to violence.

One of the most disturbing examples of this dynamic can be seen in Rapaport's (2003) analysis of the pornographic portrayal of the Holocaust, *Ilsa, She-Wolf of the SS*. While the film suggests that it constitutes a historical warning about the trauma experienced in the camps, it simply uses the brutal depictions of torture to reaffirm some of the most banal aspects of sadomasochistic culture. According to Rapaport, in these Nazi-exploitation films, the horror of medical experimentation and torture is transformed into the substance of erotic sadism. The traumatic experience is rendered legible through a framework that ultimately colonizes these experiences through a more familiar cultural code—in this case, pornography. As such, misrecognition can result in the loss of memory as well as the inscription of these experiences through a way of looking at the wounded body that turns it into a spectacle rather than an object of sympathy.

Despite the threat that visual spectacle plays in distancing viewers from the event, can one experience the truth of six million people dying in concentration camps without seeing the visual evidence of the bodies stacked in box cars—evidence that was repressed for a decade after World War II? Baer (2002) suggested that photography makes the event real to the audience. The paradox of the visual simultaneously presences the suffering of others while also providing a barrier through which the looking subject can experience the wounding from a safe distance.

Hariman and Lucaites (2003) explored how certain pieces of violent and revolting Vietnam War iconography function to perpetuate this cycle by subjecting the nation to the dynamics of shame through a variety of cultural contexts. In their analysis of the young girl running from the napalm, they wrote that "the photograph functions as a powerful emotional and inventional resource for animating moral deliberation and democratic dissent as it mediates the stranger relationality central to public engagement" (p. 35). As the young girl circulates through public culture, her image is, at once, recognizable at a human level and estranged from the western viewer because her ambient brutality collides with the national ethos. While the picture contains pornographic shock value, her presence in the public domain forces viewers to reassess the policies that they have consciously embraced. This exchange between the hypervisible (and those components of cultural trauma that this visibility either reveals or hides) becomes the key factor in understanding how the graphic representation of trauma must balance the line between the spectacle of shock and the goals of truth-telling in the public sphere.

The Aesthetics of Trauma

Gaps from trauma within our symbolic terrain extend beyond the relationship between the traumatized subject and the moment of wounding—the wound can itself be transcribed into the literary field and create a shift in consciousness by revising aesthetic dynamics. This section articulates these dynamics.

Literary Ambiguity   In his classic work on the Holocaust, Blanchot (1986) described trauma as unknowable, using the boundary between art and science to emphasize the limitations of history to understand intense pain or to capture the disjuncture that these types of events represent. Blanchot suggested that the attempt to grasp the Holocaust represents a failure in the traditional modes of knowing—cultural, scientific, or historical. As the open wound calls for ritual repetition and reenactment, these reenactments can function to obfuscate rather than know the event. Hartman (1995) noted that this symbolic violence can be marked by the punctures left in the aesthetic terrain of a given culture as individuals strive to imagine the event now lost to history. When events (such as war, military defeat, or genocide) plague a particular culture, the symbolic damage left fosters alienation and psychological congestion.

The suggestion that art may have an epistemic function in these contexts has not gone unnoticed in ethnographic work within traumatized societies. In a discussion of the complementary roles that conventional healthcare and artistic performance play in dealing with the effects of violence at a national level, Weine (1996) observed, within the field of aesthetics:

> As opposed to the work of health care professionals or journalists or
> social scientists who construct objective documentation of traumatic
> events, creative artists seek to produce art that will provide a compelling
> experience that communicates a highly complex and nuanced form of
> knowledge. (p. 168)

Because the event cannot be grasped using traditional vocabularies,
aesthetics emerge as an alternative mode of expression that attempts
to capture the traumatic event as a human experience (see earlier
discussion of public memorials and museums).

In a work that predates Blanchot's observations about the unknowable nature of atrocity, Alain Resnais produced one of the first
documentaries dealing with the Holocaust, entitled *Night and Fog*
(1955)—a film that uses the languid repetition of the death camps
combined with allied file footage to create more of a montage than a
narrative. Often this "unknowability" represents not so much a failure to apprehend the past fully, but rather an effort to employ this
aesthetic medium by prompting meditation upon the metaphysics
of representation itself. Borrowing heavily from the literary style of
Margurite Duras, Resnais attempted to express the inexpressible by
creating an emotive or psychological effect (Crowley, 2000). Trauma
within novels or short stories usually takes the form of a fragmented
consciousness unable to reassemble itself (Whitehead, 2004). While
the American literary culture abounds with many examples of this
literary form, texts that grapple with the memories of violence are
most likely to deploy this style—particularly those linking personal
trauma to the wounds shared by the entire culture.

In *Ceremony*, Silko (1977) traced the formative events surrounding the life of a Native American World War II vet returning home
from the Pacific after being imprisoned by the Japanese and forced
to participate in the death of his brother in a POW camp. As he
descended into sickness and alcoholism, Silko sought to capture
the miasmal confusion that he experienced, writing in a disjointed
form of prose that jumps around sporadically in time and place.
This form of literary nausea (which also finds its roots in the work of
Duras) suggests that the opening of the wound comprises a process
that never ends—that it perpetuates itself throughout the life of the
individual and leaves him or her in multiple places at once (Crowley,
2000). This fragmentation thus inscribes itself within the field of literary aesthetics, leaving itself as a perpetual trace that both links and
disconnects the culture to and from its past.

Capturing traumatic moments through aesthetic formats has led some scholars to conclude that new literary genres respond to this impulse. For example, Gilmore (2001a) suggested that the recent surge in memoir writing demonstrates a systematic focus on the ego-response of individuals who find themselves in extraordinary circumstances. She explained that cultural critics must pay careful attention to the "coincidence of trauma and self-representation and what it reveals about the cultural and psychic work of autobiography, its internally fractured histories, and especially, its limits" (p. 129).

In many ways, the emergence of the therapeutic memoir may present certain problems for the articulation of trauma. In a cautionary note about the limits of these genres such as autobiography, Berlant (2001) observed that rendering traumatic events through an eloquent prose may, in fact, cause memories to lose their original meaning. This standpoint challenges the idea that trauma can be represented in a seamless, stylistically pleasing format. If the experience itself is jagged, ugly, and visceral, does a unified prose style betray these memories? In response to these ruptures and literary violence, stylistically open or ambiguous performances serve as responses to these events that do not constrain the author or designer in a traditional format—relying instead upon strategic ambiguity to open the field of interpretation to other voices.

Poetic Teleology   Within the narrative and poetic dynamics that inform most modern societies, political and cultural actors frequently arrange dynamics of space and time to articulate the boundaries of progress. According to Enlightenment ideology, individual subjectivity is coded along an event trajectory that leads eventually toward resolution or perfection—that history as a logical unfolding of events shapes what will become a desirable future (Tarral, 1998). The aesthetic dynamics of resolution shape the action and potential action that human actors may take when confronted with catastrophe by sowing their understanding of history with moral consciousness. Ruptures in the cultural consciousness lead to aesthetic action that informs our shared reality and the lexicons that we use to know these events.

The term *catastrophe* originally signified the resolution of a literary text—usually a transition for the worse as in the case of tragedy (see, for example, *The American Heritage Dictionary*, 2000). Terms such as catastrophe demonstrate the fluid relationship between the fields of aesthetics and knowledge, particularly the interpenetration between the two spheres through the field of symbolic rupture (Tansman, 2003). This *telos*, the endpoint toward which all literary action strives, emerges in cultural texts as markers that trace the aesthetic dynamics that subsequently inform cultural definitions of healing and progress.

While responses to Hurricane Katrina varied, the reemergence of the blues culture contributed to defining this natural disaster. Woods (2005) argued that this "indigenous knowledge system has been used repeatedly by multiple generations of working-class African Americans to organize communities of consciousness" (p. 1008). Yet, at the same time, the essential narrative that these songs elaborate posits the individual as one who is subject to the often overpowering caprice of nature.

While the stories told by blues performers rely heavily upon resignation, other narrative forms can inspire cultural transformations that enhance a culture's ability to move forward. One potential example of this research emerges in the work of Zerubavel (2002), who examined the mythic terrain of Israel in its post-Diaspora period. He asserted that the younger constituents of this culture resist early exile myths where Jewish identity is viewed as the product of a conservative, easily victimized individual (Galut) and instead embrace the "young and robust, daring and resourceful, direct and down to earth, honest and loyal, ideologically committed and ready to defend his people to the bitter end" (p. 116). These types of transitions are facilitated by one literary form being laid across another, creating ethical shifts in these vocabularies as old forms are repressed and new representations emerge. Such revisions in collective mythology may respond to shifting material conditions, providing new directions for managing the past that compel future actions by linking their mythic terrain with political necessity.

Given this elision between aesthetics and epistemology through history, it is not unfair to say that the rhetorical critic adopts the role of archaeologist, probing back through the stratified layers of discourse that compose the current cultural consciousness. One of the foundational literary forms that functions as a cornerstone of western literature, romanticism has roots in the expression of cultural trauma. Jenson (2001) noted that this aesthetic construct emerged as a vehicle for inscribing pain onto the existing mythopoetic frame in postrevolutionary France. By integrating human consciousness and action into a workable aesthetic teleology, romanticism can infuse fragmented or failing epistemologies with moral force. Grey (2002) argued that the complementary forces of realism and romanticism combine within the *hibakusha* (atomic bomb survivor) literature so that, rather than challenging the moral efficacy of atomic weapons, these texts deify nuclear technology as a legitimate force for creating social transformation.

Tracing the aesthetic dynamics of trauma within the literary field of a particular culture often reveals subtexts within symbolic activity that have their basis in historical action. Thus, narratives of atomic annihilation filter into and emerge through literature, science, and religion to create an ideal endpoint through which past and present intersect—managing the violence of symbolic ruptures by fusing them through both new and old aesthetic formats. When these authors code their personal experience with the blast and subsequent radiation sickness as moments of spiritual awakening, they create a progress narrative. From this standpoint, aesthetic teleologies drive the literary action of the text and subsequently influence the beliefs and patterns of thought that constitute cultural visions of the future.

Traumatic (In)Visibility and the Unconscious

In his work entitled *The Political Unconscious*, a treatise on the historical undercurrents that inform literary texts, Jameson (1981) situated the critic as one who excavates in order to understand the meanings and frameworks that inform these historical enactments. Once a traumatic event occurs, its rendering within the cultural consciousness may continue to impact the traumatized, yet they may remain essentially invisible (see Hartman, 1995). This section reviews some of the implications of post-Marxist and poststructual thought for the study of trauma and the ways in which concepts of the cultural unconscious—the sphere of absence and negation—frame our understanding of this phenomenon.

The Poststructural Detour In many ways, Blanchot's (1986) work foreshadows the emergence of poststructuralism as a paradigm for understanding the unknowable repetitions of signifiers as they lose their connection with the event through continual circulation. The assumption that events such as the Holocaust represent an end to history because they cannot be represented has drawn challenges from those scholars who grapple with this discourse. Mandel (2001) cautioned against the use of terms such as "unspeakable" because distancing "the Holocaust from contemporary culture eradicates our responsibility toward, and even our complicity with, what has been deemed beyond the range of human thought" (p. 206). Rothberg (2000) attempted to find a middle ground between these empirical and poststructural perspectives by suggesting that the antirealism of Blanchot can be supplemented with the recognition that certain epistemic vocabularies avoid rendering evil as either natural or banal. For poststructural thought, the focus upon that which is absent in the text leads the critic to view the text as an artificial veneer that only establishes its own presence via the negation of its opposite—in this case, an unwanted memory.

The tendency to render trauma as an absent (non)event even when visible is particularly powerful in American popular culture. For example, popular films (especially in the genre of war films) employ glossy Hollywood aesthetics to present stories in an appealing and consumable manner that reduces the amount of psychic disruption the events produce (Vickroy, 2002).

The film *Windtalkers* (Woo, 2002), a depiction of the Navajo code-talkers from World War II, depicts a series of highly traumatic experiences from the perspective of a GI who suffers from a severe head wound. These representations of trauma are ultimately circumvented and the trauma rendered (un)real by the glossy Hollywood battle scenes. Similar dynamics have been traced in the field of popular television. Lee (2003) examined the U.S. television show *Law and Order*, observing that "the true spectacle in this series, the principal story told, is not the characters' dramatic response to crime, but the absence of response—the absence of psychic commotion and unrest" (p. 83). Rather than deal directly with the trauma, shows feature episodic moments, each with its own sense of closure that ignores the damage done by the violence, essentially turning the trauma into an absent phantom.

Zelizer's (1998) research on the Holocaust traces the contours of presence and absence in the marketplace of visibility. She argued that the photograph directly impacts the representation of events such as the Holocaust in our collective memory by excising certain realities. If, for example, the primary photos used to depict this event focus primarily upon the liberation of the camps, this type of remembrance systematically forgets other aspects of this experience. While examining how both graphic and historical accounts of this event evolve over time, Zelizer noted that "subtle lexical changes—such as the transformation of Holocaust to holocaust and of genocide to genocidal—further flatten the term's original reference" (p. 197). This "flattening" fosters a situation where the event cannot be known, and it reduces the legitimacy of those who experienced the trauma by denying presence within the text.

Haunting, Absence, and/or Return   In his analysis of the war film *Saving Private Ryan*, Ehrenhaus (2001) argued that the text masks Holocaust memory by using a more romantic veneer that functioned to reaffirm American culture. Ehrenhaus pointed to "the indisputable recognition that these very foundations were found wanting, and more distressingly, were part of the landscape of memory upon which the Holocaust was carried out" (p. 334). This film drives the memory itself underground, becoming a repressed *other* that must return or surface in indirect ways to ensure that the nation's own eugenicist past remains submerged.

A brief exploration of a literary metaphor illustrates this dynamic. Gutierrez-Jones (2001) suggested that wounds left upon the body politic by events such as slavery divide the self between legitimate and illegitimate terrains. As noted in the last section, many artists attempt to capture this division in their work. For example, Toni Morrison frequently channels the trauma induced by racist violence through fictional phantoms and unseen spirits who become a meta-discourse on ethnic shame (Bouson, 2000). As much as her characters struggle to free themselves from the fetters of the past, these phantoms manifest themselves in the world as a material presence and pull the subject back into the past despite efforts to move forward. While the past remains invisible, its presence can be felt when these spirits erupt into the realm of consciousness to torment those who would forget them. Pursuing these ghosts requires a gestalt shift for critics because they are charged with probing language for unconscious traces rather than simply accepting the text at face value, a process that requires an enhanced sensitivity to the subterranean layers that these symbols often possess.

Given the prevalence of these issues throughout the cultural terrain, popular media such as film exhibit the ideologies used to manage these tensions and often provide suggestive snapshots for gauging the level of anxiety produced by these memories at a given moment (Griffin & Shaikat, 1995; Rasmussen & Downey, 1991). These analyses frequently focus upon the dynamics of repression to explain the ongoing trauma: As particular cultural forms are read through the larger culture, the disruptive event brings them back to that consciousness in explosively indirect ways. Gunn (2004) examined the World Trade Center attacks in just such a manner, arguing that they prompted a cultural panic that generated mass hallucinations as primitive iconography erupted from the unconscious into the visible world.

For the critics who attune themselves to these dynamics, the process of unpacking deflected reverberations that emerge through discourse mandates the use of an interpretive process that deploys historiography as a means to excavate the aesthetic sedimentation of the present. Frentz and Rushing (1993) offer some of the most vivid research in this area. They pursued how repressed cultural conflicts and wounds can resurface indirectly through cinematic narratives, requiring the critics to unmask the text to access the underlying trauma. As painful memories acquire symbolic form throughout the popular and political culture, various aesthetic conventions give license to those voices from the past that, for some reason, have been either temporarily silenced or whose message has been deflected through images and narratives that hide their original form.

In their work on *Jaws*, Frentz and Rushing (1993) detailed how the original wound has become a key factor in defining modern masculinity, that male identity stems from an essential trauma that can be resolved only by killing or repressing the feminine. While this symbolic violence provides an illusory transcendence or resolution of contending components, it comes at profound social cost. Extending this textual analysis outward, the dynamics of trauma are keenly illustrated in the reactionary men's movements of the 1990s. Fearful that feminism was symbolically castrating men by forcing them to adopt more emotional vocabularies, Bly (1990) created a mythical male archetype in *Iron John*, a man whose identity is linked to his childhood wounding. Therefore, Bly suggested that men's identity is linked to trauma, that violence and wounding are essential to the development of their gender identity. If one extends these observations, masculinity itself becomes a cover that hides trauma, casting men as repressed wounded subjects who function only when their pain is rendered invisible through a veneer of violence and rationality.

Hirsch (2002) asserted that, "for post-memorial artists, the challenge is to define an aesthetic based on a form of identification and projection that can include the transmission of the bodily memory of trauma without leading to the self-wounding and retraumatization that is rememory" (p. 77). Ripples related to trauma may circulate throughout a culture for decades via art, film, literature, music, and politics. These disruptions haunt a particular society, reemerging in texts that abruptly revise our understanding of the event as well as the language that we use to gain access to it. While these critics remain aware of the ways that unconscious dynamics are produced, they have yet to develop any consensus for creating a discourse that does not render some component of the traumatic experience invisible. Perhaps the concept of equilibrium—that one should maintain an open boundary between the spheres of visual legitimacy and the unconscious—might provide the basis for a new template for healing. As it is, critics must excavate these dynamics of (in)visibility that seem to be an inevitable by-product of the symbolic management of trauma. In these cases, trauma is personified as a repressed specter that haunts the consciousness of a culture and, while right in front of our eyes, is virtually unrecognizable.

Conclusion

Much like the Gordian knot referenced earlier, identifying and categorizing the workings of trauma lead one through multiple discursive fields as one idea or dynamic folds into the next. This journey wraps around itself, proceeds down seemingly linear pathways, and then doubles back on what suddenly becomes unfamiliar terrain. The preceding pages have attempted to move beyond simply outlining a discrete academic history of trauma as it pertains to the field of communication. Instead, this chapter provides a heuristic for articulating trauma using the theoretical nuances that animate our discipline. With attention on discursive processes that span the range of contexts from interpersonal and organizational dynamics to the rhetorical analysis of politics and culture, communication researchers can offer valuable perspectives on exploring and resolving these psychic tensions.

Trauma begins at the localized level, but it quickly expands to encompass an entire culture at every level. Its reverberations can be felt through intersubjective networks, as well as the mass-mediated forums that attempt to represent identity at the national and international levels. While we experience trauma personally, it can be interpreted only through symbolic networks. By recognizing trauma studies as a unique and legitimate domain within communication research, we embrace an opportunity to provide valuable insight into important cultural processes as well as to address highly relevant and complex questions spanning local and global contexts.

Because the psychological and physical experience of trauma is so profound, it can leave scars upon the symbolic terrain that are experienced on multiple levels. Whether the event is evoked again and again through language (or is systematically repressed or masked through indirect linguistic codes), it seems to necessitate symbolic response. In fact, one interesting question for future investigation might address why particular events seem to cause such powerful ruptures and others do not (Hume, 2000).

One lingering question involves the potential of trauma to break old linguistic codes or ethical frameworks and foster new ways of looking at the world. As individuals grapple with disease and personal violence in a world where global violence appears to be increasing, the marks that these bodily experiences leave upon both local networks and the larger culture must be excavated and known in order to provide discernable pathways through an increasingly complex and pathological world. These fissures in human consciousness force reconfigurations in the symbolic codes that provide our roadmap to future political action.

At its core, the experience of trauma has created a crisis in epistemology. Whether one proceeds from the psychoanalytic perspective that codes trauma as a neurotic experience or embraces Blanchot's (1986) rhetoric of the unspeakable where trauma represents an end to knowledge itself, these frameworks each suffer because they delegitimate the traumatized subject or render it illegible within the larger field of signs and representations. Scholars who focus upon the discursive nature of these definitions can create a new epistemological framework for grappling with these experiences.

The present heuristic suggests that the profound impact that traumatic histories continue to have upon their respective cultures necessitates some form of *praxis*, the application of theoretical insight into the social realm where political action is determined. This revision in the epistemology of trauma moves us away from crippling metaphysical discussions while at the same time acknowledging that traditional knowledge codes such as psychology offer limited insights. Through interpersonal, institutional, health, political, intercultural, environmental, and mass-mediated contexts (among others) that animate the discipline of communication, trauma emerges as a powerful and consequential phenomenon that can be articulated and managed through flexible frameworks. To follow the traumatized subject through its linguistic pathways, one must sustain attention to the lexical nuance present in the theoretical systems used to describe it.

Acknowledgments

The author would like to thank the editor and reviewers for their thoughtful commentary and guidance. She would also like to acknowledge the sacrifice and courage of the people of the Gulf Coast and the City of New Orleans as they heal their wounds and martial their resources for an uncertain future.

References

Acheson, K. (2007). Silence in dispute. In C. S. Beck (Ed.), *Communication yearbook 31* (pp. 1–59). New York, NY: Lawrence Erlbaum Associates.

Acton, C. (2004). Diverting the gaze: The unseen text in women's war writing. *College Literature, 31,* 53–79.

Agelarakis, A. (2006). Artful surgery. *Archeology, 59,* 18–23.

Ainslie, R., & Brabeck K. (2003). Race murder and community trauma: Psychoanalysis and ethnography in exploring the impact of the killing of James Byrd in Jasper, Texas. *Journal for the Psychoanalysis of Culture and Society, 8,* 42–50.

Alexander, J., Eyerman, R., Giesen, B., Smelser, N., & Sztompka, P. (2004). *Cultural trauma and collective identity.* Berkeley: University of California Press.

American Heritage Dictionary of the English Language (4th ed.). (2000). Catastrophe. Retrieved November 8, 2006, from www.bartleby.com/61/

Anderson, L. (2006, October 3). "Horrific" attack kills Amish girls: Gunman shoots 11 at school, commits suicide. *Chicago Tribune.* Retrieved November 6, 2006, from http://www.chicagotribune.com/news/nationworld// chi-0610030152oct03,1,807069.story?coll=chi-newsnationworld-hed

Armada, B. J. (1998). Memorial agon: An interpretive tour of the National Civil Rights Museum. *Southern Communication Journal, 63,* 235–243.

Baer, U. (2002). *Spectral evidence: The photography of trauma.* Cambridge, MA: MIT Press.

Balakian, P. (2003). *The burning Tigris: The Armenian genocide and the American response*. New York: Perennial.

Beck, C. (2005). Personal stories and public activism: The implications of Michael J. Fox's public health narrative for policy and perspectives. In E. B. Ray (Ed.), *Case studies in health communication* (pp. 335–346). Mahwah, NJ: Lawrence Erlbaum Associates.

Belau, L. (2001). Trauma and the material signifier. *Postmodern Culture, 11*, 1–40.

Berlant, L. (2001). Trauma and ineloquence. *Cultural Values, 5*, 41–58.

Berman, L. (2000). Surviving on the streets of Java: Homeless children's narratives of violence. *Discourse and Society, 11*, 149–171.

Berrington, E., & Jemphrey, A. (2003). Pressures on the press: Reflections on reporting tragedy. *Journalism, 4*, 225–248.

Blair, C., Jeppeson, M. S., & Pucci, E. (1991). Public memorializing postmodernity: The Vietnam Veterans Memorial as prototype. *Quarterly Journal of Speech, 77*, 263–288.

Blanchot, M. (1986). *The writing of the disaster* (A. Smock, Trans.). Lincoln: University of Nebraska Press.

Bly, R. (1990). *Iron John: A book about men*. New York: Addison–Wesley.

Bouson, J. (2000). *Quiet as it's kept: Shame, trauma, and race in the novels of Toni Morrison*. Albany: State University of New York Press.

Braithwaite, C. A. (1997). Were YOU there? A ritual of legitimacy among Vietnam veterans. *Western Journal of Communication, 61*, 423–447.

Breitweiser, K. (2006). *Wake-up call: The political education of a 9/11 widow*. New York: Warner Books.

Brown, J. E. (1987). News photography and the pornography of grief. *Journal of Mass Media Ethics, 2*, 75–81.

Brown, W. J., Basil, M. D., & Bocarnea, M. C. (2003). Social influence of an international celebrity: Responses to the death of Princess Diana. *Journal of Communication, 53*, 587–605.

Bucy, E. P. (2003). Emotion, presidential communication, and traumatic news: Processing the World Trade Center attacks. *Harvard International Review of Press and Politics, 8*, 76–96.

Burke, B. (2001). Anatolian origins of the Gordian knot legend. *Greek, Roman, and Byzantine Studies, 42*, 255–263.

Carabas, T., & Harter, L. (2005). State-induced illness and forbidden stories: The role of storytelling in healing individual and social traumas in Romania. In L. Harter, P. Japp, & C. Beck (Eds.), *Narratives, health, and healing*. Mahwah, NJ: Lawrence Erlbaum Associates.

Carawan, G., & Carawan, C. (Eds.). (1990). *Sing for freedom: The story of the civil rights movement through its songs*. Bethlehem, PA: Sing Out Publications.

Carlson, A. C., & Hocking, J. E. (1988). Strategies of redemption at the Vietnam Veterans Memorial. *Western Journal of Speech Communication, 52,* 203–215.

Carrington, P., Collins, J., Gerbasi, C., Haynes, A., & Charles, E. (2006). *Love you, mean it: A true story of love, loss, and friendship.* New York: Hyperion.

Caruth, C. (1995). Trauma and experience: An introduction. In C. Caruth (Ed.), *Trauma: Explorations in memory* (pp. 3–11). Baltimore: Johns Hopkins University Press.

Caruth, C. (1996). *Unclaimed experience: Trauma, narrative and history.* Baltimore, MD: Johns Hopkins University Press.

Caruth, C. (2001). An interview with Jean Laplanche. *Postmodern Culture, 11,* 1–21.

Chaitin, J. (2002). Issues and interpersonal values among three generations in families of Holocaust survivors. *Journal of Social and Personal Relationships, 19,* 379–402.

Clark, M. (2005). Resisting attrition in stories of trauma. *Narrative, 13,* 294–298.

Coates, L., & Wade, A. (2004). Telling it like it isn't: Obscuring perpetrator responsibility for violent crime. *Discourse and Society, 15,* 499–526.

Cohen, E. L., & Willis, C. (2004). One nation under radio: Digital and public memory after September 11. *New Media and Society, 6,* 591–610.

Colley, L. (2005). Imperial trauma: The powerlessness of the powerful. *Common Knowledge, 11,* 198–214.

Coulter, A. (2006). *Godless: The church of liberalism.* New York: Crown Forum.

Crowley, M. (2000). *Duras, writing and the ethical: Making the ethical whole.* Oxford, England: Clarendon.

Cvetkovich, A. (2003). *An archive of feelings: Trauma, sexuality and lesbian public cultures.* Durham, NC: Duke University Press.

Dewan, S., & Hamill, S. D. (2006, October 5). Survivors struggle to come to terms with killing of 5 Amish girls. *New York Times,* p. A20.

Du Bois, W. E. B. (1903). *The souls of Black folk.* New York: McClurg & Company.

Dutta-Bergman, M. J. (2004). Interpersonal communication after 9/11 via telephone and Internet: A theory of channel complementarity. *New Media and Society, 6,* 659–673.

Ehrenhaus, P. (1988). Silence and symbolic expression. *Communication Monographs, 55,* 41–57.

Ehrenhaus, P. (2001). Why we fought: Holocaust memory in Spielberg's *Saving Private Ryan. Critical Studies in Media Communication, 18,* 321–337.

Englehardt, K. J., Sallot, L. M., & Springston, J. K. (2004). Compassion without blame: Testing the accident decision flow chart with the crash of Valujet Flight 592. *Journal of Public Relations Research, 16,* 127–156.

Eyal, G. (2004). Identity and trauma: Two forms of the will to memory. *History and Memory, 16,* 5–36.

Eyerman, R. (2001). *Cultural trauma: Slavery and the formation of African American identity.* Cambridge, England: Cambridge University Press.

Farrell, K. (1998). *Post-traumatic culture: Injury and interpretation in the nineties.* Baltimore: Johns Hopkins University Press.

Feldman, A. (2004). Memory theaters, virtual witnessing, and the trauma-aesthetic. *Biography, 27,* 163–202.

Foss, K. A., & Domenici, K. L. (2001). Haunting Argentina: Synecdoche in the protests of the mothers of the Plaza de Mayo. *Quarterly Journal of Speech, 87,* 237–258.

Foss, S. (1986). Ambiguity as persuasion: The Vietnam Veterans Memorial. *Communication Quarterly, 34,* 326–340.

Foucault, M. (1965). *Madness and civilization: A history of insanity in the age of reason.* New York: Random House.

Frank, A. W. (1995). *The wounded storyteller: Body, illness, and ethics.* Chicago: University of Chicago.

Frank, D. A., & McPhail, M. L. (2005). Barack Obama's address to the 2004 Democratic National Convention: Trauma, compromise, consilience, and the (im)possibility of racial reconciliation. *Rhetoric and Public Affairs, 8,* 571–593.

Frank, J. (2003). Bearing proxy-witness. *Biography, 25,* 58–72.

Frentz, T. S., & Rushing, J. H. (1993). Integrating ideology and archetype in rhetorical criticism: A case study of *Jaws. Quarterly Journal of Speech, 79,* 61–81.

Gallagher, M. (2006, November 4). Project daffodils: Alexander students, staff send flowers to Pennsylvania Amish. *Athens Messenger,* A1, A5.

Gilmore, L. (2001a). Limit cases: Trauma, self-representation, and the jurisdictions of identity. *Biography, 24,* 128–139.

Gilmore, L. (2001b). *The limits of autobiography: Trauma and testimony.* Ithaca, NY: Cornell University Press.

Greenberg, J. (Ed.). (2003). *Trauma at home: After 9/11.* Lincoln: University of Nebraska Press.

Greene, K., Frey, L. R., & Derlega, V. J. (2002). Interpersonalizing AIDS: Attending to the personal and social relationships of individuals living with HIV and/or AIDS. *Journal of Social and Personal Relationships, 19,* 5–17.

Grey, S. H. (2002). Writing redemption: Trauma and the authentication of the moral order in the *hibakusha* literature. *Text and Performance Quarterly, 22,* 1–23.

Griffin, R. J., & Shaikat, S. (1995). Causal communication: Movie portrayals and audience attributions for Vietnam Veterans' problems. *Journalism and Mass Communication Quarterly, 72,* 511–524.

Gunn, J. (2004). The rhetoric of exorcism: George W. Bush and the return of political demonology. *Western Journal of Communication, 68,* 1–23.

Gutierrez-Jones, C. (2001). *Critical race narratives: A study of race, rhetoric, and injury.* New York: New York University Press.

Haridakis, P. M., & Rubin, A. M. (2005). Third-person effects in the aftermath of terrorism. *Communication and Society, 8,* 39–59.

Hariman, R., & Lucaites, J. L. (2003). Public identity and collective memory in U.S. photography: The image of the accidental napalm. *Critical Studies in Media Communication, 20,* 35–66.

Harris, M. (1998). *Trauma, recovery, and empowerment: A clinician's guide for working with women in groups.* New York: Free Press.

Harter, L., Stephens, R., & Japp, P. (2000). President Clinton's apology for the Tuskegee syphilis experiment: A narrative of remembrance, redefinition, and reconciliation. *The Howard Journal of Communication, 11,* 19–34.

Hartman, G. (1995). On traumatic knowledge and literary studies. *New Literary History, 26,* 537–563.

Hasian, M. (2004). Remembering and forgetting the final solution: A rhetorical pilgrimage through the U.S. Holocaust Memorial Museum. *Critical Studies in Media Communication, 21,* 64–92.

Hastings, D. (2006, October 7). Murder visits an Amish school house. *The Washington Post.* Retrieved November 6, 2006. from http://www.washingtonpost.com/wp-dyn/content/article/2006/10/070AR2006100700394.html

Hesford, W. (2004). Documenting violations: Rhetorical witnessing and the spectacle of distant suffering. *Biography, 27,* 104–144.

Higonnet, M. (2002). Authenticity and art in trauma narratives of World War I. *Modernism/Modernity, 9,* 91–107.

Hirsch, M. (2002). Marked by memory: Feminist reflections on trauma and transmission. In N. Miller & J. Tougaw (Eds.), *Extremities: Trauma, testimony, and community* (pp. 71–91). Urbana, IL: University of Chicago Press.

Homans, M. (2006). Adoption narratives, trauma, and origins. *Narrative, 14,* 4–26.

Howard, C., Tuffin, K., & Stephens, C. (2000). Unspeakable emotions: A discourse analysis of police talk about reactions to trauma. *Journal of Language and Social Psychology, 19,* 295–314.

Horvitz, D. (2000). *Literary trauma: Sadism, memory, and sexual violence in American women's fiction.* Albany: State University of New York Press.

Hubbard, B., & Hasian, M. (1998). Atomic memories of the *Enola Gay*: Strategies of remembrance at the National Air and Space Museum. *Rhetoric and Public Affairs, 1,* 363–385.

Hume, J. (2000). The forgotten 1918 influenza epidemic and the press portrayal of public anxiety. *Journalism and Mass Communication Quarterly, 77,* 898–915.

Illich, I. (1976). *Medical nemesis: The expropriation of health.* New York: Pantheon.

Jameson, F. (1981). *The political unconscious: Narrative as social symbolic act.* New York: Cornell University Press.

Jenson, D. (2001). *Trauma and its representations: The social life of mimesis in post-revolutionary France.* Baltimore, MD: Johns Hopkins University Press.

Jones, J. H. (1993). *Bad blood: The Tuskegee syphilis experiment.* New York: Free Press.

Jorgensen-Earp, C. R., & Lanzilotti, L. A. (1998). Public memory and private grief: The construction of shrines at the sites of public tragedy. *Quarterly Journal of Speech, 84,* 150–170.

Katriel, T. (1993). Our future is where our past is: Studying heritage museums as ideological performative arenas. *Communication Monographs, 60,* 69–75.

Katriel, T. (1994). Sites of memory: Discourses of the past in Israeli pioneering settlement museums. *Quarterly Journal of Speech, 80,* 1–20.

Kennerly, E. (1987). Mass media and mass murder: American coverage of the Holocaust. *Journal of Mass Media Ethics, 2,* 61–70.

Langellier, K. M. (2001). "You're marked": Breast cancer, tattoo, and the narrative performance of identity. In J. Brockmeier & D. Carbaugh (Eds.), *Narrative and identity: Studies in autobiography, self, and culture* (pp. 145–184). Amsterdam: John Benjamins.

Laplanche, J., & Pontalis, J. (1973). *The language of psychoanalysis* (D. Nicholson-Smith, Trans.). New York: Norton.

Laub, D. (2005). From speechlessness to narrative: The cases of Holocaust historians and of psychiatrically hospitalized survivors. *Literature and Medicine, 24,* 253–265.

Layton, L. (1995). Trauma, gender identity and sexuality: Discourses of fragmentation. *American Imago, 52,* 107–125.

Lee, S. (2003). These are our stories: Trauma, form, and the screen phenomenon of *Law and Order*. *Discourse, 25,* 81–97.

Lerner, P. (2003). *Hysterical men: War, psychiatry, and the politics of trauma in Germany, 1890–1930.* Ithaca, NY: Cornell University Press.

Levi, P. (1988). *The drowned and the saved* (R. Rosenthal, Trans.). New York: Summit.

Leys, R. (2000). *Trauma: A genealogy.* Chicago: University of Chicago Press.

Linenthal, E., & Englehardt, T. (Eds.). (1996). *History wars: The* Enola Gay *and other battles for the American past.* New York: Henry Holt.

Loffreda, B. (2000). *Losing Matt Shepard: Life and politics in the aftermath of anti-gay murder.* New York: Columbia University Press.

Mahoney, D. B. (2001). A normative construction of Gulf War syndrome. *Perspectives in Biology and Medicine, 44,* 575–584.

Mandel, N. (2001). Rethinking "After Auschwitz": Against a rhetoric of the unspeakable in Holocaust writing. *boundary 2, 28,* (2), 203–228.

McAdams, D. P., & Bowman, P. (2001). Narrating life's turning points: Redemption and contamination. In D. P. McAdams, R., Josselson, & A. Lieblich (Eds.), *Turns in the road: Narrative studies of lives in transition* (pp. 3–34). Washington, DC: American Psychological Association.

McMahon, R. J. (1999). Rationalizing defeat: The Vietnam War in American presidential discourse, 1975–1995. *Rhetoric and Public Affairs, 2,* 529–549.

Miller, N. (2003). Portraits of grief: Telling details and the testimony of trauma. *differences, 14,* 112–135.

Mister, S. M. (1986). Reagan's *Challenger* tribute: Combining generic constraints and situational demands. *Communication Studies, 37,* 158–165.

Moeller, S. (1999). *Compassion fatigue: How the media sell disease, famine, war and death.* New York: Routledge.

Moore, J., & Slater, W. (2003). *Bush's brain: How Karl Rove made George W. Bush presidential.* Hoboken, NJ: Wiley Sons.

Nelson, H. L. (2001). *Damaged identities, narrative repair.* Ithaca, NY: Cornell University Press.

Pennebaker, J. W., & Beall, S. K. (1986). Confronting a traumatic event: Toward an understanding of inhibition and disease. *Journal of Abnormal Psychology, 95,* 274–281.

Pennebaker, J. W., & O'Heeron, R. C. (1984). Confiding in others and illness rate among spouses of suicide and accidental-death victims. *Journal of Abnormal Psychology, 93,* 473–476.

Petronio, S. (2002). *Boundaries of privacy: Dialectics of discourse.* Albany: State University of New York Press.

Petronio, S. (2004). Road to developing communication privacy management theory: Narrative in progress, please stand by. *Journal of Family Communication, 4,* 193–208.

Petronio, S., Reeder, S., Hecht, M., & Ros-Mendoza, M. (1996). Disclosure of sexual abuse by children and adolescents. *Journal of Applied Communication Research, 24,* 181–199.

Place, N. (1992). Journalists and trauma: The need for counseling. *Australian Studies in Journalism, 1,* 113–158.

Planalp, S., Rutherford, D. K., & Honeycutt, J. M. (1988). Events that increase uncertainty in personal relationships II: Replication and extension. *Human Communication Research, 14,* 516–547.

Prosise, T. (1998). The collective memory of the atomic bombings misrecognized as objective history: The case of the public opposition to the National Air and Space Museum's atom bomb exhibit. *Western Journal of Communication, 62,* 316–347.

Prosise, T. (2003). Prejudiced, historical witness, and responsible: Collective memory and liminality in the Beit Hashoah Museum of Tolerance. *Communication Quarterly, 51,* 351–366.

Ragland-Sullivan, E. (2001). The psychical nature of trauma: Freud's Dora, the young homosexual woman, and the fort!da! paradigm. *Postmodern Culture, 11,* 1–32.

Ramadanovic, P. (2001). From haunting to trauma: Nietzsche's active forgetting and Blanchot's writing of the disaster. *Postmodern Culture, 11,* 1–63.

Rapaport, L. (2003). Holocaust pornography: Profaning the sacred in *Ilsa, She-Wolf of the SS. Shofar, 22,* 53–79.

Rasmussen, K., & Downey, S. D. (1991). Dialectical disorientation in Vietnam War films: Subversion of the mythology of war. *Quarterly Journal of Speech, 77,* 176–195.

Rauch, A. (1998). Post-traumatic hermeneutics: Melancholia in the wake of trauma. *Diacritics, 28,* 111–120.

Reading, A. (2003). Digital interactivity in public memory institutions: The uses of new technologies in Holocaust museums. *Media, Culture and Society, 25,* 67–85.

Resnais, A. (producer and director). (1955). *Night and fog* [motion picture]. Canada: Criterion Studies. [Review of the book *Love you, mean it: A true story*]. *Publishers Weekly, 253*(24), 40.

Rothberg, M. (2000). *Traumatic realism: The demands of Holocaust representation.* Minneapolis: University of Minnesota Press.

Sattler, D. N. (2002). *The September 11th attacks on America: Relationships among psychological distress, post-traumatic growth, and social support in New York.* Boulder, CO: National Hazard Center.

Scarry, E. (1985). *The body in pain: The making and unmaking of the world.* New York: Oxford.

Segall, K. (2005). Stories and song in Iraq and South Africa: From individual to collective mourning performances. *Comparative Studies of South Asia, African and the Middle East, 25,* 138–151.

Sharf, B. (1997). Out of the closet and into the legislature: The impact of communicating breast cancer narratives on health policy. *Health Affairs, 20,* 213–218.

Sharf, B., Friemuth, V. S., Greenspon, P., & Plotnick, C. (1993). Confronting cancer on *thirtysomething*: Audience response to health content on entertainment television. *Health Communication, 1,* 157–172.

Shay, J. (1994). *Achilles in Vietnam: Combat trauma and the undoing of character.* New York: Atheneum.

Shuman, A., & Bohmer, C. (2004). Representing trauma: Political asylum narrative. *Journal of American Folklore, 11,* 294–314.

Sicher, E. (2001). The future of the past: Countermemory and post-memory in contemporary American post-Holocaust narratives. *History and Memory, 12,* 56–91.

Silko, L. (1977). *Ceremony.* New York: Penguin.

Soloman, M. (1985). The rhetoric of dehumanization: An analysis of medical reports of the Tuskegee syphilis project. *Western Journal of Speech Communication, 49,* 233–247.

Steyn, M. E. (2004). Rehabilitating whiteness disgraced: Afrikaner white talk in post-apartheid South Africa. *Communication Quarterly, 52,* 143–169.

Sturken, M. (1992). *Tangled memories: The Vietnam War, the AIDS epidemic, and the politics of remembering.* Berkeley: University of California Press.

Tansman, A. (2003). Catastrophe, memory and narrative: Teaching Japanese and Jewish responses to twentieth century atrocity. *Discourse, 25,* 248–271.

Tarral, M. (1998). Heroic narratives of quest and discovery. *Configurations, 6,* 223–242.

Taylor, B. (1998). The bodies of August: Photographic realism and controversy at the National Air and Space Museum. *Rhetoric and Public Affairs, 1,* 331–361.

Taylor, B. (2003). Our bruised arms hung up as monuments: Hiroshima iconography in post-cold-war culture. *Critical Studies in Media Communication, 20,* 1–34.

Trujillo, N. (1993). Interpreting November 22: A critical ethnography of an assassination site. *Quarterly Journal of Speech, 79,* 447–466.

Vanderford, M. L., & Smith, D. H. (1996). *The silicone breast implant story: Communication and uncertainty.* Mahwah, NJ: Lawrence Erlbaum Associates.

Vansant, J. (2001). *Reclaiming Heimat: Trauma and mourning in memoirs by Jewish Austrian reémigrés.* Detroit, MI: Wayne State University Press.

Vickroy, L. (2002). *Trauma and survival in contemporary fiction.* Charlottesville: University of Virginia Press.

Warner, M. (1993). The mass public and the mass subject. In B. Robbins (Ed.), *The phantom public sphere* (pp. 234–256). Minneapolis: University of Minnesota Press.

Weine, S. (1996). The witnessing imagination: Social trauma, creative artists, and witnessing professionals. *Literature and Medicine, 15,* 167–182.

Whitehead, A. (2004). *Trauma fiction.* Edinburgh, Scotland: Edinburgh University Press.

Woo, J. (Producer/director). (2002). *Windtalkers* [Motion picture]. United States: MGM.

Woods, C. (2005). Do you know what it means to miss New Orleans? Katrina, trap economics, and the rebirth of the blues. *American Quarterly, 57,* 1005–1018.

Yoo, D. (1996). Captivating memories: Museology, concentration camps, and Japanese American history. *American Quarterly, 48,* 680–699.

Young, N. (2007). Identity trans/formations. In C. S. Beck (Ed.), *Communication yearbook 31* (pp. 223–272). New York, NY: Lawrence Erlbaum Associates.

Zavestoski, S., Brown, P., McCormick, S., Mayer, B., D'Ottavi, M., & Lucove, J. (2004). Patient activism and the struggle for diagnosis: Gulf War illnesses and other medically unexplained physical symptoms in the U.S. *Social Science & Medicine, 58,* 161–175.

Zelizer, B. (1998). *Remembering to forget: Holocaust memory through the camera's eye.* Chicago: University of Chicago Press.

Zerubavel, Y. (2002). The mythological Sabra and Jewish past: Trauma, memory, and contested identities. *Israel Studies, 7,* 115–144.

Zwarg, C. (2002). Du Bois on trauma psychoanalysis and the would-be black savant. *Cultural Critique, 51,* 1–39.

Chapter 5 Contents

5

Identity Trans/formations

Niki L. Young
Western Oregon University

The tension between identification and separation, the opposing functions of identity, profoundly influences the ways that scholars understand and study identity. Identities can be shared or disputed, accepted or rejected, hidden or transformed. In this review, I discuss theories of identity in communication studies, examining identity as cultural text, impression management, cultural enactment, language acts, and boundary management. I offer an approach to communicating identity that spans disciplinary boundaries, focusing on the processes of identity transformation and trans/formations and illuminating the ways that individuals and groups confer and resist identities.

This topic is of great interest to scholars throughout the field; yet, because of the vastness of the literature, establishing inter- and transdisciplinary dialogue about identity is fraught with difficulty. I conclude the chapter with an analysis of our research and identify areas in need of additional investigation. As such, this chapter provides a framework for developing a meaningful framework for studying identity.

Life is given texture by countless acts of recognition.
From everyday interactions to the far-reaching deliberations
of legislatures and courts, people are constantly asking
the interconnected questions:
Who are you? Who am I? Who are we?
Patchen Markell

The questions of recognition, isolation, connection, identity, community, diaspora, and displacement resonate strongly in our mobile and often fragmented world. These questions achieved particular importance following Hurricane Katrina. In the aftermath of the storm, neighborhoods vanished, and residents scattered. Victims of this natural disaster lost not only their homes but also important parts of their identity. The story of Keith Calhoun and his wife Chandra McCormick serves as a poignant reminder of complex answers to these questions. Calhoun and McCormick, "both photographers who grew up in the mostly African-American Lower Ninth Ward," dedicated themselves to documenting and preserving the "small-town way of life in black Louisiana" (Sontag, 2006, p. B1). Sontag described them as keepers of the culture:

> compiling a historical record as they took pictures of the pleasure clubs, the prisoners, the dockworkers, the bluesmen, the river baptisms, the sugar cane fields, the voodoo priestesses, the Mardi Gras Indians, and so on … But they did not expect their living history of the Lower Ninth Ward to become actual history in their lifetime. And they did not prepare for disaster … And so, when the hurricane destroyed their house at the corner of Chartres and Flood streets, they lost two-thirds of their life's work. (p. B8)

Displaced by the flood, the two photographers have "shifted their focus for the moment to Mexican day laborers in Texas" (Sontag, p. B8), where they currently reside in a mostly White suburb of Houston. Some of their photos survived, and the couple recently exhibited several in a gallery in Manhattan, hoping that the project will be a catalyst for the redevelopment of the neighborhood. Calhoun wonders, however, if the Lower Ninth will reclaim its identity and if the spirit of the neighborhood will ever return.

While the floodwaters have receded and much debris has been cleared, entire neighborhoods in New Orleans remain empty. Similar to the losses of those suffering across the globe due to earthquakes, tsunamis, floods, drought, and disease, the magnitude of the losses incurred by victims of Hurricane Katrina is enormous. Photographers Calhoun and McCormick still maintain their professional identities but no longer possess their connection to place and community. The poignant revelations of their loss are also a rhetorical exigence (Bitzer, 1968) that others hope will catalyze redevelopment.

The issue of identity pervades contemporary life and scholarly discussions. Identity "has become a key word; there are conferences, lectures, books and articles on every aspect of identity that one can think of" (Sarup & Raja, 1998, p. 1). Philosophers (Gutmann, 2003; Taylor, 1989), psychologists (Wetherell, 1996), social psychologists (Côté & Levine, 2002), sociologists (Hewitt, 1989), political scientists (Markell, 2003), educators (Chickering & Reisser, 1993; Gutmann, 1987), and lawyers (Friedman, 1999) have all written about identity. Gutmann (2003) asserted that "[l]iving the life of a free person means being free to express one's identity" (p. 200). Educators and researchers need to be aware of the multiple identities that we will encounter in our increasingly global communities. Educators as well as researchers observing and reporting in the field have ethical obligations to be truthful and treat identity respectfully. According to Lindquist (2001), "When people learn they take on a new identity" (p. 267). Identity holds special significance for communication scholars because communication is both constituent and reflective of identity, the means by which we express and understand identity.

This review of the literature on identity within the discipline indicates that identities are expressed, negotiated, formed, and defined through discourse. Notably, identities change and transform as individuals progress through their life spans and encounter varying circumstances, jobs, living situations, etc. Indeed, Gergen (1991) described the complexities of enacting self in the postmodern era, characterizing identities as fragmented and fluid (rather than singular and static) (see also Rayner, 2006). Like a chameleon changing colors to blend into the background, individual identities change and morph in response to the context.

Communication in health care settings, for example, abides by certain constraints not present in other settings. Public and private identities may differ. Representations of identity in performance and the media can act like mirrors in a carnival fun house, exaggerating some qualities while minimizing others. Some identity representations are culturally taboo to some while, at the same time, affirming to others. The recent violence in Denmark over cartoon depictions of the prophet Muhammad provides an important reminder that individuals interpret actions differently in various locales around the world as varied people identify (or not) with images and, in so doing, assert their own identities as members of particular cultures. Given such complexities (and corresponding potential for relational, health, social, and political challenges), identity constitutes an important consideration for communication scholars.

In this chapter, I clarify key terms and underscore the importance of related work on identification and division. Building on that discussion, I situate identity as a communicative accomplishment and review identity research across the communication discipline.[1] By teasing out the tensions between modernist and postmodernist perspectives on identity, I offer an approach to communicating identity that spans disciplinary boundaries, focusing on the processes of identity transformation and trans/formations and illuminating the ways that individuals confer and resist identities. Developing a communication-centered approach to studying identity is vital because the complexity of identity and its relationship to communication create a wealth of possibilities for scholarly research. The immense quantity of identity literature creates challenges and opportunities for future researchers. In the conclusion, I reflect on what we have learned about identity and suggest areas that would benefit from additional research.

Identity, Identification, and Separation

Identity makes us unique and distinct, reflecting our "oneness," and connects and binds us, reflecting our "sameness." The tensions between identification and separation, the two opposing functions of identity, profoundly influence the way scholars study and understand identity. Kenneth Burke (1960) acknowledged this tension in his "Dialectician's Prayer":

> And may we have neither the mania of the One
> Nor the delirium of the Many—
> But both the Union and the Diversity. (p. 283)

Identification, also called *consubstantiation* (Burke, 1962, 1966, 1969a, 1969b), can be ideological, demographic, empathic, and phenomenological (Byker & Anderson, 1975; Woodward, 2003).[2] According to Woodward, it comprises "a rhetorical form of superconductivity" (p. x) that connects individuals. Identification can create a shared identity, connoting belonging and creating community. The Latin root *com* in community means "jointly or entirely" (A. Morehead & L. Morehead, 1995, p. 141; see related arguments by underwood and Frey, this volume).

Identity and identification are closely related. As Woodward (2003) observed, the threshold that divides identification from identity is thin and illusive. Sweet's (2005) analysis of Goth culture provides an interesting example of the ways in which identity and identification intersect. According to Sweet, asserting identity constitutes a way of celebrating individuality that simultaneously facilitates the possibility of group identity. In the Goth subculture, individuals attempt to set themselves apart from others through their distinctive choices regarding appearance (asserting individual identity), yet the markers of difference that they embrace also indicate similarity, a means of finding others with similar ideologies. Their distinctive choices of markers of difference function like uniforms, creating an affective identity based on shared preferences. The rules of dress and behavior that encompass belonging to a group are norms (Hogg & Reid, 2006).

These markers of difference that assert Goth identity enable members to establish connections and form a shared identity through identification. Creating shared identity through identification is important for social action. Rhetorical advocacy in social movements, argued Stewart (1999), involves a search for a new identity. According to Stewart, "Group identity provide[s] movement members with a critical sense of unity, togetherness, solidarity and community" (p. 94).

Smith (1994) and Marshall (1997) elaborated on different types of identification established cinematically. Smith described the different levels of engagement that audiences can experience with characters: recognition, alignment, and allegiance. Marshall's scheme includes *associative identification*, based on the initial connection between audience and actor; *admiring identification*, analogous to referential power; *sympathetic identification*, which incorporates empathy and perspective-taking, and *cathartic identification*, a form of transference in which the audience achieves a sense of emancipation through their involvement with the character. The typologies proposed by Smith and Marshall provide scholars with a means of discussing the varying levels of strength of identification.

Separation, also called division by Burke (1950/1969b), prompts an individual identity based on difference. A complex process, separation isolates people from each other. When we organize our perceptions and categorize others, we engage in division. Categorizing often involves valuing (and devaluing) others utilizing hierarchy. Communication processes, argued Carbaugh (1996), "model not play, but competition and stratification" (p. 193). When we define others as being similar to or different from us and value that which is like us (and devalue that which is unlike us), we practice what Burke termed the *negative*.

Division sparks separate identity that connotes difference, creating distance, dissonance, and disunity. The Latin root *dis* in "distance" and "dissonance" means "separate, not joined" and "not, or negation in the active sense" (A. Morehead & L. Morehead, 1995, p. 199). Both defining others by their differences and failing to recognize difference can lead to negation. Tajfel and Turner's (1979) social identity theory described the process of social categorization that depersonalizes people. Thus, according to Hogg and Reid (2006), "We see them not as unique individuals but as embodiments of their group" (p. 10). Interpersonal negation, displayed in bullying (Pörhölä, Karhunen, & Rainivaara, 2006), can escalate. Prejudice and discrimination institutionalized in the American South and mirrored in the practice of apartheid in South Africa constitute two examples of escalation. The terrorizing of Black Americans by the Ku Klux Klan, the dehumanizing treatment of prisoners in the Abu Ghraib prison in Iraq, ethnic cleansing in Bosnia, the civil war in Rwanda between the Tutsi and Hutu, and the Holocaust exemplify troubling types of negation as well. Discrimination, alienation, deviance, dominance, anomie, and hegemony comprise binary processes that allocate power and status to one while taking power away from the other.

The thread that connects identity, identification, and separation is power. Questions of dominance and power reflect the scholarship of postmodern philosophers such as Michel Foucault (1969/1972); modern scholars such as Kenneth Burke (1962, 1966, 1969a, 1969b) have focused on the processes of identification and division expressed through colonialism, racism, and efforts to resist hegemony. Thus, negotiation and expression of (and resistance to) identity comprise central issues for communication scholars.

Theoretical Orientations to Identity

Theoretical explanations of identity range from static (modernist) to fluid (postmodern) and from cognitive to interactional accomplishments. For example, Orbe and Harris (2001) observed that the predominant approaches to studying identity in communication studies come from psychology (i.e., Erikson, 1963) or social psychology (Mead, 1934). These approaches emphasize personal and relational identity. Henri Tajfel's social identity theory offers another perspective (Tajfel & Turner, 1979). According to Callero (2006, p. 4417), "For Tajfel the key to understanding prejudice, discrimination and intergroup conflict is found in an individual's social identity as defined by group membership." Social identity refers to the individual's understanding of group membership. Individual commitment to the group positively correlates with positive bias toward the group or in-group favoritism. Scholars investigating identity from these perspectives tend to employ empirical social scientific research methods.

In 1993, Hecht outlined a communication theory of identity that acknowledged that individuals perform and enact identities symbolically. Hecht discussed personal, relational, and shared/communal identities, and he noted several paradoxes with regard to identity— for example, identities are both enduring and changing.

Orbe and Harris (2001) researched interracial identity. Their comprehensive analysis included theories of interracial communication and a well-developed history of the construct of race. They addressed contemporary issues such as interracial romantic relationships and friendships as well as media representations of racial identities. Drawing from Collier's (1997) cultural identity theory, Orbe and Harris concluded that individuals negotiate and define identities, possess multiple identities, and form identities through discourse with others.

Eisenberg (2001) proffered a communication theory of identity in health communication. Building on Becker's (1997) analysis of mortality, Eisenberg's theory asserts the perspective that humans inherently live with uncertainty and make sense of their own mortality. He argued these sense-making activities are at the core of one's identity, encompassing biological, cultural, spiritual, interpersonal, and economic concerns.

A growing number of researchers explore identity from the perspective of anthropology (Geertz, 1973) and sociolinguistics (Hymes, 1974), utilizing ethnography. Philipsen (1975, 1976, 1987, 1989, 1992) was one of the first communication scholars to make use of ethnography and focus on situated identity. In "Speaking 'Like a Man' in Teamsterville," Philipsen (1975) encouraged scholars to examine communication as practice. Philipsen described culture as a "socially constructed and historically transmitted pattern of symbols, meanings, premises, and rules" (1992, pp. 7–8). Uncovering the meanings, premises, and rules embedded in our speech codes reveals the particular and culturally meaningful ways that humans communicate, for "wherever there is a distinctive culture, there is to be found a distinctive code of communicative conduct" (Philipsen, 1992, p. 125).

Dollar and Merrigan (2002) described ethnographic practices in group communication research, and they discussed ways in which ethnography of communication could inform scholarship. They noted that "[f]ocusing attention on context, form, and meaning" contributes to understanding such issues as "symbols and forms for communicating, rules and norms for communicating, and the relationship between communication and group identity" (p. 61).

Carbaugh developed a theory of situated identity to connect the social identities that people advance with the social interaction that shapes them (1988, 1991, 1993, 1995, 1996). He argued that "[e]very social scene involves agents in action" (1996, p. 3). Carbaugh examined the situated self and communication in a variety of settings or contexts, including the playful self at college basketball games, the working self making television, the marital self and naming, and the gendered self in television talk shows. He also acknowledged the tension between individual and shared identity, which arise from the tensions between the processes of identification and separation/division. In that book, Carbaugh contended:

> As individualized meanings are being voiced, the cultural forms and moral imperatives necessary for the creation of those meanings are silenced. Put differently, discursively coding the person in terms of dignity amplifies meanings of individual and self, while muting the common cultural features that make meaning possible. (1996, p. 136)

Côté and Levine (2002) asserted that the burgeoning interest in identity at least partially stems from the importance of individual choice and negotiation in identity formation. Notably, individual choice and agency influence (and get influenced by) our social interactions, and communication scholars remain keenly interested in questions of identity because identity emerges through (and becomes evident by) communicative practices. Reactions to identity impact social concerns, such as HIV/AIDS and poverty, as well as social behavior.

Identity Research Across the Communication Discipline

Theories of identity tell us that identity can be personal, relational, and/or shared and communal. Identity is socially constructed and communicated symbolically, via narrative, performance, and other rhetorical efforts by agents in action in specific situations or scenes. Notably, identities can be enacted and communicated in many different contexts. According to Hewitt (1989, p. 174), "Identity has community and culture as its guarantors, but it is inevitably the product of particular situations." Hewitt's observation acknowledges the underlying tension between identification (that which is shared) and separation (the unique and individual). Because it constitutes a core component of our interactions in a plethora of contexts, identity holds special significance for communication scholars.

Researchers across the communication discipline (such as political communication, cultural and critical studies, feminism, popular culture, media studies, health communication, interpersonal communication, intercultural communication, organizational communication, legal communication, and family communication) continue to explore important issues of identity. As I detail in the following sections, they explore identity from both modern and postmodern perspectives, examining identity as cultural texts and representations, impression management, cultural enactment, language acts, and boundary management.

Identity as Cultural Texts and Representations

Employing a postmodern perspective, identities can be read as cultural texts that embody ideologies. Holland (2006) examined how the body comes to matter in the rescue of Jessica Lynch. A hyperfeminine icon, the media depicted Lynch as a primary casualty of war, unable to perform effectively as a solider, whose ineptness is signified by her female body. According to Holland, the media cast her as a heroine with a tragic flaw (her femininity) who had to be rescued by her male protectors. Grindstaff and DeLuca (2004) considered representations of the corpus of Daniel Pearl, and they discussed the role of his body, an agent without agency, as a rhetorical resource. Pearl's body became a text that was forced to testify on behalf of Islamic fundamentalism. Notably, audiences differed in their reactions, illustrating their respective identifications with the mediated text. To Pakistani nationals, Pearl was the embodied voice of ideology; to Americans, Pearl emerged as a hero.

Questions of identity are central to representations that encompass issues of naming, definition, and interpretation—key concerns for researchers in critical and cultural studies, feminism, popular culture, media studies, and rhetorical and performance studies. When we name, define, and interpret actions and/or others, we inevitably invoke the processes of identification and separation. Parameswaran (2004) studied representations of feminine agency in narratives about Indian beauty queens. She found that the media represents the beauty queen as an emerging hero with whom audiences can identify and in whose story of success is embedded a hegemonic construction of class, gender, and nation. Western representations of gender, race, class, and cultural identity spread around the world through globalization. Darling-Wolf (2004) examined popular cultural texts and discussed ways that Japanese women negotiate Westernized representations of feminine beauty. Even as Japanese women critiqued Western influence, Darling-Wolf asserted that their own views of feminine beauty were clearly shaped by and conformed to Western global hegemony. Negotiating required the women to assert a unique individual Japanese identity while simultaneously recognizing and affirming (via identification) Western views of beauty.

Cloud (1996) analyzed the cultural production of Oprah Winfrey as an authentic hero. She identified a "rhetoric of tokenism" (p. 115) in Winfrey's biography, which authorizes a person from a marginalized or oppressed group to speak as a cultural hero. Hip-hop music's representations of African-American identity stem from autobiography (individual identity) and Black culture (shared identity established through identification). Hess (2005) analyzed the way in which White rap artists negotiate to establish a legitimate identity and confront a view of Whites as socially privileged and not credible. According to Hess, the rap artist Vanilla Ice tried to imitate Black rap identities and create a "social blackness" (p. 374) to establish credibility, but his creation of a false biography ultimately cost him. In contrast, the performer Eminem inverted Black narratives to capitalize on how his Whiteness hindered his acceptance as a rapper. Eminem utilized his identity as a minority to establish his credibility. According to K. H. Wilson (2003), the racial politics of imitation prevalent in the nineteenth century, in which some forms of imitation were deemed permissible for African Americans and some were not, still remains with us.

Representations also function as political imperatives. Morris and Sloop (2006) studied cultural representations of gay kissing. Kissing, they argued, comprises a performative act and involves a transformative combustion that has become a queer juggernaut. While representations of same sex kissing have increased in the U.S. mainstream media and the shock value of the gay kiss has decreased, many still view gay kissing as deviant sexual behavior. Morris and Sloop argued that gay kissing constitutes the final front in the battle for a queer world. A politics of visibility surrounds representations of gay identity. The current debate in the United States over legislative efforts to define marriage as existing only between a man and woman provides evidence that a clash of ideologies persists with regard to sexual identity.

Questions about sexual identity reverberate globally as well. Altman (1996) pondered the existence of a universal gay identity linked to modernity versus a more postmodern common consciousness of sexual identity based on homosexuality. Amid the increasing influence of globalization, Altman found that identities emerge differently in various parts of the world. Indeed, he argued that scholarly discussions of the experience of sexuality cannot be separated from the social and political contexts in which these individuals express (or repress) these identities.

Identity as Impression Management

The use of identity to strategically accomplish goals interests scholars from both the modern and postmodern traditions. Within the modern tradition, scholars have explored identity as impression management. Often synonymous with self-presentation, impression management comprises goal-directed behavior to influence others' perceptions of self. Erving Goffman (1959) utilized the imagery of the theatre to describe human interaction. To Goffman (1959, 1961, 1963, 1967, 1971, 1974), social life can be understood as a series of performances. His dramaturgy "focuses on the sense of individuality that persons acquire through interacting with others" (Brissett & Edgley, 1990, p. 14).

Communicating an image to a public audience is especially important in politics. Sigelman (2001) examined presentation of self in presidential life, focusing on the public (or shared) and private (or individual) personas of Lyndon B. Johnson and Richard Nixon. Backstage, both presidents asserted their respective individual identities, displaying traits considered unsuitable for a general audience; however, while onstage, they strived to create identification, presenting a "presidential" presence that communicated shared values. Public image is important not only on stage but also online. Verser and Wicks' (2006) analysis of the Gore and Bush Web sites in the 2000 election demonstrates the power of visual communication to exemplify positive impressions of the candidates, such as competency, motivation, and productivity (see also related arguments in this volume by Southwell and Yzer).

Face   Some scholars interested in impression management focus more narrowly on face. Goffman (1967) defined face as "an image of self delineated in terms of approved social attributes—albeit an image that others may share" (p. 5). Ting-Toomey's (1988) face negotiation theory follows Goffman's dramaturgical tradition, and it extends that perspective by considering identity or face management across cultures, connecting interpersonal and intercultural communication.

Face negotiation theory assumes that maintaining and negotiating face in communication situations occurs universally across cultures, consideration of face increases when uncertainty increases, and face and other expressions of culture can influence conflict styles in interpersonal and intergroup conflict (Hofstede, 1991; Hui & Triandis, 1986; Ting-Toomey & Kurogi, 1998; Triandis, 1995).

Identity and face needs merge in certain health communication encounters. In their study of patients' self-disclosure of HIV status to health care providers, Agne, Thompson, and Cusella (2000) concluded that patients' face needs relate to their satisfaction. The authors suggested that health care providers need to address patients' face needs. In this volume, Goldsmith, Miller, and Caughlin noted the implications of open communication for couples struggling to enact preferred fact amid a cancer diagnosis.

From a more psychological perspective, other scholars have described the implications of self-perception for constructing and enacting face. Self-construals comprise "the perceptions that individuals have about their thoughts, feelings and actions" (Hsu, 2002, p. 124) or their self-image (Oetzel, 1998). This research applies the cultural framework of independence and interdependence to self-perception, mediating "the influence of cultural individualism–collectivism on an individual's behavior" (Oetzel, p. 134). According to Hsu, research participants with independent self-construals viewed the self as a "unique, distinct, and autonomous entity" (p. 125); whereas, persons with interdependent self-construals sought to maintain harmony in relationships (see also Markus & Kitayama, 1991) and expressed more concern with promoting in-group goals (Singelis, 1994).

Research indicates that both dimensions of self, independent and interdependent, exist within each individual, regardless of cultural identity (Gudykunst et al., 1996; M. S. Kim et al., 1996; Singelis, 1994; Singelis & Brown, 1995), and self-construal appears to interact in complex ways with other aspects of cultural identity (M. S. Kim et al., 1996, 2000; M. S. Kim, Shin, & Cai, 1998; Park & Levine, 1999; Ting-Toomey, Oeztel, & Yee-Jung, 2001). Oetzel suggested self-construal serves as a better predictor of conflict styles than cultural-ethnic background.

Role Enactment   Face and facework influence both intercultural communication and interpersonal interaction in a variety of contexts. Goffman (1959) noted that individuals must be aware of and able to respond effectively to role expectations in different situations to manage their impressions effectively. The ways in which individuals conform to societal norms influence the degree to which others identify with them. Expectations as well as power differentials impact how we perceive others in educational and health care settings, as well as in private spheres such as the home.

Role expectations encumber many professional identities (for related arguments about organizational roles and expectations, see Ballard & Gossett, this volume, and Waldeck & Myers, this volume). Physicians assume different roles depending on the nature of the physician–patient encounter (John, 1996). According to John, in medical emergency encounters, physicians dominate and assert total control; in acute illness encounters, the physician assumes the role of guide, and, in chronic illness encounters, physicians become partners with patients. Tensions between professional identity and role expectations required nurses to negotiate issues of hierarchy and status, according to Apker, Propp, and Zabava Ford (2005). Educators also assume many roles (Hendrix, Jackson, & Warren, 2003). Instructional communication scholars have investigated the instructor role (see, for example, Chesebro & McCroskey, 2002; Cooper & Simonds, 2003).

Role expectations can also encumber relational roles. Foster (2005) explored the ways in which private/individual and public/cultural roles intersect in discourse about motherhood. Motherhood, she argued, simultaneously encompasses an aspect of individual identity, a relational identity, and a social institution endowed with cultural and political value. Contemporary discourses about motherhood implicate gender roles, social roles, and power (see, for example, Harter, Kirby, Edwards, & McClanahan, 2005, as well as Medved & Rawlins, 2006, for related arguments about stay-at-home fathers). Indeed, as Golden, Kirby, and Jorgenson (2006) observed, stakeholders across the globe continue to dispute and co-negotiate legitimate enactments of roles as parent and as employee.

Strategic Interactions   Impression management is a concern not only of individuals but also of larger entities, such as businesses and organizations, that seek to maintain a positive public image (see related review of research on organizational rhetoric by Meisenbach & McMillan, 2006). Persuasion underscores all impression management, even if unintentionally, encompassing both interpersonal and public communication.

J. D. Patterson and Allen (1997) examined accounts of stakeholders in an organizational communication framework in response to the strategic communication of environmental activist organizations. These researchers looked at how stakeholders perceived the legitimacy of various impression management strategies. They concluded that different audiences perceived legitimacy differently and that four components influence legitimacy: value consistency, truthfulness, sufficiency of explanations, and sustenance. When the impression management strategy matched audience members' values more closely, identification increased, and they perceived the strategy more positively.

Allen and Caillouet (1994) studied impression management strategies used by organizations in response to a crisis. They contended that crises threaten legitimacy and, in periods of crisis, corporate actors need to communicate multiple images. The researchers examined messages designed to gain audience approval and create identification. They developed a typology of strategies that included justification, ingratiation, denouncement, and distortions. Other research on identity management has focused on teacher communication activities that relate to student motivation (Kerssen-Griep, 2001) and teaching identity management with the drama *Death of a Salesman* (Zorn, 1991).

Relatedly, source credibility has long been of interest to scholars of persuasion (Stiff, 1994), and it intersects with this discussion of identity and strategic interactions. Identity can be used strategically to accomplish goals, mirroring Aristotle's (1954) conception of communication as concerned with persuasion. Logue and Miller (1995) characterized rhetorical status as identity communicators based on particular contexts that affect how we perceive ourselves and others.

Identity as Cultural Enactment

Incorporating a postmodern perspective, Fong and Chuang (2004) described cultural identity as simultaneously relational and contextual as well as ambiguous and fragmented. They argued that our cultural identities constantly evolve. As populations become increasingly diverse through the process of globalization, deepening our understanding of cultural identities assumes ever greater importance. Several anthologies offer ethnographic and autoethno-graphic portraits of various racial and ethnic identities that function as "thick descriptions" (Geertz, 1973, p. 14).

In Fong and Chuang's (2004) *Communicating Ethnic and Cultural Identity*, Fong (2004b) defined different social and cultural identities including gender, age, spiritual, class, national, and regional identities. This work also highlights distinguishing features of ethnic and cultural identity such as names (Fong, 2004a). Other descriptions in the collection include maintenance of ethnic identity through daily interactions in an African-American–owned beauty salon (Bailey & Oetzel, 2004), reflections on Latina identity (Olivas, 2004), and descriptions of Franco-American identity (Langellier, 2004) and Asian American identity (Chuang, 2004).

Another collection, edited by Samovar and Porter (2003), also references postmodern thought. Notably, the authors acknowledge that identities are negotiated, and they recognize that many individuals reside in more than one culture (Y. Y. Kim, 2003). This work also included a discussion of the relationship of language and culture (Fong, 2003; Zhong, 2003) as well as a discussion of ethical considerations (Shuter, 2003). Other contributors examined cultural identities in various contexts, including business (Lindsley & C. Braithwaite, 2003; Quasha & McDaniel, 2003) and health care (Rao, 2003).

Lustig and Koester's (2000) edited volume highlighted the interplay of identity and difference, similarly reflecting postmodern concerns. For example, in her essay on names, Kroll (2000) acknowledged that "I know my identity and who I am because I know what I am not" (p. 23). Newsome (2000) discussed boundaries and margins created by racism and argued that African Americans are socialized to forget their heritage and to embrace the ideology of the dominant group. Edelman (2000) noted that, for Jews, identity has not always been a matter of choice. According to Edelman, "Each wave of immigrants, and the successive generations of their children, has had to choose between passing as non-Jews or publicly embracing and maintaining their Jewish roots as Jewish Americans" (p. 236). This collection also proffered a multifaceted picture of various cultural identities, including Thai (Knutson, 2000), Micronesian (Marie, 2000), and Navajo (C. Braithwaite, 2000).

Language and culture relate closely. The intricate relationship of communication, language, and identity complicates research on identity. According to Tabouret-Keller (1997, p. 317), "The language spoken by somebody and his or her identity as a speaker of this language are inseparable. This surely is a piece of knowledge as old as human speech itself: Language acts are acts of identity."

Identity as Language Acts

Language connects people to their culture, history, and tradition (House, 2003). Individuals who speak multiple languages inhabit multiple worlds and experience multiple identities. Sandra Cisneros (1991) observed that speaking another language encompasses another way of seeing. B. Wilson (1993) explained:

> It is one of the remarkable aspects of language that we appear to take on different personalities simply by making different sounds than the ones to which we are accustomed. For those who are truly bilingual this seems so obvious as to hardly bear mentioning: they flit easily between tongues ... they will talk casually about "my Pakistani self" and "my English persona." ... When I speak Spanish, the language I know best besides English, I find my facial muscles set in a different pattern, and new, yet familiar gestures taking over my hands. I find myself shrugging and tossing my head back, pulling down the corners of my mouth and lifting my eyebrows. I touch people all the time ... I speak more rapidly and fluently and I use expressions that have no counterpart in English ... To speak another language is to lead a parallel life ... (pp. 159–160)

While our textbooks discuss the influence of the language one speaks on one's identity, little work appears in our journals on bi- and multilingualism.

Employing a postmodern perspective, Giroux (2003) noted that "[l]anguage is more than a mode of communication or a symbolic practice that produces real effects: It is also a site of contestation and struggle" (p. 195). The dominant social order often determines the language spoken in a particular area. According to Marlow and Giles (2006, p. 343), "Throughout history, multiple indigenous groups have had their cultural, linguistic, and communicative identities supplanted by dominant groups' norms." Over 1,000 separate languages were in use in the New World when the first colonizers and explorers arrived—a number that is estimated to have declined by at least 40% since then (Berlitz, 1982). A Hawaiian proverb states, "In the language there is life, and in the language there is death" (Marlow & Giles, p. 343). Today, globalization threatens many languages. The commodification of culture and language (du Gay, Evans, &

Redman, 2001; Hall & du Gay, 1996) transforms language from a means of communication to a means of production, and it pressures individuals to perform a marketable identity that may exclude their native tongue.

Language revitalization movements, a means of re-establishing individual and shared identity, have developed in a variety of locations. Hebrew is one of the most successful re-established languages (Berlitz, 1982). Marlow and Giles (2006) found that language revitalization efforts in Hawaii were successful at increasing language vitality. C. Braithwaite (1997) researched Navajo educational communication practices to learn how Navajo Community College integrates Navajo culture into courses. Several courses at the college are taught in the Navajo language, and the courses instructed in English integrated Navajo culture through sense of place, duality of life, Diné identity, and enactment. The role of language and identity constitutes an area that certainly warrants further research.

Identity as Boundary Management

Just as our cultural backgrounds impact identities, communication scholars have discovered that place and space constrain and enable achievement of identities by social actors. According to Hall and du Gay (1996), who assumed a postmodern view, "Identity has a pivotal relationship to the politics of location" (p. 1). Rhetorical theory abounds with references to location. For example, Aristotle (1954) provided "topoi" or places to look for arguments in the *Rhetoric*. Modern scholars such as Toulmin (1964), Burke (1969a), and Bitzer (1968) also discussed the influence of space and place. Kenneth Burke included the scene in his pentad, observing that the scene contains both the agent and the act. Bitzer's rhetorical situation derives "from the Latin *situs* ('situation' or 'site')" (Darsey, 2004, p. 6). Carbaugh's (1996) theory of situated identity also connects identity and place.

Dollar and Zimmers (1998) argued that identity entails an interactional accomplishment grounded in a cultural landscape. They studied social identity and communicative boundaries among young adult homeless. Harter, Berquist, Titsworth, Novak, and Brokaw (2005) also investigated the politics of space, stigma, and identity construction with homeless youth. Dollar and Zimmers contended that the stigma of being homeless revealed a number of communicative boundaries and that speakers adopted specific codes to manage their social identity. Harter and her colleagues found that youth without homes embody invisible subjectivities and that social discourses about community space involve youth without homes and function as barriers to intervention by educators and service providers.

Young (1994) explored the rhetoric of homelessness. She discovered that the site or location of communication conferred and denied speaker legitimacy. Drawing from the work of Michel Foucault (1969/1972), who was concerned with the institutional sites from which speakers make their discourse, Young examined speech by and for homeless people on the public streets, in the legislative hearing room, and in the courts. Congressional hearings and courtrooms comprise sites of institutional authority in which only certain types of speech by certain people are allowed; whereas, "[l]ike 'the heath' in Shakespeare's time, 'the street' in our own time has come to signify a close repository of things evil and alien" (Hopper, 1991, p. 129). Young discovered that politicians treated homeless individuals speaking in congressional hearing rooms as legitimate while they ignored homeless speakers on the street. A mother's recollection of an encounter with a homeless man demonstrates how the street denies identity: "My son asked, 'Mommy, why is that man lying on the sidewalk?' ... I didn't really notice him. To me, he was part of the landscape" (Manning, 1992, p. 6D).

Kruse (2005) examined the relationship of identity and location with respect to John Lennon. A cultural geographer, Kruse's research links communication, place, and celebrity. He studied places and the spatial practices that occurred within them, elaborating on ways that meaning is constructed in memory through the ascription of meanings to place. Kruse argued that John Lennon cannot be defined in a single discourse but rather can be read as a cultural text. Lennon, argued Kruse, holds several identities associated with particular places.

According to Dickinson, Ott, and Aoki (2006), "Museums, memorials, and other historical places are key sites in the construction of collective memory and national identity" (p. 27). Trujillo (1993) argued that these locations (such as Dealy Plaza, the site where John Kennedy was assassinated, or Ground Zero of 9/11 fame) are imbued by the public with a rich cultural significance (see related review by Grey, this volume).

Identity Transformations

As the analysis of John Lennon attests, individuals perform multiple and diverse identities throughout their lives. Such identities shift, change, and even clash. As such, we now turn our attention to the processes of identity change through transformation and trans/formation, illuminating the ways in which individuals confer and resist identities. In this section, I discuss transformation (the modernist-oriented shifting from one identity to another) in terms of forced change and individual empowerment.

Forced Change in Identity

Identity can be transformed due to unexpected changes in circumstances, requiring individuals to adapt their understanding of self and others. Medical diagnoses encompass one such example (see related review in this volume by Goldsmith et al.). Physician and oncologist Rachel Naomi Remen (1996) shared moving stories about the ways that cancer transformed identities in *Kitchen Table Wisdom: Stories that Heal*. Scholars Roth and Nelson (1997) examined the construction of HIV diagnoses in narratives about physician–patient interactions and stressed the importance of HIV-positive communities in the construction of HIV-positive identities.

Additionally, identity can be unexpectedly transformed through "outing." Outing occurs when others publicly proclaim an individual's hidden and private identity. Some journalists and activists denounce outing as a violation of the right of privacy, while others defend outing as a political tactic (Gross, 1991).

Displacement can also change one's identity. Growing interest in diaspora (see D. Boyarin & J. Boyarin, 1993; Kelley & Lemelle, 1994; T. R. Patterson & Kelley, 2000) is reflected in the journal *Diaspora: A Journal of Transnational Studies*. According to T. R. Patterson and Kelley, the journal "has tended to focus on issues of migration and globalization" (p. 13). These authors asserted that diaspora comprises both a process and a condition, and the processes of diaspora (such as imperialism, colonialism, and racial capitalism) have shaped both African and Western culture. Regarding the Jewish Diaspora, D. Boyarin and J. Boyarin observed that "the place of *difference* increasingly becomes the Jewish place" (p. 697, emphasis added).

The more recent relocation of 80% of the citizens of New Orleans following Hurricane Katrina is another testament to the connection between identity and place. Patterson and Kelley characterize diaspora as an unfinished migration.

Ana Menendez (2001) compellingly captured the experience of immigrants to the United States, who take on new identities when they come to live in a different country, in the story of Juanito the dog. Just off the boat from Cuba, Juanito, a feisty dog, sees a beautiful poodle and tries to engage her in conversation. The poodle exclaims that she is a refined breed of considerable class, orders Juanito to speak in English, and tells him he is nothing but a short, insignificant mutt. Struggling to express his thoughts in the foreign language of English, Juanito responds, "Pardon me, your highness. Here in America I may be a short, insignificant mutt, but in Cuba I was a German shepherd" (Menendez, p. 28).

As such, more powerful others often impose identity on unwilling (but relatively powerless) immigrants. Flores (2003) examined representations of Mexican immigrants in the 1920s and 1930s, during a deportation drive and repatriation campaign that resulted in a mass exodus of Mexican Americans. A narrative of immigrant need prevailed in the national consciousness before the Depression, in which U.S. employers envisioned Mexican Americans as the ideal labor force. According to Flores, they defined Mexican Americans as peons, perceived to be ignorant, docile, and willing to work for very little. In the years following the Depression, however, the very presence of Mexican Americans was used as evidence in restrictionist narratives that portrayed immigrants as taking American jobs and as threatening, suspect, and dangerous. These narratives continue to clash today. Sergio Arau, writer and director of the film *A Day Without a Mexican,* used absence to show the importance of immigrants to the U.S. economy. The film explored what would happen if all the immigrants in a state were to disappear suddenly and used absence to make the invisible visible (Artenstein & Arau, 2004).

According to Chang and Aoki (1998), "How a nation treats immigrants speaks volumes about the nation" (p. 310). The current debates over immigration in the United States, the Bush administration's proposals to make English the official national language of the United States, efforts to fence the U.S. border with Mexico, issues such as racial profiling and electronic surveillance in this post-9/11 world, and the recent decision by the French government to ban the wearing of any religious dress all relate to modernist treatments of identity—one of us (or not), for us (or against us)—as well as underscore the pivotal nature of power in constructing identities.

Choosing Change in Identity

Although complicated by circumstance, degree of communicative skill, and cohesiveness of community, individuals and groups can seize agency to alter or invoke identities. Indeed, scholars spanning the communication discipline (including communication and disability, interracial communication, organizational communication, health communication, and feminism) continue to note the ways in which individuals empower themselves to advance preferred identities through discursive practices.

D. Braithwaite and C. Braithwaite (2003) explored communication with persons with disabilities. They noted that "persons with disabilities use a distinctive speech that implicates specific models of personhood, society and strategic life" (p. 166). This form of speech contributes a specific identity that, in turn, serves as a basis for identity change and redefinition. The authors conducted interviews with persons with disabilities, and they discovered three ways of engaging in redefinition. Individuals can redefine themselves as part of a new culture, redefine the concept of disability, and/or redefine disability for the dominant culture. This research underlines the importance of the way that we frame and define our own identities. Establishing a shared and empowered identity can galvanize social movements. As Coopman (2003) argued, viewing disability as a cultural identity and community provides a means of empowerment for persons with disabilities to participate fully in the social construction of their life experience.

Ellingson (2004) studied identity and women cancer survivors, a group that "occupies a position at the intersection of (at least) three marginalizing identities" (p. 79). The marginalized identities of patient, woman, and cancer survivor stigmatized these women in various ways. The women in this investigation discussed complementary and alternative medicine. Talking with others and exploring options offered agency, allowing the women to gain a feeling of control and empowerment as agents of their own health. It also fostered identification. Ellingson concluded that women who asserted their identity through talking were "defying the mandate to be silent about our embodied experiences and values" (p. 97). Physicians, she argued, should pay greater attention to the voice of the life world.

Other examples of deliberate identity transformation through assuming disguises, adopting personas, or establishing alternate identities occur both in popular culture and in the groves of academe. When she discovered that her own notoriety as the restaurant critic of the *New York Times* interfered with her ability to write reviews, Ruth Reichl (2005) donned a variety of disguises to reclaim the anonymity necessary to do her job. Scholars have adopted alternate personas and identities as well. The academic blogger Bitch Ph.D. created an online persona that has taken on a life of her own (McClellan, 2004). Gloria Watkins employs the name *bell hooks* as an alternate identity to explore difficult questions and speak in a different voice. Anthropologist Cathy Small, writing under the pseudonym Rebekah Nathan (2005), has been both criticized and praised for going undercover as a student to report on the state of American colleges and universities in *My Freshman Year: What the Professor Learned by Becoming a Student*. Indeed, passing as someone else may also function as a disguise.

In the film *Osama* (Barmak, Fraser, LeBrocquy, & Barmak, 2004), an Afghan woman dressed her daughter as a boy so that, as a male, the child could work to support his (her) mother. The film juxtaposed the roles and responsibilities that the child had as a boy with the lack of choices and freedoms that she experienced as a girl. In *Reading Lolita in Tehran*, Azar Nafisi (2004) also explored hidden identities and transformations. Defying the edicts of the fundamentalist regime in power in Iran, Nafisi secretly taught Western literature in her home to a small group of female students, creating a shared identity through identification while simultaneously being ostracized by the larger society/culture. Nafisi's memoir is an example of narrative theorizing and instructional communication set in a politicized atmosphere constrained by religion. The story also comprises a form of political communication and a call for social change.

Changes in group names and the use of different labels reflect variations in how groups negotiate identity over time (Orbe & Harris, 2001). Orbe and Harris noted that several variations have been used over time to describe racial identity, including African, colored, Negro, Black, Afro-American and African American. Conversely, they observed, "European Americans have historically remained unnamed because of their positions of privilege in the United States" (p. 58). Growing interest in communicating Whiteness (Warren, 2003) comprises a response to heightened awareness of this privileged position.

Lucas and Buzzanell (2004), in their study of blue-collar work, career, and success, examined occupational narratives of underground miners. Occupational narratives, they argued, comprise cultural artifacts that were used to socialize miners into blue-collar work and to reinforce work identities. According to these researchers, "In work and organizational contexts, narrative possesses the transformative power to mold individual and organizational identities" (p. 277).

Identity Trans/formation

As communication scholars continue to examine identity (and its implications for health, relationships, community, etc.), our theoretical conceptualizations and methodological approaches become increasingly important. Quintanilla, Cano, and Ivy (2004) discovered that identities can be defined, constrained, and limited by models and paradigms. These authors discussed the significance of the biomedical, social/culture, and feminist models of menopause. The biomedical model defines menopause as a deficiency disease or disorder, and it has been used to convince women that they suffer from an illness. The social/culture model presents menopause through the context of cultural, social, political, and economic factors. The feminist model depicts menopause as a normal and natural transition, and it employs an integrative perspective that centers on the point of view of the woman experiencing it. While the feminist approach draws from both the biomedical and social/culture models, the focus is also distinctively phenomenological. This perspective reflects the increased attention given to the body and embodied discourse (see, for example, Conquergood, 1991).

Aristotle's (1954) notion of communication as strategic and goal oriented still influences communication scholarship even as our understanding of the means of attaining such goals continues to evolve. Modernist-oriented models are dualistic, and they focus on transformation or change from one identity to another. We now need a pluralistic, elastic model that permits acknowledgment of postmodern fluidity and fragmentation. As Gergen (1991) explained, individuals can advance and juxtapose multiple (and potentially contradictory) identities. In this section, I argue that the process of identity transformation is fundamental to persuasion and social action, reflecting the poststructuralist influence on boundaries, borders, and the margin that redefine identity. Identity operates in the interval "between reversal and emergence; an idea which cannot be thought in the old way, but without certain key questions cannot be thought of at all" (Hall & du Gay, 1996, p. 2; Markell, 2003).

The postmodern emphasis on deconstructing power and authority to reveal hegemony (Foucault, 1969/1972), I argue, results in a more knowing communication that operates from metacognitive awareness so that social actors operate strategically and deliberately. In a world in which change is the only constant, they employ change strategically to accomplish their goals. When identity is trans/formed, social actors create and change it. Identity trans/formations are enacted/performed discursively by and within groups and scholarly communities. Examining these trans/formations can create new understandings of the tactics that social actors utilize to express and negotiate identity.

Trans/formations by Social Movements or Groups

The second half of the twentieth century witnessed the emergence of large-scale political and social movements, including second-wave feminism, civil rights, American Indian Movement, disability rights, and gay and lesbian liberation. Trans/forming as a mode of organizing by social or movement groups is inextricably connected to the idea that one's identity makes one peculiarly vulnerable to violence, marginalization, exploitation, cultural imperialism, and powerlessness. In recent years, communication scholars have focused their attention on illuminating the tensions between identity and difference in social movements and groups.

Communication scholars have examined how the civil rights movement successfully trans/formed the identity of Black Americans. They moved from the margin to the mainstream, from invisible to being visible, and from being silent to having a voice. The juxtaposition of identities marked an important part of social change. The contrast during the March to Selma, when morally superior and passive African-American marchers were physically and forcefully resisted by Alabama state troopers, made a powerful argument (The First March, n.d.; Young, 2005).

In spite of the tremendous achievements of the civil rights movement, racial identity continues to pose problems. Many scholars continue to cite W. E. B. Du Bois's prescient observation that "the problem of the 20th century is the problem of the color line" (1965, p. 221). In reality, the dominant culture often resists identity change because it may impose alternate identities unwillingly on others.

Following Anzaldúa (1987), J. A. Scott (2006) explored the "borderland" between the civil rights movement and the women's rights movement in her work on the Combahee River Collective (1975–1980), one of the leading Black feminist organizations in the nation. By examining the cross-fertilization of these two movements, J. A. Scott argued that "[w]hat made Combahee so unique was its range of vision; the organization viewed race, class, gender, and sexuality as the connective tissue between various social reform movements rather than the wedge that divides them" (p. 4). This vision was encapsulated in the Combahee River Collective's founding statement:

> The most general statement of our politics ... would be that we are actively committed to struggling against the racial, sexual, heterosexual, and class oppression and see as our particular task the development of an integrated analysis and practice based upon the fact that the major systems are interlocking. The synthesis of these oppressions creates the conditions of our lives. (Combahee River Collective, 1982, pp. 2–3)

J. A. Scott concluded that "the openness of Combahee's mission and the permeability of multiple identities inspired black feminists to engage in collaborations that expanded the very meaning of 'we' and 'community' in the process" (p. 4).

Giroux (2003) examined pedagogies of denial, and he argued that a new racism is operating in American society. The discourse of color-blindness, he contends, produces a neoliberal racism. The language of color-blindness makes racial conflict and discrimination a thing of the past, and it assumes "that race has no valence as a marker of identity or power" (p. 198). Furthermore, changes in social values, which emphasize commerce and economic power, diminish the influence of race (and shared identity) as "an essential category for examining the relationship between justice and democratic society" (p. 200). Giroux argued for continued trans/formation, noting that "[a]ny attempt to address the politics of the new racism in the United States must begin by reclaiming the language of the social and affirming the project of an inclusive and just democracy" (p. 206).

Morris (1997) also considered rhetorical identity trans/formation, within the frame of the education of Native Americans. Morris explored the transformational mimesis, or rhetorical and cultural transformations that were used to trans/form Native American identity. Over time, through education, acculturation, and assimilation, Native Americans' cultural identities were erased and called into question to be replaced with "a readily available, 'superior identity' provided by the dominant society" (p. 155). Such practices encompass the legacy of what Hendrix et al. (2003) termed restrictive pedagogies that seldom call into question harmful educative practices. Morris explained the harmful consequences to Native American students, asserting that "transformational mimesis ... puts identity under erasure. The children become both Indian and White and neither Indian nor White. Everything in their world is now in conflict" (p. 161). Morris also suggested that "transformational mimesis manifests itself in the lives of other marginalized groups" (p. 168) and called for additional research of this issue.

An interesting response to this hegemony was expressed in what Morris (1997) labeled texts of resistance. These texts reject the discourse of the dominant culture and celebrate key virtues (establishing an individual identity) of the resident culture. While they serve as a warning to others, these texts also function as a badge of honor for survivors, a means of identification, and a place for healing the wounds of self and community (see related arguments by Grey, this volume). Young (2005) examined identity trans/formation regarding the homeless. She argued that the "need for transformation is particularly acute for the homeless" (p. 9) because society defines them by what they lack and excludes them from community. As such, they remain marginalized and voiceless. The space in which the homeless dwell (the street) renders speakers illegitimate, deviant, and alien. This hegemony makes it easy for us to ignore homeless people, effectively making them invisible (Young, 1994; see also Harter, Berquist, et al., 2005).

The concept of presence, first developed in *The New Rhetoric* by Perelman and Olbrechts-Tyteca (1969), sheds light on identity trans/formations within homeless rhetoric. The presence of homeless people disturbs others, often underlying legislation and regulations to banish the homeless or make homelessness a status crime (Hastings, 1992; Powell, 2004). Yet presence can be trans/formed into an argument to address homelessness as a social problem. The organization

SHARE/WHEEL has successfully staged "tent cities" that make large numbers of homeless people visible as an effective vehicle for social change (Freeman, 2002). According to Freeman, the organization asks, "After all, what is more motivating? Invisible homeless people, or visible homeless people?" (¶ 25). Young (2005) argued that presence can make a material argument for social change, and that presence can be established phenomenologically through narrative, to make a rhetorical argument. In each of the preceding examples, identity involves more than "the personal." Identities also express status, power, legitimacy, and control. As Brody (2003) observed, "The performance of the personal is [also] political" (p. 207).

Disability studies also explore tensions between identity and difference. According to Harter, Scott, Novak, Leeman, and Morris (2006, p. 4), "Communication scholars are uniquely situated to explore the articulation of disability and difference." Harter and her colleagues utilized narrative theorizing and ethnographic fieldwork to investigate how members of Passion Works—an alternative discourse community characterized by embodied rhetoricity—performed a counternarrative of disability. Lindemann-Nelson (2001) coined the term "counternarrative" to describe "a story that resists an oppressive identity and attempts to replace it with one that commands respect" (p. 6). Following Lindeman-Nelson, Harter et al. explained that "[n]arratives represent a performative strategy with particular significance for individuals marginalized or otherwise absent from dominant discourse" (p. 6). Members of Passion Works redefined themselves and established a different identity from the one that the prevailing culture assigned, effectively repositioning and trans/forming their identity through a counternarrative. This trans/formation resembles the texts of resistance in Native American re-education and the counterpresence that was employed so effectively in the civil rights movement. Like the tent cities used to confront homelessness, Harter et al. explained that Passion Works "transforms the societal forces that, in part, led to its emergence in the first place" (p. 7).

Trans/formational Pedagogies

Critical and progressive pedagogies also provide scholars with ways of trans/forming student understanding of identity issues. Several scholars have written about critical and progressive pedagogies

(Cooks, 2003; Giroux, 2003; Hendrix et al., 2003; Howard, 2004; Johnson & Bhatt, 2003). Cooks developed a critical pedagogy to teach about Whiteness, which she defined as "a set of rhetorical strategies employed to construct and maintain a dominant White culture and identities" (p. 246). She sought to provide pedagogies and strategies that would highlight White invisibility and normalcy. Critical and radical pedagogy "has begun to shift its focus increasingly to the body and performance of identity" (p. 247). Cooks added emotions to this framework and examined the fears and emotions that underlie discussions of democracy and citizenship, exploring a pedagogy of discomfort. Students explored their racial identity through individual narratives that created a Whiteness narrative as a pedagogical story. This metanarrative heightened students' understanding of issues of race and positionality.

Giroux's (2003) discussion of the new racism evolving within the language of color-blindness ended with a call to action based on pedagogy. According to Giroux, "Any viable antiracist pedagogy must make the political more pedagogical by recognizing how public pedagogy works to determine and secure racial identity" (p. 208). Communication educators must "draw attention between critique and social transformations" (p. 209).

Hendrix et al. (2003) worked to integrate identities into classroom pedagogy. They noted that "the majority of the research still does not address how the multiple identities of professor/teacher and student are negotiated on a daily basis in the ever-changing U.S. American classrooms" (p. 178). These researchers saw "the classroom as a nexus where identities co-mingle" (p. 179). Their critical pedagogy began by recognizing that each individual has multiple identities, and it acknowledged that identities may be complicated and contradictory. According to Hendrix et al., "It is through our multiple definitions of the self that we are connected to the world, and conversely, the world is connected to us" (p. 183). They suggested three methods for investigating identity: critical pedagogy, identity negotiation, and cultural contracts theory. Each of these perspectives focused on the processes that trans/form identity.

Howard (2004) combined critical pedagogy and interactive performance practice as a method of instigating identity trans/formation. She grounded her work in Dwight Conquergood's (1991, 1998) summons for performance that revolutionizes. Conquergood (1998) used the term *kinesis* to convey an urgent motivation to break and remake oppressive social structures. Howard adapted Boal's Theatre of the Oppressed techniques to stimulate identity trans/formation with regard to eating and body image. This approach led to increased personal awareness and action and extended students' personal learning to a cultural critique. She concluded that "interactive performance becomes a mechanism for student empowerment" (p. 228).

Johnson and Bhatt (2003) developed an innovative critical pedagogy, based on "the kind of relational and autoethnographic exploration we engage" (p. 231). The two researchers formed an alliance that enabled them to "encourage students to 'step back' from their lenses and broaden their world views" (p. 233). The researchers explicitly acknowledged and incorporated their own identities (as a South Asian woman and a U.S.–born White, middle-class lesbian) as a means of examining the intersections of identity. Johnson and Bhatt's critical pedagogy allowed them to address how individuals can experience both privilege and oppression simultaneously.

Trans/formation of Texts

Queer(ing) constitutes a relatively new methodology (Brody, 2003; Brookey & Westerfelhaus, 2001; Johnson, 2001) that "critically interrogates notions of selfhood, agency, and experience" (Johnson, p. 3). Henderson (2001) noted in her review of the literature on gay, lesbian, bisexual, and transgender studies that "the exploration of sexual indeterminacy and performance is sometimes the marker of 'queer studies'" and referred to this work as a "postmodern approach to scholarship" (p. 481).

Carpenter (2003) applied queer theory to Robert O'Hara's play, *Insurrection: Holding History*. According to Carpenter, "The play questions the sanctity of written historical narratives and encourages us to reassess the authority granted to the written word" (p. 186), especially with regard to race, sex, and gender. O'Hara "uses the fantastical to emancipate African American history and identity from the bondage of compulsive white heteronomativity" (p. 187). The play presents identity as a fluid experience that cannot be confined to an authoritative text. The analysis attempts to de-privilege absolute authoritarian discourses.

Carpenter (2003) used the term *queer* as a play upon words, observing that queer has been redefined and is now used to (1) discuss the politics of the personal, (2) question a spectrum of personal identities, (3) resist the imposition of certain identities, and (4) act against the hegemony of a particular worldview. This methodology mirrors critical theory, wherein the author queers (questions or critiques) history by emphasizing history's own performativity. In other words, by employing a metacognitive awareness of performance and using that perspective and awareness as a spotlight, critics are able to identify and dismantle ideologies. Queer theory, like critical theory, seeks to enact social change. Carpenter remarked that O'Hara's work constitutes a "fervent attempt to liberate the marginalized African American experience from the sidebars of history" (p. 201).

Carpenter (2003) examined shared identity and how a queer perspective can help liberate an historical experience. This approach differs from that employed by Brody (2003), who examined the actions of a single agent or actor and the ways that the refusal to perform an expected role functions as the "performance of the possibility of another identity" (p. 220). For Brody, queering operates as a particular way of reading a text or performance. Brody studied Angelina Grimke's *The Closing Door*. She envisioned the text as queer because the performance of the personal is political and because it performs Black queer difference. Brody read the text as a racialized, gendered performance of motherhood that queers racial reproduction.

Brody's (2003) analysis began by noting the limited freedom and choices of African-American women in the early 1900s (the time Grimke's story was published). The dominant culture expected them to produce (male) offspring (and, thus, the African-American labor force so important to the U.S. economy). At the same time, large numbers of African-American males were killed by lynching. Together, these two forces created significant dilemmas for African-American women. Why would women want to bring children into a world that would eventually kill them?

Brody (2003) found the answer to this dilemma in Grimke's story, which "relies on the anguish of repudiated and devastated motherhood to give expression to racial protest" (p. 209). Choosing not to reproduce, not to foster the next generation, argued Brody, comprised a queer act. The very pressures on women that sparked the refusal emerged as the forces that "open the door to a new form of queer, feminist subjectivity" (p. 208). The refusal to act in prescribed ways became an act of liberation and the performance of the possibility of another identity.

Brookey and Westerfelhaus (2001) argued that positive portrayals of identity also demand critical scrutiny. According to them, the queer critique and queer media studies hold two purposes: (1) "to challenge negative representations of the queer experience," and (2) to "uncover subtextual queer experience in mass mediated texts" (p. 143). The authors examined media portrayals of gay drag queens in the film *To Wong Foo, Thanks for Everything! Julie Newmar.* Their analysis illuminated how positive portrayals can simultaneously be constraining. Brookey and Westerfelhaus examined the discourse of deification and ways that a positive depiction puts the character above and removes him or her from the mainstream. Deification constitutes the opposite of demonization in that, instead of focusing on negative behaviors, deification portrays best behaviors that "depict the culturally marginalized as 'unrealistically superior'" (p. 143).

The cult of true womanhood (which invested women with a spiritual piety and sexual purity that demanded they remain in the home to care for the family, removed and away from the public sphere) serves as an example of unrealistically superior expectations that put women above the norm and removed them from the mainstream. Brookey and Westerfelhaus (2001) concluded that, while the film elevated and celebrated one kind of queer experience, it also limited and contained that experience. The positive portrayal itself became another way of marginalizing the characters that it purported to celebrate.

Identities can be conferred, denied, accepted or rejected, and changed in a variety of ways as a result of interaction with others. The questions raised by Patchen Markell in the epigraph to this chapter (2003)—Who am I? Who are you? Who are we?—resonate as scholars attempt to understand and resolve identity tensions in organizations, in health care, in classrooms, and among and between social groups. Identity is central to communication studies, and communication studies can make unique contributions to the understanding of identity.

Challenges and Opportunities

Examining the relation of communication and identity is crucial, and the time is right to reflect and cast new light on the way that identity has been pursued and dispatched in our discipline. In these concluding pages, I discuss the challenges to studying identity and specify areas in need of additional research. I urge future scholars to consider these opportunities.

The question of identity is ancient, but the notion of the self is modern (Crable, 2006). With the advent of postmodernism, tension exists between those who see identity as fabricated, constructed, fragmented, and capable of multiple constructions (Dyske, 2001; Gergen, 1991; Hall, 1990; Hedge, 1998; Sarup & Raja, 1998) and those who view identity as relatively stable (Harrison, 2006). Crusius (1997, ¶ 12) argued, "Poststructuralists view identity as, at best, a fiction. If it is a fiction, I would only insist that it is a necessary one … we … require identities of some sort for the *dramatis personae* of our world."

Pursue Postmodern Paradoxes and Connections

The postmodern view of identity as elastic and fluid encouraged the metaphors of migration and diaspora. The metaphor of migration refers to movement, while diaspora is defined as scattering. These metaphors hold particular relevance not only in the aftermath of Hurricane Katrina but also with respect to postmodern tendencies to relocate and migrate by choice due to career or for other reasons. As Gergen (1991) observed, we have become quite transient again.

We might even ask how the literature in communication has been a migration, a journey through territories in which identities, locations, and bodies interact. As Cindy Patton (1996) explained, "Space and identity converge in complex ways; a body names a place, a body takes names to a place, a body's presence transforms—new names and a new sense of place arise" (p. 143).

In response to the isolation and fragmentation of the postmodern world, its migration and diaspora (Kirby, 1989), the other metaphor the postmodern paradigm fosters is home. People long to reclaim lost places or spaces that represent home and community (King, 2001). King observed that "[o]ur journals proclaim that there is a hunger for connection and a new recognition of the deep human need to belong somewhere" (p. vi). The need for belonging may be especially strong for those who are displaced. For many victims of Hurricane Katrina, the words of the legendary Louis Armstrong continue to resonate: "Do you know what it means to miss New Orleans, and miss it each night and day? I know I'm not wrong, this feelings getting stronger the longer I stay away" (Lange and Alter, 1946).

The metaphor of the pilgrimage is perhaps a more fitting one, which connects identity with both movement and belonging. Aden (1999) employed this metaphor in his analysis of the film *Field of Dreams*. In his conception, the pilgrimage involves four stages: entering the liminoid, building a sacred place/community, gaining respect for others, and returning home (see also related work on the metaphor of the borderland by Anzaldúa, 1987; Flores, 2003).

The literature review reveals that our understanding of the processes that isolate us (such as discrimination, prejudice, distance, deviance, anomie, and hegemony) is better developed than our understanding of the processes that create community, such as identification. According to Phelan (1988, p. 347), "The idea of community and the practice of communication are connected not only in root meaning but in everyday life on a variety of scales." Future research should adopt a plenary model, in which dualities, intersections, and paradoxes combine to create new understandings. John Hewitt (1989, p. 152) asked, "What does it mean to have 'identity' in our contemporary, everyday usage of the term? It is to be like others and yet also have qualities that are different from them." Identity is characterized by dualities. We define what and who we are vis-à-vis what and who we are not. The comic Carlos Mencia, interviewed about questions of identity on the National Public Radio program *Morning Edition*, explained that growing up, "I was always an insider and an outsider at the same time" (Inskeep, 2006). The trick involves looking at these binary elements, borders, or boundaries with new lenses and redefining them as opportunities to establish new identities.

Barker's (1997) exploration of the production of multiple, hybrid identities amongst British Asian girls exemplifies research focusing on dualities. The subjects of the study found themselves simultaneously both in and out of British society and Asian culture. Coping with this situation required them to construct identities from a variety of sites and discourses. The resources for constructing identity are multiplying through the influence of globalization.

Focusing on the places that identities intersect is also a fruitful approach. Doxtader's (2003) theory of reconciliation "opposes definition in a non-definite way. Its defining question is how human beings can invent and express the potential to be(come) by standing between what they are and what they are not" (p. 267). Reconciliation is a step on the pilgrim's journey, requiring entry into what Victor Turner (1969) termed liminal states, betwixt and between the firmly defined.

Hecht (1993) advised scholars interested in identity to consider contradictions or paradoxes and to go beyond simply recognizing opposites through layering ideas and methods. According to Hecht, this approach befits identity because "[l]ayering implies that there are alternate ways of knowing that are continually juxtaposed and played off each other and/or blended together" (p. 76). Johnson and Bhatt (2003) noted that "we cannot simply discuss race, gender, sexual identity, class, ability, religion or nationality in isolation. Rather, we must study how each and all of these (as well as other identities) intersect and inform each other" (p. 234).

Two recent studies exemplify research that examines intersections and paradoxes. Harter et al. (2006) discovered that counternarratives of disability not only resisted an identity but also established community, observing that "[m]embers of Passion Works reweave the tattered fabric of exclusion as they engage in communal collaboration and integration" (p. 4). In an interesting twist, Harter et al. explained that "[t]he expression of solidarity paradoxically [became] a source of community" (p. 21). Writing in a similar vein, Rose (1997) raised the intriguing possibility that one can simultaneously create through performance both a collective and an individualized self. Rose examined identity production in an American Sign Language performance. She argued that "[t]he body signing in performance is a conflicted site of identity production, creating, minimally, both a collective and individualized self" (p. 333).

The tension between the opposing functions of identity, identification, and separation strongly influences the way that we understand and research identity. Crable (2006) argued that identity arises out of this tension. According to Crable, identity functions as armor against existential anxiety. Many scholars agree that identification can only be understood in relation to separation or division (S. K. Foss, K. A. Foss, & Trapp, 2002; Woodward, 2003). Pepper and Larson's (2006) examination of identity negotiation in a postacquisitional culture exemplifies research from this perspective. They concluded that members negotiate identities in a cultural performance arising from the tension between identification and separation or what they term *disidentification*.

Conclusion

Pollock (1998, p. 21) argued that texts are "inseparable from the processes by which they are made, understood and deployed." Similarly, identity is inseparable from the processes by which it is negotiated, constructed, and expressed. Like the phoenix emerging from the ash, identity arises out of tensions—the tensions between belonging and separation or division. This unique space creates new possibilities; it is a location of genesis. This tension is illustrated by Kenneth Burke (1968), one of the leading authorities on identity, who acknowledged that he lived on the fringes, "yet he required the margins as a place to think freely, without disciplinary constraints" (Crusius, 1997, ¶ 5). Burke's scholarly identity emerged from the tension created by separation and his sense of not belonging to a specific disciplinary community.

This literature review reveals that identity is both something we have and something we do, that identity functions as both a condition and a process, emerging through (and becoming evidenced by) communicative practices. Although paradigmatic differences exist within our field—modernists view identity as relatively stable and postmodernists perceive identity as fluid and capable of infinite (re)constructions—neither can deny the centrality of identity to communication studies. We use identity to create meaning and make sense of the world. Focusing attention on context, form, and meaning in which identity is implicated is important because identity pervades contemporary life and scholarly discussions. As Crusius concluded:

> We can discard identity in theory but never in practice, where it matters little whether we make our identities or they are made for us. Whatever the case, we cannot interpret our world except by attributing identity, and these attributions matter because they have ethical, political and rhetorical consequences. (1997, ¶ 12)

Acknowledgments

Portions of this chapter were presented in a paper at the National Communication Association Convention in Boston, November 19, 2005. The author wishes to thank Christina S. Beck and the three anonymous reviewers for their insightful comments and suggestions.

Notes

1. I offer examples of bodies of literature throughout this chapter. These exemplars illustrate my points but they are not intended to represent all works in these various areas.
2. Interested readers should also refer to George Cheney's important extension of Burke's work on identification in the organizational context (see, e.g., Cheney, 1983a, 1983b; Cheney & Tompkins, 1987; C. Scott, Corman, & Cheney, 1998).

References

Aden, R. C. (1999). *Popular stories and promised lands: Fan cultures and symbolic pilgrimages.* Tuscaloosa, AL: University of Alabama Press.

Agne, R. R., Thompson, R. L., & Cusella, L. P. (2000). Stigma in the line of face: Self-disclosure of patients' HIV status to health care providers. *Journal of Applied Communication Research, 28,* 235–261.

Allen, M. W., & Caillouet, R. H. (1994). Legitimation endeavors: Impression management strategies used by an organization in crisis. *Communication Monographs, 61,* 44–64.

Altman, D. (1996). Rupture or continuity? The internationalization of gay identities. *Social Text, 48,* 77–94.

Anzaldúa, G. (1987). *Borderlands: The new mesitza = la frontera.* San Francisco: Aunt Lute Books.

Apker, J., Propp, K. J., & Zabava Ford, W. S. (2005). Negotiating status and identity tensions in healthcare team interactions: An exploration of nurse role dialectics. *Journal of Applied Communication Research, 33,* 93–115.

Aristotle (1954). *The rhetoric and poetics of Aristotle.* (W. R. Roberts & I. Bywater, Trans.). New York: The Modern Library.

Artenstein, I. (Producer), & Arau, S. (Writer/director). (2004). *A Day Without a Mexican* [motion picture]. United States: Eye on the Ball Films.

Bailey, C. L., & Oeztel, J. (2004). Tighten me up: Reflecting and maintaining ethnic identity through daily interactions in an African-American-owned beauty salon. In M. Fong & R. Chuang (Eds.), *Communicating ethnic and cultural identity* (pp. 217–229). Lanham, MD: Rowman & Littlefield Publishers, Inc.

Ballard, D., & Gossett, L. (2007). Alternative times: The temporal perceptions, processes, and practices defining the nonstandard work relationship. In C. S. Beck (Ed.), *Communication yearbook 31* (pp. 273–320). New York, NY: Lawrence Erlbaum Associates.

Barker, C. (1997). Television and the reflexive project of self: Soaps, teenage talk and hybrid identities. *British Journal of Sociology, 48,* 611–628.

Barmak, S., Fraser, J., & LeBrocquy, J. (Producers), & Barmak, S. (Director). (2004, February 6). *Osama* [Motion picture]. United States. MGM.

Becker, E. (1997). *The denial of death.* New York: Free Press.

Berlitz, C. (1982). *Native tongues.* New York: Grosset & Dunlap.

Bitzer, L. F. (1968). The rhetorical situation. *Philosophy and Rhetoric, 1,* 1–14.

Boyarin. D., & Boyarin, J. (1993). Diaspora: Generation and the ground of Jewish identity. *Critical Inquiry, 19,* 693–725.

Braithwaite, C. A. (1997). Sa'ah Naaghai Bik'eh Hozhoon: An ethnography of Navajo educational communication practices. *Communication Education, 46,* 219–233.

Braithwaite C. (2000). Roast mutton, fry bread, and tilt-a-whirls: Cultural and intercultural communication at the Navajo national fair. In M. W. Lustig and J. Koester (Eds.), *Among US: Essays on identity, belonging and intercultural competence* (pp. 232–239). New York: Longman.

Braithwaite, D. O., & Braithwaite, C. A. (2003). "Which is my good leg?" Cultural communication of persons with disabilities. In L. A. Samovar & R. E. Porter (Eds.), *Intercultural communication: A reader* (10th ed., pp. 165–176). Belmont, CA: Thomson Wadsworth.

Brissett, D., & Edgley, C. (1990). (Eds.) *Life as theater: A dramaturgical sourcebook.* New York: Aldine de Gruyter.

Brody, J. D. (2003). Queering racial reproduction: "Unnatural acts" in Angelina Weld Grimke's *The Closing Door. Text and Performance Quarterly, 23,* 205–224.

Brookey, R. A., & Westerfelhaus, R. (2001). Pistols and petticoats, piety and purity: *To Wong Foo,* the queering of the American monomyth, and the marginalizing discourse of deification. *Critical Studies in Media Communication, 18,* 141–157.

Burke, K. (1960). Myth, poetry, and philosophy. *Journal of American Folklore, 73,* 283–306.

Burke, K. (1962). *A rhetoric of religion.* Berkeley: University of California Press.

Burke, K. (1966). *Language as symbolic interaction.* Berkeley: University of California Press.

Burke, K. (1968). *Collected Poems, 1915–1967.* Berkeley: University of California Press.

Burke, K. (1969a). *A grammar of motives.* Berkeley: University of California Press. (Original work published 1945.)

Burke, K. (1969b). *Rhetoric of motives.* Berkeley: University of California. (Original work published 1950.)

Byker, D., & Anderson, L. J. (1975). *Communication as identification: An introductory view.* New York: Harper & Row.

Callero, P. (2006). Social identity theory. In G. Ritzer (Ed.), *Blackwell encyclopedia of sociology.* (pp. 4417–4420). Oxford, England: Blackwell Publishing.

Carbaugh, D. (1988). *Talking American.* Norwood, NJ: Ablex.

Carbaugh, D. (1991). Communication and cultural interpretation. *Quarterly Journal of Speech, 77,* 336–341.

Carbaugh, D. (1993). Communal voices: An ethnographic view of social interaction and conversation. *Quarterly Journal of Speech, 79,* 99–130.

Carbaugh, D. (1995). The ethnographic communication theory of Philipsen and associates. In D. P. Cushman & B. Kovacic (Eds.), *Watershed research tradition in human communication theory* (pp. 269–297). Albany: State University of New York Press.

Carbaugh, D. (1996). *Situated selves: The communication of social identities in American scenes.* Albany: State University of New York Press.

Carpenter, F. C. (2003). Robert O'Hara's insurrection: "Que(e)rying" history. *Text and Performance Quarterly, 23,* 186–205.

Chang, R. S., & Aoki, K. (1998). Centering the immigrant in the inter/national imagination. *La Raza Law Journal, 10,* 309–361.

Cheney, G. (1983a). On the various and changing meanings of organizational membership: A field study of organizational identification, *Communication Monographs, 50,* 343–363.

Cheney, G. (1983b). The rhetoric of identification and the study of organizational communication. *Quarterly Journal of Speech, 69,* 143–158.

Cheney, G., & Tompkins, P. (1987). Coming to terms with organizational identification and commitment. *Central States Speech Journal, 38,* 1–15.

Chesebro, J. L., & McCroskey, J. C. (2002). *Communication for teachers.* Boston: Allyn and Bacon.

Chickering, A.W., & Reisser, L. (1993). *Education and identity* (2nd ed.). San Francisco: Jossey–Bass.

Chuang, R. (2004). "Perpetual foreigner": In search of Asian Americans' identity and otherness. In M. Fong & R. Chuang (Eds.), *Communicating ethnic and cultural identity* (pp. 345–359). Lanham, MD: Rowman & Littlefield.

Cisneros, S. (1991). *The house on Mango Street.* New York: Vintage Books.

Cloud, D. (1996). Hegemony or concordance? The rhetoric of tokenism in "Oprah" Winfrey's rags-to-riches biography. *Critical Studies in Mass Communication, 13,* 115–137.

Collier, M. J. (1997). Cultural identity and intercultural communication. In L.A. Samovar & R. E. Porter (Eds.), *Intercultural communication: A reader* (pp. 36–44). Belmont, CA: Wadsworth.

Combahee River Collective. (1982). The Combahee River Collective Statement: Black feminist organizing in the seventies and eighties. In G. Hull, P. Bell-Scott, & B. Smith (Eds.), *All the women are white, all the blacks are men, but some of us are brave: Black women's studies* (pp. 13–22). Old Westbury, NY: Feminist Press.

Conquergood, D. (1991). Rethinking ethnography: Towards a critical cultural politics. *Communication Monographs, 58,* 179–194.

Conquergood, D. (1998). Beyond the text: Toward a performative cultural politics. In S. Dailey (Ed.), *The future of performance studies: Visions and revisions* (pp. 25–36).

Cooks, L. (2003). Pedagogy, performance and positionality: Teaching about Whiteness in interracial communication. *Communication Education, 52,* 245–258.

Cooper, P. J., & Simonds, C. J. (2003). *Communication for the classroom teacher* (7th ed.). Boston: Allyn & Bacon.

Coopman, S. J. (2003). Communicating disability: Metaphors of oppression, metaphors of empowerment. In P. J. Kalbfleisch (Ed.), *Communication yearbook 27* (pp. 337–394). Mahwah, NJ: Lawrence Erlbaum Associates.

Côté, J. E., & Levine, C. G. (2002). *Identity formation, agency, and culture: A social psychological synthesis.* Mahwah, NJ: Lawrence Erlbaum Associates.

Crable, B. (2006). Rhetoric, anxiety, and character armor: Burke's interactional rhetoric of identity. *Western Journal of Communication, 70,* 1–22.

Crusius, T. (1997, March). *The question of Kenneth Burke's identity—and* Permanence and Change. Paper presented at the Conference on College Composition and Communication, Phoenix, AZ. Retrieved November 1, 2006, from http:www.cla.purdue.edu/dblakesely/burke/crusius.html

Darling-Wolf, F. (2004). Sites of attractiveness: Japanese women and Westernized representations of feminine beauty. *Critical Studies in Media Communication, 21,* 325–345.

Darsey, J. (2004). James Baldwin's *Topoi.* In P. A. Sullivan & S. R. Goldzwig (Eds.), *New approaches to rhetoric* (pp. 5–29). Thousand Oaks, CA: Sage.

Dickinson, G., Ott, B. L., & Aoki, E. (2006). Spaces of remembering and forgetting: The reverent eye/I at the Plains Indian museum. *Communication and Critical/Cultural Studies, 3,* 27–48.

Dollar, N. J., & Merrigan, G. M. (2002). Ethnographic practices in group communication research. In L. R. Frey (Ed.), *New directions in group communication* (pp. 59–78). Thousand Oaks, CA: Sage.

Dollar, N. J., & Zimmers, B. G. (1998). Social identity and communicative boundaries: An analysis of youth and young adult street speakers in a U.S. American community. *Communication Research, 25,* 596–617.

Doxtader, E. (2003). Reconciliation—A rhetorical concept/ion. *Quarterly Journal of Speech, 89,* 267–292.

Du Bois, W .E. B. (1965). *The souls of Black folk in three Negro classics*. New York: Avon Books.

du Gay, P., Evans, J., & Redman, P. (Eds.) (2001) *Identity: A reader*. London: Sage.

Dyske, S. (2001, May 20). Postmodern self. Retrieved June 14, 2006, from http://www/dyske.com

Edelman, S. M. (2000). To pass or not to pass, that is the question: Jewish cultural identity in the United States. In M. W. Lustig & J. Koester (Eds.), *Among US: Essays on identity, belonging and intercultural competence* (pp. 232–239). New York: Longman.

Eisenberg, E. M. (2001). Building a mystery: Toward a new theory of communication identity. *Journal of Communication, 51,* 534–552.

Ellingson, L. L. (2004). Women cancer survivors: Making meaning of chronic illness, disability, and complementary medicine. In P. M. Buzzannell, H. Sterk, & L. H. Turner (Eds.), *Gender in applied communication contexts* (pp. 79–98). Thousand Oaks, CA: Sage.

Erikson, E. (1963). *Childhood and society* (2nd ed.). New York: Norton.

Flores, L. A. (2003). Constructing rhetorical borders: Peons, illegal aliens, and competing narratives of immigration. *Critical Studies in Media Communication, 20,* 362–387.

Fong, M. (2003). The nexus of language, communication, and culture. In L. A. Samovar & R. E. Porter (Eds.), *Intercultural communication: A reader* (10th ed., pp. 198–205). Belmont, CA: Thomson Wadsworth.

Fong, M. (2004a). Ethnic and cultural identity: Distinguishing features. In M. Fong & R. Chuang (Eds.), *Communicating ethnic and cultural identity* (pp. 35–50). Lanham, MD: Rowman & Littlefield.

Fong, M. (2004b). Multiple dimensions of identity. In M. Fong and R. Chuang (Eds.), *Communicating ethnic and cultural identity* (pp. 19–34). Lanham, MD: Rowman &Littlefield.

Fong, M., & Chuang, R. (Eds.). (2004). *Communicating ethnic and cultural identity*. Lanham, MD: Rowman & Littlefield.

Foss, S. K., Foss, K. A., & Trapp, R. (2002). *Contemporary perspectives on rhetoric* (3rd ed.). Prospect Heights, IL: Waveland.

Foster, E. (2005). Desiring dialectical discourse: A feminist ponders the transition to motherhood. *Women's Studies in Communication, 28,* 57–83.

Foucault, M. (1972). *The archaeology of knowledge and the discourse on language* (A. M. Sheridan Smith, Trans.). New York: Pantheon Books. (Original work published 1969.)

Freeman, A. L. (2002). Tent cities: The SHARE/WHEEL tent city project. Retrieved January 7, 2005, from http:// anitraweb.org/homelessness/faqs/tentcities.html

Friedman, L. M. (1999). *The horizontal society*. New Haven, CT: Yale University Press.

Geertz, C. (1973). *Thick description: Toward an interpretive theory of culture*. New York: Basic Books.

Gergen, K. J. (1991). *The saturated self: Dilemmas of identity in contemporary life*. New York: Basic Books.

Giroux, H. A. (2003). Spectacles of race and pedagogies of denial: Anti-Black racist pedagogy under the reign of neoliberalism. *Communication Education, 52*, 191–211.

Goffman, E. (1959). *The presentation of self in everyday life*. Garden City, NY: Doubleday.

Goffman, E. (1961). *Encounters: Two studies in the sociology of interaction*. Indianapolis, IN: Bobbs–Merrill.

Goffman, E. (1963). *Behavior in public places*. New York: Free Press.

Goffman, E. (1967). *Interaction ritual: Essays on face-to-face behavior*. Garden City, NY: Doubleday.

Goffman, E. (1971). *Relations in public*. New York: Basic Books.

Goffman, E. (1974). *Frame analysis: An essay on the organization of experience*. Cambridge, MA: Harvard University Press.

Golden, A. G., Kirby, E. L., & Jorgenson, J. (2006). Work-life research from both sides now: An integrative perspective for organizational and family communication. In C. S. Beck (Ed.), *Communication yearbook 30* (pp. 143–196). Mahwah, NJ: Lawrence Erlbaum Associates.

Goldsmith, D., Miller, L., & Caughlin, J. (2007). Openness and avoidance in couples communicating about cancer. In C. S. Beck (2007), *Communication yearbook 31* (pp. 61–115). New York, NY: Lawrence Erlbaum Associates.

Grey, S. (2007). Wounds not easily healed: Exploring trauma in communication studies. In C. S. Beck (Ed.), *Communication yearbook 31* (pp. 173–222). New York, NY: Lawrence Erlbaum Associates.

Grindstaff, D. A., & DeLuca, K. M. (2004). The corpus of Daniel Pearl. *Critical Studies in Media Communication, 21*, 305–324.

Gross, L. (1991). The contested closet: The ethics and politics of outing. *Critical Studies in Mass Communication, 8*, 352–389.

Gudykunst, W. B., Matsumoto, Y., Ting-Toomey, S., Nishida, T., Kim, K. S., & Heyman, S. (1996). The influence of cultural individualism-collectivism, self construals, and individual values on communication styles across cultures. *Human Communication Research, 22*, 510–543.

Gutmann, A. (1987). *Democratic education*. Princeton, NJ: Princeton University Press.

Gutmann, A. (2003). *Identity in democracy*. Princeton, NJ: Princeton University Press.

Hall, S. (1990). Cultural identity and diaspora. In J. Rutherford (Ed.), *Identity, community, culture, difference* (pp. 222–237). London: Lawrences & Wishart.

Hall, S., & du Gay, P. (Eds.) (1996). *Questions of cultural identity*. London: Sage.

Harrison, K. (2006). Scope of self: Toward a model of television's effects on self-complexity in adolescence. *Communication Theory, 16,* 251–279.

Harter, L. J., Berquist, C., Titsworth, B. S., Novak, D., & Brokaw, T. (2005). The structuring of invisibility among the hidden homeless: The politics of space, stigma, and identity construction. *Journal of Applied Communication Research, 33,* 305–327.

Harter, L. M., Kirby, E. L., Edwards, A., & McClanahan, A. (2005). Time, technology, and meritocracy: The disciplining of women's bodies in narrative construction of age-related infertility. In L. M. Harter, P. M. Japp, & C. S. Beck (Eds.), *Narratives, health, and healing* (pp. 83–106). Mahwah, NJ: Lawrence Erlbaum Associates.

Harter, L. M., Scott, J. A., Novak, D. R., Leeman, J., & Morris, J. F. (2006). Freedom from flight: Performing a counter-narrative of disability. *Journal of Applied Communication Research, 34,* 3–29.

Hastings, D. (1992, December 27). Frustrated communities trying to outlaw homelessness. *Sunday Baton Rouge Advocate,* p. 10C.

Hecht, M. L. (1993). 2002—A research odyssey: Toward the development of a communication theory of identity. *Communication Monographs, 60,* 76–81.

Hedge, R. S. (1998). Swinging the trapeze: The negotiation of identity among Asian Indian immigrant women in the United States. In D. V. Tanno & A. Gonzalez, (Eds.), *Communication and identity across cultures* (pp. 34–55). Thousand Oaks, CA: Sage.

Henderson, L. (2001). Queer communication studies. In W. B. Gudykunst (Ed.), *Communication yearbook 24* (pp. 465–484). Thousand Oaks, CA: Sage.

Hendrix, K. G., Jackson, R. L., & Warren, J. R. (2003). Shifting academic landscapes: Exploring co-identities, identity negotiation, and critical progressive pedagogy. *Communication Education, 52,* 177–190.

Hess, M. (2005). Hip-hop realness and the white performer. *Critical Studies in Media Communication, 22,* 372–389.

Hewitt, J. P. (1989). *Dilemmas of the American self.* Philadelphia: Temple University Press.

Hofstede, G. (1991). *Culture and organizations: Software of the mind.* London: McGraw–Hill.

Hogg, M. A., & Reid, S. A. (2006). Social identity, self-categorization, and the communication of group norms. *Communication Theory, 16,* 7–30.

Holland, S. L. (2006). The dangers of playing dress-up: Popular representations of Jessica Lynch and the controversy regarding women in combat. *Quarterly Journal of Speech, 92*, 27–50.

Hopper, K. (1991). A poor apart: The distancing of homeless men in New York's history. *Social Research, 58*, 107–140.

House, J. (2003). English as a lingua franca: A threat to multilingualism? *Journal of Sociolinguistics, 7*, 556–578.

Howard, L. A. (2004). Speaking theatre/doing pedagogy: Revisiting theatre of the oppressed. *Communication Education, 53*, 217–233.

Hsu, C. F. (2002). The influence of self-construals, family and teacher communication patterns on communication apprehension among college students in Taiwan. *Communication Reports, 15*, 123–132.

Hui, C. H., & Triandis, H.C. (1986). Individualism–collectivism: A study of cross-cultural researchers. *Journal of Cross-Cultural Psychology, 17*, 225–248.

Hymes, D. (1974). *Foundations in sociolinguistics: An ethnographic approach*. Philadelphia: University of Pennsylvania Press.

Inskeep, S. (Writer). (2006, June 12). Conversations on immigration: Carlos Mencia [radio broadcast episode]. In E. McDonnell (Producer), *Morning Edition*. Washington, DC: National Public Radio.

John, J. (1996). A dramaturgical view of the health care service encounter. *European Journal of Marketing, 30*, 60–74.

Johnson, E. P. (2001). "Quare" studies, or (almost) everything I know about queer studies I learned from my grandmother. *Text and Performance Quarterly, 21*, 1–25.

Johnson, J. R., & Bhatt, A. J. (2003). Gendered and racialized identities and alliances in the classroom: Formations in/of resistive space. *Communication Education, 52*, 230–244.

Kelley, R. D. G., & Lemelle, S. J. (Eds.) (1994). *Imagining home: Class, culture and nationalism in the African Diaspora*. London, England: Verso.

Kerssen-Griep, J. (2001). Teacher communication activities relevant to student motivation: Classroom facework and instructional communication competence. *Communication Education, 50*, 256–273.

Kim, M. S., Hunter, J. E., Miyahara, A., Horvath, A., Bresnahan, M., & Yoon, J. (1996). Individual versus cultural-level dimensions of individualism and collectivism: Effects on preferred conversational styles. *Communication Monographs, 63*, 28–49.

Kim, M. S., Klingle, R. S., Sharkey, W. F., Park, H. E., Smith, D. H., & Cai, D. (2000). A test of a cultural model of patients' motivation for verbal communication in patient–doctor interactions. *Communication Monographs, 67*, 262–283.

Kim, M. S., Shin, H. C., & Cai, D. (1998). Cultural influences on preferred forms of requesting and re-requesting. *Communication Monographs, 65,* 45–67.

Kim, Y. Y. (2003). *Unum* and *Pluribus:* Ideological underpinnings of inter-ethnic communication in the United States. In L. A. Samovar & R. E. Porter (Eds.), *Intercultural communication: A reader* (10th ed., pp. 108–119). Belmont, CA: Thomson Wadsworth.

King, A. (2001). Editorial. *Quarterly Journal of Speech, 87,* vi.

Kirby, A. (1989). A sense of place. *Critical Studies in Mass Communication, 6,* 322–326.

Knutson, T. J. (2000). Tales from Thailand: Lessons from the land of smile. In M. W. Lustig & J. Koester (Eds.), *Among US: Essays on identity, belonging and intercultural competence* (pp. 221–231). New York: Longman.

Kroll, M. L. S. (2000). My name is.... In M. W. Lustig & J. Koester (Eds.), *Among US: Essays on identity, belonging and intercultural competence* (pp. 18–23). New York: Longman.

Kruse, R. J., II (2005). Contemporary geographies of John Lennon. *Critical Studies in Media Communication, 22,* 456–461.

Lange, E., & Alter, L. (1946). Do you know what it means to miss New Orleans? [Recorded by Louis Armstrong]. On *Sixteen Most Requested Songs* [CD]. New York: Sony (1994).

Langellier, K. M. (2004). "Where I come from is where I want to be": Com-municating Franco American ethnicity. In M. Fong & R. Chuang (Eds.), *Communicating ethnic and cultural identity* (pp. 297–312). Lanham, MD: Rowman & Littlefield.

Lindemann-Nelson, H. (2001). *Damaged identities: Narrative repair.* Ithaca, NY: Cornell University Press.

Lindquist, J. (2001). Hoods in the polis. *Pedagogy, 1,* 261–275.

Lindsley, S. L., & Braithwaite, C. (2003). U.S. Americans and Mexicans working together: Five core Mexican concepts for enhancing effec-tiveness. In L. A. Samovar and R. E. Porter (Eds.), *Intercultural com-munication: A reader* (10th ed., pp. 293–299). Belmont, CA: Thomson Wadsworth.

Logue, C. M., & Miller, E. F. (1995). Rhetorical status: A study of its origins, functions, and consequences. *Quarterly Journal of Speech, 81,* 20–48.

Lucas, K., & Buzzanell, P. M. (2004). Blue collar work, career and success: Occupational narratives of Sisu. *Journal of Applied Communication Research, 32,* 273–292.

Lustig, M. W., &, Koester, J. (2000). *Among US: Essays on identity, belonging and intercultural competence.* New York: Longman.

Manning, A. (1992, February 5). Explaining plight of homeless to your kids. *USA Today,* p. 6D.

Marie, V. (2000). Living in paradise: An inside look at the Micronesian culture. In M. W. Lustig and J. Koester (Eds.), *Among US: Essays on identity, belonging and intercultural competence* (pp. 239–253). New York: Longman.

Markell, P. (2003). *Bound by recognition.* Princeton, NJ: Princeton University Press.

Markus, H. R., & Kitayama, S. (1991). Culture and the self: Implications for cognition, emotion, and motivation. *Psychological Review, 98,* 224–253.

Marlow, M. L., & Giles, H. (2006). From the roots to the shoots: A Hawaiian case study of language revitalization and modes of communication. In C. S. Beck (Ed.), *Communication yearbook 30* (pp. 343–385). Mahwah, NJ: Lawrence Erlbaum Associates.

Marshall, P. D. (1997). *Celebrity and power: Fame in contemporary culture.* Minneapolis: University of Minnesota Press.

McClellan, J. (2004, October 7). Spilling the beans. *Guardian Unlimited.* Retrieved September 8, 2006 from http://technology.guardian.co.uk/online/story/ 0,3605,1320832,00.html

Mead, G. H. (1934). *Mind, self, and society.* Chicago: University of Chicago Press.

Medved, C., & Rawlins, W. K. (2006). *Investigating the discourses and practices of at-home fathers/breadwinning mother couples: Stances, tensions, and ironies.* Manuscript submitted for publication.

Meisenbach, R., & McMillan, J. (2006). Blurring the boundaries: Historical developments and future directions in organizational rhetoric. In C. S. Beck (Ed.), *Communication yearbook 30* (pp. 99–142). Mahwah, NJ: Lawrence Erlbaum Associates.

Menendez, A. (2001). *In Cuba I was a German Shepherd.* New York: Grove Press.

Morehead, A., & Morehead, L. (Eds.). (1995). *The new American Webster handy college dictionary* (3rd ed.). New York: Signet.

Morris, C. E., III, & Sloop, J. M. (2006). "What these lips have kissed": Refiguring the politics of queer public kissing. *Communication and Critical/Cultural Studies, 3,* 1–26.

Morris, R. (1997). Educating savages. *Quarterly Journal of Speech, 83,* 152–172.

Nafisi, A. (2004). *Reading Lolita in Tehran: A memoir in books.* New York: Random House Trade Paperback.

Nathan, R. (2005). *My freshman year: What a professor learned by becoming a student.* Ithaca, NY: Cornell University Press.

Newsome, C. (2000). Finding one's self in the margins. In M. W. Lustig & J. Koester (Eds.), *Among US: Essays on identity, belonging, and intercultural competence* (pp. 93–99). New York: Longman.

Oetzel, J. G. (1998). The effects of self-construals and ethnicity on self-reported conflict styles. *Communication Reports, 11,* 133–144.

Olivas, M. R. (2004). Communicating a Latina identity: Becoming different, doing difference, and being different. In M. Fong & R. Chuang (Eds.), *Communicating ethnic and cultural identity* (pp. 231–246). Lanham, MD: Rowman & Littlefield Publishers, Inc.

Orbe, M. P., & Harris, T. M. (2001). *Interracial communication: Theory into practice.* Belmont, CA: Wadsworth/Thomson Learning.

Parameswaran, R. (2004). Global queens, national celebrities: Tales of feminine triumph in post-liberalization India. *Critical Studies in Media Communication, 21,* 346–370.

Park, H. S., & Levine, T. R. (1999). The theory of reasoned action and self-construal: Evidence from three cultures. *Communication Monographs, 66,* 199–219.

Patterson, J. D., & Allen, M. W. (1997). Accounting for your actions: How stakeholders respond to the strategic communication of environmental activist organizations. *Journal of Applied Communication Research, 25,* 293–321.

Patterson, T. R., & Kelley, R. D. G. (2000). Unfinished migrations: Reflections on the African Diaspora and the making of the modern world. *African Studies Review, 43,* 11–45.

Patton, C. (1996). *Fatal advice: How safe sex education went wrong.* Durham, NC: Duke University Press.

Pepper, G. L., & Larson, G. S. (2006). Cultural identity tensions in a post-acquisition organization. *Journal of Applied Communication Research, 34,* 49–71.

Perelman, C., & Olbrechts-Tyteca, L. (1969). *The new rhetoric: A treatise on argumentation* (J. Wilkinson & P. Weaver, Trans.). Notre Dame, IN: University of Notre Dame Press.

Phelan, J. M. (1988). Communing in isolation. *Critical Studies in Mass Communication, 4,* 347–351.

Philipsen, G. (1975). Speaking "like a man" in Teamsterville: Culture patterns of role enactment in an urban neighborhood. *Quarterly Journal of Speech, 61,* 13–22.

Philipsen, G. (1976). Places for speaking in Teamsterville. *Quarterly Journal of Speech, 62,* 15–25.

Philipsen, G. (1987). The prospect for cultural communication. In D. L. Kincaid (Ed.), *Communication theory from Eastern and Western perspectives* (pp. 245–254). New York: Academic Press.

Philipsen, G. (1989). Speech and the communal function in four cultures. In S. Ting-Toomey & F. Korzenny (Eds.), *Language, communication and culture: Current directions* (pp. 79–92). Newbury Park, CA: Sage.

Philipsen, G. (1992). *Speaking culturally: Explorations in social communication*. Albany: State University of New York Press.

Pollock, D. (1998). Introduction: Making history go. In D. Pollock (Ed.), *Exceptional spaces: Essays in performance and history* (pp. 1–45). Chapel Hill: University of North Carolina Press.

Pörhölä, M., Karhunen, S., & Rainivaara, S. (2006). Bullying at school and in the workplace: A challenge for communication research. In C. S. Beck (Ed.), *Communication yearbook 30* (pp. 249–301). Mahwah, NJ: Lawrence Erlbaum Associates.

Powell, R. W. (2004, November 19). Lawsuit challenges ticketing of homeless. *San Diego Union Tribune*, pp. B1, B3.

Quasha, S., & McDaniel, E. R. (2003). Reinterpreting Japanese business communication in the information age. In L. A. Samovar & R. E. Porter (Eds.), *Intercultural communication: A reader* (10th ed., pp. 283–292). Belmont, CA: Thomson Wadsworth.

Quintanilla, K., Cano, N. F., & Ivy, D. K. (2004). The defining of menopause. In P. M. Buzzannell, H. Sterk, & L. H. Turner (Eds.), *Gender in applied communication contexts* (pp. 79–98). Thousand Oaks, CA: Sage.

Rao, N. (2003). "Half-truths" in Argentina, Brazil, and India: An intercultural analysis of physician–patient communication. In L. A. Samovar & R. E. Porter (Eds.), *Intercultural communication: A reader* (10th ed., pp. 309–319). Belmont, CA: Thomson Wadsworth.

Rayner, P. (2006). A need for postmodern fluidity? *Critical Studies in Media Communication, 23*, 345–349.

Reichl, R. (2005). *Garlic and sapphires: The secret life of a critic in disguise*. New York: Penguin Press.

Remen, R. N. (1996). *Kitchen table wisdom: Stories that heal*. New York: Riverhead Books.

Rose, H. M. (1997). Julianna Fjeld's *The Journey*: Identity production in an ASL performance. *Text and Performance Quarterly, 17*, 331–342.

Roth, N. L., & Nelson, M. S. (1997). HIV diagnosis rituals and identity narratives. *AIDS Care, 9*, 161–180.

Samovar, L. A., & Porter, R. E. (Eds.). (2003). *Intercultural communication: A reader* (10th ed.). Belmont, CA: Thomson Wadsworth.

Sarup, M., & Raja, T. (1998). *Identity, culture, and the postmodern world*. Edinburgh, Scotland: Edinburgh University Press.

Scott, C., Corman, S., & Cheney, G. (1998). A structurational model of identification in the organization. *Communication Theory, 8*, 298–336.

Scott, J. A. (2006). *"Then, I rose to her/my/our defense": Re-envisioning the history and legacy of the Combahee River Collective in Give Us Each Day: The Diary of Alice Dunbar-Nelson*. Paper presented at the annual convention of the National Communication Association, San Antonio, TX.

Shuter, R. (2003). Ethics, culture, and communication: An intercultural perspective. In L. A. Samovar & R. E. Porter (Eds.), *Intercultural communication: A reader* (10th ed., pp. 449–455). Belmont, CA: Thomson Wadsworth.

Sigelman, L. (2001). The presentation of self in presidential life: Onstage and backstage with Johnson and Nixon. *Political Communication, 18,* 1–22.

Singelis, T. M. (1994). The measurement of independent and interdependent self-construals. *Personality and Social Psychology Bulletin, 20,* 580–591.

Singelis, T. M., & Brown, W. (1995). Culture, self, and collectivist communication: Linking culture to individual behavior. *Human Communication Research, 21,* 354–389.

Smith, M. (1994). Altered states: Character and emotional response to the cinema. *Cinema Journal, 33,* 39–41.

Sontag, D. (2006, February 9). When the Lower Ninth posed proudly. *New York Times,* B1, B8.

Southwell, B., & Yzer, M. (2007). The roles of interpersonal communication in media campaigns. In C. S. Beck (Ed.), *Communication yearbook 31* (pp. 419–462). New York, NY: Lawrence Erlbaum Associates.

Stewart, C. (1999). Championing the rights of others and challenging evil: The ego function the protest of other-directed social movements. *Southern Communication Journal, 64,* 91–105.

Stiff, J. B. (1994). *Persuasive communication.* New York: Guilford Press.

Sweet, D. R. (2005). More than Goth: The rhetorical reclamation of the subcultural self. *Popular Communication, 3,* 239–264.

Tabouret-Keller, A. (1997). Language and identity. In F. Coulmas (Ed.), *The handbook of sociolinguistics* (pp. 315–326). Oxford, England: Blackwell.

Tajfel, H., & Turner, J. C. (1979). An integrative theory of intergroup conflict. In W. G. Austin & S. Worcher (Eds.), *The social psychology of intergroup relations* (pp. 33–47). Montereau, CA: Brooks/Cole.

Taylor, C. (1989). *Sources of the self: The making of modern identity.* Cambridge, MA: Harvard University Press.

The First March, (n.d.) *America's story from America's library.* Retrieved March 1, 2005 from http://www.americaslibrary.gove/cgi-bin/page.cgi/jb/modern/selma_1

Ting-Toomey, S. (1988). Intercultural conflict styles: A face-negotiation theory. In Y. Y. Kim & W. Gudykunst (Eds.), *Theories in intercultural communication* (pp. 213–235). Newbury Park, CA: Sage.

Ting-Toomey, S., & Kurogi, A. (1998). Facework competence in intercultural conflict: An updated face-negotiation theory. *International Journal of Intercultural Relations, 22,* 187–225.

Ting-Toomey, S., Oetzel, J. G., & Yee-Jung, K. (2001). Self-construal types and conflict management styles. *Communication Reports, 14,* 87–104.

Toulmin, S. (1964). *The uses of argument.* Cambridge, England: Cambridge University Press.

Triandis, H. (1995). *Individualism and collectivism.* Boulder, CO: Westview.

Trujillo, N. (1993). Interpreting November 22: A critical ethnography of an assassination site. *Quarterly Journal of Speech, 79,* 447–466.

Turner, V. (1969). *The ritual process.* Ithaca, NY: Cornell University Press.

Verser, R., & Wicks, R. H. (2006). Managing voter impressions: The use of images on presidential candidate Web sites during the 2000 campaign. *Journal of Communication, 56,* 178–197.

Waldeck, J., & Myers, K. (2007). Organizational assimilation theory, research, and implications for multiple areas of the discipline. In C. S. Beck (Ed.), *Communication yearbook 31* (pp. 361–367). New York, NY: Lawrence Erlbaum Associates.

Warren, J. T. (2003). *Performing purity: Whiteness, pedagogy, and the reconstitution of power.* New York: Peter Lang.

Wetherell, M. (Ed.). (1996). *Identities, groups and social issues.* London: Sage.

Wilson, B. (1993). *Trouble in Transylvania: A Cassandra Reilly mystery.* Seattle: Seal Press.

Wilson, K. H. (2003). The racial politics of imitation in the nineteenth century. *Quarterly Journal of Speech, 89,* 89–108.

Woodward, G. (2003). *The idea of identification.* Albany: State University of New York Press.

Young, N. L. (1994). There's no place like home: An analysis of the rhetoric of the homeless in a judicial opinion, an advocate's congressional testimony, and testimonial narratives by the homeless (Doctoral dissertation, Louisiana State University, 1994). *Dissertation Abstracts International, 55,* 243.

Young, N. L. (2005). Presence and praxis: Trans/forming identity for social change. *International Journal of Communication, 15,* 9–19.

Zhong, M. (2003). Contemporary social and political movements and their imprints on the Chinese language. In L. A. Samovar & R. E. Porter (Eds.), *Intercultural communication: A reader* (10th ed., pp. 206–216). Belmont, CA: Thomson Wadsworth.

Zorn, T. E. (1991). Willy Loman's lesson: Teaching identity management with *Death of a Salesman. Communication Education, 40,* 219–225.

Chapter 6 Contents

6

Alternative Times: Temporal Perceptions, Processes, and Practices Defining the Nonstandard Work Relationship

Dawna I. Ballard and Loril M. Gossett
University of Texas at Austin

Alternative notions of temporality are the defining quality of nonstandard work relationships such as temporary jobs, contract labor, part-time employment, and various forms of telework. These arrangements challenge traditional boundaries of personal versus work time, call into question unlimited versus conditional time limits for membership, and highlight seasonal versus steady-state orientations toward production. This chapter focuses on the unique temporal perceptions, processes, and practices associated with nonstandard work arrangements that shape and are shaped by communication in local and global circumstances, spanning multiple levels of organizational analysis and, indeed, diverse areas of our discipline. Given the position of time as a constitutive communication construct, examining the intersection of time and nonstandard work relationships lends value to investigations on a wide variety of important "life" issues. For instance, contemporary stakeholder conversations surrounding issues of work–life balance, a changing life span and lifestyle, and global community have all been accompanied by increased discussion of nonstandard work relationships. The temporal dimension of these discourses foregrounds the role of communication in shaping the quality of members' lives in both professional and personal domains.

Time represents a unifying theme among nonstandard work relationships—part-timers, temps, teleworkers, and independent contractors all share nontraditional temporal relationships with their employing organizations. More than a coincidence, time is one of the constituent elements signifying the "alternative" nature of these labor arrangements because temporal norms and assumptions shape the very process of communicating and organizing (Ballard & Seibold, 2003; Bourdieu, 1977; Hall, 1983; Schein, 1992). These nonstandard forms of employment challenge traditional boundaries of personal versus work time, call into question unlimited versus conditional time limits for membership, and highlight seasonal versus steady-state orientations toward production. As such, the "time" of these arrangements presents an opportunity for us to consider vital communication and organizational processes. The need to problematize basic

communication and organizational aspects of nonstandard membership is underscored by the fact that, despite their fairly long-standing position in modern organizational life, extant organizational and
communication theories continue to presume traditional membership roles (see related reviews on identity by Young, this volume, and
on organizational assimilation by Waldeck & Myers, this volume).

Time remains critical to understanding communication across
a range of settings and divisional boundaries. Bruneau (1974, 1977)
addressed the far-reaching importance of time in the study of communication more than a quarter of a century ago. Termed chronemics
(following Poyatos, 1976), Bruneau (1979) encouraged scholars to concentrate on "the meaning of human time experiencing as it influences
and is influenced by human communication" (p. 429). Bruneau underscored two important assumptions regarding the relationship between
time and communication in this definition. First, time and communication are recursively constituted. Our experience of time impacts
our communication patterns and, in turn, such communication patterns help frame our experience of time. Second, the focus on meaning implies that intersubjective—or shared—experiences of time, and
not solely objective measures of temporal behavior or individual (subjective) orientations, should inform communication scholarship. To
wit, the study of human temporality is inherently the study of human
communication. Social constructions of time exist intersubjectively
through persons' interaction and coordination with others, as well
as in their shared symbolic representations of temporality (Bourdieu,
1977; Giddens, 1984). As elaborated in this chapter, our experience of
time is dynamic and molded through the process of communication
in a variety of work, family, interpersonal, and global settings.

In the following pages, we theoretically ground the present discussion in terms of both temporality and communication. We draw
together three complementary frameworks—McPhee and Zaug's
(2000) framework of the communicative constitution of organizations; Ancona, Okhuysen, and Perlow's (2001) integrative interdisciplinary framework of organizational temporality; and Ballard
and Seibold's (2003) multilevel communication-based framework of
organizational temporality—to accomplish this goal. McPhee and
Zaug's work attracts our attention to key communicative aspects of
nonstandard work arrangements and assists development of a typology of these arrangements as a means of synthesizing a currently
fragmented literature. We then introduce Ancona and colleagues'

framework to offer a broad temporal perspective on nonstandard work and the role of temporal perceptions, processes, and practices in its social construction. Finally, we employ Ballard and Seibold's model to identify specific factors that have been theorized as impacting the status of nonstandard work and the members who hold these arrangements, as well as specific temporal dimensions that shed light on their unique position in the organizational landscape. In the remaining pages, we integrate these three models to explore the unique temporal perceptions, processes, and practices associated with alternative work arrangements that impact (and are impacted by) human interaction. Throughout the chapter, we reference several analogous findings and/or questions relevant to topics of scholarly interest across the field of communication. As such, we point to potential research directions in a variety of areas—including interpersonal, family, health, small-group, technology, conflict, religious, critical, and feminist communication scholars—that can help inform (and be informed by) research on nonstandard work relationships.

Theoretical Background and Outline of Chapter

Theorizing Nonstandard Membership

McPhee and Zaug (2000) identified *membership negotiation* and *activity coordination* as two of the four message flows or interaction processes (in addition to *self-structuring* and *institutional positioning*) contributing to the communicative constitution of organizations. These message flows shed light on the nature of nonstandard work relationships. By definition, compared to standard arrangements, nonstandard work features unique member negotiation flows (messages about the meaning of membership) and forms of activity coordination (messages about the time and timing of work). These two flows foster understanding of relationships that individuals have with (or in relation to) formal organizations and serve as an important boundary condition for our discussion. The other two flows—self-structuring and institutional positioning—examine macrolevel issues, such as the structure of the organization as a system (self-structuring) and the identity of the organization within the larger environment (institutional positioning). Thus, by focusing on member negotiation and activity coordination, we distinguish alternative *work relationships* (mesostructures) from alternative *forms of organizing* (macrostructures), a separate, albeit important, topic.

As McPhee and Zaug (2000) indicated, "These flows are arenas in which organizations do vary and can be changed in their fundamental nature" (¶ 13). They added:

> Many authors have claimed, over the decades, that new forms of organizations have emerged, as a result of various social and technological developments. A theory such as this one gives us a template by which to detect, diagnose, and assess novel organizational phenomena. (¶ 13)

Their theoretical framework stems from the assumption that examining the relatedness of these interaction processes in organizational life encompasses essential background to an informed understanding of organizations and their members. Nonstandard work arrangements provide an ideal context in which to explore the relatedness of membership negotiation and activity coordination and, in so doing, reveal fundamental assumptions about the connection of work, time, and communication in our lives. The growing body of literature on nonstandard work arrangements, however, lacks a clear organizing framework to facilitate analysis of the similarities and differences among the various types of nonstandard work arrangements.

According to Kalleberg, Reskin, and Hudson (2000), standard employment arrangements involve "the exchange of a worker's labor for monetary compensation from an employer, with work done on a fixed schedule—usually full time—at the employer's place of business, under the employer's control, and with the mutual expectation of continued employment" (p. 258). In contrast, nonstandard work arrangements entail positions that are part time, temporary in nature, or oblige employees to work in a different space or time than their co-workers and supervisors. McPhee and Zaug's (2000) *membership negotiation* and *activity coordination* communication flows offer a theoretical lens to identify and compare both standard and nonstandard organizational memberships. These two mesolevel flows particularly pertain to the study of nonstandard work arrangements because they highlight the ways in which organizational members establish their identities and learn how to function within the organization.

McPhee and Zaug (2000) discussed the process of membership negotiation as communication within the organization that "recounts the struggle of individuals to master or influence their member roles, statuses, and relations to the organization" (¶ 42). Specific interactions that typify the membership negotiation flow include recruiting, social-izing, and positioning the individual within the larger organizational framework. These membership negotiation processes differ based on the degree to which the organization treats an individual as a "per-manent" or "temporary" member of the organizational system (for related argument on organizational assimilation, also see Waldeck & Myers, this volume). In contrast, according to McPhee and Zaug, activity coordination concerns the interactions within the organi-zation that focus on "members engaging in interdependent work or deviating from pure collaborative engagement" (¶ 42). The activity coordination flow emphasizes day-to-day interactions and negotia-tions that take place among members in order to meet the practical demands and situations of daily organizational life and differ based on the degree to which an individual maintains a "fixed" or "flexible" spatial and temporal presence in the organization.

These two communication flows (membership negotiation and activity coordination) represent the key dimensions that distin-guish varied types of work arrangements. We use them here to cre-ate a typology illustrated in Figure 6.1 that depicts four membership types, allowing us to distinguish among standard (i.e., "real" mem-bership) and nonstandard relationships as well as between two types

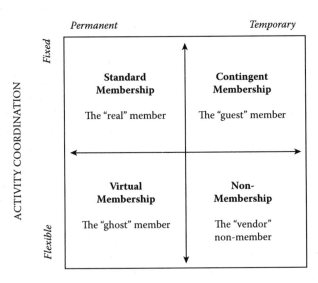

Figure 6.1   Typology of nonstandard work relationships.

of nonstandard arrangements (i.e., contingent "guest" membership and virtual "ghost" membership) and to provide a boundary that signifies where membership ends (i.e., "vendor" nonmembership). Notably, drawing from McPhee and Zaug's (2000) focus on *organizing* as a process—as opposed to *organizations* as entities—this typology pertains to a variety of organized social collectives (including family units and religious communities) and, potentially, to interpersonal, family, small-group, conflict, health, religious, feminist, and critical communication scholarship. We will detail such possible connections throughout the chapter.

The "Real" Member Versus "Vendor" Nonmember: Traditional Relationships Standard membership consists of persons treated as *real* members who occupy fixed physical and/or temporal space and unrestricted membership expectations. Examples of standard organizational membership include traditional employment relationships as well as associates of work cooperatives (Cheney, 1999). Family communication and conflict scholars might recognize discourse about "real" membership in terms of parents who occupy the same physical and temporal space as their children, thus constructing the noncustodial parent's family as nonstandard and less real, due to the lack of shared time and space (Braithwaite & Baxter, 2006).

In contrast, nonmember *vendor* status reflects the absence of any fixed physical or temporal organizational presence within the system, a true outsider, including third-party service providers such as property appraisers or lawyers hired to perform specific tasks. Nonmembership might also encompass home-based businesses, such as the new discourse on "mamapreneurs"—women who start their own businesses as a way to stay at home with their children while maintaining an income source (Ellison, 1999). The nonmember comprises an important distinction in an era of increasingly nontraditional work forms and arrangements, where nonmembership often gets confused with nonstandard membership. In health communication and small-group contexts, the distinction in online social support groups between members and "lurkers" exemplifies the difference between a member and nonmember (Alexander, Peterson, & Hollingshead, 2003, p. 313).

The "Guest" Member: Contingent Relationships Contingent membership consists of "guests" who occupy fixed physical and/or temporal space but are bound by conditional membership, including temporary employees, independent contractors, interns, substitute teachers, and seasonal workers. For example, guest members may work within the regular organizational system with respect to activity coordination but know a pre-established departure date or expect to leave upon the completion of a particular set of duties. The *Oxford English Dictionary* (OED) defines a guest variously as "one who is entertained at the house or table of another" and "a stranger" (Simpson & Weiner, 2006, ¶ 1). This definition reflects a conditional association, and it implies relational and communicative distance.

For instance, in religious communities, church attendees may judge membership status, in part, based on spatiotemporal regularity (i.e., by formally or informally tracking attendance). Regular and irregular attendees may be discursively regarded as real and guest members, respectively (Association of Religion data archives, 2006). Similarly, according to Simpson and Weiner (2006, ¶ 1), the OED defines *contingent* as "dependent for its occurrence or character on or upon some prior occurrence or condition" and "nonessential." Thus, the common use of terms like contingent to depict this part of the workforce reflects a superfluous orientation to their membership. Gossett (2002) employed the term *guest* to describe how organizations keep contingent members "at arm's length" in many settings (p. 385).

Communication scholars identify a variety of ways in which temporary relationships impact human interaction. For example, conflict theorists argue that people more likely engage in competitive rather than collaborative strategies when negotiating with someone they do not expect to see or work with in the future (Hocker & Wilmot, 1991). Temporary relationships allow people to engage in communicative strategies that may not be sustainable over the long term, but provide them with some short-term advantage. In the organizational context, temporary workers can afford to make mistakes at a job assignment because they are unlikely to follow them to their next job (Gossett, 2006; Henson, 1996).

Likewise, some employers treat contingent workers in a way that they would not be able to treat their permanent staff—subjecting them to abusive work conditions or sexual harassment (Gottfried, 1991; Rogers & Henson, 1997). Employers often perceive the temp as disposable, and he or she therefore may not receive the organizational considerations that a firm might offer to regular employees.

Additionally, in this volume, Miller, Roloff, and Malis's theorizing about ongoing conflicts raises the specter that new temps or interns might actually be participating in conflicts that began with previous members in their position. For example, we co-direct our department's internship program, and we routinely find that our students inherit conflicts that began before their arrival, especially in circumstances where others refer to them only as "the intern." This notion of "naming" members as a position, instead of a person, comprises an important communication phenomenon associated with contingent relationships.

The "Ghost" Member: Virtual Relationships   Virtual membership consists of "ghost" members who occupy permanent positions within the organization but who differ from others in the organization with respect to the way that they navigate the spatiotemporal boundaries of the system. Such organizational members encompass telecommuters, virtual team members (that are members of brick-and-mortar firms), part-timers, and job sharers. These members hold a flexible physical and/or temporal presence, but long-term membership expectations. The definition of *virtual* in the OED originally referenced being "possessed of certain physical virtues or capacities" and now more commonly suggests "that is so in essence or effect, although not formally or actually; admitting of being called by the name so far as the effect or result is concerned" (Simpson & Weiner, 2006, ¶ 1). Thus, the physical absence of these members (for at least some of the time) distinguishes them from their standard counterparts, particularly in the discourse of their colleagues.

For example, Ostrom (2003) described confusion about time and space as a common issue associated with job-sharing arrangements. As a job sharer herself in a newsroom setting, she recounted:

> Despite our constructing giant charts, plastering them everywhere and peppering our various editors with them, there always seemed to be confusion about who was where when ... which inevitably led to the 5th "W": "Why?" As in, "Why the hell are they doing this????!!!!" (p. 151)

The situation that brought on this tirade by her editor reflects her status as a *ghost*, defined as "an incorporeal being" (Simpson & Weiner, 2006, ¶ 1). Connotatively, describing a person as a ghost means that he or she remains conspicuously absent from normal, day-to-day interaction.

In contrast to organizational contexts where those working in conventional settings sometimes see ghost members as deserters, in relational and interpersonal communication contexts, ghost membership sometimes leads to greater intimacy due to idealized perceptions of the real persona. For example, research on long-distance romantic relationships indicates that these couples often feel more committed to each other than co-located couples. According to Dainton and Aylor (2002), while the lack of regular physical intimacy or casual interaction is difficult, these communicative challenges can encourage committed partners to emphasize the positive over the negative.

Similarly, virtual organizational members often find value in their alternative labor arrangement despite the fact that these employees also report greater social isolation and fewer advancement opportunities than their "real" co-workers. Committed virtual workers tend to emphasize the temporal flexibility and personal freedoms (e.g., the ability to wear casual clothes, no commute time, etc.) created by their long-distance organizational memberships—advantages not similarly available to "standard" employees of the firm.

The present discussion focuses on contingent and virtual work arrangements and the distinct temporal perceptions, processes, and practices that define them. Having established the phenomena of interest as well as their origins in McPhee and Zaug's (2000) communication flows, we turn next to the temporal aspects of the analysis.

Theorizing Organizational Temporality

Ancona and colleagues (2001) offered an integrative framework designed to provide a common set of terms and points of reference for the study of temporality in the workplace. Used here to order our analysis, they described three interrelated categories of temporal constructs—*conceptions of time, mapping activities to time,* and *actors relating to time*—that allow researchers simultaneously to clarify the focus of a given analysis as well as to consider multiple aspects and interrelationships concerning said constructs. They recommended that researchers specify a category (from among these three) when using a term in order to set the context of the conversation. Because "our understanding of a variable in one category affects and is affected by variables in the other two categories" (p. 521), they suggested that investigations should be described in terms of each of the three categories, highlighting the interrelationships. The concurrent clarity and insight of this practice should foster more fruitful conversations with greater synergistic potential. Locating the ensuing analysis within this broader framework facilitates such dialogue as well as underscores the mutually constitutive nature of temporal perceptions, processes, and practices.

In the following sections of the chapter, we link each of these aspects of temporality—the perceptions, processes and practices—associated with nonstandard work relationships to Ancona and colleagues' (2001) framework concerning broader conceptions of time, how persons and organizations map activities to time, and the ways in which actors relate to time, respectively. Within this larger metaframework, we use Ballard and Seibold's (2003) mesolevel model to identify temporal perceptions at the individual, group, organizational, and cultural levels that give rise to nonstandard work relationships; examine how members' diverse *construals of time* impact temporal processes surrounding membership issues, and explore the *enactments of time* most pivotal to the temporal practices of alternative organizing. We address each of these issues (i.e., temporal perceptions, processes, and practices) in turn and employ them as the organizing framework for the remainder of this chapter.

Temporal Perceptions Associated With Nonstandard Relationships

The unique temporal perceptions associated with nonstandard relationships extend from members' *conceptions of time* (Ancona et al., 2001). Variables in this category concern the different types of time organizations and their member experiences, and how these conceptions influence (and are influenced by) the ways in which members *map activities to time* (e.g., their temporal enactments that reflect unique temporal practices associated with activity coordination) as well as *relate to time* (e.g., their temporal construals, which alter or forestall the temporal processes associated with traditional membership negotiation). Three types of temporal conceptions through which members discern what counts as nonstandard include objective, subjective, and intersubjective (Hernadi, 1992).

Objective time references external pacers in the organizational environment, such as market forces that dictate product life cycles.

Subjective time inheres in individuals' unique temporal experience associated with individual characteristics such as personal influences, professional–personal conflicts, and social identity. Finally, *intersubjective time* concerns shared experiences of time by a group of people, including dominant cultural patterns, industry norms, occupational norms, organizational culture, and work group norms as related to time. Hernadi (1992) explained that "[a]s social role-players, natural organisms and personal selves we always exist at the intersections of those *intersubjective, objective,* and *subjective* lifetimes through which each of us participates in a variety of world times" [italics added] (p. 151). While time is never solely objective, subjective, or intersubjective—as each one shapes the other—these distinctions help us to reflect on how varied conceptions of time impact perceptions of nonstandard work arrangements. Ballard and Seibold (2003) addressed each of these varied temporal conceptions in their mesolevel model of organizational temporality. Their model offers an integrative perspective on the role of cultural, environmental, organizational, group, and individual level influences in shaping organizational members' temporal experience. We detail each of these sources in the following section.

Cultural-Level Influences

As elaborated below, *dominant cultural patterns* frame the broader conversation about members' orientation to employment, in general, and their relationship with their employing organization, in particular. For example, cultural norms surrounding temporal compression, speed, long- versus short-term expectations, face time, and downtime and leisure work to shape perceptions of nonstandard arrangements.

Temporal Compression   While researchers have established differences in time across cultures (Bruneau, 1979; Hall, 1983; Hofstede & Bond, 1988), the increasing use of nonstandard work arrangements represents a global spatiotemporal phenomenon in industrial culture. For example, organizational and national borders do not bind independent contractors or teleworkers—they rely on communication technologies to work virtually throughout the globe. The proliferation of communication technologies enables and constrains this intersubjective experience of temporal "boundarylessness," and it reflects the larger postmodern theme of temporal compression articulated by Hassard (2002). The temporal compression that characterizes members' lives at work and home often makes alternative work arrangements that rely on such compression more culturally accepted—even if the coordinative and self-structuring interaction processes can cost more for organizations and create more physical and emotional demands on their members than traditional arrangements (Shockley-Zalabak, 2002). The rapid growth of this industry illustrates a global transformation of the temporal contract between the worker and the employer and shapes perceptions of their conventionality.

Related to the boundarylessness created by advanced communication information technologies (ACITs) is the fact that, because it is always 8:00 a.m. somewhere and the Internet is always "on," nonstandard members (such as independent contractors or teleworkers) must adapt their home or local schedules in order to be available whenever needed by organizations. Increasing discussion around the Blackberry phenomenon (also called "Crackberries") and their associated 24–7 work demands raises questions for critical scholarship about where power resides in these arrangements. A related study of governing in operating rooms suggests that, regardless of formal power positions, the persons that control the time and scheduling can exert significant power and influence over others (Riley & Manias, 2006). While telework, job sharing, and independent contracting can constitute forms of employee control, critical scholars are well situated to problematize the distribution of power in such relationships. Similarly, communication technology scholars may explore the intersection of ACITs and temporality.

Speed   Contingent employment, in the form of temporary labor, is rapidly expanding in nearly every industrial economy due, in part, to the speed with which such relationships can be formed and the related lack of long-term obligation. While staffing firms employ only 2% of all U.S. workers, they comprise the nation's fifth fastest growing industry (Berchem, 2004). This field represents one of the most rapidly growing types of nonstandard employment in the European Union (Townsley & Stohl, 2003; Van Breugel, Van Olffen,

& Olie, 2005). Since 1992, temporary work has "increased five-fold in Denmark, Spain, Italy, and Sweden and just under four-fold in Austria" (Storrie, 2002, p. 28).

Temporary staffing has become a fully multinational industry, with firms such as Manpower Staffing maintaining offices in 68 countries, including locales as diverse as the United States, China, and Morocco. Manpower's expansion into China is particularly interesting; the agency established its Beijing office through a joint venture with the Chinese government. According to Parker (1994), "Like the U.S. offices, the purpose of the Chinese unit is to provide clerical and technical workers to Western and Japanese companies operating in China" (p. 32). The increasingly globalized nature of the temporary help industry allows multinational firms to move quickly into new countries and take advantage of the local labor pool, without altering the contingent labor practices of their home culture. Here, a culture of speed leads to positive perceptions of contingent relationships.

Long- Versus Short-Term Expectations   Despite a broad shift toward contingent labor around the world, facilitated by a shared experience of temporal compression, differences in temporal perceptions associated with contingent work still persist across countries due to an intersection of economic and cultural differences concerning the temporal nature of work itself. For example, Houseman and Osawa (2003) noted national differences in the growth of nonstandard work arrangements. In countries with high employment taxes or expectations of lifetime employment, such as Japan, companies have increasingly embraced the use of part-time rather than full-time employees. This labor arrangement has the advantage of maintaining a degree of employment stability within the organizational system while reducing the financial burden of maintaining a large "standard" workforce.

In the United States, the advantages from the employer perspective include the absence of benefits, retirement plans, and insurance programs for nonstandard members; only an elite group of permanent employees are afforded such resources (Jorgensen & Riemer, 2000; Wiens-Tuers, 2001). This economic incentive for companies encourages the long-term use of nonstandard labor arrangements. It also explains why, in Europe (where governments often require companies to provide equal pay and benefits for their nonstandard and standard employees), vendor relationships are more common, forcing the division between members and nonmembers to become more explicit (Houseman & Osawa, 2003).

The growth in contingent labor (temporary and contract work, in particular) in countries like Singapore relates both to a need for companies to attract employees in a tight market as well as to cultural values of long-term membership for standard members (Van Dyne & Ang, 1998). In Singapore, a country with chronic labor shortages due to low birthrates and an aging population, contingent work arrangements draw people into the organization rather than pushing them away. Thus, offering flexible work conditions to young workers as a low risk way to try out an organization comprises a strategy that firms use to attract and retain valuable members.

Related to the intersection of cultural values and economic policy, unions in Europe remain strong and labor laws make it difficult to terminate employees without cause (e.g., downsizing); as such, workers still expect organizations to offer stable and somewhat permanent employment relationships (Amuedo-Dorantes, 2000). The European Foundation for the Improvement of Living and Working Conditions (2006) offered one example:

> In Spain, job security has been, and is still, one of the principles underlying labour regulations, and has led to regulations such as the preference for contracts of employment of indefinite duration, the prohibition on repeated renewal of temporary contracts, continuation of the contract of employment in the event of transfer of undertaking, and the requirement for justified reasons for dismissal. (¶ 1)

Job security was at the heart of the 2006 youth riots in France after employers wanted the right to dismiss employees under 26 years of age without cause during the first 2 years of employment (Ford, 2006). While 2 years at the same firm may seem like a somewhat permanent job to U.S. workers, French youth perceive such a work arrangement as inherently "temporary" (even though they may not be terminated after 2 years). In contrast, after experiencing several decades of corporate downsizings in the United States, workers have come to accept the notion that organizations no longer offer long-term employment stability. Buzzanell and Turner (2003) argued that job loss has become so common that Americans view all jobs as somewhat temporary and "redefine career as a series of employer–employee contracts" (p. 28). Thus, different cultural attitudes about the temporal nature of work and related economic policies shape how workers perceive guest versus real membership.

Face Time   Cultural differences toward the meaning of work relationships also impact perceptions of virtual work and the frequency with which companies and individuals make these arrangements. For example, some U.S. employees may view virtual work arrangements (such as telecommuting) as desirable because these situations allow them to spend more time at home while still maintaining a degree of organizational presence (constituting a *ghost* membership) (Hylmö & Buzzanell, 2002; Kraut, 1989). For these members, time spent in the workplace does not hold symbolic value as long as the job gets done—a specific cultural orientation that regards a strict demarcation between work and home (A. G. Golden, Kirby, & Jorgenson, 2006; E. P. Thompson, 1967).

However, in cultures where work and life are not so carefully divided (E. P. Thompson, 1967), members treat virtual work arrangements as less socially acceptable. For example, Claus Bang Møller, a Danish employment expert, noted that workers in his country are expected to develop strong ties with their organizational colleagues and become part of the work community. Face time and socializing entail important aspects of employment in that culture, and, as such, they do not consider telecommuting to be an appropriate work arrangement (C. Møller, personal communication, March 27, 2006).[1] They envision members' time as a shared commodity that permits the organization to function as a whole.

Downtime and Leisure   Part of the popularity and desire for virtual work arrangements in the United States may stem from the fact that the country has one of the longest average work weeks and the fewest vacation days compared to other industrialized countries (De Graaf, 2003). The temporal demands of U.S. companies continue to be so great that workers may need to negotiate for "part-time" status simply to be assured of a 40-hour work week (Catalyst, 1993; Goldstein, 2006). Increasingly, this challenge has created a discursive environment where organizational members talk openly about the need for decreased work hours.

Citizens in the United States and Canada celebrated the first annual "Take Back Your Time" day" on October 24, 2003. As described on their Web site (www.timeday.org, ¶ 1), "Take Back Your

Time is a major U.S./Canadian initiative to challenge the epidemic of overwork, over-scheduling and time famine that now threatens our health, our families and relationships, our communities and our environment." As a bona-fide political movement, initiatives such as Time Day make a perfect site for studying the role of discourse in engaging civic participation. In marked contrast to U.S. working conditions, the European Union has a "Working Time Directive" that mandates a 48-hour limit to the work week (Millar, 2005). Additionally, France and parts of Germany have attempted to further limit the work week to 35 hours (Hermann, 2005). Many European countries also offer six or more weeks of annual vacation time, all of which may make it easier for employees to see full-time employment as reasonable rather than a familial or lifestyle sacrifice (Houseman & Osawa, 2003; Knox, 2004).

Environmental-Level Influences

Technical Environment The technical environment (Scott, 1987) within which an organization exists contains fairly objective temporal pacers, or *zeitgebers* (a German word literally meaning "time givers") (Bluedorn, 2002), that influence perceptions of nonstandard work arrangements. Aside from the intersubjective temporality, organizations must also deal with objective temporal markers that indicate things like average time to market for their competitors as well as observed fiscal markers for reporting quarterly performance. Because of market speed and other pacers in the environment, various forms of virtual work have come to be utilized by contemporary organizations as a way to meet these challenges. While variations on this theme are not novel, the increased use of this work arrangement and its particular reliance on communication technology encompass some of the factors that distinguish it as a new and nonstandard work relationship. Environmental zeitgebers have contributed to its increasing prevalence and its status as a preferred alternative in certain contexts and industries (Shockley-Zalabak, 2002).

Members of virtual teams confront their own circadian rhythms, another zeitgeber in addition to the environmental one, which draws attention to the disadvantages of certain virtual arrangements (McGrath & Kelly, 1986; Shockley-Zalabak, 2002). Unfortunately, coordinating across time zones means a disruption in traditional sleep cycles. While Shockley-Zalabak characterized this situation as an inconvenience, depending on the regularity of such disruption, it can actually represent a potential health risk for participants in these arrangements. In fact, medical professionals have recognized that the health risks associated with ignoring the body's circadian rhythms may extend beyond the employee. Not surprisingly, extended work shifts for medical residents are dangerous for patients (Humphries, 2004). Downplaying the health risks of a variety of time-related stressors, including nonstandard work arrangements, comprises an area that health communication researchers are well situated to interrogate these messages. Further, examining the ways that organizations normalize and downplay these health risks in everyday discourse would be a valuable contribution to the literature.

Institutional Environment   Related to the notion of a zeitgeber, some organizations hire temporary workers to act as "rate busters" and speed up production or increase the effort exerted by their regular workforce. Coupled with decreased job security, this type of cultural practice can shape the institutional character of members' work environment as even less secure and more competitive. Temporary members interested in obtaining permanent positions learn to work at a faster pace and take fewer breaks than their permanent counterparts in order to demonstrate their value to the company (Gottfried, 1991; Henson, 1996). These behaviors can threaten the job security of permanent workers, pressuring them to match the pace of the temps in order to maintain their position in the organization. This rate-buster effect has also been found with part-time workers, who use high productivity as a way to compensate for the lack of physical time that they spend in the office environment (Kropf, 1998).

Organizational-Level Influences

Industry and Occupational Norms
Industry Norms   Depending on shared conceptions of time, we should note that members do not always label virtual work relationships as "alternative," and these arrangements may even be common in certain industries, such as day trading and insurance sales. Additionally, nursing and other types of "shift" work occupations common in certain industries now embrace part-time and job-sharing

arrangements (Goldstein, 2006; Thornicroft & Strathdee, 1992). Acceptance may extend from the fact that shift work already draws clear temporal boundary lines between those who are on and off the clock, regardless of their status as professional or managerial employees. Even the notion of being "on call" discursively represents that times exist when one is not available (aside from exceptional circumstances). Thus, the lack of shared space and time (i.e., the physical absence of some members while others work) may be more expected and acceptable in some occupations than in others. Future research may seek to compare the negotiation of nonstandard work arrangements in 24-hour or shift-based occupations (healthcare, manufacturing, hotels, etc.) with professions that organize labor around a more traditional 40-hour week (office administration, banking, etc.).

Occupational Norms   The perceptions associated with contingent work arrangements also differ based on occupational members' intersubjective experience of time. As an occupational group, managers and executives must take a long-term perspective on short-term decisions and be strategic about the types of work arrangements that best suit their organization (Lawrence & Lorsch, 1967). Accordingly, the long-term implications of entering into contingent (i.e., short-term) labor agreements shape their perceptions of this work practice. For instance, in the volatile U.S. economy, organizations often use guest workers (temps, contract labor, interns, etc.) to enable core-periphery management models where "real" organizational members are protected from organizational downsizing by a layer of easily excisable contingent members (Aaronson, Rissman, & Sullivan, 2004; Wiens-Tuers, 2001). This "just-in-time" approach to staffing permits managers to keep a degree of distance from their contingent employees and makes them easier to terminate (Gossett, 2002). Used in this way, contingent work arrangements serve as a management strategy for keeping guest workers separated from the rest of the organization.

Organizational Culture   In addition to broad cultural norms, varying organizational cultures also shape (and are shaped by) members' intersubjective temporal experience, which informs perceptions regarding nonstandard work. Specifically, notions of face time and normative career trajectories comprise sociotemporal issues that inform our conversations about nonstandard work relationships such as telework, job sharing, and part-time employment. These virtual arrangements can meet with resistance precisely because they violate the spatiotemporal norms of an organization (Feldman & Doerping-haus, 1992). For example, Glass's (2004) study of work-family policies used by women found that "months spent working from home or working fewer than 30 hours per week (accommodations that reduce the physical time employees spend at their workplace) were heavily penalized [on wage growth], though only for managerial and professional women" (p. 387). Staff employees might be able to manage ghost membership, but managers and professional female employees needed to be constantly and physically present within the work environment to avoid negative salary consequences. Organizational norms that place a high value on face time and physical presence can intervene to frame virtual arrangements as marginal and, thus, the participants less committed or promotable (Ellison, 1999; Hylmö & Buzzanell, 2002; Kropf, 1998).

Shared beliefs and norms associated with time and perceptions of contingent and virtual work practices vary widely across a given occupation within the same environmental and national context. For example, stories about senior colleagues discouraging tenure-track female faculty from "setting back their clock" (analogous to going part time or job sharing) to have children prior to promotion and denying tenure to others for the same reason exist alongside accounts of university departments where multiple assistant professors have young children and receive support from colleagues to do so (Story, 2005). Face-time norms fluctuate a great deal as well. Whereas some academic departments expect assistant professors to work from campus and be visible at all hours of the day (and night), face-time requirements might be nonexistent at a sister department in another location. Therefore, organizations' and work groups' experiences of time strongly influence perceptions of ghost members (those engaged in arrangements like telework, part-time employment, or job sharing).

Group-Level Influences

The Group Guest The process of group development places a premium on member stability (Arrow, Poole, Henry, Wheelan, & Moreland, 2004). Relatedly, group norms surrounding temporal continuity influence perceptions of members with discontinuous histories and/or without expectations for a future with the group (for related reviews of research on community and identity, respectively, see underwood & Frey, this volume; Young, this volume). As a result, guest members can find themselves defined as outsiders and not allowed to participate fully in the group (Barker, 1999; Galup, Saunders, Nelson, & Cerveny, 1997; Gossett, 2002).

While new standard employees might be quickly socialized into the group, organizations can marginalize contingent employees by treating them as outsiders with limited interaction opportunities (for related discussion of organizational assimilation, see Waldeck & Myers, this volume). For example, Sias, Kramer, and Jenkins (1997) found new temporary workers less likely than their new standard counterparts to engage in regular interaction with their co-workers (i.e., asking or giving information). These guest members may have difficulty communicating with their permanent co-workers and fellow temporary employees because they lack a past or an expectation of a future relationship with each other (Putnam & Stohl, 1990). As such, these members struggle with significant challenges as they strive to be integrated into work groups and develop the social norms that might govern their interactions with others.

Contingent workers may not be communicatively isolated within the group environment, but their interpersonal interactions can look different from those of their permanent co-workers because of their short-term membership expectations. For example, Nelkin (1970) concluded that migrant workers tend to form affective rather than instrumental friendships with one another since they do not perceive value in an instrumental friendship but affective relationships make the environment more pleasant.

As co-directors of the internship program for our own department, we find that student journal entries based on their internship experiences regularly reflect frustration with feeling excluded from ordinary member rituals, despite receiving messages about their wonderful performances as contingent group members. In more than one instance, interns described exclusion from staff parties, even after actually helping to plan and execute the event. Nonetheless, in other cases (though certainly not the norm), students felt welcomed into the fold and given full membership privileges immediately upon arrival, evidence in support of the moderating role of group norms. Thus, at the group level, intersubjective temporal norms concerning continuity intercede to shape the meaning ascribed to nonstandard work relationships.

Finally, the presence of contingent workers can have an impact on the entire group environment and not just on individual workers. For example, Pearce (1993) determined that the inclusion of contract employees on workplace teams lowered the level of trust permanent employees had in their employer. Additionally, Cheney (1999) noted that the addition of temporary members in Basque work cooperatives challenged group norms of full participation and organizational ownership. Nelkin's (1970) study of migrant work groups found that tension and mistrust were common characteristics of these work groups because the workers did not necessarily know each other and had no clear expectation of a future relationship after the season was over. Contingent work relationships frame perceptions about the meaning of group membership and the nature of interactions between co-workers, mirroring the "support" attributes of community described by underwood and Frey elsewhere in this volume.

The Group Ghost Similar to the challenges of guest members, ghost members who may be longtime employees of the organization also report feeling communicatively isolated from their work groups as a result of their nonstandard work arrangement (Kraut, 1989; Meyers & Hearn, 2000). Teleworkers and part-timers can lose touch with group norms by lacking a physical presence in the office at the same time as their co-workers—missing out on lunches, gossip over coffee, and spontaneous hallway interactions. Hylmö (2004) equated the transition to telework with the loss associated with organizational downsizing. In both situations, co-workers "lose" the day-to-day interactions that they had with one another and may mourn the loss of daily contact (p. 62). The telework experience feels so distinct that many of the virtual members in Hylmö's study referred to themselves as "independent contractors" (p. 54). Thus, the ghost member may come to feel like a guest as well because of the change in group dynamics. Similar to contingent members, virtual members' perceptions of group dynamics and interactions often change with their transitions to this alternative work arrangement.

The family communication literature discusses related group norm challenges created by divorce and remarriage (Braithwaite, Olson, Golish, Soukup, & Turman, 2001). Blended family communication dynamics are particularly complicated because they highlight the fact that members cannot presume stability within the family system. As a result, some members may be defined as more "ghost" than "real" (e.g., the parent living outside the home) or treated inherently as "guest" (e.g., a parent's most recent spouse) (Braithwaite & Baxter, 2006). Blended families experience group norms that are uniquely flexible; members cannot take their relationship and status with the others in the system as stable or permanent. Related to the absence of stability in a family unit, migrating agricultural workers must physically move between regional and national boundaries in order to keep up with seasonal and crop changes. They must adapt to the temporal norms of their various employers (work hours, growing seasons, pace of labor, holidays, etc.) to stay on an assignment. In the case of parents who hold these work arrangements, this instability directly affects their families.

Individual-Level Influences

Personal Influences: Life Cycle Stages
Early and Late Career   In addition to intersubjective temporal constructions at cultural, organizational, and group levels, organizational members' own subjective experiences of time reinforce the alternative nature of certain work relationships. Age constitutes one such temporal variable that, while objective in and of itself, takes on a subjective meaning for individuals. Age-based social norms often moderate members' perceptions of participating in nonstandard employment relationships. For example, a contingent work arrangement shifts in its meaning and significance depending on the time in a worker's life that it occurs (Hassard, 1991). For a younger worker, contingent employment (internships, temping, etc.) may provide an opportunity to experiment with different occupations without a corresponding perception of commitment or obligation to the employing organizations (Kurlantzick, 2001). Relatedly, contingent work can allow older workers to downshift into more flexible employment arrangements while still remaining active and earning an income (Hignite, 2000; Parker, 1994). Individuals nearing retirement (as well as those in early career stages) can perceive contingent work arrangements as boundary spanning, allowing them to move gradually from organizational outsiders to insiders and then back to outsiders (see, e.g., Riggs, 2004).

Midcareer   In contrast to perceptions of nonstandard employment during early and late career stages, workers perceive temporary work quite differently during the middle stages of life or when such situations unfold involuntarily. For example, mid-career professionals

who have been downsized often report difficulty finding employment despite their many years of work experience (Riggs, 2004). In
a study by Buzzanell and Turner (2003), some downsized men felt
unable to navigate the challenges of finding work after they had been
let go from their former employer. One gentleman indicated that he
was "'dumbfounded' and felt victimized by bureaucracy and age discrimination because he was in his 50s ... [H]is preparations and his
job search, while resulting in part-time work with career potential,
were perceived as unsuccessful" (p. 38).

Age-based cohort differences can also lead to interpersonal problems on the job for employees who suddenly become the generational
minority. Once hired, older members can struggle to be defined as
legitimate subordinates by their (sometimes younger) organizational
superiors (Riggs, 2004). As a result of these factors and because of
broader culturally based attributions that associate seniority in age
with organizational seniority, older workers re-entering the workforce
face age-based hiring discrimination (Chan & Stevens, 2001; McCann
& Giles, 2002). While part-time and temporary employment may be
desirable for younger and preretirement workers, these arrangements
typically do not satisfy mid-career professionals who expected to be
at the height of their earning power and organizational status during their 40s and 50s (Buzzanell & Turner, 2003). Thus, perceptions
of nonstandard work can be shaped both by members' subjective
temporal experience as well as their colleagues' intersubjective (i.e.,
cultural) constructions of time.

Work–Home Conflict: Professional Versus Personal Time   In addition to issues associated with age, individuals' subjective temporal
experiences with conflicts between their professional and personal
time can lead them to seek out nonstandard work relationships
(Bailyn, 1993; Edley, Hylmö, & Newsom, 2004). Similar to the dialectics that communication scholars use to examine the nature of
interpersonal and familial relationships (Baxter & Montgomery,
1996) and, in the current volume, that Acheson uses to explicate
silence, the formation and performance of nonstandard arrangements can be understood as a negotiation between multiple and
competing notions of membership.

These arrangements make explicit the fact that memberships
extend beyond organizational borders to family, friends, civic groups,
religious communities, and other non-work-related entities. They

prompt organizational scholars to extend their boundaries outside the workplace and, similarly, encourage others to consider how professional issues shape (and are shaped by) personal ones. Notably, we find "work–life balance" discourse to be problematic because it reflects and reinforces a tension between "working" and "living." Rather than broadening scholars' range of inquiry outside work-related issues, it actually creates a false dichotomy and continues to privilege work. Instead, we choose to describe this dialectic as a tension between the professional and personal—which we constantly negotiate in our day-to-day interactions across settings and contexts.

Job sharing, shifting to part-time status, becoming an independent contractor, and engaging in telework constitute some of the ways that individuals use alternative work forms to negotiate issues of professional/personal balance and (re)define their temporal relationship with their employing organization (A. G. Golden et al., 2006; Kirby & Krone, 2002; Solomon, 1994). For example, people who wish to stay home to care for children or the elderly, attend school, or pursue another avocation need to attain personal flexibility without compromising economic stability. Nonstandard employment can facilitate accomplishment of both goals. Nonetheless, as described next, cultural differences impact the degree to which individuals envision this choice as a viable option.

Hantrais (1993) noted that the United Kingdom boasts one of the highest rates of part-time work in Europe. She argued that the prominence of this particular nonstandard arrangement can be partly attributed to the preference of British mothers to work part time in order to be home to care for their children. In contrast, according to Hantrais, "French women in professional occupations more readily accept that a child's mother is not necessarily the only person who could look after him/her in the early formative years" (p. 154). Additionally, Warner (2005) found that French society considers work to be "a normal part, even a desirable part, of a modern mother's life" (p. 10), and women do not feel guilty about maintaining a full-time career after they have children.

Related to the cultural and economic intersections described earlier, many Scandinavian countries provide state support for childcare facilities, making it cost effective for both parents to work full time rather than for one parent to stay at home to look after the children, according to Birte Asmuss, a professor of business communication in Denmark (B. Asmuss, personal communication, March 27,

2006).² Conversely, "the rapid growth of part-time employment among Japanese women has been linked to a tax structure with strong financial incentives for married women to keep their earnings below certain thresholds" (Houseman & Osawa, 2003, p. 11). Therefore, according to Houseman and Osawa, Japanese women often leave the workforce entirely when raising young children, and they only work part time when their offspring reach adulthood because their extra income is offset with the cost of child care and taxes.

Consistent with these findings, the Japanese employment model encourages a strong divide between personal and professional responsibilities, with one spouse fully responsible for parenting and the other for wage earning. However, parenting is expected to be a shared duty in many Scandinavian countries. For example, in Sweden, a couple can only get full family leave by sharing it between the father and mother (Eriksson, 2005). Additionally, both parents possess the right to shortened work hours until their children reach 8 years of age. Such policies encourage both men and women to make adjustments in their work arrangements as a way to balance personal and occupational demands, shaping positive perceptions of nonstandard work relationships (Houseman & Osawa, 2003).

In cultures such as the United States, where couples do not necessarily divide family-care expectations equally, women may be more likely to pursue family leave than men (Kirby & Krone, 2002). Thus, when home life becomes demanding, women, rather than men, tend to make the occupational and temporal adjustments. The predominance of women in part-time and job-sharing positions marks these work arrangements as more than simply "nonstandard" in these cultures. Instead, nonstandard arrangements become gendered, defining the part-timer or teleworker as someone on the "mommy track" and no longer a full-fledged member of the organization (Buzzanell & Lucas, 2006; Ellison, 1999; Rogers, 2000). Such discursive formations serve to differentiate this work relationship, and the subjective temporal experiences that give rise to it, as nonstandard.

Social Identity

Separate Identities   While group norms concerning temporal continuity and stability often marginalize short-term members, these same members—such as independent contractors, interns, and temporary employees—often possess a distinct social identity that impacts their own subjective experience of time and perceptions of their status as different from others (Henson, 1996; Jordan, 2003). Gossett (2006) found that, just as employing organizations may keep their temporary employees at arm's length, the temps themselves can draw boundaries and forestall their complete assimilation into the organization. The short-term nature of many temp assignments allows these workers to experience time as well as perceptions of their membership as highly punctuated and enables them to maintain social identities separate from their various employers (Gossett, 2001).

Multiple Identities   Independent contractors also experience unique temporal challenges to their social identity. Contractors may work for multiple organizations at the same time by contributing to several different projects at once. The overlapping temporal nature of these work relationships challenges the ability of contractors to define their identities clearly as members of one firm or another. Additionally, in the case of job loss, adopting the nonstandard identity of an independent contractor or consultant can provide persons with an occupational identity to replace the organizational one that they lost. Contractors and consultants are never really out of work. They just continually search for new clients (Evans, Kunda, & Barley, 2004). Thus, the fluid temporal boundaries frame their perceptions of this work arrangement.

Threatened Identities   The role of social identity in shaping perceptions of nonstandard work has a great deal to do with the degree to which these arrangements are voluntary or involuntary. For example, Buzzanell and Goldzwig (1991) observed that "linear thinking and talk" dominate the career literature (p. 475). Persons who deviate from this norm by choice can find their nonstandard work identities empowering and uniquely satisfying. However, as members feel forced into the nonlinear trajectory associated with nonstandard employment due to job loss or lack of other opportunities, these work arrangements can threaten their sense of social worth and self-esteem. Despite the fact that downsizing has become common enough to lose some of its stigma, workers still do not always know how to process the negative emotions associated with job loss (Buzzanell & Turner, 2003). In this case, they perceive nonstandard work as inherently problematic.

Further, in the United States, relying on nonstandard work can place the health and safety of a person's family at risk, contributing to negative perceptions of certain virtual and contingent arrangements.

American workers typically count on their employers to provide health insurance, retirement benefits, and other key services. However, temporary and part-time positions in the United States rarely come with benefits similar to those enjoyed by full-time employees (Rogers, 2000; Smith, 2001). In countries where the government provides affordable public health care, child care, and strong unemployment benefits (i.e., most of Europe), individuals perceive nonstandard arrangements as less threatening because they do not prevent them from providing for the basic needs or welfare of their families (B. Asmuss, personal communication, March 27, 2006).

Mistaken Identities   Virtual workers also struggle with social identity issues related to their nonstandard work arrangements. Hylmö (2004) noted that teleworkers start to feel defined by the technological tools they use to interface with their co-workers. While these workers maintain a virtual presence through e-mail, instant messaging, and phone calls, they find that their relationships and identities within their respective organizations fundamentally change. These workers can start to feel that they no longer constitute full-fledged members of the firm and instead occupy a more *ghostly* organizational persona. These workers may morph into a type of organizational "cyborg," connected and identified by communication technology rather than their physical person.

Additionally, virtual workers must negotiate their identities within the home environment. Children, neighbors, and other diversions must be managed by the individual worker without the boundaries of the formal organization to help define when and how work and play get negotiated. One telecommuting friend of the second author had to repeatedly refuse neighbor requests for babysitting and other considerations when they saw her "home alone all day." Also, family members may not treat the teleworker as an organizational employee when they are in the house, requiring the employee to navigate different types of familial relationships in order to occupy both roles in the home (Ellison, 1999). At least in part, virtual members' perceptions of nonstandard work can be constructed through their frequently mistaken identities.

Ancona and colleagues (2001) proposed that organizational members' conceptions of time shape (and are shaped by) the ways in which actors relate to time. We consider these issues next by explicating the temporal processes associated with nonstandard work relationships.

Temporal Processes in Nonstandard Relationships

The temporal processes that typify nonstandard relationships reflect differences in how actors relate to time compared to traditional arrangements. Variables in this category concern the actors themselves (Ancona et al., 2001), and they include members' temporal construals, or the ways in which they orient to time (Ballard & Seibold, 2003). For instance, their orientations to time as fleeting or limited or interests in long-term plans or immediate concerns reflect how group members construe time.

Organizational members' construals of time impact (and often get impacted by) the communication structures that enable and constrain members' work processes (Ballard & Seibold, 2003), including mesolevel structures such as coordination methods, feedback cycles, and workplace technologies (Barley, 1988; Dubinskas, 1988; Lawrence & Lorsch, 1967; Orlikowski, 2000; J. D. Thompson, 1967). A distinguishing characteristic of the temporal processes that guide nonstandard work relationships resides in the brief feedback cycles within which organizations undertake basic membership negotiation message flows (McPhee & Zaug, 2000) and the ways in which these cycles shape the distinct temporal perspectives members hold toward the present and future.

Feedback cycles comprise the time horizons across which organizations hold units accountable for their performance (Cusella, 1987). While the notion of feedback typically implies that some assessment or information will be provided at the end of that horizon, the communicative power of these structures does not reside in such outcomes. Rather, feedback cycles, or loops, enable and constrain members' behavior through the symbolic functions that they serve. They communicate the expected timing of members' actions and thus serve as a standard to give meaning to members' time at micro- and macrolevels. The expectations associated with this cyclic process frame perceptions of the present and future in jobs with conditional time limits for membership. Jones (1988) described the difference between construals of the present and future:

> We can distinguish between time as a structured, unitized measure of the sequence of unfolding events, *compelled toward some distant outcome*, and time as the backdrop for behaviors, thoughts, and feelings. The former is a conception of action that occurs within a time that flows linearly, inexorably, and necessarily forward. It is a perspective that is

strongly guided by the future. The latter is a feeling of behavior that occurs *in-time*, where time consciousness is suspended and action occurs in the infinite present. (p. 26)

Because membership negotiation message flows concern relationships between organizations and their members, the issue of present and future becomes central to (temporally bound) relational processes. McPhee and Zaug (2000) asserted that "one process vital to an organization is the communication that establishes and maintains or transforms its relationship with each of its members" (¶ 23). The very notion of a relationship includes an explicit temporal dimension (Fisher & Drecksel, 1985). In many nonstandard work arrangements, such as temporary employment or contract labor, a stable, future-focused temporal construal may be absent on the part of the employer or the employee (Henson, 1996; Jordan, 2003; Parker, 1994). Such a void poses implications for communication processes, such as identity formation. In his social theory of learning, Wenger (1998) detailed multiple modes of belonging that members might assume. For example, according to Wenger, imagination involves a process of expanding oneself in time and space to produce new images of the world and oneself. As such, it explicitly concerns the future (and past). Given that temporary and contract workers often share a limited past and future with their employing organizations, this process is forestalled. Thus, the impossibility of temporally bound membership processes constitutes a hallmark of the alternative status of particular work relationships.

Many guest work arrangements feature a tension between present and future time orientations of the workers and their employers. As organizational guests, contingent workers (contractors, temps, etc.) know that they may be asked to leave at any time, with little or no warning. Transitory members must get used to living in the present rather than plan for futures with particular organizations. In a study of migrant labor, Nelkin (1970) asserted:

> Time is not perceived as a continuous and predictable process, but as a series of disconnected periods; of good seasons and bad seasons, good weeks and bad weeks. What happens during the current week or season is not perceived as having much to do with what will happen during a future period. (p. 480)

Contingent workers seldom receive feedback or performance evaluations from the organizations that employ them, underscoring this present-centered focus (Gossett, 2006). Evaluations constitute training tools that organizations use to improve member performance for the future. These evaluative processes may not be considered necessary for guest members who can be dismissed easily or lack a clear future within the organization. Future research might explore the extent to which a lack of consistent feedback for contingent workers reinforces the "here today, gone tomorrow" quality of this nonstandard work arrangement.

Related to the process of membership negotiation and its evaluative dimensions, based on their unique activity coordination patterns, virtual members employing innovative solutions to their personal time quandaries often find themselves under more regular organizational scrutiny than their standard counterparts (Ostrom, 2003). Virtual relationships, such as job sharing and teleworking, may hold an (explicitly or implicitly) experimental quality, which may be renegotiated at any time. Organizations often enter these *ghostly* membership arrangements as a means to retain valuable employees who need additional flexibility in their work schedules. Therefore, the organization communicates a long-term orientation toward these individuals by making nonstandard work an alternative to leaving the system entirely. However, subsequent evaluations often concern both the work performed by the employee and the value of the work arrangement itself (Cunningham & Murray, 2005; Kurland & Egan, 1999; Solomon, 1994). The long-term success and acceptance of these virtual work arrangements require that they survive this additional degree of scrutiny.

In contrast to the goals of job sharing and telecommuting (i.e., to retain more talented employees), organizations frequently conceptualize *guest* members (i.e., temporary and contract work) as a disposable workforce (Henson, 1996; Smith, 2001). Seemingly, these work arrangements encourage all parties involved to adopt an exclusively present-focused orientation toward their respective work relationships. However, the U.S. Bureau of Labor statistics (2005) indicate that 56% of temporary employees would prefer a permanent, secure (i.e., standard) work arrangement. As a result, employers can use a temp's desire for a stable future as a unique motivational strategy: *If you work hard enough as a temp, we might make you a permanent employee* (Smith, 1998). The stakes remain even higher for many foreign contractors, who need their work assignments to last long enough for them to complete their U.S. citizenship paperwork. At a

personal level, these foreign contractors possess a long-term orientation toward their relationships with clients. However, these workers
must also struggle with the daily reality of little job security, and, as
such, they can be let go and deported at any time (Alarcon, 1999).
Thus, a central tension in many of these nonstandard work relationships comprises the highly contested nature of the present and future
orientation for both the worker and the employer.

Importantly, existing models of communication processes now
commonly assume long-term relationships. Given the unique temporal expectations associated with contingent relationships, examining
relational processes in this context can expand existing models of
development. Fisher and Drecksel's (1985) cyclical model of developing relationships depicts the ebb and flow of relational processes, and
Waldeck and Meyers's review of assimilation issues in this volume
highlights the temporal aspects of assimilation.

Of related interest for interpersonal communication contexts,
self-disclosure scholars note that people may reveal a great deal of
personal information to total strangers whom they never expect
to see again (Rosenfeld & Kendrick, 1984). Although inconsistent
with traditional self-disclosure processes, this occurs commonly in
temporary situations (e.g., talking to fellow passengers on a plane).
Hence, self-disclosure processes in relationships across varying time
scales can be informed by research on nonstandard work.

Temporal Practices Related to Nonstandard Relationships

The unique temporal practices related to various nonstandard relationships reflect differences in how members map activities to time
compared with traditional arrangements. Variables in this category
concern the creation of order (Ancona et al., 2001) and include members' temporal enactments, or the way that they "perform" time (Ballard & Seibold, 2003). For instance, a group's flexibility regarding work
plans and timing, the tendency of members to multitask or juggle several things at once, the pace at which the group usually works, punc-
tuality of members in beginning or carrying out their work, degree of
scheduling, and member ability to focus on work encompass different
dimensions of the ways that organizational members enact time.

Organizational members' day-to-day temporal enactments frame
(and are framed by) the communication structures that enable and

constrain members' work processes (Ballard & Seibold, 2003). Two of the most distinguishing characteristics of nonstandard work relationships reside in the coordination methods and workplace technologies upon which they rely to accomplish basic activity coordination message flows (McPhee & Zaug, 2000). These structures contribute to the unique temporal *flexibility* and *separation* associated with both virtual and contingent arrangements such as telework, independent contracting, job sharing, and virtual teams.

Flexibility

The type of activity coordination required among organizational groups prescribes and delineates the communication processes involved (McPhee & Zaug, 2000). In J. D. Thompson's (1967) view, varying coordination needs linked to internal task interdependencies foster specific organizational communicative requirements. These requirements, in turn, give rise to particular temporal enactments. The minimal, or pooled, nature of interdependence mandated by certain jobs affords members the ability to work in flexibly designed work arrangements, including telework, job sharing, and independent contracting. Flexibility refers to the degree of rigidity in time structuring and task completion plans and occurs in work that permits relative temporal autonomy (Ballard & Seibold, 2000, 2004). Nonstandard work relationships take advantage of this flexibility to form new arrangements.

For example, job sharing permits individuals to divide responsibilities for a single job temporally so that they can make more fluid task commitments. This virtual work arrangement does not simply constitute two people who alternate the times that they work in a part-time capacity; rather, job-sharing requires two people to share fully the responsibilities of a regular organizational position. This arrangement allows nonstandard workers to avoid being reduced to marginal part-time jobs that may not offer desired advancement opportunities and intellectual challenges. The job-share partners have flexibility in how they negotiate the duties of the position between them, but they do not have flexibility in the degree to which they are expected to adapt and respond to the temporal demands of the larger system.

Cynthia R. Cunningham and Shelley S. Murray (2005), two women who successfully negotiated a job-share position within the banking industry, discussed the unique challenges of this type of nonstandard work relationship. Some of their "standard" co-workers attempted to exploit their alternating absence from the office and pit them against each other in meetings where only one was present or to cut out one of the partners in favor of the other when making decisions. Such communicative tactics resemble children who try to play one parent off another in order to gain an advantage in the relationship. To keep their employment arrangement intact, Cunningham and Murray remained in constant communication with each other, regardless of their physical location. According to Cunningham and Murray, "[W]e did regular 'data dumps,' leaving each other voice-mails—sometimes 15 to 20 daily ... We knew if anything fell through the cracks, there would be no more job-share" (p. 128). While job-share arrangements may not always offer microlevel flexibility in terms of what Evans et al. (2004) described as fine-grained time (immediate time concerns within a given day, hour, or minute), they can facilitate macrolevel flexibility by providing one partner with needed downtime, or beach time, a positive connotation for time off between projects or days in the office.

In contrast with job sharing, telework explicitly promises a great deal of flexibility within fine-grained time, and workers rely on particular types of coordination and new communication technologies. Thus, new workplace technologies—including e-mail, instant messaging, cellular phones, and virtual meeting applications, to name a few—comprise central enabling structures. This fine-grained flexibility, resulting from working at home and making connections through various technologies, can be questioned by co-located organizational members who emphasize the lack of precise accounting for teleworkers' time (Hylmö & Buzzanell, 2002). They advance this suspicion despite member accessibility (which, ironically, serves to weaken promised flexibility). In spite of these perceptions, the actual practice of teleworking often becomes more temporally expansive (in terms of longer working hours) than traditional work. L. Golden and Figart (2002) argued that teleworkers regularly work longer hours than their counterparts due to a blurring of the lines between work and home. As a result, temporal rigidity gets traded for temporal overload, and many members find themselves overworked and isolated.

In their study of technical contractors, Evans et al. (2004) sought to contrast the temporal flexibility of permanent employees, like teleworkers and job sharers, with independent contractors who can do as

they please. However, despite the flexibility afforded by the coordinative requirements and workplace technologies connected with their
jobs, they discovered that many contractors fail to take advantage of
this temporal practice for a number of reasons. For instance, people
who go into contracting tend to feel a high sense of professionalism
or love of their "craft" and are likely to be workaholics. Additionally, contractors may be called in during times of organizational crisis for their particular specialty, so the arrangement fundamentally
restricts flexibility. Finally, they perceive the need to enact traditional
"hard-working" behaviors due to their reliance on referrals for future
business. In Evans and colleagues' study, approximately one fourth
of the independent contractors interviewed scheduled downtime as
a way of enacting coarse-grained flexibility; whereas, only 14% of
participants enacted fine-grained flexibility. Evans et al. noted that,
"unlike insisting on temporal autonomy within a contract, taking
time off between contracts might lower contractors' annual incomes
and deplete their savings, but it did not jeopardize their reputations"
(p. 29), supporting Ancona and colleagues' (2001) assertion that
members mapping of activities to time intersects with their conceptions of time.

Ciulla (2000) argued that craftspeople in the pre-industrial era
enjoyed a great deal of flexibility in their work schedule. They got
their work done but did not necessarily punch a clock. Instead,
Ciulla explained, skilled, pre-industrial workers lived a life "a bit like
the life of a college student—irregular eating and sleeping, intermin-
gled with intense drinking, partying, and all-night work sessions"
(p. 177). In short, these workers integrated their work with the rest of
their lives. Nonstandard work arrangements recall some of the flexible aspects of this pre-industrial work ethic. According to Ciulla,
industrialization moved organizational members toward Fordist
models of management, with everyone in the same place and time to
ensure maximum efficiency and production.

Virtual work arrangements challenge the activity coordination
norms that encourage employees to work at the same location and
period of time. Contingent work arrangements complicate membership norms that encourage employees to commit to a single
system for an indefinite period of time. By examining the nonstandard labor practices of negotiating *how much time* a job should take
(part-timers, contract jobs) and *where* it should be done (telecommuters, migrating workers) as well as *how long* membership will last

(temporary workers, interns), researchers can explore the ways in which these labor arrangements may embrace some pre-industrial attitudes about work and time.

Separation

Temporal separation concerns the degree to which stakeholders eliminate or allow extraneous factors in the process of task accomplishment. Members display low levels of separation in practices that make their time expressly available to others with few boundaries (Ballard & Seibold, 2004). In contrast to nonstandard work arrangements that permit high levels of flexibility, arrangements characterized by low levels of separation provide members with little ownership over their time. Virtual teams exemplify this temporal practice, owed to the communication technologies that facilitate interaction with members around the globe as well as the different time zones that members must cross to coordinate synchronously (e.g., DeSanctis & Monge, 1999; Lipnack & Stamps, 1997).

These issues constitute the protean places detailed by Shockley-Zalabak (2002). In her study of the communication processes of a virtual team, one manager confirmed that each team member had been chosen specifically because of his or her demonstrated ability to manage high-pressure situations. A key aspect of the high-pressure task environment stems from the temporal simultaneity required to function successfully in the team. According to Shockley-Zalabak, members were routinely woken in the middle of the night to offer troubleshooting advice to members in other parts of the world and "concluded they were not really engaged in self management but continuous reactions to customer demands" (p. 247). In response to this almost total lack of temporal separation, one member protested that "[w]e work across time and space, but we don't want to be boundaryless" (p. 247).

Flexibility–Separation Dialectic

Communication tools (cell phones, pagers, the Internet, etc.) act as technological leashes, keeping the worker tied to the organizational environment. Ciulla (2000) noted that employees who are informally "always on call" never truly separate from their work and become prisoners of the organization. In this way, the flexible work environment can also develop into the inescapable work environment. A variety of nonstandard work arrangements simultaneously struggle with issues of temporal separation and flexibility.

For example, migrant workers constantly manage their personal lives in response to the transitory nature of their occupation. Migrants comprise a unique form of contingent labor in the sense that they often bring a specific skill set that employers demand for a limited period of time in a particular location. Once they complete a project, these workers need to be able to move to another place where they can utilize their abilities. Migrant workers must be flexible enough to travel wherever and whenever potential employers require their skills (Nelkin, 1970; Thornburgh, 2006). The temporal and spatial flexibility mandated for this particular contingent occupation overwhelms all other aspects of the worker's life, determining where the employee lives, in what conditions, and for how long (U.S. Department of Labor, 2000). Migrating workers from foreign countries face additional challenges adjusting to their constantly changing work environments. New host communities do not necessarily embrace foreign workers; instead, residents often define them as criminals (Flores, 2003) or accuse them of taking jobs away from local workers (Seper, 2006). As such, these workers may come to feel like *unwelcome guests* within the organizations that they serve and communities in which they live.

Time in a distant location coupled with the low-tech environments in which they often work complicates connections with friends and family back home. This separation can cause migrating workers (often forced to leave their families behind) to suffer from anxiety and other mental health problems (Grzywacz et al., 2006). The threat of estranged marriages, the challenges of remote childrearing, and the difficulty of crossing national borders to stay in regular contact with their loved ones can encourage migrant workers to bring their families with them (Schneider, 2004; Thornburgh, 2006). As a result, these workers and their families struggle to separate their personal lives fully from this nonstandard work arrangement.

While the term *migrant worker* is often associated with low-skilled, manual labor positions (e.g., agriculture, construction, ranching, etc.), increasingly, a variety of professional occupations require workers to move frequently in order to stay employed

(Schneider, 2004). These workers face significant adjustments to their personal lives (constant travel, long-distance relationships, etc.) in order to meet the geographic demands of their various employment arrangements (Ciulla, 2000). As such, people in these highly skilled occupations (e.g., health care, information technology workers, organizational consultants, etc.) may experience familial separation challenges similar to those traditionally associated with migrating farm workers and day laborers. Future research might explore the ways in which various migratory work arrangements impact family dynamics or local community engagement.

Conclusion

Nonstandard work relationships encompass a wide range of employment options in contemporary organizations. Despite their prevalence, communication scholars have not interrogated these arrangements and their related theoretical and practical concerns. In order to facilitate inquiry into these important changing membership forms, this chapter joined three compatible and complementary perspectives to engage these issues from a communication perspective and informed by a temporal outlook. Notably, we used McPhee and Zaug's (2000) theoretical framework of the communicative constitution of organizations to advance a typology of nonstandard work relationships that distinguishes among standard "real" members, contingent "guest" members, virtual "ghost" members, and "vendor" nonmembers. Throughout the chapter, we have pointed to similarities in the temporality of nonstandard work and communication issues across a variety of divisional boundaries.

As we have stressed, stakeholders construct nonstandard work relationships via alternative times. These "times" reside in members' temporal perceptions associated with the arrangement, the temporal processes that are precluded by it, or the temporal practices that define it. While *membership negotiation* explicitly concerns the process, and *activity coordination* speaks to the practice, organizational members' temporal perceptions about nonstandard work arrangements emerge through message flows as *organizational self-structuring* (communication concerning internal relations and norms that become the basis for work processes) and *institutional positioning* (communication with outside entities that serves to establish an organization's identity and its place within the larger system of other organizations).

For example, as a part of their institutional positioning, organizations might self-structure through nonstandard work arrangements like virtual teams, a dispersed workforce, network organizing, and immigrant labor in order to manage the challenge of global relevance. In recent years, this practice has been reflected in the increased prevalence of migrant labor in the form of international, highly skilled, semipermanent workers in the high-tech and medical industries (Alarcon, 1999) and the expanding use of a dispersed workforce in the form of network organizing and cross-national virtual teams (Shockley-Zalabak, 2002).

Additionally, during times of a labor shortage, an organization may self-structure using multiple "family-friendly" policies such as telework and job sharing in order to affect institutional positioning message flows designed to attract and retain the most talented members. In this case, organizations design these microlevel aspects of activity coordination to improve membership negotiation processes. In contrast, underlying temporal perceptions, based on long-standing cultural values concerning face time, often limit such policies during times of a labor surplus when organizations tend to neglect membership negotiation message flows (Hochschild, 1997). Thus, the relatedness of these flows—and of the temporal issues constituting nonstandard work relationships—remains essential to understanding these work arrangements and the communication processes that give rise to them. We have interrogated the mesolevel flows in the present chapter. We recommend that researchers pursue the macroflows described by McPhee and Zaug (2000) in future research.

Given the position of time as a constitutive communication construct, examining the intersection of time and nonstandard relationships lends value to investigations on a variety of "life" issues that span traditional divides. While *perceptions* of time shape (and are shaped by) these arrangements, and unique temporal *practices* call attention to their use, an often overlooked aspect concerns the ways in which they impact basic communication *processes* that unfold over time. The intersection of temporality and nonstandard work has been overlooked in the literature, but it reflects a natural marriage of two timely organizational and societal matters. Through our synthesis of these two literatures, we hope to provide communication scholars with a compelling research agenda that will drive scholarship in multiple areas of the discipline.

Acknowledgments

The authors gratefully acknowledge Christina S. Beck, Laurie K. Lewis, Patrice Buzzanell, and three anonymous reviewers for their insightful comments and suggestions. An earlier version of this paper was presented at the 2005 convention of the National Communication Association, Boston, MA.

Notes

1. Claus Bang Møller is an adviser for EURES Denmark, an organization that serves Danish and other European employers, job seekers, and students who wish to work in Denmark or any other European country.
2. Birte Asmuss, Ph.D., is an assistant professor at the Centre for Business Communication at the Aarhus School of Business, Denmark. Dr. Asmuss uses conversation analysis, interviews, and linguistic anthropology to examine talk at work (job appraisal interviews, meetings, etc.) and related issues of organizational and intercultural communication.

References

Aaronson, D., Rissman, E., & Sullivan, D. (2004). Assessing the jobless recovery. *Economic Perspectives, 28,* 2–21.

Alarcon, R. (1999). Recruitment processes among foreign-born engineers and scientists in Silicon Valley. *American Behavioral Scientist, 42,* 1381–1397.

Alexander, S. C., Peterson, J. L., & Hollingshead, A. B. (2003). Help is at your keyboard: Support groups on the Internet. In L. Frey (Ed.), *Group communication in context: Studies of bona fide groups* (2nd ed., pp. 309–334). Mahwah, NJ: Lawrence Erlbaum Associates.

Amuedo-Dorantes, C. (2000). Work transitions into and out of involuntary temporary employment in a segmented market: Evidence from Spain. *Industrial and Labor Relations Review, 53,* 309–325.

Ancona, D. G., Okhuysen, G. A., & Perlow, L. A. (2001). Taking time to integrate temporal research. *Academy of Management Review, 28,* 512–529.

Arrow, H., Poole, M. S., Henry, K. B., Wheelan, S., & Moreland, R. (2004). Time, change, and development: The temporal perspective on groups. *Small Group Research, 35,* 73–105.

Association of Religion Data Archives. (2006). Religious service attendance data based on the General Social Survey. Retrieved October 11, 2006, from http://www.thearda.com/quickstats/qs_55.asp

Bailyn, L. (1993). *Breaking the mold: Women, men and time in the new corporate world.* New York: The Free Press.

Ballard, D. I., & Seibold, D. R. (2000). Time orientation and temporal variation across work groups: Implications for group and organizational communication. *Western Journal of Communication, 64,* 218–242.

Ballard, D. I., & Seibold, D. R. (2003). Communicating and organizing in time: A meso level model of organizational temporality. *Management Communication Quarterly, 16,* 380–415.

Ballard, D. I., & Seibold, D. R. (2004). Communication-related organizational structures and work group members' temporal experience: The effects of interdependence, type of technology, and feedback cycle on members' views and enactments of time. *Communication Monographs, 71,* 1–27.

Barker, J. R. (1999). *The discipline of teamwork: Participation and concertive control.* Thousand Oaks, CA: Sage.

Barley, S. R. (1988). On technology, time, and social order: Technically induced change in the temporal organization of radiological work. In F. Dubinskas (Ed.), *Making time: Ethnographies of high-technology organizations* (pp. 123–169). Philadelphia: Temple University Press.

Baxter, L. A., & Montgomery, B. M. (1996). *Relating: Dialogues and dialectics.* New York: The Guilford Press.

Berchem, S. P. (2004, May–June). The bright spot: ASA's annual economic analysis of the staffing industry. *American Staffing Association.* Retrieved August 19, 2004, from http://www.staffingtoday.net/staffstats/annualanalysis04.pdf

Bluedorn, A. C. (2002). *The human organization of time: Temporal realities and experience.* Stanford, CA: Stanford Business Books.

Bourdieu, P. (1977). *Outline of a theory of practice.* Cambridge, England: Cambridge University Press.

Braithwaite, D. O., & Baxter, L. A. (2006). "You're my parent but you're not": Dialectical tensions in stepchildren's perceptions about communicating with the nonresidential parent. *Journal of Applied Communication Research, 34,* 30–49.

Braithwaite, D. O., Olson, L., Golish, T., Soukup, C., & Turman, P. (2001). "Becoming a family": Developmental processes represented in blended family discourse. *Journal of Applied Communication Research, 29,* 221–247.

Bruneau, T. (1974). Time and nonverbal communication. *Journal of Popular Culture, 8,* 658–666.

Bruneau, T. (1977). Chronemics: The study of time in human interaction (with a glossary of chronemic terminology). *Communication, Journal of the Communication Association of the Pacific, 6,* 1–30.

Bruneau, T. (1979). The time dimension in intercultural communication. In D. Nimmo (Ed.), *Communication yearbook 3* (pp. 423–433). New Brunswick, NJ: Transaction Books.

Buzzanell, P. M., & Goldzwig, S. R. (1991). Linear and nonlinear career models: Metaphors, paradigms, and ideologies. *Management Communication Quarterly, 4,* 466–505.

Buzzanell, P. M., & Lucas, K. (2006). Gendered stories of career: Unfolding discourses of time, space, and identity. In B. J. Dow & J. T. Wood (Eds.), *The Sage handbook on gender and communication* (pp. 161–178). Thousand Oaks, CA: Sage.

Buzzanell, P. M., & Turner, L. (2003). Emotion work revealed by job loss discourse: Backgrounding–foregrounding of feelings, construction of normalcy, and (re)instituting of traditional masculinities. *Journal of Applied Communication Research, 31,* 27–57.

Catalyst (1993). *Flexible work arrangements II: Succeeding with part-time options.* New York: Catalyst.

Chan, S., & Stevens, A. (2001). Job loss and employment patterns of older workers. *Journal of Labor Economics, 19,* 484–521.

Cheney, G. (1999). *Values at work: Employee participation meets market pressure at Mondragon.* Ithaca, NY: ILR Press.

Ciulla, J.B. (2000). *The working life: The promise and betrayal of modern work.* New York: Times Books.

Cunningham, C. R., & Murray, S. S. (2005). Two executives, one career. *Harvard Business Review, 83*(2), 125–131.

Cusella, L. P. (1987). Feedback, motivation, and performance. In F. M. Jablin, L. L. Putnam, K. H. Roberts, & L. W. Porter (Eds.), *The handbook of organizational communication* (pp. 624–678). Newbury Park, CA: Sage.

Dainton, M., & Aylor, B. (2002). Patterns of communication channel use in the maintenance of long-distance relationships. *Communication Research Reports, 19,* 118–129.

De Graaf, J. (Ed.). (2003). *Take back your time: Fighting overwork and time poverty in America.* San Francisco: Berrett–Koehler Publishers.

DeSanctis, G., & Monge, P. (1999). Special issue: Communication processes for virtual organizations. *Organizational Science, 10,* 693–703.

Dubinskas, F. (1988). Janus organizations: Scientists and managers in genetic engineering firms. In F. Dubinskas (Ed.), *Making time: Ethnographies of high-technology organizations* (pp. 170–232). Philadelphia: Temple University Press.

Edley, P. P., Hylmö, A., & Newsom, V. A. (2004). Alternative organizing communities: Collectivist organizing, telework, home-based internet businesses, and online communities. In P. Kalbfleisch (Ed.), *Communication yearbook 28* (pp. 87–126). Mahwah, NJ: Lawrence Erlbaum Associates.

Ellison, N. B. (1999). Social impacts: New perspectives on telework. *Social Science Computer Review, 17,* 338–356.

Eriksson, R. (2005, September). *Parental leave in Sweden: The effects of the second daddy month.* (Swedish Institute for Social Research, SOFI). Stockholm, Sweden: Stockholm University.

European Foundation for the Improvement of Living and Working Conditions. (2006). Job security: Spain. Retrieved March 23, 2006, from http://www.eurofound.eu.int/emire/SPAIN/JOBSECURITY-ES.html

Evans, J. A., Kunda, G., & Barley, S. R. (2004). Beach time, bridge time, and billable hours: The temporal structure of technical contracting. *Administrative Science Quarterly, 49,* 1–38.

Feldman, D. C., & Doerpinghaus, H. I. (1992). Missing persons no longer: Managing part-time workers in the '90s. *Organizational Dynamics, 21*(1), 59–72.

Fisher, B. A., & Drecksel, G. L. (1985). A cyclical model of developing relationships: A study of relational control interaction. *Communication Monographs, 50,* 66–78.

Flores, L. A. (2003). Constructing rhetorical borders: Peons, illegal aliens, and competing narratives of immigration. *Critical Studies in Media Communication, 20,* 362–387.

Ford, P. (2006, March 8). French youth want jobs with security: Masses protested a bill that would make it easier to get hired and fired. *Christian Science Monitor, 98*(70), 6.

Galup, S., Saunders, C., Nelson, R., and Cerveny, R. (1997). The use of temporary staff and managers in a local government environment. *Communication Research, 24,* 698–730.

Giddens, A. (1984). *The constitution of society.* Berkeley: University of California Press.

Glass, J. (2004). Blessing or curse? Work-family policies and mother's wage growth over time. *Work and Occupations, 31,* 367–394.

Golden, A. G., Kirby, E. L., & Jorgenson, J. (2006). Work-life research from both sides now: An integrative perspective for organizational and family communication. In C. S. Beck (Ed.), *Communication yearbook 30* (pp. 143–196). Mahwah, NJ: Lawrence Erlbaum Associates.

Golden, L., & Figart, D. M. (2000). *Working time: International trends, theory, and policy perspectives.* New York: Routledge.

Goldstein, R. L. (2006). *Women and part time work: The mommy track or a flexible career alternative? Exploring the transition from full to part time.* Unpublished master's thesis, University of Texas, Austin.

Gossett, L. M. (2001). The long-term impact of short-term workers: The work life concerns posed by the growth of the contingent workforce. *Management Communication Quarterly, 15*, 115–120.

Gossett, L. M. (2002). Kept at arm's length: Questioning the organizational desirability of member identification. *Communication Monographs, 69*, 385–404.

Gossett, L. M. (2006). Falling between the cracks: Control challenges of a contingent workforce. *Management Communication Quarterly, 19*, 376–415.

Gottfried, H. (1991). Mechanisms of control in the temporary help service industry. *Sociological Forum, 6*, 699–713.

Grzywacz, J. G., Quandt, S. A., Early, J., Tapia, J., Graham, C. N., & Arcury, T. A. (2006). Leaving family for work: Ambivalence and mental health among Mexican migrant farmworker men. *Journal of Immigrant and Minority Health, 8*, 85–97

Hall, E. T. (1983). *The dance of life.* New York: Doubleday.

Hantrais, L. (1993). The gender of time in professional occupations. *Time & Society, 2*, 139–157.

Hassard, J. (1991). Aspects of time in organization. *Human Relations, 44*, 105–125.

Hassard, J. (2002). Essai: Organizational time: Modern, symbolic, and postmodern reflections. *Organization Studies, 23*, 885–892.

Henson, K. D. (1996). *Just a temp.* Philadelphia: Temple University Press.

Hermann, C. (2005). Why is the 35-hour work week in retreat? *Canadian Dimension, 39*(3), 37.

Hernadi, P. (1992). Objective, subjective, intersubjective times: Guest editor's introduction. *Time & Society, 1*, 147–158.

Hignite, K. B. (2000). Aging gracefully. *Association Management.* Retrieved March 29, 2006, from http://www.allbusiness.com/periodicals/article/621431-1

Hochschild, A. R. (1997). *The time bind: When work becomes home and home becomes work.* New York: Henry Holt and Company.

Hocker, J. L., & Wilmot, W. W. (1991). *Interpersonal conflict* (3rd ed.). Dubuque, IA: Wm. C. Brown.

Hofstede, G., & Bond, M. H. (1988). The Confucius connection: From cultural roots to economic growth. *Organizational Dynamics, 16*(4), 4–21.

Houseman, S., & Osawa, M. (2003). *Non-standard work in developed economies: Causes and consequences.* Kalamazoo, MI: W. E. Upjohn Institute for Employment Research.

Humphries, C. (2004, November 12). Sleep medicine: Extended shifts for residents called risky for patients. *Focus Online: News from Harvard Medical, Dental and Public Health Schools.* Retrieved October 11, 2006, from http://focus.hms.harvard.edu/2004/Nov12_2004/sleep_medicine.html

Hylmö, A. (2004). Women, men, and changing organizations: An organizational culture examination of gendered experiences of telecommuting. In P. M. Buzzanell, H. Sterk, & L. H. Turner (Eds.), *Gender in applied communication contexts* (pp. 47–68). Thousand Oaks, CA: Sage.

Hylmö, A., & Buzzanell, P. M. (2002). Telecommuting as viewed through cultural lenses: An empirical investigation of the discourses of utopia, identity, and mystery. *Communication Monographs, 69,* 329–356.

Jones, J. M. (1988). Cultural difference in temporal perspectives: Instrumental and expressive behaviors in time. In J. E. McGrath (Ed.), *The social psychology of time: New perspectives* (pp. 21–38). Newbury Park, CA: Sage.

Jordan, J. W. (2003). Sabotage or performed compliance: Rhetorics of resistance in temp worker discourse. *Quarterly Journal of Speech, 89,* 19–40.

Jorgensen, H., & Riemer, H. (2000). Permatemps: Young temp workers as permanent second-class employees. *The American Prospect, 11*(18), 115–117.

Kalleberg, A., Reskin, B., & Hudson, K. (2000). Bad jobs in America: Standard and non-standard employment relations and job quality in the United States. *American Sociological Review, 65,* 256–278.

Kirby, E. L., & Krone, K. J. (2002). "The policy exists but you can't really use it": Communication and the structuration of work-family policies. *Journal of Applied Communication Research, 30,* 50–77.

Knox, N. (2004, July 27). Longer work weeks likely in Europe. *USA Today,* p. 4B.

Kraut, R. E. (1989). Telecommuting: The trade-offs of home work. *Journal of Communication, 39*(3), 19–47.

Kropf, M. B. (1998). Women's career development and part-time arrangements. *New Directions for Adult and Continuing Education, 80,* 43–51.

Kurland, N. B. & Egan, T. D. (1999). Telecommuting: Justice and control in the virtual organization. *Organization Science, 10,* 500–513.

Kurlantzick, J. (2001, March 19). A temporary boom in the job market. *US News & World Report, 130*(11), 40.

Lawrence, P. R., & Lorsch, J. W. (1967). *Organization and environment: Managing differentiation and integration.* Boston: Harvard University Press.

Lipnack, J., & Stamps, J. (1997). *Virtual teams: Reaching across space, time and organizations with technology.* New York: John Wiley & Sons.

McCann, R., & Giles, H. (2002). Ageism in the workplace: A communication perspective. In T. D. Nelson (Ed.), *Ageism: Stereotyping and prejudice against older persons* (pp. 163–199). Cambridge, MA: MIT Press.

McGrath, J. E., & Kelly, J. R. (1986). *Time and human interaction: Toward a social psychology of time.* New York: Guilford Press.

McPhee, R. D., & Zaug, P. (2000). The communicative constitution of organizations: A framework for explanation. *The Electronic Journal of Communication, 10,* Article MCPHEE V10N1200. Retrieved August 16, 2002, from http://www.cios.org/getfile\McPhee_V10n1200

Meyers, N., & Hearn, G. (2000). Communication and control: Case studies in Australian telecommuting. *Australian Journal of Communication, 27*(2), 39–64.

Millar, M. (2005, December 6). U.K. to push for WTD fix. *Personnel Today,* p. 1.

Miller, C., Roloff, M., & Malis, R. (2007). Understanding interpersonal conflicts that are difficult to resolve. In C. S. Beck (Ed.), *Communication yearbook 31* (pp. 117–171). New York, NY: Lawrence Erlbaum Associates.

Nelkin, D. (1970). Unpredictability and lifestyle in a migrant labor camp. *Social Problems, 17,* 472–487.

Orlikowski, W. J. (2000). Using technology and constituting structures: A practice lens for studying technology in organizations. *Organization Science, 11,* 404–428.

Ostrom, C. (2003). Jobs to share. In J. de Graaf (Ed.), *Take back your time: Fighting overwork and time poverty in America* (pp. 146–153). San Francisco: Berrett–Koehler Publishers.

Parker, R. E. (1994). *Flesh peddlers and warm bodies: The temporary help industry and its workers.* New Brunswick, NJ: Rutgers University Press.

Pearce, J. L. (1993). Toward an organizational behavior of contract laborers: Their psychological involvement and effects on employee co-workers. *Academy of Management Journal, 36,* 1082–1096.

Poyatos, F. (1976). *Man beyond words: Theory and methodology of nonverbal communication.* Oswego, NY: New York State English Council.

Putnam, L. L., & Stohl, C. (1990). Bona fide groups: A reconceptualization of groups in context. *Communication Studies, 41,* 248–265.

Riggs, K. (2004). *Granny@work: Aging and new technology on the job in America.* New York: Routledge.

Riley, R., & Mania, E. (2006). Governing time in operating rooms. *Issues in Clinical Nursing, 15,* 546–553.

Rogers, J. K. (2000). *Temps: The many faces of the changing workplace.* Ithaca, NY: Cornell University Press.

Rogers, J. K., & Henson, H. D. (1997). "Hey, why don't you wear a shorter skirt?" Structural vulnerability and the organization of sexual harassment in temporary clerical employment. *Gender and Society, 11,* 215–237.

Rosenfeld, L. B., & Kendrick, W. L. (1984). Choosing to be open: An empirical investigation of subjective reasons for self-disclosing. *Western Journal of Speech Communication, 48,* 326–343.

Schein, E. H. (1992). *Organizational culture and leadership.* San Francisco: Jossey-Bass.

Schneider, G. (2004, November 15). The new migrants: More tech workers have to keep moving to find work. *Austin American-Statesman,* D1, D4.

Scott, W. R. (1987). *Organizations: Rational, natural, & open systems.* Englewood Cliffs, NJ: Prentice Hall.

Seper, J. (2006, April 10). Arrival of aliens ousts U.S. workers. *The Washington Times.* Retrieved October 23, 2006, from http://www.washtimes.com/functions/print.php?StoryID=20060410-123506-1297r

Shockley-Zalabak, P. (2002). Protean places: Teams across time and space. *Journal of Applied Communication Research, 30,* 231–250.

Sias, P. M., Kramer, M. W., & Jenkins, E. (1997). A comparison of the communication behaviors of temporary employees and new hires. *Communication Research, 24,* 731–754.

Simpson, J. A., & Weiner, S. C. (Eds.). (2006). *The Oxford English dictionary* (2nd ed.) [Electronic version]. London: Oxford University Press. Retrieved November 11, 2006, from the OED database.

Smith, V. (1998). The fractured world of the temporary worker: Power, participation, and fragmentation in the contemporary workplace. *Social Problems, 45,* 411–430.

Smith, V. (2001). *Crossing the great divide: Worker risk and opportunity in the new economy.* Ithaca, NY: ILR Press.

Solomon, C. M. (1994). Job sharing: One job, double headache? *Personnel Journal, 73*(9), 88–93. Retrieved March, 8 2005, from the Business Source Premier database. http://search.epnet.com.content.lib.utexas.edu:2048/login.aspx?direct=true&db=bth&an=9409231644

Storrie, D. (2002). *Temporary agency work in the European Union.* Dublin, Ireland: European Foundation for the Improvement of Living and Working Conditions.

Story, L. (2005, September 20). Many women at elite colleges set career path to motherhood. *New York Times.* Retrieved October 11, 2006, from http://www.nytimes.com

Thompson, E. P. (1967). Time, work-discipline and industrial capitalism. *Past and Present, 38,* 56–97.

Thompson, J. D. (1967). *Organizations in action.* New York: McGraw–Hill.

Thornburgh, N. (2006, February 6). Inside the life of the immigrants next door. *Time, 167*(6), 34–45.

Thornicroft, G., & Strathdee, G. (1992). Job share a consultant post. *British Medical Journal, 305,* 1–3.

Townsley, N. C., & Stohl, C. (2003). Contracting corporate social responsibility: Swedish expansions in global temporary agency work. *Management Communication Quarterly, 16,* 599–605.

underwood, d., & Frey, L. (2007). Communication and community: Clarifying the connection across the communication contexts. In C. S. Beck (Ed.), *Communication yearbook 31* (pp. 369–418). New York, NY: Lawrence Erlbaum Associates.

U.S. Bureau of Labor Statistics. (2005, February). *Contingent and alternative employment arrangements.* Retrieved September, 1 2005, from http://www.bls.gov/news.release/conemp.nr0.htm

U.S. Department of Labor. (2000, March). Findings from the National Agricultural Workers Survey (NAWS) 1997–1998: A demographic and employment profile of United States farm workers. (DOL Research Report No. 8). Washington, DC: U.S. Department of Labor.

Van Breugel, G., Van Olffen, W., & Olie, R. (2005). Temporary liaisons: The commitment of "temps" towards their agencies. *Journal of Management Studies, 42,* 539–566.

Van Dyne, L., & Ang, S. (1998). Organizational citizenship behavior of contingent workers in Singapore. *Academy of Management Journal, 41,* 692–703.

Waldeck, J., & Myers, K. (2007). A state of the art review: Organizational assimilation theory, research, and implications for multiple divisions of the discipline. In C. S. Beck (Ed.), *Communication yearbook 31* (pp. 321–367). New York, NY: Lawrence Erlbaum Associates.

Warner, J. (2005). *Perfect madness: Motherhood in the age of anxiety.* New York: Riverhead Books.

Wenger, E. (1998). *Communities of practice: Learning, meaning, and identity.* New York: Cambridge University Press.

Wiens-Tuers, B. A. (2001). Employee attachment and temporary workers. *Journal of Economic Issues, 25,* 45–60.

Young, N. (2007). Identity trans/formation. In C. S. Beck (Ed.), *Communication yearbook 31* (pp. 223–272). New York, NY: Lawrence Erlbaum Associates.

Chapter 7 Contents

7

Organizational Assimilation Theory, Research, and Implications for Multiple Areas of the Discipline: A State of the Art Review

Jennifer H. Waldeck
Chapman University

Karen K. Myers
University of California, Santa Barbara

In examining the state of the art in organizational assimilation studies, we explicate specific linkages between work on assimilation in organizational contexts and other areas of the communication discipline. We define the construct, present an overview of the primary theoretical models that have directed research on organizational assimilation since the 1970s, and identify the major areas of research, discussing representative studies within each area. Throughout, we illustrate ways in which communication scholars in the areas of instructional/developmental, technology, mass media, health, intercultural/developmental, and group communication might draw from organizational assimilation research for a heightened understanding of their own variables of interest. Finally, based on an in-depth review of the literature in this area, the authors recommend intensified research attention to the antecedents to particular assimilation processes, development of research methods that would capture the dynamic and interactive nature of assimilation, and conscientious efforts by assimilation scholars to promote the utility of their work to researchers working in other areas of the field.

Overview

Organizational assimilation is a key construct that encompasses the process by which individuals become integrated into the culture of organizations (Jablin, 2001). Although assimilation has been primarily the domain of organizational scholars, the concept holds significance for numerous other areas of the field of communication. Thus, in this chapter, we strive to illustrate how and why assimilation constitutes a key construct across the discipline, with important metatheoretical and practical implications for human communication. Toward that end, we pose four related goals for this chapter.

First, we discuss the primary definitions of socialization and assimilation within organizations. Second, we review the theories and models of organizational assimilation. Third, we identify major areas of research focusing on assimilation and discuss representative studies and methodological approaches. Fourth, throughout this discussion, we take a broad view of assimilation, proposing new linkages to other areas of the field and ways to consider assimilation research. Craig (1999) observed that, because commonalities as well as tensions exist among communication theories, "these different types of theory cannot develop in total isolation from each other but must engage each other in argument" (p. 124). Therefore, we suggest that assimilation comprises a construct that spans traditional discipline divides and methodological approaches. We argue that study of assimilation from multiple disciplinary perspectives can simultaneously enhance its explanatory power, elevate the status and credibility of communication researchers' work in this area, and provide a powerful construct with implications for a metatheory of human communication.

Although people usually enter organizations with some training preparing them for their jobs, many organization- and job-learning-specific tasks take place after entry. Organizational members in both work and nonwork settings often learn from inside their organizations as they interact with one another and apprehend the norms and day-to-day contextual nuances (Waldeck, Seibold, & Flanagin, 2004). Similar to interpersonal communication, the ability to communicate in ways that result in effective assimilation is an acquired skill (Porter, Lawler, & Hackman, 1975). As individuals encounter unfamiliar situations for which they lack behavioral or cognitive referents, engage in intercultural experiences, deal with new forms of technology, and so on, they learn and relearn to communicate effectively. Therefore, the investigation of inputs, processes, and products of assimilation may guide researchers who seek to understand how people communicate in response to new or changing stimuli in their environments.

Defining the Construct: Organizational Assimilation

Scholars typically frame the process of learning about and adjusting to normative organizational practices as *organizational assimilation*, a term that commonly encompasses a number of related and often interchanged constructs (Kramer & V. D. Miller, 1999). Early research in organizational entry and adjustment processes emphasized the organization's perspective on how members learn their roles and responsibilities. Much of this work examined outcomes associated with various organizational training techniques and means of communicating orienting information (e.g., Putnam, Murray, & Hill, 1981; St. John, 1980; Van Maanen, 1978; Van Maanen & Schein, 1979). Most of these scholars used the term *socialization*, referring to the ongoing process by which individuals learn "the values, norms, and required behaviors that allow them to participate as members of organizations" (Van Maanen, 1978, p. 27).

Others (Graen, 1976; Jablin, 1982; Katz & Kahn, 1966; Porter et al. 1975) have pointed out that Van Maanen's (1978) definition and this narrow focus limit the range of experiences that, in practice, encompass the learning, negotiation, and adjustment process. These authors noted that the definition of socialization fails to acknowledge how individuals actively innovate and create roles for themselves within the organization. Thus, Porter et al. coined the term *individualization* to characterize socialization experiences that result in creativity, innovation, and contributions to the organization (as opposed to passive acceptance of existing organizational norms). Alternatively, Katz and Kahn introduced the terms *role taking* (socialization) and *role making* (individualization) to describe the process by which people become functioning organizational members.

However, the terms socialization and assimilation often appear interchangeably within the literature, and the definitions even oppose each other (Moreland & Levine, 1982). Moreland and Levine suggested that socialization includes the organization's efforts to acquaint and develop members as well as the mutual adjustment as the "group accommodates itself to the individual, who in turn is assimilated into the group" (p. 162). Meanwhile, Jablin (1982) and Kramer and V. D. Miller (1999) employed a blanket term for organizational assimilation, emphasizing both "learning and adapting to the norms, expectations, and perspectives of the organization" (Jablin, p. 260) (socialization/role taking) and "taking an active part in defining their organizational roles" (Jablin, p. 261) (individualization/ role making). In our research, and in this chapter, we use the term "organizational assimilation."

Conceptual Conclusions

Myers and Oetzel (2003) and Myers (2005) synthesized the preceding perspectives by discussing assimilation as a reciprocal process in which both individuals and organizational structures have power. They defined assimilation as an experience during which persons become familiar with others in the organization, acculturate, feel involved in and recognized as a contributing member, attain a level of job competency, and negotiate roles through reciprocal influence communication; notably, both organizational veterans and newcomers assimilate as they negotiate membership, define their roles, and attempt to influence their organizations (Jablin & Krone, 1987; Jones, 1986). As a result of assimilation, organizational members often reduce anxiety associated with uncertainty regarding their roles in the organization (Katz & Kahn, 1966).

In this section, we have overviewed organizational assimilation and noted that most scholars describe assimilation as a process through which organizational members influence the organizations in which they work, thus creating change within those organizations, and become affected by existing organizational practices and norms, thus changing as individuals (see also related review by Ballard & Gossett, this volume). Further, we reviewed and advanced initial conclusions about the conceptual confusion resulting from the interchangeable use of unique terms in the organizational communication literature. Next, we move to a discussion of theoretical developments in the area of assimilation.

Theoretical Models of Assimilation

Guiding Theories

Noting the number of variable analytic studies within the socialization literature, Saks and Ashforth (1997) argued that "there is no theory" (p. 235) of socialization. Indeed, many socialization and assimilation researchers have studied variables in an attempt to demonstrate statistical relationships and predictive models of effective assimilation. However, theoretical frameworks guide many studies.

Assimilation literature most prominently extends from uncertainty reduction theory (Berger & Calabrese, 1975). In fact, some studies presume that organizational assimilation essentially *is* the process newcomers engage in to reduce uncertainties about how to do their jobs, how to relate to other people in their organization, and what others expect of them with regard to their performance (Waldeck et al., 2004). Members experience anxiety when they cannot communicate effectively (i.e., by learning desirable behaviors and assimilating appropriately) (Black & Ashford, 1995). Conversely, the ability to engage in communication that reduces one's uncertainties can reduce stress and result in a heightened state of organizational assimilation that ostensibly improves one's attachment and contributions to the organization and overall satisfaction (V. D. Miller & Jablin, 1991).

Organizational members may amass an array of important concerns regarding their ability to perform adequately and integrate successfully. For example, newcomers and incumbents develop uncertainties regarding how to fit in, do their jobs, understand performance evaluation, relate to others socially, and select their friends at work, among others (see Kramer, 1989, 1993, 2004; Kramer, Callister, & Turban, 1995; Kramer & Noland, 1999, on concerns of incumbents, and Feldman, 1976; V. D. Miller, 1997; V. D. Miller & Jablin, 1991, on newcomers' issues). Indeed, these issues concern communicators in any context, and as we shall explore within this chapter, the knowledge that we obtain regarding individuals' assimilation into organizational cultures brings much to bear on the process of communicating competently in other situations. In numerous social, family, and professional contexts, individuals need to learn normative, expected behaviors, exert social influence, participate in socially acceptable ways, and contribute to explicit and implicit objectives of the situation.

Sense-making also provides a useful theory for explaining assimilation processes (see Louis, 1980). Louis argued that newcomers experience surprise and disillusionment at organizational entry and that sense-making enables them to cope with surprise, contrast, and change. As a result, organizational newcomers may cognitively restructure and reorder beliefs about their work, organizations, and associated relationships. For example, V. D. Miller and Jablin (1991) concluded that their model of information-seeking tactics will help in understanding "the manner by which newcomers cope with or make sense of their new organizational environments" (p. 114). Sense-making comprises a potentially underused theoretical framework for assimilation research in communication because, according to Louis, it primarily features a cognitive process rather than a behavioral (communicative) one.

Role theory offers a third theoretical contextualization for many assimilation studies. Roles encompass a social structure's set of behavioral expectations associated with a given position and therefore integral in assimilation (Ebaugh, 1988). Thus, a primary purpose of organizational assimilation involves shaping members into organizationally determined roles. For example, Apker, Propp, and Ford's (2005) study of nurses' assimilation into healthcare teams detailed the process by which the nurses negotiated their role status and identified with other members of the team. According to role theory, individuals adapt behaviors to fulfill the expectations associated with their roles. Indeed, for some, work becomes not just a means for earning a living; rather, work makes one's life (Drucker, 1973). Similarly, Kanter (1993) suggested that a person's role (and its accompanying opportunity, power, and social ties) begins to define him or her. Apker et al., for instance, found that role dialectics, or tensions, arise as nurses communicate their professional identities and relate to others in terms of hierarchy and status and that strong role identification, perhaps to the extent that Drucker and Kanter theorized, helps to reduce those tensions.

Social exchange theory may also be useful to assimilation researchers. This theory suggests that individuals choose to interact with others when they perceive rewards from that interaction (Homans, 1959; Thibaut & Kelley, 1959). Therefore, according to this perspective, organizational members communicate more frequently and substantively with those from whom they perceive they will receive rewards (tangible or intangible) relative to their investment. For example, Kramer (2005) employed social exchange theory to examine individuals' participation in community theater groups, and he discovered that rewards (such as positive audience reaction, social interaction, and peer support) predicted theater members' satisfaction and commitment.

Application of these theories within the assimilation literature, and resulting new knowledge claims, should draw new connections to other areas of communication research. For example, the reader can draw links from uncertainty reduction that occurs in organizations to the active, passive, and interactive uncertainty reduction strategies that individuals use during the formation of personal relationships that Berger (1987) discussed and to the process of reciprocal self-disclosure that results in the development of relational history and shared interpersonal norms studied by Vangelisti,

Caughlin, and Timmerman (2001). More specifically, assimilation resembles a construct known as *relationship viability* (discussed primarily by interpersonal scholars), and that linkage demonstrates how organizational assimilation comprises an interpersonal experience and how interpersonal relationships require assimilation.

In other words, individuals both learn and create relational structures that permit relationship satisfaction and viability. More specifically, Werner and Baxter's (1994) definition of relationship viability reflects an underlying conceptualization of interpersonal relationships as the outcome of effective assimilation. They suggested that "relationship viability is the extent to which the individual or group can function effectively to stay alive psychologically and socially, to flourish, to grow and change, and to achieve short- and long-term goals" (p. 324). In Moreland and Levine's (2001) group socialization model, the first step is mutual evaluation of relational costs and benefits, a process similar to the one that takes place within close interpersonal relationships.

A Tactical Theory of Organizational Socialization

Most of the work on organizational assimilation/socialization stems from seminal discussions of socialization by Van Maanen and Schein (1979), which focused on how newcomers adjust to organizations—primarily through experiences afforded to them by their organizations. In their theory, Van Maanen and Schein argued that organizations use six primary tactics to structure the socialization experiences of newcomers. Each of these tactics exists on a bipolar continuum. First, *fixed* tactics offer the new member precise knowledge of the time required to complete a given step of socialization and/or the entire process. Conversely, *variable* tactics do not provide newcomers with any advance notice of their expected transition timetable. Second, *sequential* tactics prescribe a fixed sequence of steps that leads to role competence, compared to *random* tactics that keep the sequence ambiguous or frequently changing. Third, experienced members, either individually or in groups, utilize *serial* tactics when they mentor newcomers about to assume similar roles in the organization. *Disjunctive* tactics do not employ explicit role models for newcomers. Rather, newcomers are left alone to determine how the socialization process will proceed and how they will learn.

Fourth, according to Van Maanen and Schein (1979), socialization strategies may be either *formal* or *informal*. Organizations segregate formal socialization experiences from the ongoing work context in settings such as corporate "universities" or classroom training sessions. Less formal programs typically involve little instruction, allowing the member to sink or swim. Fifth, *individual* socialization encompasses one-on-one newcomer/senior partnering, and self- or organization-imposed newcomer isolation. Conversely, *collective* tactics involve placing an individual newcomer in a cohort of individuals who participate in an identical set of experiences, resulting in relatively similar outcomes for each member. Finally, Van Maanen (1978, p. 34) asserted that *investiture* tactics validate the "viability and usefulness" of the professional identity that a newcomer already possesses, as opposed to *divestiture* strategies that "deny and strip away certain entering characteristics of a recruit." Several important lines of research have developed and enhanced our understanding of this early theory of socialization and led researchers to acceptance of the more integrative assimilation construct. A review of two such developments follows.

Development 1: Socialization Is an Interactive Process   Researchers have developed the Van Maanen and Schein (1979) theory of socialization tactics in ways that underscore the interactive nature of socialization. Rather than viewing socialization simply as training and orientation—something organizations "do" for newcomers—researchers have underscored that newcomers often act proactively in their attempts to become assimilated; they do not just wait for socialization experiences to happen (Griffin, Colella, & Goparaju, 2000; Jablin, 2001; Myers & Oetzel, 2003; Saks & Ashforth, 1996). Further, members frequently attempt to individualize or negotiate their roles and influence organizations and each other in important ways with their prior experiences, attitudes, and knowledge (as opposed to the traditional socialization view that newcomers arrive as "blank slates," ready to be written upon by institutional procedures, norms, and existing culture that effectively allows organizations to shape their attitudes and behaviors) (Jablin & Krone, 1994; T. Y. Kim, Cable, & S. P. Kim, 2005; Klein & Weaver, 2000; Waldeck et al., 2004).

In the group communication literature, Moreland and Levine's (1982) model of group socialization illustrates the interactivity of fitting in at the group level of analysis. Specifically, Moreland and

Levine's model describes a three-step process in which, first, members mutually evaluate each another. Following mutual evaluation, members can develop feelings of commitment to the group (and vise versa), which may rise and fall throughout membership. When mutual commitment reaches sufficient levels, they can transition to become accepted members of the workgroup.

In the 1990s, several studies of newcomer proactivity focused on members' attempts to acquire information (Bauer & Green, 1994; Morrison, 1993a). For example, Morrison linked proactive information seeking to positive socialization outcomes. Specifically, she found that the frequency with which 135 new accountants sought job-related information corresponded to how well they mastered their jobs, defined their roles, internalized their organization's culture norms, and became socially integrated. Similarly, Bauer and Green reported that interactivity among organizational members (especially newcomers and incumbents) was positively associated with the information seeker's performance, satisfaction, and organizational commitment. Taken together, these works support the view that assimilation constitutes an interactive activity over which newcomers may exercise some control.

The theoretical notion of assimilation interactivity relates to communication research beyond the organizational context. For example, in their analysis of how technology facilitates the development of community, Edley, Hylmo, and Newsom (2004) described how members of online communities interact and the functions that their Web-based relationships serve. Edley et al. reported that individuals use online communities to facilitate supportive discourse among family, friends, neighbors, and other individuals that help them to learn how to manage the tensions associated with balancing work and personal concerns. In other words, as people interact, they learn appropriate and normative behavioral responses to the challenges that they discuss in these online communities. Similarly, in his theory of innovation, Rogers (1995) noted that the diffusion (the popularization and widespread use) of innovations, such as new technologies, comprises a social process involving user work with, and modification of, the meaning and purpose of the technology.

Elsewhere, researchers have described intercultural communication encounters as "complex and dynamic" (Begley, 2006) and as interactive learning and coping experiences (Witte, 1993). As a result, intercultural and organizational scholars might benefit by investigating each other's theories on the processes of entry, adaptation, and negotiation. For example, intercultural theory might be advanced by exploring how overt and covert attempts to discover normative practices can translate to improved functioning in the new culture. Conversely, the work on immigrant or sojourner acculturation (e.g., Hanne, 2005, as well as related review by Ballard & Gossett, this volume) could provide a deeper understanding of the role of power (and powerlessness) in the organizational adjustment process.

Development 2: Outcomes of Socialization Tactics   Scholars also have advanced our understanding of Van Maanen and Schein's (1979) perspective by demonstrating a number of specific outcomes of socialization tactics. For instance, individualized socialization has been positively associated with innovation (N. J. Allen & Meyer, 1990; Ashforth & Saks, 1996; Jones, 1986). Conversely, institutional tactics that allow for newcomer interaction with peers and organizational members result in more rapid socialization than do individual tactics (which do not promote collegial interaction) (N. J. Allen & Meyer, 1990; Reichers, 1987). Several studies have linked institutional tactics with custodial outcomes (in which newcomers, heavily influenced by the organization, sustained the status quo) (N. J. Allen & Meyer, 1990; Ashforth & Saks, 1996; Jones, 1986). According to N. J. Allen and Meyer, collective, formal, sequential, fixed, serial, and divestiture tactics correlated with high levels of newcomer commitment to the organization. In a reanalysis of N. J. Allen and Meyer's data, Baker (1995) found socialization tactics that promote interaction impact member role clarity and organizational commitment more strongly than strategies advancing individualization—especially for newcomers.

Not surprisingly, Hart, V. D. Miller, and Johnson (1998) found that institutional tactics are related to superior–subordinate openness. Organizational members with high status play key roles in "indoctrinating" newcomers or members of lesser status with institutional socialization tactics, resulting in a high level of superior/subordinate communication. However, research on interpersonal bullying in organizational contexts provides a caveat that a fine line exists between a high-status organizational member providing "suggestive" advice to a lower status member or newcomer and being perceived as uncivilized or abusive with his or her directives, therefore rendering the use of institutional socialization tactics possibly problematic and risky. Tracy, Lutgen-Sandvik, and Alberts (2005) demonstrated that bullying often takes place in situations with a power disparity between the "aggressor" and the "victim" (see also related review by Pörhölä, Karhunen, & Rainivaara, 2006).

Clearly, socialization tactics that exacerbate the potential for both power imbalances and resulting patterns of negative communication exist in many types of relationships of interest to communication scholars, especially in the areas of political communication, feminist scholarship, interpersonal and intercultural communication, and instructional communication. When newcomers face the challenge of learning group norms, and existing members of the social structure desire to preserve those norms, the potential for negative indoctrination lingers. In situations where mediated forms of communication (such as online bulletin boards, company intranet chat rooms, and discussion forums) permit anonymity of communicators, the risk of abusive, uncivil, or bullying communication patterns increases (Williamson & Pierson, 2003). With the proliferation of communication technologies that facilitate interpersonal, group, and organizational communication both locally and globally, the positive and negative potential assimilation-related effects of mediated communication require research attention from empirical, theoretical, and practical perspectives.

Recent research demonstrates the relationship of institutionalized socialization tactics to a variety of membership outcomes. Institutionalized tactics appear to be associated with lower role ambiguity, role conflict, person–job/organizational fit, task mastery, job satisfaction, organizational commitment, and intentions to quit (Hart & V. D. Miller, 2005; Hart, V. D. Miller, & Johnson, 2003; Kim et al., 2005; Riordan, Weatherly, Vandenberg, & Self, 2001; Saks & Ashforth, 1997; Seibert, 1999). For example, Hart and V. D. Miller found that fixed and serial tactics lead to information about performance proficiency, and Klein and Weaver (2000) discovered that orientation programs (a formal tactic) relate positively to learning about goals/values, organizational history, and people.

Instructional and developmental communication scholars provide evidence of similar outcomes in classroom learning contexts. For instance, Bippus, Kearney, Plax, & Brooks (2003) discovered that faculty and staff in mentoring relationships engage in frequent interaction, and, when students perceive and recognize faculty encouragement, students begin to think critically about their courses and their future plans. Notably, Bippus et al. also concluded that students evaluate their learning experiences much more positively than in the absence of such socializing interactions and relationships. This research regarding the outcomes of institutionalized socialization in multiple contexts suggests that, although individuals play a role in their own assimilation, they still appreciate and respond to structure and formal relationships for helping them to learn preferred normative behaviors.

Developmental Theory of Assimilation

Early work (Jablin, 1987; Porter et al., 1975; Van Maanen & Schein, 1979) relies on the theory that assimilation occurs in several stages. However, Smith and Turner (1995) contended that stage models of organizational socialization are "more likely to disable than enable efforts to generate understandings" (p. 173). Furthermore, Bullis (1993) and Clair (1996) argued that the use of phase models is limiting and inappropriate in that they devalue individuals and privilege a managerial/institutional perspective. Although the developmental theory of assimilation stages has been controversial within the field, Kramer and V. D. Miller (1999) defended it, and a number of important seminal works (Feldman, 1981; Schein, 1969; Van Maanen, 1976) have relied upon this framework as a useful tool to understand what members face as they assimilate.

The first phase, *anticipatory socialization*, involves two interrelated processes: occupational choice/entry and choosing/entering a particular organization (Jablin & Krone, 1987). The former, anticipatory *vocational* socialization, entails the gathering and processing of occupational information from family, educational institutions, part-time employment, peers and friends, and the media (Jablin, 2001), and it occurs through messages that appear to influence young peoples' lifelong attitudes toward work (Medved, Brogan, McClanahan, Morris, & Shepherd, 2006). In anticipatory *organizational* socialization, Jablin argued that prospective employees exchange information with interviewers and recruiters, other members of the organization, and sources outside the organization (e.g., friends, family, teachers). During this period, the primary activities for prospective newcomers include forming expectations about the job, information transmitting and processing, and making decisions regarding employment.

The second phase of organizational socialization, *accommodation* or *encounter* (Feldman, 1976), includes the period in which a newcomer observes the actual organization (versus her or his expectations) and attempts to become a participating member. During this time, according to Feldman, new members (a) learn their tasks, (b) define roles, and (c) determine, jointly with their supervisors, criteria for evaluating progress in the organization. Jablin (2001) specified the relationships and communicative structures that enable the attainment of these objectives through interactivity: role negotiation, peer and supervisory relationship development, information giving, information seeking, informal mentoring, formal mentoring, training, and orienting. All of these organizational relationship structures underscore the critical importance of information exchange and overall underlying uncertainty reduction issues in predicting successful assimilation.

In the third stage, uncertainty-reducing behaviors target enacting organizational norms. This stage of organizational assimilation, *role management* or *metamorphosis*, comprises a new employee's effort to obtain some consistency among his or her own "attitudes, beliefs, and values and those prevailing in the organization ... and begins to make shifts to adapt to these incongruencies" (Jablin, 1982, p. 268). Such information comes from three primary sources: official (often media-related sources in the organization), managers, and members of an individual's workgroup. Absence of communication from any of these sources, Jablin noted, may result in challenges to a person's assimilation efforts.

Finally, Jablin (2001) asserted that the process of *organizational disengagement* encompasses a challenge for the individual taking leave and those who remain in the work environment. Exiting an organization involves voluntarily or involuntarily giving up a role and its related identity, and even though the individual may choose to exit, he or she may experience periods of mental and communicative disassociation, even periods of grief (Ebaugh, 1988). Although Jablin provided initial insight into the disengagement/exit stage, in light of the dynamic economic, social, and political nature of contemporary organizations, urgent need mandates systematic examination of exit process. For example, Pfann (2006) examined the displacement of 3,650 people during a mass layoff in the Netherlands and noted the importance of such work in view of a global trend toward downsizing and outsourcing. In the United States, the massive workforce reduction and plant closures associated with the financial crisis of General Motors, one of America's largest employers, and the concomitant stress that it places on those who leave, their families and communities, those who stay, and the organization itself exemplify why a renewed focus on the exit process is critical (see Hakim, 2005).

Similarly, mergers, acquisitions, and other changes require assimilation as well. Hart et al. (2003) pointed out the need for understanding assimilation related to organizational change, and Cartwright and Schoenberg (2006) noted that, as the number of mergers and acquisitions increases globally, the failure rate remains consistently high.

Because assimilation models describe the challenges that individuals confront throughout their efforts to relate to others, behave normatively, and accomplish organizational objectives, they may offer some insights into the overall life cycle of interpersonal relationships (see related arguments in Knapp, 1984; Rawlins, 1992). For instance, through processes similar to the ones through which children gain anticipatory/vocational socialization information from adults (Gibson & Papa, 2000), they may also acquire key messages and lessons about participating in interpersonal relationships. More specifically, Gibson and Papa used the term *cultural osmosis* to describe the process by which parents expose children to a strong work ethic and enable them to develop values about work based on familial influences. As a result, people who have absorbed cultural information through "osmosis" enter organizations and occupations readily accepting normative practices and values. Gibson and Papa's work could serve as a basis for understanding some of the modeling that influences young people's understanding of how to participate in interpersonal relationships—particularly difficult, largely uncertain ones. Moreover, their research could illuminate the experience of entry and assimilation into the culture of illness, described by Adelman and Frey (1997).

Criticisms of the Developmental Approach   The explication of assimilation as a developmental process has been a useful and heuristic way of studying how communication facilitates person–organization fit, despite that, in some of his earliest work, Jablin (1987) indicated that assimilation is not a linear process. However, importantly, this perspective focuses on an individual's life span with regard to organizational involvement (e.g., beginning with childhood and early orientation to work and addressing entry, adjustment, and even exit from an organization) (Bullis, 1993; Jablin & Krone, 1994; Kramer & V. D. Miller, 1999). Therefore, the developmental approach comprises a systematic and linear model for understanding complex personal and relational issues surrounding assimilation. Despite that fact, however, some scholars criticized developmental or stage models because they may inaccurately depict assimilation processes as linear (Bullis, 1993; Clair, 1996; Smith & Turner, 1995). Furthermore, as Fisher (1986) and Bauer, Morrison, and Callister (1998) argued, stage models do not adequately demonstrate *how* transition from one phase to another occurs.

However, Kramer and V. D. Miller (1999) countered that a time-based model provides a useful way of organizing our observations of the process that the aggregate of working individuals experience. Even critics of the developmental model acknowledge that this perspective has contributed to our understanding of socialization (Bullis, 1993; Clair, 1996). The value of a developmental model might be limited to answering questions in practice, rather than theoretical questions, which will advance assimilation as an area of study. For example, it serves as a worthwhile pedagogical tool for sharing some of the emotions, interactions, and activities that might occur across the first few months of employment with newcomers. Yet, because assimilation experiences can focus on so many issues, occur across the life span, and become framed by organizational culture, it may be impossible to understand particular assimilation activities according to stages. Thus, in terms of advancing a theory of organizational assimilation, the developmental model may lack explanatory power and heuristic value.

Research-Based Responses to Criticisms of the Developmental Approach   Accordingly, Hart et al. (2003) explored perceptions of organizational veterans at two points in time during an organizational change. In this important move to consider the assimilation experiences of persons other than newcomers, Hart et al. learned that role ambiguity and role conflict decrease over time and that commitment to organizational goals increases between early socialization experiences and later ones. Kramer (1993) similarly employed multiple data collection periods. Waldeck et al. (2004) sought to examine the ongoing nature of assimilation for newcomers and seasoned members experiencing change at the individual, group, and/or organizational levels by broadly defining circumstances that require assimilation among both newcomers and veterans. These studies represent important steps away from a narrow conceptualization of socialization toward one in which researchers consider varied and dynamic individual, group, and organizational factors.

Future studies must take up these tasks of pursuing assimilation longitudinally and conceptualizing assimilation activities broadly to include ones that reduce uncertainty at any time of organizational change or individual uncertainty. Tidwell and Sias (2005) further noted the necessity of longitudinal methods for assessing the role of *personality traits* in predicting information-seeking behaviors during assimilation. Through such investigations, "investigators gather data that indicate how the process unfolds over time" (Poole, Van de Ven, Dooley, & Holmes, 2000, p. 12). Such studies could provide rich insights about the progression of events that impact assimilation. However, as K. Miller (2001) acknowledged, the difficulties with measuring overtime activities (such as assimilation) pose a challenge to organizational scholars in that "most of our theories of organizational communication are ... processual, but our research methods have lagged behind these theories by considering cross-sectional data" (p. 147). As K. Miller observed, "it is a rare study that includes multiple data collection periods, let alone the observation and analytic procedures that would allow for a full mapping and understanding of the assimilation process" (p. 147).

Thus, although we might have a richer picture of assimilation as a result of longitudinal designs than from static, cross-sectional studies, a number of conceptual and methodological concerns continue to limit this area of study. Despite these challenges, Kramer (1993) and Hart et al. (2003) established the groundwork for future longitudinal design implementation in assimilation studies. In another area, longitudinal studies employing the developmental model might shed light on the complex process of political socialization and the development and change of partisan attitudes over time. For example, Holbert and Hansen (2006) found that the priming effect of Michael Moore's film *Fahrenheit 911* differed among audiences based on their political party identification, as well as the strength of that identification. Interestingly, Holbert and Hansen noted that strength of political party identification is fluid for many Americans and changes over time. Thus, a developmental assimilation study of these phenomena could enhance our understanding of the effects of media on political attitudes and voting behavior.

Contemporary Theories of Organizational Assimilation

A Theory of the Dimensions of Organizational Assimilation   Considering the developments described earlier, Myers and Oetzel (2003) explicated a theory of the communicative dimensions of organizational assimilation. They developed this model based on data collected from a diverse sample of individuals from various organizations. As such, they constructed a widely generalizable model of six communicative processes that individuals experience as they assume their roles: becoming familiar with others in the organization, acculturating into the organization, feeling recognized as a contributing member, feeling involved, attaining a level of job competency, and role negotiating. The Myers and Oetzel model should provide future direction by guiding researchers to examining specific functions of assimilating communication.

Information-Seeking From a Contemporary Perspective   Recent work exploring information-seeking processes reflects the complex environments in which they occur. For example, Flanagin and Waldeck (2004) developed a framework that specifies how individuals use advanced communication and information technologies (ACITs)—devices that transmit, manipulate, or analyze information, often relying on a computer, and that have been widely used since 1970 to aid in communication—to access information and facilitate interpersonal relationships that contribute to successful organizational assimilation. ACITs might include e-mail, cell phone, PDAs, Internet, and intranet. Flanagin and Waldeck proposed a number of factors that may predict organizational members' selection and use of technologies for socializing purposes, including features of their socialization experiences (the identifiable stage at which the information need occurs, the type of information required, and prevalent organizational socialization tactics), individual attitudes and personality characteristics (levels of self-monitoring and communication apprehension), and group and organizational norms for technology use (social influences to utilize technology, observation of group and organizational norms regarding such resources, and feedback regarding use).

In one test of elements advanced by Flanagin and Waldeck (2004), Waldeck et al. (2004) asserted that members consider the feedback that they receive about their assimilation-related use of ACITs and then enact the same or different information-seeking behaviors. They could continue using the ACIT for the same or similar purposes, supplement the information they acquired through an ACIT with information from another source or channel, discontinue use of the ACIT in response to their assimilation-related ACIT experience, expand use of the ACIT, and/or discover new functions of an ACIT that they already employ for other purposes "by accident" and begin to use the technology for information-seeking or uncertainty reduction.

Flanagin and Waldeck's (2004) model requires further testing in varied contexts because it offers a thorough proposition of how and why ACITs assist organizational members in their information-seeking efforts. Accounting for variables at the individual, group, and organizational levels of analysis, as well as being grounded in theories of media selection and use, Flanagin and Waldeck's model contributes to the study of information-seeking and uncertainty reduction. Given the prevalence of ACITs in nearly all communicative contexts and their role in facilitating interpersonal (Walther & Anderson, 1994), family (Kraut & Mukhopadhyay, 1999), intercultural (Zhu, Gareis, Bazzoni, Rolland, & Sokuvitz, 2005), health (Ginossar, 2005; Lewis, 2006), and instructional (reviewed in Waldeck, Kearney, & Plax, 2001) communication, Flanagin and Waldeck's model holds important implications for understanding the role of digital communication in diverse communication contexts.

Tidwell and Sias (2005) provided another model of individual differences regarding information-seeking behavior. They maintained that a preponderance of studies examining antecedents of information-seeking consider only situational variables. Instead, Tidwell and Sias argued for the importance of more stable variables—personality traits. Employing Costa and McCrae's (1994) big five personality constructs (neuroticism, extroversion, openness to experience, agreeableness, and conscientiousness) as their independent variables, Tidwell and Sias investigated the relationship between personality traits and relational, performance, and/or task information-seeking and the role of perceived social costs in newcomer information-seeking behaviors. They found evidence of specific links between personality traits and both covert and overt information-seeking behaviors of newcomers.

This study further enriches assimilation theory by framing newcomer perceptions of social costs as mediators between traits and information-seeking behaviors, rather than fixed situational constituents solely dependent on the situation itself. Responses to that information may be illuminated by David, Cappella, and Fishbein's (2006) study on the influence of group interaction following exposure to antidrug advertisements. They found that personality traits most greatly influenced antidrug beliefs, but that discussion among peer groups directly related to more favorable impressions of marijuana use. Taken together, the studies by Flanagin and Waldeck (2004), Tidwell and Sias (2005), and David et al. represent a contemporary theoretical perspective on the complex individual- and macrolevel variables that influence information-seeking and resulting responses.

Assimilation as Discourse That Occurs Within and Outside the Organization   To discover the role that discourse plays in organizational socialization, Barge and Schlueter (2004) examined the content of messages that newcomers recalled from entry into organizations and the socialization-related functions that these messages served. They employed Stohl's (1986) memorable message framework for eliciting the kinds of short discursive units that individuals remembered hearing that impacted their work life when they first entered the organization (from sources within and outside) and learning how organizational newcomers actually used these messages in their organizational lives. Barge and Schlueter delineated eight categories of messages that served socialization-related functions for the newcomers in their sample. These categories included discursive formations that (1) told the newcomer what it meant to behave professionally within the work context, (2) communicated both formal and unwritten work expectations and rules, (3) emphasized the values of a strong work ethic, (4) alerted the newcomer to the importance of office politics, (5) underscored the importance of customer service, (6) centered on the metaphor of the team and emphasized that the newcomer should feel part of the "organizational family," (7) stressed the value of the newcomer to the organization, and (8) reflected the importance of giving input and communicating openly at work.

Newcomers perceived these messages to function in a variety of ways. Specifically, according to Barge and Schlueter (2004), respondents reported that memorable messages influenced them to (1) develop personal abilities and grow, (2) do their best, (3) be organized, (4) be positive and have fun, (5) adhere to company expectations, (6) deliver high-quality services to customers, and (7) reflect on the work process. Barge and Schlueter emphasized the theoretical importance of these findings, noting that discourse during organizational entry serves both organizational socialization functions (i.e., some messages encourage newcomers to fit into existing organizational patterns) and individuation functions (i.e., some messages encourage newcomers to develop individual abilities). Indeed, 76% of the memorable messages functioned to motivate the newcomer to "stand out" and build his or her personal abilities as a way of enhancing performance.

Barge and Schlueter conceded several problematic aspects of their findings. For example, newcomers confront tensions to both "fit in" and "stand out" and encouragement to "do one's best," thus privileging organizational needs over individual needs. However, we see some positive implications of their findings regarding memorable messages and their functions. They reveal evidence of organizations encouraging individuals to be innovative. Overall, Barge and Schlueter's important contribution to the literature details the implications of discourse for newcomers and sets the foundation for more analyses by communication scholars of the conversational practices that support assimilation.

Beyond organizational communication, memorable messages hold interesting implications for the study of intercultural and interpersonal communication. Described as rules of thumb (Stohl, 1986), the messages that individuals receive and process as memorable should be telling predictors of their behavior within a given context. A number of researchers have reported the influence of the mass media (Bradford, Rhodes, & Edison, 2005; Greenberg & Busselle, 1996) and social norms or expectations (Burgoon, Stern, & Dillman, 1995) on individuals' expectations for, and behavior within, interpersonal relationships. Memorable messages may explain the effects of key social others (e.g., parents, grandparents, teachers, and other role models) and popular media characterization on persons' perceptions of what to expect from (and how to behave in) interpersonal interactions.

The establishment of family norms and interaction patterns might be better understood through an analysis of memorable messages as well. For example, Braithwaite, Olson, Golish, Soukup, and Turman (2001) identified five trajectories of family development among blended families attempting to establish appropriate boundaries, solidarity, and roles. Potentially, the study of memorable messages that members of blended families recall—and persons to whom they go for advice or counsel, such as others who have had previous experience blending a family, the blended family, or their own families of origin—might reveal underlying beliefs about family and blended family communication that predict the ease or difficulty with which these persons assimilate into a successfully blended family.

In the area of mass media, researchers have established that parents can protect their children from harmful media effects through coviewing (parental supervision of children during exposure to mass media) (Nathanson, 1998) and that the positive effects of parental coviewing earlier in life wane when children reach adolescence and interact with communication media in the company of peers (Nathanson, 2001). Examination and comparison of memorable messages from parents and peers about mediated images may yield useful information regarding the differential impacts of parental and peer influence on the way that young people respond to media exposure. Just as members rely on memorable messages to know how to act appropriately within the organization, we expect that people depend on similar messages for assimilating into an array of social and intercultural situations, and research attention on such messages would further our understanding of the roles of discourse and information attention, selection, and retention in communicative behavior across communication contexts.

In this section, we have highlighted the theoretical frameworks from which assimilation research has emerged and discussed representative empirical tests of these models. Additionally, we specified other areas throughout the communication discipline that could benefit from these models and ways that diverse communication scholars could profit from incorporating one or more of these theoretical underpinnings into their research. Next, we describe the primary themes of research. Indeed, the implications of assimilation research span our discipline.

Major Areas of Recent Research
and Methodological Perspectives

Introductory Note

Jablin (2001) provided a comprehensive historical review of the assimilation/socialization literature. Therefore, we refer readers to Jablin's chapter and, in this section, strive to assess the lines of research as a basis for drawing conclusions about the present state and future of this area of study. Our review and analysis of research published in the communication, business, management, and organizational behavior/psychology fields revealed that assimilation research can be classified according to eight primary themes. This section of the chapter highlights each theme as well as representative studies within each respective category. Because several of these studies were not mutually exclusive to one theme, we reference them in more than one category.

Antecedents and Correlates to Assimilation Effectiveness

Research in this category examines the factors that predict, and relate to, assimilation effectiveness. Although Jablin (2001) reported many of the research studies on antecedents and correlates to assimilation effectiveness, they remain important to this chapter as the rationale and basis for the development of the other seven major areas of research on this topic. Therefore, we briefly review this research here.

Needs. The seminal works (Graen, 1976; Louis, 1980; Van Maanen & Schein, 1979) and more recent studies (Ashforth & Saks, 1996; Chao, O'Leary-Kelly, Wolf, Klein, & Gardner, 1994; V. D. Miller, 1997; Orpen, 1995; Tidwell & Sias, 2005) discuss needs as precursors to communication-related assimilation experiences. First, *individual-level* needs for information and affiliation influence newcomer communication behavior (Ashford & Cummings, 1983; Teboul, 1994), individual alignment with colleagues or peers for collegial support (Kalbfleisch & Keyton, 1995), and mentoring (Waldeck, Orrego, Plax, & Kearney, 1997), as well as the enactment of particular socialization tactics by experienced organizational members (Ashforth & Saks, 1996). According to Ashforth and Saks, *group-level* needs for leadership, cohesion, and supportive/confirming communication climates elicit the enactment of certain socialization tactics; in particular, high needs for leadership, cohesion, and support relate to institutionalized socialization tactics. Finally, *organizational-level* needs for stability, coordination, control, power, and conscientious/competent role performance correspond to specific assimilation processes (Barge & Schlueter, 2004; Jablin, 1987; Robbins, 1983). For example, Rynes (1991) found that experienced members tend to perceive newcomers as a threat in organizations with high stability needs, often resulting in a strained relationship between newcomers and veterans.

Learning. Learning remains key to members' organizational performance and social adjustment. Several studies emphasized the influence or mediating effect of learning in assimilation and indicators of adjustment. For example, among service employees, learning partially mediated the relationship between curiosity and performance (Reio & Wiswell, 2000). In Klein and Weaver's (2000) study, learning also impacted the influence of socialization efforts on newcomer commitment and job satisfaction. Further, Klein, Fan, and Preacher (2006) found that learning partially mediated the impact of realistic pre-entry knowledge and the newcomers' perceptions of socialization agent helpfulness on role clarity, commitment, and job satisfaction. Among British Army recruits, learning fully mediated the impact of the Army's socialization tactics on commitment and satisfaction (Cooper-Thomas & Anderson, 2002). These studies provide evidence for a long-standing assumption that members' ability to learn influences assimilation.

Proactivity and self-presentation/regulating. Proactivity interacts with learning and adjustment in terms of information seeking, controlling (Ashford and Black, 1996), and self-regulating (Porath & Bateman, 2006; Saks & Ashforth, 1996) and the ways in which such behavior influences assimilation outcomes. For example, newcomer proactivity corresponds positively with increased newcomer learning, role clarity, job performance, commitment, and satisfaction, but also with decreased stress, task-specific anxiety, and intentions to quit (Ashford & Black, 1996; Holder, 1996; Morrison, 1993a, 1993b; Saks & Ashforth, 1996). In their study of new accountants, Saks and Ashforth discovered that newcomers employed six types of self-regulating behaviors, including self-goal setting, self-observation, cueing strategies, self-reward, self-punishment, and rehearsal to manage their experiences strategically. Similarly, Maier and Brunstein (2001) found that personal goal setting predicted higher job satisfaction and commitment. More specifically, when members set goals but did not believe that they could attain them, commitment and other assimilation-related outcomes suffered. Yet, when members believed that they could achieve their goals, the act of goal setting positively impacted assimilation-related outcomes.

Context may also play a role in the influence of proactivity on assimilation. In a recent study of probationary firefighters, demonstrating proactivity comprised a requirement for becoming accepted by others in the department (Myers, 2005). In part, Myers argued, this necessity relates to the traditional, paramilitary culture of the fire service. However, another important contextual implication involves the nature of the occupation. In dangerous situations, firefighters need to know that they can depend on fellow crew members to be proactive problem solvers. Proactivity may be important, but not as essential, for other organizations that require teamwork.

Assimilation and Identification

This category of research explores the intersection between assimilation outcomes and organizational identification. *Identification* is the degree to which membership within an organization or team comprises an "emotionally significant aspect of one's identity" (Van Der Vegt & Bunderson, 2005, p. 535).[1] In organizations or groups with high levels of identification, individuals remain committed to the organization (or the group) and its goals rather than (or in addition to) their own goals (Cheney & Tompkins, 1987). For example, Cheney (1983) found that individuals view identification as a motivating factor in their work lives, and as such, they generally appreciate organizational messages that promote member identification. He further concluded that, when identification is strong, individuals likely use institutional information in the decision-making process. Assimilation studies from an identification perspective thus pursue the (a) complexities of managing multiple organizational identifications during organizational transition—a time in which assimilation needs are particularly high (Larson & Pepper, 2003), (b) relationship between socialization tactics and experiences and resulting levels of identification (Gibson & Papa, 2000), and (c) relationship between identification and individual- and team-level learning and performance outcomes during assimilation experiences (Van Der Vegt & Bunderson, 2005).

Taken as a whole, these studies indicate the reciprocal relationship between organizational and/or team identification levels and assimilation effectiveness. For example, in a study of identification with and assimilation to blue-collar work groups, Gibson and Papa (2000) asserted that persons' anticipatory socialization experiences (e.g., interactions in adolescence and early adulthood with significant family members, friends, and teachers regarding work and organizational membership) predicted their identification with an organization. Van Der Vegt and Bunderson (2005) found that individuals who identified with multiple divisions within an organization perceived more effective assimilation experiences than those who did not achieve identification. Consistent with a social identity perspective, members whose roles provide higher levels of salience for their self-identity more likely adopt normative group behaviors (Hogg & Reid, 2006) than others. Thus, this category of research attests that organizational identification marks an important component of assimilation and that successful and effective assimilation experiences might also influence greater levels of identification with organizations and work groups.

Similar to the ways in which organizational members must manage their affiliation with groups, subgroups, the larger organization, and third-party stakeholders, family members must manage relationship issues that span across family and organizational boundaries (Golden, Kirby, & Jorgenson, 2006) and juggle their ties with one another. More specifically, several interpersonal communication researchers have been interested in the changing nature of contemporary American families—blended, boomerang, and multicultural families that often struggle to cultivate loyalty, flexible boundaries, role definition, support, and trust in view of their complexities (Braithwaite & Baxter, 2006; Braithwaite et al., 2001; Graham, 2003). A study of identification and its relationship to family dynamics, such as successful blending (see, for example, Braithwaite et al.), might reveal an important aspect of family functioning. Similarly, a study of identification as it relates to assimilation into intimate relationships might shed light on why some couples are able to form a tightly knit, highly satisfying "culture of two" (Bruess & Pearson, 1993, p. 613) that distinguishes them from less satisfied couples. Indeed, organizational assimilation research could shed light on other marital relationship issues such as how differences in religious backgrounds affect marital satisfaction (Hughes & Dickson, 2005) or, as Graham observed, how individuals can work through dialectical tensions following breakup of their marriages.

Assimilation as a Social Construct

This category of research investigates how patterns of relationships affect assimilation. Early work (Louis, 1980; Reichers, 1987) indicated that social interactions provide the means to effective assimilation ends. Thus, Morrison (2002) employed network analysis to examine the relationship of newcomers' network characteristics (size, density, strength, range, and status) to three types of assimilation outcomes: organizational knowledge, task mastery, and role clarity. This study shed new light on the role of relationship in assimilation outcomes by analyzing the overall structure and function of relational patterns. Morrison demonstrated that organizational members' informational and friendship networks systematically relate to discrete assimilation outcomes. For example, newcomers with larger networks spanning organizational units revealed greater organizational knowledge, and those with denser and stronger networks reported greater mastery of their jobs and greater role clarity. Similarly, Maitlis (2005) noted a positive relationship between organizational members' sense-making abilities and organizational leaders' "sense-giving" (attempts to guide, influence, or assist in another's understanding of an issue) efforts—further illustrating the necessity of social relationships for assimilation.

In her examination of communication in healthcare settings, Coopman (2001) noted the importance of cooperative relationships for establishing productive hospice care teams. Lammers and Krikorian (1997) employed the bona fide group framework (see Putnam & Stohl, 1990) to understand the interactivity and performance outcomes of surgical teams, thereby defining key membership-related conceptual elements of the construct. We argue that both of these studies also examined aspects of assimilation, given their focus on group members' positioning to achieve common goals and effective ways of interacting in teams with outcomes of significant real-world importance.

Yet, still other areas could benefit from greater attention to how their dependent variables of interest might be influenced by relational constructs. For example, in their review of instructional and developmental research in the 1990s, Waldeck et al. (2001) noted that, "although we know about 'teacher' behaviors and 'student' behaviors ... we know very little about how teacher–student *interactions* influence learning. Thus, we need more investigations of relational constructs ... to uncover the dynamic interplay between teachers and students" (p. 224). We contend that conceptualization of learning as a process of assimilation for both teachers and students could be valuable to instructional researchers. For example, in a study of student question asking, West and Pearson (1994) identified categories of questions, as well as teacher antecedents and consequents to each type. The use of a relational framework that incorporates other aspects of teacher–student interaction (e.g., mentoring or extraclass communication) as predictors of student questioning and teacher responses would be a fruitful next step in this line of research.

Assimilation as a Psychological Contract

Studies in this category explore assimilation as the result of psychological contracts between individuals and organizations. Rousseau (1989) defined *psychological contracts* as the beliefs that individuals hold regarding the terms and conditions of the exchange agreement between themselves and their organizations. Numerous studies have demonstrated the importance of psychological contracts in explaining member behaviors such as commitment, turnover, and citizenship (see, for example, Conway & Briner, 2002; Lester, Turnley, Bloodgood, & Bolino, 2002; Robinson & Morrison, 1995). Consequently, De Vos, Buyens, and Schalk (2003) found that changes in newcomers' perceptions of the promises that they made to their employers were affected by views of their own contributions as well as perceptions of inducements received by their employer. This line of research offers an important overall understanding of assimilation because it (a) sheds light on reasons why assimilation might be ineffective (e.g., employers change their part of the contract after the anticipatory stage) and (b) demonstrates that psychological contracts between individuals and organizations must be reciprocal and adaptive in order to provide a realistic preview and successful encounter process resulting in long-term assimilation effectiveness.

Psychological contracts could play a similar role in assimilation in nonorganizational experiences, such as in expectations that individuals develop related to intimate relationships. Assimilation research can contribute insights into how individuals negotiate such contracts in all types of relationships through message exchange. In an extension of the communication competence construct, Lakey and Canary (2002) investigated relational partners' abilities to simultaneously achieve their own relationship goals and to be sensitive to their significant other's goals. They determined that the ability to enact integrative patterns of communication that reflect both concern for self and other's goals within relationships results in partner perceptions of support and enhanced ability to manage conflict.

This study suggests that research on psychological contracts and interpersonal communication competence may inform one another and serve as a basis for understanding assimilation to relationships in a variety of contexts, including organizational, interpersonal, instructional and developmental, and group situations. Messages should serve as an important tool for the negotiation of explicit, rather than implicit, psychological contracts in any situation where multiple communicator goals and expectations exist. Lakey and Canary's (2002) work offers evidence that the more explicit partners are in their communication about conflict management—in effect, executing oral, in addition to psychological, contracts—the more effective and successful that their assimilation, learning, and uncertainty reduction will be within the relational context.

Assimilation to Work Groups and Teams

As we noted earlier, Moreland and Levine (1982, 2001) proposed that most socialization takes place at the level of the workgroup. Within organizations, newcomers come to understand the environment and develop relationships with those closest to them—the members of their workgroup (Anderson, Riddle, & Martin, 1999). Unique group characteristics may influence member assimilation more so than the broader organization-level socialization influences (Cini, Moreland, & Levine, 1993; Hennessy & West, 1999). By extension, in organizations with multiple workgroups, groups' distinctive influences on members' assimilation may cause group-to-group variation in members' assimilation.

In a test of these propositions, Myers and McPhee (2006) used Moreland and Levine's (1982) workgroup model as a framework, yet added trust to determine the impact of firefighting crew interaction and its effect on individual-level membership variables and crew assimilation. Their results indicated that involvement and trust influenced or supported later assimilation stages of commitment and acceptance. Crew performance, a key group-level process in firefighting crews, affected individual members' levels of commitment. Importantly, this study concluded that assimilation processes and intervariable relationships vary across groups, even in groups as homogeneous in task role composition and dedication as firefighters.

Similarly, Chen and Klimoski (2003) and Chen (2005) studied newcomer adaptation and team socialization in high-technology workers. Chen and Klomoski identified six role domains of newcomer performance on project teams: job (performing the expected tasks of the job), career (developing the ability to make progress in one's career), innovation (being innovative and creative), customer service (communicating effectively with customers), team (satisfactorily working well with teammates), and organization (performing beyond the organization's expectations). Subsequently, Chen found that early performance predicted empowerment and turnover. Comparable to Myers and McPhee's (2006) findings, outcomes differed from group to group, confirming that group-level differences translate to individual assimilation variation.

These studies offer relevant implications for unity and performance of many types of groups. For example, in the area of health communication, surgical and other medical teams must develop long- or short-term task-related roles and interdependencies to work quickly while avoiding accidents and unnecessary pain and injury to patients (Apker et al., 2005; Lammers & Krikorian, 1997). Further, studies of group assimilation may explain why some group-based learning experiences succeed and why participants fail to benefit as much from others. For example, T. H. Allen and Plax (2002) suggested that classroom-based learning groups could be affected by a number of group tensions. Assimilation studies of group socialization may inform our understanding of these tensions and drive research on ways to reduce them and, consequently, improve learning outcomes. Similarly, Web-based communities of practice enable knowledge sharing and management, connecting people with similar interests or concerns (Vestal, 2006). Vestal noted that the "true value of these communities ... and whether they succeed or fail, comes from the ongoing interaction and work of the group" (p. 8). Therefore, an examination of group socialization as a means to assimilation and effective group functioning may be important for understanding the value and function of increasingly common Web-enabled communities.

Assimilation Research in Intact, Applied Organizational Contexts

A goal of any organizational research should be to test the validity of theory in a variety of situations to determine its usefulness. Several studies tested theories in field settings to expand understanding of assimilation in context, to identify scope conditions, and to field-test theorized implications of socialization practices. Although one can argue that most organizational research is "applied" in that researchers collect data from members of actual organizations, the studies that compose this category report findings collected from intact workgroups within real organizations and may reflect unique characteristics of the organizational type or industry. For example, during an organizational restructuring, Hart et al. (2003) discovered that members responded to institutional and individual tactics in similar ways and that organizational change necessitated resocializing existing employees who transitioned with the organization. Hart and V. D. Miller's (2005) longitudinal study of new hotel managers explored the relationship of socialization contexts, the content of received messages, and worker adjustment. Based on their findings, they argued that informal socialization (such as informal initiation, shared stories, and trial-by-fire experiences) complement more formal organizational socialization efforts, significantly affecting role ambiguity and role innovation.

Zorn and Gregory (2005) demonstrated the influence of peer friendships as first-year students assimilate into medical school. They concluded that those relationships were instrumental in the socialization process because they offered invaluable socioemotional support to medical students that could not be obtained elsewhere. In another high-stress occupation, Myers (2005) tested the utility of the Myers and Oetzel (2003) model of organizational assimilation in a municipal fire department. Firefighters did become familiar with others, acculturate, increase involvement, feel recognized, and develop job competency. However, contrary to the Myers and Oetzel model, the probationary firefighters did not role negotiate. In this high-reliability organization, the firefighters exerted considerable effort in developing trustworthiness within the crew and organization.

Measures of Assimilation Effectiveness

Measuring assimilation constitutes a complex task because assimilation is multidimensional as members adapt, individualize roles, and position themselves into their new environments (Fisher, 1986; Van Maanen & Schein, 1979). Several instruments have operationalized and measured: (a) the types of information (content areas) that members attain as they integrate, (b) domains of socialization, and (c) assimilation processes.

Chao et al. (1994) posited that members become socialized by acquiring knowledge relative to six areas: (1) history of the organization, (2) people of the organization, (3) performance proficiency, (4) goals and values, (5) language, and (6) politics. They validated their six-dimension scale (including 34 items) by examining data from entry-level accounting professionals. They assessed convergent and discriminate validity by comparing correlations within and across items in the six subscales and by comparing the subscales to five career effectiveness measures (personal income, career involvement, identity resolution, adaptability, and job satisfaction). The Chao et al. socialization subscales are widely used in communication, management, social psychology, and other disciplines. In the field of communication, its usefulness remains limited because it does not enable researchers to investigate *how* members learn about these six content areas of socialization; thus, researchers often use this scale in conjunction with instruments that evaluate communication processes.

Similarly, Taormina (2004) assessed four dimensions of socialization: (a) training, (b) understanding, (c) co-worker support, and (d) beliefs about the future. He established convergent validity by comparing the four subscales to three subscales (work involvement, communication patterns, and financial rewards) from Taormina's (1994) Performance-Maintenance Questionnaire. Taormina (2004) described his 20-item instrument as more generic than Chao and colleagues' (1994), but he argued that his scale provides more comprehensive information because it also assesses more knowledge domains, such as rules and regulations. Primarily, the instrument measures assimilation outcomes, and like Chao and colleagues' instrument, it specifies some learning content areas.

In the field of communication, Myers and Oetzel (2003) asserted an instrument to assess assimilation processes. They developed their six dimensions and questionnaire by reviewing literature and interviewing individuals from a variety of for-profit and nonprofit organizations. Their six dimensions include: (1) becoming familiar with others, (2) acculturating and adapting, (3) becoming involved, (4) feeling recognized, (5) developing job competency, and (6) role negotiation. They validated their 20-item questionnaire by collecting data from 342 individuals in a variety of industries. They evaluated divergent validity by comparing correlations between subscales and with propensity to leave. They determined convergent reliability with interitem correlations and comparisons to job satisfaction and organizational identification. Similarities between the Chao et al. (1994) and Myers and Oetzel dimensions are not surprising since many of the communicative processes described in the Myers and Oetzel model enable the acquisition of the specific assimilation content areas described by Chao et al.

The Role of Advanced Communication and Information Technologies

This category of research examined the role of ACITs in the assimilation process as well as the importance of appropriate socialization to organizational media. In one representative study from this category, Waldeck et al. (2004), working from an uncertainty reduction/information acquisition perspective, reviewed face-to-face communication, traditional technologies, and ACITs as predictors of effective assimilation-related uncertainty reduction. Reasoning that reliance on these traditional channels alone is unlikely in contemporary organizations that enable and require use of ACITs, Waldeck et al. found that, although face-to-face communication best predicted effective assimilation, organizational members also valued advanced technologies for assimilation-related uncertainty reduction more than traditional ones.

This study lays the groundwork for future examinations of pervasive ACITs in assimilation experiences across contexts outside organizational assimilation. For example, scholars interested in online matchmaking (Heino, Ellison, & Gibbs, 2005) may adapt the findings of Waldeck et al. to learn how couples strategically manage the information that they share online, versus in person, and how online daters identify the "right" time to meet face to face. Elsewhere, these findings might illuminate how and why online instruction and e-mail communication between teachers and students enable positive learning outcomes. Assimilation research provides insight into the role of online technology in one's ability to form successful relationships to people, tasks, and organizational structure, and these findings could be used as a framework for how people use online communication for forming and sustaining other personal relationships.

Summary

During the past 15 years, research on organizational assimilation has flourished. Despite some disagreements regarding the conceptualization of the construct, the appropriate theoretical framework for describing the process, and valid measurement techniques, we can make several important intellectual claims from this body of research.

First, we know what effective assimilation is and how it happens across varied organizational contexts. Furthermore, scholars have advanced several important theoretical frameworks from which to offer predictions about other aspects of organizational functioning. These theories address assimilation tactics, the interactivity and outcomes of the process, dimensions of assimilation, information acquisition (through both traditional and contemporary media), and the types of discourse that enable assimilation. A vast body of empirical research has revealed important correlates to assimilation, and a number of studies explicate the relationship between assimilation and identification and the social and psychological nature of the process. Researchers have tested claims about assimilation in specific applied contexts and developed several key measures of socialization and assimilation. Further, we know a limited amount about the changing role that interactive digital communication technologies (such as e-mail, Internet, intranet, voice mail, and cell phones) play in effective assimilation.

These theories and empirical findings provide rich insights beyond the organizational context. Effective assimilation processes remain necessary for communication in nearly any context—not just organizations. Effective assimilation comprises an essential component of positive learning outcomes in classrooms, successful life-span transitions and development, processing and responses to mediated messages by children and adults, participation in social, political, and work-related groups and teams, and satisfying dyadic relationships. As such, assimilation contributes a robust construct that spans the communication discipline.

The Future of Assimilation Research From a Communication Perspective

Although theory and research in the area of assimilation have been characterized by significant growth and development over the last 15 years, we see three specific areas ripe for future investigation by communication scholars. Attention to these three issues should enhance our understanding of assimilation in organizational contexts as well as the utility of this research beyond organizations. First, our review and analysis of existing studies indicates that substantial research has been conducted on the processes and outcomes of assimilation, but less work has been done to reveal the antecedent conditions that predict assimilation experiences. To move forward, future work should illuminate (a) what predicts the use of particular assimilation tactics; (b) what individual, group, and organizational factors forecast proactive information seeking (versus observation); and (c) under what conditions socialization tactics are both effective and ineffective.

Second, we recognize a need for development of research designs that can capture the dynamic and interactive nature of the assimilation construct. Inquiries into organizational assimilation typically focus on individual, group, or organizational level variables, but they have fallen short to the extent that they do not examine interactions among these three levels of analysis. Since assimilation involves negotiations, adaptation, and outcomes at and across all three levels, research that features all three levels of analysis (and their interactions) is critical. As we have demonstrated in this chapter, assimilation comprises a dynamic, interactive experience for members, their work groups, their organizations, and numerous important third parties. Building on the work of Rousseau and House (1994), who argued for the use of multiple levels of analysis in order to illuminate complex organizational dynamics, we recommend research on interactions within and across individual, group, and organizational levels that bear on the process and outcomes of assimilation. Such work would offer a prescriptive approach for individuals to engage in situationally appropriate behaviors as they strive to learn the norms and values of their organizations and for other organizational members to offer experiences that meet the unique needs of newcomers and those in transition.

Finally, and perhaps most importantly, organizational communication scholars certainly should disseminate their work widely and draw explicit linkages between their theories, constructs, and empirical findings to other areas of research within the discipline. Likewise, researchers working from diverse methodological and contextual perspectives should recognize the richness of assimilation theory and research.

As we have asserted, assimilation constitutes a construct that bridges diverse contexts within the communication discipline—both to the extent that the work of varied communication scholars can inform our understanding of organizational assimilation and that literature on organizational assimilation can be relevant and valuable to others beyond organizational communication. Whenever individuals must or desire to come together to interact for a shared goal (e.g., completion of work-related task, resolving a medical problem, electing a political candidate, developing a relationship), elements of the assimilation process occur. Earlier in the chapter, we noted that our understanding of assimilation has been enhanced by incorporating theories of media use (Waldeck et al., 2004), health communication (Zorn & Gregory, 2005), interpersonal communication (V. D. Miller & Jablin, 1991), family communication (Gibson & Papa, 2000), intercultural communication (Barge & Schuleter, 2004), and instructional communication (Waldeck et al., 1997). However, examination of assimilation by those researchers could similarly benefit their work and enable the field, as a whole, to enhance its knowledge claims about assimilation processes in an array of communicative contexts.

Notes

1. See also related chapters in this volume on identity (Young, 2007), community (underwood & Frey, 2007), and nonstandard work relationships (Ballard & Gossett, 2007).

References

Adelman, M. B., & Frey, L. R. (1997). *The fragile community: Living together with AIDS.* Mahwah, NJ: Lawrence Erlbaum Associates.

Allen, N. J., & Meyer, J. P. (1990). Organizational socialization tactics: A longitudinal analysis of links to newcomers' commitment and role orientation. *Academy of Management Journal, 33,* 847–858.

Allen, T. H., & Plax, T. G. (2002). Exploring consequences of communication in the classroom: Unraveling relational learning. In L. R. Frey (Ed.), *New directions in group communication* (pp. 219–234). Thousand Oaks, CA: Sage.

Anderson, C. M., Riddle, B. L., & Martin, M. M. (1999). Socialization processes in groups. In L. R. Frey (Ed.), *The handbook of group communication theory and research* (pp. 139–166). Thousand Oaks, CA: Sage.

Apker, J., Propp, K. M., & Ford, W. S. Z. (2005). Negotiating status and identity tensions in healthcare team interactions: An exploration of nurse role dialectics. *Journal of Applied Communication Research, 33,* 93–115.

Ashford, S.J., & Black, J.S. (1996). Proactivity during organizational entry: The role of desire for control. *Journal of Applied Psychology, 81,* 199–214.

Ashford, S. J., & Cummings, L. L. (1983). Feedback as an individual resource: Personal strategies of creating information. *Organizational Behavior and Human Performance, 32,* 370–398.

Ashforth, B. E., & Saks, A. M. (1996). Socialization tactics: Longitudinal effects on newcomer adjustment. *Academy of Management Journal, 39,* 148–178.

Baker, W. K. (1995). Allen and Meyer's 1990 longitudinal study: A reanalysis and reinterpretation using structural equation modeling. *Human Relations, 48,* 169–188.

Ballard, D., & Gossett, L. (2007). Alternative times: The temporal perceptions, processes, and practices defining the nonstandard work relationship. In C. S. Beck (Ed.), *Communication yearbook 31* (pp. 273–320). New York, NY: Lawrence Erlbaum Associates.

Barge, J. K., & Schlueter, D. W. (2004). Memorable messages and newcomer socialization. *Western Journal of Communication, 68,* 233–256.

Bauer, T. N., & Green, S. (1994). Effect of newcomer involvement in work-related activities: A longitudinal study of socialization. *Journal of Applied Psychology, 79,* 211–223.

Bauer, T. N., Morrison, E. W., & Callister, R. R. (1998). Organizational socialization: A review and directions for future research. In G. R. Ferris (Ed.), *Research in personnel and human resources management* (Vol. 16, pp. 149–214). Greenwich, CT: JAI Press.

Begley, P. (2006). Sojourner adaptation. In L. A. Samovar, R. E. Porter, & E. R. McDaniel (Eds.), *Intercultural communication: A reader* (11th ed., pp. 387–393). Belmont, CA: Thomson.

Berger, C. R. (1987). Communicating under uncertainty. In M. Roloff & G. R. Miller (Eds.), *New directions in communication research* (pp. 39–62). Newbury Park, CA: Sage.

Berger, C. R., & Calabrese, R. J. (1975). Some explorations in initial interaction and beyond: Toward a developmental theory of interpersonal communication. *Human Communication Research, 1,* 99–112.

Bippus, A. M., Kearney, P., Plax, T. G., & Brooks, C. F. (2003). Teacher access and mentoring abilities: Predicting the outcome value of extra class communication. *Journal of Applied Communication Research, 31,* 260–275.

Black, J. S., & Ashford, S. J. (1995). Fitting in or making jobs fit: Factors affecting mode of adjustment for new hires. *Human Relations, 48,* 421–437.

Bradford, M. B., Rhodes, N., & Edison, A. (2005, May). *Cultivation of relationship expectations through accessibility.* Paper presented at the annual meeting of the International Communication Association, New York.

Braithwaite, D. O., & Baxter, B. A. (2006). "You're my parent but you're not": Dialectical tensions in stepchildren's perceptions about communicating with the nonresidential parent. *Journal of Applied Communication Research, 34,* 30–48.

Braithwaite, D. O., Olson, L. N., Golish, T. D., Soukup, C., & Turman, P. (2001). "Becoming a family": Developmental processes represented in blended family discourse. *Journal of Applied Communication Research, 29,* 221–247.

Bruess, C. J. S., & Pearson, J. C. (1993). "Sweet pea" and "pussy cat": An examination of idiom use and marital satisfaction over the life cycle. *Journal of Social and Personal Relationships, 10,* 609–615.

Bullis, C. (1993). Organizational socialization research: Enabling, constraining, and shifting perspectives. *Communication Monographs, 60,* 10–18.

Burgoon, J.K., Stern, L. A., & Dillman, L. (1995). *Interpersonal adaptation: Dyadic interaction patterns.* New York: Cambridge University Press.

Cartwright, S., & Schoenberg, R. (2006). Thirty years of mergers and acquisitions research: Recent advances and future opportunities. *British Journal of Management, 17,* S1–S5.

Chao, G., O'Leary-Kelly, A., Wolf, S., Klein, H., & Gardner, P. (1994). Organizational socialization: Its content and consequences. *Journal of Applied Psychology, 79,* 730–743.

Chen, G. (2005). Newcomer adaptation in teams: Multilevel antecedents and outcomes. *Academy of Management Journal, 48,* 101–116.

Chen, G., & Klimoski, R. J. (2003). The impact of expectations on newcomer performance in teams as mediated by work characteristics, social exchanges, and empowerment. *Academy of Management Journal, 46,* 591–607.

Cheney, G. (1983). On the various and changing meanings of organizational membership: A field study of organizational identification. *Communication Monographs, 50,* 342–383.

Cheney, G., & Tompkins, P. K. (1987). Coming to terms with organizational identification and commitment. *Central States Speech Journal, 38,* 1–15.

Cini, M., Moreland, R. L., & Levine, J. M. (1993). Group staffing levels and responses to prospective and new group members. *Journal of Personality and Social Psychology, 65,* 723–734.

Clair, R. (1996). The political nature of the colloquialism, "a real job": Implications for organization socialization. *Communication Monographs, 63,* 249–267.

Conway, N., & Briner, R. (2002). A daily diary study of affective responses to psychological contract breach and exceeded promises. *Journal of Organizational Behavior, 23,* 287–302.

Cooper-Thomas, H., & Anderson, N. (2002). Newcomer adjustment: The relationship between organizational socialization tactics, information acquisition and attitudes. *Journal of Occupational and Organizational Psychology, 75,* 423–437.

Coopman, S. J. (2001). Democracy, performance, and outcomes in interdisciplinary health care teams. *The Journal of Business Communication, 38,* 261–284.

Costa, P. T., & McCrae, R. R. (1994). "Set like plaster?" Evidence for the stability of adult personality. In T. F. Heatherton & J. L. Weinberger (Eds.), *Can personality change?* Washington, DC: American Psychological Association.

Craig, R. T. (1999). Communication theory as a field. *Communication Theory, 9,* 119–161.

David, C., Cappella, J. N., & Fishbein, M. (2006). The social diffusion of influence among adolescents: Group interaction in a chat room environment about antidrug advertisements. *Communication Theory, 16,* 118–140.

De Vos, A., Buyens, D., & Schalk, R. (2003). Psychological contract development during organizational socialization: Adaptation to reality and the role of reciprocity. *Journal of Organizational Behavior, 24,* 537–559.

Drucker, P. (1973). *Management: Tasks, responsibilities, practices.* New York: Harper & Row.

Ebaugh, H. (1988). *Becoming an ex: The process of role exit.* Chicago: University of Chicago Press.

Edley, P. P., Hylmo, A., & Newsom, V. A. (2004). Alternative organizing communities: Collectivist organizing, telework, home-based Internet businesses, and online communities. In P. Kalbfleisch (Ed.), *Communication yearbook 28* (pp. 87–124). Mahwah, NJ: Lawrence Erlbaum Associates.

Feldman, D. (1976). A contingency theory of socialization. *Administrative Science Quarterly, 21,* 433–452.

Feldman, D. C. (1981). The multiple socialization of organization members. *Academy of Management Review, 6,* 309–318.

Fisher, C. D. (1986). Organizational socialization: An integrative review. In K. M. Rowland & G. Ferris (Eds.), *Research in personnel and human resource management* (Vol. 4, pp. 101–145). Greenwich, CT: JAI Press.

Flanagin, A. F., & Waldeck, J. H. (2004). Technology use and organizational socialization. *Journal of Business Communication, 41,* 137–165.

Gibson, M. K., & Papa, M. J. (2000). The mud, the blood, and the beer guys: Organizational osmosis in blue-collar work groups. *Journal of Applied Communication Research, 28,* 68–88.

Ginossar, T. (2005, May). *Exploring participation in cancer-related virtual communities.* Paper presented at the annual meeting of the International Communication Association, New York.

Golden, A. G., Kirby, E. L., & Jorgenson, J. (2006). Work-life research from both sides now: An integrative perspective for organizational and family communication. In C. S. Beck (Ed.), *Communication yearbook 30* (pp. 143–196). Mahwah, NJ: Lawrence Erlbaum Associates.

Graen, G. B. (1976). Role-making processes within complex organizations. In M. D. Dunnette (Ed.), *Handbook of industrial and organizational psychology* (pp. 1201–1245). Chicago: Rand McNally.

Graham, E. E. (2003). Dialectic contradictions in postmarital relationships. *Journal of Family Communication, 3,* 193–214.

Greenberg, B. S., & Busselle, R. (1996). What's old, what's new: Sexuality on the soaps. *Siecus Report, 24,* 14–16.

Griffin, A. E. C., Colella, A., & Goparaju, S. (2000). Newcomer and organizational socialization tactics: An interactionist perspective. *Human Resource Management Review, 10,* 453–474.

Hakim, D. (2005, November 18). For a G.M. family, the American dream vanishes. *The New York Times,* p. A1.

Hanne, T. (2005). In a cultural no man's land: Or, how long does culture shock last? *Journal of Intercultural Communication, 10,* 2–20.

Hart, Z. P., & Miller, V. D. (2005). Context and message content during organizational socialization: A research note. *Human Communication Research, 31,* 295–309.

Hart, Z. P., Miller, V. D., & Johnson, J. (1998, November). *The socialization of new hires and resocialization of incumbents: The role of tactics and communication relationships.* Paper presented at the annual meeting of the National Communication Association, New York.

Hart, Z. P., Miller, V. D., & Johnson, J. R. (2003). Socialization, resocialization, and communication relationships in the context of an organizational change. *Communication Studies, 54,* 483–495.

Heino, R. D., Ellison, N. B., & Gibbs, J. L. (2005, May). *Are we a "match"? Choosing partners in the online dating market.* Paper presented at annual meeting of the International Communication Association, New York.

Hennessy, J., & West, M. A. (1999). Intergroup behavior in organizations: A field test of social identity theory. *Small Group Research, 30,* 361–382.

Hogg, M. A., & Reid, S. A. (2006). Social identity, self-categorization, and the communication of group norms. *Communication Theory, 16,* 7–30.

Holbert, R. L., & Hansen, G. J. (2006). *Fahrenheit 911,* need for closure and the priming of affective ambivalence: An assessment of intra-affective structures by party identification. *Human Communication Research, 32,* 109–129.

Holder, T. (1996). Women in nontraditional occupations: Information-seeking during organizational entry. *Journal of Business Communication, 33,* 9–26.

Homans, G. C. (1959). *Social behavior: Its elementary forms.* New York: Harcourt Brace Jovanovich.

Hughes, P. C., & Dickson, F. C. (2005). Communication, marital satisfaction, and religious orientation in interfaith marriages. *Journal of Family Communication, 5,* 25–41.

Jablin, F. M. (1982). Organizational communication: An assimilation approach. In M. Roloff & C. Berger (Eds.), *Social cognition and communication* (pp. 255–286). Newbury Park, CA: Sage.

Jablin, F. M. (1987). Organizational entry, assimilation, and exit. In L. Putnam, K. Roberts, & L. Porter (Eds.), *Handbook of organizational communication* (pp. 679–740). Newbury Park, CA: Sage.

Jablin, F. M. (2001). Organizational entry, assimilation, and exit. In F. Jablin & L. Putnam (Eds.), *The new handbook of organizational communication* (pp. 732–818). Thousand Oaks, CA: Sage.

Jablin, F. M., & Krone, K. J. (1987). Organizational assimilation. In C. Berger & S. Chaffee (Eds.), *Handbook of communication science* (pp. 711–746). Newbury Park, CA: Sage.

Jablin, F. M., & Krone, K. J. (1994). Task/work relationships: A life-span perspective. In M. L. Knapp, & G. R. Miller (Eds.), *Handbook of interpersonal communication* (2nd ed., pp. 621–675). Thousand Oaks, CA: Sage.

Jones, G. (1986). Socialization tactics, self-efficacy, and newcomers' adjustments to organizations. *Academy of Management Journal, 29,* 262–279.

Kalbfleisch, P. J., & Keyton, J. (1995). Power and equality in mentoring relationships. In P. J. Kalbfleisch & M. J. Cody (Eds.), *Gender, power, and communication in human relationships* (pp. 189–212). Hillsdale, NJ: Lawrence Erlbaum Associates.

Kanter, R. M. (1993). *Men and women of the corporation* (2nd ed.). New York: Basic Books.

Katz, D., & Kahn, R. L. (1966). *The social psychology of organizations.* New York: Wiley.

Kim, T.-Y., Cable, D.M., & Kim, S.-P. (2005). Socialization tactics, employee proactivity, and person–organization fit. *Journal of Applied Psychology, 90,* 232–241.

Klein, H. J., Fan, J., & Preacher, K.J. (2006). The effects of early socialization experiences on content mastery and outcomes: A mediational approach. *Journal of Vocational Behavior, 68,* 96–115.

Klein, H. J., & Weaver, N.A. (2000). The effectiveness of an organizational-level orientation training program in the socialization of new hires. *Personnel Psychology, 53,* 47–66.

Knapp, M. L. (1984). *Interpersonal communication and human relationships.* Boston: Allyn and Bacon.

Kramer, M. W. (1989). Communication during intraorganizational transfers. *Management Communication Quarterly, 3,* 213–248.

Kramer, M. W. (1993). Communication and uncertainty reduction during job transfers: Leaving and joining processes. *Communication Monographs, 60,* 178–198.

Kramer, M. W. (2004). *Managing uncertainty in organizational communication.* Mahwah, NJ: Lawrence Erlbaum Associates.

Kramer, M. W. (2005). Communication and social exchange processes in community theater groups. *Journal of Applied Communication Research, 33,* 159–182.

Kramer, M. W., Callister, R., & Turban, D. (1995). Information-receiving and information-giving during job transitions. *Western Journal of Communication, 59,* 151–170.

Kramer, M. W., & Miller, V. D. (1999). A response to criticisms of organizational socialization research: In support of contemporary conceptualizations of organizational assimilation. *Communication Monographs, 66,* 358–367.

Kramer, M. W., & Noland, T. L. (1999). Communication during job promotions: A case of ongoing assimilation. *Journal of Applied Communication Research, 27,* 335–355.

Kraut, R., & Mukhopadhyay, T. (1999). Information and communication: Alternative uses of the Internet in households. *Information Systems Research, 10,* 287–304.

Lakey, L. G., & Canary, D. J. (2002). Actor goal achievement and sensitivity to partner as critical factors in understanding interpersonal communication competence and conflict strategies. *Communication Monographs, 69,* 217–236.

Lammers, J. C., & Krikorian, D. H. (1997). Theoretical extension and operationalization of the bona fide group construct with an application to surgical teams. *Journal of Applied Communication Research, 25,* 17–38.

Larson, G. S., & Pepper, G. L. (2003). Strategies for managing multiple organizational identifications. *Management Communication Quarterly, 16,* 528–558.

Lester, S. W., Turnley, W. H., Bloodgood, J. M., & Bolino, M. C. (2002). Not seeing eye to eye: Differences in supervisor and subordinate perceptions of and attributions for psychological contract breach. *Journal of Organizational Behavior, 23,* 39–56.

Lewis, T. (2006). Seeking health information on the Internet: Lifestyle choice or a bad attack of cyberchondria? *Media, Culture, and Society, 28,* 521–539.

Louis, M. (1980). Surprise and sense-making: What newcomers experience when entering unfamiliar organizational settings. *Administrative Science Quarterly, 23,* 225–251.

Maier, G. W., & Brunstein, J.C. (2001). The role of personal work goals in newcomer's job satisfaction and organizational commitment: A longitudinal analysis. *Journal of Applied Psychology, 86,* 1034–1042.

Maitlis, S. (2005). The social processes of organizational sensemaking. *Academy of Management Journal, 48,* 21–49.

Medved, C. E., Brogan, S., McClanahan, A. M., Morris, J. F., & Shepherd, G. J. (2006). Family and work socializing communication: Messages, gender, and ideological implications. *Journal of Family Communication, 6,* 161–180.

Miller, K. (2001). Quantitative research methods. In F. M. Jablin & L. L. Putnam (Eds.), *The new handbook of organizational communication: Advances in theory, research, and methods* (pp. 137–160). Thousand Oaks, CA: Sage.

Miller, V. D. (1997). An experimental study of newcomers' information seeking behaviors during organizational entry. *Communication Studies, 47,* 1–24.

Miller, V. D., & Jablin, F. (1991). Information seeking during organizational entry: Influences, tactics, and a model of the process. *Academy of Management Review, 16,* 92–120.

Moreland, R. L., & Levine, J. M. (1982). Group socialization: Temporal changes in individual-group relations. In L. Berkowitz (Ed.), *Advances in experimental social psychology* (Vol. 15, pp. 137–192). New York: Academic Press.

Moreland, R. L., & Levine, J. M. (2001). Socialization in organizations and work groups. In M. E. Turner (Ed.), *Groups at work: Theories and research* (pp. 69–112). Mahwah, NJ: Lawrence Erlbaum Associates.

Morrison, E. W. (1993a). Longitudinal study of the effects of information seeking on newcomer socialization. *Journal of Applied Psychology, 77,* 173–183.

Morrison, E. W. (1993b). Newcomer information seeking: Exploring types, modes, sources, and outcomes. *Academy of Management Journal, 36,* 557–589.

Morrison, E. W. (2002). Newcomers' relationships: The role of social network ties during socialization. *Academy of Management Journal, 45,* 1149–1160.

Myers, K. K. (2005). A burning desire. *Management Communication Quarterly, 18,* 344–384.

Myers, K. K., & McPhee, R. D. (2006). Influences on member assimilation in workgroups in high reliability organizations: A multilevel analysis. *Human Communication Research, 32,* 440–468.

Myers, K. K., & Oetzel, J. G. (2003). Exploring the dimensions of organizational assimilation: Creating and validating a measure. *Communication Quarterly, 51,* 438–457.

Nathanson, A. I. (1998). Identifying and explaining the relationship between parental mediation and children's aggression. *Communication Research, 26,* 124–143.

Nathanson, A. I. (2001). Parents versus peers: Exploring the significance of peer mediation of antisocial television. *Communication Research, 28,* 251–275.

Orpen, C. (1995). The effect of socialization tactics on career success and satisfaction: A longitudinal study. *Psychological Studies, 40,* 93–96.

Pfann, G. A. (2006). Downsizing and heterogeneous firing costs. *Review of Economics and Statistics, 88,* 158–179.

Poole, M. S., Van de Ven, A., Dooley, K., & Holmes, M. (2000). *Organizational change and innovation processes.* New York: Oxford University Press.

Porath, C.L., & Bateman, T.S. (2006). Self-regulation: From goal orientation to job performance. *Journal of Applied Psychology, 91,* 185–192.

Pörhölä, M., Karhunen, S., & Rainivaara, S. (2006). Bullying at school and in the workplace: A challenge for communication research. In C. S. Beck (Ed.), *Communication yearbook 30* (pp. 249–302). Mahwah, NJ: Lawrence Erlbaum Associates.

Porter, L. W., Lawler, E. E., & Hackman, J. R. (1975). *Behavior in organizations*. New York: McGraw–Hill.

Putnam, L. L., Murray, E., & Hill, B. (1981). *Mode of communication in the encounter phase of organizational socialization*. Paper presented at the annual meeting of the Central States Speech Association, Chicago.

Putnam, L., & Stohl, C. (1990). Bona fide groups: A reconceptualization of groups in context. *Communication Studies, 41*, 248–265.

Rawlins, W. K. (1992). *Friendship matters: Communication, dialectics, and the life course*. Hawthorne, NY: Aldine de Gruyter.

Reichers, A. E. (1987). An interactionist perspective on newcomer socialization rates. *Academy of Management Review, 12*, 278–287.

Reio, T. G., & Wiswell, A. (2000). Field investigation of the relationship among adult curiosity, workplace learning, and job performance. *Human Resource Development Quarterly, 11*, 5–30.

Riordan, C. M., Weatherly E. W., Vandenberg, R. J., & Self, R. M. (2001). The effects of pre-entry experiences and socialization tactics on newcomer attitudes and turnover. *Journal of Managerial Issues, 13*, 159–176.

Robbins, S. P. (1983). *Organization theory: The structure and design of organizations*. Englewood Cliffs, NJ: Prentice Hall.

Robinson, S. L., & Morrison, E. W. (1995). Psychological contracts and OCB: The effect of unfulfilled obligations on civic virtue behavior. *Journal of Organizational Behavior, 16*, 289–298.

Rogers, E. M. (1995). *The diffusion of innovations* (4th ed.). New York: Free Press.

Rousseau, D. M. (1989). Psychological and implied contracts in organizations. *Employee Responsibilities and Rights Journal, 2*, 121–139.

Rousseau, D. M., & House, R. J. (1994). Meso organization behavior: Avoiding three fundamental biases. In C. L. Cooper & D. M. Rousseau (Eds.), *Trends in organizational behavior* (Vol. 1, pp. 13–30). New York: Wiley.

Rynes, S. L. (1991). Recruitment, job choice, and post-hire consequences: A call for new research directions. In M. D. Dunnette & L. M. Hough (Eds.), *Handbook of industrial and organizational psychology* (Vol. 2, pp. 399–444). Palo Alto, CA: Consulting Psychologists.

Saks, A. M., & Ashforth, B. E. (1996). Proactive socialization and behavioral self-management. *Journal of Vocational Behavior, 48*, 301–323.

Saks, A. M., & Ashforth, B. E. (1997). Organizational socialization: Making sense of the past and present as a prologue for the future. *Journal of Vocational Behavior, 51,* 234–279.

Schein, E. H. (1969). Organizational socialization and the profession of management. *Industrial Management Review, 9,* 1–16.

Seibert, S. (1999). The effectiveness of facilitated mentoring: A longitudinal quasi-experiment. *Journal of Vocational Behavior, 54,* 483–502.

Smith, R. C., & Turner, P. K. (1995). A social constructionist reconfiguration of metaphor analysis: An application of "SCMA" to organizational socialization theorizing. *Communication Monographs, 62,* 152–181.

St. John, W. D. (1980). The complete employee orientation program. *Personnel Journal, 59,* 373–378.

Stohl, C. (1986). Quality circles and changing patterns of communication. In M. McLaughlin (Ed.), *Communication yearbook 9* (pp. 511–531). Beverly Hills, CA: Sage.

Taormina, R. J. (1994). The organizational socialization inventory. *International Journal of Selection and Assessment, 2,* 133–145.

Taormina, R. J. (2004). Convergent validation of two measures of organizational socialization. *International Journal of Human Resource Management, 15,* 76–94.

Teboul, J. C. B. (1994). Facing and coping with uncertainty during organizational encounter. *Management Communication Quarterly, 8,* 190–224.

Thibaut, J. W., & Kelley, H. H. (1959). *The social psychology of groups.* New York: Wiley.

Tidwell, M., & Sias, P. (2005). Personality and information seeking: Understanding how traits influence information-seeking behaviors. *Journal of Business Communication, 42,* 51–77.

Tracy, S., Lutgen-Sandvik, P., & Alberts, J. (2005, May). *Escalated incivility: Analyzing workplace bullying as a communication phenomenon.* Paper presented at the annual meeting of the International Communication Association, New York.

underwood, e. d., & Frey, L. R. (2007). Communication and community: Clarifying the connection across the communication discipline. In C. S. Beck (Ed.), *Communication yearbook 31* (pp. 369–418). New York, NY: Lawrence Erlbaum Associates.

Van Der Vegt, G. S., & Bunderson, S. (2005). Learning and performance in multidisciplinary teams: The importance of collective team identification. *Academy of Management Journal, 48,* 532–547.

Vangelisti, A. L., Caughlin, J. P., & Timmerman, L. (2001). Criteria for revealing family secrets. *Communication Monographs, 68,* 1–27.

Van Maanen, J. (1976). Breaking-in: Socialization to work. In R. Dubin (Ed.), *Handbook of work, organization, and society* (pp. 67–130). Chicago: Rand McNally.

Van Maanen, J. (1978). People processing: Strategies of organizational socialization. *Organizational Dynamics, 7,* 19–36.

Van Maanen, J., & Schein, E. (1979). Toward a theory of organizational socialization. *Research in Organizational Behavior, 1,* 209–264.

Vestal, W. (2006, March). Sustaining communities of practice. *KM World, 15*(3), 8–40.

Waldeck, J. H., Kearney, P., & Plax, T. G. (2001). Instructional and developmental communication theory and research in the 1990s: Extending the agenda for the 21st century. In W. B. Gudykunst (Ed.), *Communication yearbook 24* (pp. 207–230). Thousand Oaks, CA: Sage.

Waldeck, J. H., Orrego, V. O., Plax, T. G., & Kearney, P. (1997). Graduate student/faculty mentoring: Who gets mentored, how it happens, and to what end. *Communication Quarterly, 45,* 93–109.

Waldeck, J. H., Seibold, D. R., & Flanagin, A. F. (2004). Organizational assimilation and communication technology use. *Communication Monographs, 71,* 161–183.

Walther, J. B., & Anderson, J. F. (1994). Interpersonal effects in computer-mediated interaction. *Communication Research, 21,* 460–488.

Werner, C. M., & Baxter, L. A. (1994). Temporal qualities of relationships: Organismic, transactional, and dialectical views. In M. L. Knapp & G. R. Miller (Eds.), *Handbook of organizational communication* (2nd ed., pp. 323–379). Thousand Oaks, CA: Sage.

West, R., & Pearson, J. C. (1994). Antecedent and consequent conditions of student questioning: An analysis of classroom discourse across the university. *Communication Education, 43,* 299–311.

Williamson, L., & Pierson, E. (2003). The rhetoric of hate on the Internet: Hateporn's challenge to modern media ethics. *Journal of Mass Media Ethics, 18,* 250–267.

Witte, K. (1993). A theory of cognition and negative affect: Extending Gudykunst and Hammer's theory of uncertainty and anxiety reduction. *International Journal Intercultural Relations, 17,* 197–215.

Young, N. (2007). Identity trans/formations. In C. S. Beck (Ed.), *Communication yearbook 31* (pp. 223–272). New York, NY: Lawrence Erlbaum Associates.

Zhu, Y., Gareis, E., Bazzoni, J. O, Rolland, D., & Sokuvitz, S. (2005). A collaborative online project between New Zealand and New York. *Business Communication Quarterly, 68,* 81–96.

Zorn, T. E., & Gregory, K. W. (2005). Learning the ropes together: Assimilation and friendship development among first-year medical students. *Health Communication, 17,* 211–231.

Chapter 8 Contents

8

Communication and Community: Clarifying the Connection Across the Communication Community

erin daina underwood and Lawrence R. Frey
University of Colorado at Boulder

Community is a compelling, but elusive, concept that spans many areas
of the communication discipline and methodologies employed by communication scholars. However, no systematic attempt has been made to
synthesize studies of community across the communication discipline.
This state-of-the-discipline review examines contemporary empirical
communication research studies to reveal ways in which community, and
its relationship to communication, have been conceived and operationalized. Examining this literature clarifies the concept of community and its
connection to communication and suggests profitable directions for future
research.

Introduction

Community comprises one of the most overused terms employed in
contemporary discourse by scholars, practitioners, and the general
public alike; indeed, the Library of Congress lists 5,231 books with
community in the title, and a Google search of the term produced
more than 4.8 billion web sites! In part, the extensive use of this
term reflects questions, issues, and concerns about the relationship
between the individual and the collective grappled with by philosophers (especially Western philosophers) over the centuries. Scholars
have also argued that the concept is particularly compelling in contemporary, postmodern life (especially in the United States), where
we seemingly search for a sense of place (Meyrowitz, 1985), struggle
with a saturated self (Gergen, 1991), and lack an ability to conceive of
the common good (Bellah, Madsen, Sullivan, Swidler, & Tipton, 1985,
1991). "In such a world," contended Adelman and Frey (1997), "community bespeaks what we have lost and are trying to regain" (p. 1).

The extensive use of community also undoubtedly occurs because
of the wide range of phenomena to which the term can refer. People
employ the term to describe everything from physical (e.g., geographical

neighborhoods) and virtual (e.g., internet chat rooms) locations, to perceptions (e.g., feeling part of an interpersonal network) and interpersonal relationships (e.g., the close relationships that often develop in support groups), to symbolic practices (e.g., bereavement rituals that help people to cope with the loss of community members and to "re-member" as a community). People, thus, view community as a noun (e.g., a gated community), an adjective (e.g., community theatre), and an adverb (e.g., community building).

The extensive quantitative and qualitative use of the term community results in what Hayakawa (1949, p. 44) once called a *purr word*— a word that sounds nice (like a cat purring) and conveys pleasant connotative thoughts, but a word that has virtually lost its substantive denotative meaning because of the many different conceptions that people have of it. Indeed, more than 40 years ago, Hillery (1963) claimed that "'community' has become an omnibus word. The full spectrum of its meanings embraces a motley assortment of concepts and qualitatively different phenomena" (p. 779).

Reflecting the widespread fascination with the concept of community, and the many uses to which it can be put, communication scholars, like their colleagues across the social sciences and humanities, have gravitated toward the study of community. Indeed, the study of community dates back to the very beginning of the formal discipline of communication, when researchers investigated how theatre could serve local communities (see Arvold, 1915; Chorpenning, 1919; Thorpe, 1925).[1] Since that time, community has been studied by scholars in virtually every area of the communication discipline. Communication scholars have focused, for instance, on:

interpersonal and group communication practices in communal settings, such as residential settings (e.g., Adelman & Frey, 1994, 1997; Alemán, 2001, 2003; Frey, Adelman, Flint, & Query, 2000; Frey, Adelman, & Query, 1996; Frey, Query, Flint, & Adelman, 1998; Query & James, 1989; Williams & Guendouzi, 2000)

organizational communication that promotes community (e.g., Barge, 2003; Della-Piana & Anderson, 1995; Ruud, 1995)[2]

community health communication (e.g., Clean, 1997; Dutta-Bergman, 2004; Eisenberg, Baglia, & Pynes, 2006; Medved et al., 2001; Stephens, Rimal, & Flora, 2004)

communication and community in educational contexts (e.g., Goldberg, Kole, Shields, & Hutchinson, 1984; Kim, Brunner, & Fitch-Hauser, 2006)

communication in cultural, intercultural, and multicultural communities (e.g., C. A. Braithwaite, 1997; Darling-Wolf, 2004; Philipsen, 1975, 1976; Quinlisk, 2004)
newspaper and other media use and community ties (e.g., Bramlett-
Solomon & Merrill, 1991; Finnegan & Viswanath, 1988; Stamm,
1985; Stamm & Weiss, 1986; Viswanath, Finnegan, Rooney, &
Potter, 1990)
community media practices (e.g., Glascock, 2004; Higgins, 1999a,
1999b; E. B. Hindman, 1998; King & Mele, 1999; Pollock & Yulis,
2004; see also Southwell & Yzer, this volume)
communication in online communities (e.g., Baym, 1993, 2000; Bird,
1999; Boczkowski, 1999; Bostdorff, 2004; Cooks, 2002; Cooks,
Scharrer, & Paredes, 2003; Jordan, 2005; Lindemann, 2005; S. J.
Patterson & Kavanaugh, 2001; Waltman, 2003; Wright, 2000)

Moreover, this research has employed a variety of methodological
approaches, including quantitative, qualitative, and rhetorical methods.
Community, thus, offers a compelling concept that spans some traditional dividing lines drawn in the communication disciplinary sand.[3]

Although communication scholarship on community and state-of-
the-art literature review essays have focused on particular aspects of
communication and community—such as meetings as sites for building and fragmenting community (K. Tracy & Dimmock, 2004), alternative organizing communities (Edley, Hylmö, & Newsom, 2004),
community collaboration (Heath & Frey, 2004), community and
public relations (Hallahan, 2004), and mediated communication and
community (Katz, Rice, Acord, Dasgupta, & David, 2004)—no review
of this important literature exists that cuts across the communication
discipline. This essay, therefore, reviews contemporary empirical communication research studies focused on community to help clarify
ways in which the concept is employed in communication research,
explain how communication and community are related, and shape
future scholarship. Such a review may even provide some common
language for referencing, understanding, and studying the ubiquitous
concept of community so that it does not remain a purr word.

We begin this review by explaining the selection of research studies that we included. We then examine two general conceptions of
communication—the transmission perspective and the constitutive
perspective—that inform the general study of community, specific
conceptions of community in communication scholarship, and
the relationship between these conceptions of communication and

community from a dialectical perspective. We conclude with some general claims about what this literature shows about communication and community and offer suggestions for future research.

Methods

We base this study on a review of empirical research studies of communication and community published in scholarly communication journals. First, we were interested in empirical research that had been conducted to see how scholars have studied communication and community, as opposed to essays that offer conceptual, theoretical, methodological, critical, or other similar perspectives on this topic. Second, we limited this review to research studies published in scholarly journals because scholars widely regard journals as upholding rigorous standards that include blind peer review by experts in the field and that typically result in significant revision of original submissions and relatively high rejection rates of manuscripts.[4] Moreover, as Allen, Gotcher, and Siebert (1993) observed in their review of organizational communication studies published in scholarly journals from 1980 to 1991, journal articles are "accessible, up-to-date, and shared" (p. 253). Allen et al. also suggested that reviewing journal articles enables scholars to make sense of an eclectic and ill-defined field, a description that certainly applies to the study of communication and community.

Third, to ascertain the state of communication scholarship on the topic of interest, this review focuses on articles in communication journals (e.g., those published by the international, national, and regional communication associations), as opposed to other disciplinary journals. Restricting the review to communication journals follows other state-of-the-discipline reviews, such as the reviews of organizational communication journal articles by Allen et al. and by Meyers, Brashers, Center, Beck, and Wert-Gray (1992) and the review of health communication journal articles by Beck et al. (2004).[5] Fourth, to review contemporary research conducted on communication and community, we analyzed journal articles published during the last 20 years (1985–2005). Although any time frame chosen is arbitrary, a 20-year period seemed more than sufficient for meeting the purposes of this review, and it provides a longer time frame than the other reviews of communication journal articles just cited.

To acquire relevant communication journal articles that focused on community, we employed a number of search procedures. First, we consulted Matlon and Ortiz's (1997) *Index to Journals in Communication Studies Through 1995*, which references 24 journals from their conception through 1995, for articles on community.[6] Using this index as one means of locating relevant communication journal articles is typical in literature reviews (see, e.g., Beck et al., 2004); indeed, Meyers et al. (1992) claimed that the journals included in this index "are the principle [*sic*] communication journals" (p. 243). Second, we searched for articles on communication and community in the ComAbstracts database, sponsored by the Communication Institute for Online Scholarship, which references 100 journals, most of which start with the first issue published.[7] Once we acquired the full text of an article, we examined its references and obtained relevant full-text articles. We also expanded the list of articles based on feedback from the reviewers of the original draft of this essay and other experts in various areas of the communication discipline (e.g., rhetoric and media studies) to whom we sent the list and asked for suggestions.

In enacting these search procedures, we made a number of decisions about what types of articles to include and exclude. Our first priority involved finding articles that incorporated community in the title; subsequently, we considered use of that term in the abstract, a separate section, or in the discussion/conclusion portion of an article to be potentially relevant. We excluded articles that used the term community solely to reference research participants studied (e.g., research that described nonstudent research participants as community members or community health communication campaigns that were labeled as such because they targeted people other than students), as well as articles that linked a relatively large population of people together into a so-called community simply because they shared a common characteristic, with no primary focus on community practices or processes per se (e.g., research on the beliefs of the scientific community), and articles that focused on a particular contemporary individual and his or her attempts to promote community (e.g., Dobris, 1996; Jensen & Hammerback, 2000; Lee, 1995).

In addition, we chose not to include historical essays about community in other centuries (e.g., Browne, 1996; Mackin, 1991; Simonson, 2003); articles on community as portrayed in films, television shows, music, visual imagery (e.g., tapestry), magazines, and books (e.g., Aden, 1995; Cooks & Aden, 1995; Gourgey & Smith, 1996;

Graves, 2001; Ingram, 2003; Jasinski, 1993; P. Johnson, 2004; Larson & Oravec, 1987; Sefcovic, 2002; Sexton & McKee, 2001), and articles that might be called "communications and community" that examined information and technical features of mediated communication and community (e.g., Pigg, 2001; Slack & Williams, 2000; Zucchermaglio & Talamo, 2003).

Finally, we acknowledge a number of important concepts related (some more closely than others) to community but that constitute separate fields of investigation. Hence, we did not incorporate these concepts in this review unless the study dealt explicitly with community as already articulated; these topics include civic/political participation/citizenship (e.g., Asen, 2004; Hariman & Lucaites, 2002; O'Sullivan, 1995; M. J. Patterson & Hall, 1998; Schmitz, Rogers, Phillips, & Paschal, 1995; Schrool, 1999; Shah, Cho, Eveland, & Kwak, 2005; Zaeske, 2002), collective/public memory (e.g., Haskins, 2003; Jorgensen-Earp & Lanzilotti, 1998; Katriel, 1994), deliberative democracy (e.g., Hauser & Benoit-Barne, 2002; Hicks, 2002), public dialogue (K. A. Pearce & W. B. Pearce, 2001; W. B. Pearce & K. A. Pearce, 2000), public goods (e.g., Fulk, Flanagin, Kalman, Monge, & Ryan, 1996; Rafaeli & LaRose, 1993), public space (e.g., Georgiou, 2001), and social capital (e.g., Beaudoin & Thorson, 2004; Scheufele & Shah, 2000; Shah, 1998).

These search criteria and selection procedures produced a total of 105 journal articles addressing communication and community that we considered to be most relevant for the purposes of this review.[8] Twenty-eight of those articles were conceptual, theoretical, methodological, applied (e.g., overviews of community intervention programs), or literature review essays[9]; the remaining 77 articles selected for this analysis constituted empirical research studies.[10] Although we do not claim to feature an exhaustive list, we believe that this corpus of journal articles is sufficiently large enough to address the contemporary study of communication and community.[11] Indeed, this literature spans the communication discipline, attracting scholars from, for instance, interpersonal, group, organizational, and media studies.

The methods used to study communication and community also varied; using Frey, Botan, and Kreps's (2000) classification scheme, 36 studies employed naturalistic inquiry (qualitative methods, such as participant observation and in-depth interviews, to study communicative behavior in natural settings); 23 studies utilized survey methods (quantitative questionnaires and interviews designed to describe characteristics of respondents and the populations they represent); 14 studies used textual analysis (to describe and interpret the characteristics of a recorded or visual message, with 10 of those studies employing rhetorical analysis/criticism to describe, analyze, interpret, and evaluate the persuasive force of messages in texts and 4 studies using content analysis to identify, enumerate, and analyze occurrences of specific messages and message characteristics in texts), and 4 studies applied a mixed-method design (specifically, rhetorical and content analysis; survey and content analysis, naturalistic and rhetorical, and survey and naturalistic).[12]

This body of literature tells much about the study of community from a communication perspective. Specifically, as explicated next, the literature reveals ways in which scholars' conceptualizations of communication influence how they approach the study of community and conceive of community, and the practices and processes on which they focus their research.

Communication Perspectives on Community

Community may appeal to a great many scholars across the communication discipline because of the assumed intimate and intricate relationship between these concepts. At one level, this relationship can be traced to the shared etymological basis for the two terms. As Shepherd (2001) explained:

> The word *communication* ... arose from the Latin *munia*, meaning gifts or services. Communication, then, might be understood ... as an activity of mutual giving and servicing. (The prefix, "co-" implies mutuality; the suffix, "-tion" denotes an act or process.) ... Community [also] arises from the same Latin root of *munia*, where the reciprocal giving and mutual service that takes place in communication works to make a common people, or *communis*, a community which is bound together through gifts of service.... *Munia* (or communication) to the common group is required so that a community can be made and maintained. (p. 30)

In addition to common linguistic roots, scholars have discussed the historical and political links between communication and community. For instance, rhetoricians (e.g., Depew & Peters, 2001) have traced the connection between communication and community at least as far back as Aristotle, who viewed speech as the means by which private households were bound into a public community that created commonality, and media scholars (e.g., Carey, 1989, drawing on Cooley, Dewey, the Chicago School, and others) have argued that the development of mass communication was central to connecting dispersed people together to enact the democratic community envisioned by the founders of the United States.

However, although communication and community may be intimately connected, communication scholars differ on the conceptual perspective or lens through which they view this relationship. Two general conceptual perspectives relevant for understanding how communication scholars approach the study of community include: (a) the *transmission perspective* (also called the *linear-flow, instrumental,* or *information-exchange* perspective, among other terms), in which communication involves the transfer of messages from one person to another person (see, e.g., the account of the origins of communication by Peters, 1989; Shepherd, 2001); and (b) the *constitutive perspective* (also called the *ritual, cultural,* or *meaning-based* perspective, among other terms), in which scholars view communication as the primary social process that creates reality (see, e.g., Carey, 1989; Mokros & Deetz, 1996).

Transmission Perspective

With regard to the study of communication and community, scholars who adopt a transmission perspective explore how communities use communication (albeit, sometimes unintentionally) as a tool to accomplish particular purposes. These scholars tend to assume that a community already exists and that individual members and/or the collective group employ communication to meet particular needs and goals. Not surprisingly, given the extensive use of mediated forms of communication to transmit information, some media scholars, and especially journalism researchers, often adopt this perspective. For instance, based on a textual (rhetorical) analysis of 1.5 years of opinion-page content in a newspaper, *The Jasper NewsBoy*, concerning the dragging death of James Byrd, Jr. in June 1998, Glascock (2004) showed that this coverage played an important role in helping the community where the crime occurred to successfully restore its image.

In a related manner, but using a different form of textual analysis (content analysis) to study a sample of newspapers and reversing the flow of influence between newspapers and communities, D. B. Hindman (1996) demonstrated how newspaper content during periods of change reflects the concerns of powerful groups within and beyond the community. D. B. Hindman, Littlefield, Preston, and Nuemann

(1999) later determined, using survey methods (interviews), that local newspaper editors in more ethnically pluralistic communities were more likely to value news about ethnic groups. Examples illustrating the transmission perspective as applied to internet-based communities include two textual (rhetorical) analyses of Ku Klux Klan (KKK) web sites: Waltman's (2003, p. 22) analysis of communication techniques (reliance on trickery and the encouragement of superficial message processing) used on the KKK's "Just for Kids" web site to recruit children to this "community of hate" and Bostdorff's (2004) study of how KKK web sites employed rhetoric (an angry style of discourse) to unite KKK community members through opposition to minority groups (particularly Jews). In each case, community comprises a taken-for-granted concept that exists prior to the communication being examined, with communication functioning as a tool to accomplish particular community goals, such as restoring community image or promoting connection between community members.

Another application of the transmission communication perspective to the study of community occurs in the quantitative survey research conducted to understand the relationship between communication and community variables. For instance, on the basis of telephone interviews conducted with adults in Madison, Wisconsin, McLeod, Scheufele, and Moy (1999) found that individuals' orientation toward the larger community rather than their orientation to the local neighborhood positively related to their participation in a civic forum. Rothenbuhler's (1991) telephone survey of adult Iowa residents demonstrated that the communication variables of keeping up with local news and getting together with other people correlated highly to a measure of community involvement. Rothenbuhler, Mullen, DeLarell, and Ryul (1996) subsequently noted, based on another telephone survey of adult Iowa residents, that newspaper reading corresponded to readers' community attachment and involvement, whereas television news viewing did not. In each of these studies, scholars assumed that community variables existed and could be linked to communication practices.

Constitutive Perspective

In contrast to those who adopt a transmission perspective, scholars who maintain a constitutive communication perspective focus on how communication creates—is constitutive of—community. From such a perspective, scholars do not assume that community exists prior to communication, nor is communication "a variable contained within a community; community itself is best regarded as a phenomenon that emerges from communication" (Adelman & Frey, 1997, p. 5). Communication, consequently, "is a means for the accomplishment of community rather than a medium of relation to it or information about it" (Rothenbuhler, 2001, p. 159). Indeed, Depew and Peters (2001) went so far as to claim that "prior to communicative interaction there are no individual [*sic*]; posterior to communicative interaction, there are only individuals who are members of communities" (p. 11). "Such a conception of communication," argued Shepherd (2001), "turns the modern metaphor of 'transference' into a postmodern one of 'transcendence'" (p. 32).

Scholars who approach community from a constitutive perspective, thus, explore how communication creates and maintains community.[13] One of the best examples of this approach is the media research conducted on the creation of *interpretive communities*, or how participation in social groups provides members with frames and strategies for interpreting mediated texts (see del Río, 2006; Lindlof, 1988). Although scholars certainly can and have looked at interpretive communities from a transmission perspective by studying how a priori frames and strategies provided by such communities affect members' views of mediated texts, Beck (1995), using naturalistic inquiry of television viewers of a sports team in a college dormitory, described how communication practices, such as display of knowledge of shared terms, overt identification of allegiance to the sports team watched, and participation in ongoing commentary of a jointly viewed television show, helped to create community interpretively. As another example, Lindemann's (2005) textual (rhetorical) analysis of online journals detailed how skill/competence in narrative performances served as the primary way that members created and sustained community. Perhaps Fuoss's (1995) textual (rhetorical) analysis of the 1936–1937 Flint, Michigan, autoworkers' sit-down strike captured the constitutive perspective best when he concluded:

> A dialectical relationship exists between [communication] performance and community whereby communities not only produce but are produced by performances.... First, performances articulate community by putting into circulation particular interpretations of community. Second, performances articulate community by enacting communal relationships in the

> very process of gathering persons for a performance event and engaging
> those persons either as actors in or audience members for a performance.
> (pp. 93–94)

Fuoss's (1995) conclusion points to an important reason that these studies elude easy classification with respect to the communication perspective adopted. Although most authors do not overtly articulate their conception of communication in their research reports, some scholars explicitly explore how communication is both constitutive of community and simultaneously employed by a community as a tool. Frey, Adelman, et al.'s (2000) examination of the role of communication practices in the symbolic construction of community in a residential facility for people living with AIDS provides one example of this approach. In one sense, the researchers assumed that residents utilized particular communication practices to govern their community. However, in keeping with a constitutive perspective, they explained how those communication practices helped residents to construct a perception of the residence as a community instead of, for instance, a facility or an institution. Their survey of residents revealed that both everyday/special and governance/support communication practices related to members' perceptions of the residence as a community and their satisfaction in living there.

With this understanding of communication scholars' approaches to the relationship between communication and community, we now turn to how they have conceptualized community. In exploring these conceptualizations, we reveal how the transmission and constitutive perspectives offer one way of operationalizing conceptualizations of communication and community in research practice. We then examine how communication scholars have employed a dialectical perspective to study community attributes.

Conceptualizations of Community in Communication Scholarship

This literature review reveals particular ways in which community has been conceptualized in contemporary communication scholarship. Specifically, communication scholars have focused on four general attributes of community: physical, support, influence, and meaning-making attributes.[14] These conceptualizations, which emerged organically from analyzing this set of studies, parallel other disciplinary research on community (e.g., in sociology). In particular, these attributes flesh out what scholars studying community have identified as a distinguishing feature—social interaction. As K. P. Wilkinson (1991) explained, "In sociological definitions of community (Hillery, 1955) and in actual uses of the term in ordinary language and thought (Plant, 1974), one element stands out: the substance of community is social interaction" (p. 13; see also Hillery, 1982; S. G. Jones, 1995b). This interactional theory of community (see Kaufman, 1959, 1985; Warren, 1978; K. P. Wilkinson, 1970, 1986) resonates well with the extant communication scholarship because all of the conceptualizations of community identified here are grounded in social interaction.

Physical Attributes

First, communication scholars conceptualize community according to its *physical attributes*, which include community as a site, group, or virtual location. Most of these studies focus on a physical *site* where scholars assumed that community exists, could be observed/empirically studied, or created. These physical sites ranged from relatively large geographical areas, such as the seven residential community areas in Los Angeles surveyed by Ball-Rokeach, Kim, and Matei (2001), to a relatively defined piece of land, such as the investigation of the formation of interpretive community at the *Field of Dreams* baseball site outside the small town of Dyersville, Iowa, by Aden, Rahoi, and Beck (1995), to a particular building, such as the retirement community studied by Alemán (2001, 2003). A second set of studies concentrate on a particular *group*, such as community theatre groups (see Kramer, 2002, 2004, 2005) and Imagine Chicago, a community-based organization devoted to fostering the hope and imagination of Chicago residents regarding their future (Barge, 2003). A third set of studies focus on *virtual* communities in cyberspace, such as Bird's (1999) study of an internet e-mail fan group.

Scholars, of course, must study community in some physical setting. In fact, sociologists, anthropologists, and other social scientists agree that community refers to some physical location or spatial milieu (see, e.g., Bender, 1978; Hawley, 1950; Hiller, 1941; Hillery, 1955; Parsons, 1960; Poplin, 1979; K. P. Wilkinson, 1991). This same understanding applies to the general public. As I. M. Young (1995) noted, "In ordinary speech for most people in the U.S., the term community refers to people with whom I identify in a locale" (p. 244). Indeed, the German word *Gemeinschaft* (community) originally referred to common community land (see Konig, 1968), and to this day, one of the first definitions offered in most dictionaries for the term community refers to a group of people who live in the same locality.

However, in addition to establishing how physically instantiated communities employ communication practices to achieve their goals, scholars working from a constitutive perspective have also revealed how people's interpretations of a physical site or group is constructed as a community via their communication practices. For instance, using naturalistic inquiry to understand the interplay of symbolic and material landscapes in two rural Kansas counties, Procter (1995) described how converting space to place involved a symbolic transformation process that occurred through storytelling and how such *place attachment*—the emotional bonding of people and groups to places (see, e.g., Altman & Low, 1992)—intensified people's "commitment to community and to the preservation of that community's culture" (Procter, p. 232; see also Carbaugh, 1999).

Support Attributes

Second, communication scholars conceptualize community according to its *support attributes*, including psychological belonging, social bonding, meeting safety and protection needs, and emotional aid. *Psychological belonging*, in the sense of individuals feeling part of a group, long has been identified as an important element of community. For instance, D. McMillan and Chavis (1986) defined community, in large measure, as emotional connections between people who feel a sense of belonging to a particular site or group (see also Cohen, 1985; Tinder, 1995). Psychological bonding relates strongly to *social bonding*, which occurs as meaningful interpersonal relationships and community ties form. Gusfield (1975) talked about a defining feature of community as the "relational ... quality or character of human relationships" (p. xvi; see also Hummon, 1992; K. P. Wilkinson, 1991). Psychological belonging and social bonding can help to achieve feelings of *safety and protection* and relate to community members providing *emotional aid* to one another.

Wright's (2000) communication study of the support attributes of community exemplifies research from the transmission perspective. Wright examined a stratified random sample of social support messages generated by members of the SeniorNet community, an internet group for older individuals. He concluded that the downloaded conversations revealed three support themes: promoting community support (e.g., conversations mentioning how helpful the web site was), providing advice disguised as self-disclosure, and sharing life events. Wright, thus, showed how members of this assumed community employed social support communication strategies to meet their needs, primarily to provide one another with emotional aid.

Ball-Rokeach et al. (2001) offered a complementary example of research focusing on the support attributes of community from a constitutive perspective. They developed and tested, using survey methods, a communication infrastructure model of belonging among dwellers of urban residential environments. Specifically, the researchers examined how storytelling functioned as an intervening variable between the physical locale of urban space and residents' sense of belonging to a neighborhood. In so doing, their study detailed how the support communication process of storytelling created a sense of community, or what they called the "storytelling neighborhood" (p. 392).

Influence Attributes

Third, communication scholars have conceptualized community with respect to *influence attributes*, which have been identified by many other scholars as an inherent feature of community life (see, e.g., Kanter, 1968; D. McMillan & Chavis, 1986). Influence attributes include *behavioral norms* (e.g., promoting conformity), *identification* (e.g., constructing a sense of us versus them), *regulation of social order* (e.g., creating institutional patterns of appropriateness), and *collective action* (e.g., engaging in community protest).

In terms of the transmission perspective, Vrooman's (2001) naturalistic inquiry of the creation of a norm in a virtual community against flaming (the sending of virulent insults via e-mail) to provide a more equitable space for harassed women focused on the influence attributes of community (specifically, behavioral norms and identification). Silver (2005) noted that, although the dominant discourse used by developers of the Blacksburg Electronic Village (BEV), an online community network, concentrated on community (especially in terms of promoting civic participation), the implementation of the BEV attempted to regulate social order via a "highly commercialized agenda ... [of] building an electronic shopping mall under the banner of an electronic town hall" (p. 187). Weitzel and Geist's (1998) study of community groups' use of parliamentary procedures underscored how those procedures functioned as a set of rules to influence the vigilance of collective decision making in groups.

With respect to the constitutive nature of influence on community, Rogers et al.'s (1995) naturalistic inquiry indicated how HIV and AIDS and the communication responses to them (specifically, prevention campaigns) in San Francisco altered socially constructed notions about community through changes in personal and interpersonal behavior (e.g., prevention practices) and in organizational activities (e.g., harnessing the power of peer networks to engage in collective action that regulated social order). As another example, Ruud (1995) examined how the organizational discourse that characterized a regional symphony promoted both solidarity among the musicians and division among the musicians, board of directors, and the administration. As Ruud concluded:

> The clash of organizational identities hindered the Symphony's efforts to move toward what Bellah et al. (1985) describe as a genuine community. As Symphony members highlighted their individual memberships with the musicians, the board of directors, or the administration, the notion of community became a secondary concern. (p. 218)

Meaning-Making Attributes

Fourth, communication scholars conceptualize community with respect to its *meaning-making attributes*, which include *common beliefs, values, attitudes,* and *identities* (e.g., Hart, Jennings, & Dixson, 2003; Jacobs & Yousman, 1999; McLean, 1997; Shah, Kwak, & Holbert, 2001; Shah, McLeod, & Yoon, 2001; Simpson, 1995; Stavitsky, 1994), *collectively recognizable future or ideal* (e.g., Rakow et al., 2003; Schely-Newman, 1997; Yu & Sears, 1996), *sense of everyday purpose* (e.g., Hill, 2003; Riggs, 1996; Rucinski, 2004; Shue & Beck, 2001), and *shared semiotic structure* (e.g., Benson, 1996; Berkowitz & TerKeurst, 1999; Ray, 1987; Wright, 2002). Scholars in other disciplines have commented on this aspect of community. Hummon

(1990), for example, explained community ideology as a cultural system in which "people, in adopting such ideologies, incorporate assumptions, beliefs, and values that enable them to ... *make sense* of reality and their place in the everyday world" (p. 5; see also Cohen, 1985). However, because of the emphasis on symbolic practices, communication scholars appear to be at the forefront of articulating the meaning-making capacities of what Hunter (1974), in the title to his book, called "symbolic communities."

From a transmission perspective, communication comprises the primary tool that communities utilize to make meaning. For instance, Jeffres, Atkin, and Neuendorf (2002), using survey methods, determined how grassroots print media practices (e.g., number of neighborhood newspapers read) had more impact than other communication practices (e.g., interpersonal communication and exposure to local television news) in forming people's beliefs about community, particularly shared convictions about community assets. Dollar and Zimmers's (1998) study, using naturalistic inquiry, specified how youth and young adult street persons in one locale acted as a speech community, employing communication strategies to express their identity and challenge more powerful community members.

From a constitutive perspective, the very meaning of community emerges through communication. For example, Pezzullo's (2003) naturalistic inquiry showed how "toxic tours" of "Cancer Alley," the region between Baton Rouge and New Orleans, Louisiana, conducted by environmental justice activists functioned rhetorically "as cultural performances to help build communities of resistance through acts of politicizing memory" (p. 228). By promoting common beliefs, attitudes, and values about unjust environmental practices, these tours created resistance communities that had a clear sense of what remains to be done to promote a collectively recognizable ideal future in that region. In a similar vein, Peeples (2003) engaged in textual (rhetorical) analysis of a community conflict in South-Central Los Angeles, where residents opposed the construction of a garbage incinerator. Peeples detailed how residents' rhetoric reconstructed the boundaries of community regarding "insiders" and "outsiders" to transcend county divisions of community for the purpose of including all of the people located in the potential sites for the incinerator. This work on environmental justice and community also illustrates well the intersections among all four attributes of community.

A Dialectical Conceptualization of Communication and Community

In studying these four attributes of community, communication scholars, like their colleagues in other areas of the discipline,[15] often employ, either explicitly or implicitly, a dialectical perspective to explore how tensions of community life are managed by (from a transmission perspective) and created through (from a constitutive perspective) communication. Dialectical tensions result from simultaneously holding two interdependent, contradictory ideas that "are not merely different from one another or in conflict with one another; they are the underlying opposing tendencies in a phenomenon which mutually exclude and simultaneously presuppose one another" (Goldsmith, 1990, p. 538; see also N. Young, this volume).

A dialectical perspective is particularly appropriate for studying the relationship between communication and community because, as Adelman and Frey (1997) observed:

> Community life is like a tightrope, held taut by the sustained tensions of daily living.... This metaphor, unlike more romanticized, stable images of community, captures the precarious collective structures and relationships that sustain group living. Human relationships are riddled with contradictions, inconsistencies, and paradoxes; fluctuations between regularity and change are thus more like a tightrope than a featherbed. (pp. 17–18)

Based on this review, scholars studying communication and community have concentrated, either explicitly or implicitly, on six major dialectical tensions.[16] In this section, we list them in order from most to least, based on the number of studies that seemed to address them. Notably, studies often focus on several dialectical tensions, some of which represent dialectical tensions that have been examined in other areas of communication scholarship[17]: (a) *consumer–producer tension* of accepting community in its current state and contributing to its changing meaning, (b) *individual–collective tension* that privileges both personal autonomy and commitment to a larger group/community, (c) *place–space tension* of connection to but not constrained by a particular physical locale, (d) *ideal future–everyday present tension* of a collective ideal regarding what a community should be in the future coupled with the vernacular reality of what exists in the present, (e) *participation–apathy tension* of simultaneously valuing community members' involvement and accepting their indifference, and (f) *us-them tension* of seeking similarity with and differentiating from others.

Virtually all of these dialectical tensions are studied across the four community attributes.[18] However, for the purposes of explicating this perspective within the conceptualizations of communication and community previously articulated, we examine some research examples that collectively illustrate these six tensions as they apply to the two communication perspectives and each of the four community attributes.

Alemán (2001) conceptualized a retirement community with respect to physical attributes. Working from a transmission communication perspective, Alemán indicated how residents' complaining behaviors communicatively managed the individual–collective dialectical tensions of independence and (a) social constraint, (b) dependence, and (c) interdependence. Working from a constitutive perspective, Peeples's (2003) study showed how residents' communication practices negotiated the place–space dialectic to reconstruct the boundaries of community to fight the construction of a garbage incinerator.

With regard to support attributes of community, Quinlisk (2004), working from a transmission perspective by studying a university as an assumed multicultural community, found that students demonstrated both participation and apathy by expressing support for multiculturalism and diversity but revealing little willingness to actually engage in intercultural interactions. Fuoss's (1995) analysis of an autoworkers' sit-down strike from a constitutive perspective described ways in which the autoworkers' communication performances articulated "the limits of community by constructing, maintaining, reinforcing, or renegotiating the boundary between communication and other, insider and outsider, 'us' and 'them'" (pp. 93–94).

In terms of influence attributes, Kramer's (2004) study of a community theatre group specified how members used communication to manage the individual–collective tension of their commitment to the group and their commitment to other life activities. Della-Piana and Anderson's (1995) study of a community service organization suggested how members' social construction of community (through their explicit use of the community term) both enabled and constrained their current and potential future organizing practices.

Finally, with respect to a meaning-making conception of community, Jordan (2005) examined how the inability of online blogging community members to construct rhetorical arguments that were community oriented to make sense of a member's act of betrayal led to the demise of the community. From a transmission perspective, this study illustrated the potential result of not effectively managing the ideal future–everyday present tension. Aden et al.'s (1995) constitutive investigation of the interpretive community formed at the site in Iowa made popular by the movie *Field of Dreams* detailed how participants negotiated the individual–collective tension such that "individuals at once can converge and diverge symbolically within the confines of an interpretive community" so that "individuals can feel unique yet part of a larger congregation" (pp. 368, 377).

Communication and Community: Continuing the Conversation

As this review of the literature shows, the study of communication and community has been a central concern of scholars from across the communication discipline employing different methodological approaches. However, no corresponding attempt has been made to take stock of this literature, leaving communication scholars studying community, paradoxically, in a potentially isolated environment and not in conversation with one another. This review of contemporary research literature sought to fill that gap by clarifying how communication scholars have empirically studied community. This review reveals the state of that conversation and suggests ways in which the conversation might be continued in future research.

First, communication scholars have discovered much about the relationship between communication and community. From the transmission perspective of communication as a tool, scholars have shown the significance of face-to-face and mediated communication practices for accomplishing community goals; from a constitutive perspective, scholars have demonstrated how, as Rothenbuhler (1991) eloquently claimed, "communication and community grow in each other's shadows; the possibilities of one are structured by the possibilities of the other" (p. 76). However, communication scholars have not always been clear about the communication perspective that they employ to study community and its relative advantages and limitations. Communication scholars also could devote more attention to the interplay between these two perspectives to articulate, dialectically, how communication practices simultaneously "build communities" and are employed by "built communities."

Revealing that interplay may well necessitate engaging in longitudinal, multimethodological research programs that track the development of community from its "starting point" (assuming that can
be identified) to its cessation. Kramer's (2002, 2004, 2005) research
program on community theatre groups, utilizing naturalistic inquiry
and survey methods and studying those groups from a relatively
early beginning point (e.g., the open call for cast members), serves as
a good example. Most communication researchers enter communities some time after they have been established, and such research
undoubtedly will continue; in those cases, though, researchers
might strive to situate the community within its historical context
by asking members how they understand the development of their
community and the communication practices that contributed to it.

Second, communication scholars' conceptualizations of community verify, concretize, and extend previous conceptions. The
community attributes on which communication scholars have
focused—physical, support, influence, and meaning-making attributes—reflect, in large measure, attributes that have been historically
studied by scholars in other disciplines—locale; emotional connection; social interaction; influence; and shared symbols, identity, and
culture. By confirming these characteristics of community in communication practice, communication scholars have affirmed how
"abstract ideals of brotherhood and harmony, of love and union must
be translated into concrete social practices" (Kanter, 1972, p. 75).
Communication scholars, consequently, have helped to reveal how
community, to use Geertz's (1973) famous metaphor for culture, constitutes a web spun of physical, support, influence, and meaning-making attributes. Those who work from a constitutive perspective focus
on the communication processes of spinning that web; those who work
from a transmission perspective concentrate on the communication
practices employed to strengthen strands of an existing web.

Although communication scholars have helped to clarify the contours, parameters, and boundaries of the elusive concept of community, they could be clearer in their research reports regarding the
attributes of community on which they focus. Poplin (1979, p. 4)
claimed that one glaring problem with scholarship on community
involves "lack of conceptual rigor" regarding the central construct;
consequently, Poplin urged scholars to fit their conceptualization of
community into some recognized typology. The four community
attributes that emerged from this review of the extant empirical

research offer one such typology—a system of thinking about community from the perspective of communication theory that differs from how a sociologist, for example, would organize these same concepts and observations—that communication scholars can potentially use to classify their study of community conceptually. In so doing, scholars from across the many areas of the communication discipline who study community could more easily recognize how they treat community in similar and dissimilar ways.

The typology also encourages communication scholars to take a holistic view of community by studying multiple attributes—potentially, all four attributes. Many communication studies did investigate multiple attributes, but very few examined all four. Alemán's (2001) study of complaining communication among the elderly in a retirement community exemplifies how scholars can investigate all four attributes in a single study—in this case, how the sharing of a semiotic structure among residents (a meaning-making attribute of community) related to social bonding (a support attribute) and regulated social order (an influence attribute) within this particular site (a physical attribute).

Third, in studying these attributes, communication scholars have viewed community through a dialectical lens in which participants grapple with ongoing tensions that remain at the heart of everyday communal life as opposed to viewing community as a stable site that provides protection from these tensions. Although communication scholars seldom explicitly frame community in dialectical terms, they have embraced the complexity of community life by focusing on the simultaneous competing needs, goals, expectations, and experiences that "form the pulse of routine as well as volatile and transitional moments ... [and are] the fundamental properties of social life" (Rawlins, 1992, p. 7). In that regard, communication scholars have recognized that community concepts "must be understood in their context of contrasts, by what they point away from as well as what they point toward" (Gusfield, 1975, p. xv).

Extending from a dialectical perspective, no single, dominant ideal of community exists; instead, community comprises an "essentially contested concept" (Gallie, 1964, p. 158) expressed through a variety of oppositional views. As Fuoss (1995) explained, "Community and contestation are not oppositional forces but flip sides of the same social process as indivisible from one another as the front and back sides of a sheet of paper" (p. 94). Such a perspective contrasts sharply with more romantic, utopian notions of community that reflect "a way of life long since passed in the progress of civilization" (K. P. Wilkinson, 1991, p. 1).[19]

However, because of the lack of longitudinal research programs on communication and community, with most studies comprising single investigations, we know little about how dialectical tensions emerge, shift, and change over the course of community life, especially in relation to individual and collective communication practices. Moreover, communication scholars have only begun to explore dialectical tensions associated with power that pervade community life and how communication "creates space for the multiple and oppositional voices to be heard" (Adelman & Frey, 1997, p. 106). We lack insight, for instance, about communication in marginalized communities or communities of resistance, although Hill (2003), Peeples (2003), and Pezzullo (2003) provide a valuable start in that direction.

The study of communication and community is alive and well in the communication discipline. We have sought to contribute to that important area of study by describing the state of empirical research literature across the communication discipline and, thereby, clarifying and making common the discourse of scholars who study communication and community and how we might continue that conversation.

Notes

1. Although a number of universities and colleges may include communication and theatre in the same department or school, and although the National Communication Association (NCA) has a theatre division, the two disciplines have parted ways substantially (although performance studies remains a strong element of the communication discipline, as reflected in the research included in this chapter). A focus on theatre as a communicative means of affecting communities, however, remains vibrant in the theatre discipline (see, e.g., recent work by Billingham, 2005; Cohen-Cruz, 2006; Haedicke & Nellhaus, 2001; Inomata & Cohen, 2006; Kuftinec, 2003; Taylor, 2003) and, to a more limited degree, continues in the communication discipline as well (see, e.g., Schoell, 1953; Starmer, 1946; Toc, 1971; Wegner, 1985; B. Wilkinson, 1976; for examples of recent scholarship, see Conquergood, 2002; Harter, Sharma, Pant, Singhal, & Sharma, 2007; Park-Fuller, 2003; Rich & Rodríguez, 2007).

2. Some communication scholars, however, question whether community can be enacted in workplaces and view the use of this term in that context as a means of exercising organizational control (see, e.g., Gossett & Tompkins, 2001).

3. Interestingly, unlike other social formations studied by communication scholars (e.g., groups or organizations), no division or interest group concentrates on the study of community in the NCA, International Communication Association, or any regional communication association. The lack of such a group simply could be the result of no one yet initiating it, but it also might reflect that the study of community cuts across the communication discipline.

4. Chesebro (1993), for instance, reported that 95% of manuscripts were revised before being published (see also Knapp & Daly, 2004), and Eadie (1999) found that, across the six NCA journals at that time, the mean acceptance rate, calculated on the last completed 3-year editorial term for each journal, was 18.3%.

5. We recognize that scholarly books and chapters in edited scholarly books on communication and community may well meet the high standards employed by scholarly journals. However, limited databases exist for acquiring those sources, especially chapters in edited scholarly books, compared to databases for acquiring journal articles. We also acknowledge important critiques of the dominant ideologies and disciplinary practices associated with the journal publishing system, including communication journals (see, e.g., Bach, Blair, Nothstine, & Pym, 1996; Blair, Brown, & Baxter, 1994; Schwartzman, 1997; Swartz, 1997). Still, despite their problems, scholarly journals remain, at least perceptually among scholars (e.g., in making tenure and promotion decisions), one of the most important sources, if not the most important source, of primary research reports; as LaFollette (1992) claimed, "Journals represent the *principal* means of *formal* communication among scientists and social scientists through which research is made public and through which it is evaluated and authenticated by other experts, before and after publication" (p. 75). Consequently, we examined communication journals for the purposes of this review.

6. Journals (both their current and past titles) in this index include: *Argumentation and Advocacy/Journal of the American Forensic Association, Communication Education/Speech Teacher, Communication Monographs/Speech Monographs, Communication Quarterly/Today's Speech, Communication Reports, Communication Research, Communication Research Reports, Communication Studies/Central States Speech Journal, Communication Theory, Critical Studies in Mass Communication, Human Communication Research, Howard Journal of Communications, Journal of Applied Communications Research/Journal of Applied Communications Research, Journal of the Association for Communication Administration/Bulletin of the Association of Departments and Administrators in Speech Communication, Journal of Broadcasting & Electronic Media/Journal of Broadcasting, Journal of Communication,*

Journal of Communication and Religion/Religious Communication Today, Journalism & Mass Communication Quarterly/Journalism Quarterly/Journalism Bulletin, Philosophy and Rhetoric, Quarterly Journal of Speech/Quarterly Journal of Public Speaking/Quarterly Journal of Speech Education, Southern Communication Journal/Southern Speech Communication Journal/Southern Speech/Southern Speech Bulletin, Text and Performance Quarterly, Western Journal of Communication/Western Journal of Speech Communication/Western Speech Communication/Western Speech, and *Women's Studies in Communication/ORWAC Bulletin: Women's Studies in Communication.*

7. In addition to the journals covered by Matlon and Ortiz's (1997) index, ComAbstracts includes the following journals and yearly publications (both their current and past titles): *Advances in Discourse Processes, Advances in Telematics, American Journalism, Argumentation and Advocacy/Journal of the American Forensic Association, Asian Journal of Communication, Atlantic Journal of Communication, Australian Journal of Communication, Australian Studies in Journalism, Canadian Journal of Communication, Communicatie, Communication, Communication Education/Speech Teacher, Communication Law and Policy, Communication Review, Communication Yearbook, Communications: The European Journal of Communication Research, Convergence, Critical Studies in Media Communication/Critical Studies in Mass Communication, Discourse and Society, Discourse Processes, Electronic Journal of Communication, European Journal of Communication, Free Speech Yearbook, Gazette, Global Media and Communication, Harvard International Journal of Press/Politics, Health Communication, Historical Journal of Television, Information Communication & Society, International Journal of Listening, International Journal on Media Management, Issues in Applied Linguistics, Journal of Business Communication, Journal of Business and Technical Communication/Iowa State Journal of Business and Technical Communication, Journal of Family Communication, Journal of Health Communication: International Perspectives, Journal of Language and Social Psychology, Journal of Marketing Communication, Journal of Mass Media Ethics, Journal of Media Economics, Journal of Media and Religion, Journal of Public Relations Research, Journal of Radio Studies, Journal of Social and Personal Relationships, Journalism, Journalism History, Journalism and Communication Monographs/Journalism Monographs, Language and Communication, Management Communication Quarterly, Mass Comm Review, Mass Communication Research, Mass Communication & Society, Media Psychology, Media Studies Journal/Gannett Center Journal, New Media and Society, Newspaper Research Journal, Nordicom Review, Operant Subjectivity,*

Organization Communication: Emerging Perspectives, Philosophy and Rhetoric, Political Communication/Political Communication and Persuasion, Popular Communication/Progress in Communication Sciences, Public Opinion Quarterly, Public Relations Research and Education, Public Relations Review, Research on Language and Social Interaction, Rhetoric and Public Affairs, Rhetoric Review, Semiotica, Small Group Research/Small Group Behavior/Comparative Group Studies, Studies in Communications, Television & New Media, Visual Communication, Westminister Papers in Communication and Culture, Written Communication.

8. To give some indication of the winnowing process involved in this search, ComAbstracts listed 272 articles with communication and community in the title for the 1985–2005 time period.

9. Conceptual/theoretical/methodological/applied/literature review essays included: Beniger (1987), Donovan (2002), Dutta-Bergman (2005), Friedland (2001), Galegher, Sproull, and Kiesler (1998), Gaziano (1988), Goodall (1999), Gumpert and Drucker (2001), Ingram (2003), S. Jones (1998b), Kelemen and Smith (2001), Lindlof (2002), Makagon (2004), Matei, Ball-Rokeach, Wilson, Gibbs, and Hoyt (2001), McKerrow (1998), McLeod et al. (1996), Medved et al. (2001), Nossek (2003), Penman (1996), Pinkett and O'Bryant (2003), Schaefer (1999), Schuler (2001), Stamm, Emig, and Hesse (1997), Steeves (1993), Viswanath, Kosicki, Fredin, and Park (2000), Wolff et al. (2004), Zappen, Gurak, and Doheny-Farina (1997), and Zelizer (1993). Our search procedures also discovered 14 authored texts (Anderson, Dardenne, & Killenberg, 1994; Arnett, 1986; Arnett & Arneson, 1999; Berg & Boguslaw, 1985; Cohen, 1985; Dardene, 1996; Duff, 2001; Felkins, 2002; Howley, 2005; Jankowski, 2002; Katriel, 1991; Mackin, 1997; Sheras & Koch-Sheras, 2006; Steele, 1986) and 11 edited texts (Anderson, Cissna, & Arnett, 1994; Brier & Lovelock, 1996; DeSanctis & Fulk, 1999; Giles, 2002; Hogan, 1998; S. G. Jones, 1995a, 1998a; McDonald, Orbe, & Ford-Ahmed, 2002; Nasimento, 1998; Olson, 2000; Shepherd & Rothenbuhler, 2001) published over the last 20 years that focused on communication and community, including *Communication Yearbook 28* (Kalbfleisch, 2004). Examples of other authored texts and chapters in edited texts that constitute original empirical research studies of communication and community but not considered in this review of journal articles include Adelman and Frey (1994, 1997), Brock and Howell (1994), Conquergood (1994), Frey et al. (1998), Goodall (1996), Howell, Brock, and Hauser (2003), Johnstone (1990), S. U. Phillips (1983), and Spano (2001). We use these and other sources in this essay to discuss the empirical research studies conducted on communication and community.

10. In alphabetical order, these studies include: Aden et al. (1995), Alemán (2001, 2003), Ball-Rokeach et al. (2001), Barge (2003), Beck (1995), Benson (1996), Berkowitz & TerKeurst (1999), Bird (1999), Boczkowski (1999), Bostdorff (2004), Cooks (2002), Cooks et al. (2003), Darling-Wolf (2004), Della-Piana and Anderson (1995), Dollar and Zimmers (1998), Dutta-Bergman (2004), Frey, Adelman, et al. (1996, 2000), Fuoss (1995), Glascock (2004), Hart et al. (2003), Higgins (1999a, 1999b), Hill (2003), D. B. Hindman (1996), D. B. Hindman et al. (1999), E. B. Hindman (1998), Jeffres et al. (2002), Jeffres, Dobos, and Sweeney (1987), Jordan (2005), King and Mele (1999), Kramer (2002, 2004, 2005), Lindemann (2005), Matei, Ball-Rokeach, and Qui (2001), McLean (1997), McLeod, Scheufele, and Moy (1999), McLeod, Scheufele, Moy, Horowitz, et al. (1999), S. McMillan (2001), Neuwirth, Salmon, and Neff (1989), S. J. Patterson and Kavanaugh (2001), Peeples (2003), Pezzullo (2003), Pollock and Yulis (2004), Procter (1995), Query and James (1989), Quinlisk (2004), Rakow et al. (2003), Ray (1987), Riggs (1996), Rogers et al. (1995), Rothenbuhler (1991), Rothenbuhler et al. (1996), Rucinski (2004), Ruud (1995), Schely-Newman (1997), Shah, Kwak, et al. (2001), Shah, McLeod, et al. (2001), Shue and Beck (2001), Silver (2005), Simpson (1995), Stamm and Guest (1991), Stamm and Weiss (1986), Stavitsky (1994), Stephens et al. (2004), Trujillo (1993), Vrooman (2001), Waltman (2003), Weitzel and Geist (1998), Williams and Guendouzi (2000), Wright (2000, 2002), Yu and Sears (1996), and Zoller (2000). Contact the first author for a table that provides the authors, focus of study, methods employed, and relevant findings about communication and community (erin.underwood@colorado.edu).

11. We apologize to anyone whose relevant article we might somehow have overlooked in conducting this search.

12. A number of studies employing naturalistic inquiry also engaged in some form of document analysis, but they were not classified as using a mixed-method design because qualitative document analysis often is an integral part of that type of research, such as in ethnography.

13. The lack of communication (e.g., silence; see Acheson, this volume) can also affect our understanding of a lack of community.

14. Both these four attributes and their subcategories are not discrete conceptualizations but ways of describing how communication scholars have conceptualized community; consequently, many studies employ multiple and overlapping conceptions. These attributes and their subcategories also probably reflect more of a speech communication perspective than a mass communication perspective because of the literature that we included.

15. A dialectical perspective has been used, for instance, to empirically study (a) interpersonal/relational communication (e.g., Baxter, 1990;

Baxter & Simon, 1993; Goldsmith, 1990; A. J. Johnson, Wittenberg, Villagran, Mazur, & Villagran, 2003; Pawlowski, 1998; Rawlins, 1983; see also the conceptual work by Baxter, 1988, 1993, 2006; Baxter & Montgomery, 1996, 1997, 1998; Brown, Altman, & Werner, 1992; Dindia, 1994; Montgomery & Baxter, 1998; Petronio, 2002; Rawlins, 1992; Werner & Baxter, 1994); (b) family communication (e.g., Baxter, Braithwaite, Bryant, & Wagner, 2004; D. O. Braithwaite & Baxter, 2006; D. O. Braithwaite, Baxter, & Harper, 1998; Cissna, Cox, & Bochner, 1990; Ford, Ray, & Ellis, 1999; Graham, 2003; Sabourin & Stamp, 1995; Toller, 2005; see also the conceptual essay by Baxter, 2004); (c) group communication (e.g., Adelman & Frey, 1994, 1997; Kramer, 2004; see also the conceptual work by Barge, 1996; Frey & Barge, 1997; S. D. Johnson & Long, 2002); (d) organizational communication (e.g., Harter, 2004; Jameson, 2004; Kellett, 1999; S. J. Tracy, 2004; Trethewey & Ashcraft, 2004; Vaughn & Stamp, 2003; see also the conceptual work by Mumby & Stohl, 1991; Stohl & Cheney, 2001); (e) health communication (e.g., Apker, Propp, & Ford, 2005; Chay-Nemeth, 1998); (f) environmental communication (e.g., Ruud & Sprague, 2000); (g) intercultural/international communication (e.g., Chen, Drzewiecka, & Sias, 2001; Erbert, Pérez, & Gareis, 2003; T. S. Jones & Bodtker, 1998; see also the conceptual work by Martin & Nakayama, 1999; Martin, Nakayama, & Flores, 1998; Yep, Lovaas, & Ho, 2001); and (h) media (e.g., Meyer, 2003; Rasmussen & Downey, 1989, 1991).

16. Many other dialectical tensions were investigated in the studies, but each of the tensions featured in this chapter was addressed in more than 25 studies. Some scholars studying these tensions might prefer to call them issues, (phenomenological) problems, variables, dualities, or another appropriate label.

17. As two examples of dialectical tensions studied in other areas of the communication discipline, Werner and Baxter (1994) identified three general clusters of dialectic themes (and specific dialectical tensions within each theme) in interpersonal communication scholarship—(a) integration-separation (e.g., communal-individual), (b) expression-nonexpression (e.g., openness-closedness), and (c) stability-change (e.g., certainty-novelty)—and Martin and Nakayama (1999) specified six dialectics in intercultural communication research—(a) cultural-individual, (b) person/social-contextual, (c) differences-similarities, (d) static-dynamic, (e) present-future/history-past, and (f) privilege-disadvantage.

18. Our read of this set of articles revealed that all six tensions were studied across the four community attributes, except for the following: physical attributes—us-them tension, support attributes—ideal future-everyday present tension, and meaning-making attributes—participation-apathy tension.

19. Communitarianism (see, e.g., Etzioni, 1993, 1995, 1998; Eztioni, Volmert, & Rothchild, 2004; Tam, 1998), for instance, has been critiqued in this way (see, e.g., Bell, 1993; Frazer & Lacey, 1993; D. L. Phillips, 1993).

References

Acheson, K. (2007). Silence in dispute. In C. S. Beck (Ed.), *Communication yearbook 31* (pp. 1–59). New York, NY: Lawrence Erlbaum Associates.

Adelman, M. B., & Frey, L. R. (1994). The pilgrim must embark: Creating and sustaining community in a residential facility for people with AIDS. In L. R. Frey (Ed.), *Group communication in context: Studies of natural groups* (pp. 3–22). Hillsdale, NJ: Lawrence Erlbaum Associates.

Adelman, M. B., & Frey, L. R. (1997). *The fragile community: Living together with AIDS*. Mahwah, NJ: Lawrence Erlbaum Associates.

Aden, R. C. (1995). Nostalgic communication as temporal escape: *When It Was a Game*'s reconstruction of a baseball/work community. *Western Journal of Communication, 59,* 20–38.

Aden, R. C., Rahoi, R. L., & Beck, C. S. (1995). "Dreams are born on places like this": The process of interpretive community formation at the *Field of Dreams* site. *Communication Quarterly, 43,* 368–380.

Alemán, M. W. (2001). Complaining about the elderly: Examining multiple dialectical oppositions to independence in a retirement community. *Western Journal of Communication, 65,* 89–112.

Alemán, M. W. (2003). "You should get yourself a boyfriend" but "let's not get serious": Communicating a code of romance in a retirement community. *Qualitative Research Reports in Communication, 4,* 31–37.

Allen, M. W., Gotcher, A. J. M., & Siebert, J. H. (1993). A decade of organizational communication research: Journal articles 1980–1991. In S. A. Deetz (Ed.), *Communication yearbook 16* (pp. 252–330). Newbury Park, CA: Sage.

Altman, I., & Low, S. M. (Eds.). (1992). *Place attachment.* New York: Plenum Press.

Anderson, R., Cissna, K. N., & Arnett, R. C. (Eds.). (1994). *The reach of dialogue: Confirmation, voice, and community.* Cresskill, NJ: Hampton Press.

Anderson, R., Dardenne, R., & Killenberg, G. M. (1994). *The conversation of journalism: Communication, community, and the news.* Westport, CT: Praeger.

Apker, J., Propp, W. M., & Ford, W. S. Z. (2005). Negotiating status and identity tensions in healthcare team interactions: An exploration of nurse role dialectics. *Journal of Applied Communication Research, 33,* 93–115.

Arnett, R. C. (1986). *Communication and community: Implications of Martin Buber's dialogue.* Carbondale: Southern Illinois University Press.

Arnett, R. C., & Arneson, P. (1999). *Dialogic civility in a cynical age: Community, hope, and interpersonal relationships.* Albany: State University of New York Press.

Arvold, A. G. (1915). The little country theater. *Quarterly Journal of Speech, 1*, 65–73.

Asen, R. (2004). A discourse theory of citizenship. *Quarterly Journal of Speech, 90*, 189–211.

Bach, T. E., Blair, C., Nothstine, W. L., & Pym, A. L. (1996). How to read "How to Get Published." *Communication Quarterly, 44*, 399–422.

Ball-Rokeach, S. J., Kim, Y-C., & Matei, S. (2001). Storytelling neighborhood: Paths to belonging in diverse urban environments. *Communication Research, 28*, 392–428.

Barge, J. K. (1996). Leadership skills and the dialectics of leadership in group decision making. In R. Y. Hirokawa & M. S. Poole (Eds.), *Communication and group decision making* (2nd ed., pp. 301–342). Thousand Oaks, CA: Sage.

Barge, J. K. (2003). Hope, communication, and community building. *Southern Communication Journal, 69*, 63–81.

Baxter, L. A. (1988). A dialectical perspective on communication strategies in relationship development. In S. Duck (Ed.), *Handbook of personal relationships: Theory, research, and interventions* (pp. 257–273). New York: Wiley.

Baxter, L. A. (1990). Dialectical contradictions in relationship development. *Journal of Social and Personal Relationships, 7*, 69–88.

Baxter, L. A. (1993). The social side of personal relationships: A dialectical perspective. In S. Duck (Ed.), *Social context and relationships: Understanding relationship processes* (Vol. 3, pp. 139–165). Newbury Park, CA: Sage.

Baxter, L. A. (2004). A tale of two voices: Relational dialectics theory. *Journal of Family Communication, 4*, 181–192.

Baxter, L. A. (2006). Relational dialectics: Multivocal dialogues of family communication. In D. O. Braithwaite & L. A. Baxter (Eds.), *Engaging theories in family communication: Multiple perspectives* (pp. 130–145). Thousand Oaks, CA: Sage.

Baxter, L. A., Braithwaite, D. O., Bryant, L. E., & Wagner, A. E. (2004). Stepchildren's perceptions of the contradictions in communication with stepparents. *Journal of Social and Personal Relationships, 21*, 447–467.

Baxter, L. A., & Montgomery, B. M. (1996). *Relating: Dialogues and dialectics.* New York: Guilford Press.

Baxter, L. A., & Montgomery, B. M. (1997). Rethinking communication in personal relationships from a dialectical perspective. In S. Duck (Ed.), *Handbook of personal relationships: Theory, research, and interventions* (2nd ed., pp. 325–349). New York: John Wiley & Sons.

Baxter, L. A., & Montgomery, B. M. (1998). A guide to dialectical approaches to studying personal relationships. In B. M. Montgomery & L. A. Baxter (Eds.), *Dialectical approaches to studying personal relationships* (pp. 1–16). Mahwah, NJ: Lawrence Erlbaum Associates.

Baxter, L. A., & Simon, E. P. (1993). Relationship maintenance strategies and dialectical contradictions in social networks. *Journal of Social and Personal Relationships, 10,* 225–242.

Baym, N. K. (1993) Interpreting soap operas and creating community: Inside a computer-mediated fan culture. *Journal of Folklore Research, 30,* 143–177.

Baym, N. K. (2000). *Tune in, log on: Soaps, fandom, and online community.* Thousand Oaks, CA: Sage.

Beaudoin, C. E., & Thorson, E. (2004). Social capital in rural and urban communities: Testing differences in media effects and models. *Journalism & Mass Communication Quarterly, 81,* 378–399.

Beck, C. S. (1995). You make the call: The co-creation of media text through interaction in an interpretive community of "Giants' fans." *Electronic Journal of Communication, 5*(1). Retrieved March 28, 2006, from http://www.cios.org/getfile/Beck_V5N195

Beck, C. S., Benitez, J. L., Edwards, A., Olson, A., Pai, A., & Torres, N. B. (2004). Enacting "health communication": The field of health communication as constructed through publication in scholarly journals. *Health Communication, 16,* 475–492.

Bell, D. (1993). *Communitarianism and its critics.* Oxford, England: Clarendon Press.

Bellah, R. N., Madsen, R., Sullivan, M. W., Swidler, A., & Tipton, S. M. (1985). *Habits of the heart: Individualism and commitment in American life.* New York: Harper & Row.

Bellah, R. N., Madsen, R., Sullivan, M. W., Swidler, A., & Tipton, S. M. (1991). *The good society.* New York: Knopf.

Bender, T. (1978). *Community and social change in America.* New Brunswick, NJ: Rutgers University Press.

Beniger, J. (1987). Personalization of the mass media and the growth of pseudo-community. *Communication Research, 14,* 352–371.

Benson, T. W. (1996). Rhetoric, civility, and community: Political debate on computer bulletin boards. *Communication Quarterly, 44,* 359–378.

Berg, W. M., & Boguslaw, R. (1985). *Communication and community: An approach to social psychology.* Englewood Cliffs, NJ: Prentice-Hall.

Berkowitz, D., & TerKeurst, J. V. (1999). Community as interpretive community: Rethinking the journalist–source relationship. *Journal of Communication, 49*(3), 125–136.

Billingham, P. (Ed.). (2005). *Radical initiatives in interventionist and community drama.* Portland, OR: Intellect.

Bird, S. E. (1999). Chatting on Cynthia's porch: Creating community in an e-mail fan group. *Southern Communication Journal, 65,* 49–65.

Blair, C., Brown, J. R., & Baxter, L. A. (1994). Disciplining the feminine. *Quarterly Journal of Speech, 80,* 383–409.

Boczkowski, P. J. (1999). Mutual shaping of users and technologies in a national virtual community. *Journal of Communication, 49*(2), 86–108.

Bostdorff, D. M. (2004). The internet rhetoric of the Ku Klux Klan: Study in web site community building run amok. *Communication Studies, 55,* 340–361.

Bramlett-Solomon, S., & Merrill, B. (1991). Newspaper use and community ties in a model retirement community. *Newspaper Research Journal, 12,* 60–69.

Braithwaite, C. A. (1997). Sa'ah Naaghai Bik'eh Hozhoon: An ethnography of Navajo educational communication practices. *Communication Education, 46,* 219–233.

Braithwaite, D. O., & Baxter, L. A. (2006). "You're my parent but you're not": Dialectical tensions in stepchildren's perceptions about communicating with the nonresidential parent. *Journal of Applied Communication Research, 34,* 30–48.

Braithwaite, D. O., Baxter, L. A., & Harper, A. M. (1998). The role of rituals in the management of the dialectical tensions of "old" and "new" blended families. *Communication Studies, 49,* 101–120.

Brier, A., & Lovelock, R. (Eds.). (1996). *Communication and community: Anglo-German perspectives.* Brookfield, VT: Avebury.

Brock, B. L., & Howell, S. (1994). Leadership in the evolution of a community-based political action group. In L. R. Frey (Ed.), *Group communication in context: Studies of natural groups* (pp. 135–152). Hillsdale, NJ: Lawrence Erlbaum Associates.

Brown, B. B., Altman, I., & Werner, C. M. (1992). Close relationships in the physical and social world: Dialectical and transactional analysis. In J. A. Anderson (Ed.), *Communication yearbook 13* (pp. 508–521). Newbury Park, CA: Sage.

Browne, S. H. (1996). Encountering Angelina Grimké: Violence, identity, and the creation of radical community. *Quarterly Journal of Speech, 82,* 55–73.

Carbaugh, D. (1999). "Just listen": "Listening" and landscape among the Blackfeet. *Western Journal of Communication, 63,* 250–270.

Carey, J. W. (1989). *Communication as culture: Essays on media and society.* Boston: Unwin Hyman.

Chay-Nemeth, C. (1998). Demystifying AIDS in Thailand: A dialectical analysis of the Thai sex industry. *Journal of Health Communication: International Perspectives, 3,* 217–232.

Chen, T. C-C., Drzewiecka, J. A., & Sias, P. M. (2001). Dialectical tensions in Taiwanese international student friendships. *Qualitative Research Reports in Communication, 2,* 57–65.

Chesebro, J. W. (1993). How to get published. *Communication Quarterly, 41,* 373–382.

Chorpenning, C. B. (1919). Putting on a community play. *Quarterly Journal of Speech, 5,* 45–53.

Cissna, K. N., Cox, D. E., & Bochner, A. P. (1990). The dialectic of marital and parental relationships within the stepfamily. *Communication Monographs, 57,* 44–61.

Clean, S. M. (1997). A communication analysis of community mobilization on the Warm Springs Indian Reservation. *Journal of Health Communication: International Perspectives, 2,* 113–125.

Cohen, A. P. (1985). *The symbolic construction of community.* New York: Tavistock.

Cohen-Cruz, J. (2006). The problem democracy is supposed to solve: The politics of community-based performance. In D. S. Madison & J. Hamera (Eds.), *The Sage handbook of performance studies* (pp. 427–445). Thousand Oaks, CA: Sage.

Conquergood, D. (1994). Homeboys and hoods: Gang communication and cultural space. In L. R. Frey (Ed.), *Group communication in context: Studies of natural groups* (pp. 23–55). Hillsdale, NJ: Lawrence Erlbaum Associates.

Conquergood, D. (2002). Lethal theatre: Performance, punishment, and the death penalty. *Theatre Journal, 54,* 339–367.

Cooks, L. (2002). Zonians in cyberspace: The imagining of individual, community and nation on the *Panama-L* listserv. *Communication Quarterly, 50,* 467–490.

Cooks, L., & Aden, R. C. (1995). *Northern Exposure*'s sense of place: Constructing and marginalizing the matriarchal community. *Women's Studies in Communication, 18*(2), 1–17.

Cooks, L., Scharrer, E., & Paredes, M. (2003). Creating a space for "every woman" at Oprah.com. *Electronic Journal of Communication, 9*(2–4). Retrieved March 28, 2006, from http://www.cios.org/getfile/cooks_v13n1

Dardene, R. (1996). *A free and responsible student press: An ideal vision of how community and communication can preserve scholastic journalism.* St. Petersburg, FL: Poynter Institute for Media Studies.

Darling-Wolf, F. (2004). Virtually multicultural: Trans-Asian identity and gender in an international fan community of a Japanese star. *New Media & Society, 6,* 507–528.

Della-Piana, C. K., & Anderson, J. A. (1995). Performing community: Community service as cultural conversation. *Communication Studies, 46,* 187–200.

del Río, E. (2006). The Latina/o problematic: Categories and questions in media communication research. In C. S. Beck (Ed.), *Communication yearbook 30* (pp. 387–430). Mahwah, NJ: Lawrence Erlbaum Associates.

Depew, D., & Peters, J. D. (2001). Community and community: The conceptual background. In G. J. Shepherd & E. W. Rothenbuhler (Eds.), *Communication and community* (pp. 3–21). Mahwah, NJ: Lawrence Erlbaum Associates.

DeSanctis, G., & Fulk, J. (Eds.). (1999). *Shaping organization form: Communication, connection, and community.* Thousand Oaks, CA: Sage.

Dindia, K. (1994). The intrapersonal–interpersonal dialectical process of self-disclosure. In S. Duck (Ed.), *Dynamics of relationships* (pp. 27–56). Thousand Oaks, CA: Sage.

Dobris, C. A. (1996). Maya Angelou: Writing the "Black Voice" for the multicultural community. *Howard Journal of Communications, 7,* 1–12.

Dollar, N. J., & Zimmers, B. G. (1998). Social identity and communicative boundaries: An analysis of youth and young adult street speakers in a U.S. American community. *Communication Research, 25,* 596–617.

Donovan, T. (2002). Community, assimilation, and the unfamiliar. *Philosophy & Rhetoric, 35,* 244–265.

Duff, R. A. (2001). *Punishment, communication, and community.* New York: Oxford University Press.

Dutta-Bergman, M. J. (2004). An alternative approach to social capital: Exploring the linkage between health consciousness and community participation. *Health Communication, 16,* 393–410.

Dutta-Bergman, M. J. (2005). Access to the internet in the context of community participation and community satisfaction. *New Media & Society, 7,* 89–109.

Eadie, B. (1999, January 20). NCA journal acceptance rates. *CRTNET News.* Retrieved March 30, 2006, from http://lists1.cac.psu.edu/cgi-bin/wa?A2=ind9901&L=crtnet&T=0&P=6232

Edley, P. P., Hylmö, A., & Newsom, V. A. (2004). Alternative organizing communities: Collectivist organizing, telework, home-based internet business, and online communities. In P. J. Kalbfleisch (Ed.), *Communication yearbook 28* (pp. 87–124). Mahwah, NJ: Lawrence Erlbaum Associates.

Eisenberg, E. M., Baglia, J., & Pynes, J. E. (2006). Transforming emergency medicine through narrative: Qualitative action research at a community hospital. *Health Communication, 19,* 197–208.

Erbert, L. A., Pérez, F. G., & Gareis, E. (2003). Turning points and dialectical interpretations of immigrant experiences in the United States. *Western Journal of Communication, 67,* 113–137.

Etzioni, A. (1993). *The spirit of community: Rights, responsibilities, and the communitarian agenda.* New York: Crown.

Etzioni, A. (Ed.). (1995). *New communitarian thinking: Persons, virtues, institutions, and communities.* Charlottesville: University Press of Virginia.

Etzioni, A. (Ed.). (1998). *The essential communitarian reader.* Lanham, MD: Rowman & Littlefield.

Etzioni, A., Volmert, A., & Rothchild, E. (Eds.). (2004). *The communitarian reader: Beyond the essentials.* Lanham, MD: Rowman & Littlefield.

Felkins, P. K. (2002). *Community at work: Creating and celebrating community in organizational life.* Cresskill, NJ: Hampton Press.

Finnegan, J. R., Jr., & Viswanath, K. (1988). Community ties and use of cable TV and newspapers in a Midwest suburb. *Journalism Quarterly, 65,* 456–473.

Ford, L. A., Ray, E. B., & Ellis, B. H. (1999). Translating scholarship on intrafamilial sexual abuse: The utility of a dialectical perspective for adult survivors. *Journal of Applied Communication Research, 27,* 139–157.

Frazer, E., & Lacey, N. (1993). *The politics of community: A feminist critique of the liberal-communitarian debate.* Toronto, Canada: University of Toronto Press.

Frey, L. R., Adelman, M. B., Flint, L. J., & Query, J. L., Jr. (2000). Weaving meanings together in an AIDS residence: Communicative practices, perceived health outcomes, and the symbolic construction of community. *Journal of Health Communication: International Perspectives, 5,* 53–72.

Frey, L. R., Adelman, M. B., & Query, J. L., Jr. (1996). Communication practices in the social construction of health in an AIDS residence. *Journal of Health Psychology, 1,* 383–397.

Frey, L. R., & Barge, J. K. (Eds.). (1997). *Managing group life: Communicating in decision-making groups.* Boston: Houghton Mifflin.

Frey, L. R., Botan, C. H., & Kreps, G. L. (2000). *Investigating communication: An introduction to research methods* (2nd ed.). Boston: Allyn and Bacon.

Frey, L. R., Query, J. L., Jr., Flint, L. J., & Adelman, M. B. (1998). Living together with AIDS: Social support processes in a residential facility. In V. J. Derlega & A. P. Barbee (Eds.), *HIV and social interaction* (pp. 129–146). Thousand Oaks, CA: Sage.

Friedland, L. A. (2001). Communication, community, and democracy: Toward a theory of the communicatively integrated community. *Communication Research, 28,* 358–391.

Fulk, J., Flanagin, A. J., Kalman, M. E., Monge, P. R., & Ryan, T. (1996). Connective and communal public goods in interactive communication systems. *Communication Theory, 6,* 60–87.

Fuoss, K. W. (1995). "Community" contested, imagined, and performed: Cultural performance, contestation, and community in an organized-labor social drama. *Text and Performance Quarterly, 15,* 79–98.

Galegher, J., Sproull, L., & Kiesler, S. (1998). Legitimacy, authority, and community in electronic support groups. *Written Communication, 15,* 493–530.

Gallie, W. B. (1964). *Philosophy and the historical understanding.* New York: Schocken Books.

Gaziano, C. (1988). Community knowledge gaps. *Critical Studies in Mass Communication, 5,* 351–357.

Geertz, C. (1973). *The interpretation of cultures.* New York: Basic Books.

Georgiou, M. (2001). Crossing the boundaries of the ethnic home: Media consumption and ethnic identity construction in the public space: The case of the Cypriot Community Centre in North London. *Gazette, 63,* 311–329.

Gergen, K. J. (1991). *The saturated self: Dilemmas of identity in contemporary life.* New York: Basic Books.

Giles, H. (Ed.). (2002). *Law enforcement, communication, and community.* Philadelphia: John Benjamins.

Glascock, J. (2004). The Jasper dragging death: Crisis communication and the community newspaper. *Communication Studies, 55,* 29–47.

Goldberg, J. H., Kole, J. S., & Hutchinson, J. A. (1984). Back to our roots through speech communication: Focusing on community in the community college. *Communication Education, 33,* 19–24.

Goldsmith, D. (1990). A dialectical perspective on the expression of autonomy and connection in romantic relationships. *Western Journal of Speech Communication, 54,* 537–556.

Goodall, H. L., Jr. (1996). *Divine signs: Connecting spirit to community.* Carbondale: Southern Illinois University Press.

Goodall, H. L., Jr. (1999). Casing the academy for community. *Communication Theory, 9,* 465–494.

Gossett, L. M., & Tompkins, P. K. (2001). Community as a means of organizational control. In G. J. Shepherd & E. W. Rothenbuhler (Eds.), *Communication and community* (pp. 111–133). Mahwah, NJ: Lawrence Erlbaum Associates.

Gourgey, H., & Smith, E. B. (1996). "Consensual hallucination": Cyberspace and the creation of an interpretive community. *Text and Performance Quarterly, 16,* 233–247.

Graham, E. E. (2003). Dialectical contradictions in postmarital relationships. *Journal of Family Communication, 3,* 193–214.

Graves, M. P. (2001). The Quaker tapestry: An artistic attempt to stitch together a diverse religious community. *Journal of Communication and Religion, 24,* 1–42.

Gumpert, G., & Drucker, S. J. (2001). A plea for chaos: Controlled unpredictability, uncertainty and serendipitous life in the urban community. *Qualitative Research Reports in Communication, 2,* 25–32.

Gusfield, J. (1975). *Community: A critical response.* New York: Harper & Row.

Haedicke, S. C., & Nellhaus, T. (Eds.). (2001). *Performing democracy: Interactional perspectives on urban community-based performance.* Ann Arbor: University of Michigan Press.

Hallahan, K. (2004). "Community" as a foundation for public relations theory and research. In P. J. Kalbfleisch (Ed.), *Communication yearbook 28* (pp. 233–279). Mahwah, NJ: Lawrence Erlbaum Associates.

Hariman, R., & Lucaites, J. L. (2002). Performing civic identity: The iconic photograph of the flag raising on Iwo Jima. *Quarterly Journal of Speech, 88,* 363–382.

Hart, R. P., Jennings, W. P., & Dixson, M. J. (2003). Imagining the American people: Strategies for building political community. *Journal of Communication, 53,* 138–164.

Harter, L. M. (2004). Maculinity(s), the agrarian frontier myth, and cooperative ways of organizing: Contradictions and tensions in the experience and enactment of democracy. *Journal of Applied Communication Research, 32,* 89–118.

Harter, L., Sharma, D., Pant, S., Singhal, A., & Sharma, Y. (2007). Catalyzing social reform through participatory folk performances in rural India. In L. R. Frey & K. M. Carragee (Eds.), *Communication activism: Volume 2. Media and performance activism* (pp. 285–314). Cresskill, NJ: Hampton Press.

Haskins, E. V. (2003). "Put your stamp on history": The USPS commemorative program "Celebrate the Century" and postmodern collective memory. *Quarterly Journal of Speech, 89,* 1–18.

Hauser, G. A., & Benoit-Barne, C. (2002). Reflections on rhetoric, deliberative democracy, civil society, and trust. *Rhetoric & Public Affairs, 5,* 261–275.

Hawley, A. H. (1950). *Human ecology: A theory of community structure.* New York: Ronald Press.

Hayakawa, S. I. (1949). *Language in thought and action.* New York: Harcourt, Brace.

Heath, R. G., & Frey, L. R. (2004). Ideal collaboration: A conceptual framework of community collaboration. In P. J. Kalbfleisch (Ed.), *Communication yearbook 28* (pp. 189–230). Mahwah, NJ: Lawrence Erlbaum Associates.

Hicks, D. (2002). The promise(s) of deliberative democracy. *Rhetoric & Public Affairs, 5,* 223–260.

Higgins, J. W. (1999a). Community television and the vision of media literacy, social action, and empowerment. *Journal of Broadcasting & Electronic Media, 43,* 624–644.

Higgins, J. W. (1999b). Sense-making and empowerment: A study of the "vision" of community television. *Electronic Journal of Communication, 9*(2–4). Retrieved March 28, 2006, from http://www.cios.org/getfile/Higgins_V9N23499

Hill, P. S. (2003). And still I rise: Communicative resistance of African American women in a culturally diverse community. *Electronic Journal of Communication, 13*(2–3). Retrieved March 29, 2006, from http://www.cios.org/getfile/01327_EJC

Hiller, E. T. (1941). The community as a social group. *American Sociological Review, 6,* 189–202.

Hillery, G. A., Jr. (1955). Definitions of community: Areas of agreement. *Rural Sociology, 20,* 111–122.

Hillery, G. A., Jr. (1963). Villages, cities, and total institutions. *American Sociological Review, 28,* 779–791.

Hillery, G. A., Jr. (1982). *A research odyssey: Developing and testing a community theory.* New Brunswick, NJ: Transaction Books.

Hindman, D. B. (1996). Community newspapers, community structural pluralism, and local conflict with nonlocal groups. *Journalism & Mass Communication Quarterly, 73,* 708–721.

Hindman, D. B., Littlefield, R., Preston, A., & Nuemann, D. (1999). Structural pluralism, ethnic pluralism, and community newspapers. *Journalism & Mass Communication Quarterly, 76,* 250–263.

Hindman, E. B. (1998). Community, democracy, and neighborhood news. *Journal of Communication, 48*(2), 27–29.

Hogan, J. M. (Ed.). (1998). *Rhetoric and community: Studies in unity and fragmentation.* Columbia: University of South Carolina Press.

Howell, S., Brock, B., & Hauser, E. (2003). A multicultural, intergenerational youth program: Creating and sustaining a youth community group. In L. R. Frey (Ed.), *Group communication in context: Studies of bona fide groups* (2nd ed., pp. 85–108). Mahwah, NJ: Lawrence Erlbaum Associates.

Howley, K. (2005). *Community media: People, places, and communication technologies.* New York: Cambridge University Press.

Hummon, D. M. (1990). *Commonplaces: Community ideology and identity in American culture.* Albany: State University of New York Press.

Hummon, D. M. (1992). Community attachment: Local sentiment and sense of place. In I. Altman & S. M. Low (Eds.), *Place attachment* (pp. 253–278). New York: Plenum Press.

Hunter, A. (1974). *Symbolic communities: The persistence and change of Chicago's local communities.* Chicago: University of Chicago Press.

Ingram, J. (2003). Once upon a time in Hong Kong: The construction of community as collective agency. *Southern Communication Journal, 69*, 51–62.

Inomata, T., & Cohen, L. S. (Eds.). (2006). *Archaeology of performance: Theaters of power, community, and politics*. Lanham, MD: Altamira Press.

Jacobs, R., & Yousman, W. (1999). Understanding cable television community access viewership. *Communication Research Reports, 16*, 305–316.

Jameson, J. K. (2004). Negotiating autonomy and connection through politeness: A dialectical approach to organizational conflict management. *Western Journal of Communication, 68*, 257–277.

Jankowski, N. W. (with Prehn, O.). (Eds.). (2002). *Community media in the information age: Perspectives and prospects*. Cresskill, NJ: Hampton Press.

Jasinski, J. (1993). (Re)constituting community through narrative argument: *Eros* and *philia* in *The Big Chill*. *Quarterly Journal of Speech, 79*, 467–486.

Jeffres, L. W., Atkin, D., & Neuendorf, K. A. (2002). A model linking community activity and communication with political attitudes and involvement in neighborhoods. *Political Communication, 19*, 387–421.

Jeffres, L. W., Dobos, J., & Sweeney, M. (1987). Communication and commitment to community. *Communication Research, 14*, 619–643.

Jensen, R. J., & Hammerback, J. C. (2000). Working in "quiet places": The community organizing rhetoric of Robert Parris Moses. *Howard Journal of Communications, 11*, 1–18.

Johnson, A. J., Wittenberg, E., Villagran, M. M., Mazur, M., & Villagran, P. (2003). Relational progression as a dialectic: Examining turning points in communication among friends. *Communication Monographs, 70*, 230–249.

Johnson, P. (2004). Black radio politically defined: Communicating community and political empowerment through Stevie Wonder's KJLH-FM, 1992–2002. *Political Communication, 21*, 353–367.

Johnson, S. D., & Long, L. M. (2002). "Being a part and being apart": Dialectics and group communication. In L. R. Frey (Ed.), *New directions in group communication* (pp. 25–41). Thousand Oaks, CA: Sage.

Johnstone, B. (1990). *Stories, community, and place: Narratives from middle America*. Bloomington: Indiana University Press.

Jones, S. G. (Ed.). (1995a). *CyberSociety: Computer-mediated communication and community*. Thousand Oaks, CA: Sage.

Jones, S. G. (1995b). Understanding community in the information age. In S. G. Jones (Ed.), *CyberSociety: Computer-mediated communication and community* (pp. 12–29). Thousand Oaks, CA: Sage.

Jones, S. G. (Ed.). (1998a). *CyberSociety 2.0: Revisiting computer-mediated communication and community*. Thousand Oaks, CA: Sage.

Jones, S. G. (1998b). Understanding micropolis and community. *Electronic Journal of Communication, 8*(3). Retrieved April 2, 2006, from http://www.cios.org/getfile/Jones_V8N398

Jones, T. S., & Bodtker, A. (1998). A dialectical analysis of a social justice process: International collaboration in South Africa. *Journal of Applied Communication Research, 26,* 357–373.

Jordan, J. W. (2005). A virtual death and a real dilemma: Identity, trust, and community in cyberspace. *Southern Communication Journal, 70,* 200–218.

Jorgensen-Earp, C. R., & Lanzilotti, L. A. (1998). Public memory and private grief: The construction of shrines at the sites of public tragedy. *Quarterly Journal of Speech, 84,* 150–170.

Kalbfleisch, P. J. (Ed.). (2004). *Communication yearbook 28.* Mahwah, NJ: Lawrence Erlbaum Associates.

Kanter, R. M. (1968). Commitment and social organization: A study of commitment mechanisms in utopian communities. *American Sociological Review, 33,* 499–517.

Kanter, R. M. (1972). *Commitment and community: Communes and utopias in sociological perspective.* Cambridge, MA: Harvard University Press.

Katriel, T. (1991). *Communal webs: Communication and culture in contemporary Israel.* Albany: State University of New York Press.

Katriel, T. (1994). Sites of memory: Discourse of the past in Israeli pioneering settlement museums. *Quarterly Journal of Speech, 80,* 1–20.

Katz, J. E., Rice, R. E., Acord, S., Dasgupta, K., & David, K. (2004). Personal mediated communication and the concept of community in theory and practice. In P. J. Kalbfleisch (Ed.), *Communication yearbook 28* (pp. 315–370). Mahwah, NJ: Lawrence Erlbaum Associates.

Kaufman, H. F. (1959). Toward an interactional conception of community. *Social Forces, 38,* 8–17.

Kaufman, H. F. (1985). An action approach to community development. In F. A. Fear & H. K. Schwarzweller (Eds.), *Focus on community* (pp. 53–65). Greenwich, CT: JAI Press.

Kelemen, M., & Smith, W. (2001). Community and its "virtual" promises: A critique of cyberlibertarian rhetoric. *Information, Communication & Society, 4,* 370–387.

Kellett, P. M. (1999). Dialogue and dialectics in managing organizational change: The case of a mission-based transformation. *Southern Communication Journal, 64,* 211–231.

Kim, S-H., Brunner, B. R., & Fitch-Hauser, M. (2006). Exploring community relations in a university setting. *Public Relations Review, 32,* 191–193.

King, D. L., & Mele, C. (1999). Making public access television: Community participation, media literacy and the public sphere. *Journal of Broadcasting & Electronic Media, 43,* 603–623.

Knapp, M. L., & Daly, J. A. (2004). *A guide to publishing in scholarly communication journals* (3rd ed.). Mahwah, NJ: Lawrence Erlbaum Associates.

Konig, R. (1968). *The community* (E. Fitzgerald, Trans.). New York: Schocken Books.

Kramer, M. W. (2002). Communication in a community theater group: Managing multiple group roles. *Communication Studies, 53,* 151–170.

Kramer, M. W. (2004). Toward a communication theory of group dialectics: An ethnographic study of a community theater group. *Communication Monographs, 71,* 311–332.

Kramer, M. W. (2005). Communication and social exchange processes in community theater groups. *Journal of Applied Communication Research, 33,* 159–182.

Kuftinec, S. (2003). *Staging America: Cornerstone and community-based theater.* Carbondale: Southern Illinois University Press.

LaFollette, M. C. (1992). *Stealing into print: Fraud, plagiarism, and misconduct in scientific publishing.* Berkeley: University of California Press.

Larson, C. U., & Oravec, C. (1987). *A Prairie Home Companion* and the fabrication of community. *Critical Studies in Mass Communication, 4,* 221–244.

Lee, R. (1995). Electoral politics and visions of community: Jimmy Carter, virtue, and the small town myth. *Western Journal of Communication, 59,* 39–60.

Lindemann, K. (2005). Live(s) online: Narrative performance, presence, and community in LiveJournal.com. *Text and Performance Quarterly, 25,* 354–372.

Lindlof, T. R. (1988). Media audiences as interpretive communities. In J. A. Anderson (Ed.), *Communication yearbook 11* (pp. 87–107). Newbury Park, CA: Sage.

Lindlof, T. R. (2002). Interpretive community: An approach to media and religion. *Journal of Media and Religion, 1,* 61–74.

Mackin, J. A., Jr. (1991). Schismogenesis and community: Pericles' funeral oration. *Quarterly Journal of Speech, 77,* 251–262.

Mackin, J. A., Jr. (1997). *Community over chaos: An ecological perspective on communication ethics.* Tuscaloosa: University of Alabama Press.

Makagon, D. (2004). A search for social connection in America's town square: Times Square and urban public life. *Southern Communication Journal, 69,* 1–21.

Martin, J. N., & Nakayama, T. K. (1999). Thinking dialectically about culture and community. *Communication Theory, 9,* 1–25.

Martin, J. N., Nakayama, T. K., & Flores, L. A. (1998). A dialectical approach to intercultural communication. In J. N. Martin, T. K. Nakayama, & L. A. Flores (Eds.), *Readings in cultural contexts* (pp. 5–14). Mountain View, CA: Mayfield.

Matei, S., Ball-Rokeach, S. J., & Qiu, J. L (2001). Fear and misperception of Los Angeles urban space: A spatial-statistical study of communication-shaped mental maps. *Communication Research, 28,* 429–463.

Matei, S., Ball-Rokeach, S. J., Wilson, M. E., Gibbs, J., & Hoyt, E. G. (2001). Metamorphosis: A field research methodology for studying communication technology and community. *Electronic Journal of Communication, 11*(2). Retrieved March 30, 2006, from http://www.cios.org/getfile/matei_V11n201

Matlon, R. J. (Ed.), & Ortiz, S. P. (Assoc. Ed.). (1997). *Index to journals in communication studies through 1995.* Annandale, VA: National Communication Association.

McDonald, T. A., Orbe, M. P., & Ford-Ahmed, T. (Eds.). (2002). *Building diverse communities: Applications of communication research.* Cresskill, NJ: Hampton Press.

McKerrow, R. E. (1998). Rhetoric and the construction of a deliberative community. *Southern Communication Journal, 63,* 350–356.

McLean, S. (1997). A communication analysis of community mobilization on the Warm Springs Indian Reservation. *Journal of Health Communication: International Perspectives, 2,* 113–125.

McLeod, J. M., Daily, K., Guo, Z., Eveland, E. P., Jr., Bayer, J., Yang, S., et al. (1996). Community integration, local media use, and democratic processes. *Communication Research, 23,* 179–209.

McLeod, J. M., Scheufele, D. A., & Moy, P. (1999). Community, communication, and participation: The role of mass media and interpersonal discussion in local political participation. *Political Communication, 16,* 315–336.

McLeod, J. M., Scheufele, D. A., Moy, P., Horowitz, E. M., Holbert, R. L., Zhang, W., et al. (1999). Understanding deliberation: The effects of discussion networks on participation in a public forum. *Communication Research, 26,* 743–774.

McMillan, D., & Chavis, D. M. (1986). Sense of community: A definition and theory. *Journal of Community Psychology, 14,* 6–23.

McMillan, S. (2001). Virtual community: Boundary crossings at health-related web sites. *Electronic Journal of Communication, 11*(2). Retrieved March 29, 2006, from http://www.cios.org/getfile/mcmill_v11n201

Medved, C. E., Morrison, K., Dearing, J. W., Larson, R. S., Cline, G., & Brummans, B. H. J. M. (2001). Tensions in community health improvement initiatives: Communication and collaboration in a managed care environment. *Journal of Applied Communication Research, 29,* 137–152.

Meyer, M. D. E. (2003). "It's me. I'm it": Defining adolescent sexual identity through relational dialectics in *Dawson's Creek*. *Communication Quarterly, 51*, 262–276.

Meyers, R., Brashers, D., Center, C., Beck, C., & Wert-Gray, S. (1992). A citation analysis of organizational communication research. *Southern Communication Journal, 57*, 241–246.

Meyrowitz, J. (1985). *No sense of place: The impact of electronic media on social behavior*. New York: Oxford University Press.

Mokros, H. B., & Deetz, S. (1996). What counts as real? A constitutive view of communication and the disenfranchised in the context of health. In E. B. Ray (Ed.), *Communication and disenfranchisement: Social health issues and implications* (pp. 29–44). Mahwah, NJ: Lawrence Erlbaum Associates.

Montgomery, B. M., & Baxter, L. A. (Eds.). (1998). *Dialectical approaches to studying personal relationships*. Mahwah, NJ: Lawrence Erlbaum Associates.

Mumby, D., & Stohl, C. (1991). Power and discourse in organization studies: Absence and the dialectic of control. *Discourse and Society, 2*, 313–332.

Nasimento, A. (Ed.). (1998). *A matter of discourse: Community and communication in contemporary philosophies*. Brookfield, VT: Ashgate.

Neuwirth, K., Salmon, C. T., & Neff, M. (1989). Community orientation and media use. *Journalism Quarterly, 66*, 31–39.

Nossek, H. (2003). Active research as a bridge between theory and practice: A suggested model for playing an active role in organizing community television as a tool of empowerment in the community. *Communications: The European Journal of Communication Research, 28*, 305–321.

Olson, M. E. (Ed.). (2000). *Feminism, community, and communication*. New York: Haworth Press.

O'Sullivan, P. B. (1995). Computer networks and political participation: Santa Monica's teledemocracy project. *Journal of Applied Communication Research, 23*, 93–107.

Park-Fuller, L. (2003). Audiencing the audience: Playback Theatre, performative writing, and social activism. *Text and Performance Quarterly, 23*, 288–310.

Parsons, T. (1960). *Structure and process in modern societies*. Glencoe, IL: Free Press.

Patterson, M. J., & Hall, M. W. (1998). Abortion, moral maturity, and civic journalism. *Critical Studies in Mass Communication, 15*, 91–115.

Patterson, S. J., & Kavanaugh, A. L. (2001). Building a sustainable community network: An application of critical mass theory. *Electronic Journal of Communication, 11*(2). Retrieved March 28, 2006, from http://www.cios.org/getfile/patter_v11n201

Pawlowski, D. R. (1998). Dialectical tensions in marital partners' accounts of their relationships. *Communication Quarterly, 46,* 396–416.

Pearce, K. A., & Pearce, W. B. (2001). The Public Dialogue Consortium's school-wide dialogue process: A communication approach to develop citizenship skills and enhance school climate. *Communication Theory, 11,* 105–123.

Pearce, W. B., & Pearce, K. A. (2000). Extending the theory of the coordinated management of meaning (CMM) through a community dialogue process. *Communication Theory, 10,* 405–423.

Peeples, J. A. (2003). Trashing South-Central: Place and identity in a community-level environmental justice dispute. *Southern Communication Journal, 69,* 82–95.

Penman, R. (1996). Imagining conversation and community. *Australian Journal of Communication, 23,* 16–23.

Peters, J. D. (1989). John Locke, the individual, and the origin of communication. *Quarterly Journal of Speech, 75,* 387–399.

Petronio, S. (2002). *Boundaries of privacy: Dialectics of disclosure.* Albany: State University of New York Press.

Pezzullo, P. C. (2003). Touring "Cancer Alley," Louisiana: Performances of community and memory for environmental justice. *Text and Performance Quarterly, 23,* 226–252.

Philipsen, G. (1975). Speaking "like a man" in Teamsterville: Culture patterns of role enactment in an urban neighborhood. *Quarterly Journal of Speech, 61,* 13–23.

Philipsen, G. (1976). Places for speaking in Teamsterville. *Quarterly Journal of Speech, 61,* 13–22.

Phillips, D. L. (1993). *Looking backward: A critical appraisal of communitarian thought.* Princeton, NJ: Princeton University Press.

Phillips, S. U. (1983). *The invisible culture: Communication in classroom and community on the Warm Springs Indian Reservation.* New York: Longman.

Pigg, K. E. (2001). Applications of community informatics for building community and enhancing civic society. *Information, Communication & Society, 4,* 507–527.

Pinkett, R., & O'Bryant, R. (2003). Building community, empowerment and self-sufficiency. *Information, Communication & Society, 6,* 187–210.

Plant, R. (1974). *Community and ideology: An essay in applied social philosophy.* Boston: Routledge and Kegan Paul.

Pollock, J. C., & Yulis, S. G. (2004). Nationwide newspaper coverage of physician-assisted suicide: A community structure approach. *Journal of Health Communication: International Perspectives, 9,* 281–308.

Poplin, D. E. (1979). *Communities: A survey of theories and methods of research* (2nd ed.). New York: Macmillan.

Procter, D. E. (1995). Placing Lincoln and Mitchell counties: A cultural study. *Communication Studies, 46,* 222–233.

Query, J. L., Jr., & James, A. C. (1989). The relationship between interpersonal communication competence and social support among elderly support groups in retirement communities. *Health Communication, 1,* 165–184.

Quinlisk, C. C. (2004). Communicator status and expectations in intercultural communication: Implications for language learning in a multicultural community. *Communication Research Reports, 21,* 84–91.

Rafaeli, S., & LaRose, R. (1993). Electronic bulletin boards and "public goods" explanations of collaborative mass media. *Communication Research, 20,* 277–297.

Rakow, L. F., Belter, B., Dyrstad, H., Hallsten, J., Johnson, J., & Indvik, K. (2003). The talk of movers and shakers: Class conflict in the making of a community disaster. *Southern Communication Journal, 69,* 37–50.

Rasmussen, K., & Downey, S. D. (1989). Dialectical disorientation in *Agnes of God. Western Journal of Speech Communication, 53,* 66–84.

Rasmussen, K., & Downey, S. D. (1991). Dialectical disorientation in Vietnam War films: Subversion of the mythology of war. *Quarterly Journal of Speech, 77,* 176–195.

Rawlins, W. K. (1983). Negotiating close friendship: The dialectic of conjunctive freedoms. *Human Communication Research, 9,* 255–266.

Rawlins, W. K. (1992). *Friendship matters: Communication, dialectics, and the life course.* New York: Aldine de Gruyter.

Ray, G. B. (1987). An ethnography of nonverbal communication in an Appalachian community. *Research on Language and Social Interaction, 21,* 171–188.

Rich, M. D., & Rodríguez, J. I. (2007). A proactive approach to peer education: The efficacy of a sexual assault intervention program. In L. R. Frey & K. M. Carragee (Eds.), *Communication activism: Volume 2. Media and performance activism* (pp. 315–344). Cresskill, NJ: Hampton Press.

Riggs, K. E. (1996). Television use in a retirement community. *Journal of Communication, 46*(1), 144–156.

Rogers, E. M., Dearing, J. W., Rao, N., Campo, S., Meyer, G., Betts, G. J. F., et al. (1995). Communication and community in a city under siege: The AIDS epidemic in San Francisco. *Communication Research, 22,* 664–678.

Rothenbuhler, E. (1991). The process of community involvement. *Communication Monographs, 58,* 63–78.

Rothenbuhler, E. W. (2001). Revising communication research for working on community. In G. J. Shepherd & E. W. Rothenbuhler (Eds.), *Communication and community* (pp. 159–179). Mahwah, NJ: Lawrence Erlbaum Associates.

Rothenbuhler, E., Mullen, L., DeLarell, R., & Ryul, C. (1996). Communication, community attachment, and involvement. *Journalism & Mass Communication Quarterly, 73,* 445–464.

Rucinski, D. (2004). Community boundedness, personal relevance, and the knowledge gap. *Communication Research, 31,* 472–495.

Ruud, G. (1995). The symbolic construction of organizational identities and community in a regional symphony. *Communication Studies, 46,* 201–221.

Ruud, G., & Sprague, J. (2000). Can't see the (old growth) forest for the logs: Dialectical tensions in the interpretive practices of environmentalists and loggers. *Communication Reports, 13,* 55–65.

Sabourin, T. C., & Stamp, G. H. (1995). Communication and the experience of dialectical tensions in family life: An examination of abusive and nonabusive families. *Communication Monographs, 62,* 213–242.

Schaefer, D. J. (1999). From community to community-ings: Making sense of electronic discussion groups. *Electronic Journal of Communication, 9*(2–4). Retrieved March 29, 2006, from http://www.cios.org/getfile/schaefer_V9N23499

Schely-Newman, E. (1997). Finding one's place: Locale narratives in an Israeli moshav. *Quarterly Journal of Speech, 83,* 401–415.

Scheufele, D. A., & Shah, D. V. (2000). Personality strength and social capital: The role of dispositional and informational variables in the production of civic participation. *Communication Research, 27,* 107–131.

Schmitz, J., Rogers, E. M., Phillips, K., & Paschal, D. (1995). The Public Electronic Network (PEN) and the homeless in Santa Monica. *Journal of Applied Communication Research, 23,* 26–43.

Schoell, E. R. (1953). The changing community theatre. *Western Journal of Communication, 17,* 37–44.

Schrool, C. J. (1999). Theorizing the flip side of civic journalism: Democratic citizenship and ethical readership. *Communication Theory, 9,* 321–345.

Schuler, D. (2001). Community *networking* versus community *networks*: A short note on their interrelationships. *Electronic Journal of Communication, 5*(1). Retrieved March 29, 2006, from http://www.cios.org/getfile/Schuler_V11n201

Schwartzman, R. (1997). Peer review as the enforcement of disciplinary orthodoxy. *Southern Communication Journal, 63,* 69–75.

Sefcovic, E. M. I. (2002). Cultural memory and the cultural legacy of individualism and community in two classic films about labor unions. *Critical Studies in Media Communication, 19,* 329–351.

Sexton, G., & McKee, A. (2001). The place of media in community formation for homeless youth: A case study of *Gibber* magazine. *Australian Journal of Communication, 28*(2), 63–76.

Shah, D. V. (1998). Civic engagement, interpersonal trust, and television use: An individual level assessment of social capital. *Political Psychology, 19*, 469–496.

Shah, D. V., Cho, J., Eveland, W. P., Jr., & Kwak, N. (2005). Information and expression in a digital age: Modeling internet effects on civic participation. *Communication Research, 32*, 531–565.

Shah, D. V., Kwak, N., & Holbert, R. L. (2001). "Connecting" and "disconnecting" with civic life: Patterns of internet use and the production of social capital. *Political Communication, 18*, 141–162.

Shah, D., McLeod, J. M., & Yoon, S-H. (2001). Communication, context, and community: An exploration of print, broadcast, and internet influences. *Communication Research, 28*, 464–506.

Shepherd, G. J. (2001). Community as the interpersonal accomplishment of communication. In G. J. Shepherd & E. W. Rothenbuhler (Eds.), *Communication and community* (pp. 25–52). Mahwah, NJ: Lawrence Erlbaum Associates.

Shepherd, G. J., & Rothenbuhler, E. W. (Eds.). (2001). *Communication and community*. Mahwah, NJ: Lawrence Erlbaum Associates.

Sheras, P. L., & Koch-Sheras, P. R. (2006). *Couple power therapy: Building commitment, cooperation, communication, and community in relationships*. Washington, DC: American Psychological Association.

Shue, L. L., & Beck, C. S. (2001). Stepping out of bounds: Performing feminist pedagogy within a dance education community. *Communication Education, 50*, 125–143.

Silver, D. (2005). Selling cyberspace: Constructing and destructing the rhetoric of community. *Southern Communication Journal, 70*, 187–199.

Simonson, P. (2003). Assembly, rhetoric, and widespread community: Mass communication in Paul of Tarsus. *Journal of Media and Religion, 2*, 165–182.

Simpson, T. A. (1995). Communication, conflict, and community in an urban industrial ruin. *Communication Research, 22*, 700–719.

Slack, R., & Williams, R. A. (2000). The dialectics of place and space: On community in the "information age." *New Media & Society, 2*, 313–334.

Southwell, B. C., & Yzer, M. C. (2007). The roles of interpersonal communication in media campaigns. In C. S. Beck (Ed.), *Communication yearbook 31* (pp. 419–462). New York, NY: Lawrence Erlbaum Associates.

Spano, S. (2001). *Public dialogue and participatory democracy: The Cupertino community project*. Cresskill, NJ: Hampton Press.

Stamm, K. R. (1985). *Newspaper use and community ties: Toward a dynamic theory*. Norwood, NJ: Ablex.

Stamm, K. R., Emig, A. G., & Hesse, M. B. (1997). The contribution of local media to community involvement. *Journalism & Mass Communication Quarterly, 74*, 97–107.

Stamm, K. R., & Guest, A. M. (1991). Communication and community integration: An analysis of the communication behavior of newcomers. *Journalism Quarterly, 68*, 644–656.

Stamm, K. R., & Weiss, R. (1986). The newspaper and community integration: A study of ties to a local church community. *Communication Research, 13*, 125–137.

Starmer, G. L. (1946). College-community dramatics and the G.I. student. *Southern Communication Journal, 12*, 21–24.

Stavitsky, A. (1994). The changing perception of localism in U.S. public radio. *Journal of Broadcasting & Electronic Media, 38*, 19–33.

Steele, I. K. (1986). *The English Atlantic, 1675–1740: An exploration of communication and community.* New York: Oxford University Press.

Steeves, L. H. (1993). Creating imagined communities: Development communication and the challenge of feminism. *Journal of Communication, 43*(3), 218–229.

Stephens, K. K., Rimal, R. N., & Flora, J. A. (2004). Expanding the reach of health campaigns: Community organizations as metachannels for the dissemination of health information. *Journal of Health Communication: International Perspectives, 9*, 97–111.

Stohl, C., & Cheney, G. (2001). Participatory processes/paradoxical practices: Communication and the dilemmas of organizational democracy. *Management Communication Quarterly, 14*, 349–407.

Swartz, O. (1997). Disciplining the "other": Engaging Blair, Brown, and Baxter. *Southern Communication Journal, 62*, 253–256.

Tam, G. (1998). *Communitarianism: A new agenda for politics and citizenship.* New York: New York University Press.

Taylor, P. (2003). *Applied theatre: Creating transformative encounters in the community.* Portsmouth, NH: Heinemann.

Thorpe, C. D. (1925). The Oxford Players, the cherry orchard, and the playhouse. *Quarterly Journal of Speech, 11*, 360–363.

Tinder, G. (1995). *Tolerance and community.* Columbia: University of Missouri Press.

Toc, H. (1971). "I shot an arrow in the air ..." The performing arts as weapons of social change. *Journal of Communication, 21*, 115–135.

Toller, P. W. (2005). Negotiation of dialectical contradictions by parents who have experienced the death of a child. *Journal of Applied Communication Research, 33*, 46–66.

Tracy, K., & Dimmock, A. (2004). Meetings: Discursive sites for building and fragmenting community. In P. J. Kalbfleisch (Ed.), *Communication yearbook 28* (pp. 127–164). Mahwah, NJ: Lawrence Erlbaum Associates.

Tracy, S. J. (2004). Dialectic, contradiction, or double bind? Analyzing and theorizing employee reactions to organizational tensions. *Journal of Applied Communication Research, 32,* 119–170.

Trethewey, A., & Ashcraft, K. L. (2004). Practicing disorganization: The development of applied perspectives on living with tension. *Journal of Applied Communication Research, 32,* 81–88.

Trujillo, N. (1993). Interpreting November 22: A critical ethnography of an assassination site. *Quarterly Journal of Speech, 79,* 447–466.

Vaughn, M., & Stamp, G. H. (2003). The empowerment dilemma: The dialectic of emancipation and control in staff/client interaction at shelters for battered women. *Communication Studies, 54,* 154–168.

Viswanath, K., Finnegan, J. R., Jr., Rooney, B., & Potter, J. (1990). Community ties in a rural Midwest community and use of newspapers and cable television. *Journalism Quarterly, 67,* 899–911.

Viswanath, K., Kosicki, G. M., Fredin, E. S., & Park, E. (2000). Local community ties, community-boundedness, and local public affairs knowledge gaps. *Communication Research, 27,* 27–50.

Vrooman, S. S. (2001). Flamethrowers, slashers and witches: Gendered communication in a virtual community. *Qualitative Research Reports in Communication, 2,* 33–41.

Waltman, M. S. (2003). Strategems and heuristics in the recruitment of children into communities of hate: The fabric of our future nightmares. *Southern Communication Journal, 69,* 22–36.

Warren, R. L. (1978). *The community in America* (3rd ed.). Chicago: Rand McNally.

Wegner, P. S. (1985). Strange bedfellows: The small college and community theatre. *Journal of the Association for Communication Administration, 54,* 73–75.

Weitzel, A., & Geist, P. (1998). Parliamentary procedure in a community group: Communication and vigilant decision making. *Communication Monographs, 65,* 244–259.

Werner, C. M., & Baxter, L. A. (1994). Temporal qualities of relationships: Organismic, transactional, and dialectical views. In M. L. Knapp & G. R. Miller (Eds.), *Handbook of interpersonal communication* (2nd ed., pp. 323–379). Thousand Oaks, CA: Sage.

Wilkinson, B. (1976). Bringing dinner theatre to the college and community. *Journal of the Association for Communication Administration, 15,* 48–49.

Wilkinson, K. P. (1970). The community as a social field. *Social Forces, 48,* 311–322.

Wilkinson, K. P. (1986). In search of the community in the changing countryside. *Rural Sociology, 51,* 1–17.

Wilkinson, K. P. (1991). *The community in rural America*. Westport, CT: Greenwood Press.

Williams, A., & Guendouzi, J. (2000). Adjusting to "the home": Dialectical dilemmas and personal relationships in a retirement community. *Journal of Communication, 50*(3), 65–82.

Wolff, M., Young, S., Beck, B., Maurana, C. A., Murphy, M., Holfield, J., et al. (2004). Leadership in a public housing community. *Journal of Health Communication: International Perspectives, 9,* 119–126.

Wright, K. (2000). The communication of social support within an on-line community for older adults: A qualitative analysis of the Senior Net community. *Qualitative Research Reports in Communication, 1,* 33–43.

Wright, K. (2002). Social support within an on-line cancer community: An assessment of emotional support, perceptions of advantages and disadvantages, and motives for using the community from a communication perspective. *Journal of Applied Communication Research, 30,* 195–209.

Yep, G. A., Lovaas, K. E., & Ho, P. C. (2001). Communication in "Asian American" families with queer members: A relational dialectics perspective. In M. Bernstein & R. Reimann (Eds.), *Queer families, queer politics: Challenging culture and the state* (pp. 152–172). New York: Columbia University Press.

Young, I. M. (1995). The ideal of community and the politics of difference. In P. A. Weiss & M. Friedman (Eds.), *Feminism and community* (pp. 233–257). Philadelphia: Temple University Press.

Young, N. L. (2007). Identity trans/formations. In C. S. Beck (Ed.), *Communication yearbook 31* (pp. 223–272). New York, NY: Lawrence Erlbaum Associates.

Yu, X., & Sears, A. (1996). "Localism" in Chinese media context: An examination of a closed circuit community cable system. *Journal of Broadcasting & Electronic Media, 40,* 208–226.

Zaeske, S. (2002). Signatures of citizenship: The rhetorics of women's antislavery petitions. *Quarterly Journal of Speech, 88,* 147–168.

Zappen, J. P., Gurak, L. J., & Doheny-Farina, S. (1997). Rhetoric, community, and cyberspace. *Rhetoric Review, 15,* 400–419.

Zelizer, B. (1993). Journalists as interpretive communities. *Critical Studies in Mass Communication, 19,* 219–237.

Zoller, H. M. (2000). "A place you haven't visited before": Creating the conditions for community dialogue. *Southern Communication Journal, 65,* 191–207.

Zucchermaglio, C., & Talamo, A. (2003). The development of a virtual community of practices using electronic mail and communicative genres. *Journal of Business and Technical Communication, 17,* 259–284.

Chapter 9 Contents

9

The Roles of Interpersonal Communication in Mass Media Campaigns

Brian G. Southwell and Marco C. Yzer
University of Minnesota

Communication scholarship has witnessed an explosion of disciplinary divisions and specific topic interest groups in the past 50 years that represents either noteworthy maturation or a troubling splintering, depending on your vantage point. As a result, important intersections remain for us to explore. In this review, we seek to highlight connections between interpersonal communication and mass media campaigns by identifying related streams of research that help us to explain how and why interpersonal talk and mass media efforts routinely affect each other. In doing so, we identify three general categories of roles of interpersonal communication: (planned or unintended) media campaign outcome, mediator of media campaign effects, and moderator of campaign effects.

The Roles of Interpersonal Communication in Mass
Media Campaigns

Half a century ago, Katz and Lazarsfeld's (1955) *Personal Influence* presaged the trajectory of late twentieth-century mass communication research and its move away from an assumption that mass media messages dictate people's behavior directly. In that frequently cited volume, they noted that information often does not flow from media outlets directly to audience members, but instead travels via intermediary opinion leaders. In doing so, they highlighted the importance of understanding interpersonal communication in order to grasp media effects.

In recent decades, a diverse array of scholars has continued to acknowledge that engagement with mass media does not occur in a vacuum free of interpersonal networks. Researchers voicing such a stance range from Katz and Lazarsfeld (1955) and other sociologists such as Wright (1986) to political scientists, such as Druckman and Nelson (2003), to critical theorists, such as Hagen and Wasko (2000), to health communication campaign evaluators (e.g., Hornik, 1989; Hornik et al., 2000; T. Korhonen, Uutela, H. Korhonen, & Puska, 1998). Despite this widespread acknowledgment, however, our discipline lacks a systematic review of the specific potential roles that interpersonal interaction can play with regard to mass media campaign effects.

We can attribute this gap in knowledge partially to a divide that has existed for decades between interpersonal communication researchers and those focused on mass media effects. In this chapter, we begin to bridge these areas of research by discussing the (potential and documented) roles of interpersonal communication in media effects that relate to strategic campaigns. While our ultimate attention concerns the impact of conversation for campaign efforts, we draw, by necessity, from a range of scholarship on human engagement with media content and the potential influence of talking with other people before, after, or during that process.

In order to accomplish these tasks, we begin by addressing fundamental questions about the nature of interpersonal communication, and we locate it in the past century's work on information flow among mass audiences. That discussion provides a foundation upon which we can explore three specific roles for interpersonal interaction: as an outcome of campaign effects, as a mediator of campaign effects, and as a moderator of campaign effects. We then highlight what we know about each of the roles that talk might play and about key limitations. We focus largely on issues related to media-based political advocacy, health promotion, and science communication because several keenly relevant and illustrative examples lay in those domains. At the same time, we also intend our discussion to be applicable to scholars studying mass communication, interpersonal communication, language and social interaction, organizational communication, public relations and advertising, and social networks.

Conceptualizing Interpersonal Communication and Mass Media Campaigns

Ultimately, we seek to bolster our understanding of why media campaigns experience varying degrees of success and the role of interpersonal communication in those efforts. To establish necessary foundation for that exploration, we start by clarifying key terms.

Interpersonal Communication

In their review of interpersonal communication research, Roloff and Anastasiou (2001) speculated that "interpersonal communication researchers will increasingly tie their scholarship to the significant issues facing society" (p. 65). By moving beyond assessment of isolated dyadic experience to place interpersonal communication in a larger context, researchers can acknowledge both the ways in which the environment affects such interaction and the ways in which understanding interpersonal communication can help illuminate macrolevel patterns of information flow.

Approximately two decades ago, however, Cappella (1987) noted the importance, and difficulty, of defining interpersonal interaction. Given the range of scholarly approaches to interpersonal communication, Roloff and Anastasiou (2001) acknowledged that "we are doubtful that there will ever be consensus about a definition of the field or a central theory" (p. 65). Indeed, in his more recent review of theorizing on interpersonal communication, Berger (2005) noted that "[i]t is possible to organize theoretical activity within the interpersonal communication domain into at least six distinct areas" (p. 417).

Because a complete exploration of the many orientations to interpersonal communication extends beyond the scope of this review, we focus here on two key characteristics of interpersonal communication that are most central to this chapter.[1] In particular, we suggest that interpersonal communication is consequential behavior and that it occurs in diverse contexts. (Admittedly, we also largely focus here on conversation between two people rather than the full array of phenomena that might fall under the heading of interpersonal communication.)

Interpersonal Communication as Consequential Behavior   According to Cappella (1987), interaction occurs when person A's trajectory of behavior is influenced by person B over and above the behavior that we would expect based on baseline data from person A. Although interpersonal communication can yield both intended and unintended outcomes, it necessarily involves mutually co-oriented participants and affects those participants' choices for subsequent actions (see foundational work by Watzlawick, Bavelas, & Jackson, 1967, as well as an excellent survey of this body of research in Knapp & Daly, 2002).

As such, conversation not only constitutes a mechanism for information repetition and exposure among participants, but it also comprises a relatively complex dyadic or group variable likely to be influenced by an array of factors that relate to human needs and desires and environmental constraints (e.g., Berger, 2002; Daly, 2002; Dillard, Anderson, & Knobloch, 2002; Poole, McPhee, Canary, &

Morr, 2002; Walther & Parks, 2002, as well as related review by Roloff & Anastasiou, 2001). Most importantly, we regard conversation not just as simple information delivery between people but rather as relationally and socially consequential behavior, albeit sometimes in response to evolving circumstances as conversations unfold (see related arguments by Berger, 2005). Moreover, those exchanges can happen in a variety of contexts.

An Array of Contexts for Interpersonal Communication   Although early research on interpersonal communication focused on face-to-face interaction (see Knapp, Daly, Albada, & Miller, 2002), many agree that interpersonal communication can occur in a variety of settings. In light of this idea, scholars have begun to explore similarities and differences among and between those communication contexts, as discussed later. Whether those differences matter for campaigns, however, is of central concern here.

With the dawn of the Internet, a number of scholars have investigated online communication (e.g., Baym, Zhang, & Lin, 2004; Herring, 1999; Price & Cappella, 2002; Price, Nir, & Cappella, 2006; Walther & Parks, 2002; Weger & Aakhus, 2003; see also discussion in review by Berger, 2005). For example, Duffy, Smith, Terhanian, and Bremer (2005) sought to elucidate differences between online and face-to-face survey data, and Matsuba (2006) distinguished between face-to-face and online relationships. That range of work suggests online communication itself is not monolithic and comprises several categories of interaction. Herring, for example, delineated between chat and more gradual sequences of bulletin board postings or e-mail exchanges.

Following her assessment of numerous chat streams, Herring (1999) also concluded that online chat, one example of online communication, is often incoherent and disjointed. Yet, Baym and colleagues (2004) reported that college students perceived Internet-based conversation as only slightly lower in quality than face-to-face interaction. Moreover, Papacharissi (2005) made a similar point in her review of online interaction scholarship, claiming that both online and face-to-face interactions reflect human needs and desires and thus are not necessarily distinct.

In light of these ideas, the question of whether the range of available interpersonal communication contexts matters merits empirical exploration, especially in terms of mass media effects. Available evidence suggests that both online and face-to-face interaction can affect outcomes that matter to mass communication scholars. For example, Price, Cappella, and Nir (2002) discovered that online dialogue conducted through a WebTV project appeared to facilitate opinion change, just as face-to-face discussion sometimes can. Hardy and Scheufele (2005) directly compared the effects of reported face-to-face discussion about politics and relevant computer-mediated interactions such as chat and found similar effects in both cases. As a result, it appears that we can now find conversation occurring between people in a variety of contexts and that many of these contexts might yield effects worthy for our consideration of how talk relates to media campaigns.

Mass Media   Defining mass media can involve a relatively simple exercise in listing types of information technologies (e.g., newspapers, radio, or television). Even in recent years, many introductory textbooks (e.g., Turow, 2003; Vivian, 2006) have continued to organize chapters in this way. Such categorization, however, has lost some of its utility in the face of contemporary blurring of boundaries between media types in terms of modes of information presentation and organizational ownership (see related arguments by Rayner, 2006). Bryant and Miron (2004) have observed:

> For example, (a) all of the media of mass communication are undergoing dramatic changes in form, content, and substance ... (b) newer forms of interactive media ... are altering the traditional mass communication model from that of communication of one-to-many to communication of many-to-many ... (c) media ownership patterns are shifting dramatically ... (d) the viewing patterns and habits of audiences worldwide are changing so rapidly to be almost mercurial. (p. 662)

Chaffee and Metzger (2001) openly asked recently whether we were witnessing the "end of mass communication" (p. 365). The answer to that question is not a definite yes. Instead, perhaps we are experiencing an explosion of alternatives and possibilities for mass media (see Rayner, 2006, and review by Rubin & Haridakis, 2001). Even the authors of Web logs, or blogs, typically seek to maintain a mass audience of sorts, though, of course, they do not often attain it (Lawson-Borders & Kirk, 2005). According to Rubin and Haridakis, "[N]ewer media have mass, interpersonal, organizational, political, economic, and cultural dimensions" (p. 73).

Whether we are witnessing the end of mass media organizations in general, then, is an open question. Economic considerations alone suggest that audiences will continue to be massive for the foreseeable future, even if they have decreased in size somewhat (Webster, Phalen, & Lichty, 2000). Moreover, if we consider mass communication from a functional perspective, as advocated by Wright (1986), mass media institutions will not likely fade for reasons of obsolescence (see review by Roessler, this volume). Mass media serve and address mass audiences, and that relationship will likely continue in some form, especially as available technology continues to evolve.

Mass Media Campaigns

Use of mass media for strategic campaigns boasts a history almost as long as the history of mass media technologies. This section situates campaigns as strategic enterprises that can address specific social issues.

Campaigns as Strategic Enterprises   As Paisley (1989) observed, the story of campaigns in the United States can be traced back to numerous examples in the eighteenth and nineteenth centuries. In fact, individuals were attempting to influence others' behavior through media messages even before 1776. In the 1720s, Cotton Mather attempted to promote inoculation during Boston's smallpox epidemic, in part through the distribution of pamphlets that highlighted the effectiveness of immunization. Later, in the nineteenth century, Paisley noted that a variety of social change organizations attempted to reach mass audiences through print media. The abolitionist movement, which sought to eliminate slavery, actively printed material intended to change beliefs and attitudes toward the practice and succeeded in that approach, incurring the wrath of protesters who destroyed printing facilities. Undoubtedly, such strategic use of media played an important role in shifting public opinion at the time.

Rogers and Storey (1987) noted that planners intend campaigns to generate specific outcomes or effects among a relatively large group of people through an organized set of communication activities, usually within a specific period of time. Such efforts are not the sole domain of advertisers. Public relations specialists, for example, conventionally conceptualize mass media campaigns as part of their work, for they perceive campaigns as time-limited efforts to present a limited set of messages intended to affect audience beliefs (see Coombs, 2001; Heath, 2001; Vasquez & Taylor, 2001). Whether promoting a corporate image (Pinkleton & Austin, 2006) or a non-profit agenda, such as that of Planned Parenthood (Bostdorff, 1992), public relations professionals have routinely conducted organized efforts in this vein.

Contemporary media campaigns have featured advertisements, public service announcements, and, more recently, Internet-based tools and other interactive digital applications. Trammell, Williams, Postelnicu, and Landreville (2006), for example, noted the rise of candidate Web sites and Web logs in political campaigns (see also Taylor, Kent, & White, 2001). In the health domain, interactive video comprises an increasingly popular campaign tool. Interactive video, in a sense, can take the form of an educational movie that allows an audience partially to control its part in that movie. Read and his colleagues (2006), for example, recently demonstrated that men potentially at risk for HIV infection reduced risky sexual behaviors after they participated in an interactive video intervention more than men who were not assigned to watch the treatment.

The Varied Foci of Media Campaigns   Media campaigns have been conducted around the globe in the past century for a variety of persuasive purposes. Examples include electoral campaigns in the world's democracies (Bolivar, 2001; Trent & Friedenberg, 2000) and efforts to organize populations for political action other than going to the polls, such as public opinion in the context of national referendums in the European Union (de Vreese & Semetko, 2004) or mobilization in the People's Republic of China in the second half of the twentieth century (Latham, 2000).

Yet another critical focus of campaigns concerns health outcomes, particularly those that result from risk behaviors associated with public health threats. Rogers and colleagues, for example, described at least two radio campaigns in Tanzania: the Mtu ni Afya ("Man Is Health") health literacy project in the early 1970s (Rogers & Storey, 1987) and the Twende na Wakati ("Let's Go With the Times") family planning project in the 1990s (Vaughan & Rogers, 2000). Hornik and colleagues (2000) reported on the National Youth Anti-Drug Media Campaign in the United States; Mudde and de Vries (1999) addressed a multimedia smoking cessation campaign in the Netherlands, and Wellings (2002) discussed mass media safer sex campaigns in Europe and noted six different countries where mass media campaigns contributed to increased condom use.

Wellings' (2002) analysis, in fact, reflects a critical explanation for the popularity of mass media campaigns. Organizations pay for campaigns based on their potential to foster obvious and consequential behavior change. At the same time, this contention has not been accepted universally, given a long-standing debate on the actual potential for campaigns to affect audiences in this way. In fact, during the last five decades, the prevailing view of the impact of campaigns has evolved from a so-called limited effects view to a period of renewed confidence in campaigns and, more recently, to a view of likely effects as moderate and nuanced (Maibach, 1993; Roberts & Maccoby, 1985; Wallack, 1990).

H. Mendelsohn (1973), for example, refuted skepticism about campaigns by observing that earlier studies did not find mass media campaign effects because, among other reasons, campaigns often did not target relevant factors, and evaluation research unrealistically attempted to demonstrate immediate, large, and direct campaign effects on behavior. Fifteen years later, Rogers and Storey (1987) fine-tuned Mendelsohn's contention by observing that many successful campaigns share an ability to induce interpersonal communication about the campaign topic, an intermediate outcome that, in turn, might affect behavioral outcomes. Here we see one of the many important connections between the interpersonal and campaign literatures relevant to our discussion.

Indeed, a number of scholars writing about strategic communication in recent years have drawn a connection to interpersonal scholarship. Based on their state of the discipline review of public relations scholarship, for example, Botan and Taylor (2004) argued that "[t]he most striking trend in public relations over the past 20 years ... is its transition from a functional perspective to a cocreational one" that emphasizes the role of publics in creating shared meaning (p. 651). They also argued that "public relations scholars have revisited interpersonal communication to understand relationship building better" (p. 652; see also Taylor et al., 2001; Vasquez & Taylor, 2001).

Moreover, such a general emphasis on the necessity of treating individuals as part of social groups and networks in order to understand media effects actually fits with a wide array of scholarship beyond campaign evaluation, including research on interpretive communities (e.g., Aden, Rahoi, & Beck, 1995; Fish, 1980; Lindlof, 1988). Lindlof, for example, argued that interpretation of media content is at least partly a function of community membership. Accordingly, campaign material interpretation might be a partial function of community interaction. How community members collectively engage a campaign might tell us much about the ultimate success of that effort. A better understanding of mass media campaign effects requires consideration of the relationship between interpersonal communication and the sharing (and co-construction) of information from media campaigns.

Interpersonal Communication and Information Flows

In this section, we discuss the roots of intersections between interpersonal communication and media effects. In that vein, we begin with a brief overview of the long history of investigation of talk as a vital part of the information flow process. We will not focus exclusively on campaign research in this section. Instead, we set the stage for our later discussion by exploring how sociologists, epidemiologists, and mass communication scholars have traced information spread.

The Two-Step Flow and Diffusion Research

Katz and Lazarsfeld (1955), unsurprisingly, offer an appropriate starting point in terms of scholarship, if not purely in terms of chronology. Drawing upon earlier speculation by Lazarsfeld, Berelson, and Gaudet (1944), Katz and Lazarsfeld asserted that interpersonal conversation mediates between the general broadcast of information and individual engagement of and action upon that information. Specifically, these researchers observed the pivotal role played by opinion leaders as individuals who both engage news and elite media sources and, in turn, dispense information from those sources to their networks of followers. Scholars subsequently extended the original notion of a two-step flow by pointing to the possibility of a multistep flow; however, the basic idea remains as a prominent account of media effects (see Brosius and Weimann, 1996, or Katz, 1987, for further discussion).

Following in the wake of this initial observation, one important strain of related scholarship has been work to model the spread of ideas among populations. A variety of scholars have applied the idea that information could be traced from media through various interpersonal pathways to a host of studies that might be characterized as diffusion research. One actually can trace the intellectual roots of most diffusion studies back much further than the Katz and Lazars-feld (1955) book. For example, early observations by Tarde (1903) at the end of the nineteenth century on imitation and the spread of ideas shed light on the notion that the social nature of humans and their tendency to converse offer a key route for information diffusion. In the early twentieth century, numerous examples emerged of information quickly spreading via interpersonal channels, including telephone conversations. For example, Scanlon (1998) noted how quickly news of the 1917 Halifax explosion spread across Canada, at least in part as telephone switchboards lit up.

Thinking about which channels promote information spread also predates *Personal Influence*. As DeFleur (1987) noted, several studies in the *American Sociological Review* in the 1940s and 1950s provided a complicated array of evidence on this issue. D. C. Miller (1945), for example, claimed that more than 90% of a college student population heard about the death of U.S. President Franklin D. Roosevelt within a half hour of official news reports, a phenomenon that he attributed to the quick spread of news through interpersonal channels. Somewhat contrasting evidence about channel roles, however, can be found in Larsen and Hill's (1954) study of how people in the U.S. state of Washington found out about the death of Ohio Senator Robert Taft. In the Taft case, individuals cited radio, rather than word of mouth, as their source of information.

As DeFleur (1987) observed, even this simple contrast suggested that the spread of ideas and information cannot be treated as a uniform phenomenon. Different contexts and circumstances likely contribute to diverse patterns of information spread, and individual-level variables also potentially play a role. Recognition of such complexity, in turn, inspired a generation of diffusion studies (e.g., DeFleur & Larsen, 1958; Rogers, 1962; Rosengren, 1973) that sought to go beyond simple documentation of information spread to understandings about who adopts innovative beliefs and how exactly certain innovations gain prominence after their initial introduction.

Rogers's (1962) famous volume, called simply *Diffusion of Innovations*, focused squarely on the question of whether individuals vary in their openness to new information. In that initial volume, Rogers answered that question affirmatively. He demonstrated individual-level variance in the time required for agricultural innovation adoption among individuals. In turn, he characterized people as being more or less likely to adopt particular innovations.

Later work on diffusion and, in some ways, even Rogers's later editions (1995 or 2003) have tended to focus less on characterizing individual receptivity, instead explicitly tracking information flow through social networks. Recently, Fan and Yu (2005) even questioned whether we need—and attempted to refute empirically—an assumption of individual difference in openness to new ideas in order to explain patterns of information spread. Milgram's (1967) study on the small-world phenomenon indicated that impressive information flows often involve only a limited number of communication agents. On a similar plane, Granovetter (1974) determined that important outcomes—for example, getting a job—more often occur through communication with other network members than through direct exposure to formal information sources. Such studies have fueled other research that has approached information flow from a perspective more akin to epidemiological studies of infection. For example, Valente (1995) emphasized the utility of understanding social networks for studying diffusion, a point emphasized in his recent collaborations (e.g., Schuster et al., 2006). We can expect information to spread most quickly when established social connections exist among members of a population.

Under some circumstances, social networks can even offer a powerful rival to media outlets. Rawan (2001) highlighted the example of Iran in the 1970s, where information crucial to the Iranian Revolution of 1979 spread largely through social networks connected to mosques rather than through electronic media channels controlled by the Shah regime. In fact, Rawan suggested that the Shah government may not have fully grasped the importance of such traditional and oral means of communication. More recently, in a piece on political information flow, de Vreese and Boomgaarden (2006) contended that interpersonal channels might matter more than media exposure for questions of opinion change among "politically sophisticated" individuals (p. 19).

Such ideas have penetrated the thinking of marketing research as well. Reingen and Kernan (1986) explored the importance of referral networks for marketing outcomes. Recent popular writing on the notions of viral marketing (Rosen, 2002) or "word-of-mouth epidemics" (Gladwell, 2000, p. 32) also clearly takes a cue from earlier scholarly thinking about the relevance of infection models for communication campaigns. The core message of such marketing tomes and popular commentary is that information spread might mimic other natural patterns, such as the spread of disease.

Clearly, then, thinking on diffusion has evolved to produce a range of studies. This research includes both studies of technological or behavioral innovation diffusion and of news diffusion, which DeFleur (1987) argued represent two distinct bodies of work. After all, the spread of a piece of information likely entails a simpler process than the widespread adoption of a behavior, a process undoubtedly underpinned by changes in knowledge and beliefs but nonetheless at least a step removed from simply hearing about a particular idea or news item.

Beyond Information Flow: Other Roles for Interpersonal Communication

Whether people largely learn new information about specialized topics from talking with other people in their social networks or they primarily seek information about topics so that they might talk with other people, of course, also remains an open question. Interpersonal communication is not always particularly informative per se. Sometimes it constitutes a ritualistic activity for which people undoubtedly draw upon information from media but through which people do not necessarily transmit and learn large volumes of completely new information. As such, pure diffusion notions do not sufficiently account for all conversations relevant to mediated information.

Eveland (2004) cautioned against assuming that interpersonal interaction always acts as a diffusion mechanism, suggesting that interpersonal communication can be related to key variables such as knowledge without necessarily serving as a link through which new information flows. In reviewing relevant political communication research (e.g., Lenart, 1994; Scheufele, 2002), Eveland noted at least three plausible explanations for the documented relationship between knowledge about politics and talk about politics: simple exposure (consistent with the aforementioned notion of a two-step flow), anticipatory elaboration, and discussion-generated elaboration. According to Eveland, a simple exposure explanation suggests that talking with a person exposes others to information to which that person has been exposed; one person passes information to the next. Elaboration explanations offer a somewhat different account of the process. In a situation of anticipatory elaboration, people are motivated to process political information from news content more deeply when they anticipate impending conversations with others. In slight contrast to anticipatory elaboration, Eveland argued that discussion-generated elaboration focuses on information processing at the actual time of the conversation in question.

Using data from U.S. election surveys, Eveland (2004) found the most support for the elaboration explanations, suggesting that people prepare for talk by elaborating on information and also that discussion itself encourages information elaboration. Anticipation of future conversations, as well as actual discussion with others, apparently can affect engagement with mass media. The simple exposure account, however, was largely not supported. While Eveland discovered a positive relationship between political discussion and political knowledge, he did not identify any additional boost in knowledge from speaking with a relatively knowledgeable partner.

Eveland's (2004) work does not suggest that the two-step flow account of the relationship of mass communication and interpersonal communication is not plausible under some circumstances, of course. Instead, it suggests that we need to take the nature of the discourse in question into account before estimating the potential for relevant interpersonal communication to act as a conduit for information and knowledge gain. Sometimes, anticipated interaction prompts media use and information seeking—as in the case in which individuals want to be prepared to talk with a relative with whom they always disagree politically—rather than acting as a source of new information.

With these distinctions in mind, we now turn our attention to the various roles that interpersonal communication might play with specific regard to media campaigns. In looking at organized efforts to use media to affect behavior, we argue that information diffusion comprises but one part of the picture. We need to understand how talk between individuals affects, and is affected by, campaign efforts to change or reinforce behavior.

Interpersonal Communication as an Outcome of Campaign Exposure

Is there a connection between media campaign exposure and people's tendency to talk to each other? When would we expect people to talk with others about what they have encountered while engaging media content? Why would people bother discussing media content in the first place?

These specific questions are not new. Roughly two decades ago, G. R. Miller (1986) noted "a neglected connection" (p. 132) between mass media exposure and interpersonal communication. Simply seeing a television advertisement will not always lead a person to talk with his or her friends about it, and yet we also know that people sometimes discuss such ads (e.g., Hornik & Yanovitzky, 2003), just as they interact with other media programming (e.g., Rogers et al., 1999). Sometimes, these instances are the intentional consequence of planned campaign efforts; in other cases, people share information that they have gleaned from media sources in ways that campaign staff might view as undesirable. Here we can ask what types of content generate talk and under what circumstances this happens.

Interpersonal Communication as a Planned Outcome

Direct-to-consumer advertising of prescription drugs (DTCA) provides a good example of campaigns that aim to induce conversation. Health insurance regulations in the United States have reduced patient voice in prescription decision making. As a result, DTCA campaigns in recent years have taken advantage of loosened requirements to directly urge patients to talk with their doctor in order to obtain the prescription for the advertised drug (Lyles, 2002). (Whether that effort is ethical or helpful for broader society, of course, remains an open question.)

In recent decades, a number of health promotion efforts also have attempted to engage social networks as a part of their strategies. Kelly et al. (1992) adapted the notion of opinion leaders to the realm of HIV prevention. For example, Kelly and colleagues found evidence that so-called popular people often served as vital network hubs in urban homosexual communities and thus assisted with the endorsement and spread of prevention skills information and risk information. By identifying and working directly with those opinion leaders rather than solely broadcasting messages, Kelly and others concluded that interpersonal communication can be an important tool. Moreover, their work suggests that some individuals might be more well connected to others and also more likely to talk actively with them about media content than their peers.

In many ways, such efforts extend aforementioned thinking about the diffusion of innovations. Singhal and colleagues (e.g., Singhal & Rogers, 2003; Svenkerud, Singhal, & Papa, 1998) have demonstrated the extent to which early enthusiasm for the diffusion of innovation approach has been translated in recent decades into health campaign efforts around the globe. Svenkerud et al., for example, offered a relevant review of efforts in Thailand to curb the spread of HIV/AIDS. They claimed that targeted social networks made a vital difference between relatively successful intervention efforts and less successful activities in Bangkok. Efforts to work with respected and influential housewives in Bangkok's Klong Toey neighborhoods appeared more effective than attempts to collaborate with motor-cycle taxi drivers. Both housewives and taxi drivers often spoke with other people, but housewives could be perceived as hubs in more well-established social networks. Moreover, Svenkerud et al. determined that housewives enjoyed greater reputations of credibility among their conversation partners than taxi drivers. As such, efforts to employ social networks for diffusion efforts cannot be treated as equal. We need to consider the context and nature of those networks in understanding the role of interpersonal communication in health promotion.

In addition to our earlier examples, a number of media-based strategic communication efforts have attempted to stimulate conversation as an outcome (e.g., Afifi et al., 2006; Hafstad & Aaro, 1997; Hornik et al., 2000; Piotrow, Kincaid, Rimon, & Rinehart, 1997; Rogers et al., 1999). The development of conversational skills has been an explicit goal of numerous media campaigns. According to Hornik et al., a major strategy of the U.S. Office of National Drug Control Policy's national media campaign against marijuana use in the late 1990s and early 2000s involved facilitating interactions between parents and their teenage children about drugs. In that case, campaign planners hoped to encourage parents who found themselves unmotivated to talk with their children about drugs or unsure of their ability to do so. Teaching people how to discuss sensitive topics has also been an explicit goal of many organ donation efforts. For example, Afifi and colleagues claimed that organized campaign efforts to prompt family discussion about organ donation could be improved by paying closer attention to the ways in which families seek and share information.

Reasons Why People Talk About Campaigns

Some of the extant research on mass media prompting of interaction suggests specific ways that such content can facilitate talk. Hafstad and Aaro (1997) documented an antismoking campaign in Norway that employed provocative, emotional appeals in order to stimulate conversation among adolescent viewers and their peers. According to Hafstad and Aaro, such efforts assume that people (and perhaps specifically adolescents) tend to tell their friends, family, and neighbors about particularly startling media content that they encounter to establish community boundaries and interpersonal bonding. Further, G. R. Miller (1986) proposed that media exposure might serve either to dampen or spur conversation by affecting conversational competency and providing fodder for dialogue.

Previous research suggests that motivations for conversation vary. To harness motivations for campaign purposes, we need frameworks with which to predict conversational occurrence. A functional view of interpersonal conversation as exchange between two or more people can guide our search for a general theory of circumstances in which talk should stem from media exposure. People talk with each other for a variety of specific reasons, ranging from strategic identity management to persuasion of others to simple task accomplishment (Berger, 1995; Seibold, Cantrill, & Meyers, 1985).

Strack and Deutsch (2004) noted in their exhaustive review that social behavior results from both reflective consideration (of beliefs about the behavior in question) and impulsive processes (that involve immediate spreading activation of readily available schemata in the brain in response to stimuli). Initiation of interpersonal communication, as a social behavior, sometimes will reflect reasoning about its utility (e.g., consideration of whether to ask someone to go to dinner) and other times simply constitute a reaction stemming from biological need (e.g., asking for food when desperately hungry).

With regard to reflective consideration, frameworks for understanding and predicting behavior such as Fishbein's (2000; see also Fishbein & Yzer, 2003) integrated model of behavior prediction, which builds upon the earlier theory of reasoned action (Fishbein & Ajzen, 1975; Ajzen & Fishbein, 1980) and theory of planned behavior (Ajzen, 1991) are useful. From this perspective, social behavior (such as interpersonal communication) ultimately extends from attitudinal, normative, and efficacy beliefs that people hold about performing that behavior. Campaign content might variously affect those beliefs and thus spur conversation.

Whether media campaign messages can sometimes act in such a manner, then, is a suitable topic for exploration here. Yzer, Siero, and Buunk's (2001) work on discussing condom use with a new partner offers relevant evidence in this regard. Importantly, Yzer and associates carefully distinguished the act of bringing up condom use with a partner from other behaviors, such as actual condom use. Moreover, after modeling such conversation as a function of intention and past behavior, they specifically highlighted the indirect role that conversational *norms*—or perceptions that important others value and condone talking about a particular topic—play in encouraging talk. Insofar as conversational norms are vulnerable to campaign efforts, such work allows us to assess the types of messages that might be most useful in facilitating conversation on this topic.

Perceived efficacy to engage in conversation comprises another factor relevant under this general framework. Experiencing some types of educational media content might boost one's own sense of topical understanding and conversational competency. By extension, if exposure raises a person's confidence (accurately or not) in their ability to understand and talk about a particular topic, then, all else being equal, we can expect that talk about that topic will be more likely to ensue, a claim for which Southwell and Torres (2006) found some recent support.

Southwell and Torres (2006) evaluated a media-based project specifically focused on bolstering conversational competence about science, engineering, technology, and mathematics. Experimental data from that study demonstrated that science news exposure can indirectly affect conversation about science by bolstering perceived understanding of science. Southwell and Torres recruited regular television news viewers from a midsize designated market area (a television viewing area) in the United States using random digit dialing and randomly assigned them to one of three science news exposure conditions. As hypothesized, science television news exposure appeared to boost perceived ability to understand science. In addition, perceived ability to understand science predicted conversations about science, suggesting that perceived understanding of science acts as a partial mediator of the relationship between media exposure and subsequent conversation about science and technology.

In short, then, we would expect interpersonal communication to stem from media exposure when that content affects perceptions of the personal utility and value of interacting with others on a topic or changes perceptions of one's conversational abilities. Media content might spur persons to learn more, empower them with information they feel compelled to share with others, loosen normative constraints on talking about taboo subjects, or even affect their perception that they can engage in conversation. At the same time, campaigns also might affect such perceptions in unintended fashion.

Unintended Talk About Campaign Content

People can talk about media campaign content in a way not intended by campaign planners. For example, Visser and Mirabile's (2004) work underscores the idea that diffusion-through-social-network approaches harbor important limitations and weaknesses. They demonstrated that communication between network members about attitude objects actually negatively impacted persuasion efforts. In attitudinally congruent networks (i.e., networks in which most members hold similar preexisting views), resistance to persuasion attempts was stronger than in attitudinally incongruent networks, suggesting that the strength of ties among network members may actually pose a barrier to campaign attempts in some cases.

Conversation in networks might help a person to assess his or her original opinion rather than simply to provide new information from a campaign (Festinger, 1950). To inform diffusion-through-social-network approaches more effectively, we need to better understand the circumstances under which individuals resist and respond adversely to the network majority (Visser & Mirabile, 2004), an opinion leader (Katz & Lazarsfeld, 1955), or referents who are not very influential network members (Granovetter, 1973).

David, Cappella, and Fishbein (2006) highlighted another prime example of how interpersonal communication can undermine campaign persuasion goals. David and colleagues studied interaction about campaign messages with an experimental design in which they assigned some participants to chat with other participants in an online chat forum following exposure to antidrug campaign advertisements. In this case, again, group discussion apparently functioned in a way not anticipated by campaign planners.

Participants assigned to talk with others actually reported attitudes and normative beliefs more strongly in favor of marijuana use than their counterparts who simply watched the ads. According to David et al. (2006), individuals most likely to process antidrug ads in a biased fashion also tended to speak up in group discussions. As a result, many of the comments in the group discussions favored drug use. Consequently, participants exposed to such discussions heard numerous prodrug viewpoints, a pattern that affected both attitudinal and normative perceptions. For example, individuals experimentally assigned to discuss the ads subsequently reported more normative pressure to use marijuana.

As David et al. (2006) discovered, discussion can, at times, be an uncooperative partner for campaign planners. Even if a campaign manages to generate conversation, campaign staff cannot guarantee that resulting talk will coincide with campaign goals, especially when recipients engage in biased processing of campaign materials. Regardless, we should consider alternative reactions to all campaigns, particularly those that intentionally strive to generate conversation.

In addition, a tangential but undoubtedly relevant area of research involves work on rumor or gossip. Research on rumors extends back at least to Allport and Postman's (1947) classic book, *The Psychology of Rumor*, in which they point to the perceived relevance and importance of a topic and the ambiguity of available information as predictors of the likelihood of a rumor spreading. Rosnow (1991, 2001) took this view further to suggest that people generate or spread rumors as a means of coping with anxiety or uncertainty. Rumors essentially constitute stories or embellishments that help to explain uncertain situations and provide a rationale for behavior. As Allport and Postman (1946/1947) observed in an early article in *Public Opinion Quarterly*, rumors can function to relieve urges, justify feelings, and explain circumstances. Walker and Gibbons (2006) recently reached a similar conclusion. As a result, we can predict that rumor creation and spread constitutes a relatively frequent phenomenon in human experience (see also Grey, this volume, for discussion of societal trauma).

Interpersonal communication about rumors can occur in face-to-face contexts, but, building on our earlier discussion, little reason exists to restrict our attention there. In fact, investigation of the spread of rumors on the Internet (e.g., Bordia & DiFonzo, 2004) represents an important new area of inquiry. One might even argue that the availability of the Internet has quickened the pace of rumor-mongering and extended the geographic reach of rumors to an extent that the spread of rumors now rivals resource-limited campaign efforts as an information source in some circumstances. Richardson (2005), writing about the global information environment in the wake of discovering severe acute respiratory syndrome (SARS) in Asia a few years ago, noted that the architecture of the Internet facilitated publication of a wild array of conspiracy theories and general hyperbole through newsgroups and blogs. According to Richardson, for a short period of time, official Web sites, such as that of the World Health Organization, were isolated hubs of balanced information amid a wider information environment awash in inaccurate information.

How might rumors be related to organized campaign efforts? In short, we might expect rumors to arise, and potentially to act as impediments, under certain conditions. The importance of ambiguity and uncertainty in the emergence and spread of rumors suggests that certain types of campaign efforts are particularly likely to be plagued. Specifically, instances in which campaign officials are unable or unwilling to provide key pieces of information seem ripe for rumor mongering. In the aforementioned SARS case documented by Richardson (2005), Chinese government officials could have moved more quickly to stem the rising tide of rumors. Scanlon (1977) also documented this phenomenon in his description of postdisaster rumor chains.

Disaster communication, then, in which officials use mass media to organize populations for evacuation or to communicate other public health and safety messages, is likely to be especially vulnerable (see Gale, 1987; Sood, Stockdale, & Rogers, 1987). The 2005 experience in the United States with Hurricane Katrina or the 2004 earthquake recovery efforts in south and southeastern Asia highlight the vital role that short-term communication campaigns could play if successfully implemented to move people and keep them away from certain harms. Such efforts nonetheless must contend with public discussion and interpretation as people hear official announcements and then seek to fill in the information gaps left open by the incomplete nature of those announcements.

Interpersonal Communication as Mediator of Campaign Effects

If campaigns can generate talk, for better or worse, then it also makes sense for us to consider the possibility that such conversations, in turn, can spur desired behaviors among audiences. If that is the case, we can consider conversations also to serve sometimes as a mediating link between campaign exposure and particular campaign goals. In light of that possibility, even if campaign planners do not explicitly attempt to generate talk, campaign evaluators should consider the potential role of interpersonal communication in explaining campaign effects, an argument largely consistent with recent prominent calls to reassess evaluation design (e.g., Hornik & Yanovitzky, 2003; Valente & Saba, 2001).

In simplest terms, interpersonal conversation can potentially extend necessary message reach and frequency—particularly important when advertising budgets are not spectacularly high. On a different plane, campaign-induced conversation might also lead to social norm discovery that indirectly leads to behavior change. We discuss support for both possibilities later, especially in the specific realm of health and science communication.

Parrott (2004) has gone so far as to suggest that the recent lack of focus on interpersonal communication as a potential explanation for outcomes represents an important oversight by health campaign scholars. Talk with others, after all, appears to be an important part of the array of channels claimed by individuals as influential with regard to science and health decision-making (Morton & Duck, 2001; O'Keefe, Ward, & Shepard, 2002; Trumbo, 1998; Wilkin & Ball-Rokeach, 2006). O'Keefe and colleagues, for example, found that landowners in Wisconsin tended to rely on a diverse set of information sources, sometimes including only conversation with other people who kept track of the news, in monitoring developments related to the local watershed. Wilkin and Ball-Rokeach found that Latinos in Los Angeles reported interpersonal networks of friends and family to be important sources of health information, along with health professionals and media content specifically designed for them. The question, however, is whether such dependence on interpersonal channels might be tapped to facilitate indirect campaign effects.

In proposing their model of health campaign effects in the context of illicit drug use, Hornik and Yanovitzky (2003) discussed at least two plausible ways in which conversation could serve as a mediator. Each of these paths pertains to the specific case of the antidrug campaign that they highlight and also more broadly to our general discussion. At the community level, Hornik and Yanovitzky pointed to the possibility of "social diffusion" of campaign messages (p. 215), paralleling the core ideas suggested by our earlier discussion of the two-step flow and diffusion traditions: Information plausibly flows from mass media through individuals and on to other individuals who interact with the initially exposed. In this way, interpersonal communication serves as an exposure bridge that facilitates exposure of a large part of community to key campaign messages.

At the same time, Hornik and Yanovitzky (2003) stressed another mediation possibility at the individual level by noting the possibility that campaign exposure might lead a person to talk with others about campaign messages and to discover normative support (or lack thereof, in an alternate case) for campaign-relevant behaviors. By acting as a conversational prompt, campaigns might lead individuals to find out that others support particular health behaviors more than they originally supposed and thus indirectly encourage behavior change.

Some recent empirical evidence from the health campaign literature coincides with this possibility. Valente and Saba (1998, 2001) assessed a mid-1990s contraceptive promotion campaign in Bolivia. They argued strongly in favor of acknowledging the role that social networks play in information diffusion. They also presented evidence from the Bolivian case that illustrates a positive link between media campaign exposure and change over time in perceptions that other people in particular social networks actually use contraceptives. This potential norm discovery or norm sensitization effect echoes Hornik and Yanovitzky's (2003) contentions. (Whether media exposure alone might be sufficient to boost perceptions of social norms or whether such exposure prompts actual conversations that, in turn, boost perceptions of relevant norms, of course, remain open questions, though the two possibilities also are not mutually exclusive.)

The possibility of a mediating role for interpersonal communication in explaining campaign effects holds important implications for the practice of campaign evaluation. Envisioning interpersonal communication as at least a partial mediator suggests that we need to track whether a campaign stimulates some of those exposed to converse with others about the campaign. In all likelihood, not all conversation partners receive direct messages from campaigns. Some learn about it through conversation.

Typical campaign evaluations, however, find a measure of exposure to the campaign and simply correlate it with outcome variables, such as knowledge, beliefs, and attitudes. Do and Kincaid

(2006), for example, looked at the relationship between viewing of an entertainment-education program, relevant knowledge, and health clinic visits in Bangladesh without explicit consideration of conversation. Researchers in such situations tend to classify those who were not exposed directly to the campaign (but who may have talked about it with others) as generally nonexposed to campaign messages; as a result, they likely underestimate the true effect of the campaign.

This trend might stem in part from the tendency of mass media campaign developers to concentrate on individual-level, psychological models of behavior change that tend to treat conversation only as a distal variable (DiClemente, Crosby, Sionean, & Holtgrave, 2004). Under such an approach, the role of interpersonal communication resembles demographic background variables or prior experience variables whose only impact is a function of individual belief change. Although useful for many campaign planning efforts, these approaches do not explicitly focus on the specific roles that it can play.

In the health communication domain, we have witnessed a promising trend toward theory-driven formative research to inform message design and campaign development (J. D. Fisher & W. A. Fisher, 2000; Parrott, Wilson, Buttram, Jones, & Steiner, 1999; Silk & Parrott, 2003). Based on social-psychological theories of behavior change, such research can identify the critical determinants of the recommended behavior in the particular target audience. According to behavior change theories, a campaign message more successfully improves behavior when it changes those critical determinants (Aggleton, 1997; Fishbein & Yzer, 2003; J. D. Fisher & W. A. Fisher, 1992; Flay & Burton, 1990). Although encouraging, the trend toward focusing on behavioral theory for campaign development nonetheless comes at a cost. Theories of health behavior change can usefully be applied to informing message content, but they were not designed to specify the exact communication vehicles that bring about change. As a result, mass media campaigns and evaluation research of these campaigns typically do not consider unofficial communication channels, such as conversation, as relevant to track in order to explain how information spreads as a function of a planned mass media campaign (see Yzer & van den Putte, 2006, for relevant discussion).

In other words, thinking of interpersonal communication as a mediator implies that campaign effects can be indirect, and failure to model conversation in evaluation analyses restricts one's ability to demonstrate those indirect effects adequately. Conversely, accepting a possible mediating role for conversation might better reveal actual campaign effects. It also should move planners beyond thinking solely in terms of maximizing direct exposure to a campaign.

Interpersonal Communication as Moderator of Campaign Effects

Not all mass communication researchers conceptualize interpersonal conversation solely as a simple outcome or as a conduit of information from media to individuals. Following Chaffee (1986), for example, some researchers (e.g., Eveland, 2004, or Tsfati, 2003) have explored whether interpersonal communication might offer a competing channel of information, as we noted above, or even might act in an amplifying (rather than directly mediating) fashion in political or civic contexts. In a political communication example, M. Mendelsohn (1996) found that Canadian voters were primed by election campaign materials to evaluate candidates in terms of overall leadership perceptions, whereas interpersonal conversation tended to activate thinking about salient issues. Voter engagement with mass media not only led to simple information exposure differences, but it also apparently posed consequences for subsequent information processing different from those of interpersonal conversations. In other words, interpersonal channels performed differently than mass media channels and demonstrated the potential to interact with other types of information seeking and exposure to jointly affect issue evaluation.

In some of these studies, in contrast to most diffusion approaches, scholars argue that conversation can facilitate, amplify, or dampen campaign effects. For example, Druckman (2004) questioned whether political campaigns and interpersonal discussions might sometimes prime alternative or orthogonal criteria for candidate judgment. In this way, the absence of competing talk might be viewed as a facilitating condition for media effects while the presence of consonant talk might also boost effects.

In recent years, a number of scholars have built on these studies to explore the possibility that interpersonal communication actually moderates media effects (e.g., Druckman, 2004; Hardy & Scheufele, 2005; Southwell, 2005; van den Putte, Southwell, & Yzer, 2006). Based on this research, talk could facilitate or hamper media effect outcomes in at least two key ways: memory and behavior change. When might such moderation matter? This possibility seems particularly acute with regard to any topic likely to enjoy relatively uneven levels of discussion across general populations. Some people likely talk about politics more than others, for example. Insofar as some groups talk about a topic a lot and others do not, any conception of related mass media effects as uniform phenomena should be tempered by the potential moderating influence of widely varying conversational networks.

Interpersonal Communication, Media, and Memory

A growing literature on the relationships between conversation and memory (e.g., Dickinson & Givón, 1997; Edwards & Middleton, 1987; Southwell, 2005) suggests that people do not accept and store information directly from media outlets and then simply retrieve that information later in unmitigated fashion. The presence or absence of conversation about a topic around the water cooler or the dinner table or the chat room might augment or affect the degree to which people report remembering any information about the topic initially encoded from mass media exposure.

Why should conversation matter with regard to memory? Theoretically, memory comprises a complex of subsystems vulnerable to a variety of influences (Bower, 2000). We can, and should, view memory as encompassing at least the act of encoding and the dynamics of information retrieval. Retrieval, in turn, offers a prime site for the influence of conversation.

Fuster (1999) offered a useful overview of the retrieval process. While we know that the general concept of memory might better be categorized in terms of different variant tasks such as recognition or recall, some basic ideas about retrieval appear to be valid for memory as a whole. Primarily, retrieval almost never results in a perfectly efficient procurement of a single representation. Instead, a retrieval-prompting stimulus, such as an element of a conversation with another person, invites remembering an array of related thoughts. As Fuster succinctly noted, "[t]hat stimulus, in a broad sense, is like the hand in the basket that picks out one cherry and makes others follow" (p. 199).

This metaphorical perspective parallels network models of memory (see Anderson, 1983, 1990, for discussion), which posit that people share and access information in the brain through activation of interconnected neural nodes. That architecture of nodes, in turn, allows for spillover activation. As Anderson's work highlights, activation of one specific node also will enhance the salience of related information in adjacent nodes.

With these perspectives in mind, we logically can expect that interpersonal communication should arouse related representations of media content that have been previously encoded and formed in the brain. Extending from research on the brain, this notion poses direct implications for our view of campaign audiences. Rather than seeing them as stand-alone addresses for information delivery and encoding, we should view people who engage media content as being interconnected pieces of a larger community that, in turn, might need to be addressed as a whole because of the potential for interpersonal exchange to impact campaign message reception.

For example, general conversation about the specific public health dangers of hurricanes, flooding, or earthquakes could reinforce or amplify memory for connected material gleaned from mass media reports on those topics. Interpersonal communication about the actual media content in question could also reinforce memory for that content. Robinson and Davis (1990), for example, surmised that conversation about news stories may facilitate the long-term storage and retrieval of information from those stories.

Southwell (2005) recently revealed an impact of conversation on memory for advertisements from a health communication campaign by demonstrating a cross-level interaction between the amount of relevant conversation in a respondent's environment and the sheer prevalence of an advertisement in explaining recognition memory for that advertisement. In general, Southwell found a positive relationship between the frequency of an antidrug advertisement on television and the degree that people later remembered viewing that advertisement. The extent to which advertisement prevalence translated into memory, however, depended on the existence of social networks rich in conversation about drugs. People who often engaged in relevant conversation about drugs also tended to be those who later remembered prevalent campaign advertisements.

On a different plane, Druckman (2004) discovered that campaign priming effects in a U.S. Senate election relied upon reinforcement from interpersonal communication. Media campaign emphasis on Social Security and integrity apparently had the strongest priming effect on those who also experienced reinforcement from discussions about the campaign. Such a finding underscores the need for political campaigns to be evaluated with this contextual interaction in mind. We may need to curb our expectations of impact for those campaigns that do not enjoy the presence of supportive social networks to reinforce effects.

The Southwell (2005) and Druckman (2004) studies also point out the difficulty of teasing out such moderating effects empirically. Both studies are noteworthy for their potential external generalizability, as neither relies solely on laboratory results. Each study reports data from actual campaign experiences, lessening their vulnerability to criticism about the contrived nature of effects often lodged at experimental work. Because of the uncontrolled setting of each, however, more work remains to be done to identify the exact mechanisms at play in producing these interactions. Future work could combine experimental design with realistic contexts to further investigate how talk moderates memory effects.

Interpersonal Communication, Media, and Behavior

What about behavior change? Is it conceivable that interpersonal talk could affect the relationship between media exposure and behavior? Recent work by Scheufele and colleagues begins to address this question, at least with regard to political participation. Scheufele (2001, 2002; see also Hardy & Scheufele, 2005) argued that citizens experience differential gains from media content related to politics and civic engagement as a function of their interpersonal interaction patterns. In other words, he asserted—and found some evidence to suggest—that interpersonal communication moderates the relationship between mass media exposure and political behavior. Such discussion ostensibly provides motive, incentive, and skills to discern the information from media reports necessary to mobilize and to act upon media messages.

These claims, while consistent with evidence gathered to date, also call for further clarification. Perhaps the moderation occurs at the point of information processing and retention rather than somewhere more proximal to intention formation and behavioral performance. In that way, such results might be more consonant with the memory-related interaction noted earlier than with true moderation of direct campaign effects on behavior per se. As Hardy and Scheufele (2005) contended, people might process media-based information more carefully because of anticipated conversation or be better able to engage and encode information because of knowledge structures developed through past conversation.

Caveats and Future Directions

To this point in our discussion, we have largely dealt with interpersonal communication as a monolithic entity, as though it was a uniform resource that might affect media campaign results in a dose–effect manner. Such an assumption, while convenient for summary discussion, surely is limited; interpersonal communication researchers will readily observe that much more nuance exists to discuss. As Cappella (1985) noted, conversations are exceptionally complex phenomena, consisting of behaviors, stimuli, and perceptions. We also know that interpersonal interactions vary in quality and type, just as social networks vary in size and other characteristics.

Characterizing Conversations

How might interpersonal communications differ in theoretically important ways beyond their simple existence or absence? If conversation acts as a mediator, functioning as a link between campaign exposure in a community and behavior change, then the degree of direct replication of media content in conversation could be an important factor in judging the likely impact of a conversation. If conversation serves as a moderator, affecting the nature of relationships between exposure and belief and behavior outcomes, then general topic consonance between conversation and media messages (regardless of whether people employ specific information from the campaign in discussions) might be sufficient under some circumstances to produce, for example, memory amplification effects. What other conversation variables might matter?

To date, of the various researchers working at the intersection of interpersonal communication, mass media, and campaign outcomes, political communication scholars have been perhaps the most active in attempting to assess relevant quality or content differences in conversation. Some scholars have attempted to code conversations for logical coherence (Herring, 1999) or deliberativeness (Dahlberg, 2001; Graham & Witschge, 2003; Stromer-Galley & LeBret, 2005). Graham and Witschge, for example, used textual analysis to assess whether Internet forums meet the criteria of critical debate, reciprocity, and reflexivity. That tendency to assess conversation's quality is understandable, given the centrality of concepts such as deliberation and opinion heterogeneity for theorists who care about democratic systems.

We also might assess interpersonal communication in terms of agreement or disagreement between participants (Visser & Mirabile, 2004). Disagreement (either on the part of an audience member in response to something he or she encountered via mass media or between two or more viewers subsequent to watching, reading, or listening) might well influence how individuals interpret messages relevant to a media campaign. Price et al. (2002) highlighted the potential role of disagreement for actually improving the deliberative nature of opinion among group members. On a different plane, exposure to conversational disagreement or to a partner who expresses views that conflict with his or her own also might provide the sort of inoculation against later media campaign persuasion attempts discussed by Pfau and colleagues (e.g., Godbold & Pfau, 2000; Pfau et al., 2003), although Visser and Mirabile (2004) also demonstrated that social network agreement can increase resistance to persuasion. Overall, the content of talk between conversational partners may affect the impact that interpersonal communication can have relative to media exposure. We need more work in this vein.

Measuring Conversation

The preceding comments on the character of interpersonal communication directly relate to thinking about measurement issues. A review of mass communication research that addresses interpersonal communication illustrates that researchers often conceptualize it in terms of simple self-report (e.g., de Vreese & Boomgaarden, 2006; O'Keefe et al., 2002; Southwell, 2005; van den Putte, Yzer, & Brunsting, 2005). Such self-reported interpersonal communication typically refers solely to whether or not interaction occurred. For example, van den Putte and colleagues asked participants in their panel study about the extent to which they spoke with others about smoking cessation education campaigns. In that study, participants wanted to quit more if they engaged in such conversations. Insofar as we are concerned with simple mediating effects in which interpersonal communication extends campaign reach or simple moderating effects in which any relevant conversation amplifies individual retrieval ability for campaign messages, such measures are likely adequate, if imperfect.

We should note limitations of such measures, however. When used in simple cross-sectional settings, they technically risk confounding memory (and all of its complications) and actual past behavior. Even when researchers use questions that include time-frame references or conduct time-order analyses, self-report measures have limits. For example, consistent with our earlier discussion, self-report measures alone typically do not sufficiently assess the character or nature of the conversation. Because the content of the conversation can vary in its consistency with campaign goals, we need to go further to develop conversation content measures in some circumstances.

Self-report measures of interpersonal communication can assess the (remembered) overall valence of past relevant interaction, though often campaign researchers who do measure interpersonal communication focus on talk that is supportive of the campaign or assume that any talk about the campaign would be supportive. The effects that van den Putte and colleagues (2005) found, for example, likely reflect the prevalence of conversations that, for the most part, supported smoking cessation; if the content of such conversations had been mixed or largely counter to campaign goals, they likely would not have demonstrated such a relationship, as the David et al. (2006) study suggests.

A different approach is to focus on measuring the quality of conversations, which can manifest itself as, for example, disruption (Leathers, 1969) and other normative pressure by conversational partners (David et al., 2006), conversational competence (Ellis, Duran & Kelly, 1994), or compliance with majority positions (Price et al., 2006; Visser & Mirabile, 2004). Researchers tapping conversational content and quality often have employed direct observation more than self-report measures. Typically, researchers log conversational entries, describe observed processes, and submit those data to a content analysis (e.g., Price et al., 2006).

Some might argue that such extensive measurement may not be practical for many formal mass media campaign evaluations in which conversations often cannot be readily observed among mass audiences. As we discussed earlier, however, technological advancements have changed conversation from strictly face-to-face oral exchanges to possibilities for interpersonal engagement across a range of modalities, including digital conversation (e.g., Price et al., 2006). It seems then that new media technologies actually are a boon in this regard, as they offer at least some possibilities for large-scale direct observational measurement (see Donath, Karahalios, & Viégas, 1999). For investigation of the full range of effects that we have proposed in this overview, then, we need to continue to explore these possibilities.

Conclusions

Interpersonal communication likely plays a series of insufficiently appreciated and important roles in media campaign effects. Based on theory and evidence, it could be a noteworthy outcome, act as a mediator of campaign effects, or either reinforce or dampen campaign effects. While we can expect interpersonal communication to be a regular part of the campaign audience landscape, we probably cannot expect it always to be an ally for campaign efforts.

We have much to learn about these roles, however. Future work should investigate the circumstances in which interpersonal communication is most powerful and determine appropriate variables regarding interpersonal communication and media campaigns, such as the extent of disagreement or topical consonance with campaign content, that matter in this arena. Moreover, we might be able to improve our understanding of these dynamics with improved measurement possibilities that move beyond self-report items. In addition, confirmation of these dynamics in contexts around the globe will be worthwhile.

Nonetheless, by explicating an array of roles for interpersonal communication in the context of campaigns, we hope to have outlined some new avenues for campaign evaluation. At a minimum, we should be able to assess effects more exhaustively with this framework by emphasizing important interaction possibilities and potential indirect effects. At the same time, this review also should serve as a call for greater collaboration between researchers (such as interpersonal and mass communication scholars) who typically do not view themselves as inhabiting the same terrain. Moreover, numerous groups of relevant researchers (in areas such as social psychology, organizational behavior, and public relations) should join this scholarly discussion. Collectively invoking conversation as a variable will not offer any of those researchers a universal panacea in the search for campaign effects, but including the concept in campaign research undoubtedly will enrich our theoretical understanding of when and how campaigns work.

Notes

1. We acknowledge the many diverse traditions in interpersonal communication research. The space and scope of this chapter restricted our ability to offer an overview of the many references relevant to those traditions. For more complete reviews, please see Berger (2005), Knapp and Daly (2002), or Roloff and Anastasiou (2001).

References

Aden, R. C., Rahoi, R. L., & Beck, C. S. (1995). "Dreams are born on places like this": The process of community formation at the *Field of Dreams* site. *Communication Quarterly, 43,* 368–380.

Afifi, W. A., Morgan, S. E., Stephenson, M. T., Morse, C., Harrison, T., Reichert, T., et al. (2006). Examining the decision to talk with family about organ donation: Applying the theory of motivated information management. *Communication Monographs, 73,* 188–215.

Aggleton, P. (1997). Behavior change communication strategies. *AIDS Education and Prevention, 9,* 111–123.

Ajzen, I. (1991). The theory of planned behavior. *Organizational Behavior and Human Decision Processes, 50,* 179–211.

Ajzen, I., & Fishbein, M. (1980). *Understanding attitudes and predicting social behavior.* Englewood Cliffs, NJ: Prentice Hall.

Allport, G. W., & Postman, L. J. (1946/1947). An analysis of rumor. *Public Opinion Quarterly, 10,* 501–517.

Allport, G. W., & Postman, L. J. (1947). *The psychology of rumor.* New York: Holt, Rinehart & Winston.

Anderson, J. R. (1983). *The architecture of cognition.* Cambridge, MA: Harvard University Press.

Anderson, J. R. (1990). *Cognitive psychology and its implications* (3rd ed.). New York: W. H. Freeman.

Baym, N. K., Zhang, Y. B., & Lin, M.-C. (2004). Social interactions across media: Interpersonal communication on the Internet, telephone, and face-to-face *New Media & Society, 6,* 299–318.

Berger, C. R. (1995). Inscrutable goals, uncertain plans, and the production of communicative action. In C. R. Berger & M. Burgoon (Eds.), *Communication and social influence processes* (pp. 1–28). East Lansing: Michigan State University Press.

Berger, C. R. (2002). Goals and knowledge structures in social interaction. In M. L. Knapp & J. A. Daly (Eds.), *Handbook of interpersonal communication* (3rd ed., pp. 181–212). Thousand Oaks, CA: Sage.

Berger, C. R. (2005). Interpersonal communication: Theoretical perspectives, future prospects. *Journal of Communication, 55,* 415–447.

Bolivar, A. (2001). Changes in Venezuelan political dialogue: The role of advertising during electoral campaigns. *Discourse & Society, 12,* 23–45.

Bordia, P., & DiFonzo, N. (2004). Problem solving in social interactions on the Internet: Rumor as social cognition. *Social Psychology Quarterly, 67,* 33–49.

Bostdorff, D. M. (1992). "The Decision Is Yours" campaign: Planned Parenthood's characteristic argument of moral virtue. In E. L. Toth & R. L. Heath (Eds.), *Rhetorical and critical approaches to public relations* (pp. 301–313). Hillsdale, NJ: Lawrence Erlbaum Associates.

Botan, C. H., & Taylor, M. (2004). Public relations: State of the field. *Journal of Communication, 54,* 645–661.

Bower, G. H. (2000). A brief history of memory research. In E. Tulving & F. I. M. Craik (Eds.), *The Oxford handbook of memory* (pp. 3–32). New York: Oxford University Press.

Brosius, H. B., & Weimann, G. (1996). Who sets the agenda? Agenda-setting as two-step flow. *Communication Research, 23,* 561–580.

Bryant, J., & Miron, D. (2004). Theory and research in mass communication. *Journal of Communication, 54,* 662–704.

Cappella, J. N. (1985). The management of conversations. In M. L. Knapp, & G. R. Miller (Eds.), *Handbook of interpersonal communication* (pp. 393–438). Beverly Hills, CA.: Sage.

Cappella, J. N. (1987). Interpersonal communication: Definitions and fundamental questions. In C. R. Berger & S. H. Chaffee (Eds.), *Handbook of communication science* (pp. 184–238). Newbury Park, CA: Sage.

Chaffee, S. H. (1986). Mass media and interpersonal channels: Competitive, convergent, or complementary? In G. Gumpert & R. Cathcart (Eds.), *Inter/media: Interpersonal communication in a media world* (pp. 62–80). New York: Oxford University Press.

Chaffee, S. H., & Metzger, M. J. (2001). The end of mass communication? *Mass Communication & Society, 4,* 365–379.

Coombs, W. T. (2001). Interpersonal communication and public relations. In R. L. Heath (Ed.), *Handbook of public relations* (pp. 105–114). Thousand Oaks, CA: Sage.

Dahlberg, L. (2001). The Internet and democratic discourse: Exploring the prospects of online deliberative forums extending the public sphere. *Information, Communication, and Society, 4*, 615–633.

Daly, J. A. (2002). Personality and interpersonal communication. In M. L. Knapp & J. A. Daly (Eds.), *Handbook of interpersonal communication* (3rd ed., pp. 133–180). Thousand Oaks, CA: Sage.

David, C., Cappella, J. N., & Fishbein, M. (2006). The social diffusion of influence among adolescents: Group interaction in a chat room environment about anti-drug advertisements. *Communication Theory, 26*, 118–140.

DeFleur, M. L. (1987). The growth and decline of research on the diffusion of news, 1945–1985. *Communication Research, 14*, 109–130.

DeFleur, M. L., & Larsen, O. N. (1958). *The flow of information.* New York: Harper & Brothers.

de Vreese, C. H., & Boomgaarden, H. G. (2006). Media message flows and interpersonal communication: The conditional nature of effects on public opinion. *Communication Research, 33*, 19–37.

de Vreese, C. H., & Semetko, H. A. (2004). *Political campaigning in referendums: Framing the referendum issue.* London: Routledge.

Dickinson, C., & Givón, T. (1997). Memory and conversation: Toward an experimental paradigm. In T. Givón (Ed.), *Conversation: Cognitive, communicative, and social perspectives* (pp. 91–132). Amsterdam: John Benjamins.

DiClemente, R. J., Crosby, R. A., Sionean, C., & Holtgrave, D. (2004). Community intervention trials: Theoretical and methodological considerations. In D. S. Blumenthal & R. J. DiClemente (Eds.), *Community-based health research: Issues and methods* (pp. 171–197). New York: Springer Publishing Company.

Dillard, J. P., Anderson, J. W., & Knobloch, L. K. (2002). Interpersonal influence. In M. L. Knapp & J. A. Daly (Eds.), *Handbook of interpersonal communication* (3rd ed., pp. 423–474). Thousand Oaks, CA: Sage.

Do, M. P., and Kincaid, D. L. (2006). Impact of an entertainment-education television drama on health knowledge and behavior in Bangladesh: An application of propensity score matching. *Journal of Health Communication, 11*, 301–325.

Donath, J., Karahalios, K., and Viégas, F. (1999). Visualizing conversation. *Journal of Computer-Mediated Communication, 4*(4). Retrieved July 28, 2006, from http://jcmc.indiana.edu/vol4/issue4/donath.html

Druckman, J. N. (2004). Priming the vote: Campaign effects in a U.S. Senate election. *Political Psychology, 25*, 577–594.

Druckman, J. N., & Nelson, K. R. (2003). Framing and deliberation: How citizens' conversations limit elite influence. *American Journal of Political Science, 47*, 729–745.

Duffy, B., Smith, K., Terhanian, G., & Bremer, J. (2005). Comparing data from online and face-to-face surveys. *International Journal of Market Research, 47,* 615–639.

Edwards, D., & Middleton, D. (1987). Conversation and remembering: Bartlett revisited. *Applied Cognitive Psychology, 1,* 77–92.

Ellis, D. G., Duran, R. L., & Kelly, L. (1994). Discourse strategies of competent communicators: Selected cohesive and linguistic devices. *Research on Language and Social Interaction, 27,* 145–170.

Eveland, W. P. (2004). The effect of political discussion in producing informed citizens: The roles of information, motivation, and elaboration. *Political Communication, 21,* 177–193.

Fan, D. P., & Yu, H. (2005, November) *A unified model for the diffusion of innovations, mass media effects, and the spiral of silence within the contexts of social networks and paradigms.* Paper presented at the annual meeting of the Midwest Association of Public Opinion Research, Chicago.

Festinger, L. (1950). Informal social communication. *Psychological Review, 14,* 271–282.

Fish, S. (1980). *Is there a text in this class? The authority of interpretive communities.* Cambridge, MA: Harvard University Press.

Fishbein, M. (2000). The role of theory in HIV prevention. *AIDS Care, 12,* 273–278.

Fishbein, M., & Ajzen, I. (1975). *Belief, attitude, intention, and behavior: An introduction to theory and research.* Reading, MA: Addison–Wesley.

Fishbein, M., & Yzer, M. C. (2003). Using theory to develop effective health behavior interventions. *Communication Theory, 13,* 164–183.

Fisher, J. D., & Fisher, W. A. (1992). Changing AIDS risk behavior. *Psychological Bulletin, 111,* 455–474.

Fisher, J. D., & Fisher, W. A. (2000). Theoretical approaches to individual level change in HIV-risk behavior. In J. Peterson & R. DiClemente (Eds.), *Handbook of HIV prevention* (pp. 3–55). New York: Plenum.

Flay, B. R., & Burton, D. (1990). Effective mass communication strategies for health campaigns. In C. Atkin & L. Wallack (Eds.), *Mass communication and public health: Complexities and conflicts* (pp. 129–146). Newbury Park, CA: Sage.

Fuster, J. M. (1999). *Memory in the cerebral cortex: An empirical approach to neural networks in the human and nonhuman primate.* Cambridge, MA: The MIT Press.

Gale, R. P. (1987). Calculating risk: Radiation and Chernobyl. *Journal of Communication, 37,* 68–79.

Gladwell, M. (2000). *The tipping point: How little things can make a big difference.* New York: Little, Brown and Company.

Godbold, L. C., & Pfau, M. (2000). Conferring resistance to peer pressure among adolescents: Using inoculation theory to discourage alcohol use. *Communication Research, 27,* 411–437.

Graham, T., & Witschge, T. (2003). In search of online deliberation: Towards a new method for examining the quality of online discussions. *Communications, 28,* 173–204.

Granovetter, M. (1973). The strength of weak ties. *American Journal of Sociology, 78,* 1360–1380.

Granovetter, M. (1974). *Getting a job: A study of contacts and careers.* Cambridge, MA: Harvard University Press.

Grey, S. (2007). Wounds not easily healed: Exploring trauma in communication studies. In C. S. Beck (Ed.), *Communication yearbook 31* (pp. 173–222). New York, NY: Lawrence Erlbaum Associates.

Hafstad, A., & Aaro, L. E. (1997). Activating interpersonal influence through provocative appeals: Evaluation of a mass media-based antismoking campaign targeting adolescents. *Health Communication, 9,* 253–272.

Hagen, I., & Wasko, J. (2000). Introduction. In I. Hagen & J. Wasko (Eds.), *Consuming audiences? Production and reception in media research* (pp. 3–28). Cresskill, NJ: Hampton Press.

Hardy, B. W., & Scheufele, D. A. (2005). Examining differential gains from Internet use: Comparing the moderating role of talk and online interactions. *Journal of Communication, 55,* 71–84.

Heath, R. L. (Ed.) (2001). *Handbook of public relations.* Thousand Oaks, CA: Sage.

Herring, S. (1999). Interactional coherence in CMC. *Journal of Computer-Mediated Communication, 4*(4). Retrieved July 28, 2006, from http://jcmc.indiana.edu/vol4/issue4/herring.html

Hornik, R. (1989). The knowledge–behavior gap in public information campaigns: A development communication view. In C. T. Salmon (Ed.), *Information campaigns: Balancing social values and social change* (pp. 113–138). Newbury Park, CA: Sage.

Hornik, R., Maklan, D., Cadell, D., Judkins, D., Sayeed, S., Zador, P., et al. (2000). *Evaluation of the National Youth Anti-Drug Media Campaign: Campaign exposure and baseline measurement of correlates of illicit drug use from November 1999 through May 2000.* Bethesda, MD: National Institute on Drug Abuse.

Hornik, R., & Yanovitzky, I. (2003). Using theory to design evaluations of communication campaigns: The case of the National Youth Anti-Drug Media Campaign. *Communication Theory, 13,* 204–224.

Katz, E. (1987). Communications research since Lazarsfeld. *Public Opinion Quarterly, 51,* s25–s45.

Katz, E., & Lazarsfeld, P. F. (1955). *Personal influence.* Glencoe, IL: Free Press.

Kelly, J. A., St. Lawrence, J. S., Stevenson, L.Y., Hauth, A.C., Kalichman, S.C., Diaz, Y.E., et al. (1992). Community AIDS/HIV risk reduction: The effects of endorsements by popular people in three cities. *American Journal of Public Health, 82,* 1483–1489.

Knapp, M. L., & Daly, J. A. (Eds.). (2002). *Handbook of interpersonal communication* (2nd ed.). Thousand Oaks, CA: Sage.

Knapp, M. L., Daly, J. A., Albada, K. F., & Miller, G. R. (2002). Background and current trends in the study of interpersonal communication. In M. L. Knapp & J. A. Daly (Eds.), *Handbook of interpersonal communication* (3rd ed., pp. 3–20).Thousand Oaks, CA: Sage.

Korhonen, T., Uutela, A., Korhonen, H., & Puska, P. (1998). Impact of mass media and interpersonal health communication on smoking cessation attempts: A study in North Karelia, 1989–1996. *Journal of Health Communication, 3,* 105–118.

Larsen, O. N., & Hill, R. J. (1954). Mass media and interpersonal communication in the diffusion of a news event. *American Sociological Review, 19,* 426–433.

Latham, K. (2000). Nothing but the truth: News media, power and hegemony in South China. *The China Quarterly, 163,* 633–654.

Lawson-Borders, G., & Kirk, R. (2005). Blogs in campaign communication. *American Behavioral Scientist, 49,* 548–559.

Lazarsfeld, P. F., Berelson, B., & Gaudet, H. (1944). *The people's choice: How the voter makes up his mind in a presidential campaign.* New York: Columbia University Press.

Leathers, D. G. (1969). Process disruption and measurement in small group communication. *Quarterly Journal of Speech, 55,* 287–301.

Lenart, S. (1994). *Shaping political attitudes: The impact of interpersonal communication and mass media.* Thousand Oaks, CA: Sage.

Lindlof, T. R. (1988). Media audiences as interpretive communities. In J. A. Anderson (Ed.), *Communication yearbook 11* (pp. 81–107). Thousand Oaks, CA: Sage.

Lyles, A. (2002). Direct marketing of pharmaceuticals to consumers. *American Review of Public Health, 23,* 73–91.

Maibach, E. (1993). Social marketing for the environment: Using information campaigns to promote environmental awareness and behavior change. *Health Promotion International, 8,* 209–224.

Matsuba, M. K. (2006). Searching for self and relationships online. *Cyber-Psychology & Behavior, 9,* 275–284.

Mendelsohn, H. (1973). Some reasons why information campaigns can succeed. *Public Opinion Quarterly, 37,* 50–61.

Mendelsohn, M. (1996). The media and interpersonal communications: The priming of issues, leaders, and party identification. *Journal of Politics, 58,* 112–125.

Milgram, S. (1967). The small world problem. *Psychology Today, 2,* 60–67.

Miller, D. C. (1945). A research note on mass communication. *American Sociological Review, 10,* 691–694.

Miller, G. R. (1986). A neglected connection: Mass media exposure and interpersonal communicative competency. In G. Gumpert & R. Cathcart (Eds.), *Inter/media: Interpersonal communication in a media world* (pp. 132–139). New York: Oxford University Press.

Morton, T. A., & Duck, J. M. (2001). Communication and health beliefs: Mass and interpersonal influences on perceptions of risk to self and others. *Communication Research, 28,* 602–626.

Mudde, A. N. & de Vries, H. (1999). The reach and effectiveness of a national mass media-led smoking cessation campaign in The Netherlands. *American Journal of Public Health, 89,* 346–350.

O'Keefe, G. J., Ward, H. J., & Shepard, R. (2002). A repertoire approach to environmental information channels. *Science Communication, 23,* 392–409.

Paisley, W. (1989). Public communication campaigns: The American experience. In R. E. Rice & C. K. Atkin (Eds.), *Public communication campaigns* (2nd ed., pp. 15–38). Newbury Park, CA: Sage.

Papacharissi, Z. (2005). The real-virtual dichotomy in online interaction: New media uses and consequences revisited. In P. J. Kalbfleisch (Ed.), *Communication yearbook 29* (pp. 215–237). Mahwah, NJ: Lawrence Erlbaum Associates.

Parrott, R. (2004). Emphasizing "communication" in health communication. *Journal of Communication, 54,* 751–787.

Parrott, R., Wilson, K., Buttram, C., Jones, K., & Steiner, C. (1999). Migrant farm workers' access to pesticide protection and information: Cultivando Buenos Habitos campaign development. *Journal of Health Communication, 4,* 49–64.

Pfau, M., Roskos-Ewoldsen, D., Wood, M., Yin, S., Cho, J., Lu, K.-H., et al. (2003). Attitude accessibility as an alternative explanation for how inoculation confers resistance. *Communication Monographs, 70,* 39–51.

Pinkleton, B. E. & Austin, E. W. (2006). *Strategic public relations management: Planning and managing effective communication programs* (2nd ed.). Mahwah, NJ: Lawrence Erlbaum Associates.

Piotrow, P. T., Kincaid, D. L., Rimon, J. & Rinehart, W. (1997). *Family planning communication: Lessons for public health.* New York, NY: Praeger.

Poole, M. S., McPhee, R. D., Canary, D. J., & Morr, M. C. (2002). Hypothesis testing and modeling perspectives on inquiry. In M. L. Knapp & J. A. Daly (Eds.), *Handbook of interpersonal communication* (3rd ed., pp. 23–72). Thousand Oaks, CA: Sage.

Price, V., & Cappella, J. N. (2002). Online deliberation and its influence: The electronic dialogue project in Campaign 2000. *IT & Society, 1,* 303–329.

Price, V., Cappella, J. N., & Nir, L. (2002). Does disagreement contribute to more deliberative opinion? *Political Communication, 19,* 95–112.

Price, V., Nir, L., & Cappella, J. N. (2006). Normative and informational influences in online political discussions. *Communication Theory, 16,* 47–74.

Rawan, S. M. (2001). Interaction between traditional communication and modern media: Implications for social change in Iran and Pakistan. In K. Hafez (Ed.), *Mass media, politics, and society in the Middle East* (pp. 175–196). Cresskill, NJ: Hampton Press.

Rayner, P. (2006). A need for postmodern fluidity? *Critical Studies in Media Communication, 23,* 345–349.

Read, S. J., Miller, L. C., Appleby, P. R., Nwosu, M. E., Reynaldo, S., Lauren, A., et al. (2006). Socially optimized learning in a virtual environment: Reducing risky sexual behavior among men who have sex with men. *Human Communication Research, 32,* 1–34.

Reingen, P. H., & Kernan, J. B. (1986). Analysis of referral networks in marketing: Methods and illustration. *Journal of Marketing Research, 23,* 370–378.

Richardson, K. (2005). *Internet discourse and health debates.* New York: Palgrave Macmillan.

Roberts, D. F., & Maccoby, N. (1985). Effects of mass communication. In G. Lindzey & E. Aronson (Eds.), *Handbook of social psychology* (Vol. 2, pp. 539–598). New York: Random House.

Robinson, J. P., & Davis, D. K. (1990). Television news and the informed public: An information-processing approach. *Journal of Communication, 40*(3), 106–119.

Roessler, P. (2007). Media content diversity. In C. S. Beck (Ed.), *Communication yearbook 31* (pp. 463–520). New York, NY: Lawrence Erlbaum Associates.

Rogers, E. M. (1962). *Diffusion of innovations* (1st ed.). New York: The Free Press.

Rogers, E. M. (1995). *Diffusion of innovations* (4th ed.). New York: The Free Press.

Rogers, E. M. (2003). *Diffusion of innovations* (5th ed.). New York: The Free Press.

Rogers, E. M., & Storey, J. D. (1987). Communication campaigns. In C. R. Berger & S. H. Chaffee (Eds.), *Handbook of communication science* (pp. 817–846). Newbury Park, CA: Sage.

Rogers, E. M., Vaughan, P. W., Swalehe, R. A., Rao, N., Svenkerud, P., & Sood, S. (1999). Effects of an entertainment-education radio soap opera on family planning in Tanzania. *Studies in Family Planning, 30,* 193–211.

Roloff, M. E., & Anastasiou, L. (2001). Interpersonal communication research: An overview. In W. B. Gudykunst (Ed.), *Communication yearbook 24* (pp. 51–70). Thousand Oaks, CA: Sage.

Rosen, E. (2002). *The anatomy of buzz: How to create word-of-mouth marketing.* New York: Doubleday.

Rosengren, K. E. (1973). News diffusion: An overview. *Journalism Quarterly, 50,* 83–91.

Rosnow, R. L. (1991). Inside rumor: A personal journey. *American Psychologist, 46,* 484–496.

Rosnow, R. L. (2001). Rumor and gossip in interpersonal interaction and beyond: A social exchange perspective. In R. M. Kowalski (Ed.), *Behaving badly: Aversive behaviors in interpersonal relationships* (pp. 203–232). Washington, DC: American Psychological Association.

Rubin, A. M., & Haridakis, P. (2001). Mass communication research at the dawn of the 21st century (pp. 73–97). In W. B. Gudykunst (Ed.), *Communication yearbook 24* (pp. 73–97). Thousand Oaks, CA: Sage.

Scanlon, J. (1998). The search for nonexistent facts in the reporting of disasters. *Journalism & Mass Communication Educator, 53*(2), 45–53.

Scanlon, T. J. (1977). Post-disaster rumor chains: A case study. *Mass Emergencies, 2,* 121–126.

Scheufele, D. A. (2001). Democracy for some? How political talk both informs and polarizes the electorate. In R. P. Hart & D. Shaw (Eds.), *Communication and U.S. elections: New agendas* (pp. 19–32). Lanham, MD: Rowman & Littlefield.

Scheufele, D. A. (2002). Examining differential gains from mass media and their implication for participatory behavior. *Communication Research, 29,* 46–65.

Schuster, D. V., Valente, T. W., Skara, S. N., Wenten, M. R., Unger, J. B., Cruz, T. B., et al. (2006). Intermedia processes in the adoption of tobacco control activities among opinion leaders in California. *Communication Theory, 16,* 91–117.

Seibold, D. R., Cantrill, J. G., & Meyers, R. A. (1985). Communication and interpersonal influence. In M. L. Knapp & G. R. Miller (Eds.), *Handbook of interpersonal communication* (pp. 551–611). Beverly Hills, CA: Sage.

Silk, K. J., & Parrott, R. L. (2003, November). *Health message design: Testing the effectiveness of statistical evidence in messages about "Franken-food."* Paper presented at the annual meeting of the National Communication Association, Miami Beach, FL.

Singhal, A., & Rogers, E. M. (2003). *Combating AIDS: Communication strategies in action.* Thousand Oaks, CA: Sage.

Sood, R., Stockdale, G., & Rogers, E. (1987). How the news media operate in natural disasters. *Journal of Communication, 37,* 27–41.

Southwell, B. G. (2005). Between messages and people: A multilevel model of memory for television content. *Communication Research, 32,* 112–140.

Southwell, B. G., & Torres, A. (2006). Connecting interpersonal and mass communication: Science news exposure, perceived ability to understand science, and conversation. *Communication Monographs, 73,* 334–350.

Strack, F., & Deutsch, R. (2004). Reflective and impulsive determinants of social behavior. *Personality and Social Psychology Review, 8,* 220–247.

Stromer-Galley, J., & LeBret, J. (2005, October). *The best and worst of political chat online.* Paper presented at Internet Research 6.0: Internet Generations. Chicago.

Svenkerud, P. J., Singhal, A., & Papa, M. J. (1998). Diffusion of innovations theory and effective targeting of HIV/AIDS programmes in Thailand. *Asian Journal of Communication, 8,* 1–30.

Tarde, G. (1903). *The laws of imitation* (E. W. C. Parsons, Trans.). New York: H. Holt and Company.

Taylor, M., Kent, M. L., & White, W. J. (2001). How activist organizations are using the Internet to build relationships. *Public Relations Review, 27,* 263–284.

Trammell, K. D., Williams, A. P., Postelnicu, M., & Landreville, K. D. (2006). Evolution of online campaigning: Increasing interactivity in candidate Web sites and blogs through text and technical features. *Mass Communication and Society, 9,* 21–44.

Trent, J. S., & Friedenberg, R. V. (2000). *Political campaign communication: Principles and practices.* Westport, CT: Praeger.

Trumbo, C. (1998). Communication channels and risk information: A cost-utility model. *Science Communication, 20,* 190–203.

Tsfati, Y. (2003). Debating the debate: The impact of exposure to debate news coverage and its interaction with exposure to the actual debate. *Harvard International Journal of Press/Politics, 8,* 70–86.

Turow, J. (2003). *Media today: An introduction to mass communication.* Boston: Houghton Mifflin.

Valente, T. W. (1995). *Network models of the diffusion of innovations.* Cresskill, NJ: Hampton Press, Inc.

Valente, T. W., & Saba, W. P. (1998). Mass media and interpersonal influence in a reproductive health communication campaign in Bolivia. *Communication Research, 25,* 96–124.

Valente, T. W., & Saba, W. P. (2001). Campaign exposure and interpersonal communication as factors in contraceptive use in Bolivia. *Journal of Health Communication, 6,* 303–322.

van den Putte, B., Southwell, B. G., & Yzer, M. C. (2006, July). *Can talk amplify normative effects in health campaigns?* Paper presented at the annual meeting of the International Communication Association, Dresden, Germany.

van den Putte, B., Yzer, M. C., & Brunsting, S. (2005). Social influences on smoking cessation: A comparison of the effects of six social influence variables. *Preventive Medicine, 41,* 186–193.

Vasquez, G. M., & Taylor, M. (2001). Public relations: An emerging social science enters the new millennium. In W. B. Gudykunst (Ed.), *Communication yearbook 24* (pp. 319–342). Thousand Oaks, CA: Sage.

Vaughan, P. W., & Rogers, E. M. (2000). A staged model of communication effects: Evidence from an entertainment–education radio soap opera in Tanzania. *Journal of Health Communication, 5,* 203–227.

Visser, P. S., & Mirabile, R. R. (2004). Attitudes in the social context: The impact of social network composition on individual-level attitude strength. *Journal of Personality and Social Psychology, 87,* 779–795.

Vivian, J. (2006). *The media of mass communication (2006 update)* (7th ed.). Boston: Pearson.

Walker, W. R., & Gibbons, J. A. (2006). Rumor mongering as a collective coping strategy for traumatic public events: Evidence from face to face interactions and rumors on the Internet. *International Journal of Cognitive Technology, 11,* 31–35.

Wallack, L. (1990). Improving health promotion: Media advocacy and social marketing approaches. In C. Atkin & L. Wallack (Eds.), *Mass communication and public health: Complexities and conflicts* (pp. 147–163). Newbury Park, CA: Sage.

Walther, J. B., & Parks, M. R. (2002). Cues filtered out, cues filtered in: Computer-mediated communication and relationships. In M. L. Knapp & J. A. Daly (Eds.), *Handbook of interpersonal communication* (3rd ed., pp. 529–563). Thousand Oaks, CA: Sage.

Watzlawick, P., Bavelas, J. H. B., & Jackson, D. D. (1967). *Pragmatics of human communication: A study of interactional patterns, pathologies, and paradoxes.* New York: Norton.

Webster, J. G., Phalen, P. F., & Lichty, L. W. (2000). *Ratings analysis: The theory and practice of audience research.* Mahwah, NJ: Lawrence Erlbaum Associates.

Weger, H. J., & Aakhus, M. (2003). Arguing in Internet chat rooms: Argumentative adaptations to chat room design and some consequences for public deliberation at a distance. *Argumentation and Advocacy, 40*(2), 23–38.

Wellings, K. (2002). Evaluating AIDS public education in Europe: A cross-national comparison. In R. Hornik (Ed.), *Public health communication: Evidence for behavior change* (pp. 131–146). Mahwah, NJ: Lawrence Erlbaum Associates.

Wilkin, H. A., & Ball-Rokeach, S. J. (2006). Reaching at risk groups: The importance of health storytelling in Los Angeles Latino media. *Journalism, 7,* 299–320.

Wright, C. R. (1986). *Mass communication: A sociological perspective.* New York: McGraw–Hill.

Yzer, M. C., Siero, F. W., & Buunk, B. P. (2001). Bringing up condom use and using condoms with new sexual partners: Intentional or habitual? *Psychology and Health, 16,* 409–421.

Yzer, M. C., & van den Putte, B. (2006, July). *Conversation as a mediator of smoking cessation campaign effects.* Paper presented at the annual meeting of the International Communication Association, Dresden, Germany.

Chapter 10 Contents

10

Media Content Diversity: Conceptual Issues and Future Directions for Communication Research

Patrick Roessler
University of Erfurt

The notion of diversity is crucial for our view of mass media as part of a pluralistic society. On the one hand, mass media integrates individuals by "providing a common set of values, ideas and information" (McQuail, 2000, p. 71) as the media focus on those issues relevant for public discussion. At the same time, media coverage must consider the broad variety of events and positions that emerge continuously. The diversity of issues, opinions, and actors seems to be a prerequisite for a pluralistic society. For both perspectives—integration and diversity—"too much" can be dysfunctional for society. Focusing too closely on particular issues can result in control and censorship; whereas, an extremely diversified coverage may lead to fragmentation of audiences.

This chapter overviews research efforts related to the diversity issue that remain largely unconnected in scholarly discussions so far. With its focus on content diversity in the mass media, this chapter presents empirical evidence regarding different types of media systems, media outlets, genres, and subject areas, with a special emphasis on journalistic media coverage. Thus, it provides a comprehensive insight into diversity research from the United States and, particularly, European countries.

Media Content Diversity: Conceptual Issues and Future Directions for Communication Research

Cuban citizen Fariñas Hernández stopped eating on January 31, 2006. The head of the independent news agency, Cubanácan Press, went on a hunger strike because the government closed the office's Internet access, one of the few opportunities to break through the strong media control exercised by the regime. Hernández stated that any Cuban citizen should have the right to acquire information, despite the conformity imposed on the island's media by state authorities, and that he was ready to die as a martyr for that objective (Rüb, 2006). Beyond its obvious reference to freedom of speech and related values, this example also illustrates how crucial content diversity seems to be for our view of mass media as part of a pluralistic society. Hernández's main argument is not the right to publish his own ideas without censorship but the opportunity to be informed by a wide and diverse range of sources. In other words, for mass media to contribute effectively and ethically to a pluralistic society, it must exhibit content diversity. In the past, communication scholars have studied content diversity from different perspectives. This chapter reviews both theoretical and empirical work on content diversity, representing research from diverse frameworks and levels of assessment.

After defining media diversity, I describe the relevance of diversity in media content, focusing on politics and the democratic process as well as on the economic view of diversity in a given media market. As demonstrated by the introductory case, this notion of diversity usually refers to societies of the Western hemisphere; however, the global dimension of content diversity deserves further consideration here. The main part of the manuscript organizes existing research in the field of content diversity on macro-, meso-, and micro-levels of measurement. This classification distinguishes between diversity assessment in terms of the media system and its overall structure (macro), the meso-level of single media outlets or genre representation in a given media system, and finally (and most prominently featured in this chapter) the micro-level of issues and protagonists. This review covers all types of media, with an accent on television because regulation has stimulated diversity research in this area. While, on the meso-level, I consider all types of genres encountered in the mass media (from entertainment to informational and educational content), analysis on the micro-level emphasizes the journalistic coverage of current events, which remains particularly relevant for the development and maintenance of pluralism in politics and society.

A final section discusses the implications of these results for our general view on content diversity as well as opportunities for further research, including prospects regarding the future role of digital media, such as the Internet and satellite TV, which multiply the number and accessibility of media sources dramatically.

This chapter addresses a construct that obviously concerns the heart of media studies and mass communication because it depicts the reality portrayed by mass media from an aggregate viewpoint (content diversity). Further, the interfaces between content diversity

in mass media and a whole range of problems in the field of communication seem obvious. First, diversity comprises an important
aspect of media regulation, involving permanent disputes in media
policy and media economy literature. However, in a broader sense,
the extensiveness of content diversity in mass media reaches far
beyond legal matters. Given that the omnipresent and ubiquitous
media pervade our everyday lives, content diversity needs to be considered in many contexts. As the studies reviewed in this chapter
indicate, it influences the effectiveness of health communication
campaigns, it impacts social and political problems, and it relates to
our understanding of foreign cultures.

Finally, the underlying principles of any content diversity analysis—the antagonism between diversity and integration, fragmentation and uniformity, and the problem of reaching the optimum
between the different poles—can be applied to reasoning in interpersonal and organizational communication as well. The distribution
of knowledge and information constitutes, for instance, a crucial
issue in organizations. In this realm, members also strive to keep the
balance between the diversification required to fulfill occupational
tasks and affirming a common set of values and goals that keep the
employees motivated and related to the organization (see related
arguments by Waldeck & Myers, this volume).

Content Diversity Defined and Measured

Content Diversity in Mass Communication: A Definition

Content diversity focuses on the representation of contents in mass
media, particularly at the degree of variety on different levels of analysis. Following Teachman's (1980) general definition, diversity constitutes the distribution of population elements along a continuum
of homogeneity to heterogeneity with respect to one or more variables. Notably, one weakness of this concept is that it seems rather
empty of a specific meaning beyond that of mere differentiation itself
(McQuail, 2005). This chapter provides interpretations for varying
degrees of content diversity by reviewing the body of research in
this field and connecting it to broader frameworks that offer specific
views of how to identify the value of diversity—the political, social,
and economic values, in particular.

Empirical research addresses both views with two constructs rather similarly measured but reflecting the two perspectives. *Diversity*, on the one hand, means the variety or breadth of media content available to media consumers, with higher consumer welfare provided by high diversity. *Diversification*, on the other hand, refers to the supply side of media firms, particularly to the number of business areas in which the firm is involved, the variety of its product offerings, or the range of geographic regions in which it does business. Measurement of both constructs usually expresses the respective degree of homogeneity or heterogeneity by a standardized coefficient that allows for comparisons over time or between relevant units in the market (see Dimmick, 2004).

Before turning to the mathematical procedures for obtaining these coefficients, three dimensions need to be considered theoretically because they influence the assessment of diversity in a substantial way: categorical variety, disparity of units, and balance of distribution (Moreau & Peltier, 2004). The first aspect could sound trivial, but it exerts an immediate influence on the result of diversity calculations: The *number of categories* included predetermines the possible variety distribution. More opportunities for diversity exist with more detailed categories.

With a rising number of categories, the *disparity of units* deserves further attention. Diversity researchers should give reason for what they consider to be similar in terms of classifying units into categories. Further, researchers should establish a meaningful taxonomy. Since such taxonomies tend to concentrate on simple categorical data, they implicitly treat the distance between each of the units coded in different categories as equal. According to Moreau and Peltier (2004), "For example, we would consider ... the disparity between a comedy and a drama is identical to that between a cartoon and a thriller" (p. 126).

Finally, the *balance of a distribution* that represents the optimum of diversity needs careful thought.[1] The most popular view suggests that we achieve optimum diversity if all given categories are represented with a similar share (*open diversity*)—a notion that is questionable at least (van Cuilenburg, 2000a). Vettehen (2005) illustrated that diversity statistically increases even when unfavorable categories gain as much weight as favorable ones. Instead, the concept of *reflective diversity*, introduced by McQuail and van Cuilenburg (1983) and also applied by van der Wurff (2004), stresses that the optimum strikes a perfect match between the diversity on the supply side and the diversity on the demand side. According to van der Wurff, "It exists when broadcasters provide the exact combination of programmes that audiences demand" (p. 218).

McQuail and van Cuilenburg (1983) as well as van der Wurff (2004) imply that audience demand comprises an empirical unit, but one might argue that researchers could determine a distribution appropriate for a society based on normative considerations, too, in order to develop a taxonomy for diversity assessment. At present, the tension between the two concepts of open versus reflective diversity can be easily observed in political campaigns. On the one hand, policies often mandate equal representation (i.e., the amount of time allowed for each candidate during TV debates). On the other hand, in Germany, the allocation of time slots for political parties to broadcast their TV ads strictly follows their relevance in the political field, usually measured by recent election results (Holtz-Bacha, 2000). Another type of reflective diversity refers to normative standards—for example, in health communication. Public service institutions and medical experts have agreed upon several guidelines for healthy nutrition behavior. To attain reflective diversity, one could, for instance, demand that TV represent types of food in the same proportions recommended for consumption. In contrast, empirical studies could prove that the diet displayed on TV strongly emphasizes unhealthy products (sweets, snacks, alcohol, etc.) while ignoring more valuable nutrition (Roessler, Lücke, Linzmaier, Steinhilper, & Willhöft, 2006).

Strategies for Diversity Measurement

Researchers have developed several types of coefficients in order to express the degree of diversity, and these numerical values obviously need to integrate the two dimensions linked most closely to the empirical distribution: Measurement of diversity constitutes an interaction between the number of categories with the assignment of elements to these categories (*dual-concept diversity*; see McDonald & Dimmick, 2003). To estimate this interaction, empirical studies mostly fall back on measures of concentration like the entropy index (e.g., Hellman, 2001; Hillve, Majanen, & Rosengren, 1997; Kambara, 1992). This procedure implies an *open diversity* perspective; the coefficient indicates highest diversity when the distribution is flat (i.e., an equal share of objects allocated to each category). Diversity is lowest when all objects are allocated to one category (for a special open diversity coefficient OD, see Vettehen, 2005).

The most popular coefficient to express entropy is the Herfindahl–Hirschman index (HHI) often employed in economic studies to measure concentration (as an opposite to diversity). The HHI results from adding up the squared percentages for each category, and it runs from 0 to 10,000 (in the case where all objects are gathered in one single category). According to Litman (1979), "The higher the Herfindahl index, the greater the concentration of programming into a few program types, and hence the less the diversity" (p. 403). If we define diversity as open diversity, the HHI provides an appropriate measure. For purpose of interpretation, the U.S. Department of Justice issued a guideline according to which an industry is not concentrated with an HHI below 1,000, moderately concentrated with an HHI between 1,000 and 1,800, and highly concentrated with an HHI above 1,800 (see Einstein, 2004b). However, if a specialized use requires, for example, sensitivity to the presence of small proportions in certain categories to protect minority interests, other coefficients are available (for a methodological overview and a typology, see, most recently, McDonald & Dimmick, 2003; Stark, 2006).

McDonald and Lin (2004) promoted a simple but expressive measure of diversity that balances several desirable characteristics. They favor the calculation of Simpson's D, based on random probability estimations. Simpson's D is obtained by summing the squared shares of each category and subtracting that sum from 1; thus, it equals the procedure for HHI, and the values can be transformed easily (D = 1 − HHI/10,000). According to McDonald and Lin, Simpson's D can be transformed into a standardized version that reflects the number of categories and into other refined measures controlling for special distribution characteristics. Altogether, the advantages of Simpson's D and its related coefficients include ease of calculation, ease of interpretability (ranging from 0 to 1), and comparability across studies (in the standardized version).

It should be emphasized here that the present notion of diversity obviously differs from another track of research also pursued in sociology and political science: diversity in terms of cultural or ethnic representations in societies, communities, or the media. This broad field of inquiry (which always includes the question of equality and inequality of opportunities) contributes to the present review only as far as matters of media representation of characters, indicating a very special form of variety in content. Relevant arguments based on these representations (often relying on interpretative methods rather than on the calculation of diversity coefficients) emerged from the area of critical cultural studies (see, e.g., Downing & Husband, 2005; Gentz & Kramer, 2006; Kamalipour & Carilli, 1998).

Content Diversity as a Political and Social Value

Democratic Principles versus Regulation Efforts

Media performance in democratic nations extends from a broader principle of diversity, which frequently guides the goals of communications policy (McQuail, 1992). At least in Western democracies, it seems widely accepted that the distribution of information and shared cultural values depends on the diversity of communication content and should be a major goal of any media system (Hoffmann-Riem, 1987; for an overview of regulations intended to safeguard diversity in European countries, see Holznagel, 1997). As de Jong and Bates (1991) noted, "The promotion of diversity among media sources has been one of the oldest and most consistent of the stated goals of American media policy" (p. 159). However, diversity may not constitute a desirable condition under all circumstances because it may create tension with other values (such as the unity or cohesion of a society or community with strong belief systems, whether religious or secular) (McQuail, 2005).

One main function of mass media in modern societies involves a capacity to integrate individuals by "providing a common set of values, ideas and information" (McQuail, 2000, p. 71). The media focus on issues relevant for a public discussion—a process addressed in the context of the agenda-setting approach (see, e.g., Roessler, 1999)—as they draw audience attention toward the problems to be solved. Consequently, media coverage plays an important role for social integration, forming a basis for discourse between individuals, groups, and other entities in society (see Jarren, 2000; Vlasic, 2004).

At the same time, media coverage must consider the broad variety of events and positions that emerge continuously. The diversity of issues, opinions, and actors seems to be a prerequisite for a pluralistic society, and from a normative point of view, this diversity should be visible particularly in the political content of mass media (see, e.g., Ishikawa & Muramatsu, 1996). They should represent an appropriate sample of topics as well as political positions, due to their importance for public information and opinion formation (see, e.g., McQuail & van Cuilenburg, 1983; Roessler, 2000, 2005a). In their apodictic statement, Ishikawa and Muramatsu observed:

> Each member of the audience, with differing interests and concerns, should have equal rights for selection. Therefore, even if individual viewers/listeners may not come into contact with broadcasting in its entirety, broadcasting as a whole should strive to be diverse enough in its contents to serve all interests.... We feel that each member of the audience should have the opportunity to come into contact with other individuals with different personalities or viewpoints. In order to build a democratic society, each citizen must be aware of the existence of other citizens who may have quite different values and attitudes. (pp. 200–201)

Arguments promoting content diversity need to be framed in a historical perspective, as early twentieth-century nations faced different attempts to abuse mass media for propaganda purposes, in order to maintain the power of undemocratic regimes. Early theorists on mass society recognized diversity as a value under threat from the universalizing and connected centralizing tendencies with emerging mass appeal media (McQuail & van Cuilenburg, 1983). One instrument comprised the "gleichschaltung" in Nazi Germany, meaning that censorship reducing the variety of media coverage according to standards set by the ruling class united the nation under a common set of values. Within this context,

> [Diversity] stands opposed to control, because control imposes uniformity. It can be equated, if not with freedom itself, then with the fruits of freedom, since freedom should lead to a multiplicity of voices and where is no diversity, we may suspect freedom to be restricted, whatever it may say in law or constitution. (McQuail, 2005, p. 2)

Nevertheless, a measurable degree of diversity does not ensure the development of free and informed opinion per se. Studies exploring issue diversity in German newspapers from 1936 to 1938 found that regional and local newspapers covered a broad range of issues that varied substantially between the different outlets (see review by Pohl, 2006). Although the Nazi regime imposed a rigid system to exert control over mass media coverage, diversity of coverage on the level of current events amounted to 40% and more—indicating that, on a given day, almost half of newspaper topics were unique in the sense that they were not addressed by any other newspaper of the same market. Obviously, the "gleichschaltung" did not aim primarily at limiting the diversity of issues, but censorship became more influential regarding the evaluation and interpretation of these events, as several case studies reported by Pohl prove. Hence, issue diversity alone did not ensure freedom, given that public opinion reportedly remained rather uniform those days, emphasizing once more that diversity constitutes a multidimensional construct operating on various levels.

As a consequence, governmental action in democratic countries strives to maintain diversity, supervised by institutions such as the Federal Communications Commission (FCC) in the United States (Einstein, 2004a), the Kommission zur Ermittlung der Konzentration im Medienbereich (KEK) in Germany (Humphreys, 1994), or the media commissions in Sweden (Gustafsson, 1992). Their regulation efforts are political in nature, but they usually operate with instruments directed toward the media market, based by and large on the interplay of subsidies and antitrust laws. Officials justify legal action given the state's responsibility to secure diversity in media (Branahl, 1992; Saxer, 1992).

Positive and Negative Outcomes of Diversity

Notably, both perspectives—integration and diversity—treat "too much" as dysfunctional for society. Focusing too closely on particular issues, the danger of control and censorship, or an "over-integration" (Maletzke, 1980, p. 205) cannot be ruled out; an extremely diversified coverage may lead to fragmentation of audiences. For analytical purposes, McQuail (2000) proposed organizing these processes in a two-by-two matrix. One dimension refers to the direction of the effect—either centrifugal or centripetal. The second dimension represents a more optimistic or more pessimistic interpretation of these effects, depending on one's normative perspective. For example, freedom and diversity would point to an optimistic view of centrifugal tendencies based on diversity in media content, while dominance and uniformity comprise the pessimistic view of centripetal effects, which also could be interpreted in terms of solidarity and integration.

However, the crucial question involves the position of the climax. In other terms, which relationship of centrifugal and centripetal tendencies represents the optimum for a society? Sometimes, shifts in regulation policies and societal values displace the political and social value of diversity (in terms of variety in information, education, and culture) by market mechanisms. However, is it really true, as argued by economists, that a free market does not produce maximum diversity, but always an optimum level of diversity (e.g., Heinrich, 1992)? Given the ever-expanding range and capacity of distribution technologies, this research reveals the obvious fallacy that diversity should not be a problem anymore (McQuail, 2005).

Moreover, the notion of content diversity as a political and social value usually implies the diversity of "valuable" content. German scholars Manfred Knoche (1980) and Günther Rager (1982) coined the term *publizistische Vielfalt,* which might best be translated as diversity in the journalistic content of mass media, with regard to substantial information on matters of political or social relevance. *Journalistic diversity* is achieved when media content across different segments of the media market represents the greatest possible quantity and variety of information and opinions (Rager & Weber, 1992). Thus, diversity in terms of serving democratic processes of opinion forming obviously means journalistic diversity, whereas the broader view of diversity, independent from a particular type of content, refers to the audience's freedom of choice from a diverse supply of media content provided in a certain market.

Notably, most of the discussion so far exclusively addresses the conditions in Western democracies guided by the idea of freedom of speech in order to create an informed citizenship. Obviously, the value of content diversity "tends to be closely linked to one particular, albeit dominant, model of democratic society and procedure, namely that of individualistic pluralism" (McQuail, 2005, p. 29). Moreover, according to McQuail, diversity is not disposable anywhere but limited to "favoured locations that benefit from a long established civic culture, not to mention the wealth that buys the rich a variety of media choice that may not be available to others" (p. 29). In societies based on different principles and forms of government (e.g., totalitarian regimes), media fulfill different functions, indicating a significant alternative perspective on diversity.

Content Diversity as an Economic Value

The idea of diversity remains central to free market economics because, without a diversity of products and suppliers, no true competition exists (see, e.g., McQuail, 2005). Conversely, diversity does not always result from a free market, given market failures, market deficits, and media regulation deficits (Ludwig, 2004). Economic theory attributes a small degree of diversity in a media market only partly to the strategies of media companies, while consumers should accept responsibility for stimulating a diverse range of media offerings (Sjurts, 2004). Hence, a basic conceptual distinction entails media diversity as access to the media market (as opposed to choice for the audience). Iosifides (1999) argued:

> Regarding diversity of access, the key question is whether the possibility of establishing new media companies leads to the situation where all legitimate interests in a given society have an equal (or proportional) share of access to media channels. Regarding diversity as choice, the key question is whether an increase in channels actually leads to greater choice for the audience. (p. 155)

Economists tend to reduce the question of diversity to the first aspect, with diversification representing another important construct. Consequently, recent developments on regional and global markets clearly illustrate that a diversified media company has better opportunities because it appears less vulnerable to current trends, may apply economies of scale to its range of products, and can develop new marketing areas (Dimmick, 2004).

Nevertheless, the economic processes leading to or preventing diversity differ between the markets under study. In his comprehensive overview, van der Wurff (2005) described the mechanisms for broadcasting, trade magazines, and the newspaper industry. He concluded that too little and too much economic competition can reduce diversity and that relevant factors include the balance between subscription and advertising revenues as well as the opportunities to realize economies of scale or scope. In any case, van der Wurff contended that "optimal levels of competition or concentration therefore vary from media market to market and cannot be determined once and for all" (p. 299). However, the question remains open regarding how this "optimal level" should be defined theoretically; from economic theory, one may speculate that aspects of democratic representation and integration probably play a minor role here. Additionally, future regulation policies will need to define the media markets required to be diverse in terms of geography, technologies, types of content, or a combination of all three (van Cuilenburg, 2005).

In recent years, the rise of the Internet gave hope that content diversity might become distributed more equally, given the ubiquity of digital media. Multiplying the already existing abundance of media channels, Internet sources were expected to provide the final deliberation of the information market (Bagdikian, 2004). Yet, again, more does not necessarily mean different or even better, and recent studies warn that the existing mainstream media conglomerates have already begun the "colonization of cyberspace" (Blevins, 2002, p. 95). Based on observations in Canada, authors from a critical studies point of view predict the "rise of what we can call 'Machiavellian media'" with the Internet being nothing more than a further element of a "self-referentially enclosed information system governed by multimedia conglomerates" (Winseck, 2002, p. 795).

Critical scholars dispute a naïve economic perspective that, as an outcome of diversification, content diversity may result implicitly from entrepreneurial decisions if they involve successful market strategy (Bagdikian, 2004; Blevins, 2002; Winseck, 2002). As opposed to the social and political perspective, the market model of diversity treats diversification as a valued end in itself, "leaving the allocation of value essentially to the judgment (or behavior) of consumers" (McQuail, 2005, p. 7). Economic rationality guides the balance between uniformity and variety of content available, and revenues could just as well be maximized by producing only a few blockbuster movies, books, Web sites, and so on. However, according to McQuail, the link between the two relevant constructs—or, in other terms, how diversity of access may translate to choice for the audience—results from diversity in media content as an outcome of certain structures. Communication scholars (who improved the method of content analysis substantially in recent years) have collected some empirical evidence for content diversity on different levels that will be presented in the following section.

Levels of Analysis in Content Diversity Research: Empirical Results

A Typology of Research: Macro-, Meso-, and Micro-Levels

For any assessment of content diversity in mass media, the level of analysis becomes crucial. Media content can be analyzed on different

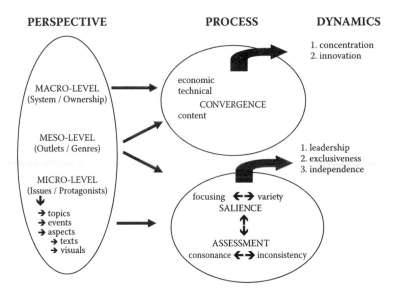

Figure 10.1   Processes and dynamics involved in media diversity perspectives on different levels of analysis. (Based on Roessler, P., 2000, p. 171. In O. Jarren, K. Imhof, & R. Blum, Eds., *Zerfall der Öffentlichkeit?* [pp. 168–186]. Opladen, Germany: Westdeutscher Verlag.)

levels of aggregation, from the overall number of channels in a media system down to the representation of single arguments or persons resulting in the coverage. In an initial typology, Knoche (1980); McQuail and van Cuilenburg (1983), as well as McQuail (1992); and, more recently, Schulz and Ihle (2005), described three levels for the measurement of diversity.[2] Each of these levels encompasses varying processes and different dynamics (see Figure 10.1). Diversity can be assessed on the macro-level of the media system as a whole, looking at such issues as ownership and market shares. As such, researchers explore the process of economic or technical convergence, described by the mutual adaptation of technologies (e.g., on a digital basis) and economic players (e.g., in mergers) and caused by dynamics of concentration or innovation.

On the meso-level of single media outlets or genre representation, convergence in terms of content may result. Scholars locate further processes with respect to content perception prominently on the micro-level of issues and protagonists (Knoche, 1980, p. 132). A range exists between focusing and variety, especially in terms of salience. The media also present a continuum of consonance in opinions. Media research identified dynamics such as media leadership and co-orientation, exclusiveness of coverage, and outlets covering the same issues by independent decisions.

These levels may overlap, at least in part. However, each of these levels can be the subject of an empirical measurement of diversity and may serve as a heuristic to organize the literature in this field.

Diversity on the Macro-Level: Media System Structures

One main line of discussion about diversity corresponds to the conditions for the access to the media market. The level of media system structures only implicitly relates to the notion of content diversity. If diversity of players comprises a precondition for content diversity, empirical data for system level assessment use indicators measuring on the meso-level. However, this dimension remains the realm where governmental actions and regulation policies may exert an immediate influence on the media market. Furthermore, global media players representing a strong voice in the public arena (see, e.g., Rust, 1992) impact media diversity on the macro-level as well as powerful institutions like the FCC, which leads to an ongoing discussion about media ownership and diversity (Hoffman-Riem, 1996; for a recent overview, see Einstein, 2004a).

Journalists, as well as the public, often suspect the demise of diversity, assuming that "when power is concentrated in a handful of giants, some kind of Orwellian total control of information is inevitable" (McCarthy, 2000, p. 13; see also Bagdikian, 2004). Also, what contribution to program diversity is made by legislative steps like the Telecommunications Act of 1996 or the 1992 Cable Act (Roof, Trauth, & Huffman, 1993), which stipulated a must-carry regulation for cable system operators to broadcast local channels (Kim, 1999)? Current regulations in the United States include (1) a so-called diversity index (DI) based on the logic of the HHI, which considers all media in a given market but remains controversial in terms of application (Baker & Kübler, 2004), and (2) for the TV market, a threshold that limits concentration to 39% of potential viewers that must not be exceeded by any provider. The latter rule is easy to supervise, but its shortcomings are obvious as it emphasizes the technical range of a provider's offerings but not their actual use (Kübler, 2005).

Analysis of Regional Markets   Oscillating between the poles of legislative intervention and the idea of a free marketplace, technological progress with the advent of cable and satellite television has led to a focus on deregulation, adjusting the TV market to that of the printed press (see, e.g., Bruck, 1993). However, observations from other media markets, such as the music-recording industry (Dowd, 2004), or from countries all over the world (e.g., Hoffmann-Riem, 1987) imply that market dynamics follow their own rules.

On the one hand, economic models and data from local newspaper markets suggest that the quality of coverage increases with competition (Lacy, 1987, 1989). In her in-depth analysis of daily newspaper markets, George (2002) applied an imaginative empirical approach. As indicators for newspaper content, she coded dictionaries of newspaper staff according to the job titles of about 20,000 reporters and editors. Comparing data from 1993 and 1999, she established a relationship between the number of different reporting beats and the amount of newspaper owners in a market. Her regression analysis indicated, in fact, that a decreasing number of owners increased the number of beats covered in a market. She argued that, as soon as an owner accounts for a new paper, he or she has to take care that the coverage of the new paper does not compete too much with his or her other papers. George asserted that readership usually did not decline in this process of consolidation; nevertheless, she admitted that duplicate coverage (in terms of beats) from varying sources might be an important source for viewpoint diversity within these beats.

Berry and Waldfogel (2001) found similar results for local radio markets in the United States. Looking at the effects of the 1996 Telecommunications Act, these researchers analyzed how the number of stations interacted with the variety of programming formats between 1993 and 1997. Their panel data on 243 radio broadcast markets revealed each station's audience, owner identity, and programming format. The researchers assigned each of the more than 5,000 stations to one of 46 programming formats. Their evidence suggests that increased concentration may cause owners to space their stations differently and thus the consolidation of markets increased the overall variety of formats available in a market.

A good example of the interface between political and economic values of diversity occurred in early 2006 in Germany when the Federal Cartel Office prohibited a merger between Springer, a leading publisher, and the ProSiebenSat.1 TV group. The KEK, representing a national board of media control, prevented the takeover because it feared that the new conglomerate would reduce diversity and possess the power to exert a dominant influence on public opinion (see, e.g., Anonymous, 2006). Within the decision-making process, politicians and media experts argued whether free enterprise (protecting German media outlets against takeovers from multinational players) can be restricted based on a threshold rule that lacks any empirical evidence. The KEK, which strives to ensure media diversity in Germany, developed a measure based on audience shares to indicate diversity, but it has not yet linked this indicator to criteria of media content.

Global Markets: Comparative Evidence   Global players offering their media products to a worldwide audience on a variety of markets heavily influence cross-national diversity of media content. Regarding the publishing industry in general, van Kranenburg, Hagedoorn, and Pennings (2004) monitored the activities of 32 large-size companies from the United States, Australia, and Europe between 1999 and 2002. Eight types of industrial engagements in the field of media accounted for a diversity assessment: books, magazines, newspapers, entertainment, marketing, education, the Internet, and others. Their data suggested that all businesses felt a strong need for diversification, which remained rather stable over time. Companies coming from different geographic regions did not differ much in terms of product diversification, but they differed substantially when investigating international diversification strategies. Due to their large domestic market, North American firms mainly focused their operations on their home country, while the leading European companies, in particular, had already gone through a transition looking for competitive advantages on the international stage.

In the case of television, scholars assumed some impact of imported programs on local viewers, according to the notion of cultural imperialism (see Elasmar, 2003, for a detailed review). Currently, under conditions of outlet multiplication on cable and satellite television, foreign channels, as a whole, may be viewed internationally as well, serving the needs of ethnic minorities in a society—including efforts to establish cross-border television channels operated from different countries (e.g., Chalaby, 2005). The more traditional view focuses on the influence of American movies and television on audiences all over the world. For instance, A. Tan, G. Tan, and Gibson (2003) studied the implications of American television for the worldview of

Russian audiences. Based on the cultivation approach (and controlling for English proficiency and personal experience), Tan et al. confirmed that audiences turned to specific program types most likely
to depict American values, and the researchers predicted acceptance
of those values.

Moreau and Peltier (2004) measured cultural diversity in the movie
business, comparing the United States, Mexico, South Korea, France,
Hungary, and the European Union for the time period between 1990
and 2000. While the selection of nations reflects different strategies
of market regulations, they included both supply and consumption of
movies from different countries as well as other data on the respective
movie markets. The authors drew a differentiated picture of cultural
diversity, dependent on the indicators used. For example, the United
States ranked high in the variety of supply, given a high number of
different films from countries all over the world released per year and
most screens per capita available. Yet, the cultural balance of movies
both supplied and consumed heavily skewed toward domestic products. In contrast, the strictly regulated South Korean market consisted
of a high supplied and consumed diversity in terms of geographical
origin. Altogether, cultural diversity emerged as highest in France
and the European Union across all indicators, and the gaps between
the countries seemed to be widening rather than closing.

Diversification Versus Diversity   Studies from the television market also indicate that media commercialization, leading to a larger
number of media outlets, does not inevitably strengthen the space
for new, creative programming, but it may lead to more mass appeal
programming instead (see Iosifides, 1999, with a summary for different countries). Over many years, a worldwide trend toward concentration within the media market became visible, dominated by
spectacular takeovers, mergers, and other acquisitions. While global
media representatives claim concentration to be a safeguard to diversity because it may strengthen the positions of a firm in the market and against political and advertiser power, empirical evidence
points in another direction. According to Iosifides, "Concentration,
internationalization, and commercialization have resulted in more
emphasis on profitability than on cultural quality.... Market incentives may not be adequate to provide the optimal level of cultural and
political diversity" (pp. 157–158). In her groundbreaking study on
the structure of the television market in the United States, Einstein

(2004a) examined American regulation policies in detail. Her conclusion, after a close inspection of market structures and their reactions to FCC decisions, seems pretty clear. Television regulation based on a multiplication of outlets has proven to be ineffective in creating diversity, mainly because of the industry's dependence on advertising revenues. Indeed, Sjurts (2004) reported the same result for the German market.

As a consequence, the elegant (and simple) argument that access diversity on a macro-level (see Figure 10.1), resulting in a variety of outlets, will prompt diversity in audience choices can no longer be made. The substantial concern raised here cannot be brushed aside as a "myth of 'big media'" that "confuses size with power" (Samuelson, 2003, p. 42). This line of argument needs additional evidence from the examination of media performance itself. Apart from the question of ownership, to what degree does the mass media content available to a broader audience depict a diverse picture of social reality? Is the assumption true that, as an article in *Business Week* asserted, "even as media ownership consolidates, media content is fragmented, adding to the diversity and quality of programming, both news and entertainment" (Anonymous, 2004, p. 140)?

As mentioned before, evidence for diversity on the macro-level of media structures is methodologically generated from data analysis on the meso-level by aggregating results that refer to the representation of outlets and genres in a given media environment. Thus, the bulk of empirical research addresses the meso-level and investigates similarities and differences in content provided by the relevant channels assigned to the respective media system.

Diversity on the Meso-Level: Outlets and Genres

Vertical and Horizontal Diversity   On the meso-level of single media outlets (e.g., a certain TV channel or a newspaper) or content genres (e.g., entertainment programs or news coverage), processes of diversification correspond to content development. Yet, their focus lies on the qualitative diversity of media content provided rather than mere quantitative diversity in terms of variety of channels or broadcasting stations (Hoffmann-Riem, 1987). Media try to match the needs of their audience by providing what has proven a success (and even by copying other outlets). At the same time, they constantly struggle to develop innovative formats, occasionally leading to new categories of programming, expressed by genre labels such as "edutainment" or "infotainment." Such genre categories standing for a certain program type indicate the measure of media diversity on the meso-level (for a summary, see Hellman, 2001).

Following the argument of McQuail and van Cuilenburg (1983) and Hillve et al. (1997), two different perspectives must be distinguished: *channel diversity* (also called *internal* or *vertical diversity*), referring to the choice of program types provided by any single outlet over a certain period of time, and *system diversity* (also identified as *external* or *horizontal diversity*), depicting the variety of program types offered by all outlets in a defined market at one given point in time. From an economic point of view, external diversity equates diversity protection by competition, while internal diversity can be described as a business strategy (Feldmann, 2004). Hence, the meso-level analysis may result in evidence on the macro-level of content convergence within the system under study (see Figure 10.1). The notion behind it resembles the access diversity argument detailed earlier in this chapter. According to Levin (1971), "The wider the range of available program types, the greater the number of possible choices and the more varied the tastes and audiences accommodated" (p. 81).

In the case of television, channel diversity usually remains larger for networks than for special-interest channels, but the latter may contribute heavily to a system's overall diversity because it offers content not prominently featured by other stations. In fact, multiple ways exist to achieve diversity in the television landscape. For example, McDonald and Lin (2004) argued that "[h]igh system-level diversity can be achieved if all the programs are generalists, all specialists, or some generalists and some specialists" (p. 109).

Empirical Evidence From Europe   Empirical studies focusing explicitly on internal and external diversity were conducted almost exclusively for the United States, where the emergence of new nationwide television network systems was also discussed in terms of content diversity, and for Europe, where the competition between public and private stations fuels an ongoing debate about media regulation (Hoffmann-Riem, 1996; for an earlier summary of empirical results, see Woldt, 1992). Taking Germany as an example, some scholars have suggested that the implementation of a so-called dual system of television (where both public and private stations factor into media diversity) contributes to external diversity of the system as a whole and compensates for a limited internal diversity of singular channels (Holtz-Bacha, 1997; Humphreys, 1994). Consequently, the legitimacy of the entire system connects to the question of whether media can maintain a reasonable amount of diversity, leading to substantial research efforts in order to track convergent tendencies between public and private programs (e.g., Merten, 1994).

Other work directly addressed the standards of internal and external diversity regarding program types. In two sequential studies, longterm trends revealed a constantly high degree of external diversity in the German television system, whereas public broadcasting exhibited a slightly reduced internal diversity, and special interest channels seemed to catch up (Brosius & Zubayr, 1996; Rossmann, Brandl, & Brosius, 2003). A recent long-term study covering the trends in German network television programming between 1992 and 2001 calculated external diversity for eight nationwide stations and differentiated between the open diversity and the reflective diversity notion. HHI coefficients indicate a higher value for reflective compared to open diversity; nevertheless, both trends paralleled over the years and displayed little variance over time (Schulz & Ihle, 2005).

Accordingly, a longitudinal study based on data from Finland indicated a very high overall diversity of the channel system, as a whole, while diversity within single channels stagnated. Further, due to program scheduling patterns, even increasing channel diversity did not necessarily enhance system diversity because of content duplications at some given points in time (Aslama, 2006; Aslama, Hellman, & Sauri, 2004; Hellman, 2001). Similar studies from Sweden (Hillve et al., 1997; Hillve & Rosengern, 1996) concluded that both system and channel diversity increased between 1985 and 1996. Conversely, researchers in the Netherlands found a decline (Roth, 2004; van Cuilenburg, 2000b; van der Wurff, 2004). Their results indicate a "ruinous competition" according to which television stations tended to focus on short-term savings by providing a mainstream program. As a consequence, the overall television offerings would likely become less diverse and "more of the same" (van der Wurff & van Cuilenburg, 2001; van der Wurff, van Cuilenburg, & Keune, 2000). However, a highly concentrated television market in the Netherlands still produced a high degree of media diversity (DeBens, 1998; van Cuilenburg, 2005). Interestingly, at least for the Dutch television market, it made no difference whether researchers calculated open diversity for single 1-hour time slots or for larger periods of time (weekdays, months) because the index values were almost identical regardless of the level of aggregation (Vergeer, 2005).

Empirical Evidence From the United States and Comparative Studies   Several longitudinal studies were conducted in the United States investigating the program type diversity of the national networks in prime time. Evidence covers the periods between 1948 and 1956 (Long, 1979), 1953 and 1974 (Dominick & Pearce, 1976), 1973 and 1978 (Litman, 1979), 1950 and 1982 (Wakshlag & Adams, 1985), 1980 and 1989 (Lin, 1995), and, more recently, 1986 to 2000 (McDonald & Lin, 2004) as well as 1955 and 2003 (Einstein, 2004b). Due to different methods in sampling and, especially, a varying number of genre categories used, results are not fully coherent. On the one hand, after a slow but steady decrease since 1953, Dominick and Pearce discovered that a sharp decline in network diversity coincided with the Prime Time Access Rule introduced in 1971 (see also Wakshlag & Adams). On the other hand, Litman's data from the 1970s showed that, with the emergence of a new competitor (ABC), all networks took chances on new types of programming and opted to counterprogram against their rivals, leading to higher amounts of vertical and horizontal diversity. During the 1980s, when the emergence of alternative program sources was expected to trigger program type diversity, Lin found that coefficients remained on a rather constant level.

In her comprehensive view of the period between 1955 and 2003, Einstein (2004b) observed that the overwhelming conclusion of these studies is a decline of diversity and, particularly, "that there has been no definitive relationship established between source diversity and the programming produced" (p. 145). In her own empirical work, she related the long-term decrease of diversity in U.S. network programming to changes in the advertising environment (e.g., the target group orientation and stronger competition of cable competitors). Looking at the summer of 2003, when networks scheduled original programming in a competitive way to target the same viewer group (young adults), she identified very low diversity figures due to virtually identical programs appearing on all the networks. This trend contributes to a "ruinous competition" where viewers turn to cable because of the lack of diversity on networks (Einstein, 2004b, p. 152).

Nevertheless, looking beyond the nationwide networks, the overall number of channels offered in a market can be expected to relate positively to program type diversity (Grant, 1994). For networks as well as for cable or satellite, the increase in the number of stations usually enhances diversity. In an initial assessment of channel diversity in cable television, de Jong and Bates (1991) categorized whole channels according to a set of 32 programming types, without looking at single programs. On the level of mere channel characteristics, diversity increased between 1976 and 1986, and it expanded at an accelerating rate. This result was further specified on the program level by McDonald and Lin (2004). They investigated the influence of new (cable) networks both on overall system diversity and the diversity of traditional network programming in the United States (ABC, NBC, CBS). Based on 24 single program types, their data suggested two things. First, overall system diversity increased slightly between 1986 and 2000, with now seven networks' 196 original first-run programs (instead of three traditional networks broadcasting 81 programs in 1986). Second, the diversity among traditional networks remained fairly stable, while new channels surpassed their competitors rather quickly in this respect.

Yet, discerning voices urge caution toward these results, claiming that outlet diversity may have been a poor replacement for content diversity. Many new channels—often owned by networks as secondary distribution channels—consist only of off-network reruns that may contribute to diversity at a given point in time but, overall, do not constitute a new and diverse program choice. Furthermore, genre-specific channels like Nickelodeon or the History Channel simply provide the same content for the entire day (see Einstein, 2004a).

The search for internationally comparative description on television system diversity led to the 1992 Quality Assessment of Public Broadcasting project (QAPB). Here, researchers gathered data from Canada, Great Britain, Japan, Sweden, and the United States to assess the degree of internal and external diversity at a given point in time (for a detailed report, see Ishikawa et al., 1996). Three results can be highlighted from this study. First, with regard to all-day program diversity, researchers found the highest value in Great Britain, followed by broadcasters in Sweden, Japan, and Canada. In comparison, U.S. channels scored lowest on the entropy measures, indicating little diversity, particularly during prime time. Second, public service channels showed higher diversity in all countries, leading all private channels by far and being even more pronounced during prime time. Third, on the system level, all countries displayed a high degree of diversity, but mainly due to the diverse program content of public broadcasting. Particularly in the United States, PBS assured diversity that was otherwise not provided by the other main commercial networks (Litman & Hasegawa, 1996), a fact underscored by earlier studies (Grant, 1994).

Diversity on the Micro-Level of Coverage

Obviously, it seems imperative to move beyond this program type diversity on the level of genres and formats to truly assess media content diversity. According to Einstein (2004a), "Clearly, if you want diverse content then you have to regulate the content, not everything around it" (p. 211). In other terms, it can be useful to look at structural features if we question content diversity, but these indicators hold limited validity compared to a close inspection of the media content itself that is supposed to create diversity. Thus, the focus of attention shifts to the *micro-level* of journalistic coverage, which includes *diversity of contents* and *person and group diversity* (see Hoffmann-Riem, 1987). From an economic point of view, media outlets in a competitive market likely "will choose to remain substitutes in the types and topics of news and try to differentiate in the quality and depth of coverage of these areas" (Lacy, 1987, p. 290). The subsequent sections organize research following this micro-level perspective, with an emphasis on journalistic coverage represented in the mass media, including the workflow in newsrooms and the representation of issues, events, or protagonists.

Journalistic Workflow, Quality Assessment, and Diversity   Media coverage on current events results from journalistic work, and, not surprisingly, diversity on its various levels also qualifies as a normative criterion of quality in the field of journalism (Blumler, 1991). For example, if we look at the set of news factors that guide the selection of news items for publication, current issues remain as important as established ones. Producing media coverage involves novelty and innovation as well as routine and repetition (McQuail, 2005). As a consequence, the numerous attempts to define quality of media performance consistently refer to diversity representing one important dimension within a larger set of different indicators. Yet, again, the value of diversity for quality assessment depends on the level of analysis under study. If the quality of a single program or outlet is controversial, diversity comprises an insufficient indicator because, in most cases, it is pointless to blame a single offering for a lack of diversity (with the exception of internal diversity in the case of channel quality assessment).

How does a contribution to media diversity emerge from journalistic practice? An observational study recorded the workflow in 30 German newsrooms of different types of media (Roessler, 2006). Results illustrated the presence of diversity considerations in everyday newsroom routines. According to Roessler, media persons closely track their own coverage as well as their competitors' but with varying results. Sometimes, journalists quickly adopt a "hot" topic appearing elsewhere, often with a different "spin;" in other cases, they neglect issues because competitors reported on them a little earlier. Roessler asserted that clear patterns emerged regarding the type of media. All television newsrooms included numerous TV sets, showing the current news flow on different channels, while journalists monitored newspapers, magazines, other print media, and the Internet for inspiration. Alternatively, radio journalists drew on wire service reports but turned on their television sets to record sound bites of sources and other material suited for broadcasting. Print media, and local newspapers in particular, constantly play television sets and radios, but mostly for entertainment purposes; primarily, they turned to other print media and interpersonal sources for orientation. Hence, diversity affected all fields of the journalistic workflow: investigation, selection, and presentation (Blöbaum, 1992).

Roessler's (2006) study included a standardized measure of media use patterns of the individual journalists observed (see also Reinemann, 2003). As Roessler noted, their days typically start with mass media, such as radio alarm clocks or morning newspapers for German reporters. The individual amount of media use almost doubles the average of German audience members, with the main news show of the oldest public television station as a focal point. According to Roessler, other influential media for journalists include quality newspapers and magazines, while they judged tabloids to be untrustworthy but relevant for the work of "other journalists."

Cross-national data from the United States, Sweden, Italy, Germany, and the United Kingdom point in the same direction. A majority of journalists stated that they observe the wire services as well as other journalists in their own newsrooms, leading national media, and leading competitors. Clearly, orientation toward national "opinion leader media" seems the rule and not the exception among journalists (Donsbach, 2004, p. 140). Nevertheless, wire services also play a key role. Currently, few outlets would be able to survive without this continuous stream of information fed by global sources and transmitted instantaneously via the Internet. Because many newsrooms are not capable of maintaining a larger network of correspondents all over the globe and in areas of special interest, manufactured and available news from wire services become increasingly important (see, e.g., Wilke, 2000). Wire services transmit news minutes after an event, ready to be used for coverage. Thus, it seems reasonable to assume a substantial share of overlapping news due to wire service reports (Roessler, 2002).

Empirical evidence indicates a rather diverse output of wire services that may be surprising if we consider their claims as a broad and comprehensive source of news. Three services under study (the national *dpa* and *ddp* and the German service of *Associated Press*) devoted a quarter of the whole output to issues that were present in all three sources. Yet, 75% of reports were not covered by all three primary German outlets. At the same time, this apparently broad range of news items is severely reduced if we look at the stories selected by journalists. An analysis of 12 German newspapers revealed that coverage tends to focus on events represented in more than one wire service report, thus reducing the impact of exclusive wire news. The "publicity ratio" (PR), representing the share of newspapers reached by each event covered by any of the wire services, remained considerably low on average (6.1%) but amounted to 32.8% when only the 152 events reported by all wire services were considered (Roessler, 2002). Based on these findings, a consensus among wire service reports enhances the probability that an event will be covered by a large number of newspapers.

Processes on the Micro-Level: Issue Diversity   Micro-level coverage constitutes an important field for empirical research because similarities on the meso-level of program types, genres, etc., may conceal substantial differences in the presentation of content. Early criticism has already pointed out that characteristics other than the "general type" measures could be relevant for the audience and that, from a viewer's standpoint, it is highly questionable why presentation of Oliver's *Hamlet*, a Marx brothers film, and *High Noon* should be defined as no diversity because all are "Feature Films," while the addition of *I Love Lucy* ("situation comedy"?) and *Bonanza* ("serial melodrama"?) constitute a double increment of diversity. (Greenberg & Barnett, 1971, p. 91)

Hallenberger (1997) as well as Einstein (2004b) also complained that diversity on the program type level does not always mean a true multiplicity of viewpoints because substantial differences may be hidden behind general genre labels. In other words, as Owen (1978) explained, "There may be as much 'diversity' *within* traditional program types as *among* program types" (p. 44). This notion challenges both dimensions of the diversity assessments mentioned before: the definition of categories as well as the classification of items according to these categories.

The *differentiation of issues* on the micro-level becomes important as a determinant for social cognition and our mapping of the "world outside" that turns into "the pictures in our head" (Lippmann, 1922, p. 11). It may refer to diversity of overall topics, single events, or even certain aspects of these events (e.g., arguments within a text or pictures depicted in the case of visuals). Hence, coverage of two given media outlets may vary in the topics represented; if they cover the same topic, the events reported may be different, and, even if they depict the same event, each outlet may emphasize certain aspects, like the pros, cons, or attributes of a person in selected pictures (see Figure 10.1). Such emphasis remains crucial to *framing*, which explores how journalistic coverage links arguments, positions, and news items to a framework for issue interpretation (see, e.g., Reese, Gandy, & Grant, 2001).

On each of these sublevels, one may further distinguish between processes on a more cognitive and evaluative dimension: (1) Is the item covered by many or few outlets, indicating the salience of an item? (2) Do outlets assess an item in the same way or differently? Following Noelle-Neumann and Mathes (1987), this distinction between the two dimensions refers to two different processes: *focusing*, if news coverage agrees on a common set of problems, and *consonance*, if coverage shares the same tone. According to Noelle-Neumann and Mathes, "Consonance in this sense can be described as uniform or similar tendencies in reporting by different media" (p. 404). As Noelle-Neumann and Mathes asserted, this evaluative dimension underscores the *diversity of opinion* notion, in which the media should represent all relevant opinions in an appropriate way to ensure a high level of public information. I suggest the terms *variety* and *inconsistency,* respectively, for the opposite outcome of these processes.

Finally, at least three types of dynamics leading to a certain degree of focusing or consonance have been identified (Roessler, 2000). First, *exclusiveness* (with one outlet controlling coverage) often indicates a low degree of focusing or consonance between the media on a lower level but may contribute to stronger agreement on the events or topics level. Second, over time, the original exclusiveness turns to a *leadership* dynamic where other media follow the coverage of an opinion leader medium (see Mathes & Pfetsch, 1991); the time frame for leadership may be rather short (e.g., if newspaper journalists observe current television coverage) or, in some cases, rather long (e.g., in the Watergate case or for HIV coverage). Third, most important and often the rule, outlets take publishing decisions independent of each other but leading to the same results, given that journalistic selection rules like those suggested by the theory of news values (e.g., Staab, 1990) tend to homogenize media coverage. However, at the same time, they still leave a considerable amount of variance unexplained (see Schoenbach, 1980, for empirical evidence related to diversity assessment). Some news stories dominate on all channels, whereas others appear only in particular programs.

Research on Diversity in Issues   Empirical evidence on the microlevel of diversity is less comprehensive than for assessments on the program-type level. Analyzing the issues of editorials in the five German quality newspapers between 1994 and 1998, Eilders (2000) found an average dissimilarity coefficient of 75.7% for every pair of newspapers. When comparing any two newspapers on a daily basis, three out of four editorials featured different *topics*, and, consequently, they only shared one out of four. For each of the 45 topical categories, Eilders calculated a mean value of the number of newspapers covering the category (focusing index). With a possible variation between one (newspaper) and five (all newspapers), the average was around 1.5 and never exceeded 2.2 (topic: political parties and movements). Regarding the special realm of editorials, Eilders found focusing on a day-by-day basis to be rather low, but turning to a weekly basis, the picture changed dramatically. Dissimilarity dropped to 53.4%, with any two newspapers sharing almost half of their editorial topics during a given week, and focusing increased to 4.24 for the political party and social movement topic. This means that nearly all of the five newspapers commented at least once on that topic during any given week.

Eilder's (2000) results already suggest that, in the case of editorials, leadership dynamics could be at work—a phenomenon addressed prominently by the concept of intermedia agenda setting (McCombs & Reynolds, 2002). In their case study of the cocaine issue in 1986, Danielian and Reese (1989) calculated week-to-week trends in coverage and identified the *New York Times* as an important outlet. The amount of its coverage led other newspapers and, particularly, the attention of television broadcast news. Yet, for a different topic (the U.S. presidential election in 1996), this role was not supported (Boyle, 2001), reminding us that general assertions remain difficult in this field. Given the reality in newsrooms and the routines in news selection and presentation (e.g., Shoemaker, 1991), explicit intermedia agenda setting seems to be the exception rather than the rule in media coverage.

Research on Diversity in Event Coverage in Television   As far as *event* coverage is concerned, a basic body of research exists under the label of *product differentiation*. Empirical studies from the United States and Germany took the single event generating a news story as their basic unit of analysis and compared the consideration of these events in competing news programs. Lemert (1974) coded the stories in the evening news of the three American networks for 2 weeks in 1971, and he found a rather impressive amount of focusing. About 58% of all weekday stories were covered on the same day by all newscasts, and nearly 70% of the stories carried by any of the networks were also covered by at least one of the other two. Even the rank order of stories showed rather high correlations, and "routine" stories were most likely to be duplicated.

A replication of this approach for 5 days in 1973, but taking a smaller segment of the news (instead of the whole news story) as the unit of analysis, yielded comparable results (Fowler & Showalter, 1974). According to Fowler and Showalter, networks allocated nearly two thirds of each network's newscasts to stories covered by at least one other network. Based on a data set from 5 days in 1982, Atwater (1984, 1986) found local television news to be more diverse, given that approximately half of the stories in each market under study were unique.[3] A 1988 sample of newscasts in three local markets in Texas supports similar conclusions: A little more than half of the stories covered identical events (56%), with variance depending on the number of different newscasts available in the market (Davie & Lee, 1993). According to Davie and Lee, electronic network news-gathering increased the level of focusing, as well as a more national or worldwide scope of the event.

Donsbach and Dupré (1994) conducted additional research in Germany, driven by the notion that, with the diffusion of cable and satellite television, the only consequence of program multipli-cation might be "more of the same" (p. 229). The German Federal Media Authorities also launched a series of broadcast studies in order to assess the local issue agendas in several German markets. The research strategy included the identification of single events and their coverage in different media outlets; nevertheless, the samples were limited to local issues in three Bavarian cities or to regional issues in Lower Saxony only (see Trebbe, 1996, 1998; Trebbe & Mau-rer, 1999; Trebbe & Weiß, 1997). The degree of diversity that can be derived from their results corresponds with findings in American local markets.

A more comprehensive study on seven TV news shows of major national networks in Germany revealed that two thirds of the sto-ries were reported exclusively by one outlet. They tended to be rather nonpolitical (see Roessler, 2005a). The channels used predomi-nantly sports, crime, disasters, and human interest stories for dis-tinguishing their profile from their competitors. Over the course of one week, only seven stories were covered by all news shows; they could be labeled as the "core news inventory" and accounted for less than 3% of stories but about 20% of program time. As duplicated stories tend to be of a higher news value (and thus longer and more prominent), studies based on mere story counts may overestimate the share of coverage devoted to exclusive reporting. The percent-age of duplicated stories dropped dramatically from 65 to 23% when Roessler considered story length rather than story counts. Linking this type of research to a media regulation framework, Schwotzer (2005) coded the diversity of news items in shows on three German channels under the same ownership (ProSiebenSAT.1 Media AG). He concluded that less than one out of three reports in a given week was broadcast by one of the stations only; whereas, two thirds of news events were duplicated in at least two of the stations.

Research on Diversity in Event Coverage: Other Media   Research on other media concentrated on regional newspapers where Haller (2000) introduced a benchmarking approach as an instrument for quality management. According to his results, a quality newspaper focusing on stories served as an indicator for diversity of local news coverage. In a different study, the comparison of political coverage in 27 German newspapers supported the assumption that, even with additional outlets under study, the balance between duplication and exclusive reporting remains stable because each additional newspaper may contribute new stories but, at the same time, likely reduces exclusivity of another one (see Roessler, 2003). According to Roessler, weighted by story length, a share of 20% of the coverage was devoted to events reported by 20 or more newspapers on the same day. In a case study on the coverage of civil protest events by German print media, Eilders (2001) calculated the overlap of coverage regarding 1,043 single events. On the other hand, of three newspapers examined, an average of 144 covered the civil protest events, leading to a remarkable share of exclusive reporting on this issue by all three outlets, based on a locally and regionally oriented selection.

In their pioneering study, McQuail and van Cuilenburg (1983) developed another benchmark for their assessment of Netherlands press coverage. They determined a "total universe of information (thus the reality)" (p. 157) derived from official records of a parliamentary debate. For this issue of rather limited scope, they were able to calculate an average share of 10% of information items that was considered by a newspaper. According to McQuail and van Cuilenburg, outlets differed heavily when the researchers compared the contribution of political parties involved in the debate to their attention in the national newspapers, as expressed by varying "reflection scores" (p. 158).

Finally, Roessler (2001b) discovered an interesting phenomenon caused by the periodicity of radio news. In Germany, radio news shows usually are broadcast every full hour, and thus, the repetition quota must be taken into account if we calculate internal diversity. In a pilot study for the radio market in Thuringia, each story was covered between two and three times per day (5 a.m. until 6 p.m.) on a given radio channel, and the repetition rate between two subsequent shows was 25% on average. Representing a rare study of diversity in radio news at the micro-level of single events, Roessler found that more than 50% of the news coverage was devoted to issues reported by all three stations in the given market at least once the very same day. According to this study, the highly structured radio format in Germany, which allows for few creative features in news presentation, seems to enhance the process of focusing on the main events.

Research on Diversity in Event Coverage: Comprehensive Perspectives   According to my review of the literature, Sasser and Russell (1972) are the only scholars who have tried thus far to assess diversity across media types within a local market. They compared coverage on local events by a newspaper, two local evening television programs, and two radio newscasts, based on a word count of stories (thus neglecting the visual component completely). Although the authors only calculated the overlap for every pair of outlets, the portion of shared stories was substantially lower than in earlier studies on the national level (see earlier discussion), which may be explained by the more frequent opportunities for diverse coverage in the local realm. Accordingly, diversity in local media coverage may depend on variations in the respective community, as it can be read from indicators of structural pluralism (see Jeffres, Cutietta, Sekerka, & Lee, 2000, for an overview of relevant studies for the relationship between media coverage and structural pluralism in communities).[4] Reporting on a variety of events is facilitated when a variety of events exist from which journalists can choose. Needless to say, particularly on the local level, the emergence of grassroots journalism; media of a counter-public, small-group communication; and other fringe media, contribute heavily to a diverse informational environment that goes beyond mass media (Eilders, 2001; Jarren, 1992; Knoche & Lindgens, 1988).

Heller (1999) collected data on the degree of diversity comparing online, television, and print output of media content providers. Heller analyzed the event coverage provided by the different outlets of *Der Spiegel, Focus,* and *Stern*. All three providers started as successful printed news magazines, extended their range by producing a television format, and, finally, launched popular Internet Web sites in the 1990s. Surprisingly, Heller discovered a rather low share of news overlap by the online medium from the printed versions. Instead, the dominating pattern revealed higher redundancy between news items on a specific channel (print, TV, online). As Heller detailed, several case studies of events attaining a high amount of public awareness supported this notion of journalistic co-orientation that focused on content provided by the same type of media.

Loosen (2005) attained similar results when she analyzed the same three content providers after the market of online newspapers consolidated. Again, overlap shares were higher within a certain type of media than within the different media related to one news provider. On average, a quarter of news items published by one provider were included in at least two of its outlets, and about 40% of event coverage could be found in the online version as well. On the other hand, the significantly larger body of Internet coverage consisted mainly of exclusive events (80%) that were not mentioned in any of the other media. Interviews with journalists confirmed that the overflow of stories that cannot be considered for the printed version is routinely handed over to the online newsroom. At the same time, the online version often fulfils the function of an electronic archive for the printed version. According to Loosen, the modularized structure of information presentation on the Internet has already changed the style of coverage in printed media that tended to follow this technique based on a compilation of different news items.

Evidence from a cross-national perspective is sparse but unequivocal. Even among countries with close relationships like those in the European Union, public agenda diversity is high (Peter & de Vreese, 2003). At the same time, almost no common background of media coverage exists, reducing the idea of a "European public" to a respectable wish (see Roessler, 2004, p. 289). Sievert (1998) supported this impression with an analysis of printed magazine coverage on the European Union in five countries. According to Sievert, the synchrony in events, regional and topical focus, and protagonists is low; domestic viewpoints, which obviously vary among the respective countries, guided most of the coverage.

The event coverage overlap with countries like the United States is even smaller, although the global marketing of video material by providers such as CNN, BBC World Service, or the European Broadcasting Union (Foote, 1995) makes an international pool of footage on current affairs widely available. This account of globalization refers to the long-standing issue of cultural imperialism with a one-way flow of content from west to east and north to south (McQuail, 2005). Nevertheless, in a global frame of reference, diversity remains overwhelmingly high (Roessler, 2004), despite the worldwide marketing of media content, unless breaking news with global implications (e.g., the death of Lady Diana or, more recently, coverage of 9/11 or the tsunami tragedy in 2005) shares an international audience.

Research on Diversity of Aspects in Media Texts Moving down to the depiction of *single aspects in text and visuals*, assessments of diversity almost completely rely on singular observations originating from case studies. One of the most prominent examples involves Halloran, Elliott, and Murdock's (1970) examination of the real-world course of a demonstration, media coverage on the event, and resulting perceptions of the audience. Their analysis included a comparison of aspects like the violence enacted during the demonstration and the (mostly negative) wording of the headlines or nature of the pictures printed and televised by several outlets. Although this study is usually cited for illustrating processes of news selection, framing, and media opinion leadership (see, e.g., Noelle-Neumann & Mathes, 1987), it contributes as well to the notion of a limited diversity on the micro-level of single aspects. The same holds true for the additional textual analysis on the cocaine issue of 1986 (Danielian & Reese, 1989), where—despite the role of the *New York Times* as leading the issue chronologically—stories in the *Washington Post* using governmental sources determined the aspects considered. Particularly for an event taking place in Bolivia, the newspapers under study referenced the same unnamed administration sources, leading Danielian and Reese to the general assumption that "when the newspapers all go in on a breaking story, they cover it in the same ways using the same themes and sources" (p. 63).

Williams and Delli Carpini (2000) provided a closer look at the dynamics of news coverage surrounding the Clinton–Lewinsky scandal. These researchers tracked the rise of this issue, assuming "the virtual elimination of the gatekeeping role of the mainstream press" (p. 61). They found initial allegations about Bill Clinton published in alternative and quasi-alternative media outlets. Together with Matt Drudge's scoop journalism on the Internet, the issue spilled over to more serious media such as the *Los Angeles Times*, with the meta-issue of Drudge's practices serving as an additional pretext for coverage. They affirmed the popular notion that an event did not truly become a "real" event until it arrived into the mainstream print press. However, their analysis suggested that the role of traditional journalists as agenda setters and issue framers was declining due to communication in the new media environment.

Research on Diversity of Aspects in Visuals Another case study referred to the German coverage on the Brent Spar scandal, and it claimed to be "the first one to apply diversity as a criterion of the text-oriented research on media quality to visuals in TV coverage" (Berens & Hagen, 1997, p. 539). Although the authors recognized a high degree of redundancy in the news coverage of private stations, where the same pictures were aired over and over again, they based their analysis on the interpretative paradigm of text analysis without developing a standardized instrument like a visual coding scheme.

Such a standardized methodological approach was introduced and applied by a German research team that created an *iconographic codebook* for visual coding (see Roessler, 2001a, for a more detailed description of the procedures). The empirical study conducted with this instrument provided the first evidence on the lowest level of TV news diversity—that of single video sequences included in coverage. Its micro-level analysis indicates a high degree of variety (Roessler, 2005a). According to Roessler, in the 7-day sample, only 10 stories could be identified that were reported the same day by all eight news shows, and less than 10% of daily events were present in more than half of the main German evening news shows.

Alternatively, in the same study, weighting the data by the length of a sequence reduced the share of unique singular sequences, and the change was noteworthy (Roessler, 2005a). Almost half of the footage was broadcast by at least two (or more) shows.

Research on Diversity of Aspects: Consonance and Geography
Little of the evidence for consonance really applies the logic of diversity analysis (see McQuail & van Cuilenburg, 1983). Most of the empirical studies conducted so far do not compare the prevalence of particular arguments in different media, but rather present aggregate data for the tone of coverage over a certain period of time to ascertain the position of a news outlet (e.g., Kepplinger, 1985). Pritchard (2002) used this strategy to assess viewpoint diversity in cross-owned media outlets during the 2000 presidential campaign in the United States. Pritchard determined the slant of newspapers and television stations belonging to the same owner in 10 local news markets. His results suggest that "common ownership of a newspaper and a television station in a community does not result in a predictable pattern of news coverage and commentary on important political events between the commonly owned outlets" (p. 13). In five of the ten newspaper–television combinations studied, the overall slant of television coverage differed noticeably from the same company's newspaper.

In contrast, Eilders (2002) calculated weekly positions for the editorials of each of five German newspapers and developed a *dissonance measure* for all weeks between 1994 and 1998. Dissonance turned out to vary between 0.5 and 0.9 on a 3-point scale, indicating little consonance between the German quality newspapers, which—although claiming to be impartial—traditionally favor either more liberal or more conservative standpoints. In the early 1960s, philosopher Hans Magnus Enzensberger (1962) discussed this problem regarding the coverage of the *Frankfurter Allgemeine Zeitung (FAZ)*. In his critical essay, he explored the main political events as depicted in 10 leading European newspapers and compared their ways of reporting to the *FAZ* coverage. Although his interpretation is ideologically based and his analysis does not meet the usual standards of an empirical content analysis, he applied the basic procedure of the micro-level aspects comparison. He contrasted the media events covered by different outlets for a limited time span and thus sharing the same historical background.

A related aspect comprises the *geographical diversity* in media coverage (see Hoffmann-Riem, 1987). The only systematic micro-level comparison of issue diversification in television news of different countries conducted thus far (Roessler, 2004) has shown that, while internal diversity is reflected by a heavy focus on domestic issues or domestication of others, the external diversity is so extreme that hardly any shared issues between media in different countries could account for the constitution of a cross-national public. Combining several of these indicators in a study on internal diversity of information formats on German TV, Bruns and Marcinkowski (1997) found a high degree of entropy over a longer period of time (1986 to 1994). They concluded that, for issues as well as for protagonists and geographical locations, channel diversification did not reduce diversity; instead, a rather balanced depiction on all three dimensions characterized coverage of channels under investigation.

Research on Diversity of Protagonists in the Media   Turning back to Figure 10.1, *diversity of protagonists* displayed in the media refers to the presence of real-world persons (politicians, athletes, etc.) or characters and their features. One prominent example involves the counting of seconds that television channels devoted to presidential candidates, based on the assumption that telepresence seems to exert a strong influence on people's decision making regarding voting decisions (e.g., Holtz-Bacha, 2000). In her study on diversity of events and protagonists in German news outlets, Mayer (2006) specified several factors that account for varying results in diversity of individuals present on the screen. According to Mayer, type of medium plays a crucial role because television makes different demands on a protagonist compared to printed media, and the selected time period for analysis is relevant because it refers to specific issue cycles and the overall news background. In sum, her results indicate that diversity remains considerably higher on the level of protagonists compared to the level of events.

Critical/cultural studies scholars widely discuss the *representation* of groups in the media, particularly in terms of race, gender, and social status (see, e.g., Dines & Humez, 2003; Gentz & Kramer, 2006; Kamalipour & Carilli, 1998). The main perspective, then, involves the distribution of power in society as reflected by these representations that encompasses an essential part of the process by which cultural members produce and exchange meaning (Hall, 1997), including the question of equality and inequality of opportunities. Literature abounds in this field, and it would constitute the topic of a chapter on its own. Still, it seems important to mention some of its conclusions here because they are highly relevant for micro-level content diversity.[5]

A well-known diversity issue stems from the under- and misrepresentation of minorities in the media, such as representation of the elderly or minorities (see, e.g., Greenberg & Brand, 1998, or a recent literature review by del Rio, 2006). Researchers have detailed the depiction of different ethnic groups in society (see, e.g., Artz, 1998; Gray, 1995). Benson (2005) focused on the presence or absence of people of color from media, reporting that, in 1997, only 112 out of 12,000 national TV network news stories focused on "Latina/o" issues, of which 64% were about crime, immigration, and affirmative action). Downing and Husband (2005) discussed the constructive versus unconstructive portrayal of minorities in the media. They called for a "recognizing diversity," which means dealing appropriately with difference—another view on reflective diversity (p. 196). In the case of sexual minorities, existing moral norms of what can be displayed by a certain type of media further enhances their under-representation. For example, for a long time, "gay people have been simply invisible in the media" (Gross, 2001, p. 410; see also Hart, 2003).

On the other hand, changes in audience demographics and usage patterns (Zook, 2003) led to a more diverse distribution of characters across various formats (e.g., in sitcoms, crime shows, etc.). This issue also relates to the nature of the visuals by which the media portrays these groups. Depicting race in stereotypes (which, in the present context, can be perceived as opposed to a diverse portrayal) works most perfectly in pictures, cartoons, or movies (Hall, 1997). Employing the cultivation approach, other scholars have addressed long-term effects of these representations (see Morgan & Shanahan, 1997, and, more recently, Hetsroni & Tukachinsky, 2006). Nevertheless, studies have not always proven that a negative presentation of racial stereotypes in the mass media translates to the audiences' perceptions and attitudes. Examining the responses to depictions in the movie *Rush Hour 2*, Park, Gabbadon, and Chernin (2006) concluded that even Asian and Black participants in the study found a positive source of pleasure in the negative portrayal of their own races, and the film did not generate oppositional discourse. In general, they suggested that comedy as a distinctive format might even naturalize racial differences rather than challenge racial stereotypes. Furthermore, Benson (2005, p. 11) claimed that the so-called "diversity journalism" may have been too successful because the equation of diversity with "race" in the public mind diverted attention from the increasing lack of diversity in other fields (e.g., ideology).

Discussion

Diversity in Pluralistic Media Systems

The general picture that can be drawn from this review of the literature on content diversity is hazy in many respects. Although a substantial body of studies is available, we lack a coherent view on how content diversity should be determined and, more importantly, on how it impacts media performance and social conditions. Deficits include (1) determining which level diversity needs to be studied and how evidence on different levels can be integrated, (2) the definition of diversity and which units should be compared to assess diversity, and, most importantly, (3) the interpretation of empirical results on diversity and their validity as indicators for social reality.

First, the results of empirical research provided in this review are not conclusive, as they vary according to time periods of data collection, region, and the level of analysis. Decreases in diversity at the macro-level should lead to decreases at the meso-level; subsequently, decreases in diversity at the meso-level should lead to decreases at the micro-level, resulting in overall lower content diversity. However, evidence so far suggests that observable decreases in diversity at the macro-level did not necessarily create decreasing diversity on the meso-level. Concentration in ownership does not inevitably reduce the range of genres, formats, or outlets available. Moreover, even if an increase on the meso-level is recorded, this change did not automatically prompt an increase in diversity on the micro-level. A multiplication of channels or introduction of formats does not always imply that media content represents a greater variety of issues, events, perspectives, opinions, regions, or protagonists (for further discussion of proposed models, see van Cuilenburg, 2005; Vlasic, 2004).

Second, from an epistemological point of view, the crucial question still remains: the definition of content diversity in a given situation (Einstein, 2004b) or, respectively, what we consider to be similar on each of the levels of analysis mentioned earlier. Deciding similarities and differences represents the core of content diversity discussions (see, e.g., Fowler & Showalter, 1974; Merten, 2001; Roessler, 2001a). It requires both theoretical and methodological reasoning, and it cannot be left to the single coder who applies an instrument, which would reduce this important issue to a matter of reliability. When deciding about similarity, the precision of measurement constitutes the framework in which a meaningful degree of coherence needs to be determined. On the macro-level of analysis, the structural indicators are often connected with channels or media outlets as units of analysis, and, in this case, usually a one-to-one correspondence of units can be demanded for coding two units as similar. On the micro-level of media coverage, the threshold obviously needs to be lower. Journalistic portrayals of reality are multilayered and many faceted; consequentially, the decision about which degree of overlap on two items should qualify as similar has to be oriented according to a presumed perception of an average media user.

Third, the most substantial deficit in diversity research thus far concerns the link between descriptive results on media performance and indicators for societal developments. Of course, the finding that media systems can be characterized by rather stable degrees of entropy on quite different levels of analysis is significant. Journalists' professional routines and standardized selection criteria do not work equally in every newsroom and thus do not lead to the same product in the end. In a competitive media market, for example, both public and private TV channels need to develop their own news profiles without leaving the common ground of widely shared, relevant events—especially in the fields of domestic and world politics. This balance can be ascertained from most empirical studies, but its ramifications still remain unclear.

The notion of diversity in media content impacts a broad variety of social issues tackled by diverse communication researchers. For instance, achieving social integration by political communication—during campaigns and beyond—represents an established issue, but so far tends to disregards the role of diversity in this process. Moreover, Vlasic's (2004) model of integration (bridging processes on the macro- and micro-levels to foster shared definitions of situations in society) could be applied to larger subsystems of society as well. For example, in the health sector, the availability of diverse information could enhance efficiency and should be supported by successful health communication—a factor that could also be included into multilevel models explaining memory for health campaign advertisements (Southwell, 2005).

Some Directions for Future Research

Alternative Media   With the emergence of new forms of journalism and public debate, observers expect content diversity to reach its peak. Earlier research on the role of alternative media already indicates that, at least in the case of issues related to protest movements, unconventional outlets such as the left-wing German newspaper *Die Tageszeitung (taz)* contribute substantially to overall content diversity in a given media market. They often succeed in covering issues neglected by traditional media and in adopting perspectives not represented in public discourse (Eilders, 2001; Knoche & Lindgens, 1988). Alternative media can focus attention on a certain issue, but to obtain a high position on the agenda, a spill-over to well-known opinion leader media of high reputation and wide circulation seems complementary (Mathes & Pfetsch, 1991; Williams & Delli Carpini, 2000).

The Internet provides an endless variety of alternative sources, opening up a new area of research that explores the interplay between traditional media and the new digital environment (for related arguments, see Croteau, 2006; Rayner, 2006). However, it should not be neglected that part of the alternative public constituted by

Internet media contributes to diversity by offering content of arguable quality, such as rumors and conspiracy theories (see, e.g., Hargrove & Stempel III, 2006a). However, the merits of the Internet as a main conveyer of content of any kind should not be disregarded because it stands for a rather unlimited and flexible communication environment indissolubly connected to the open version of diversity (see McQuail, 2005). New gatekeepers modify the traditional gatekeeping role of prestigious media, operating with different aims, standards, and professional backgrounds (see, e.g., Roessler, 2005b; Williams & Delli Carpini, 2000). The most prominent example for this trend refers to the rapidly increasing number of Web logs (blogs) that now constitute a substantial part of the online communication environment.

From the perspective of pluralism, blogs constitute a new opportunity for participation in political and social life. According to Kahn and Keller (2004), "Bloggers have demonstrated themselves as technoactivists favoring not only democratic self-expression and networking, but also global media critique and journalistic sociopolitical intervention" (p. 91). In an international study including data from the United States, Russia, China, Germany, Italy, Poland, Portugal, Sweden, and Spain, Schlobinski and Siever (2005) reported more than 70 million blogs worldwide as of July 2005, with an exponential increase since early 2004. According to these researchers, bloggers perceive their movement to be the final release from information control; Web logs are supposed to democratize information and knowledge in a new quality and quantity and thus alter access, control, and value of information.

Nevertheless, availability should not be confused with accessibility, and even less with actual use that translates into more diverse perceptions of reality, per se. Again, Weblogs may illustrate this pitfall. A recent survey of 5,246 active authors in the German blogosphere (Schmidt & Wilt, 2006) revealed that two thirds of participants claimed to update their blog several times a week, mostly for fun or to preserve ideas and experiences for themselves (diary function). Conversely, the same people assumed that mostly good friends and relatives read their blogs. According to Schmidt and Wilt, "making new contacts" rated down low in the list of possible blogging motivations. The bloggosphere can also be a source for alternative news and counterarguing, including conspiracy theories (Hargrove & Stempel III, 2006b).

On the other hand, in countries with a high level of media censorship and political repressions like Iran, an increasing number of young people use Web logs to express their opinions and discuss political matters (Aminpur, 2006). We may conclude that the Internet challenges both diversity theory and research because our way of thinking about diversity dates from the era of mass media broadcasting and may not be appropriate, given a ubiquitous digital media environment with blurring boundaries between individual and mass communication. Moreover, even in the field of television, the amount of satellite-delivered content has increased dramatically, offering the potential of a highly diverse media environment. New approaches have to be found for integrating freedom in access, choice, and choices actually realized into a common explanatory framework of content diversity.

Use of Diverse Media   The most substantial shortcoming of diversity research, according to which each degree of variety in the media system may lead to positive or negative consequences, has remained almost untreated so far by empirical research. We can only speculate whether the interplay of centrifugal and centripetal effects supports the optimistic or the pessimistic vision of society. Although we have gained some insight in the diversity provided by media coverage, the crucial question remains whether this diversity is actually consumed by media users. In other words, how does supply diversity translate into diversity in consumption (see Hallenberger, 1997)? Evidence on the audience side is limited to singular aspects like the diversity of audience agendas in political campaigns (Allen & Izcaray, 1988; Brosius & Reinemann, 1998; Wanta, King, & McCombs, 1995). The inevitability of moving to audience-centered approaches of program diversity assessment (Napoli, 1997) was recognized some time ago, but it has not yet led to substantial research efforts in this field. Vlasic's (2004) model, although designed to analyze societal integration in general, may well serve as a theoretical framework for future research.

Conclusion

This review calls for more theoretical efforts to explain diversity data rather than just collecting more empirical evidence. This analysis of content diversity in communication research has examined its relevance in social and economical terms, its measurement on different levels, and some implications of globalization and digitalization. It focused on journalistic diversity with regard to the (political) content, but it included a broader perspective of media content in its whole variety. Again, it should be emphasized that content diversity itself represents nothing more than a mere variety in media offerings. So far, research has demonstrated the varying degrees of diversity on different levels of analysis through quantitative methods, but "it has not contributed greatly to secure information about the causes and consequences of more or less diversity" (McQuail, 2005, p. 22).

The value of the concept for democracy (or within a market) is open to many definitions, but, when authors refer to a general decline in political ideology, religious belief, and communalism, the impact on the esteem for diversity appears rather obvious. McQuail (2005) asserted:

> Shared group characteristics, even those of region and community, seem to matter less to people, except for some groups under threat. In secular western societies the bases of collective identity are either weakening or changing towards more ephemeral manifestations in tastes and lifestyle, which are hardly suitable grounds for policy, although they are an expression of diversity. (p. 20)

Altogether, unlimited media diversity is not a useful prospect for a society. Maximum diversity not only threatens social integration, but it may also lead to agony of people confronted with an increasing amount of easily available information (Rager & Weber, 1992). Another important function of mass media is their capability to select and condense the informational tide. A merely diverse media offer without apparent indicators of relevance is not digestible for the audience, but the same holds true for a media environment without choices for the audience, controlled and paralyzed in conformity. Research indicates that content diversity tends to reach a point of balance between these extremes. However, it is not clear which position on this continuum needs to be considered as an optimum for society (as well as for the media market).

Notes

1. Furthermore, one could also argue that every content analysis study presenting the differences in issue coverage between several media outlets contains an assertion of diversity, although this claim is almost never made (for a recent exception, see van Lunenberg, 2002) and no coefficients for diversity are calculated.

2. See McQuail (2005, p. 13) for a more recent version of his typology, covering a broader range of diversity aspects.
3. Please note that this study used the term *consonance* for duplication on the story level (Atwater, 1986, p. 469) and not for corresponding evaluative assessments as suggested previously.
4. A German study on diversity in a local media environment was conducted in the late 1970s and assumed little diversity according several criteria, but the researcher compared only issue profiles of different outlets rather than calculating overlap shares for similar topics in different media (Rager, 1982).
5. Please note that the findings are based on a different type of evidence because this body of work relies on interpretive methods and case studies rather than on the calculation of diversity coefficients for larger media samples.

References

Allen, R. L., & Izcaray, F. (1988). Nominal agenda-diversity in a media-rich, less-developed society. *Communication Research, 15,* 29–50.

Aminpur, K. (2006, January 22). Die Jugend und die Mullahs. [The youth and the mullahs]. *Frankfurter Allgemeine Sonntagszeitung, 3,* 3.

Anonymous (2004, February 23). How to ensure media diversity. *Business Week, 3871,* 140.

Anonymous (2006). Kartellamt untersagt Fusion von Springer und ProSiebenSat.1. [Federal Cartel Office prohibits merger of Springer and ProSiebenSat.1]. *Spiegel online.* Retrieved January 23, 2006, from http://www.spiegel.de/wirtschaft/0,1518,396882,00.html

Artz, B. L. (1998). Hegemony in black and white: Interracial buddy films and the new racism. In Y. R. Kamalipour & T. Carilli (Eds.), *Cultural diversity and the U.S. media* (pp. 67–78). Albany: State University of New York Press.

Aslama, M. (2006). *The diversity challenge: Changing television markets and public service programming in Finland, 1993–2004.* Working paper, Donald McGannon Communication Research Center, Bronx, NY.

Aslama, M., Hellman, H., & Sauri, T. (2004). Does market-entry regulation matter? Competition in television broadcasting and programme diversity in Finland, 1993–2002. *Gazette, 66,* 113–132.

Atwater, T. (1984). Product differentiation in local TV news. *Journalism Quarterly, 61,* 757–762.

Atwater, T. (1986). Consonance in local television news. *Journal of Broadcasting & Electronic Media, 30,* 467–472.

Bagdikian, B. H. (2004). *The new media monopoly.* Boston: Beacon Press.

Baker, C. E., & Kübler, F. (2004). Sicherung der Meinungsvielfalt durch mehr Markt? Die rechtspolitische Entwicklung der Medienkonzentrationskontrolle in den Vereinigten Staaten [More market as a safeguard for diversity of opinions? How the control of media concentration processes develops in the U.S.]. *Media Perspektiven, 24,* 81–88.

Benson, R. (2005). American journalism and the politics of diversity. *Media, Culture & Society, 27,* 5–20.

Berens, H., & Hagen, L. (1997). Der Fall "Brent Spar" in Hauptnachrichtensendungen. Ansätze zur Operationalisierung von Qualitätskriterien für die Bildberichterstattung [The case of "Brent Spar" in evening news shows: Approaches for operationalizing criteria to assess the quality of news coverage]. In G. Bentele & M. Haller (Eds.), *Aktuelle Entstehung von Öffentlichkeit* (pp. 539–549). Konstanz, Germany: UVK.

Berry, S. T., & Waldfogel, J. (2001). Do mergers increase product variety? Evidence from radio broadcasting. *The Quarterly Journal of Economics, 116,* 1009–1025.

Blevins, J. L. (2002). Source diversity after the Telecommunications Act of 1996: Media oligarchs begin to colonize cyberspace. *Television & New Media, 3,* 95–112.

Blöbaum, B. (1992). Journalismus, Öffentlichkeit und Vielfalt [Journalism, public, and diversity]. In G. Rager & B. Weber (Eds.), *Publizistische Vielfalt zwischen Markt und Politik* (pp. 150–171). Düsseldorf, Germany: Econ.

Blumler, J. G. (1991). In pursuit of program range and quality. *Studies of Broadcasting, 27,* 191–206.

Boyle, T. P. (2001). Intermedia agenda setting in the 1996 presidential election. *Journalism & Mass Communication Quarterly, 78,* 26–44.

Branahl, U. (1992). Publizistische Vielfalt als Rechtsgebot [Media diversity as a legal command]. In G. Rager & B. Weber (Eds.), *Publizistische Vielfalt zwischen Markt und Politik* (pp. 85–109). Düsseldorf, Germany: Econ.

Brosius, H.-B., & Reinemann, C. (1998). Themenvielfalt in der Bevölkerungsagenda Ost- und Westdeutschlands [Issue diversity of the audience agenda in East and West Germany]. *Publizistik, 43,* 273–286.

Brosius, H.-B., & Zubayr, C. (1996). *Vielfalt im deutschen Fernsehprogramm. Eine Analyse der Angebotsstruktur öffentlich-rechtlicher und privater Sender* [Diversity on German TV: An analysis of public and private television channels]. Ludwigshafen, Germany: LPR-Schriftenreihe, Band 12.

Bruck, P. A. (Ed.). (1993). *Medienmanager Staat. Von den Versuchen des Staates, Medienvielfalt zu ermöglichen: Medienpolitik im internationalen Vergleich* [The nation as a media manager: Attempts to support media diversity in an international perspective]. Munich, Germany: R. Fischer.

Bruns, T., & Marcinkowski, F. (1997): *Politische Information im Fernsehen. Eine Längsschnittstudie* [Political information on television: A longterm study]. Opladen, Germany: Westdeutscher Verlag.

Chalaby, J. K. (2005). Deconstructing the transnational: A typology of cross-border television channels in Europe. *New Media & Society, 7,* 155–175.

Croteau, D. (2006). The growth of self-produced media content and the challenge to media studies. *Critical Studies in Media Communication, 23,* 340–344.

Danielian, L. H., & Reese, S. D. (1989): A closer look at intermedia influences on agenda setting: The cocaine issue of 1986. In P. Shoemaker (Ed.), *Communication campaigns about drugs* (pp. 47–66). Hillsdale, NJ: Lawrence Erlbaum Associates.

Davie, W. R., & Lee, J. (1993). Television news technology: Do more sources mean less diversity? *Journal of Broadcasting and Electronic Media, 37,* 453–464.

DeBens, E. (1998). Television programming: More diversity, more convergence? In K. Brants, J. Hermes, & L. van Zoonen (Eds.), *The media in question: Popular cultures and public interests* (pp. 27–37). London: Sage.

de Jong, A. S., & Bates, B. J. (1991). Channel diversity in cable television. *Journal of Broadcasting & Electronic Media, 35,* 159–166.

del Rio, E. (2006). The Latina/o problematic: Categories and questions in media communication research. In C. S. Beck (Ed.), *Communication yearbook 30* (pp. 387–429). Hillsdale, NJ: Lawrence Erlbaum Associates.

Dimmick, J. (2004). Introduction [special issue]. *Journal of Media Economics, 17,* 85–86.

Dines, G., & Humez, J. M. (Eds.). (2003). *Gender, race, and class in media: A text-reader* (2nd ed.). Thousand Oaks, CA: Sage.

Dominick, J. R., & Pearce, M. C. (1976). Trends in network prime-time programming, 1953–1974. *Journal of Communication, 26,* 70–80.

Donsbach, W. (2004). Psychology of news decisions: Factors behind journalists' professional behaviour. *Journalism, 5,* 131–157.

Donsbach, W., & Dupré, D. (1994). Mehr Vielfalt oder "more of the same" durch mehr Kanäle? Möglichkeiten zum Unterhaltungsslalom im deutschen Fernsehen zwischen 1983 und 1991 [More diversity or more of the same as a result of more channels? Opportunities for the use of entertainment programs on German TV, 1983–1991]. In L. Bosshart & W. Hoffmann-Riem (Eds.), *Medienlust und Mediennutz* (pp. 229–247). Munich, Germany: Ölschläger.

Dowd, T. J. (2004). Concentration and diversity revisited: Production logics and the U. S. mainstream recording market, 1940–1990. *Social Forces, 82,* 1411–1455.

Downing, J., & Husband, C. (Eds.). (2005). *Representing "race": Racism, ethnicities, and media*. London: Sage.

Eilders, C. (2000). Media as political actors? Issue focusing and selective emphasis in the German quality press. *German Politics, 9,* 181–206.

Eilders, C. (2001). Die Darstellung von Protesten in ausgewählten deutschen Tageszeitungen [The depiction of political protest in selected German newspapers]. In D. Rucht (Ed.), *Protest in der Bundesrepublik. Strukturen und Entwicklungen* (pp. 275–311). Frankfurt, Germany: Campus.

Eilders, C. (2002). Conflict and consonance in media opinion: Political positions of five German quality newspapers. *European Journal of Communication, 17,* 25–63.

Einstein, M. (2004a). *Media diversity: Economics, ownership, and the FCC.* Mahwah, NJ: Lawrence Erlbaum Associates.

Einstein, M. (2004b). Broadcast network television, 1955–2003: The pursuit of advertising and the decline of diversity. *Journal of Media Economics, 17,* 145–155.

Elasmar, M. G. (Ed.). (2003). *The impact of international television: A paradigm shift.* Mahwah, NJ: Lawrence Erlbaum Associates.

Enzensberger, H. M. (1962): Journalismus als Eiertanz. Beschreibung einer Allgemeinen Zeitung für Deutschland [Journalism as a balancing act. Description of a general newspaper for Germany]. In H. M. Enzensberger (Ed.), *Einzelheiten, Teil I* (pp. 18–73). Frankfurt, Germany: Suhrkamp.

Feldmann, V. (2004). Der Kunde als König? Zum Beitrag der Unternehmensstrategie für die Vielfalt der Medieninhalte-Produktion [Customer is king? How business strategies contribute to diversity in media content production]. In M. Friedrichsen & W. Seifert (Eds.), *Effiziente Medienregulierung. Marktdefizite oder Regierungsdefizite?* (pp. 53–70) Baden-Baden, Germany: Nomos.

Foote, J. S. (1995). The structure and marketing of global television news. *Journal of Broadcasting & Electronic Media, 39,* 127–133.

Fowler, J. S., & Showalter, S. W. (1974). Evening network news selection: A confirmation of news judgment. *Journalism Quarterly, 51,* 712–715.

Gentz, N., & Kramer, S. (Eds.). (2006). *Globalization, cultural identities, and media representations.* Albany: State University of New York Press.

George, L. M. (2002). Ownership concentration and product variety in daily newspaper markets. In L. F. Cranor & S. Greenstein (Eds.), *Communications policy and information technology: Promises, problems, prospects* (pp. 235–251). Cambridge, MA: The MIT Press.

Grant, A. E. (1994). The promise fulfilled? An empirical analysis of program diversity on television. *The Journal of Media Economics, 7,* 51–64.

Gray, H. (1995). *Watching race: Television and the struggle for "Blackness."* Minneapolis: University of Minnesota Press.

Greenberg, B. S., & Brand, J. E. (1998). U.S. minorities and the news. In Y. R. Kamalipour & T. Carilli (Eds.), *Cultural diversity and the U.S. media* (pp. 3–22). Albany: State University of New York Press.

Greenberg, E., & Barnett, H. J. (1971). TV program diversity—New evidence and old theories. *American Economic Review, 61*(2), 89–93.

Gross, L. (2001). Out of the mainstream: Sexual minorities and the mass media. In M. G. Durham & D. M. Kellner (Eds.), *Media and cultural studies: Keyworks* (pp. 405–423). Malden, MA: Blackwell.

Gustafsson, K. E. (1992). Staatliche Förderung für publizistische Vielfalt in Schweden [Governmental support for media diversity in Sweden]. In G. Rager & B. Weber (Eds.), *Publizistische Vielfalt zwischen Markt und Politik* (pp. 135–149). Düsseldorf, Germany: Econ.

Hall, S. (Ed.). (1997). *Representation: Cultural representations and signifying practices.* London: Sage.

Hallenberger, G. (1997). Dimensionen des Begriffs "Vielfalt" [Dimensions of the term "diversity"]. In H. Kohl (Ed.), *Vielfalt im Rundfunk* (pp. 10–20). Konstanz, Germany: UVK Medien.

Haller, M. (2000). TÜV für Regionalblätter [A MOT test for regional newspapers]. *Message, 4*, 44–48.

Halloran, J. D., Elliott, P., & Murdock, G. (1970). *Demonstrations and communication: A case study.* Harmondsworth, England: Penguin Books.

Hargrove, T., & Stempel III, G. H. (2006a). Anti-government anger spurs 9/11 conspiracy belief. Survey: Few American adults use blogs to get news. *newsPolls.org.* Retrieved November 11, 2006, from http://newspolls.org/story.php?story_id=55

Hargrove, T., & Stempel III, G. H. (2006b). Survey: Few American adults use blogs to get news. *ScrippsNews.* Retrieved November 11, 2006, from http://www.shns.com/shns/scrippsnews/index.cfm? action=detail&pk= BLOG-POLL-08-31-06

Hart, K.-P. R. (2003). Representing gay men on American television. In G. Dines & J. M. Humez (Eds.), *Gender, race, and class in media: A text-reader* (2nd ed., pp. 597–607). Thousand Oaks, CA: Sage.

Heinrich, J. (1992). Publizistische Vielfalt aus wirtschaftswissenschaftlicher Sicht [Media diversity from an economic perspective]. In G. Rager & B. Weber (Eds.), *Publizistische Vielfalt zwischen Markt und Politik* (pp. 232–250). Düsseldorf, Germany: Econ.

Heller, C. (1999). Die Thematisierungsleistung von Print, Fernsehen und WorldWideWeb. Ein inhaltsanalytischer Vergleich der Angebote von *Focus, Spiegel* und *Stern* [Comparing issues of print media, television, and the WorldWideWeb. A comparison of *Focus, Spiegel,* and *Stern*]. Unpublished master's thesis, University of Munich, Germany.

Hellman, H. (2001). Diversity—an end in itself? Developing a multimeasure methodology of television programme variety studies. *European Journal of Communication, 16,* 181–208.

Hetsroni, A., & Tukachinsky, R. H. (2006). Television-world estimates, real-world estimates, and television viewing: A new scheme for cultivation. *Journal of Communication, 56,* 133–156.

Hillve, P., Majanen, P., & Rosengren, K. E. (1997). Aspects of quality in TV programming: Structural diversity compared over time and space. *European Journal of Communication, 12,* 291–318.

Hillve, P., & Rosengren, K. E. (1996). Swedish public service television—Quality for sale? In S. Ishikawa (Ed.), *Quality assessment of television* (pp. 231–252). Luton, England: University of Luton Press.

Hoffmann-Riem, W. (1987). National identity and cultural values: Broadcasting safeguards. *Journal of Broadcasting & Electronic Media, 31,* 57–72.

Hoffmann-Riem, W. (1996). *Regulating media—The licensing and supervision of broadcasting in six countries.* New York: The Guilford Press.

Holtz-Bacha, C. (1997). Development of the German media market: Opportunities and challenges for U.S. media firms. *The Journal of Media Economics, 10,* 39–58.

Holtz-Bacha, C. (2000). *Wahlwerbung als politische Kultur. Parteienspots im Fernsehen 1957–1998* [Campaign ads and political culture: TV commercials in Germany 1957–1998]. Opladen, Germany: Westdeutscher Verlag.

Holznagel, B. (1997). Vielfaltskonzepte in Europa [Concepts of diversity in Europe]. In H. Kohl (Ed.), *Vielfalt im Rundfunk* (pp. 94–103). Konstanz, Germany: UVK Medien.

Humphreys, P. J. (1994). *Media and media policy in Germany. The press and broadcasting since 1945* (2nd ed.). Oxford, England: Berg.

Iosifides, P. (1999). Diversity versus concentration in the deregulated mass media domain. *Journalism and Mass Communication Quarterly, 76,* 152–162.

Ishikawa, S., Leggart, T., Litman, B., Raboy, M., Rosengren, K. E., & Kambara, N. (1996). Diversity in television programming: Comparative analysis of five countries. In S. Ishikawa (Ed.), *Quality assessment of television* (pp. 253–263). Luton, England: University of Luton Press.

Ishikawa, S., & Maramatsu, Y. (1996). Why measure diversity? In S. Ishikawa (Ed.), *Quality assessment of television* (pp. 199–202). Luton, England: University of Luton Press.

Jarren, O. (1992). Publizistische Vielfalt durch lokale und sublokale Medien? Inter-Media-Agenda-Building—Ein Systemansatz zur Realanalyse von Medienleistungen im lokalen Raum [How local and sublocal media contribute to diversity. Intermedia agenda building as a systemic approach for the re-analysis of local media performance]. In G. Rager & B. Weber (Eds.), *Publizistische Vielfalt zwischen Markt und Politik* (pp. 65–84). Düsseldorf, Germany: Econ.

Jarren, O. (2000). Gesellschaftliche Integration durch Medien? Zur Begründung normativer Anforderungen an Medien [Social integration through the media? On the justification of normative requirements for the media]. *Medien & Kommunikationswissenschaft, 48,* 22–41.

Jeffres, L. W., Cutietta, C., Sekerka, L., & Lee, J. (2000). Newspapers, pluralism, and diversity in an urban context. *Mass Communication & Society, 3,* 157–184.

Kahn, R., & Kellner, D. (2004). New media and internet activism: From the "Battle of Seattle" to blogging. *New Media & Society, 6,* 87–95.

Kamalipour, Y. R., & Carilli, T. (Eds.). (1998). *Cultural diversity and the U.S. media.* Albany: State University of New York Press.

Kambara, N. (1992, March). Study of the diversity indices used for programming analyses. *Studies of Broadcasting, 28,* 195–205.

Kepplinger, H. M. (1985). *Die aktuelle Berichterstattung des Hörfunks. Eine Inhaltsanalyse der Abendnachrichten und politischen Magazine* [Coverage on current affairs on the radio: A content analysis of evening news and political features]. Freiburg, Germany: Alber.

Kim, J. (1999). Empirical testing on an unasked question in *Turner v. FCC*: Do must-carry rules enhance diversity? *Communications and the Law, 21*(2), 55–68.

Knoche, M. (1980). Die Messbarkeit publizistischer Vielfalt [Measurability of media diversity]. In S. Klaue, M. Knoche, & A. Zerdick (Eds.), *Probleme der Pressekonzentrationsforschung* (pp. 127–138). Baden-Baden, Germany: Nomos.

Knoche, M., & Lindgens, M. (1988). Selektion, Konsonanz und Wirkungspotential der deutschen Tagespresse. Politikvermittlung am Beispiel der Agentur- und Presseberichterstattung über die GRÜNEN zur Bundestagswahl 1987 [Selectivity, consonance and impact of German newspapers: A case study of wire service and press reports on the Green Party, federal elections 1987]. *Media Perspektiven, 8,* 490–510.

Kübler, F. (2005). Konzentrationskontrolle durch Rundfunkorganisation [Concentration supervision by organizing the broadcasting system]. In C.-M. Ridder, W. R. Langenbucher, U. Saxer, & C. Steininger (Eds.), *Bausteine einer Theorie des öffentlich-rechtlichen Rundfunks* (pp. 77–89). Opladen, Germany: VS Verlag für Sozialwissenschaften.

Lacy, S. (1987). The effects of intracity competition on daily newspaper content. *Journalism Quarterly, 64,* 281–291.

Lacy, S. (1989). A model of demand for news: Impact of competition on newspaper content. *Journalism Quarterly, 66,* 40–48.

Lemert, J. B. (1974). Content duplication by the networks in competing evening newscasts. *Journalism Quarterly, 51,* 238–244.

Levin, H. J. (1971). Program duplication, diversity, and effective viewer choices: Some empirical findings. *American Economic Review, 61*(2), 81–88.

Lin, C. A. (1995). Diversity of network prime-time program formats during the 1980s. *The Journal of Media Economics, 8,* 17–28.

Lippmann, W. (1922). *Public opinion.* New York: Macmillan.

Litman, B. (1979). The television networks, competition and program diversity. *Journal of Broadcasting, 23,* 393–409.

Litman, B., & Hasegawa, K. (1996). Measuring diversity in U.S. television programming: New evidence. In S. Ishikawa (Ed.), *Quality assessment of television* (pp. 203–230). Luton, England: University of Luton Press.

Long, S. L. (1979). A fourth television network and diversity: Some historical evidence. *Journalism Quarterly, 56,* 341–345.

Loosen, W. (2005). Zur "medialen Entgrenzungsfähigkeit" journalistischer Arbeitsprozesse: Synergien zwischen Print-, TV- und Online-Redaktionen [Working routines of journalists: Synergies between newsrooms of print media, television, and the Internet]. *Publizistik, 50,* 304–319.

Ludwig, J. (2004). Mediale Vielfalt: Ein (Nicht-)Ergebnis von Anbieter-, und/oder Nachfrageinteressen, Marktdefiziten und/oder Regulierungsdefiziten? [Media diversity as a result of market mechanisms, demand and supply, or regulation deficits?]. In M. Friedrichsen & W. Seifert (Eds.), *Effiziente Medienregulierung. Marktdefizite oder Regierungsdefizite?* (pp. 11–28) Baden-Baden, Germany: Nomos.

Maletzke, G (1980). Integration—eine gesellschaftliche Funktion der Massenkommunikation [Integration—a function of mass communication in society]. *Publizistik, 25,* 199–206.

Mathes, R., & Pfetsch, B. (1991). The role of the alternative press in the agenda-building process: Spill-over effects and media opinion leadership. *European Journal of Communication, 6,* 33–62.

Mayer, M. (2006). *Konsonanz von Ereignissen und Akteuren in der Nachrichtenberichterstattung* [Consonance of events and protagonists in news coverage]. Unpublished doctoral dissertation, University of Munich, Germany.

McCarthy, J. P. (2000, May 6). Pitfalls of media-mergers. *America, 182*(16), 12–16.

McCombs, M., & Reynolds, A. (2002). News influence on our pictures of the world. In J. Bryant & D. Zillmann (Eds.), *Media effects: Advances in theory and research* (2nd ed., pp. 1–18). Mahwah, NJ: Lawrence Erlbaum Associates.

McDonald, D. G., & Dimmick, J. (2003). The conceptualization and measurement of diversity. *Communication Research, 30,* 60–79.

McDonald, D. G., & Lin, S.-F. (2004). The effect of new networks on U.S. television diversity. *The Journal of Media Economics, 17,* 105–122.

McQuail, D. (1992). *Media performance: Mass communication and the public interest.* London: Sage.

McQuail, D. (2000). *McQuail's mass communication theory* (4th ed.). London: Sage.

McQuail, D. (2005, June). *Revisiting diversity as a media policy goal.* Paper presented at the International Conference "Demokratisierung der Medien- und Informationsgesellschaft," Zurich, Switzerland.

McQuail, D., & van Cuilenburg, J. (1983). Diversity as a media policy goal: A strategy for evaluative research and a Netherlands case study. *Gazette, 31,* 145–162.

Merten, K. (1994). *Konvergenz der deutschen Fernsehprogramme. Eine Langzeituntersuchung 1985–1993* [Convergence of German TV programs. A long-term study 1985–1993]. Münster, Germany: Lit.

Merten, K. (2001). Konsensanalyse. Ein neues Instrument der Inhaltsanalyse [Consensus analysis: A new instrument of content analysis]. In W. Wirth & E. Lauf (Eds.), *Inhaltsanalyse. Perspektiven, Probleme, Potentiale* (pp. 234–243). Köln, Germany: von Halem.

Moreau, F., & Peltier, S. (2004). Cultural diversity in the movie industry: A cross-national study. *The Journal of Media Economics, 17,* 123–144.

Morgan, M., & Shanahan, J. (1997). Two decades of cultivation research: An appraisal and meta-analysis. In B. Berelson (Ed.), *Communication yearbook 20* (pp. 1–45). Thousand Oaks, CA: Sage.

Napoli, P. M. (1997). Rethinking program diversity assessment: An audience-centered approach. *The Journal of Media Economics, 10,* 59–74.

Noelle-Neumann, E., & Mathes, R. (1987). The "event as event" and the "event as news": The significance of "consonance" for media effects research. *European Journal of Communication, 2,* 391–414.

Owen, B. M. (1978). The economic view of programming. *Journal of Communication, 28,* 43–50.

Park, J. H., Gabbadon, N. G., & Chernin, A. R. (2006). Naturalizing racial differences through comedy: Asian, black, and white views on racial stereotypes in *Rush Hour 2. Journal of Communication, 56,* 157–177.

Peter, J., & de Vreese, C. H. (2003). Agenda-rich, agenda-poor: A cross-national comparative investigation of nominal and thematic public agenda diversity. *International Journal of Public Opinion Research, 15,* 44–64.

Pohl, S. (2006): *Presselenkung und Themenvielfalt im nationalsozialistischen Deutschland am Beispiel Thüringer Tageszeitunge* [Press control and issue diversity in Nazi Germany: The case of newspapers in Thuringia]. Unpublished master's thesis, University of Erfurt, Germany.

Pritchard, D. (2002). *Viewpoint diversity in cross-owned newspapers and television stations: A study of news coverage of the 2000 Presidential campaign*. Washington, DC: Federal Communications Commission.

Rager, G. (1982). *Publizistische Vielfalt im Lokalen. Eine empirische Analyse* [Media diversity in a local market: An empirical analysis] Tübingen, Germany: Vereinigung für Volkskunde.

Rager, G., & Weber, B. (Eds.). (1992). *Publizistische Vielfalt zwischen Markt und Politik. Mehr Medien—mehr Inhalte?* [Media diversity between politics and the market: More media—more content?]. Düsseldorf, Germany: Econ.

Rayner, P. (2006). A need for postmodern fluidity? *Critical Studies in Media Communication, 23,* 345–349.

Reese, S., Gandy, O. & Grant, A. (Eds.). (2001). *Framing public life: Perspectives on media and our understanding of the social world.* Mahwah, NJ: Lawrence Erlbaum Associates.

Reinemann, C. (2003). *Medienmacher als Mediennutzer. Kommunikations- und Einflussstrukturen im politischen Journalismus der Gegenwart* [Political journalists as media users: Structures of communication and influence in contemporary journalism]. Köln, Germany: Böhlau.

Roessler, P. (1999). The individual agenda-designing process: How interpersonal communication, egocentric networks and mass media shape the perception of political issues by individuals. *Communication Research, 26,* 666–700.

Roessler, P. (2000). Vielzahl = Vielfalt = Fragmentierung? Empirische Anhaltspunkte zur Differenzierung von Medienangeboten auf der Mikroebene [Multitude = diversity = fragmentation: Empirical evidence of media differentiation in contemporary journalism]. In O. Jarren, K. Imhof, & R. Blum (Eds.), *Zerfall der Öffentlichkeit?* (pp. 168–186) Opladen, Germany: Westdeutscher Verlag.

Roessler, P. (2001a). Visuelle Codierung und Vielfalts-Analysen auf Mikroebene. Kategorisierungs- und Auswertungsstrategien für die ikonographische Untersuchung journalistischer Berichterstattung [Visual coding and the analysis of diversity on a micro-level: Strategies for coding and analysis of iconographic research on media coverage]. In W. Wirth & E. Lauf (Eds.), *Inhaltsanalyse. Perspektiven, Probleme, Potentiale* (pp. 140–156). Köln, Germany: von Halem.

Roessler, P. (2001b). Vielzahl und Fokussierung im regionalen Hörfunk. Eine vergleichende Inhaltsanalyse von Nachrichtensendungen auf der Mikroebene [Diversity of local radio news. A content analysis of news shows on the micro-level]. In P. Roessler, G. Vowe, & V. Henle (Eds.), *Das Geräusch der Provinz—Radio in der Region* (pp. 159–183). Munich, Germany: Kopaed.

Roessler, P. (2002, July). *Media diversity and the flow of political news: A study of German newspaper coverage and wire service reports.* Paper presented at the annual meeting of the International Communication Association, Seoul, South Korea.

Roessler, P. (2003). Themenvielfalt im Politikressort. Ein Vergleich der Berichtsanlässe von 27 deutschen Tageszeitungen [Issue diversity of political news. A comparison of news reports in 27 German newspapers]. In W. Donsbach & O. Jandura (Eds.), *Chancen und Gefahren der Mediendemokratie* (pp. 174–187). Konstanz, Germany: UVK Medien.

Roessler, P. (2004). Political communication messages: Pictures of our world on international television news. In F. Esser & B. Pfetsch (Eds.), *Comparing political communication: Theories, cases and challenges* (pp. 271–292). Cambridge, England: Cambridge University Press.

Roessler, P. (May, 2005a). *Same pictures, same stories? Diversity on the micro-level of news coverage.* Paper presented at the annual meeting of the International Communication Association, New York.

Roessler, P. (2005b). The myth of the re-invented journalism: Functional and normative gatekeeping of web communicators. In P. Roessler & F. Krotz (Eds.), *The media society and its myths* (pp. 177–203). Konstanz, Germany: UVK.

Roessler, P. (2006). "Erstmal sehen, was die anderen machen." Vielfalt als Qualitätsmerkmal vs. mediale Koorientierung im journalistischen Alltag [Diversity as a criterion for quality versus journalistic co-orientation as a newsroom routine]. In S. Weischenberg, W. Loosen, & M. Beuthner (Eds.), *Medien-Qualitäten* (pp. 223–244). Konstanz, Germany: UVK.

Roessler, P., Lücke, S., Linzmaier, V., Steinhilper, L. & Willhöft, C. (2006). *Ernährung im Fernsehen. Darstellung und Wirkung: eine empirische Studie* [Food on German television: Representation and effects: An empirical study]. Munich, Germany: R. Fischer.

Roof, E. D., Trauth, D. M., & Huffman, J. L. (1993). Structural regulation of cable television: A formula for diversity. *Communications and the Law, 15*(2), 43–70.

Rossmann, C., Brandl, A., & Brosius, H. (2003). Der Vielfalt eine zweite Chance? Eine Analyse der Angebotsstruktur öffentlich-rechtlicher und privater Fernsehsender in den Jahren 1995, 1998 und 2001 [A second chance for program diversity? A structural analysis of the content offered by public and private television channels in 1995, 1998, and 2001]. *Publizistik, 48,* 427–453.

Roth, A. (May, 2004). *The ecology of a dual television market: competition and diversity in the Netherlands.* Paper presented at the 6th World Media Economics Conference, Montreal, Canada.

Rüb, M. (2006, February 12). Ein Leben für das Internet [A whole life for the Internet]. *Frankfurter Allgemeine Sonntagszeitung, 6,* 10.

Rust, H. (1992). Internationale Medienkonzentration und publizistische Vielfalt [Concentration of international media and diversity]. In G. Rager & B. Weber (Eds.), *Publizistische Vielfalt zwischen Markt und Politik* (pp. 27–49). Düsseldorf, Germany: Econ.

Samuelson, R. J. (2003, August 11). The myth of "big media." *Newsweek, 142*(6), 42.

Sasser, E. L., & Russell, J. T. (1972). The fallacy of news judgement. *Journalism Quarterly, 49,* 280–284.

Saxer, U. (1992). Staatliche Förderung und publizistische Vielfalt [Governmental support for media diversity]. In G. Rager & B. Weber (Eds.), *Publizistische Vielfalt zwischen Markt und Politik* (pp. 110–134). Düsseldorf, Germany: Econ.

Schlobinski, P., & Siever, T. (Eds.). (2005). Sprachliche und textuelle Merkmale in Weblogs. Ein internationales Projekt [Linguistic and textual characteristics of Weblogs: An international research project]. *Networx* (46). Retrieved November 11, 2006, from http://www.mediensprache.net/networx/networx-46.pdf

Schmidt, J., & Wilt, M. (2006). *Wie ich blogge?! Erste Ergebnisse der Weblog-Befragung 2005* [How I blog: Results of the 2005 Weblog survey]. University of Bamberg, Germany: Berichte der Forschungsstelle "Neue Kommunikationsmedien" 06-01. Retrieved November 11, 2006, from http://www.fonk-bamberg.de/pdf/fonkbericht0601.pdf

Schoenbach, K. (1980). Publizistische Vielfalt in Wettbewerbsgebieten [Media diversity in areas of competition]. In S. Klaue, M. Knoche, & A. Zerdick (Eds.), *Probleme der Pressekonzentrationsforschung* (pp. 145–161). Baden-Baden, Germany: Nomos.

Schulz, W., & Ihle, C. (2005). Wettbewerb und Vielfalt im deutschen Fernsehmarkt—Eine Analyse der Entwicklung von 1992 bis 2001 [Competition and diversity on the German TV market—an analysis of trends between 1992 and 2001]. In C.-M. Ridder, W. R. Langenbucher, U. Saxer & C. Steininger (Eds.), *Bausteine einer Theorie des öffentlich-rechtlichen Rundfunks* (272–292). Opladen, Germany: VS Verlag für Sozialwissenschaften.

Schwotzer, B. (2005). Nachrichtensynergie vs. Nachrichtenvielfalt [News synergy vs. news diversity]. In Arbeitskreis der Landesmedienanstalten ALM (Ed.), *Fernsehen in Deutschland 2005* (pp. 161–163). Berlin, Germany: Vistas.

Shoemaker, P. J. (1991). *Gatekeeping.* Newbury Park, CA: Sage.

Sievert, H. (1998). *Europäischer Journalismus. Theorie und Empirie aktueller Medienkommunikation in der Europäischen Union* [Journalism in Europe: Theoretical and empirical accounts]. Opladen, Germany: Westdeutscher Verlag.

Sjurts, I. (2004). Einfalt trotz Vielfalt in den Medienmärkten: Eine ökonomische Erklärung [Simple-mindedness in spite of diversity on the media market: An economic explanation]. In M. Friedrichsen & W. Seifert (Eds.), *Effiziente Medienregulierung. Marktdefizite oder Regierungsdefizite?* (pp. 71–87). Baden-Baden, Germany: Nomos.

Southwell, B. G. (2005). Between messages and people: A multilevel model of memory for television content. *Communication Research, 32,* 112–140.

Staab, J. F. (1990). The role of news factors in news selection: A theoretical reconsideration. *European Journal of Communication, 5,* 423–443.

Stark, B. (September, 2006). *Die Vielfalt der Messung "der Vielfalt"—Überlegungen zur methodischen Umsetzung des Vielfaltskonzepts* [Diversity in measuring "the diversity"—methodological considerations]. Paper presented at the annual DGPuK conference on methods of media studies, Zurich, Switzerland.

Tan, A., Tan, G., & Gibson, T. (2003). Socialization effects of American television on international audiences. In M. G. Elasmar (Ed.), *The impact of international television. A paradigm shift* (pp. 29–38). Mahwah, NJ: Lawrence Erlbaum Associates.

Teachman, J. D. (1980). Analysis of population diversity. *Sociological Methods & Research, 8,* 341–362.

Trebbe, J. (1996). *Der Beitrag privater Lokalradio- und Lokalfernsehprogramme zur publizistischen Vielfalt. Eine Pilotstudie am bayerischen Senderstandort Augsburg* [How private radio and TV programs contribute to media diversity: A pilot study of broadcasting in Augsburg, Bavaria]. BLM-Schriftenreihe, Band 39. Munich, Germany: R. Fischer.

Trebbe, J. (1998). *Lokale Medienleistungen im Vergleich. Untersuchungen zur publizistischen Vielfalt an den bayerischen Senderstandorten Augsburg, Landshut und Schweinfurt* [Performance of local media in comparison: Media diversity in the Bavarian regions of Augsburg, Landshut, and Schweinfurt]. Munich, Germany: R. Fischer (BLM-Schriftenreihe, Band 47).

Trebbe, J., & Maurer, T. (1999). *Hörfunklandschaft Niedersachsen 1998. Eine vergleichende Analyse der öffentlich-rechtlichen und privaten Radiosender* [Radio in Lower Saxonia 1998: A comparative analysis of public and private broadcasters]. Berlin, Germany: Vistas (Schriftenreihe der NLM, Band 6).

Trebbe, J., & Weiß, H. (1997). Lokale Thematisierungsleistungen. Der Beitrag privater Rundfunkprogramme zur publizistischen Vielfalt in lokalen Kommunikationsräumen [Issue diversity on the local level: The contribution of private broadcasting to media: diversity in local communities]. In G. Bentele & M. Haller (Eds.), *Aktuelle Entstehung von Öffentlichkeit* (pp. 445–465). Konstanz, Germany: UVK.

van Cuilenburg, J. (2000a). Media for an open and receptive society. On the economic and cultural foundation of open and receptive media diversity. In J. van Cuilenburg & R. van der Wurff (Eds.), *Media & open societies. Cultural, economic and policy foundations for media openness and diversity in East and West* (pp. 13–23). Amsterdam: Het Spinhuis.

van Cuilenburg, J. (2000b). On measuring media competition and media diversity: Concepts, theories and methods. In R. Picard (Ed.), *Measuring media content, quality and diversity* (pp. 51–84). Turku, Finland: Turku School of Economics and Business Administration.

van Cuilenburg, J. (2005). On monitoring media diversity, media profusion, and media performance: Some regulator's notes. *Communications, 30,* 301–308.

van der Wurff, R. (2004). Supplying and viewing diversity: The role of competition and viewer choice in Dutch broadcasting. *European Journal of Communication, 19,* 215–237.

van der Wurff, R. (2005). Media markets and media diversity. *Communications, 30,* 293–301.

van der Wurff, R., & van Cuilenburg, J. (2001). Impact of moderate and ruinous competition on diversity: The Dutch television market. *The Journal of Media Economics, 14,* 213–229.

van der Wurff, R., van Cuilenburg, J., & Keune, G. (2000). Competition, media innovation, and diversity in broadcasting. A case study of the TV market in the Netherlands. In J. van Cuilenburg & R. van der Wurff (Eds.), *Media & open societies: Cultural, economic and policy foundations for media openness and diversity in East and West* (pp. 119–157). Amsterdam: Het Spinhuis.

van Kranenburg, H., Hagedoorn, J., & Pennings, J. (2004). Measurement of international and product diversification in the publishing industry. *The Journal of Media Economics, 17,* 87–104.

van Lunenberg, M. A. (2002). A newspaper content analysis of Dutch industry. *Corporate Communications, 7,* 126–135.

Vergeer, M. (2005). Measuring diversity and level of aggregation. *Communications, 30,* 312–319.

Vettehen, P. H. (2005). "Open diversity" statistics: An illusion of "scientific thoroughness"? *Communications, 30,* 308–312.

Vlasic, A. (2004). *Die Integrationsfunktion der Massenmedien. Begriffsgeschichte, Modelle, Operationalisierung* [Social integration as a function of mass media: History of an idea, theoretical models, operationalization]. Opladen, Germany: Westdeutscher Verlag.

Wakshlag, J., & Adams, W. J. (1985). Trends in program variety and the prime time access rule. *Journal of Broadcasting & Electronic Media, 29,* 23–34.

Waldeck, J., & Myers, K. (2007). A state of the art review: Organizational assimilation theory, research, and implications for the discipline. In C. S. Beck (Ed.), *Communication yearbook 31* (pp. 321–367). New York, NY: Lawrence Erlbaum Associates.

Wanta, W., King, P., & McCombs, M. (1995). A comparison of factors influencing issue diversity in the U.S. and Taiwan. *International Journal of Public Opinion Research, 7,* 353–365.

Wilke, J. (Ed.). (2000). *Von der Agentur zur Redaktion. Wie Nachrichten gemacht, bewertet und verwendet werden* [Wire services and the newsroom: How news is made, assessed, and used]. Köln, Germany: Böhlau.

Williams, B. A., & Delli Carpini, M. X. (2000). Unchained reaction: The collapse of media gatekeeping and the Clinton–Lewinsky scandal. *Journalism, 1,* 61–85.

Winseck, D. (2002). Netscapes of power: Convergence, consolidation and power in the Canadian mediascape. *Media, Culture & Society, 24,* 795–819.

Woldt, R. (1992). Probleme der Messung von Vielfalt [Problems in measuring diversity]. In G. Rager & B. Weber (Eds.), *Publizistische Vielfalt zwischen Markt und Politik* (pp. 186–211). Düsseldorf, Germany: Econ.

Zook, K. B. (2003). The Fox Network and the revolution in Black television. In G. Dines & J. M. Humez (Eds.), *Gender, race, and class in media: A text-reader* (2nd ed., pp. 586–596). Thousand Oaks, CA: Sage.

Author Index

N

O

Subject Index

A

Abolitionist movement, 425
Abu Ghraib prison, 229
Academic gatekeepers, 16
Achilles in Vietnam, 192
ACITs, *see* Advanced communication
   information technologies
ACS, *see* American Cancer Society
Activity coordination, 276, 277, 278, 310
Adolescent sibling conflict, 119
Advanced communication information
   technologies (ACITs), 285, 338,
   339, 353
Advertisement prevalence, memory and, 445
Affective death, state of, 135
Affiliation, individual-level needs for, 343
Age differences, open communication
   and, 93
Alone-time, 9
Alternative media, 502
Alternative organizing, 283, 372
Alternative times, 273–320
   temporal perceptions associated with
      nonstandard relationships,
      283–300
   cultural-level influences, 284–289
   environmental-level influences,
      289–290
   organizational-level influences,
      290–300
   temporal practices related to non-
      standard relationships, 304–310
   flexibility, 305–308
   flexibility–separation dialectic,
      308–310
   separation, 308
   temporal processes in nonstandard
      relationships, 301–304

theoretical background, 276–283
   theorizing nonstandard
      membership, 276–282
   theorizing organizational
      temporality, 282–283
American Cancer Society (ACS), 70
American Indian Movement, 247
American Sign Language, 257
American Sociological Review, 429
Anger, tunnel vision associated with, 150
Anticipatory socialization, 333
Antitrust laws, 472
Arguing, *see also* Serial arguing
   adverse health effects of, 119
   negative consequence of, 149
Art, representing trauma in, 193
Assimilation
   definition of, 324
   interactivity, 330
   processes, theory for explaining, 326
Atomic bomb survivor, 207
Attribution-making, 149
Avoidance
   cancer-related issues and, 101
   consequences of, 66
   –dissatisfaction connection, 68
   predictors of, 64
   risks and benefits of, 67
Avoidant communication, 62, 63, 65
   age and, 93
   consequences of, 70
   risks and benefits of, 67

B

Balancing, 87
BBC World Service, 495

547

D

U

About the Editor

Christina S. Beck (Ph.D., University of Oklahoma, 1992) is a professor in the School of Communication Studies at Ohio University. In addition to editing *Communication Yearbook*, she contributes to the *Journal of Health Communication: International Perspectives* as book review editor and serves on the editorial boards of five communication journals. She has authored or co-authored/co-edited three award-winning books on health communication: *Communicating for Better Health: A Guide Through the Medical Mazes* (2001), *Partnership for Health: Building Relationships Between Women and Health Caregivers* (1997) (with Sandra Ragan and Athena duPre), and *Narratives, Health, and Healing: Communication Theory, Research, and Practice* (2005) (with Lynn Harter and Phyllis Japp), as well as numerous journal articles and invited book chapters. She also co-edited *The Lynching of Language: Gender, Politics, and Power in the Hill-Thomas Hearings* (1996) (with Sandra Ragan, Lynda Kaid, and Dianne Bystromm). Her research interests span the areas of health communication, language and social interaction, and mass communication. Please direct correspondence to: Christina S. Beck, Ohio University, School of Communication Studies, 210 Lasher Hall, Athens, OH 45701; E-mail: beck@ohio.edu

About the Contributors

Kris Acheson (M.A., Georgia State University, 2004) is a doctoral candidate at the Hugh Downs School of Human Communication at Arizona State University. Inspired by her experience as a high school Spanish teacher and university-level ESOL instructor, she focused her early research on the intersections of language, culture, and communication, with projects on language attitudes and ethnocentrism in foreign language classrooms. Recently, she has begun studying more critical intercultural topics related to ethnicity and gender. Communicative silence, especially in intercultural contexts, has always held great fascination for her and is an integral part of her dissertation research—a phenomenological study of communication between addicts and nonaddicts. Please direct correspondence to: Kris Acheson, College of Liberal Arts and Sciences, Arizona State University, P.O. Box 871205, Tempe, AZ 85287-1205; E-mail: Kris.Acheson@asu.edu

Dawna I. Ballard (Ph.D., University of California at Santa Barbara, 2002) is an assistant professor of communication studies at the University of Texas at Austin. Her research examines organizational temporality with particular attention to the ways in which time shapes and is shaped by a range of organizational communication processes. Her published research has appeared in *Communication Monographs, Communication Research, Management Communication Quarterly,* and *Communication Studies,* among others, and has been presented at numerous scholarly conferences, including a recent research symposium, *It's About Time: Increasing the Temporal Focus in Organizational Research,* held at the University of Maastricht by METEOR and the Department of Organization & Strategy. She teaches courses on chronemics and organizational and group communication, and co-supervises the internship program. Please direct correspondence to: Dawna I. Ballard, University of Texas at Austin, Department of Communication Studies, 1 University Station A1105, Austin, TX 78712; E-mail: diballard@mail.utexas.edu

John P. Caughlin (Ph.D., University of Texas at Austin, 1997) is an associate professor of speech communication at the University of Illinois at Urbana-Champaign. His research examines communication in families and other close relationships, focusing on the causes and consequences of avoiding communication. Recent work has appeared in journals such as *Communication Monographs, Human Communication Research, Journal of Social and Personal Relationships, Journal of Personality and Social Psychology,* and *Personal Relationships.* One of his studies on the demand/withdraw pattern of communication in marriage (which involves one person avoiding while the other nags or criticizes) won the Franklin H. Knower Article Award from the Interpersonal Division of the National Communication Association. In 2004, he received the Miller Early Career Achievement Award from the International Association for Relationship Research. Please direct correspondence to: John P. Caughlin, Department of Speech Communication, University of Illinois at Urbana-Champaign, 244 Lincoln Hall, 702 S. Wright St., Urbana, IL 60801; E-mail: caughlin@uiuc.edu

Lawrence R. Frey (Ph.D., University of Kansas, 1979) is a professor in the Department of Communication at the University of Colorado at Boulder. His teaching and research interests include group communication, applied communication (particularly social justice, community studies, and communication activism), health communication, and research methods (both quantitative and qualitative); they focus on how participation in collective communicative practices makes a difference in people's individual, relational, and collective lives. He is the author or editor of 14 books, three special journal issues, and 65 articles and chapters, as well as the recipient of 11 scholarship awards, including the 2000 Gerald M. Phillips Award for Distinguished Applied Communication Scholarship from the National Communication Association. He is a past president of the Central States Communication Association and a recipient of the Outstanding Young Teacher Award from that organization and the 2003 Master Teacher Award from the Communication and Instruction Interest Group of the Western States Communication

Association. Please direct correspondence to: Lawrence R. Frey, University of Colorado at Boulder, Department of Communication, 270 UCB, Boulder, CO 80309-0270; E-mail: Larry.Frey@Colorado. edu

Daena J. Goldsmith (Ph.D., University of Washington, 1990) is an associate professor of communication at Lewis and Clark College, Portland, Oregon. Her work examines communication dilemmas and variability in effective responses to dilemmas in interpersonal communication situations, particularly those related to social support and to management of chronic illness. Her recent book with Cambridge University Press is entitled *Communicating Social Support*. Her work has also appeared in *Human Communication Research, Communication Monographs,* and *Social Science and Medicine*. Please direct correspondence to: Daena J. Goldsmith, Lewis and Clark College, Department of Communication, 0615 Palatine Hill Road, MSC 35, Portland, Oregon 97219; E-mail: daena@lclark.edu

Loril M. Gossett (Ph.D., University of Colorado at Boulder, 2001) is an assistant professor at the University of Texas at Austin in the Department of Communication Studies. Dr. Gossett draws on a variety of qualitative methods to study nonstandard work arrangements, such as temporary employees, independent contractors, telecommuters, and volunteers. She examines how these alternative work relationships affect what it means to be or communicate as an organizational member, specifically with respect to issues of identification, power, and control. Please direct correspondence to: Loril M. Gossett, University of Texas at Austin, Department of Communication Studies, 1 University Station A1105, Austin, TX 78712; E-mail: lgossett@mail. utexas.edu

Stephanie Houston Grey is an assistant professor of rhetoric in the Department of Communication Studies at Louisiana State University. Her work explores the intersections of rhetoric, epistemology, communication theory, performance, and aesthetics. Since the dynamics of modern culture are increasingly driven by the production of knowledge, these systems of knowing have profound impact upon the discursive formation of identity. Professor Grey's research probes these intellectual systems for the moral imperatives that drive social policy. The inspiration for her present study stems from the reverberations of Hurricane Katrina, a catastrophe that continues to have economic and psychological effects across the Gulf region. Professor Grey is currently working with her dedicated colleagues at LSU to come to grips with this event and develop strategies for cultural recovery. Please direct correspondence to: Stephanie Houston Grey, Department of Communication, Studies, Louisiana State University, 136 Coates Hall, Baton Rouge, LA 70803; E-mail: houston@lsu.edu

Rachel S. Malis (Ph.D., Northwestern University, 2006) is an assistant professor in the Communication Arts and Sciences Department at Elmhurst College. She conducts research on close relationships with a focus on interpersonal conflict and health. She has published in journals such as *Human Communication Research* and *Journal of Social and Personal Relationships*. Please direct correspondence to: Rachel S. Malis, Communication Arts & Sciences Department, Elmhurst College, 190 Prospect Ave., Elmhurst, IL 60126.

Courtney Waite Miller (Ph.D., Northwestern University, 2004) is an assistant professor in the Communication Arts and Sciences Department at Elmhurst College. She focuses her research on interpersonal communication, specifically conflict in close relationships. She has authored or co-authored several book chapters and journal articles. Please direct correspondence to: Courtney Waite Miller, Communication Arts and Sciences Department, Elmhurst College, 190 Prospect Ave., Elmhurst, IL 60126; E-mail: cwmiller@elmhurst.edu

Laura E. Miller (M.A., University of Illinois at Urbana-Champaign, 2005) is a doctoral student in speech communication at the University of Illinois at Urbana-Champaign. Her research examines health communication within families and close relationships. She has published an article in *Personal Relationships,* and she was an author and presenter of a Top 4 Paper in Interpersonal Communication at the 2005 National Communication Association Convention. Please direct correspondence to: Laura Miller, Department of Speech Communication, University of Illinois at Urbana-Champaign, 244 Lincoln Hall, 702 S. Wright St., Urbana, IL 60801; E-mail: lemillrl@uiuc.edu

Karen K. Myers (Ph.D., Arizona State University, 2005) is an assistant professor of communication at the University of California, Santa Barbara. Her primary areas of research involve organizational communication with a focus on organizational socialization and assimilation, organizational knowledge, identity, emotion management, conflict, and leadership. High-reliability organizations offer a theoretically and socially important context for her investigation. Much of her work focuses on examining how group processes influence member integration and performance proficiency. Other areas of inquiry include health communication and marketing. Her work has appeared in journals such as *Management Communication Quarterly, Applied Journal of Communication Research, Human Communication Research,* and *Communication Monographs.* She is the 2006 winner of the W. Charles Redding Award for the Outstanding Dissertation in Organizational Communication. Please direct correspondence to: Karen K. Myers, Department of Communication, 4816 Ellison Hall, University of California at Santa Barbara, Santa Barbara, CA 93106-4020; E-mail: myers@comm.ucsb.edu

Patrick Roessler (Ph.D., University of Stuttgart-Hohenheim, 1996) is a professor of communication science at the University of Erfurt. His primary areas of research include media effects research, new media developments and online communication, audience research, and health communication. His research has appeared in the *Journal of Communication, Communication Research, International Journal of Public Opinion Research,* and *German Communication Yearbook.* In 2006, he was elected president of the German Communication Association. Please direct correspondence to: Patrick Roessler, University of Erfurt, Nordhaeuser Strasse, D-99080 Erfurt, Germany; E-mail: patrick.roessler@uni-erfurt.de

Michael E. Roloff (Ph.D., Michigan State University, 1975) is a professor of communication studies at Northwestern University. His research interests include bargaining and negotiation, and conflict management. He is the author of *Interpersonal Communication: The Social Exchange Approach* and co-editor of *Persuasion: New Directions in Theory and Research, Interpersonal Processes: New Directions in Communication Research, Social Cognition and Communication,* and *Communication and Negotiation.* His work has been published in such journals as *Communication Monographs, Communication Research,* and *Human Communication Research.* He is senior associate editor of the *International Journal of Conflict Management,* and he has served as editor of the *Communication Yearbook* and as co-editor of *Communication Research*. Please direct correspondence to: Michael E. Roloff, Department of Communication Studies, Northwestern University, 2240 N. Campus Drive, Evanston, IL 60208; E-mail: m-roloff@northwestern.edu

Brian G. Southwell (Ph.D., University of Pennsylvania) is an assistant professor at the University of Minnesota's School of Journalism and Mass Communication. He also holds an adjunct appointment at the university's School of Public Health. Southwell's work focuses primarily on understanding the impact of media content on memory and behavior, with an emphasis on health and science communication contexts, and it has appeared in venues such as the *Journal of Communication, Communication Research, Communication Monographs, Journalism & Mass Communication Quarterly,* and the *Journal of Health Communication.* The International Communication Association and the National Communication Association jointly named his dissertation the Health Communication Dissertation of the Year in 2003, and in 2006, the University of Minnesota awarded him the Arthur "Red" Motley Exemplary Teaching Award. Please direct correspondence to: Brian G. Southwell, School of Journalism and Mass Communication, University of Minnesota, Twin Cities, 111 Murphy Hall, 206 Church Street SE, Minneapolis, MN 55455; E-mail: south026@umn.edu

erin daina underwood is a doctoral candidate in the Department of Communication at the University of Colorado at Boulder. She has co-authored a book chapter with Gerard A. Hauser entitled "Vernacular Rhetoric and Social Movements: Performances of Resistance in the Rhetoric of the Everyday" in an edited volume by Sharon Stevens and Patricia Malesh entitled *Active Voices: Composing a Rhetoric of Social Movements.* Her scholarly interests focus on the role of rhetoric in creating and maintaining engaged public places. She is particularly interested in how rhetorics of places are related to vernacular and official rhetoric, such as in the design and use of public squares. Please direct correspondence to: erin daina underwood, University of Colorado at Boulder, Department of Communication, 270 UCB, Boulder, CO 80309-0270; E-mail: Erin.Underwood@Colorado.edu

Jennifer H. Waldeck (Ph.D., University of California, Santa Barbara) is an assistant professor of communication studies at Chapman

University, Orange, California. Her research interests are in organizational and instructional communication, with emphases on mentoring, training and development, effective assimilation of corporate employees, and how advanced communication technologies facilitate learning and performance improvement at work and in higher education. Her research has appeared in *Communication Monographs*, *Communication Education*, *The Journal of Applied Communication Research*, *Communication Yearbook*, and in several edited volumes. She has presented numerous conference papers at national and international conferences. Presently, she serves on the editorial board of *Communication Education* and is faculty advisor to Chapman University's Lambda Pi Eta chapter. She regularly teaches courses in organizational communication, persuasion, and research methods. Please direct correspondence to: Jennifer H. Waldeck, Department of Communication Studies, Chapman University, One University Drive, Orange, CA 92866; E-mail: Waldeck@chapman. edu

Niki L. Young is the director of the Center for Teaching and Learning at Western Oregon University and adjunct assistant professor of communication. Her scholarly work spans disciplinary boundaries and examines the influence of identity and communication on social change and education. She is interested in what the Greeks termed *arête*, or excellence in education, and in narratives that connect persuasion, culture, and pedagogy. She is the editor of *Faculty Voices: Volume 3*, an anthology of teaching narratives, and she was honored with an Innovative Award by the Professional and Organizational Development Network in Higher Education for her work on integrating innovative technologies in college teaching. She earned a Ph.D. in communication studies at Louisiana State University and an M.A. in rhetoric from the University of Oregon, in addition to a B.S. in education from Southern Oregon University and a B.A. in economics and law and society from Macalester College. Please direct correspondence to: Niki L. Young, Center for Teaching and Learning, Western Oregon University, 345 North Monmouth Avenue, Monmouth, OR 97361; E-mail: youngn@wou.edu

Marco C. Yzer (Ph.D., University of Groningen, 1999) is an assistant professor in the School of Journalism and Mass Communication and an adjunct professor in the School of Public Health at the University of Minnesota. His research focuses on the interplay between social psychological and communication theories as an account of persuasion processes in the context of mass-mediated health information. His work has been published in communication and psychology journals, such as *Communication Theory, Journal of Health Communication, Psychology & Health, Health Education Research, Preventive Medicine,* and *Psychology of Addictive Behaviors.* Please direct correspondence to: Marco C. Yzer, School of Journalism and Mass Communication, University of Minnesota, Twin Cities, 111 Murphy Hall, 206 Church Street SE, Minneapolis, MN 55455; E-mail: mcyzer@umn.edu

9193